The Colonial Records Of North Carolina.

William L. Saunders

The Colonial Records Of North Carolina.

The Making of Modern Law collection of legal archives constitutes a genuine revolution in historical legal research because it opens up a wealth of rare and previously inaccessible sources in legal, constitutional, administrative, political, cultural, intellectual, and social history. This unique collection consists of three extensive archives that provide insight into more than 300 years of American and British history. These collections include:

Legal Treatises, 1800-1926: over 20,000 legal treatises provide a comprehensive collection in legal history, business and economics, politics and government.

Trials, 1600-1926: nearly 10,000 titles reveal the drama of famous, infamous, and obscure courtroom cases in America and the British Empire across three centuries.

Primary Sources, 1620-1926: includes reports, statutes and regulations in American history, including early state codes, municipal ordinances, constitutional conventions and compilations, and law dictionaries.

These archives provide a unique research tool for tracking the development of our modern legal system and how it has affected our culture, government, business – nearly every aspect of our everyday life. For the first time, these high-quality digital scans of original works are available via print-on-demand, making them readily accessible to libraries, students, independent scholars, and readers of all ages.

The BiblioLife Network

This project was made possible in part by the BiblioLife Network (BLN), a project aimed at addressing some of the huge challenges facing book preservationists around the world. The BLN includes libraries, library networks, archives, subject matter experts, online communities and library service providers. We believe every book ever published should be available as a high-quality print reproduction; printed on-demand anywhere in the world. This insures the ongoing accessibility of the content and helps generate sustainable revenue for the libraries and organizations that work to preserve these important materials.

The following book is in the "public domain" and represents an authentic reproduction of the text as printed by the original publisher. While we have attempted to accurately maintain the integrity of the original work, there are sometimes problems with the original work or the micro-film from which the books were digitized. This can result in minor errors in reproduction. Possible imperfections include missing and blurred pages, poor pictures, markings and other reproduction issues beyond our control. Because this work is culturally important, we have made it available as part of our commitment to protecting, preserving, and promoting the world's literature.

GUIDE TO FOLD-OUTS MAPS and OVERSIZED IMAGES

The book you are reading was digitized from microfilm captured over the past thirty to forty years. Years after the creation of the original microfilm, the book was converted to digital files and made available in an online database.

In an online database, page images do not need to conform to the size restrictions found in a printed book. When converting these images back into a printed bound book, the page sizes are standardized in ways that maintain the detail of the original. For large images, such as fold-out maps, the original page image is split into two or more pages

Guidelines used to determine how to split the page image follows:

• Some images are split vertically; large images require vertical and horizontal splits.
• For horizontal splits, the content is split left to right.
• For vertical splits, the content is split from top to bottom.
• For both vertical and horizontal splits, the image is processed from top left to bottom right.

THE

COLONIAL RECORDS

OF

NORTH CAROLINA

PUBLISHED UNDER THE SUPERVISION OF THE TRUS-
TEES OF THE PUBLIC LIBRARIES, BY ORDER
OF THE GENERAL ASSEMBLY

COLLECTED AND EDITED

BY

WILLIAM L SAUNDERS

SECRETARY OF STATE

VOL. III—1728 TO 1734

RALEIGH
P M HALE, PRINTER TO THE STATE
1886

PRESSES OF E. M. UZZELL,
RALEIGH, N. C.

PREFATORY NOTES TO THIRD VOLUME

The third volume covers the period from the surrender of the Lords Proprietors to the end of Burrington's administration as Royal Governor, almost six years in duration

For more than two years of this period Sir Richard Everard was Governor, being allowed by the Crown to hold over until his successor under the new *régime* was ready to enter upon the discharge of his duties. During this time the Legislature met only once, in November, 1729, and enacted a number of laws, the originals of which, with all the endorsements thereon, are now preserved in the office of the Secretary of State in Raleigh The validity of these laws being called in question, as it was recited in the enacting clauses that they were passed by authority of the Lords Proprietors, the matter was referred to the Attorney-General and Solicitor-General of the Crown, and they declared them to be null and void In spite of this, however, they were regularly brought forward as valid in all of our Revisals.

On the 25th February, 1731, Burrington, who had just arrived in the colony, took the oaths of office as Governor before the Council, assembled in Edenton, and his administration terminated on the 12th November, 1734, when in the same town he received a proclamation announcing that his successor, Gabriel Johnston, had arrived at Cape Fear and qualified according to law His first Legislature met on 13th April, 1731, the second on 3d July, 1733, and the third and last on the 5th November, 1734

Historians have fallen into grave errors in regard to Governor Burrington The minutes of the last meeting of the Council held before Governor Johnston's arrival, so far as now appears, record the fact that on the 15th April, 1734, Nathaniel Rice being the oldest Councillor, took upon him the administration of the government in consequence of the departure of Governor Burrington from the province, and upon this testimony alone it would seem the historians have assumed that he left America as well and returned to England. They go on to state, also, but upon what evidence is not known, that he ended his life in a drunken brawl in the Bird-cage walk in St. James's Park in London, and the impression is created that his disgraceful death occurred soon after his return to London. The statement is certainly untrue in several material points. For example, instead of leaving America, he was in North Carolina and on duty as Governor on 1st June, 1734, and from that date until 12th November following, when he and the Legislature then in session received notice of Governor Johnston's arrival. Precisely when he returned to England does not appear, but from an entry in the Journal of the Board of Trade, it appears he was there on the 10th June, 1735. Other entries and letters show that he was in frequent communication with the Board from that time until December, 1736, after which date no reference is made to him by the Board.

Reliable evidence concerning him, however, is to be found in a manuscript volume of records in the office of the Secretary of State at Raleigh, in the shape of a copy of his last will and testament and of the probate, from which it appears that the will was made on the 8th December, 1750, and that administration with the will annexed was granted on 23d March, 1759. As the record states that the sole executor named in the will died before the testator, and does not state that the administration was *de bonis non*, the inference is that Burrington on the 23d March, 1759, had been dead but a short while. If, therefore, his statement made in 1732, that he had "served the Crown in every reign since the abdication of King James" was true he must have been a very old man at the time of his death, somewhere near eighty years old, a fact that does not seem consistent either with a drunken life or a violent death in even an occasional midnight orgy away from home.

———

Burrington's administration as Royal Governor was a stormy one in spite of the bright auspices under which it began. Welcomed with open arms and the greatest demonstrations of joy on his arrival, ninety days had not elapsed before he was in open collision, not only with the Lower House of Assembly, representing the people, but with the Chief-Justice, the Attorney-General, the Judge of the Court of Admiralty, the Secretary of the Province and the members of the Council or Upper House, all of whom were appointees and representatives of the Crown

The Chief-Justice he declared to be an ungrateful, perfidious scoundrel and an egregious sot, whose father was a smuggler and whose mother was a woman of a poor, mean family; the Attorney-General, he said, did not know law enough to be clerk to a Justice of the Peace, and was besides a man of innumerable villanies, the Secretary of the Province made it his whole business to create mischief, and attended neither the Council nor his office, and finally sought to murder him; the Judge of the Court of Admiralty was an infamous character, another member of the Council was an ungrateful villain, and still another was a disgrace to it. Nor was he less sparing in his denunciation of the Lower House of Assembly.

In some of his many quarrels the issues involved were of a purely personal character, in others they grew out of differences of opinion as to matters of public policy, but whatever the cause every difference with him resulted in a quarrel. He could tolerate no opinion that was not in accord with his own and deemed every one a personal enemy, if not a villain, who differed with him

The result of it all was that the Assembly would, as he wrote to the Board of Trade, "never pass one of the acts required or recommended in the King's Instruction nor of his proposing."

The mode of disposing of vacant lands, the powers of the Associate Justices of the Supreme Court, the regulation of fees of public officers, the provisions proper to a bill for a rent-roll for the Crown, the right to appoint clerks to the Assembly, to appoint the Public Treasurer, to create new precincts or counties with right of representation in the Lower House of Assembly, and to fix the rate of exchange, were all causes of serious difference and quarrel at one time or another within two years after his administration began. The right to create new precincts or counties he strenuously insisted belonged solely to him and the Council. The Lower House, on the contrary, quite as strenuously refused to admit members claiming to represent precincts thus formed until they had also received legislative sanction. To admit the right of the Governor and Council thus to introduce new members at will into the Lower House, would be, it was said, to put the whole government into the hands of the Governor and Council and to strip the people of all authority and control.

In the matter of the rent roll there were two points especially that never failed to provoke trouble. 1 How the rents were to be paid whether in certain productions of the country, and if so, at what price should they be rated, or in specie or currency, and if in currency, at what rate of exchange. 2 Where the rents were to be paid whether on the land or at places to be named by the agent of the Crown. The Governor insisted that these points should be settled in favor of the Crown, while the Assembly insisted upon its right to settle them as might be most conducive to the interests and convenience of the people. In the matter of public officers' fees, also, there was a wide difference of opinion, each side insisting upon its right to fix the currency in which they should be paid and the rate of exchange, or value, at which it should be taken.

Burrington was removed from office by the Lords Proprietors, and upon the intimation that he would be sent back to the province by the Crown, a paper was presented to the Board of Trade entitled "The case of the inhabitants of North Carolina in respect to Mr George Burrington's being reappointed their Governor," in which a most earnest protest was made against his appointment, based mainly upon the affidavits supporting a petition for his removal as Proprietary Governor. These affidavits, if true, show him to have been violent and lawless, both in speech and action, and given to excessive drink. The protest goes on to say, also, that he had been heard to declare that if ever he got to North Carolina as Governor again he would be the destruction of all those who aided in his removal. This paper, it would seem, was prepared in London.

On the other hand, after his removal by the Proprietors, the Lower House of the General Assembly, John Baptista Ashe being Speaker, made a formal address to the Lords Proprietors asking for his restora-

tion to the colony as its Governor, and declaring him to have been always
zealous for its welfare, on his return, too, to the colony as Royal Governor, the first grand jury that met for the whole province drew up a
formal address to the Crown in which they lauded in the highest terms
Burrington's mildness, his humanity and his tenderness to all sorts of
people, and his great impartiality in the administration of justice, and his
generous example in forgetting private differences.   The first Legislature,
too, that met after his return to the colony presented an address to the
Crown declaring that as Proprietary Governor he had rendered himself
very agreeable to the people by the great care he then shewed in his due
administration of justice and in promoting the welfare of the province,
and that his indefatigable industry and the hardships he underwent in
carrying on the settlement at Cape Fear deserved their thankful remembrance   This address was signed by Edward Moseley as Speaker   And
yet, in less than two weeks this kind-hearted, generous, mild-tempered
Governor was denouncing the Legislature in the strongest terms, comparing its members to thieves, and all because the Lower House of Assembly had passed and sent him the following resolutions

" Whereas, By the Royal Charter granted by King Charles the Second
to the Lords Proprietors of Carolina it is granted that the Inhabitants of
this Province shall have, possess and enjoy all Libertys, Franchises and
Privileges as are held, possest and enjoyed in the Kingdom of England
And Whereas it is the undoubted Right and Privilege of the People of
England that they shall not be taxed or made lyable to pay any sum or
sums of Money or Fees other than such as are by law established.   Notwithstanding which it appears by complaint made in most parts of this
Province that the Officers in General do demand take and receive from
the Inhabitants and Masters of Vessells trading to this Province four
times more than the Fees appointed by the Laws of this Province to the
great Discouragement of the Trade of this Province and the Oppression
of the People

" Resolved, That this House do wait on the Governor with this complaint and that the Council be desired to joyn with this House in requesting His Excellency to issue a Proclamation declaring such practices to be

contrary to Law and an Oppression of the subjects and strictly forbidding all officers to take larger Fees than is by Law appointed under pretence of difference of money untill such time as the officers' Fees shall be regulated by authority of Assembly, this House now having the same under consideration pursuant to His Majesty's Instructions."

Not content with abuse of its members, Burrington prorogued the Legislature from time to time, and finally dissolved it, so that there was not another session for more than two years

But the plan of governing without a Legislature by no means softened the temper of either Governor or Legislature, for in the next Legislature that met the committee appointed to draw up a reply to the Governor's speech at the opening declared the country to be laboring under oppression and perversion of justice, and specified as instances thereof that the Governor made himself the arbiter in his own quarrels, that he used force to gain possession of goods he claimed from one person, that he burnt the house of another to gain possession of land he wanted, that when attempts were made by due course of law to recover satisfaction therefor from him the Chief-Justice and his assistants gave judgment that the party injured by the Governor had no relief in their court, and, at the Governor's instigation, sought to prevent him from seeking relief elsewhere by imprisonment, excessive bail and refusing to read his petition wherein his grievances were shown that persons upon the least displeasure were called two hundred miles away to answer to trifles, that fees were unaccountably multiplied in all cases that people were turned out of their lands by those who had no right to them, that none were permitted to take up lands, though they were ready to comply with the Royal Instructions, unless they paid the Governor 2s 6d silver money for every fifty acres, a demand warranted neither by the laws of the province nor the Royal Instructions, that free people were taken up by magistrates and placed in a state of servitude little inferior to bondage, that, in short all the laws of the province were in a manner disregarded, all the courts of justice in a manner stopped, and that injustice, oppression and arbitrary rule almost overran the whole province

His reply, prompt and decided, came in the shape of a peremptory summons to the Assembly to attend him at once in the Council Chamber, where he straightway dissolved them, telling them that they had artfully and falsely represented his administration as grievous and oppressive, that certain people had "sought to pursue their own Malice and Envy under the Umbrage of an Assembly", that Burgessing had been for some years a source of lies and occasion of disturbances; that although he had offered to appoint a day for hearing charges against the Chief-Justice, the Lower House of Assembly on a sudden heat, the day before, had insolently presumed, by their Sergeant, to take him into custody for a pretended contempt, that they had also taken into custody the Receiver of the Powder Money for Roanoke Port, who had his orders not to make up any account save before the Governor in Council, that they had refused to obey the King's instructions concerning the payment of Quit Rents, and had denied they were due in any money save that of their own making, that they had offered but three bills, one so inconsiderable as not to be worth mentioning, and another that he had recommended to them, so clogged with clauses that they knew he could not assent to it, that when he proposed to them to relieve British vessels from paying powder money duty, they passed a bill exempting all vessels, and finally that they had refused to admit several members—the members from the so-called new precincts—legally chosen and returned by the proper officers, thus denying the undoubted right of the King never before contested

The next Legislature met on 6th November, 1734, but before he had time to raise an issue with it his administration came to an end

But whatever may have been the opinion of others, in his own opinion, Burrington was a man who deserved exceedingly well, both of the colony and the Crown   He said he had "served the Crown in every reign since the Abdication of King James and always was allowed to behave as a man of Honour", and that when he first came to the colony he found the inhabitants few and poor—in fact, that North Carolina was little known or mentioned before he was Governor for the Proprietors; that he took all methods to induce people to come from other countries to settle there and put himself to very great charges in making new settlements in several parts of the government, in which he succeeded according to his expectation, that the Cape Fear settlement cost him a great sum of money and infinite trouble, that during his first winter there he endured all the hardships that could happen to a man destitute of a house to live in, a hundred miles from a neighbor, in a pathless country, and obliged to have all provisions brought by sea at great charges to support the men there in his pay, that he took soundings in the inlets, bars and rivers in the province four different times, that he discovered and made known the channels of Cape Fear River and Beaufort or Topsail Inlet, before unused and unknown, that in his many journeyings by land and by water he often ran the hazard of drowning and starving, and never received any reward therefor save the thanks of two Assemblies in the province, not even his salary for the time he was Governor The character and value of his personal efforts for the development of the country, however, do not depend upon his own testimony alone, for they were formally acknowledged by the Assembly and by private individuals as well In an address to Governor Johnston, certain inhabitants of Bertie and Edgecombe precincts declared that no living man could have taken more pains and endured more fatigue than Burrington did to acquaint himself with the province in general, as his many journeys on foot in the backwoods would prove sometimes accompanied by one man only, pinched with hunger, even in danger of perishing, having but one biscuit to live on for three days, sometimes nearly naked, two hundred miles from the place he set out from, often carrying with him considerable sums of money and disposing of it to poor people to encourage them and enable them to settle the backwoods

On his return to England, he petitioned the King for the payment of the arrears of his salary and for re-imbursement for his expenditures, in having surveys and drafts made of the ports and harbors, which surveys and drafts were made under instructions from the King and sent to the Board of Trade Had he stopped there he might possibly have gotten his money, but the temptation to get another fling at his enemies was more than he could resist and he repeated the old, oft-told story of his grievances and asked that the conduct of his adversaries be examined into in order to his restoration to Royal favor Taking advantage of this, the King, at the suggestion and upon the advice of his Privy Council, dismissed the petition as being very irregular and of such a nature as could not properly receive any determination in the Privy Council

If what he says of himself be true, Burrington was indeed an exceedingly ill-used man, for, among other things, according to his statement, the Chief-Justice, the Attorney-General and the Secretary of the province, attempted to assassinate him by shooting him with a pistol, and his life was only saved by the interposition of some courageous men who came to his assistance The conspiracy to murder him was, he believed, set on foot in England, because authentic accounts of the assault upon him sent to the Board of Trade were not treated with any consideration Indictments being found against his would-be murderers, they fled by night and hid themselves in Virginia, where they remained until Governor Johnston landed in North Carolina On their return, Governor Johnston immediately distinguished the assassins with his favor, every one of them being placed in some employment.

On the other hand, as has been said, if a tithe of what his enemies said about Burrington be true, the wonder is that he got away from the colony alive, and not that an attempt was made to kill him

What, then, in view of all the facts, is the real character of Burrington? The seemingly respectful consideration given to him and to his opinions by the Board of Trade after his return to England, is by no means consistent with the theory that he was a mere drunken brawler whom they had just displaced for grave malfeasance in office His official papers, too, relating to the province, those at least unconnected with his quarrels, are well written and show an intimate knowledge of the country and the measures best adapted to promote its development Considered alone, indeed, they would present him as an active, intelligent, progressive ruler But they cannot be considered alone, and he stands out, therefore, as a man of ability, but utterly disqualified by grievous faults for the position he occupied. And yet he was a wiser ruler than his predecessor, Everard, and possessed no more faults, he was, too, to say the least, as wise as his successor, Gabriel Johnston, and no more arbitrary Certain it is, too, that the province under his administration continued to flourish and greatly prosper, both in wealth and population

It may be that Burrington was hampered by his instructions from the Crown, and that no Governor could have carried them out and kept the peace with a people who, as he said, were subtle and crafty to admiration, who could be neither outwitted nor cajoled, who always behaved insolently to their Governors, who maintained that their money could not be taken from them save by appropriations made by their own House of Assembly, a body that had always usurped more power than they ought to be allowed, with a people, in a word, who well knew their rights and dared to assert them to the full. This was, in substance, evidently the opinion of the sagacious, as well as humorous, Colonel Byrd, of Virginia, for on the 20th July, 1731, he wrote to Governor Burrington, saying: "I think, by some samples I have known of that country [North Carolina], it would cost a pretty deal of trouble to bring it into order, and a less spirit than yours will never be able to effect it. People accustomed to live without law or gospel will with great Reluctance Submit to either * * * * In the meantime I wish you all the success in the world in bringing the chaos into form and reducing that Anarchy into a regular Government. In so doing you will deserve to have your statue erected or, which perhaps is better, to have your salary doubled." But the event proved that not even Burrington's "spirit" was equal to the task of reducing North Carolina to what he and Byrd considered good order and regular government, and that unhappy Burrington got neither statue nor double salary—indeed, no salary at all.

The task was, perhaps, an impossible one, and in passing judgment upon those to whom its execution was entrusted we ought, at least, to bear in mind the difficulties in the way of its accomplishment.

The transfer of the province from the Lords Proprietors to the Crown brought about little or no change in the practical machinery of the government and no change whatever in the rights of the people, for those rights depended, not upon the will of the Proprietors nor upon that of the Crown, but upon the well-known charters of King Charles the Second. But the administration of Burrington as the first Royal Governor marks so plainly a new departure in the history of the province, that a brief view of its condition at that time may be not without interest or use as a guide in making up an opinion as to the subsequent progress of the province

The province was divided into counties, precincts and parishes, with a population of not less than 40,000 black and white, lying to the eastward of a line between the towns of Weldon and Fayetteville of the present day. The counties were two in number, divided into thirteen precincts, as follows:

1. Albemarle county, into six precincts, viz. Chowan, Perquimans, Currituck, Pasquotank, Bertie and Edgecombe

2. Bath county, divided into seven precincts, viz. Beaufort, Bladen, Carteret, Craven, Hyde, New Hanover and Onslow

Each precinct was a parish also, with a vestry and church-wardens clothed with power to raise money by poll tax not exceeding five shillings in currency on a tithable to maintain the poor and pay preachers

In the Executive department of the government there were a Governor, Council, Secretary of the Province, Receiver-General for the collection of rents due the Crown, a Surveyor-General and an Attorney-General. The power to prorogue and dissolve Legislatures and to veto their acts strengthened the hands of the Executive beyond measure almost

In the Judicial department were the Supreme Court for the province, called the General Court, consisting of a Chief-Justice and Associate Justices, and Precinct Courts that met quarterly, one for each precinct, consisting of Justices of the Peace appointed for the purpose by the Governor and Council, with power to try all personal actions under fifty pounds, to act as Orphans' Courts, appoint guardians, take securities, &c. In the General Court were combined the powers of the King's Bench, Common Pleas and Exchequer in England. The Chief-Justice and Associate Justices, together with the principal officers of the province, sat also as a Court of Oyer and Terminer and Gaol delivery. Chancery jurisdiction was vested in the Governor and Council. A list of jurors for each precinct was made up by the Assembly and the names put in a box, to be drawn at the ending of each court, by a child, for the next court. The duties since performed by sheriffs were then performed by a marshal and his deputies. There were magistrates, also, appointed by the Governor

The Legislature consisted of an Upper House, composed of the members of the Council, and a Lower House, composed of representatives from the precincts, and one each from the towns of Bath, Edenton and New Bern, the precincts in Albemarle sending five representatives each and those in Bath sending two each. The only tax imposed by the Legislature was one of five shillings in currency on each tithable, and a duty of 3s 4d per ton on vessels for powder money, as it was called, intended but not always used for pilotage and buoying out the inlets and channels. This duty was first payable in powder, shot and flints, and its purpose was to supply the demand for ammunition then so greatly needed in the conflicts with the Indians. All males not slaves, over sixteen years of age, and all slaves, whether male or female, over sixteen years of age, were tithables. There was no fixed time for the election of members of the Legislature then as now, but they were elected at such time as pleased the Governor and held office at his will, for even after they met and organized he could prorogue them at will from time to time, or might dissolve them and order a new election, if to him it seemed good. It would seem, too, that a minority had not even the power to adjourn from day to day, a prorogation by the Governor being the expedient resorted to when a minority only was present and wished to adjourn.

The currency of the province outstanding during Burrington's second administration was estimated to be £40,000, issued under an act of Assembly passed in 1729. £10,000 were set apart to be exhausted for old bills then current and the other £30,000 were distributed to the several precinct treasurers, to be let out on loan on land security, such a part of the principal with interest to be repaid annually as would sink the whole in fifteen years. There were treasurers for the province also, elected, like those for the precincts, by the Legislature.

There was a militia system also, that provided for the organization of the able-bodied men into companies and regiments. But there were neither arms, ammunition nor fortifications.

The laying out of new roads, building of new bridges, and the repair of old ones, were also provided for

---

The products of the country were tar, pitch, rosin, tobacco, indigo, rice, Indian corn, English wheat, beans, peas, flax, cotton, &c Horses, cattle, hogs and poultry were abundant, at least in the older settlements, being easily and cheaply raised Sheep, too, were raised, though perhaps not in such great numbers It was estimated that 50,000 fat hogs were driven to Virginia every year, and 10,000 fat beef cattle Pork and beef in barrels were also shipped to Virginia and elsewhere in large quantities by water But abundant as were the products of the province then, as for many years afterward, they were all needed, the surplus at least, for the purchase of negroes and "British commodities"

Saw-mills also were being put up for carrying on a trade in boards and sawed timber

---

The trade of the province was confined to New England and Virginia West India goods, sugar, molasses, rum, salt, &c , came from New England in small sloops of less than fifty tons, that went about from river to river, and for return cargoes carried back such things as could not be conveniently transported to Virginia—that is to say, the great bulk of the produce. Great complaint was made of this traffic, especially that good wheat was carried away and bad flour brought back New England rum, too, was by no means as palatable, and perhaps not as wholesome, as that of Jamaica "British commodities," as they were called, were brought from Virginia by land or in canoes in small quantities at unreasonable rates, but the bulk of the cloth used in the country whether cotton, linen or woollen, was made at home, each plantation, or at least each neighborhood, supplying its own needs from its own products and its own labor, the housewives of the country being very proficient in such matters. The staple article of this domestic manufacture was, doubtless, the cloth known as "homespun," a mixture of cotton and wool "British commodities" were so called because they were goods permitted by the British Navigation Laws to be carried into the colonies only in British vessels and from British ports, and included all articles "of ye growth, production, or manufacture of Europe, except salt for ye fishery of New England and Newfoundland, wines of the growth of Maderas or Western Islands or Azores servants and horses from Scotland and Ireland." A British vessel, in the meaning of the statute, was one built or owned in England, Ireland or one of the colonies, and owned wholly by the people thereof and navigated with the master and three-fourths of the mariners of the said places. Smuggling was an inevitable consequence of such legislation, and all along the Atlantic coast it was carried on whenever opportunity offered for doing so without too great risk of detection, and carried on, too, doubtless, without any feeling that it involved a violation of moral obligation, and looking with modern eyes upon the British Navigation Laws of early colonial days, it would be strict judgment to hold that an evasion of them by the colonists did involve the violation of any moral obligation.

The collection districts were five in number, and nominally, at least, covered the entire coast line of the colony, viz. Currituck, without any fixed place for a port of entry, Roanoke with Edenton for a port, Bath on the Pamlico, Beaufort at Topsail Inlet, and Brunswick on the Cape Fear. The towns of Bath and Edenton being far from the sea and the Currituck district having no fixed port, and there being many islands and rivers between them and the inlets, abundant opportunity was given to masters of vessels to unload goods before they saw the collectors and to take in produce after they were cleared. Of course masters of vessels did not fail to take advantage of the facilities for smuggling offered by the North Carolina coast and sounds, and great quantities of North Carolina tobacco were exported by the New England skippers without paying duty. Virginia tobacco was also sent to North Carolina and disposed of in the same way. The following is given as an instance of the way in which smuggling was carried on. In 1734 a ship loaded with French wines, brandy, tea woollen and other prohibited commodities, came in at Ocracok, and in the harbour there transferred the cargo to vessels belonging to the country, in which they were carried through Pamlico and Albemarle Sounds into Virginia and there delivered to merchants of that colony. Great search was made for the goods, but in vain The New England skippers were the chief smugglers, but Virginia and North Carolina were beneficiaries and participants also in the traffic

Virginia does not seem to have been a very favorite market with North Carolina traders Great complaint was made of the inspection law there, under which much of the tobacco was burned as unmerchantable, and of undue advantage taken by the Virginia purchasers of the Carolina drovers in the matter of charges for butchering Of course, too, complaint was made of the prices demanded for the wares the Virginia traders had for sale

There seems to be little doubt that the planters of North Carolina, and planting was almost the only occupation there, were at a great disadvantage, not only in selling, but in buying as well, even to the loss of half their goods, it was said Governor Burrington was strongly of this opinion, and constantly urged upon the government at home that the only way to put the trade of the province on a right footing was to settle a custom-house at Ocacock Island, at the south end of which he said there was sufficient water for any merchantman to come in and a secure harbour On the island was a hill, on which a small fort would command the bar, channel and harbour, and if a custom-house were settled there a town would soon grow up and serve as a depot and distributing point for a large direct trade, the goods to be sent from there to the interior in small vessels to all places not depending on the Cape Fear River for their trade, and, in a word, be the port for the Collection Districts of Roanoke, Currituck and Bath Town, create a direct trade with England, put an end to the peddling carried on by the Virginians and New Englanders and bring in ships-loads of negroes that, being much needed by the planters, could be sold well.

Something did indeed need to be done, for English goods that had been bought for 6d. would buy a bushel of wheat and a bushel and a half of corn, and similar goods that had been bought for 18d. would buy a barrel of tar

The Indians were much reduced in numbers and lived within the English settlements on reservations specially set apart for them and secure

from the attacks of foreign Indians.   There were six tribes of them, to-
wit the Mattamuskeets, the Pottasketes, the Chowans, the Tuscaroras
and the Meherrins   Of these not one nation exceeded twenty families,
except the Tuscaroras, who numbered about two hundred fighting men
These Indians were generally peaceable and quiet, though there were occasional acts of hostility between them and the Catawba Indians in hunting
on the upper parts of Cape Fear River, which the white people rather
considered to their advantage, as hostilities with their own race tended to
make the Indians keep the peace with the whites

————

Of course all roads in the northern counties, if not all in the colony,
led to Virginia, the general point of convergence being on the Nansemond River, at or near where the town of Suffolk is situated   Going
southward from Albemarle, the route was from Edenton across the sound
to Mackey's Point, some ten miles below Plymouth, a distance of about
nine miles, thence to Bath, thence across the Pamplico River, and across
the Neuse to New Bern, and thence to Wilmington   From Edenton to
Wilmington the distance, as the road ran, was near two hundred miles,
with three long ferries to cross.   To compel northern members to go to
Wilmington was a great hardship, as it was also to compel southern
members to go to Edenton   Hence the Assemblies came to meet at Bath,
as a half-way house, and then at New Bern.   Indeed, a strong effort was
made to establish the permanent seat of government at Bath, not contem-
plating, as it were, any extension of the settlement to the westward   But
try as much as might be, it was found impossible to make a town at
Bath, although it was the first chartered town in the colony

COLONIAL RECORDS.

1728.

[B. P R O Proprieties. B. T Vol. 12. No 94. R]

LETTER FROM THE SURVEYOR OF NORTH CAROLINA TO THE BOARD TRANSMITTING SEVERAL PUBLICK PAPERS

12 Dec 1728

RIGHT HONOBLE

The long contested affair of the Boundary between the Province of Carolina and his Majestys Colony of Virginia having been settled and the Line Run and Finished in October last by Commissioners appointed by either Governments pursuant to His Majestys Royall Instructions As Secretary of the Province of North Carolina I transmitted home to the Lords Proprietors the Journals of our Commissioners proceedings whilst upon the Service with a plan of the Boundary as it was agreed to by all the Commissioners on both sides which I had no sooner done than we had the joyfull news that their Lordships had surrenderd their Province to His Majesty which was received here with the most universal Satisfaction and their Governor Sir Richard Everard by his Weakness and Indiscretion had Run us unto the utmost confusion and Disorder and Rendered the Administration Contemptable and Odious to allmost every Person in the Government, but as that will be Represented to his Majesty by the Council of the Province I shall not Presume to trouble your Ldps further than to acquaint you that I have (as I am told it is a Duty now to Do) sent to your Lordps Duplicates of the Journals of of Commissioners proceedings and a Copy of the Plan which were before sent to the Lords Proprietors that if necessary they may be laid before his Majesty   I am

      Right Honoble
        Your Lordships most Obedient
        very humble Servant

              JOHN LOVICK

[B P R O PROPRIETIES B T VOL. 12—REFERRED TO IN PRECEDING LETTER]

To the Kings most Excell' Majesty

The humble Address of the Members of Councill for the Province of North Carolina

SACRED SIR

As it is with the greatest Pleasure we Receive the Notice of Your Majestys having taken this Government under Your Immediate direction, Wee humbly begg leave in the Most Dutyfull manner to Address Your Majesty on this Happy and Joyfull occasion and thus early to assure You that we as well as the People in General are intirely Devoted to Your Royall Person and Most Illustrious Family Whom God Long Preserve

And being indulged to have this access to Your Majesty we begg Leave in the humblest manner to lay before You the state of this Unhappy Province which thô of small Accompt in Respect of some others, Yet of late is very much Improved, And we have the pleasing Prospect from that Support of Authority and the Encouragement of our Trade and Commerce which we Promise ourselves now Your Majesty has taken us under Your Care that it will soon become a Flourishing Colony and Beneficial to the Crown

This Change could not have been at a more happy Juncture for us then under the Reign of a Prince beloved as the Common Father of all his Subjects and at a time when the Government here was grown so weak & Feeble that without this alteration it could not have subsisted much longer but must have Dwindled and sunk into the utmost Confusion and Disorder, and we cannot attribute the Cause of it to any thing but the great Incapacity and Weakness of our present Governor Sir Richard Everard whose Behaviour is so extraordinary that every Day Produces some Extravagant action   And it is with the greatest Sorrow we are obliged to tell Your Majesty that we Feel Oppression and Arbitrary Power, notwithstanding we have so Mild, so Gracious and so Just a Sovereign, but we assure Ourselves of Redress from Your Majesty's Known Clemency & Indulgence to all Your People, and that you will not suffer a Person to Preside over us, who has no other Notions of Government than as it gives him Power to Act as he Pleases, which bad Principles, producing as bad Actions, we must humbly Beseech Your Majesty to suffer us to Represent to You some few Instances of them

The first thing we shall begg to mention is his manner of Treating the Councill whom he frequently takes the Liberty to Abuse while sitting,

If he proposes any thing let it be ever so unreasonable or Unwarrantable it must be done and if we with the utmost good manners tell him we cannot approve of it or shew him ever so clearly that it is not Lawfull for us to Comply with him, or the injuries that would follow if we suffered many things to pass that he would have done then we are sure of having the worst of Language with threats of what he will do with us and after that he generally Leaves the Board and the Business Let it be what it will unfinished, and if any of the Officers venture to tell him of this strange Behaviour, they are sure to meet with the same ill Treatment having Quarelled with every of them purely because they wont come into his unjustifyable Measures

He ventures to make for himself what Fees he thinks proper (thö there is a Table of Fees Established by Law) and Notwithstanding the Assembly as well as the people in General having complained of his Exacting Exorbitant Fees, Yet he still continues in Defiance of Our Laws & Declared not long since (in Open Court) that he did not regard the Laws of the Country at all   It is unexpressable the Daily Quarrels that happen about his Family which seems to make of more weight then the most Important Affairs of Government, and if he fancies any one is not affected to him or his Family (which is a pack of rude Children who give offence every Day) they are sure upon the least occasion to be severely prosecuted as very lately happened to a Young Gent here who having disgusted one of the young ones the Governor took out an Action of Scandall against him and laid the Damage for Five Thousand Pounds Sterling, and gave Strict Orders to the Officer to put him into the Common Goal unless Extraordinary good Security was found, and withall gave out menacing Speeches, That he would see who dare be the Gent's Bail which Frightened many but to Prevent the Committing of so harsh a thing, the Secretary & Attorney General at last after they had in Vain Remonstrated the matter to the Governor, became Bail for the Gent, and thereby drew the Governor's heaviest Resentment upon them; After this the Governor would have this very business Examined in Councill, and after wee had Examined very narrowly into it, we found it only a very Idle Story of one of the Children and begg'd the Governor to Drop it, but he held the poor Gent to Bail till our General Court sat and then had not one word to say to it, Beside this way of Oppressing People who are so unfortunate as to fall under any of his Family's displeasure, he has found a New Method of setting up a Sort of Inquisition and when any one is noted down for an Offender the Governor Issues his Orders or Warrant for the Servants of the Person to attend at his own house, where they are Interrogated upon Oath before him and his Lady,

(and if they Boggle at the Oath they are threatened with the Goal) and
the General Questions are what they have heard their Master or Mistress
at any time say of the Governor and his Family which thõ it has hitherto amounted only to Trifling talk, yet Prosecutions has been ordered
from these examinations, and if such a Practice is not stop'd the Consequence may prove very fatall, It being a sure way to Lead Servants
into Perjury upon the least Disgust with their Masters and indeed it was
so much dreaded that one of the Councill undertook to advise the Governor against such a Wonderfull Proceeding, as what would not only
greatly Expose him but was against the usage of English Men, for which
the Gent in Return was Assaulted by the Governor and reĉed the most
injurious Language that could be uttered At other times when he has
puzled himself with these Family Disputes and Jarrs he sends his
Coõands to the Chief Justice to Commit or bind over or whatever first
comes into his head, and if the Chief Justice lets him know he cannot
Lawfully obey him, then the Judge is immediately threatened with the
Goal, & Suspension and is sure to have the most opprobious Language,
and if it happens that any thing is brought into Court that concerns even
the meanest of his Servants, he is sure to be present, and if the Court
will not act just in the manner he would have them, he immediately puts
on a face, and lets them know he is Governor, and will protest against
their Proceedings and then Affronts and Abuses them upon the Bench,
which exceedingly discourages the Court, and Spirits on others to do the
like and Weakens their Authority and greatly Obstructs the Adminis-
tring of Justice, as very lately there being a Miscreant prosecuted here
for Cursing Your Sacred Majesty and Traduceing Your Governm', upon
whose Tryall the Governor suffered his Son (as Profligate a Creature as
the Criminal) to be of Councill for him, when just as the Judge was
going to pronounce Sentance against the offender and was telling him
the heinousness of his Crime the Governor Rush'd into Court and
Pretending he had Business of His Own, Interrupted the Judge and
menaced the Court for not breaking off the Business they were upon, to
hear him, this instance we should not have been so particular in, if we
had not the most convincing reasons before to believe he had not that
Duty and Affection for Your Majesty and Your Most August House,
that all Good Subjects ought to have for he has had the Weakness as
well as the Wickedness to Boast of his being concerned (tho not Publickly Known) in the Preston Rebellion, and it has been with some Difficulty he has been prevented from signalizing the Tenth of June with
us, and on the much Lamented News of the Death of Our most Gracious

Sovereign Your Royall Father of Glorious Memory he with the greatest Exultation said upon it with an Oath Then Adieu to the Hannover Family we have done with them

We have many things more to Offer, but dare not presume to take up more of Your Majesty's time only to Beseech You, Great Sir, to consider our Miserable State, and to Relieve us from a Governor so incapable of doing Right and so altogether undeserving Your Royall Favour and Countenance.

J LOVICK	ROBERT WEST	W\" REED
THO\' HARVEY	R. SANDERSON	J WORLEY
THO\' POLLOCK	JN* PALIN	FFRAN FFOSTER
EDM\' GALE	C GALE	

Dated at the Secretary's office in N° Carolina Decem\" 12\" 1728

1729.

[B. P R O Proprieties B T Vol. 12 R 103.]

A DECLARATION BY S\" RICHARD EVERARD BART JANY 6\" 1728-9.

In Order to Convince mankind and in particular y* Inhabitants of this Province whereof I am Govern\" y* all unhappy misund\'standings & dissencons between me and the Members of Assembly and other Gent. of good note within this Government I do hereby in the most solemn manner Acknowledge to be owing to the Calumnies & false informacons given me by Chr Gale John Lovick, and W\" Little Esq\" at my arrival here & trusting too much to the Characters they gave me of Several Gent here I find those Gent the reverse \Psons of great Probity and much Sincerity This being the principal occasion of all former misunderstandings I beg as such it may be attributed and further if any Act of Governm\" since my Adm\"\" has in the least proved pernicious or detrimental to the Welfare or Repose of this Province I do hereby declare to the World it has been owing to the Advice of Gale Lovick and Little the only enemies to the Repose and quiet of this People and as they have

been so ever Since they have been in the Country their Advice for the
future shall never be regarded by

RICHARD EVERARD

Jan⁷ 6 1728-9

(Endorsed)
North Carolina
Copy of the Declaration of S⁸ Ric⁴ Everard present Deputy Gov' of North Carolina Dated 6ᵗʰ Jan⁷
1728-9 owning his having been imposed on by Mʳ
Lovick the Sec⁷ Mʳ Gale Chief Justice and Mʳ Little Attorney Gen¹

Rec̄ed from Cap' Burrington

[B. P. R. O. North Carolina Vol. 5 p 279]

To the Kings Most Excellent Majestie
The Humble Memorial of the Lords Proprietors of Carolina
Sheweth

That about twelve months agoe your Memorialists (after a treaty)
Humbly proposed to Surrender to your Majestie all their right and interest in the said Province as Lords Prop⁰ʳˢ thereof for Twenty five thousand pounds

That your Memorialists laid their several titles before Your Majesties
Attorney and Soll' General in July last and a Conveyance has been prepared with a covenant therein from your Memorialists that they should
consent to An Act of Parliament and they have for some time been in
daily expectation of having their Surrender accepted and purchase money
paid But they are now to their great surprise toll'd this can't be done till
an an Act is first obtained

That some of your Memorialists have been detained In town to attend
to attend this affair much to their prejudice and the Inhabitants and
State of the said province greatly suffers from the present unsettled condition thereof

These proceedings Your Memorialists humbly take leave to represent
to your Majestie and that every days delay is not only an hardship to
them but to all your Majesties Subjects in the said province

Wherefore they humbly pray your Majestie will be pleased in such manner as in your Royal Wisdom you shall Judge most expedient either to direct a a Surrender to be forthwith accepted from your Memorialists on payment of the Consideration mony or to give leave that your Memorialists may have the full & free exercise of all the powers granted by your Royal Predecessor King Charles the Second

All which is most Humbly submitted to your Majesties Royal Wisdom & Goodnes

---

[B. P R. O America & W Ind No. 592.]

19ᵗʰ Janⁿ 1728-9

Sir,

To-morrow Morning I must wait upon your Honour, for an Answer to the Lords Propⁿ of Carolina's Memˡ I've been the means (under the Direction of my Lord Westmoreland) of bringing, in a great measure, the Contract to bear so far, and will do every thing, an honest man can do, to Mollify the Propⁿ But indeed they think themselves ill used   I was the first that set the Notion on foot for obstructing the Spanish Plate Fleet in the Gulf of Florida, and the Drafts I have are the only ones to be depended on   I will bring them along with me to shew them yʳ Honour   I drew up the reasons justify the Prudence of the Ministers in purchasing the country as Mʳ Henry Pelham and 14 more of the House of Commons know, a copy of wᶜʰ I will present your Honour with   I would willingly in this Affair unite Zeal for the Publick Interest and Fidelity to my Principaly   I am with the greatest respect
    Sir,
     Your Honour's
      Most Obedient and
       most faithfull humble
       Servant
         THO LOWNDES

[B P R. O Proprieties. B. T Vol 12 R. 106.]

MAY IT PLEASE YOUR GRACE

Whilst I have the honour of bearing the Office of Judge of Admiralty in this Province, I think it my Duty to make Information of all such things as are manifestly prejudicial to His Majesty, It is for this reason that I humbly offer these few lines, and to Inclose to yoʳ Grace the Copy of an Original Order signed by Sir Richᵈ Everard our present Governor, to one Mʳ John Lovick acting as Secʸ under the late Proprietors of this Country, who has refused to Obey the same. Your Grace will comprehend by the Contents of that Order what Management there has been here concerning Lands for many years past.

If I mistake not there was a former Order from the Lords proprietors ever since the Year 1711, to forbid the Issuing out Warrants for Land in the Southern parts of this Government, unless the same was purchased at the rate of Twenty pounds Sterling for every Thousand Acres; Notwithstanding which, I have been informed the present Secʸ has Emitted a great number of such Warrants to the quantity of some hundred thousand Acres, & still continues to do the same, thō he well knows his Majesty has made a purchase of the Soil, which may be some thousand pounds Damage to the Crown, for if our Gracious King has purchased these proprietary Countrys, no doubt it is with the Advantages of all such former Orders as it then stood at the time of such purchase

One thing more I beg leave to acquaint your Grace with, this Mʳ Lovick Edward Moseley, Christophʳ Gale & one Willᵐ Little were lately appointed (at the expense of the Proprietʳˢ) to run the Line, or Confines, between this Governmᵗ & the Colony of Virginia, and for such service they have been carving out their own satisfaction in Lands, and at the same time, if I am not misinformed they are making application to his Majᵗʸ to be allowed in Cash for the same Service, in proportion to what the Commissʳˢ on the part of Virginia had

I thought it was proper to give your Grace this timely notice, not knowing but that such matters in respect of yoʳ Grace's Eminent Station as Secʸ of State, & principly concerned in this quarter of the World, but the same might come properly before yoʳ Grace, or some Inspecting Officer of your Appointment. And if at any time Sir you are pleased to lay your Commands on me, respecting any Affair of this Province, no man will more chearfully Obey than

> My Lord
> Your Grace's
> Most Dutifull Servant
>
> E PORTER

North Carolina
Janʸ 24ᵗʰ 1728 [1729]

[B. P R O B. T South Carolina Vol. 4 C. 48]

THO LOWNDES TO THE SECRETARY OF LDS OF TRADE

16th February 1728 (-9)

S r

Hearing that the Lords Commissioners for Trade are teazed by Pretenders to Merit in bringing about the purchase of Carolina I take the Liberty to transmit to you, a Copy of the Reasons which last year I drew, and which were presented to and approved of by the Speaker of the House of Commons and sixteen other Members, when the Demand was made for the Purchase Money in Parliament

The Proposal of attacking Fort Augustine and obstructing from Port Royal in South Carolina the Spanish Navigation was first made by me to a person of great Figure in the Administration in May next will be three years and was then licked. What service I have since done in Obviating any difficulty that might happen and in removing Obstructions that arose whilest the Bargain for Carolina was Negociating a Noble Lord of your Board (whose Justice and Honour are equal to his Title) will I doubt not readily vouch for me   And I have ample Testimony of the Pains I have since taken to keep Matters between the Crown and the Proprietors from being inflamed.

Colonel Lilly was too candid a Gentleman not to own publickly the assistance I gave him in drawing his Map of Carolina, I having the most Authentick Manuscript of that Country and of Port Royal in particular For as for poor Governour Rogers his is only an unnatural Fiction for there can be no such place as he represents Port Royal to be, till the nature of water is altered and the Globe new moulded.

I likewise inclose a Copy of a Letter from Governour Craven which I doubt not will give the Lords of Trade satisfaction, he being a Gent of known Honour, and I had a Liberty to do with it as I judged proper

I beg leave to observe to you that it is my humble Opinion that the Spaniards make their clamorous Mem** about the little Fort upon Allatamaha River to conceal their Intentions of getting from us by Treaty the Territory wee have upon the Gulf of Mexico For the Bay of Apalachia is most certainly ours   And it is highly probable there is a good Harbour, either at the Entrance of the River Quitare or the River Flint And the Country is esteemed very fertile and the Indians that did inhabit it are either chased away or killed   Of what use it may be to the Spanish Nation to have such a Concession or of what prejudice to us to grant it the Lords Commissioners for Trade are the best Judges

I am, Sir

your most obedient and most humble

servant

16ᵗʰ Febʸ
172⁴

THO LOWNDES.

P S.

There is I hear a great disposition in the rich Palatins and Germans about Leige to go to South Carolina, so a good Revenue may be made immediately to the King by Quitt Rent.

[B. P R. O B. T South Carolina Vol. 4 C. 50]

SOME REASONS TO SHEW THE ABSOLUTE NECESSITY FOR THE CROWNS BUYING THE PROPRIETY OF THE CAROLINAS AS ALSO THE ADVANTAGIOUSNESS OF THAT PURCHASE TO THE PUBLICK

[Inclosed in Mʳ Lowndes 16 Febʸ 172⁴]

South Carolina is situate between the French on the River Messissippi and the Spaniards in Florida and in the Neighbourhood of Cuba, a very strong Spanish settlement and in case of a Rupture with France or Spain and an Invasion from either must in the Condition it was in by the Disunion of the Proprietors and the Animosities between the Proprietors and Inhabitants have inevitably faln a prey, unless the British Nation had at a very great Expence rescued the Colony, which under the imediate Protection of the Crown may in a great measure be made able to defend itself upon all Occasions and of eminent use not only to all the British settlements in America, but to the Mother-Country

That South Carolina has for its contingent Charges many years last past raised about 7000ᵇ ⅌ Annum which with the Quitt Rents (which may be estimated at 1000 ⅌ annum) will under a proper Regulation and Economy go near to defray the Expence of the Government.

That had South Carolina continued a provisional Government the British Establishment could never have been freed from the Expence of the Governors Salary and the independent Company, unless the Crown had either infringed the Rights of the Proprietor or invaded the Property of the Inhabitants

That the Crown having purchased the arrears of the Quit Rents which are estimated very low in the Proprietors Account will be a means to make the Inhabitants to come into proper measures to lay upon themselves some Duty which they are well able to bear in order to defend the Province.

That had South Carolina faln into the hands of either the French or Spaniards (besides the loss of a Branch of the Revenue from enumerated Rice) the consequence would have been very fatal not only to all the settlements in North America, but also to the British Navigation to the Sugar Islands. For we should have been absolutely excluded the Navigation of the Gulf of Florida, and a communication would have lain open from all the Spanish settlements to the French Colony on the Mississippi

That by a good settlement being made at Port Royal in South Carolina where (by all accounts there is a noble harbour) the Conjunction of the Power of France and Spain will not only be prevented but as long as we are Masters of the Sea we can lay a very great restraint upon the Spanish Navigation in America. For the Spanish Plate Fleet from Mexico must of necessity pass very near our Coast and that from Peru cannot without the greatest difficulty avoid it.

That by keeping a competent number of Men of War at Port Royal (which can at a much easier Rate be accommodated with all necessaries now the whole Property is in the Crown) the British Commerce will be entirely protected from the Spanish Privateers which were always fitted out at Fort Augustine a place in the Neighbourhood of South Carolina and notorious for the mischief our Trade has even of late received.

That a station for Men of War can be at a much less Expence supported in South Carolina than at Jamaica. For South Carolina is not only productive of all sorts of Naval Stores but the provisions are better and much cheaper there than in Jamaica, and the Temperature of the Place as well as the advantagiousness of the Situation will always render it preferable to Jamaica where the Climate is so unhealthy to English Constitutions

That if North Carolina be made a district of Virginia besides the Tenths reserved upon the Whale Fishery, the Revenue of Quit Rents of that place which always bore the charge of the establishment, will bring in an immediate Profit to the Crown of about 600^l sterling yearly.

That it is acknowledged by all Persons that the most fertile and healthy Part of all America is the Tract of Land lying between Port Royal in South Carolina and Florida and well watered by Navigable Rivers and if it be lett out at a proper Quit Rent as in Maryland and Pensilvania (the Crown not being under any Obligation as to the Quit Rents for Lands not yet set out in South Carolina as it is in Virginia) t'will in a very few years not only ease the British Establishment, but bring in a competent Annual Sum of Money to be remitted to Great Britain or to be disbursed for setting on Foot in America the silk or any other Manufacture that shall be thought proper

If it is asked by way of Objection why the Proprietors surrender their Charter for so small a sum as 25,000¹ (5000¹ of which is for the arrears) if the Country be so valuable as is represented The Consideration of the number of the Proprietors, their Disunion, the Frequency of Minorities amongst them Their Inability to procure to themselves Justice from South Carolina with respect to their Quit Rents and their Want of Power to correct the great Abuses committed by the settlement about the Paper Money and other publick acts to the Prejudice of the British Commerce and an apprehension that in Case of an Invasion the Colony would be lost to the great Detriment of the Publick as well as to themselves tis humbly presumed will afford a full and satisfactory answer

THO LOWNDES.

[B. P R O B. T Virginia Vol. 18 p 107 —Extract]

LIEUT GOV GOOCH TO LORDS OF TRADE
26 MARCH 1729

My Lords,

　　*　　　　*　　　　*　　　　*　　　　*

　*　　　　*　　　　*　　　　*　　　　*　　　　*

The Commissioners appointed for settling the Boundaries between this Colony and North Carolina having finished that tedious and troublesome affair, occasioned by thick woods and rivers they were obliged to pass, I have herewith sent your Lordships their Report with the Plans of the Line as it is now run and markt out. Your Lordships will find (for which there is a Protest and an Answer) that after the Comm⁵ of Carolina had gone with ours a certain distance beyond their own Inhabitants, they refused to proceed any farther urging several reasons which I think little to the purpose, & might with equall force have been insisted on before they went so far but one of our Comm⁵ concurring with them, they returned to Carolina, & M' Fitzwilliam came back, leaving M' Byrd & M' Dandridge to discharge the more difficult part of the Duty, which they continued to do for six weeks after the separation, in which time they finished the remaining part of the Line up to the Great Mountains; and I dare to answer for it, with such exactness (as the surveyors were bound by oath to do) that I hope it will be allowed to be of equal validity with that part of the Boundary in which all parties were present. It remains that I beg your Lordships directions how the expence of this work shall be paid I find that the Comm^rs and Surveyors sent out in 1711 on the same service, were paid out of the Quit Rents by a warrant from the Treasury and though they were then out only one month the Comm^rs had one hundred pounds sterling each and the surveyors 20^s per diem a man, and the present Gentlemen expect a proportionable allowance, and they that concluded the line think and are thought to deserve more than he that left them and came home There are also sundry considerable charges for men and Provisions, some with arms for their guard, chain carryers, markers and other necessary attendants As these could not wait till their Payment was directed from England that, and the charge of the Provisions have been advanced out of the 2^s per hogshead the whole will be above 1000£ I hope to receive your Lordships signification of His Majesty's Pleasure both as to the Quantum to be allowed to the several Gentlemen, and the fund for payment thereof two Comm^rs and two Surveyors were out sixteen weeks, and one Commissioner about nine weeks.

*　　　*　　　*　　　*　　　*

*　　*　　*　　*　　*　　*

> My Lords
> > Your Lordships
> > > most dutiful most faithful &
> > > most obedient humble servant
> > > > > WILLIAM GOOCH.

Virginia
  March 26th 1729.

[B. P. R. O. Proprieties. B T Vol. 12. R 105.]

At a Court of Chancery March 31st 1729
Present
Christopher Gale Jno. Lovick Edwd Mosely
Thos Pollock Thom^s Harvey Jno Palin
Edm^d Gale Esq^rs

Gent I take this Occasion to recomend to You that speedy Care be taken to dispatch and determine such matters in this Court wherein his Majesty is anv ways Concerned, particularly what relates to a Bill ffiled some time ago by Edmund Porter Esq' against Christopher Gale and Jn° Lovick Esq^rs in the name of His Maj^ts Comm^rs of the Customs who ought not and shall not be trifled with, by unnecessary delays.

Gent' I take this Opportunity likewise to inform you of my Order of the first of Jany last past to Sec^ry Lovick, Concerning his passing or giving out anv more Warrants or Patents after the time I had appointed, having received Notice by a Letter from the Honble James Bertie and others from Great Britain, acquainting me with the Sale of this Province to his Maj^ty King George, I thought it a Duty incumbent on me to Prevent the Disposing any more of the Soil till his Majesty's Royall Pleasure was further known.   These my Resolutions I have transmitted home to the Sec^ry of State for those parts and Gent as I shall not recede from my first opinion, it is my positive commands that the said Jno. Lovick Strictly obey the said Orders and in his Majestys Name I expect every Member of this Councill will Concurr with me in proper Methods to Oblige Mr Lovick to an exact observation of the same, and that he be compelled to record the said Orders as formerly Comanded, and a true Copy thereof (attested as such) Delivered to me which hitherto the said Lovick has in a very Contemptable manner refused to do, Altho the Recording of any Judicial Matter and giving Copys thereof are not meerly (ex gratia Curia) to be granted or not to be granted at his Pleasure Whose Business it is to Record and give Copys out of His Office even of a private Letter or any other matter if so desired and paid for by the Party requesting the same much more then sure it is too observed when it is the Commands of a Governor in an affair Respecting his Majesty's Property   .

I must beg leave Gent to desire a Copy of a Complaint or Charge I am informed some of You have ex parte in a Secret and Clandestine Manner sent home to His Majesty against me in prejudice of my Character and Arraigning my Administration which it seems you composed soon after Your new fform of Governm^t when ten of you obstinately signed to a Proclamation for a Prorogation of the Genl Biennial Assembly to a longer time directly against my Consent or approbation and by that means Occasioned a totall Disolution to the great prejudice of the Inhabitants of this Country which proceedings all Mankind must needs think very extraordinary and repugnant to the known Maxims of an English Constitution

And lastly Gent I am to apprize you that a Mr Robert Route Provost Marshall under the Lords Proprietors has departed this Governm^t and the Circumstances of Affairs Making it absolutely necessary to appoint one in his Absence I have therefore Given a Commission to Mr William Williams of Edenton to Act as Provost Marsh^l for him in his Absence, and this Gent like all other Govern^m I have taken upon me to do without the necessity of acquainting you with it As to any by Laws of this Country which by the Lords prop^s orders and form of Constitution are of no Longer duration than two Years unless (Confirmed by them) gives equal Power with the Governor to every Member of the Councill to nominate and appoint Officers and Magistrates in this Province in case of a Vacancy, is a Law repugnant to the form of an English Governm^t made with no other design than to impede and Lessen the Authority of all Gov^rs and seems rather Calculated for the States of Holland or Venice & therefore in itself null and Void

I have hitherto Gent Consulted you who were proper persons to fill up Vacancys, and when I was a Stranger amongst ye I was grossly imposed, and induced to put persons into Eminent Stations who were flagrantly known (thō not at that time by me) for their Vice & Imorality Therefore Gent for the future I may Consult Your opinions as I intend to do in things of this Nature when occasion suits but I hope you will pardon me if I follow the Dictates of my own Reason in appointing such Persons in Case of Vacancy whilst I am Govr that I think most deserving and this Resolution with all the several Matters herein Contained I desire may be entered on record as it has been here read and signed by me, and Whatever this Councill or any Member thereof has to say in Answer to it, or any other Matter respecting my Conduct, I desire the same may be reduced into writing and a Copy thereof being first Publickly read and delivered to

Gent

Your Humble Servt

RICH^d EVERARD

[FROM NORTH CAROLINA LETTER BOOK OF S P G]

GOV^r EVERARD TO THE BISHOP OF LONDON

No CAROLINA April 14, 1729

MAY IT PLEASE YOUR LORDSHIP

Tis with no small concern I send this to inform you that our Church is not built, nor is it like to be gone about for those men that were

appointed commissioners for the Building it have 600£ in their hands,
are now the only opposers of building one, I was, in order to the laying the foundation, chose Churchwarden with one M' Moseley we had
several meetings to consult about Building it but could not agree, being
always hindered by our Secretary, one M' Jn° Lovick a man of no religion, fears not God nor man believes, neither, seldom seen at any place
of Divine worship, his Money is his God, ridicules all goodness, while
such a man is in power, no good can be expected, his original was bred a
Barber, brought up a foot boy & a Pimp to 2 of my Predecessors, but
enough of his Character   I lately met with a Gentleman who informs
me, one M' Sanderson who died about 10 years ago, left a will, & be-
queathed several hundred Acres of land 10 Cows & Calves 10 Sows
5 Pigs sheep & Several Household goods to maintain a clergyman in the
Precinct of Curratuck in this Province, but these are embezzled by the
management of Lovick & others of his stamp by setting the will aside,
the Gent' promised me the Copy which as soon as it comes to hand shall
be sent to your Lordship who shall command all the assistance, that
lyes in the power of my Lord

    Your most dutiful son & obd' servant

        RICH⁴ EVERARD

[B P R. O Virginia Vol. 44 p 22-23]

LORDS OF TRADE TO LIEUTENANT GOVERNOR GOOCH

        WHITEHALL May 22ⁿᵈ 1729.

SIR

  *   *   *   *   *   *

We are glad to find that the Commiss" for settling the Boundaries
between Virginia and North Carolina have made some Progress; and
we hope that the finishing this Division Line will prevent the many
Inconveniencies, which have hitherto happened for want thereof

  *   *   *   *   *   *

    Your very Loving Friends
    and humble Serv⁵

      WESTMORELAND
      P DOMINIQUE
      T PELHAM
      THO FRANKLAND

[B. P R O. VIRGINIA VOL. 44 P 32-33]

A POPPLE TO Mr SCROPE 5 JUNE 1729

To Mr Scrope Secry to the Lords of the Treasury

    SIR

My Lords Commiss^n for Trade and Plantations command me to send you the inclosed Extract of a Letter from Major Gooch Lieut Govr of Virginia dated ye 26th March 1729 wherein he desires, Orders may be sent for the payment of the Charge of the Commiss^n on behalf of the Colony of Virginia, for running a Division Line between that Colony and North Carolina.

As this service was performed in Obedience to his late Majestys Order in Council of 28th March 1727, And as the same will encourage many Grants of Land and New Settlement near those Bounds, to the great increase of his Majestys Revenue of Quit Rents in Virginia, their Lordships command me to desire, you will lay the same before the Lords Commissioners of the Treasury for her Majestys Orders what Sum shall be allowed for the charge of this Survey, and out of what Fund the same shall be paid, I am

        Sir,
      Your most humble serv^t

                      A POPPLE

Whitehall
  June 5th 1729

[B. P R. O PROPRIETIES. B. T VOL. 12. R 107]

To the most noble Thomas Duke of Newcastle Secretary of State &c

MA\ IT PLEASE \OUR GRACE

Some time ago I made bold to trouble your Grace with an Information concerning the Disposition of Lands in this Country, a Copy whereof comes here inclosed, least the Original should miscarry, since the writing of which & as I then imagined Mr Lovick and the Surveyor General one Mr Edward Moseley have gone on roundly to dispose of His Maj^ts Soil, the former by giving out Warrants and Patents, and the later surveying the same, notwithstanding the repeated Orders of Sr Richd Ever-

3

ard, our Governor to the contrary which Orders have not only been given to those two gentlemen separately but a Charge also to Mr Lovick in open Council to obey the same

Sir Richard on all these affairs has acted with the greatest regard to his Majesty's Interest, and by that means has rather chosen to lose the many Fees which accrue to him by signing Patents, than to run the hazard of doing what might be prejudicial or disliked by his Majesty, thõ his Commission is at present from under the Lords Proprietors.

This cautious way of proceeding I believe Sr Richard is in hopes will meet with your Grace's favourable opinion and Countenance and I beg your Grace will be pleased also to receive this Information and all that I have said or done herein as genuine, with a view purely for for his Majesty's Service, a Duty I shall always think incumbent on

My Lord
Your Grace's &c
E PORTER

North Carolina,
   June 15th 1729

[B P R O Proprieties. B T Vol 12. R 104.]

To the most Noble Thomas Duke of Newcastle Sec^ry of State &c

MAY IT PLEASE YOUR GRACE

As I thought my Self bound in Duty to acquaint your Grace of any Matter wch might seen prejudicial to his Maj^tys Interests in this Country, was the motive that induced me to trouble your Grace with an Account thereof, in a Letter or Memorial of the 7th of April last past, in wch was inclosed the Copy of my Charge to my Council on a Chancery Day, together with an Order to Mr John Lovick the present Secretary, that he should permit no more Warrants or Patents for Lands to pass out of his Office till His Majesty's Royal Pleasure were therein known, But if Mr Lovick being thirsty after an unreasonable Gain, & to make the most of his Office before the King's Authority took Place, has had no regard to such my Orders & Directions, & my Council not taking proper Methods in Concurrence with me as desir'd to suppress him, & there being no further Expedient left in me to prevent so unjust a Practice, as is daily carrying on by this Lovick, & Mr Edwd Mosely the Surveyor General of Lands I conceived it necessary once more to apprize your Grace with it Lovick continues hourly to fill up & give out Warrants & Patents for large Baronies of Lands, & this Moseley I am credibly informed (who is very Artful & a great Confederate of Lovick's where a Profit is in View) has lately surveyed for himself twenty thousand Acres lying contiguous on the head of a River called Trent in this Province, & has likewise surveyed twenty thousand Acres for a Gentleman in Virginia, in one body of Land on the Northern Parts of this Government for which Warrants were procured by the help of ready Cash out of the Secretary's Office I assure Y' Grace such Proceedings has been, & will be very distructive to the settlement of this Place, & the means to prevent many hundred poor People taking up small tracts of Land at a reasonable price that now will be obliged to purchase the same at second hand & at a dear Rate, for that is the view in taking up such unreasonable Bodies of Land in this Country, wch in respect of its Situation to the French and Spaniards on the Messicippy & the numerous savages living near us may prove very fatal in the End

I am lately informed notwithstanding the great exactness I have used on all Occasions since my having the Administration of this Government, to demonstrate my Affection, Duty & Loyalty to his late as well as present Maj^ty yet it seems this Lovick, Gale Chief Justice, & one Wm Little his Son in Law, agreable to their wonted Practice, have either sworn or suborn'd others to swear a Matter or Charge against me, as thö, I were disaffected to our ever happy & blessed Establishment in the most Illustrious House of Hanover, But what the particulars of the Accusations really is, or what is made Oath to by those three perfidious Men I am at a loss to Judge, having in Writing demanded a Copy thereof, as Y' Grace will perceive by the inclossed Speech to my Council, but to this Day I cannot obtain any

This Sort of Treatment my Predecessor M' Geo: Burrington received till by the help of a few ex parte Depositions, & by dint of swearing & forswearing they prevailed with the Lords Propri^rs to remove him & soon after it was my hard Fate to succeed in his Station, thö had their Lordp' then known as I believe they do since, what little Veracity ought to be put on what those Persons swore, much less on what they said, M' Burrington had not fallen under their Lordp's Displeasure To conclude I hope your Grace will excuse this tedious Representation, & believe me when I assure you three more flagrant Villains never came out of the Condemn'd Hole in New Gate for Execution at Tyburn, therefore agreable to the Prayer of the People from all Quarters of this Country in whose Name & in my own, I humbly desire & hope your Grace will be instrumental in preventing their holding any Post or Office of Profit or Trust, when we arrive to the Happiness of living under His Majesty's Auspicious Governm' w'th kind Service will perpetuate Y' Grace's Memory amongst us to future Ages, & will be an obligation of the greatest Consequence to all the Inhabitants here & in particular to

My Lord
Y' Grace's most Dutiful
& Obliged Servant

RICH'ᵈ EVERARD

North Carolina
   June 18ᵗʰ 1729

[B. P R O Virginia B. T. Vol. 44 p 34]

LORDS OF TRADE TO MAJOR GOOCH 20 JUNE 1729

Sir

*   *   *   *   *

We have likewise recommended to their Lordships what you write about the paying of the Comm'ʳˢ for laying out the Boundaries between the two Colonies of Virginia and Carolina, so that you may Shortly expect to receive his Majesty's Orders with respect thereto.

*   *   *   *   *

Your very Friends
humble serv'ᵗˢ

E ASHE
T PELHAM
THO FRANKLAND
M BLADEN
ORL'ᵒ BRIDGEMAN

Whitehall
   June 20ᵗʰ 1729

[B P R O B T Virginia Vol. 19 R 124]

WILLIAM BYRD TO THE LORDS OF TRADE

Virginia the 27ᵗʰ of June 1729

My Lords,

   The honour I have of being known to most of your Lordships gives me the confidence to trouble you with this Letter   I fear you will think it a very long one but as it is an appeal to your Justice I hope you will please to forgive me if I state my case in all its circumstances that your Lordships may be the clearer in your Determination

About 2 years since our Governour received his Majesty's Order in Council to appoint Commissioners who in conjunction with others to be named for North Carolina should run a Dividing line between the two Colonys. This line was to begin at Corotuck Inlet and run a due west course to the great mountains. In obedience to this order, our Governour was pleased to name me, Mr Fitz William and Mr Dandridge (all of the Council for the better grace of the Business) to execute such commission Two eminent surveyors were likewise named to perform the mathematical part, Mr Mayo who made the accurate Map of Barbados, and Mr Irvin, we had also a power to take as many men as we should think proper, both for the laborious part of the work and for our defence against the Indians. We had also a Chaplain allowed us, both for the benefit of Divine service and to christen the children on the Frontiers of Carolina where they are wholly destitute of a minister

Being thus appointed, we sat out on the 27th of February 172½ to Corotuck Inlet, where we met the Commissioners on the part of North Carolina and having concerted the place of beginning the allowance to be made for the variation and other necessary Preliminarys we entered on the Business the 27th of March following. T'is not easy to conceive, My Lords how much difficulty and fatigue we encountered in the low marshy grounds that lay near the sea, our course being right forward, thrô thick and thin and leading often through swamps and miry places not practicable for horses for many miles together. Our way lay through the widest part of the Dismal which is a dreadful swamp of vast extent not less than 30 miles long and 15 in breadth No humane creature ever had the Resolution to pass over this inhospitable Bogg before, and we found it so intolerable that I believe no man will ever be so hardy as to pass it again Your Lordships will incline to the same Opinion when I assure you that with the utmost diligence we cou'd use it took us up full ten days to mark and measure that small distance. However we had patience enough to overcome this and all other difficulties that stood in our way We carried on the business with very great alacrity and success til the beginning of April when the weather grew warm enough to give life and vigour to the Rattlesnakes. This obliged us to discontinue our work til the return of the cool season, which could not happen til September

Accordingly we met again on the 20th of that month at the place where we had left off and pursued the line with all the Industry we were able.

And now My Lords for variety we had quite different hardships to undergo, which were however as discouraging as those in our former Expedition. Great part of our journey lay through wild woods without path and without any Inhabitants except only Panthers, Bears, Wolves and other savage beasts. In many places we were forced to scuffle through Thickets so intolerable that it was as much as our hands cou'd do to save our Eyes in our heads. At other times our line carried us over steep hills & stony Precipices to the no small hazzard of our Necks. Nor was this all our danger but we were constrained to ford very often over unknown Rivers, where the stream was rapid, and the Bottome paved with Rocks as slippery as glass so that t'was hardly possible for horses to keep their feet. Foreseeing the difficulty of these ways for *Baggage horses* we carried no provisions with us but Biscuit, depending entirely on Providence for other subsistance. Our lodging was in the open air, and our Drink water; but what was worse than all the rest by the time we approached the mountains our horses were so jaded that we were obliged to walk great part of the way home on foot and that in Boots for fear of Bushes and vermine. However we bore up against all these Inconveniences not only with constancy but cheerfulness determining that nothing should discourage us from obeying his Majestys order in the fullest extent. And we endured it all with the more Patience because our endeavours were blest with very uncommon success. We had no Distemper no Disaster of any consequence befell any of the Company during the whole time, and we brought all the people back in better health than when they went out. Nay for 16 weeks no man that was with us ever wanted a meals meat so bountifully did Providence supply us day by day in the barren Wilderness. Our Governor has had the honor to write to your Lordships upon this subject and to transmit the Map and the Journal of our Proceedings by which you will be the better able to judge of the service we performed and of the Fatigue we underwent. But as this has happened by his Majesty's special direction he is unwilling to determine what pay we ought to have, but desires to be directed by your Lordships both as to the Quantum and by which of our 2 Revenues this Charge ought to be defrayed whether by that of the Quitrents or by that of the Two shillings ₱ Hogs head?

As to the first of these Questions, how much the Commissioners ought to have for the trouble and expence of this Expedition your Lordships have a Precedent to go by which we humbly hope will guide your Opinions in this case. In the year 1710 two Commissioners Philip Ludwell and Nathaniel Harrison Esq^rs were appointed by our Governor and

Council to do this very Business. These Gentlemen went to Corotuck Inlet in order to begin from thence but not being able to agree with the Commissioners of North Carolina they returned without performing any thing   However they having been out 4 weeks and it not being their fault that nothing was done they were paid by an order from England one hundred pounds sterling each.   Now if those Commissioners were allowed £100 for 4 weeks without enduring any hardship or doing any service I humbly submit it to your Lordships how much we ought to have, who were 16 weeks out, underwent all manner of fatigue and performed the Business faithfully & effectually which we had the honour to be imployed upon   The surveyors likewise hope they may be considered in the same proportion that the former surveyors were, namely 20 shillings a day which I think they deserve for the great fidelity & exactness with which they discharged their duty.   And our Chaplain M\u207f Peter Fontain hopes he may have as much as the surveyors, having been very diligent in his Function & having christened above an hundred children among the Gentiles of North Carolina

Then my Lords as to the second Question out of which Revenue this money ought to be paid I humbly conceive your Lordship will think it most reasonable that it be paid out of the Revenue of 2 shillings ⅌ Hogshead since that was given to defray both the constant and accidental charges of this Government   And the rather because this Fund is now in very good condition having several Thousand Pounds in Bank and in no danger of being deficient   Indeed formerly when this Revenue happened to fall in arrear (which was the case when the Payment was ordered to the Commissioners above mentioned) such services have been defrayed out of the Revenue of Quitrent.   But at present the case is quite otherwise and there is a large summ in Bank of the Two shillings ⅌ Hogshead and consequently the present charge may be more naturally born by that Revenue and the rather because the Quitrents have lately been reserved for more important services

This my Lord is a faithfull state of our case nor can I imagin that our Pretentions can be at all prejudiced by the purchase that has been since made of Carolina by the Crown Since what we did was by his Majesty's express commands   And notwithstanding such Purchase this work will still prove very advantagious to the Publick by discovering a fine Country which will soon be taken up as far as the great mountains whereby the strong Barrier will be secured to his Majesty's subjects. Besides our line will remain a lasting Boundary between the 2 Colonys which can never conveniently be united into one Government

And now I ought to ask your Lordships ten Thousand Pardons for giving so long an interruption to your attention to the Publick service   But as I could not make my case shorter without prejudicing the Justice of it I hope you will be pleased to excuse me, and to believe that I am with all the Respect in the World

> My Lords
>> Your Lordships
>>> most obedient humble servant
>>>> W BYRD

[B P R O B T Virginia Vol. 19 R 130]

LIEUT GOV GOOCH TO LORDS OF TRADE

June 29th 1729

My Lords

*   *   *   *   *   *   *   *

I forgot in my last among the allowances for the gentlemen employed in running the Boundaries to mention that of a Chaplain whom I appointed to attend that service and who deserves his Majesties consideration when the payment of that work shall be ordered   It was very necessary a Clergyman should be sent out with such a number when they were to pass through a Country where they could not have the oppertunity of attending the publick Worship and the report that a gentleman made to me sufficiently proves how well he answered my purpose in sending of him, for he Christened above an hundred children, a great many adult persons, and preached to Congregations who have never had publick Worship since their first Settlement in those Parts, such is the unhappy state of those poor Inhabitants who possess the borders of our Neighbouring Province, in which there is not one Minister

*   *   *   *   *   *   *   *

> My Lords
>> Your Lordships
>>> most faithfull and most
>>>> obedient humble servant
>>>>> WILLIAM GOOCH

[B. P R. O. B T Proprieties. Vol. 32. p 3.]

LORDS OF TRADE TO DUKE OF NEWCASTLE

8 July 1729

To his Grace the Duke of Newcastle

MY LORD,

Having received an Address from the Council of North Carolina relating to the conduct of the Governor of that Province which contains matter of a very extraordinary & heinous nature We thought it our duty without loss of time to transmit the said address to your Grace that you may lay the same before the Queen that her Majesty may signify her Royal pleasure thereupon

We are

      My Lord

         Your Grace's

           Most obedient and

              most humble Servants

                    T PELHAM
                    W BLADEN
                    W CARY

Whitehall
  July 8th 1729

[B. P R. O Proprieties B T Vol. 12. R. 99]

AT THE COUNCILL CHAMBr WHITEHALL THE 31st DAY OF JULY 1729

By a Committee of the Lords of His Majesty's Most Honoble Privy Councill

Her Majesty having been pleased to referr unto this Committee the humble Address of the Members of North Carolina, containing Complaints against Sr Richard Everard—Governor of that Province—The Lords of the Committee this day took the said Address into their Consideration, and are hereby Pleased to referr the same, to the Lords Commissioners for Trade and Plantations to Examine into the Allegations thereof, and Report their Opinion thereupon to this Committee.

                      EDWARD SOUTHWELL

[B. P. R. O Proprieties. B. T. R. 100. No. 12.]

AT THE COUNCILL CHAMB' WHITEHALL THE 31ª DAY OF JULY 1729

By a Committee of the Lords of His Majesty's Most Honoble Privy Councill

Her Majesty having been pleased to referr unto this Committee a Letter from S' Richard Everard Governor of North Carolina transmitting a Copy of his Orders and resolutions delivered to the Councill of that Province at a Court of Chancery held on the 31ª of March 1729, relating (amongst other things) to the Putting a Stop to the granting of Lands till his Majesty's Pleasure should be Known concerning them, and also to the filling up of Vacant Places within that Government The Lords of the Committee this day took the same into consideration, and are hereby pleased to referr the said Letter, together with the Copy of Governor Everard's Orders and Resolutions, to the Lords Commissioners for Trade and Plantations, to Examine into the same, and Report their Opinion thereupon to this Committee

EDWARD SOUTHWELL

[B P R O Proprieties Vol 12 R 100]

MAY IT PLEASE YOUR GRACE

In Jan' last being in such a State of Health that I could not do myself the Honour to Write to Your Grace I got M' Edm Porter our Judge of the Admiralty of this Province to transmitt to you a Copy of my Order to one M' John Lovick acting as Secretary here under the Lord Proprietors of this Country forbiding him Issuing out any more Warrants or Patents for Land till His Majesty's Pleasure were further Known which Notwithstanding the thing was a disadvantage to myself Yet I conceived it my Duty as Governor so to do after Hearing our Gracious King had made a Purchase of the Soyl tho such my Orders have been of Little or no Effect the said Lovick not regarding them as by a Letter under his hand afterwards sent me and being well informed since that he still out of an Avaritious View, continues to Emitt such Warrants and Patents for Land, I again Repeated my Comands in Open Councill the 31ª of March last Read and Delivered to be Recorded at the said Board, a true Copy thereof comes herewith Inclosed, at which time the Members of My Councill broke up in great Pett, and have not since been so mannerly as to give me an Answer, but Caviled with me concerning my Authority in case of Vacancy in appointing a Provost Marshall which occasioned an entire Overthrow of all Proceedings in Chancery I thought it necessary to give Your Grace this Information least His Majesty's Interest should suffer, there having been for severall Years past very corrupt doings in the Secretary's office of this Country Concerning the Lands Transacted by the aforesaid Lovick and Mr Edd Moseley Survr Genll as formerly set forth by Mr Ed Porters Memorial to Your Grace, and it is my humble Opinion an Officer as Receiver Genll of the Quit Rents with a Power of Inspecting into the Clandestine Disposition of Lands would be at this time Highly Necessary I'm with all due Regard and Respect

> My Lord Your Graces
> Most Obedient and Obliged
> Humble Servt
>
> RICHd EVERARD

[B. P R. O Proprieties. B. T Vol. 12. R 102]

To the Right Honble John Lord Carteret Palatin & the rest of the true & absolute Lords Proprietors of Carolina.

I did my Self the Honour about a Year & half since to send your Lordships a representation of the State & Condition of this your Province (then under my Government) containing an Exact Account of ye Scituation of all affairs relating to your Lordships Interest in particular and the Country in general, with every thing done in the Administration from my Arrival to that time, this I sent by One Mr Durley from Carolina, he also carried an Address from the Assembly to your Lordships, & some Letters I had received from the Govr of Virginia concerning the Boundarys of the Two Governments, & aboundance of Letters from other persons this Mr Durley received many other favors & Civilitys from me, therefore concluded he would faithfully perform his Promise in delivering the Letters I entrusted him with, but to my great Suprise am lately informed by some Gentlemen here (who have received Letters from London of a fresh date) that he either gave the said Writings to Lovicks Brother in London or destroyed them

At my return to this place after my first Jorney to Cape Fair River in a long Letter I sent your Lordships a Description of that part of

Carolina with my Advice & Opinion concerning the setleing thereof and
Granting the Lands Also my resolution of going there when October
Court was over, & staying till March Court came to induce & Encourage
People to settle on that River   Your Lordships had in this Letter a large
relation of the Conduct & Behaviour of Chief Justice Gale, Secretary
Lovick, & some others in the Council, of Mr Edens Will, & the Law
Suite thereupon between Mr Roderick Lloyd & Lovick Executor in Trust
of the said Will, Lovicks injustice in not paying the debts & Legacies of
Mr Eden, & detaining the residuum from the Heir at Law, I omitted
nothing worth your Lordships Notice that had passed here after the date
of my first writing, this Pacquet was recommended to the care of a Merchant in New England named Armory I am yet ignorant, whither it had
better success then the first   I must acquaint Your Lordships that dureing the two years I have been here I have received but one Letter in
Answer to some Hundreds sent to England, that Letter came into the
hands of a gentleman in Virginia who detained the same till a Messinger
from me went on purpose for it.

When I came first into Carolina there was a great Mortality among
the Cattle most Plantors lost above half their Stocks which raised the
price of Oxen & Cows double to what they had been before, a mighty
Storm in the preceeding Autumn destroyed their Corn insomuch that
there was almost a famine in the land the Year following on the 19th of
August we had another which had the same effect these mischievous
winds raised the price of Corn to five times the usual rate, Pork from
45s ℔ Barr was sold for Five & Six pounds   Never the less a Thousand
flamilys came to live in Carolina in the time of my Administration, a far
greater number would have done the same had they not heard of the Scarcity of provisions we laboured under   The Militia was in strange disorder, in most places no Officers, in other very unfit persons, this I regulated
to the satisfaction of all People.   The Justices of the precinct Courts were
mostly illeterate persons, & of no Authority for which reason I prevailed
on Coll Mosely, Coll Harvey, Coll Swan, Coll Maule, & other Gentlemen
to preside in the Courts of the precincts where they lived, by this means
Justice was duely administred, & all disorders in those Courts (very frequent before) immediately ceased, no complaint was made to me & the
Council, nor Suit brought against any Officer Civil or Military, after the
new Commissions were given out in March & April the preceeding Year

There is great plenty of provisions & Grain this year in Carolina everything is at a low rate Yet I have not heard of One man come to live in
this Country since the change of Government, We did expect five or six

hundred familys in the New Country, but I fear we shall not now be
above a tenth part of that Number S' Richard Everard your present
Govern' came into Carolina in last July he took the Government upon
him without acquainting me of his Commission, or Arrival altho' I was
in the Town when he Landed, I had made preperation to haven given
him an Entertainment but his incivility saved me that trouble, his
behaviour to me has been very unmannerly & base ever since, yet the
respect I still preserve for your Interest & the good of the Country was
the cause that I gave my Self the trouble to talk with him upon the
posture of Affairs in this province, I took an Occasion to tell him that
if he persever'd in following the Advice of Gale, Lovick & their Gang,
he would never prosper, I also assured him in the approaching benmal
Assembly I would use my Utmost to procure what Advantages I could
for him so took my Leave & went to Cape Fair, when I returned to this
Town the last of October, I was informed he had made a rediicule of my
Advice therefore I have not taken the least notice of him since I shall
not trouble your Lordships with any more about S' Richard in this paper
(the Country haveing appointed Agents to inform you at large of his
proceedings) but that he is over throwing all Order & good Government,
many Gentlemen, have given up their Commissions publickly declareing
their Contempt of him & his Actions

Great Improvements have been made since I knew the Country in
husbandry, the unsettledness of Trade has been the Subject of my discourse many days among the most Substantial Men, the conclusion ended
in a resolution to buy Vessels & carry on a sufficient Trade to Jamaica
to Supply the Country with Rum, Molossus Salt &c My removal has
put an end to this, & many other designs, several Masters who sailed
their own Vessels had bought land with design to bring their ffamilys
here have now changed their minds I must inform Your Lordships
that there is in the hands of the Publick Treasurer & Receivers above
Two thousand Pounds altho there has been no Tax besides the common
Levy of five Shillings ♜ head, which before my time did not defray the
publick Charges

I always made it my Study (while Govern') to serve Your Lordships
& this Country to the Utmost of my ability the hardships I have gone
thro by Land & Water have been very severe, I have sometimes narrowly
Escaped starving many times drowning, all my Expeditions were at my
own proper Cost and Charges, I should give your Lordships too much
trouble if I Enumerated the Losses I have sustained since I left London
for which reason shall say nothing on that head, I brought a large
ffamily of Servants which I maintained out of my own Stock, the Salary,

ffees & Perquisites of this Governm' were not more worth me in Eighteen Months then I could make of One hundred Pounds well laid out in England would produce here, this was Occasioned by some Acts of Assembly passed the November before my Evil Destiny brought me into Carolina

I know but one thing Your Lordships can take amiss from me, which was my appointing Naval Officers, Dunstans ill behaviour Obliged me to do so, besides you well know it was my Right, I have heard of many Men who have tryed matters of Property with Kings and Queens of England without being thought Ill Subjects if any Proprietor had spoken a word to me in this man's favor in respect to the Naval Officer of any Port in Carolina I should most willingly have given it him, but how he can be Naval Officer to four Ports (there being so many here) passes the understanding of all People in these parts.

I stay in this Country in Expectaōn the Complaints of Gale & Lovick against me will be sent to Carolina, which I shall be able to prove false and Scandalous, I give your Lordships my word the Law Suit between M' Lloyd and Lovick has been the chief occasion of difference here, (if not the only one) a large part of Govern' Edens Estate is reported to be gone into the hands of Affidavit Men and others as bad, it is my Opinion M' Lloyd will never get a Shilling thereof, if your Lordships make another Secretary, I think Lovick will Lovick will leave the King's Dominions, I shall tarry in these parts untill next April, have nothing to do here, its only to wait for an Oppertunity of clearing my Character if sullied by any one

Had Your Lordships been pleased to let me know the reason why you removed me, it would have been a great satisfaction, for my own part as I know not any cause you had for it, am at a loss what induced you to take so hasty a resolution of appointing a New Govern', Lovick & Gale with their Crew are Capable of acting or saying any thing, if they have accused me I think I ought to know what they have laid to my Charge if these Men Tax me with any thing unjust, or dishonourable and I am not able to justify myself I will patiently submit to be a Sacrifice to my own folly & Ignorance, but on the contrary of your Lordships find that I have behaved uprightly and in all things as becometh a Man of honour I shall receive reparation & satisfaction from Your Lordships.

I am

Your Most humble

and Most Obedient Servant

GEO BURRINGTON

[Aug, 1729]

[B. P R O B. T PROPRIETIES. VOL. 32. P 5.]

LORDS OF TRADE TO THE PRIVY COUNCIL
2 SEPTEMBER 1729

To the Right Honble the Lords of the Committee of his Maj most Honble
  Privy Council

MY LORDS,

Pursuant to your Lordships Orders of the 31st of the last month
referring to us the copy of an Address from the Members of the Council for the Province of North Carolina containing complaints against Sir
Richard Everard Deputy Governor of that Province as likewise the
copy of a letter from Sir Richard Everard to his Grace the Duke of
Newcastle with a copy of Sir Richard's Orders & Resolutions deliver'd
to the Council of North Carolina relating to the granting of Lands
there and the filling up of vacant places within that Government, We
have considered the said several papers whereupon we take leave to
inform your Lordships that upon the receipt of complaints against Governors or other Officers in His Maj Colonies in America We generally
propose that copies of these complaints should be interchangeably communicated by each party to the other for their respective answers upon
full liberty on both sides freely to examine witnesses upon the place
where no proofs are produced here in support of their allegations But
the charge against Sir Richard being of so high & heinous a nature with
respect to his Maj Royal person & government and so unbecoming a
person to whose care the said Province has been committed whereof however no proofs are transmitted to us, We humbly propose that the Governor who we presume will soon be nominated for North Carolina have
copies deliver'd to him of these complaints and be directed to make strict
enquiry into the truth thereof that exemplary justice may be done according to the nature of the offences said to have been committed

                We are
                  My Lords
                    Your Lordships
                      most obedient and
                        most humble Servants

                                          MARTIN BLADEN
                                          P DOMINIQUE
                                          W CARY
  Whitehall   T FRANKLAND
    Septr 2^d 1729.

[Reprinted from Revised Statutes of North Carolina, Vol. II, Page 466]

AN ACT FOR ESTABLISHING AN AGREEMENT WITH SEVEN OF THE LORDS PROPRIETORS OF CAROLINA, FOR THE SURRENDER OF THEIR TITLE AND INTEREST IN THAT PROVINCE TO HIS MAJESTY

Whereas, his late Majesty King Charles the second, by his letters patent under the great seal of Great Britain, bearing date at Westminster, in the fifteenth year of his reign, did grant and confirm unto Edward, then Earl of Clarendon, George, then Duke of Albemarle, William, then Lord Craven, John, then Lord Berkley, Anthony, then Lord Ashley, Sir George Carteret, Knight and Baronet, Sir William Berkley, and Sir John Colleton, Knt and Baronet, all since deceased, their heirs and assigns, all that Territory or tract of ground, situate, lying and being within his said late Majesty's dominions in America, extending from the North end of the island called Luckar island, which lieth in the Southern Virginian seas, and within six and thirty degrees of the Northern latitude, and to West as far as the South seas, and so southerly as far as the river St Matthias, which bordereth upon the Coast of Florida, and within one and thirty degrees of Northern latitude, and so West in a direct line as far as the South seas aforesaid, together with all and singular ports, harbours, bays, rivers, isles and islets, belonging unto the country aforesaid, and also all the soil, lands, fields, woods, mountains, farms, lakes, rivers, bays and islets, situate, or being within the bounds or limits aforesaid, with the fishing of all sorts of fish, whales and sturgeons, and all other royal fishes, in the seas, bays, islets and rivers within the premises, and the fish therein taken, and moreover all veins, mines, quarries, as well discovered as not discovered, of gold, silver, gems and precious stones, and all other whatsoever, whether of stones, metals or any other thing whatsoever, found or to be found, within the country, isles, and limits aforesaid, and also the patronages and advowsons of all churches and chappels, which as Christian religion should increase within the country, isles, islets and limits aforesaid, should happen thenafter to be erected, together with license and power to build and found churches, chappels, and oratories, in convenient and fit places, within the said bounds and limits, and to cause them to be dedicated and consecrated, according to the Ecclesiastical laws of the Kingdom of England, together with all and singular the like and so ample rights, jurisdictions, priviledges, royalties, prerogatives, liberties, immunities and franchises of what kind soever, within the country, isles and limits aforesaid, to have, use, exercise, and enjoy, and in as ample manner as any Bishop of Durham in the Kingdom of England, ever thentofore had, held, used or enjoyed, or of right ought or could have, use or enjoy ; and his said late Majesty did thereby for himself, his heirs and successors, make, create, and constitute the said Edward, Earl of Clarendon, George, Duke of Albemarle, William, Lord Craven, John, Lord Berkley, Anthony, Lord Ashley, Sir George Carteret, Sir William Berkley, and Sir John Colleton, their heirs and assigns, the true and absolute Lords and Proprietors of the country aforesaid, and all others the premises, (saving as therein is mentioned,) to have, hold, possess, and enjoy, the said country, isles, islets, and all and singular, other the premises, to them the said Edward, Earl of Clarendon, George, Duke of Albemarle, William, Lord Craven, John, Lord Berkley, Anthony, Lord Ashley, Sir George Carteret, Sir William Berkley, and Sir John Colleton, their heirs and assigns forever, to be holden of his late said Majesty, his heirs and successors, as of his mannor of East Greenwich in the county of Kent, in free and common soccage, and not in capite, or by knight's service And whereas, his late said Majesty, King Charles the second, by other letters patent, under the great seal of England, bearing date the thirtieth day of June, in the seventeenth year of his reign, reciting the letters patent herein first recited, did grant unto the said Edward, Earl of Clarendon, George, Duke of Albemarle, William, Lord Craven, then Earl of Craven, John, Lord Berkley, Anthony, Lord Ashley, Sir George Carteret, Sir John Colleton, and Sir William Berkley, their heirs and assigns, all that Province, territory or tract of ground, situate, lying, and being within 'his said late Majesty's Dominions of America, extending North and Eastward, as far as the North end of Carahtuke River or Gullet, upon a strait Westerly line to Wyonake Creek, which lies within or about the degress of thirtysix and thirty minutes North Latitude, and so West in a direct line as far as the South Seas, and South and Westward, as far as the degrees of twentynine inclusive, Northern latitude, and so West in a direct line, as far as the South Seas, together with all and singular ports, harbours, bays, rivers and islets belonging unto the Province or Territory aforesaid, and also all the soil, lands, fields, woods, farms, lakes, rivers, bays or islets situate or being within the bounds or limits aforesaid last before, with the fishing of all sorts of fish, whales, sturgeons, and all other royal fishes in the seas, bays, islets, and rivers, within the Premises, and the fish therein taken, together with the royalty of the

5

sea upon the coast, within the limits aforesaid, and all veins, mines and quarries, as well discovered as not discovered, of gold, silver, gems and precious stones, and all other whatsoever, be it of stones, metals, or any other things, found or to be found, within the Province, territory, islets and limits aforesaid, and furthermore the patronages and advowsons of all churches and chappels, which as Christian religion should increase within the Province, territory, isles and limits aforesaid, should happen thereafter to be erected, together with license and power to build and found churches, chappels, and oratories in convenient and fit places within the said bounds and limits, and to cause them to be dedicated and consecrated according to the Ecclesiastical laws of the Kingdom of England, together with all and singular the like, and as ample rights, jurisdictions, priviledges, prerogatives, royalties, liberties, immunities and franchises of what kind soever, within the territories, isles, islets, and limits aforesaid, to have, hold, use, exercise and enjoy the same, as amply and fully and in as ample manner, as any Bishop of Durham in the Kingdom of England ever thentofore had, held, used or enjoyed, or of right ought or could have, use or enjoy, and his said late Majesty, did thereby for himself, his heirs and successors, make, create, constitute and appoint them the said Edward, Earl of Clarendon, George, Duke of Albemarle, William, Earl of Craven, John, Lord Berkley, Anthony, Lord Ashley, Sir George Carteret, Sir John Colleton, and Sir William Berkley, their heirs and assigns, the true and absolute Lords and Proprietors of the said Province or territory, and of all other the premises, (saving as therein is mentioned,) to have, hold, possess and enjoy the said Province, territory, islets, and all and singular other the premises, to them the said Edward, Earl of Clarendon, George, Duke of Albemarle, William, Earl of Craven, John, Lord Berkley, Anthony, Lord Ashley, Sir George Carteret, Sir John Colleton and Sir William Berkley, their heirs and assigns forever, to be holden of his said Majesty, his heirs and successors, as of his mannor of East Greenwich aforesaid, in free and common soccage, and not in capite, or by Knight's service, as in and by the said several late recited letters patent, relation being thereunto had, may appear, And whereas, the part, share, interest and estate of the said Edward, late Earl of Clarendon, of and in the Provinces, territories, islets, hereditaments and premises, in and by the said several recited letters patent granted and comprised, is now come unto and vested in the Honorable James Bertie, of the parish of St John the Evangelist, in the liberty of Westminster, in the county of Middlesex, Esquire, of his own Right, and the part, share, interest and estate, of the said

George, late Duke of Albemarle, of and in the same premises, is come unto and vested in the most noble Henry now Duke of Beauford, and in the said James Bertie, and the Honourable Dodington Greville, of Bulford, in the county of Wiltz, Esquire, the two surviving Devisees named in the will of the most noble Henry late Duke of Beauford, in trust for the present Duke of Beauford, and for the right honourable Charles Noell Somerset, his brother, an infant, and the part, share, interest and estate of the said William, late Earl of Craven, of and in the same premises, is come unto and vested in the right Honourable William now Lord Craven, and the part, share, interest and estate, of the said John late Lord Berkley, of and in the same premises, is now come unto and vested in Joseph Blake, of the Province of South Carolina, in America, Esquire, and the part, share, interest and estate of the said Anthony, late Lord Ashley, of and in the same premises, is now come unto and vested in Archibald Hutcheson, of the Middle Temple, London, Esquire, (in trust for John Cotton of the Middle Temple, London, Esquire,) and the part, share, interest and estate of the said late Sir John Colleton, of and in the said premises, is now come unto and vested in Sir John Colleton, of Exmouth, in the county of Devon, Baronet, and the part, share, interest and estate of the said late Sir William Berkley, of and in the same premises, is now come unto and vested in the Honourable Henry Bertie, of Dorton, in the county of Bucks, Esquire, or in Mary Danson, of the Parish of St Andrews, Holbourne, in the county of Middlesex, Widow, or in Elizabeth Moor, of London, Widow, some or one of them, and the said Henry now Duke of Beauford, and the said James Bertie and Dodington Greville, as trustees in manner aforesaid, some or one of them, is or are seized in fee of and in one full undivided eighth part, (the whole into eight equal parts to be divided) of the premises, in and by the said recited letters patent, granted and comprized, and the same James Bertie, in his own Right, is now seized in fee, or of some other estate of inheritance, of and in one other full undivided eighth part, and each of them the said William Lord Craven, Joseph Blake, Archibald Hutcheson, as trustee for the said John Cotton, Sir John Colleton, and the said Henry Bertie, Mary Danson, and Elizabeth Moor, some or one of them, is or are respectively seized in fee, or of some other estate of inheritance, of and in one other full undivided eighth part, of and in the said Provinces, territories, and premises, islands and hereditaments, the remaining eighth part or share of and in the said Provinces, territories and premises, which formerly belonging to the said Sir George Carteret, being now vested in the right Honourable John Lord Carteret, Baron of

Hawes, his majesty's Lieutenant General and Governour of the Kingdom of Ireland, And whereas, by a Judgment or Order of the House of Lords, made the twentyseventh day of March, last past, upon the appeal of the said Mary Danson, Widow of John Danson, Esquire, deceased, from a decree of the high Court of Chancery, made the seventh day of November one thousand seven hundred and twentyone, and from a subsequent order of the fifteenth day of January, one thousand, seven hundred and twentythree, it was ordered and adjudged, that the said decree and subsequent order, complained of in the said appeal, should be reversed, and it being offered on the part of the appellant, to pay the respondent, the said Henry Bertie, the money that he paid for the purchase of the Proprietorship, in question in the said cause, together with interest for the same, it was thereby further ordered, that the Court of Chancery should direct and cause an enquiry to be made, what was the principal sum of such purchase money, and from the time of payment thereof, to compute the interest for the same, and on the appellant's payment of what shall be found due for such principal money and interest, to the said Henry Bertie, it was further ordered and adjudged, That he shall convey the said Proprietorship, to her and her heirs, and also that the respondent Elizabeth Moor, should likewise by proper conveyances, at the charge of the appellant, convey all her Right to the said Proprietorship, to the appellant, and her heirs, And whereas, since the making of the said recited several letters patent, the Lords Proprietors of the Provinces and Territories aforesaid, for the time being, have made divers grants and conveyances, under their common seal, of several Offices, and also of divers parcels of land, situate within the said Provinces and territories, to several persons, under certain quit rents, or other rents, thereby respectively reserved, and subject to several conditions, limitations or agreements, for avoiding or determining the estates of the Grantees therein mentioned, some of which may have become forfeited, and have also made divers grants of several Baronies, or large tracts of land, lying within the said Provinces or Territories, unto and for the use and benefit of several of the Lords Proprietors, or those under whom they claim, to be held and enjoyed by them and their heirs in severalty, eight of which Baronies, so granted as aforesaid, do now remain vested in the said Henry now Duke of Beaufort, or in the said James Bertie and Dodington Greville, as trustees for the purposes aforesaid, or in some or one of them, eight other of the said Baronies in the said William Lord Craven, six of the said Baronies in the present Sir John Colleton, six other Baronies in the said Archibald Hutcheson, (as trustee for the said John Cotton,)

and six other Baronies in the said Joseph Blake; each of the said Baronies containing or being mentioned or intended to contain twelve thousand acres of land, or thereabouts, except one of the said Baronies now
vested in the said William Lord Craven, which contains, or is mentioned
to contain eleven thousand acres of land or thereabouts, And whereas,
the said Henry, now Duke of Beanford, William, Lord Craven, James
Bertie, Henry Bertie, Sir John Colleton, and Archibald Hutcheson, (who
is trustee for the said John Cotton, as aforesaid,) being six of the present
Lords Proprietors of the Province and territory aforesaid, have by their
humble petition, to his Majesty in Council, offered and proposed to surrender to his Majesty, their said respective shares and interests, not only
of and in the said Government, Franchises and Royalties, in and by the
said recited letters patent granted, but also all the right and property they
have in and to the soil in the aforesaid Provinces or territories, under the
said several recited letters patent, or either of them, and also did further
propose to make an entire surrender to his Majesty of their right to all
the lands which they hold under the said grants, made by the Lords
Proprietors as aforesaid, (except only one Barony, belonging to
the present Sir John Colleton, which hath been settled and improved by his son) and also their right and interest in all lands,
granted and conveyed to other persons as aforesaid, which, by not
being improved within the time limited in the said grants or conveyances, or for any other reason, would revert to them, praying;
That in consideration of such surrender, his Majesty would be pleased
to direct, and to cause to be paid to each of them, the said Henry
Duke of Beauford, William Lord Craven, James Bertie, Henry Bertie,
Sir John Colleton, and Archibald Hutcheson, the sum of two thousand
five hundred pounds apiece, without any deduction, And whereas, Samuel Wragg, of London, Merchant, being duly authorized by letter of
attorney, under the hand and seal of the said Joseph Blake, bearing date
the eleventh day of July, one thousand seven hundred and twentyeight,
hath proposed for and on behalf of the said Joseph Blake, to surrender
and convey unto his Majesty, his heirs and successors, all the estate, right
and interest of the said Joseph Blake, in and to the premises, upon payment of the like sum of two thousand five hundred pounds, to the said
Joseph Blake without any deduction, And whereas, they the said Henry,
Duke of Beauford, William, Lord Craven, James Bertie, Henry Bertie,
Sir John Colleton and Archibald Hutcheson, who is a trustee for the
said John Cotton as aforesaid, have laid before a Committee of the Lords
of his Majesty's most honourable privy council, an estimate of all the

Arrears of quit rents and other rents, and sum and sums of money now due and owing to them and the said Joseph Blake, and to the said John, Lord Carteret, which estimate, as computed, amounts to the sum of nine thousand five hundred pounds, and they the said Henry, Duke of Beauford, Lord Craven, James Bertie, Henry Bertie, Sir John Colleton and Archibald Hutcheson, have likewise humbly proposed, That if his Majesty would please to allow the sum of five thousand pounds for the said arrears, (over and above the said several sums of two thousand five hundred pounds, to be paid to them respectively) they were willing to assign and make over to his Majesty, the right and title to the said arrears, and all other demands whatsoever, which they have or can have, upon the farmers, tenants, or inhabitants of the Provinces or territories aforesaid, or of any of them; And whereas, the said Samuel Wragg, for and on the behalf of the said Joseph Blake, hath proposed to assign to his Majesty, all the right and interest of the said Joseph Blake, in and to the said arrears and demands, upon the terms aforesaid, And whereas his Majesty, taking into his royal consideration the great importance of the said Provinces and territories, to the trade and navigation of this kingdom, and being desirous to promote the same, as well as the welfare and security of the said Provinces and territories, by taking them under the more immediate Government of his Majesty, his heirs and successors, hath been graciously pleased to accept of the said several proposals, and to agree to the same, with such variations as are hereinafter mentioned; And whereas, from the nature of the respective estates and interests, proposed and agreed to be surrendered to his Majesty as aforesaid, great difficulties may arise in the manner of conveying the same, and it is just and necessary that the parts and shares of the said Provinces and territories, so proposed and agreed to be surrendered, should be secured, to his Majesty, his heirs and successors, which cannot effectually be done and attained without the authority of Parliament; *Be it enacted*, by the King's most excellent Majesty, by and with the consent and advice of the Lords spiritual and temporal, and Commons in this present Parliament, and by the authority of the same, that all those seven undivided eighth parts, (the whole into eight equal parts or shares to be divided) and all other the part or share, parts or shares, interest and estates of them the said Henry Duke of Beauford, William Lord Craven, James Bertie, Dodington Greville, Henry Bertie, Mary Danson and Elizabeth Moor, Sir John Colleton, Archibald Hutcheson, as trustee for the said John Cotton, and Joseph Blake, and each of them, of and in the aforesaid Provinces and territories, called Carolina, and all and singular the royalties, franchises, lands,

tenements, and hereditaments and premisses, in and by the said several
recited letters patent, or either of them, granted or mentioned or intended to
be granted, by his said late Majesty, King Charles the second, to the said
Edward, Earl of Clarendon, George, Duke of Albemarle, William, Earl
of Craven, John Lord Berkley, Anthony, Lord Ashley, Sir George Carteret, Sir John Colleton, deceased, and Sir William Berkley, and their
heirs and assigns, as aforesaid, with their and every of their rights, members, and appurtenances, and also all such powers, liberties, authorities,
jurisdictions, preeminences, licenses, and priviledges, as they the said
Henry, Duke of Beauford, William, Lord Craven, James Bertie, Dodington Greville, Henry Bertie, Mary Danson, Elizabeth Moor, the present
Sir John Colleton, the said Archibald Hutcheson, as trustee for the said
John Cotton, and Joseph Blake, every or any of them, can or may
have, hold, use, exercise or enjoy, by virtue of, or under the said recited
letters patent, or either of them, and also all and singular Baronies, tracts
and parcels of land, tenements and hereditaments, which they the said
Henry, Duke of Beauford, William, Lord Craven, James Bertie, Dodington Greville, Henry Bertie, Mary Danson and Elizabeth Moor, the present Sir John Colleton, the said Archibald Hutcheson, as trustee for the
said John Cotton, and Joseph Blake, any or either of them, are or is
seized or possessed of, or entitled unto, within the said Provinces or territories, except all such tracts of land, tenements and hereditaments, as
have been at any time before the first day of January, one thousand,
seven hundred and twentyseven, granted or conveyed by, or comprised
in any grants, deeds, instruments or conveyances, under the common seal
of the said Lords and Proprietors, either in England or in the Province
aforesaid, and also, except all such plantations and lands as are now in
the possession of the said Joseph Blake, his under tenants or assigns, by
virtue of grants formerly made by the said Lords Proprietors of the said
Provinces, for the time being, to other persons, and since conveyed to, or
vested in the said Joseph Blake, And also, except all that Barony and
tract of land containing twelve thousand acres or thereabouts, the possession whereof hath some time since been delivered by the present Sir John
Colleton, unto Peter Colleton, Esquire, his second son, and all that
other Barony or tract of land, containing twelve thousand acres or thereabouts, some time since conveyed by Sir John Tyrrell, Baronet (formerly
owner of the said eighth part or share now belonging to the said Archibald Hutcheson, as trustee for the said John Cotton,) to William Wight,
Esq and his heirs. Provided, that the before mentioned exceptions or
any of them, shall not include or extend to any lands, comprised in any

grant or grants, made either in England or Carolina, under the common seal of the Lords Proprietors for the time being, which since the making such grant or grants, have become forfeited by virtue of any clauses contained therein, or to any of the Baronies, herein before recited or mentioned to be still remaining and vested in the said Henry, Duke of Beauford, and in the said James Bertie and Dodington Greville, as trustees, some or one of them, and in the said William, Lord Craven, the present Sir John Colleton, and the said Archibald Hutcheson, as trustee for the said John Cotton, respectively, nor to any rents, services, seignories, or rights to escheats, reserved upon, or incident to any such grant or grants, or any lands or estates thereby granted, all such forfeited lands, and all such rents, seignories, and rights of escheat, reserved upon or incident to any such grant or grants, or any lands and estates thereby granted, and also the Baronies last before mentioned, being hereby intended to be vested in the persons, and for the purposes hereinafter mentioned, and the reversion and reversions, remainder and remainders, yearly, and other rents, issues and profits, of the same parts or shares, Baronies, Lands, tenements, hereditaments and premises, so as aforesaid proposed and agreed to be surrendered to his Majesty, and of every part and parcel thereof, and also all the estate, title, interest, trust, property, right of action, right of entry, claim and demand whatsoever, of them the said Henry, Duke of Beauford, William, Lord Craven, James Bertie, Dodington Greville, Henry Bertie, Mary Danson and Elizabeth Moor, the present Sir John Colleton, the said Archibald Hutcheson, John Cotton and Joseph Blake, and each of them, of, in, unto or out of the same, every or any part and parcel thereof, by virtue of the said several recited letters patent, or either of them, or any grant, assignment, conveyance, or assurance, made under, or by force of the same recited letters patent, or either of them, or otherwise howsoever, shall, from and after the first day of June, one thousand seven hundred, and twentynine, be vested and settled, and the same is hereby vested and settled, in and upon Edward Bertie of Gray's Inn, in the county of Middlesex, Samuel Horsey of the Parish of St Martins in the fields, in the county of Middlesex, Henry Smith of Caversham, in the county of Oxon, and Alexius Clayton, of the Middle Temple, London, Esquires, to the only use of them the said Edward Bertie, Henry Smith, Samuel Horsey, and Alexius Clayton, their heirs and assigns, freed and discharged and absolutely acquitted, exempted and indemnified, of and from all estates, uses, trusts, intails, reversions, remainders, limitations, charges and incumbrances, titles, claims, and demands whatsoever; But nevertheless upon trust, and to the intent that they the said Edward Bertie, Samuel Horsey, Henry Smith, and Alexius Clayton, and the survivor or the survivors of them, and the heirs of such survivor, upon payment by his majesty, his heirs or successors to the said Edward Bertie, Samuel Horsey, Henry Smith, and Alexius Clayton, or to the survivors or to the survivor of them, or the executors or administrators of such survivor, of the sum of seventeen thousand, five hundred pounds, free and clear of all deductions, on or before the twentyninth day of September, in the year of our Lord, one thousand, seven hundred and twentynine, shall and do, by deed, indented, and to be enrolled in his Majesty's High Court of Chancery, surrender, convey and assure unto his Majesty, his heirs and successors, all and singular, the said seven eighth parts or shares, (the whole into eight equal parts to be divided) and all other the parts or shares, interest and estates, of and in the aforesaid Provinces or territories, and all and singular the premises, hereby vested in them the said Edward Bertie, Samuel Horsey, Henry Smith, and Alexius Clayton, and their heirs as aforesaid, which said sum of seventeen thousand five hundred pounds, they the said Edward Bertie, Samuel Horsey, Henry Smith and Alexius Clayton, the survivors or the survivor of them, or the executors and administrators of such survivor, shall immediately after receipt thereof, pay, apply, and dispose of in manner hereinafter mentioned; That is to say, the sum of two thousand five hundred pounds, part thereof, to the said James Bertie and Dodington Greville, trustees as aforesaid, or to the survivor of them, or to the executors or administrators of such survivor, two thousand five hundred pounds, or other part thereof, to the said William, Lord Craven, his executors or administrators, two thousand five hundred pounds, other part thereof, to the said James Bertie, of his own right, his executors or administrators, two thousand five hundred pounds, other part thereof, unto such person or persons, and in such shares and proportions as the same, according to the tenor, purport and true meaning of the said order or judgment of the House of Lords, ought to be paid and applied, two thousand five hundred pounds, other part thereof, to the said Sir John Colleton, his executors or administrators; two thousand five hundred pounds, other part thereof, to the said John Cotton, his executors or administrators, and two thousand five hundred pounds, the residue thereof, to the said Samuel Wragg, for the use of the said Joseph Blake, or to the said Joseph Blake, his executors or administrators.

And be it further enacted, by the authority aforesaid, that from and after payment of the said sum of seventeen thousand five hundred pounds, to the said Edward Bertie, Samuel Horsey, Henry Smith, and Alexius

6

Clayton, the survivors or the survivor of them, or the executors or administrators of such survivor, and after the execution of the said surrender
and conveyance to his Majesty, his heirs and successors, shall have,
hold and enjoy, all and singular the said seven eighth parts or shares,
(the whole into eight equal parts to be divided) and all other the parts
or shares, interests and estates, of and in the aforesaid Provinces or
territories, and all and singular the premises hereby vested in them the
said Edward Bertie, Samuel Horsey, Henry Smith and Alexius Clayton,
and their heirs as aforesaid, freed and discharged, and absolutely acquitted, exempted and indemnified of, from and against all estates, uses, trusts,
intails, reversions, remainders, limitations, charges, incumbrances, titles,
claims and demands whatsoever

And be it further enacted, by the authority aforesaid, that seven eighth
parts, (the whole into eight equal parts to be divided) of all and every
the said arrears of quit rents, and other rents, sum and sums of money,
debts, duties, accounts, reckonings, claims and demands whatsoever, now
due and owing to them the said Henry, Duke of Beauford, or the said
James Bertie and Dodington Greville, trustees as aforesaid, and to the
said John, Lord Carteret, William, Lord Craven, James Bertie in his own
right, Henry Bertie, Mary Danson and Elizabeth Moor, Sir John Colleton, Archibald Hutcheson, John Cotton or Joseph Blake, or any of them,
(whether the same be more or less, than is computed as aforesaid) and all
and every other parts or shares, of the said Henry, Duke of Beauford,
James Bertie and Dodington Greville, trustees as aforesaid, William,
Lord Craven, James Bertie in his own right, Henry Bertie, Mary Danson and Elizabeth Moor, Sir John Colleton, Archibald Hutcheson, John
Cotton and Joseph Blake, or any of them, of or in the said arrears,
or which they or any of them, their or any of their heirs, executors,
administrators or assigns, now have, or can or may have, claim, chal-
lenge or demand of or from the farmers, tenants and inhabitants, of
the Provinces or territories aforesaid, or any part thereof, or any of
them, shall, from and after the said first day of June, in the year of our
Lord, one thousand seven hundred and twentynine, be vested in the
said Edward Bertie, Samuel Horsey, Henry Smith and Alexius Clayton, the survivors and survivor of them, and the executors or administrators of such survivor, upon trust, and to the intent that they the
said Edward Bertie, Samuel Horsey, Henry Smith, and Alexius Clayton, the survivors or the survivor of them, and the executors and administrators of such survivor, shall, upon payment by his Majesty, his heirs
and successors, of the sum of five thousand pounds of lawful money of

Great Britain, free and clear of all deductions, on or before the said twenty ninth day of September, in the said year, to the said Edward Bertie, Samuel Horsey, Henry Smith and Alexius Clayton, the survivors or the survivor of them, or the executors or administrators of such survivor, by deed indented and to be enrolled in his Majesty's High Court of Chancery, grant and assign to his Majesty, his heirs and successors, all and every the said seven eighth parts or shares, (the whole into eight equal parts or shares to be divided) and all other parts or shares of the said arrears, hereby vested in them the said Edward Bertie, Samuel Horsey, Henry Smith, and Alexius Clayton

And whereas, the said Henry, Duke of Beauford, William, Lord Craven, James Bertie, Henry Bertie, Mary Danson, Dodington Greville, Sir John Colleton, John Cotton and Joseph Blake, are desirous that the said sum of five thousand pounds should be applied in manner hereinafter mentioned,

Be it further enacted, by the authority aforesaid, that the sum of five thousand pounds, after receipt thereof shall be issued and paid by the said Edward Bertie, Samuel Horsey, Henry Smith and Alexius Clayton, or the survivors and survivor of them, and the executors and administrators of such survivor, to such of the officers, agents or servants of the Lords Proprietors, or to such other person or persons, and for such purposes as the said Henry Duke of Beauford, William, Lord Craven, James Bertie, Henry Bertie, Mary Danson, Sir John Colleton, John Cotton and Joseph Blake, their executors or administrators, or any four or more of them (the executors or administrators of each of them, to be accounted only as one) shall by writing or writings, under their hands, from time to time direct and appoint.

And be it further enacted, by the authority aforesaid, that from and after payment of the said sum of five thousand pounds, unto the said Edward Bertie, Samuel Horsey, Henry Smith and Alexius Clayton, the survivors or the survivor of them, or the executors or administrators of such survivor, and after the execution of the said grant and assignment of the said parts or shares, of the said arrears, hereby directed to be made as aforesaid, his Majesty, his heirs and successors, shall and may have, receive and enjoy the said seven eighth parts or shares (the whole into eight equal parts to be divided) and all and every other parts and shares of the said arrears of quit rents, and other rents, sum and sums of money, debts, duties, accounts, reckonings, claims and demands, hereby vested in the said Edward Bertie, Samuel Horsey, Henry Smith and Alexius Clayton, and shall and may have, use and pursue such and the like remedies for recovery thereof, as fully and effectually as the said Henry, Duke of Beauford, William, Lord Craven, James Bertie, Henry Bertie, Mary Danson, Dodington Greville, Sir John Colleton, Archibald Hutcheson, John Cotton and Joseph Blake, any or either of them, might have had, used or pursued if this act had not been made

And be it further enacted, by the authority aforesaid, That the receipt or receipts of the said Edward Bertie, Samuel Horsey, Henry Smith and Alexius Clayton, the survivors or the survivor of them, or executors or administrators of such survivor, under their hands, or his hand or hands respectively, shall be a sufficient discharge to his Majesty, his heirs and successors, of and for the said several sums of seventeen thousand five hundred pounds, and five thousand pounds, or so much thereof or of either of them, as such receipts or receipt shall be given for, and that his Majesty, his heirs and successors, upon and after such receipts or receipt, given as aforesaid, shall be absolutely acquitted and discharged of and from the said monies and shall not be answerable or accountable for any loss, non-application or misapplication of the said money, or of any part thereof.

Provided always, and it is hereby declared and enacted, by the authority aforesaid, that the receipt or receipts of the said James Bertie, or Dodington Greville, or the survivor of them, his executors or administrators, under his or their hand or hands respectively, shall be a sufficient discharge to the said Edward Bertie, Samuel Horsey, Henry Smith, and Alexius Clayton, their executors or administrators, for the said sum of two thousand five hundred pounds, payable to them for the said eighth part or share of the said Provinces, territories, royalties, lands and hereditaments, which was vested in the said Henry late Duke of Beauford, and the said sum of two thousand five hundred pounds, shall be and remain subject to the trusts reposed in them by the will of the said late Duke, or otherwise, concerning the eighth part or share, but the said Edward Bertie, Samuel Horsey, Henry Smith and Alexius Clayton, their heirs, executors, or administrators, shall not be answerable or accountable for any loss or misapplication thereof, or of any part thereof

Provided also, and it is hereby declared and enacted, That the said Edward Bertie, Samuel Horsey, Henry Smith and Alexius Clayton, shall not, nor shall any of them, or the executors or administrators of any of them, be answerable or accountable for any money to be received by virtue of or under the trusts hereby reposed in them, any otherwise than each person, his executors or administrators, for such sum or sums of money as he or they shall respectively actually receive, and none of them shall be answerable or accountable for the acts, receipts, neglects, or defaults of the other of them, and also that they, the said Edward Bertie, Samuel Horsey, Henry Smith and Alexius Clayton, their executors or administrators, shall and may, out of the money hereby directed to be paid to them as aforesaid, retain and reimburse themselves for all costs, charges, damages and expenses, that they respectively shall sustain or be put unto, in and about the execution of the trusts hereby in them reposed.

And whereas there is due and owing to the King's most excellent Majesty, for arrears of rents reserved by the said several recited letters patent, or one of them, several sums of money, computed to amount to three hundred pounds or upwards, *Now it is hereby further enacted and declared*, by the authority aforesaid, that the said Henry, Duke of Beauford, William, Lord Craven, James Bertie, Dodington Greville, Henry Bertie, Mary Danson, Elizabeth Moor, the present Sir John Colleton, Archibald Hutcheson, John Cotton and Joseph Blake, and every of them, their and every of their heirs, executors and administrators, respectively, from and immediately after the said twentyninth day of September, one thousand seven hundred and twentynine, (in case the said sums of seventeen thousand five hundred pounds, and five thousand pounds, shall then be paid and satisfied, and the sale hereby intended shall be then compleated) shall be, and are hereby fully and absolutely acquitted and discharged of and from all arrears of rent whatsoever, due or owing upon or by virtue of the said recited letters patent, or either of them.

Provided always, and it is hereby further enacted and declared, by the authority aforesaid, that if his Majesty, his heirs and successors, do not or shall not, on or before the said twentyninth day of September, one thousand seven hundred and twentynine, well and truly pay or cause to be paid, both the several sums of seventeen thousand five hundred pounds, and five thousand pounds in manner aforesaid, and according to the true meaning of this act, that then they the said Edward Bertie, Samuel Horsey, Henry Smith and Alexius Clayton, or the survivors or survivor of them, or the heirs, executors or administrators of such survivor, shall not make such surrender, assignment, or conveyance of the said seven eighth parts or shares of the said Province or territories, and of the said arrears, or either of them, to his Majesty, his heirs or successors, as hereby is directed, but shall from and after the said twentyninth day of September, one thousand seven hundred and twentynine, stand and be seized of and possessed of all and singular the premises hereby in them vested, to the only proper use and behoof of them, the said Henry, Duke of Beauford, William, Lord Craven, James Bertie, Dodington Greville, Henry Bertie, Mary Danson, Elizabeth Moor, the present Sir John Colleton, John Cotton and Joseph Blake, and every of them, and of their and every of their heirs, executors, administrators and assigns, in such shares and proportions, and according to such respective rights and interests as they severally had, or could have been entitled to, in and unto the same premises, in case this act had never been made, and to and for no other use or trust, intent or purpose whatsoever

Saving and reserving to all and every person or persons, bodies politick and corporate, their heirs, successors, executors, administrators and assigns, other than and except the said Henry, Duke of Beauford, William, Lord Craven, James Bertie, Dodington Greville, Henry Bertie, Mary Danson, Elizabeth Moor, Sir John Colleton, Archibald Hutcheson, John Cotton and Joseph Blake, their respective heirs, executors or administrators, and the heirs of their respective bodies, and all and every person and persons, claiming or to claim any estate and interest in the premises, or any part thereof, in remainder or reversion, expectant upon or after the determination of any estate tail, vested in them the said Henry, Duke of Beauford, William, Lord Craven, James Bertie, Dodington Greville, Henry Bertie, Mary Danson, Elizabeth Moor, Sir John Colleton, Archibald Hutcheson, John Cotton and Joseph Blake, or any of them, and all and every person and persons claiming, or to claim any estate or interest in the premises, or any part thereof, by or under the title of the said Henry, late Duke of Beauford, deceased, such satisfaction and recompense as is hereinafter mentioned, for all such estate, right, title, interest, property, claim or demand whatsoever, in, to or out of the premises, or any part thereof, as they or any of them, now have, or might have had or been entitled to, in case this act had never been made

Provided always, and be it further enacted, by the authority aforesaid, That if any person or persons (other than and except the persons herein before excepted) who now have or shall have any estate, right, title, interest, claim or demand, either in law or in equity, of, in, to or out of the premises herein vested as aforesaid, or any part thereof, shall, within the space of seven years after the same shall be conveyed unto and vested in his Majesty, his heirs and successors as aforesaid, commence and prosecute any action or suit either in law or equity, by petition of right, English bill or otherwise, against his Majesty, his heirs or successors, or the proper officer or officers on his or their behalf, wherein such persons might or ought to have recovered the premises hereby vested as aforesaid, or any part thereof, or any estate, interest or demand, in or out of the same, the court wherein such suit or action shall be commenced or depending, shall and may adjudge or decree, that such person or persons shall recover against his Majesty, his heirs or successors, such sum or sums of money, as his or their estate, interest or demand in or about the premises hereby vested as aforesaid, shall by the same court be valued at and determined to amount unto, in full satisfaction for such estate, interest or demand; in making which valuation the said court shall estimate one full eighth part of the premises hereby vested as aforesaid, to be of the value of two thousand five hundred pounds, and no more, and shall rate and ascertain the value of such estate, interest or demand in proportion thereunto.

Saving and reserving always to the said John, Lord Carteret, his heirs, executors, administrators and Assigns, all such estate, right, title, interest, property, claim and demand whatsoever, in, unto or out of, one eighth part or share of the said Provinces or territories, with all and singular the rights, members and appurtenances thereof, and of, in and to one eighth part or share of all arrears of quit rents, and other rents, sum and sums of money, debts, duties, accounts, reckonings, claims and demands whatsoever, now due and oweing to the present Lords Proprietors of the said Provinces and territories, and all such other rights, titles, priviledges and powers whatsoever, as the said John, Lord Carteret, his heirs, executors or administrators now have or might have had or been entitled unto, in case this act, and the conveyance herein before directed to be made to his Majesty, his heirs and successors, or either of them, had not been, or should not be made

Saving also to all and every person and persons having or lawfully claiming any office or offices, place or places, employment or employments, by or under any grant or grants thereof made before the said first day of January, one thousand seven hundred and twenty seven, under the common seal of the said Lords Proprietors, either in England or in the Provinces aforesaid, all such estate, right, title and interest in or to such office or offices, place and places, employment and employments, as they or any of them now have or might have had, or been entitled unto, in case this Act had never been made

[FROM NORTH CAROLINA LETTER BOOK OF S P G]

GOV' EVERARD TO THE BISHOP OF LONDON

EDENTON Oct 12 1729

MY LORD

When I find Quakers & Baptists flourish amongst the N° Carolinians, it behoved me that am the Gov' here to enquire & look into the Original cause, which on the strictest examination & nicest scrutiny I can make, find is owing to the want of Clergymen amongst us. We in this great Province have never a one, & truly my Lord both Quakers & Baptists in this vacancy are very busy makeing Proselytes & holding meetings daily in every Part of this Gov' Indeed one New County next Virginia is well supplied by the Indefatigable Pains & industry of the Rev⁴ Mʳ Jones of Nansemond who has the Character of a Pious, Good & Worthy man but he is old & infirm My Lord, when I came first here, there was no Dissenters but Quakers in the Gov' & now by the means of one Paul Palmer the Baptist Teacher, he has gained hundreds & to prevent it, tis impossible, when I have a Secretary, one John Lovick, that makes a jest of all religion & values not noe God, man, nor Devil a true enthusiast when I promoted building the Church, he was the only man that hindered it, laid so many stumbling blocks in the way, it was impossible to go about it then, & I very much fear whilst he is in the Gov' none will be built, he may truly be called the *Remora* to all religion & goodness. His original was a footboy to the Former Gov' Mʳ Hyde, & by making friends got also to be recommended to Mʳ Eden who in the affair of Thatch the Pirate, made him act the Part of an affidavit man, but that being before my time, don't personally know it, but have it credibly attested by Honest Living Evidences of good veracity, this is the Man that at Present rules everything, Yea even our Religion &c, but hope thro' your Lordship's assistance to throw off this heavy yoke & banish him to a place where he may have less power to Perpetrate his rogueries & we have the free liberty of a good Clergy & our religion & freedom, which is the sincere & hearty Prayer of My Lord

Your Lordship's most dutiful & most Obd' son & servant

RICH⁴ EVERARD

[B. P R. O. Am & W. Ind Vol. 22 p 5.]

EXTRACT OF A LETTER FROM Mr PORTER TO GOVERNOUR BURRINGTON DATED NORTH CAROLINA 30th NOVEMBER 1729

Our Session ended last Thursday, when Sir Richard confirmed several Laws, one among the rest for raising 30000£ Paper Currency, who has a Present for so doing of 500£   How this latter Conduct will be approved of in England, in respect it breaks one of the articles of his Instructions, we are at a loss to judge.

I prevailed with him for near a Twelvemonth last past to stop Warrants and Patents for Land, till his Majesty's Pleasure was further known, himself having wrote the Duke of Newcastle his Reasons as well as his Resolutions on that occasion, which now he is every day breaking through by signing Patents

[B. P R O B. T South Carolina Vol 4 C. 71]

LORDS OF TRADE TO THO LOWNDES.
8th DECEMBER 1729

Sr

With the greatest defference I beg leave to observe to your Lordships, that exact Charts of all the Sea Coast and Bays and Soundings of all the Harbours of his Majesties American Dominions and Maps of all the Inland Territory might be procured to the great advantage of the Publick and without any additional charge   If North Carolina which (ever since t'was a seperate Government) has only been a Receptacle for Pyrates Thieves and Vagabonds of all sorts was made a District of Virginia and the Quit Rents for Lands let out duely received, there would be a competent Fond to reward a knowing and honest Man, to make such a Noble and usefull survey   The Establishment for Officers in the Proprietors time, which the Quitt Rents always discharged amounted to 480l and if a Rental was obtained (which the Proprietors could never get) would amount to a much greater Sum   The soyl of North Carolina is much better than that of Virginia, it's Timber is of the largest Growth, there is great Quantity of Iron Oar and (according to information) good reason

7

to expect Copper-Mines and the New England Traders get from thence a very great Quantity of the best Pitch and Tarr in Barter for Rum Spirits Molosses and other goods which would bear a moderate Duty to make up any Deficiency that might happen to the Fond, proposed to defray what I humbly conceive so usefull an undertaking   For besides all other advantages of such a survey wee should effectually prevent the French from Encroaching within the Limits of our Newfoundland and other Fisheries.

And when this affair is quite perfected I beg leave farther to hint that by the same Fond a Light House may easily be erected on the Point of Hilton-Head Island in the Gulf of Florida where there is a great Plenty of Noble Timber and the land high and very fit for that purpose   And this Fond may be so augmented by an easy Duty upon the Tonnage of all ships coming from Jamaica and elsewhere through the Gulf (which all the Traders for their own security would readily come into) as would maintain a competent Number of Trinity-Brothers to assist vessells that pass through that dangerous Navigation

And of what use such an Institution would be in case Port Royal should be made a Harbour for a Royal Navy and a place for stores, and of what service t'would be to the publick to have some seamen of this Nation perfectly acquainted with all the Currents and Counter-Currents in the Gulfs of Mexico and Florida and to know all the Narrow Passages to Cuba through the Bahama Islands, and all the shifting Land Banks in those Parts with a great many more advantages which would accrue to Navigation and Commerce I beg leave most humbly to submit to your Lordships great judgement and wisdom and am with the most profound respect

My Lords
　your Lordships
　　Most obedient and most
　　　faithfull humble
　　　　servant

THO· LOWNDES

P. S
If very particular and unusual Instructions are not given to the Surveyor Generall and Secretary of South Carolina the settling that Province will be much prejudiced

[B P R. O B T South Carolina Vol. 4. C 60—Extract]

COLL JOHNSON TO SEC OF B. T. DECEMBER 19th 1729.

S'

*   *   *   *   *   *

4thly That the Boundaries of South Carolina and North Carolina are absolutely necessary to be ascertained and settled to prevent any of the Inhabitants of South Carolina from running to Cape Fair and settling there to defraud their Creditors, and for the remedying this evil That Cape Fair be made a Port and a Collector of the Customs appointed to reside there, and the said place declared to be within the limits of South Carolina

*   *   *   *   *   *

S'

your most oblidged humble
servant

ROB' JOHNSON

[B P R. O Am & W Ind Vol. 22. p 6]

To the most noble Thomas Duke of New Castle Secret'y of State &c

May it please your Grace—

In my Memorial of the 15th of June last I took leave to inform your Grace of our Governour Sir Richard Everards orders to one M' John Lovick acting as Secretary respecting the Disposition of no more of the soil of this Province, until his Majestys Royal Pleasure were therein known   The occasion as I allways conceived of those orders was (as Sir Richard wrote your Grace himselfe) from a Discovery he had made of the fraudalent practice of the above John Lovick and M' Edward Moseley our Surveyor General of Lands, and notwithstanding all such convincing proofs of the same and the many resolutions Sir Richard had made of signing no more Warrants or Pattents

Yet so it is may it please your Grace, tho he knows this Country is now under the Crown, he has since broke through such his Intentions, and now every day signs both Warrants and Pattents. And what is worse was induced some time ago by the uncommon art and cunning of this Lovick and his two confederates Moseley and Will'm Little the

Receiver General to the Lords Proprietors to sign many Pattents wherein the number of acres are left Blank and on the same Pattents there is the Receiver General Littles receipt likewise in blank for the purchas money, so that the possessors of such Pattents have it in their own power to put in as much land as by our Charter might make them Landgraves or Cassicks, whereas I believe the true Intent of Sr Richard was that every pattent he so signed should contain what is by the late Lords Proprietors orders and by our own Laws distinguished to be a Tract containing six hundred and forty acres. Instead of which some people who are let into the Secrit, and that has procured such pattents has filled up the blanks with what quantity of land they pleased, one Laine of the Country of Bath put into his pattent 5000 acres others more and some less, by which means before his Majesty's commissions can take place amongst us most of the Land will be disposed of under a sham proprieterry title and the money arrising therefrom put into the pocketts of those three Messinarys Lovick, Moseley, and Little, how far such a proceedure will deserve notice, I shall submit it to your Graces opinion   As I once mentioned before if there was an officer suddenly appointed as Receiver General with a power of inspecting into such former conduct it might possibly be many thousands pounds advantage to the Crown; and if your Grace should be pleased to think me deserving of so great a trust (as I am well acquainted with the circumstance of things) no man shall more justly and faithfully discharge it, than

My Lord, your Graces most
dutifull and obedient servant
EDMOND PORTER

North Carolina
Albemarle
Desr the 22nd 1729

[FROM RECORDS OF GENERAL COURT]

NORTH CAROLINA—ss.

At a Genl Court of Over & Terminer and Genl Sessions held for the Savd province at the Courthouse in Edenton begun on Tuesday the twenty fifth day of March one thousand Seven hundred & twenty nine and continued by Adjournmt until the third of April following

Present

Christopher Gale Esq' Cheif Justice

Thomas Luton ⎫
John Alston ⎬ Esq^m Assistants
Tho' Lovick ⎪
Henry Bonner ⎭

And Severall Members of the Council (as Justices of the peace) to hold the Genl Sessions of this Government.

The following persons were impannell^d and Sworne of the Grand Jury Viz^t

Capt Benj^a Hill	Mr Robert Hicks	Mr Orlando Champion
Mr Tho' Luton Junr	Mr James Meliken	Mr Richd Willson
Mr Francis Branch	Mr John Blount	Mr James Castellaw
Mr Edward Howcot	Mr John Beverley	Mr Martin Cromen
Mr Thomas Bryan	Mr John Bonde	Mr Hill Savage
	Mr Tho' Rountree	

who being charged with things proper for their Enquiry withdrew and Consider^d thereof and on their Returne made presentm^t of the following Bills Viz^t

A Bill of Indictm^t against Solomon Smith for Felony & Murder

A Bill of Indictm^t ag^t Griffith Jones & Truman Jones for a Forcible Entry on the Estate of William Reed a minor

A Bill of Indictm^t ag^t James Bremen for assaulting Robert Pearce.

And then the Grand Jury was discharg^d from further Attendance at this Court.

And now here at this day (Viz^t &c) The aforesayd Thomas Spencer (tho' Solemnly required) came not Nor was there any return made of the Writt of Exigent

Wherefore It Consider^d by the Court here at the motion of the Attorney Genl that the same be continued returnable to the next Court on the last Tuesday in July next

And now here at this day (Viz^t &c:) came the afores^d George Allen and moved for Tryall And likewise the Attorney Genl on behalf of Our Sovereign Lord the King But the Court being given to understand that His Maj^tys most Gracious Genl Pardon was Since the offence comitted and Since the Indictm^t afores^d are of Opinion that the Sayd Offence is thereby pardon^d & that the prosecution afores^d cannot be proceeded in according to Fawcett's Case 2^d Croke 148 Do therefore Order that all further proceedings thereon be Stay^d and the Sayd Geo: Allen be discharg^d paying Costs.

And now here at this day (Viz[t] &c) came the aforesayd Joseph Jenoure by David Osheal his Attorney & moved to the Court that he might come to a legall Tryall or be discharg[d]

Whereupon the Attorney Gen[l] produced to the Court here an Order from the Governo[r] in these Words Viz[t]

NORTH CAROLINA—ss

S[r] Rich[d] Everard Bar[t] Governo[r] Cap[t] Gen[l] & Adm[ll] To W[m] Little Esq Attorney Gen[ll]

Whereas a Bill of Indictment was preferr[d] & found by the Grand Jury at July Court ag[t] Joseph Jenoure and others for a Riott, These are therefore to order & impower you to enter a Noli Prosequi on the Sayd Indictm[t] Given under my hand this first day of April 1729 in the Second year of his Maj[ty] King George y[e] second & Sign[d] Rich[d] Everard

Wherefore It is Consider[d] & by the Court here Order[d] that the sayd Joseph Jenoure & the Others mention[d] meant or intended in the sayd Indictm[t] be thereof dismist and may go without day paying Costs.

And now here at this day (Viz[t] &c) the afores[d] Nathaniel Martin in Custody of the Marshall to the Barr here brought in his proper person came and being ask[d] how of the Crime afores[d] he would acquitt himself sayd that he is not thereof Guilty & for Tryall thereof putt himself upon the Country and W[m] Little Esq[r] Atto[r] Gen[l] on behalf of our Sovereign Lord the King likewise Whereupon the Marshall was comanded to cause to come twelve &c And there came John Charlton Tho[s] Hoskins John Benbury John Champion Jo[n] Dunning Sam[l] Woodward James Smith Charles Wilkins William Handcock W[m] Branch John Carter Henderson Luton who being impannell[d] and Sworn on their Oath do say that he is not Guilty

Order[d] that the sayd Nath[l] Martin & Susanna his Wife be thereof dismist without day paying Costs

W[m] Little Esq[r] Attorney Gen[l] comes to prosecute y[e] Bill of Indictment ag[t] Solomon Smith in these Words Viz[t]

NORTH CAROLINA—ss.

To Christoph[r] Gale Esq[r] Cheif Justice and the rest of the Justices for holding the Gen[l] Court at Edenton the last Tuesday of this Instant March 1729

The Jurors for Our Sovereign Lord the King on their Oath do present that Solomon Smith late of Bertie precinct Labourer in the precinct aforesayd not having the fear of God before his Eyes but being moved

and Seduced by y⁰ instigation of the Devil on or about the first day of
November last past in the Evening of the same day at Bertie p'cinct in the
province aforesayd by force and Armes in & upon One William Coyne
in the peace of God and Our sayd Lord the King then & there being an
Assault did make And the sayd Solomon Smith with a Knife of the
value of three pence in his hand then & there drawn had & held feloniously & voluntarily the afores⁴ William Coyne at Bertie p'cinct in the
province aforesayd did Stabb & wound y⁰ Sayd William not having any
weapon then drawn nor having then there first struck the sayd Solomon
and to the sayd William Coyne of Bertie p'cinct in the province aforesayd feloniously and of his malice forethought with the aforesayd knife
One mortall wound in & upon his left breast did give about one inch &
half long and about five inches in depth with which mortall wound the
Sayd William Coyne instantly dyed and So the Jurors aforesayd upon
their Oath do say that the aforesayd Solomon Smith on the day and year
afores⁴ in Bertie p'cinct in the province aforesayd in manner & form
aforesayd killed and murder⁴ the Sayd William Coyne ag⁴ the peace of
Our sayd Lord y⁰ King his Crown & dignity &c & against the Statute
in that Case made & provided. Upon which Indictm⁴ the sayd Solomon
Smith was arraign⁴ and upon his Arraignm⁴ pleaded Not Guilty and for
Tryall thereof putt himself upon God & the Country and William Little
Esq' Att'ney Gen¹¹ on y⁰ behalf of our Sayd Lord the King likewise
Whereupon the Marshall was comanded to cause to come twelve &c. and
there came Francis Pugh William Bryan John Early James Smith John
Champion John Howell Rob' Jefferys John Dunning John Blackman
James Bate Jacob Privett & Wᵐ Charlton Jun' who being impannell⁴
and Sworne on their Oath do Say Wee Jurors do find the prisoner Solo-
mon Smith Guilty

(Sign⁴) FRANCIS PUGH Foreman

Then the sayd Solomon Smith being ask⁴ if he had any thing to Say
why Sentence Should not pass ag⁴ him as the law in that Case hath provided And he offering nothing in avoydance thereof It is Therefore Consider⁴ Sentenced & by the Court here adjudg⁴ that the sayd Solomon
Smith shall returne to the place from whence he came and from thence to
the place of Execution there to be hang⁴ by the Neck till his Body is
dead.

The Court having re⁰d from the Honoᵇˡᵉ the Governo' by the hands of
Rich⁴ Everard Esq' his Son the following paper Viz'

NORTH CAROLINA—ss.

To Chr Gale Esqr Cheif Just & to the rest of the Assistant Judges

I receiv'd a certificate yesterday sign'd by the Ch Justice in which it is Signified to me that one Sol° Smith of Bertie p'cinct Labourer stands condemn'd by this Sessions for the murther of William Coyne for which ye Sentence of the Sayd Court was for him to be hang'd As the Life of a Man is a thing of a very tender nature I am at a loss to judge if the Cheif Just means hanging till he is dead or whether it is by the Neck legg or arm for I must not guess at his meaning Besides I must tell you Gen' as the man was tryde Condemned on the twenty ninth of the last Month And the Court was Compounded of Officers not duly qualifyed to open Such Court that all proceedings therein are Extrajudiciall and Erronious Therefore cannot without Injury to my conscience Sign Such a Dead Warrant for the Execution of the unhappy prisoner till a Tryall de novo and the Court Compounded of Officers duly qualifyed and those of my Appoyntment

Given under my hand this first day of April One thousand Seven hundred & twenty nine and Sign'd Richard Everard

It was consider'd by the Court & that the Blood of an innocent person barbarously Shedd was of too great & Serious a consequence to be turn'd to Ridicule as it appears to be by the aforegoing paper or Letter to the Court Whereupon the Court came to a Resolution to certify the same again to the Hono'ble the Governo' which was done in these words Vizt

NORTH CAROLINA—ss.

Gen' Court April ye Second one thous'd Seven hundred and twenty nine By the Cheif Justice & Members of ye Gen' Court That Innocent Blood may not lye at Our Door Wee think it Our Duty once more to certify to yo' Hono' that Sol° Smith now prisoner in the Goale at Edenton has been this Sessions legally convicted for the Murder of William Coyne and that Sentence of Death was on the twenty ninth of March past pronounc'd upon him in Open Court in these Words Vizt That he should returne to the place from whence he came & from thence to the place of Execution and there be hang'd by the neck till his Body was dead. It appears to us to be a very barbarous Murder Directed to the Hono'ble Sr Rich'd Everard Gov' &c and Sign'd Chr Gale Tho' Luton Tho' Lovick & Henry Bonner

A Bill of Indictment having been presented to the Grand Jury aforesayd against Jacob Beale for killing James Beale by Misadventure and being return'd Ignoramus It was considered by the Court that he be thereof dismist and may goe with' day paying Costs

Wm Little Esqr Attorney Genl comes to prosecute a Bill of Indictment found by the Grand Jury ag^t Griffith Jones & Truman Jones in these words Viz^l

NORTH CAROLINA—ss.

To Christop^r Gale Esq. Cheif Justice & the rest of the Justices for holding the Genl Court at the Courthouse in Edenton on the last Tuesday in March Anno D^{ai} One thousand Seven hundred & twenty nine

The Jurors for Our Sovereign Lord the King on their Oath do present that Griffith Jones & Truman Jones both of pasquotank precinct having taken and associated themselves with other malefact^{rs} and disturbers of the peace of Our Sayd Lord the King being arm^d in an Hostile manner of whose names the Jurors aforesayd are wholly Ignorant upon the twelfth day of March Anno Dⁿⁱ One thousand Seven hundred & twenty eight at Pasquotank Precinct in the province aforesayd by force & Armes To witt with Swords Staves Gunns & other defensive and invasive Armes upon one Mesuage with the Appurtenances at Arenoose Creek in pasquotank p'cinct aforesayd upon the peacable possession of One Mrs Jane Reed Widow & Extrix of William Reed late of pasquotank p'cinct aforesayd Esqr dec^d did enter of which Certain Mesnage with the appurtenances the aforesayd Jane Reed Wid^o and Extrix was then & there possess^d during the minority of William Reed a Minor Son of William Reed Esqr late of the sayd p'cinct deceased to whom the freehold of the p'mises belongs And the abovesayd Griffith Jones and Truman Jones and the other malefacto^{rs} afores^d by force & Armes the aforesayd Jane from her possession aforesayd did Eject expell & amove and the Sayd Jane So being expell^d from her aforesayd Mesuage with the appurtenances unlawfully and with a Strong hand did then keep out and Still do keep & hold out against the peace of Our Sayd Lord the King that now is his Crown & dignity and Contrary to the form of the Statutes in that Case made and provided &c And on the motion of the Sayd Attorney Genl It is Consider^d & Order^d that a Capias do issue returnable to the next Court on the last Tuesday in July next

A Bill of Indictment having been preferr^d to the Grand Jury against John Perkins on Suspicion of having burnt the House of Thomas Clinson lately Situate & being in the precinct of Curratuck in the province aforesayd Which Sayd Bill of Indictm^t was return^d to the Court here Ignoramus. Therefore It is Consider^d that he give Security for his good behaviour twelve months & one day And that he continue in the Marshall's Custody untill he hath given Such Security & payd the Costs acerning by this prosecution Whereupon the sayd John Perkins in Court appear⁴ and acknowledg⁴ himself indebted to Our Sovereign Lord the King His Heirs and Successo™ in the sum of fifty pounds Sterling to be levyed on his goods & Chattells Lands and Tenem⁸ &c With Condiĉon that if the sayd John Perkins shall & do well & truly behave himself towards his Sayd Majesty and all his leige people and more especially towards Thoˢ Clinson and His Wife for twelve months & One day then this Recognizance to be voyd else to remaine of full force & Virtue

W™ Little Esq' Attorney Gen' comes to prosecute the Bill of Indictment found by the Grand Jury afores⁴ against James Bremen in these Words Viz'

NORTH CAROLINA—ss

To Christopher Gale Esq' Cheif Justice & the rest of the Justices for holding of the Gen' Court at Edenton on the last Tuesday of this instant March Anno Dˢⁱ one thousand seven hundred & twenty nine.

The Jurors for our Sovereign Lord yᵉ King upon their Oaths present that James Bremen late of Edenton in the North East parish of Chowan precinct in Albemarle County in the province aforesayd Merch' the twenty third day of this instant Moneth of March in the night time of the same day by force & Armes &c at Edenton in the parish p'cinct and County aforesayd in North Carolina aforesayd then & there by force & Armes &c the Window of the lodging room of one Robert Pearce did break open And him the sayd Robert Pearce did then & there assault & in great danger of his life did putt & Other Enormitys to the Sayd Robert Pearce then & there did offer against the peace of Our now Sayd Sovereign Lord the King his Crown & dignity &c And sign⁴ W™ Little Att'ʸ Gen' and on the Motion of the sayd Attorney Gen' It was then & there by the Court Consider⁴ and Order⁴ that he be taken into Custody of the provost Marshall and brought before the Court which was accordingly done And the sᵈ James Bremen acknowledg⁴ himself indebted to our Sovereign Lord the King His Heirs & Successo™ in the Sum of One hundred pounds Sterling & M' Edmond Porter & M™ W™ Harding Jones in the Sum of fifty pounds Sterling each to be levyed on their goods & Chattells Lands & Tenem⁸ &c With Condiĉon that if the Sayd James Bremen shall personally be & appear at the next Gen' Court to be held for this Governm' at Edenton the last Tuesday in July next then & there to answer the sayd Indictm' and in the meantime that he be of his good Behaviour then this Recognizance to be voyd else to remaine in full force &c

Whereupon Rich⁴ Everard Esq' came into Court and deliver⁴ to the Court here a Certain Writing in these Words Viz'

NORTH CAROLINA—ss.

S' Richard Everard Bar' Gov' Cap' Gen" Adm' and Comand' in Cheif
    To Christopher Gale Esq' Cheif Justice & his Assistants and to W"
    Little Esq' Attorney Gen' Greeting

Whereas a Certain Bill of Indictm' was preferr' and found by the
Grand Jury of this present Court ag' James Bremen of Edenton Merch'
for breaking open the Window of One Robert Pearce & then & there
assaulting the sayd Robert Pearce & being that I am fully assured & Satisfyed that the Sayd Indictm' was grounded upon the malice of the s'
Robert Pearce and by the instigation of Will" Badham alias Hammon
Clerk of the Gen' Court and that the Sayd James Bremen did no ways
assault Strike or any other ways hurt the Sayd Robert Pearce And that
the sayd Window was open before the Sayd James Bremen came to it
and he did not by any act whatsoever brake or disturb the peace of our
Soveraign Lord the King   This is Therefore to Command you the sayd
Christopher Gale &c to enter a Noli prosequi on the Sayd Indictment
Given under my hand and Seal this 1st day of April in the second year
of his Majesty King George y' Second Annoq D"i 1729 and Sign' Rich'
Everard and a Seale Wherefore It is Consider' & by the Court here by
& with the Consent of the Attorney Gen' that the sayd James Bremen
be thereof dismist and may go thereof without day it being the Gov-
erno" Order And It was then & there Order' that the Sayd Comand
Should be entred as aforesayd

Will am Williams of Edenton Gen' produced a Comission from the
Hono"e S' Rich' Everard Bar' Governo' &c appoynting him provost
Marshal in the room of Rob' Route Esq' who is Comissionated by the
Lords Prop" to Execute that Office in this Governm' as long as he well
behaves And the sayd W" Williams mov' to the Court here to have the
Sayd Comission admitted and himself qualify' and reçd Whereupon the
Court declared their Opinion was that the Comission aforesayd is not
good because the sayd S' Rich' Everard Governo' did not take the advice
and Consent of the Majority of the Council for granting the same as by
law he ought to have done And the Court are also of opinion that the
aforesayd Robert Route is not departed out of this Governm' as in the
Sayd Comission is Suggested And that the Deputys which act by virtue
of his Comission are good & lawfull

By direction of this Court John Parke Esq' Provost Marshall was
comanded to take into his Custody Edmond Porter & George Allen &
them safely keep until they give Security for their good behaviour
during the Sitting of this Court for a Contempt by comitting an affray

in the view and verge thereof And the sayd Geo Allen came into Court & ackrowledg⁴ himself indebted to Our Soveregn Lord the King in the Sum of ten pounds Sterling and Edmond Gale Esqʳ in the like Sum of ten pounds Sterling to be levyed on their Severall goods and Chattells Lands & Tenements &c With Condĩon that the Sayd George Allen shall be of his good behaviour during the Sitting of this Court And in further Obedience of the sayd Order and Direction the sayd Jnᵒ Parke follow⁴ the sayd Edm⁴ Porter who was fledd to the House of Mⁿ Eliza-beth Marston a publick House or Ordinary in Edenton and there told the sayd Porter he had receiv⁴ the aforesayd Order Whereupon the Honoᵇˡᵉ Sʳ Rich⁴ Everard Barᵗ Governoʳ of the province aforesaid who was at the Sayd House rose up from his Seat & comãnded him not to take any body out of his Company & further told him that he was no Marshall and that he thought he the Sayd Parke had a great .   . . . he would protect every body that was in his Company and bidd him tell the Court so Upon which the Sayd Parke imediately withdrew without the Sayd Porter and return⁴ to the Court and made report thereof

Robert Pearce came into Court and made Information upon Oath in these Words Vizᵗ Robert Pearce Sworne on the holy Evangelists upon his Oath Sayth that on Monday morning about the hours of three and four before Sunrising he this Informant being in his own Lodging room in Bed and wak⁴ out of his Sleep did hear a Noise in the next adjoining room to this Informant's And imediately thereon this Inform⁴ heard the voyce of James Bremen (to whom the sayd next adjoining room belongs & another persons voyce which this Informant takes to be Mʳ Rich⁴ Everard which Sayd Bremen & Mʳ Everard demanded this Informant to open his Door And (this Informant being silent therein) the sayd Bremen & Mʳ Everard both went round to this Informants Wooden Window which was then close shutt) which they broke open and Splitt in peices And then Mʳ Rich⁴ Everard (whose face this Informant saw by moon light) did fire in upon this Informant in his sayd Lodging room Severall times with a pistoll or pistolls thro' the Window broken open as aforesayd and took full aime to this Inform⁴ to fire at him & then went round into the Sayd Bremens Room & broke the door of the sayd room (which before was nayled) in Severall parts And Severall fires from a pistoll or pistolls were fired in upon him this Inform⁴ By which meanes he this Inform⁴ was much in danger of his life & was very much hurt in his face & hand by the Gunpowder that lodg⁴ in his Face & hand and very much burned him this Informant And further Sayth the sayd Bremen told him this Inform⁴ that he the sayd Bremen had gotten this Informants

Bullett Moole & had Cast Bulletts enough to do the business of this Informant and all the rest of em that day And Sayd See what your lisping Judge can do now to help you and the Sayd Bremen declared that he would enter into the room of this Informant and break one of his Cutlaces and then he would have but one to defend himself with, And this Informant further Saith that the Sayd James Bremen Sayd Here damne his Blood shoot his Braines out Sign⁴ Robert Pearce & thus (*) for Seale Upon which he pray⁴ Security of the Peace

Which Informaćon being Corroborated by the Oaths of John Ismas Gent and Thomas Jones Attorney at Law It is Consider⁴ that the Provost Marshall be directed to take them the sayd James Bremen and Richard Everard into his Custody and them Safely keep untill they give Security in the Sum of One hundred pounds Sterling each and two suretys for each of them in the sum of fifty pounds sterling every of them With Condićon that they be and appear at the next Gen¹ Court on the last Tuesday in July next on the third day of the sayd Court & in the mean time that they shall keep the peace of our Sovereign Lord the King as well towards his Majesty as all his leige people And particularly the Sayd Robert Pearce and not depart from the Sayd Court without Lycence &c

And then the Court }
adjourned by order }

[B. P R. O Journals. B. T Vol. 39. p 154.]

WHITEHALL Tuesday June 3ʳᵈ 1729

At a Meet⁸ of H M Comⁿ for Trade & Plant⁸
Present

Earl of Westmorland	Mʳ Pelham
Mʳ Docminique.	Mʳ Bladen
	Mʳ Ashe.

A letter was read from Maj Gooch Lieut. Gov of Virginia dated 28 Feb⁷ 172⅘ with several inclosures—including Protest of the Commⁿ of North Carolina against proceeding on the division line between the two Governments and the Virginia Comm⁸ Answer thereto. Two Plans of the Division line between Virginia and Carolina run in 1728 by the Comm⁸ & Surveyor of the two Govern⁸

Ordered that an Extract of that part of Major Gooch's letter which relates to the payment of the Virginia Comm[rs] for running the division line between that Colony and Carolina be sent to the Treasury for directions therein

[Page 160.]

WHITEHALL Wednesday June 4th 1729

A letter for enclosing an extract of M[r] Gooch letter (abovement[d]) read yesterday to M[r] Scrope Sec[ry] to the Lords of the Treasury was agreed & ordered to be sent

[Page 163.]

WHITEHALL Tuesday June 17th 1729

An Order in Councill of 26 March 1729 was read for Warrants to be prepared for M[r] Fitzwilliams Surveyor General of the Customs to be admitted into the Councils of Virginia, Carolina & Jamaica.

[Page 195.]

WHITEHALL Tuesday July 8th 1729

A letter from M[r] Lovill, Sec[ry] to the Province of North Carolina dated 12th Dec 1728 was read and the Papers therein referred to were laid before the Board, Viz

The Carolina Comm[rs] first & second Journal on the Boundary

Copy of the Plan sent to the Lords Proprietors of Carolina

Copy of an Address of the Council of the Province of North Carolina to His Majesty containing complaints against Sir Richard Everard Deputy Gov[r] of that Province

A letter for inclosing the abovement[d] Address to the Duke of Newcastle for His Majesty's directions thereon was signed.

[Page 217]

WHITEHALL Thursday August 7th 1729

An Order of the Lords of the Committee of Council dated 31st of last month referring to this Board the copy of an Address from the Members of the Council for North Carolina containing Complaints against Sir Richard Everard Deputy Gov[r] of that Province and requiring the Board to examine into the allegations thereof and report their opinion thereupon was read together with the copy of the said Address.

Another Order of the Lords of the Committee of Council of the same date referring to this Board the copy of a letter from Sir Richard Everard Deputy Governor of North Carolina to the Duke of Newcastle with a copy of Sir Richard's Orders and Resolutions delivered to the Council of that Province about granting Lands and filling vacant places in that

Goverm' and requiring the Board to examine into the same and report their opinion was read together with the said papers whereupon directions were given for enquiring who appears or solicits on behalf of Sir Richard Everard and of the Members of the Council for North Carolina in order to their bringing what Proofs they have to offer in support of their respective allegations

[Page 225.]

WHITEHALL. Tuesday Aug' 26th 1729

Capt. Burrington late Deputy Governor of North Carolina attending the undermentioned papers lately received from him concerning that Province were laid before the Board, viz'

The Journal of the Lower House of Assembly from 1st November 1725 to 14 April 1726

Copy of a letter from Capt. Burrington late Deputy Governor of North Carolina to the Lords Proprietors without date complaining of his being removed & giving some account of the affairs of that Province

Copy of the Declaration of Sir Richard Everard present Deputy Gov' of North Carolina dated 6 Jan' 172⅘ owning his having been imposed on by M' Lovick the Secretary M' Gale Chief Justice and M' Little Attorney General

The two Orders of the Lords of the Com'ee of His Maj most Hon'ble Privy Council both dated the 31st July last & mentioned in the Minutes of the 7th inst. the one referring to this Board the copy of an Address of the Council for North Carolina to His Maj containing complaints against Sir Rich. Everard Bart. Deputy Gov' there, the other referring likewise to this Board the copy of a letter from Sir Rich Everard to the Duke of Newcastle with a Copy of Sir Richard's Orders & Resolutions delivered to the Council of that Province being now again read together with the said copies of papers Their Lordships after discoursing with Capt Burrington thereupon gave directions for preparing the Draught of a Report in answer to the Orders of the Lords of the Committee of Council above mentioned.

[Page 229.]

Said Draught of Report was agreed and ordered to be transcribed 27th August.

[Page 250.]

WHITEHALL Monday October 6th 1729

A letter from M' Byrd one of the Com'rs for settling the Boundaries between Virginia and North Carolina dated in Virginia 27th June last relating to the difficulties attending that service and the pay of the persons employed therein was read And the Journal of the said Comm[n] with a chart of the Dividing Line therewith received were laid before the Board Whereupon Directions were given for preparing the Draught of a letter to M[r] Byrd in answer thereto

[Page 262.]

WHITEHALL Thursday Oct[r] 16th 1729

A letter from M[r] Vernon one of the Clerks of His Maj[y] most Honor[ble] Priv[y] to the Secretary of this Board dated yesterday was read signifying that the Lords of the Committee of Council thought it necessary & desired to discourse with the Board this Even[g] upon two of their Reports viz[t] the one made the 8th inst upon a Memorial of the House of Representatives of the Massachusetts Bay and the other upon the Address of the Members of the Council of North Carolina against Sir Richard Everard their Governor & also upon Sir Richard's letters with his Orders & Resolutions delivered to the said Council And a message being brought that the Lords of the Committee had adjourned to Monday next in the evening Their Lordships of this Board adjourned to the same time

[Page 289]

WHITEHALL Wednesday Nov[r] 26th 1729

A letter from his Grace the Duke of Newcastle of the 12th inst referring to the Board several papers as underment[d] relating to Jamaica, North Carolina and Newfoundland　　　　　　was read and the said several papers were laid before the Board, viz[t]

*　　　　*　　　　*　　　　*　　　　*　　　　*

Copy of Gov[r] Everard's letter to his Grace the Duke of Newcastle dated 18 June 1729

Copy of Gov[r] Everard's letter to the Council in his letter of 18 June 1729

Copy of a letter from M[r] Porter to His Grace the Duke of Newcastle dated 24th Jan[ry] 172⅞.

[Page 308.]

WHITEHALL Tuesday Dec[r] 16th 1729

Their Lordships then took again into consideration the North Carolina papers in answer to a complaint against the Governor & relating to Grants of Land there referred to in the Duke of Newcastle's letter of the 12th & entered in the Minutes of the 26th of last month and agreed to reconsider the same agreeable to their Report to the Lords of the Committee of 2ª Sept. last when a Governor shall be appointed for North Carolina

Order'd that a letter be wrote to Mʳ Scrope for a copy of the Surrender of Carolina from the Lords Proprietors & of such other Papers relating to the said Province as may be necessary for the Board's perusal.

1730.

[B P R O. North Carolina B T Vol. 8. A 1]

LETTER FROM THE DUKE OF NEWCASTLE TO THE LORDS OF TRADE 7ᵗʰ JANUARY 1729

Whitehall Janʳ 7ᵗʰ 17$\frac{28}{29}$

My Lords,

His Majesty having been pleased to appoint George Burrington Esqʳ Governor of North Carolina has commanded me to signify to your Lordships His Pleasure, that von prepare a Commission and Instructions for him accordingly

I am
My Lords
Your Lordships most obedient
humble servant
HOLLES NEWCASTLE

[B P R O. North Carolina B. T Vol 21 ᵖ 1]

LORDS OF TRADE TO DUKE OF NEWCASTLE 15 JANUARY 17$\frac{28}{29}$.

To His Grace the Duke of New Castle

My Lord,

Having in obedience to his Maj. commands signifyed to us by Your Grace's letter of the 7ᵗʰ inst prepared the Draught of a Commission for George Burrington Esqʳ to be his Maj. Captain General and Governor

9

in Chief of his Maj Province of North Carolina in America, We herewith transmit the same to Your Grace with our Representation thereupon
which Your Grace will be pleased to lay before his Majesty

       We are
          My Lord
             Your Grace's
                most obed^t and
                   most hum^{ble} Serv^{ts}

                         P DOCMINIQUE
                         O BRIDGEMAN
                         Wm CARY
                         F FRANKLAND
Whitehall   T PELHAM
   January 15th 17$\frac{30}{31}$.

[B P R O North Carolina B T Vol. 21 p 3.]

COMMISSION FOR CAPTAIN GEORGE BURRINGTON TO BE GOVERNOR OF NORTH CAROLINA 15 JAN^y 17$\frac{30}{31}$.

George the Second by the Grace of God of Great Britain France and Ireland King Defender of the Faith &c To Our Trusty and Welbeloved George Burrington Esqr Greeting,

We reposing especial trust and confidence in the prudence Courage
and Loyalty of you the said George Burrington of our especial grace
certain knowledge and meer motion have thought fit to constitute &
appoint and by these presents do constitute and appoint you the said
George Burrington to be our Captain General and Governor in Chief in
and over our Province of North Carolina in America.

And we do hereby require and command you to do and execute all
things in due manner that shall belong unto your said command And
the trust we have reposed in you according to the several powers & authorities granted or appointed you by this present Commission and the Instructions herewith given you or by such further powers instructions or
authorities as shall at any time hereafter be granted or appointed you
under our signet & Sign Manual or by our Order in Our Privy Council
& according to such reasonable Laws & Statutes as are now in force or
shall hereafter be made and agreed upon by you with the advice and

consent of Our Council and the Assembly of our said Province under your Govern' in such manner and form as is hereafter expressed.

And Our will and pleasure is that you the said George Burrington (after the publication of these our letters patents) do in the first place take the Oaths appointed to be taken by an Act passed in the first year of the reign of our late Royal Father of blessed memory entituled An Act for the further security of his Maj'ts person & government & the succession of the Crown in the heirs of the late Princess Sophia being Protestants & for extinguishing the hopes of the pretended Prince of Wales and his open & secret Abettors As also that you make & subscribe the Declaration mentioned in an Act of Parliament made in the 25th year of King Charles the Second, entituled An Act for preventing dangers which may happen from Popish Recusants And likewise that you take such oath as is usually taken by the Governors of our Colony of Virginia mutatis mutandis for the due execution of the Office & trust of our Capt. General & Gov' of our said Province for the due & impartial administration of Justice And further that you take the Oath required to be taken by Governors of Plantations to do their utmost that the several laws relating to the Plantations be observed which said Oath & Declaration our Council in our said Province or any three of the Members hereof have hereby full power & authority & are required to tender & administer unto you and in your absence to our Lieut. Gov' if there be any in the place All which being duly performed You shall administer unto the Members of our s'd Council as also to our Lieut. Gov' if there be any upon the place the said Oaths mentioned in the said Act entituled An Act for the further security of his Maj person & government and the succession of the Crown in the heirs of the late Princess Sophia being Protestants & for extinguishing the hopes of the pretended Prince of Wales & his open & secret abettors As also to cause & make them subscribe the aforementioned Declaration & to administer to them the Oath for the due execution of their places & trusts

And We do hereby give and grant unto you full power & authority to suspend any of the Members of our said Council from sitting voting & assisting therein if you shall find just cause for so doing

And if it shall at any time happen that by the death departure out of our said Province Suspension of any of our said Councillors or otherwise there shall be a vacancy in our said Council (any three thereof we do hereby appoint to be a quorum) Our Will & Pleasure is that you signify the same unto us by the first opportunity that We may under our Signet & Sign Manual constitute & appoint others in their stead.

But that our affairs at that distance may not suffer for want of a due number of Councillors if ever it shall happen that there shall be less than seven of them residing in our s⁴ Province We do hereby give & grant unto you the said George Burrington full power and authority to choose as many persons out of the principal Freeholders Inhabitants thereof as will make up the full number of our s⁴ Council to be seven and no more which persons so chosen & appointed by you shall be to all intents & purposes Councillors in our s⁴ Province until either they shall be confirmed by us or that by the nomination of others by us under Our Sign Manual & Signet our said Council shall have seven or more persons in it

And We do hereby give & grant unto you full power & authority with the advice & consent of Our said Council from time to time as need shall require to summon and call General Assemblies of the said Freeholders & Planters within your government according to the laws & usages of our s⁴ Province of No Carolina

And our will and pleasure is that the persons thereupon duly elected by the major part of the Freeholders according to such laws & usages as afores⁴ & of the respective Counties & places & so returned shall before their sitting take the Oaths mentioned in the said Act entituled An Act for the further security of his Maj person & the succession of the Crown in the Heirs of the late Princess Sophia being Protestants and for extinguishing the hopes of the pretended Prince of Wales & his open & secret abettors as also to make & subscribe the forementioned Declaration (which Oaths & Declaration you shall commissionate fit persons under our seal of North Carolina to render & administer to them and until the same shall be so taken & subscribed no person shall be capable of sitting tho' elected) And We do hereby declare that the persons so elected & qualifyed shall be called and deemed the General Assembly of our said Province & Territory of North Carolina

And that you the said George Burrington with the consent of the s⁴ Council & Assembly or the major part of them respectively shall have full power & authority to make constitute and ordain Laws Statutes & Ordinances for the public peace welfare & good government of our said Province and of the people & inhabitants thereof and such others as shall resort thereto & for the benefit of us our Heirs and Successors which said Laws Statutes & Ordinances are not to be repugnant but as near as may be agreeable to the Laws & Statutes of this our Kingdom of Great Britain

Provided that all such Laws Statutes & Ordinances of what nature or duration soever be within three months or sooner after the making thereof transmitted unto us under our said seal of North Carolina for our approbation or disallowance of the same as also Duplicates thereof by the next Conveyance

And in case any one or all of the said Laws Statutes & Ordinances not before confirmed shall at any time be disallowed & not approved & so signified by us our Heirs & Successors under our or their Signet & Sign Manual or by order of our or their Privy Council unto you the said George Burrington or the Commander in chief of our s⁴ Province for the time being then such & so many of the said Laws Statutes & Ordinances as shall be so disallowed & not approved shall from thenceforth cease determine & become utterly void & of none effect anything to the contrary notwithstanding

And to the end that nothing may be passed or done by our said Council or Assembly to the prejudice of us our Heirs & Successors We will and ordain that you the said George Burrington shall have & enjoy a negative voice in the making and passing of all Laws Statutes & Ordinances as aforesaid

And you shall and may likewise from time to time as you shall judge it necessary adjourn prorogue & dissolve all General Assemblies afores⁴

Our further Will and Pleasure is that you shall and may keep & use the public seal of North Carolina for sealing all things whatsoever that ought to pass the seal of our said Province under your Government

And we do further give and grant unto the said George Burrington full power and authority from time to time and at any time hereafter by yourself or by any other to be authorized in that behalf to administer & give the Oaths mentioned in the said Act for the further security of their Maj. person & government & the succession of the Crown in the heirs of the late Princess Sophia being Protestants and for extinguishing the hopes of the pretended Prince of Wales and his open & secret abettors to all and every such person or persons as you shall think fit who shall at any time or times pass into our said Province or shall be resident and abiding there

And We do by these presents give & grant unto you the said George Burrington full power & authority with the advice & consent of our said Council to erect & constitute & establish such & so many Courts of Judicature & Public Justice within our said Province & Territory you & they shall think fit & necessary for the hearing & determining of all causes as well Criminal as Civil according to law & equity & for awarding of execution thereupon with all reasonable & necessary powers & authorityes fees & privileges belonging thereunto As also to appoint & commissionate fit persons in the several parts of your Govern[t] to administer the Oaths mentioned in the afores[d] Act as also to tender and administer the afores[d] Declaration unto such persons belonging to the said Courts as shall be obliged to take the same.

And We do hereby authorize and empower you to constitute & appoint Judges & in cases requisite Commiss[rs] of Oyer & Terminer Justices of the Peace & other necessary Officers & Ministers in our said Province for the better administration of Justice & putting the Laws in execution And to administer & cause to be administered unto them such Oath or Oaths as are usually given within our said Colony of Virginia for the due execution & performance of Offices & Places & for clearing of truth in judicial causes

And we do hereby give and graunt unto you full power and authority where you shall see cause or shall judge any Offendor or Offendors in criminal matters for any fine or forfeitures due unto us fit objects of our mercy to pardon all such Offendors and remit all such offences fines and forfeitures Treason & Wilful Murder only excepted in which cases you shall likewise have power upon extraordinary occasions to grant reprieves to the Offendors until and to the intent our Royal Pleasure may be known therein

And We do by these presents authorize & empower you to collate any person or persons to any Church Chappel or other Ecclesiastical Benefices within our said Province & Territory aforesaid to which We our Heirs & Successors shall be entitled to collate as often as any of them shall happen to be void.

And We do hereby give and grant unto you the said George Burrington by yourself or by yo[r] Capt[s] & Com[rs] by you to be authorized full power & authority to levy arm muster and command all persons whatsoever residing within our said Province and Territory of North Carolina and as occasion shall serve to march from one place to another or to embark them for the resisting & withstanding all Enemies Pirates & Rebels both at sea and land and to transport such forces to any of our Plantations in America if necessity shall require for the defence of the same against the invasion or attempts of any of our Enemies and such enemies pirates and rebels (if there shall be occasion) to pursue & prosecute in or out of the limits of our said Province & Plantations or any of them   And (if it shall so please God) them to vanquish apprehend and take & being taken according to law to put to death or keep and preserve alive at your discretion and to execute Martial Law in time of invasion or other times when by law it may be executed and to do & execute all and every other thing & things which to our Capt Gen¹ or Governor in Chief doth or ought of right to belong.

And We do hereby give and grant unto you full power and authority by and with the advice and consent of our said Council of North Carolina to erect raise & build in our said Province & Territory such and so many Forts Platforms Castles Cities Boroughs Towns & Fortifications as you by the advice aforesaid shall judge necessary and the same or any of them to fortify & furnish with ordnance ammunition & all sorts of arms fit and necessary for the security & defence of our said Province and by the advice aforesaid the same again or any of them to demolish or dismantle as may be most convenient.

And for as much as divers mutinies and disorders may happen by persons shipt and employed at sea during the time of war and to the end that such as shall shipt and employed at sea during the time of war may be better governed & ordered We do hereby give and grant unto you the said George Burrington to constitute & appoint Captains Lieut⁸ Masters of Ships Commanders & other officers Commissions to execute the Law Martial according to the directions of an Act passed in the 13ᵗʰ year of the reign of King Charles the Second entituled An Act for the establishing Articles & Orders for the regulating & better government of His Maj. Navies Ships of War & forces by sea during the time of war & to use such proceedings authorities punishments corrections & executions upon any offendor or offendors who shall be mutinous seditious disorderly or any way unruly either at sea or during the time of their abode or residence in any of the forts harbours or bays of our said Province & territory as the cause shall be found to require according to Martial Law and the said directions during the time of war as aforesaid Provided that nothing herein contained shall be construed to the enabling you or any by your authority to hold plea or have any jurisdiction of any offence cause matter or thing committed or done upon the High Seas or within any of the Havens Rivers or Creeks of our said Province & Territory under your Govern⁴ by any Captain Lieut Commander Master Officer Seaman Soldier or person whatsoever who shall be in our actual service or pay in or on board any of our ships of war or other Vessels acting by immediate Commission or Warrant from our Commissioners for executing the office of our High Admiral or from our High Admiral of Great Britain for the time being under the seal of our Admiralty But that such Captain Lieut Commander Master Officer Seaman Soldier or other person so offending shall be left to be proceeded against and tryed as their offences shall require either by Commission under our Great seal of Great Britain as y* Statute of 28th Henry y* 8th directs or by Commission from our Lds Commiss[rs] for executing the Office of our High Admiral or from our High Admiral of Great Britain for the time being according to the forementioned Act for establishing Articles & Orders for the regulating and better government of His Maj. Navies Ships of War and Forces by sea and not otherwise Provided nevertheless that all disorders & misdemeanors committed on shoar by any Captain Commander Lieut Master Officer Seaman, Soldier or other person whatsoever belonging to any of our ships of war or other Vessels acting by immediate Commission or Warrant from our said Commissioner for executing the Office of High Admiral or from our High Admiral of Great Britain for the time being under the seal of our Admiralty may be tried and punished according to the Laws of the place where any such disorders offences or misdemeanors shall be committed on shoar notwithstanding such offender shall be in our actual service & born in our pay on board any such of our ships of war or other vessels acting by immediate commission or warrant from our said Commiss[rs] for executing the Office of High Admiral or Our High Admiral of Great Britain for the time being as aforesaid so as he shall not receive any protecčon for the avoiding of justice for such offences committed on shoar from any pretence of his being employed in our service at sea.

And our further Will and Pleasure is that all public money raised or which shall be raised by any Act hereafter to be made within our said Province be issued out by warrant from you by & with the advice & consent of the Council & disposed of by you for the support of the Government and according to the laws of our said Province of North Carolina and not otherwise

And We do likewise give & grant unto you full power & authority by & with the advice & consent of our said Councill to settle and agree with the inhabitants of our said Province for such lands tenements and hereditaments as now are or hereafter shall be in our power to dispose of and them to grant to any person or persons upon such terms and under such moderate quit rents services & acknowledgements to be thereupon reserved unto us as you by the advice aforesaid shall think fit which said Grants are to pass and be sealed by our public seal of our said Province & being entered upon record by such officer or officers as are or shall be appointed thereunto shall be good & effectual in law against us Our Heirs and Successors,

And We do hereby give & grant unto you the said George Burrington full power to order and appoint fairs marts & markets as also such and so many ports harbours bays havens & other places for convenience and security of shipping and for the better loading & unloading of goods and merchandizes as by you with the advice & consent of the s⁴ Council shall be thought fit & necessary.

And We do hereby require & command all Officers & Ministers Civil & Military and all other inhabitants of our s⁴ Province & Territory to be obedient aiding & assisting unto you the s⁴ George Burrington in the execution of this our Commission & of the powers & authorities herein contained and in case of yo' death or absence out of our said Province to be obedient aiding & assisting unto such person as shall be appointed by us our Heirs & Successors to be our Lieut Governor or Commander in Chief of our said Province to whom we do therefore by these presents give & grant all singular the powers & authoritys herein granted to be by him executed & enjoyed during our pleasure or until your arrival within our said Province and whom we do hereby require to take all such oaths & make such declaration as are herein before appointed to be taken & made by you Mutatis mutandis which said oaths & declaration our said Council in our said Province or any three of the Members thereof have hereby full power & are hereby required to tender & administer And if upon your death or absence out of our said Province there be no person upon the place commissionated or appointed by us to be our Lieut Governor or Commander in Chief of our said Province Our Will & Pleasure is that the eldest Councillor whose name is first placed in our Instructions to you and who shall be at the time of your death or absence residing within our said Province & Territory of North Carolina shall take upon him the administration of the Governm' & execute our said Commission & Instructions & y* several powers & authorities therein contained in y* same manner & to all intents & purposes as other our Governor or Commander in Chief should or ought to do in case of your absence until your return or in all cases until our further will and pleasure be known therein

And We do hereby declare ordain & appoint that you the s⁴ George Burrington shall and may hold execute & enjoy the office & place of our Captain General & Governor in Chief of our s⁴ Province & Territory of North Carolina with all its rights members & appurtenances whatsoever together with all & singular the powers & authorities hereby granted unto you for & during our Will & pleasure In Witness whereof We have caused these our Letters to be made Patents

Ex⁴

Witness &c.   10

[B. P R. O. NORTH CAROLINA B. T VOL. 8 A 5.]

AT THE COURT AT S⁺ JAMES'S THE 22ᵈ DAY OF JANU- ARY 1729 (-30)

Present
The King's most excellent Majesty
in Council

Upon reading this day at the Board a Draught of a Commission pre- pared by the Lords Commissioners for Trade & Plantations for George Burrington Esqʳ to be His Majᵗʸ Captain Generall and Governor in Chief of His Majesty's Province of North Carolina in America Which Draught the said Lords Commissioners have represented to be drawn in the usuall Form with the Commissions for other His Majesty's Govern- ors in America His Majesty in Councill was thereupon pleased to approve thereof and to order as it is hereby ordered that one of His Majesty's principal Secretarys of State do cause a Warrant to be prepared for His Majesty's Royall signature in order to pass the said Draught of a Com- mission (which is hereunto annexed) under the Great Seal of Great Britain

A true Copy

TEMPLE STANYAN

[B P R. O. NORTH CAROLINA B T VOL. 8. A 6]

COPY OF AN ORDER OF COUNCIL OF THE 22ᵈ JANᵛ 17²⁹⁄₃₀

At the Court at S⁺ James's the 22ᵈ day of January 1729
Present
The Kings most excellent Majesty
in Council

Whereas the Members of the Council of the Province of North Caro- lina have by an address presented to His Majesty at this Board com- plained against Sir Richard Everard appointed Deputy Governor of that Province by the late Lords Proprietors thereof as being guilty of crimes of a heinous nature with respect to His Majesty's Royal Person and Government—And whereas the said Sir Richard Everard hath by his letter to His Grace the Duke of Newcastle one of His Majesty's principal Secretarys of State complained of some of the Proceedings of the said Council and also of the Secretary of that Province, for having taken upon them to make Grants of Lands there and to fill up vacant Places in that Government His Majesty was this day pleased to take the said Papers into his Royal consideration together with two reports from the Lords of the Committee of Council and also from the Lords Commissioners for Trade & Plantations thereupon—And in regard there hath not been any proofs transmitted to support the said Complaints—His Majesty doth therefore hereby order, that copies of the said Papers be put into the hands of George Burrington Esqr His Majesty's Governor of North Carolina, to make strict enquiry into the truth thereof—And report to His Majesty at this Board the matter of fact as it shall appear to him that exemplary justice may be done according to the nature of the offences said to have been committed

A true copy

TEMPLE STANYAN

[B. P. R. O North Carolina B. T Vol. 21 p 25]

LORDS OF TRADE TO THE KING 3 FEBRUARY 17¾

To the King's most excellent Majty

MAY IT PLEASE YOUR MAJESTY

Your Majesty having been pleased to appoint a Governor over your Province of North Carolina We take leave to represent to Your Majesty that a public seal will be necessary for sealing all public instruments there according to the method practised in all other Your Maj Colonies in America, We therefore most humbly propose that Your Maj may be pleased to order a public seal for the said Province accordingly

Which is most humbly submitted

T. PELHAN
M. BLADEN.
ED ASHE
OR BRIDGEMAN

Whitehall
February 3d 17¾

[B P R. O North Carolina B. T Vol. 8. A 2.]

ORDER OF COUNCIL OF THE 21ˢᵗ FEBRUARY·17¾¾

At the Court at Sᵗ James the 21st day of February 17¾¾
Present
The King's Most Excellent Majesty in Council

Upon reading this day at the Board, a Representation from the Lords Commissioners for Trade and Plantations, setting forth, that as His Majesty hath been pleased to appoint a Governor over the Province of North Carolina, a Publick Seal will be necessary for sealing all publick Instruments there, according to the method practised in all other His Majesty's Colonys in America   And therefore humbly propose, that such a Seal may be ordered accordingly   His Majesty in Council was pleased to approve thereof, and to order as it is hereby ordered, that a Publick Seal be prepared and given to the Governor of the said Province of North Carolina, And that the said Lords Commissioners for Trade and Plantations do cause a Draft of such Seal, to be prepared and laid before His Majesty at the Board, for His Royall Approbation

JA   VERNON

[B P R O Am & W Ind No. 592.]

WARRANT APPOINTING Mʳ RICE SECRETARY OF NORTH CAROLINA FEBʸ 17¾¾

Our Will and Pleasure is that you prepare a Bill for our Royal signature to pass our Great Seal, containing our Grant of the office or Place of Secretary of our Province of North Carolina in America, unto our Trusty and Welbeloved Rice Esqʳ To have, hold, exercise and enjoy the same by himself or his sufficient Deputy or Deputies (for whom he will be answerable) during our Pleasure, and his Residence within our said Province with all Fees Rights, Profits, Priviledges & advantages whatsoever thereunto belonging in as full and ample manner as any other Secretary of our said Province hath held or of right ought to have held and enjoyed the same, and for so doing this shall be your Warrant. Given at our Court at St James the   day of February 17¾¾ in the third year of our Reign

By his Majᵗʸˢ command

To our Attorney or
  Solicitor General

[B P R. O North Carolina B T Vol. 8. A 3.]

REPRESENTATION OF GOVERNOR BURRINGTON TO THE BOARD OF TRADE

[March 1730.]

To the Right Honble the Lords Commissioners of His Majesty's Trade and Plantations.

The humble Representation of George Burrington, Governor of North Carolina vizt

The Inhabitants of said Province are exceeding poor and distressed ariseing from the calamitys of the well known warrs with the Indians of the said country whereby they were not only decreased by great numbers who therein perished, but the rem^r suffered from such incursions by the destruction of their Houses, Cattle & Plantations, which from his great care and application (when Govr for the Proprietors) together with the low price of quitt rents encouraged a multitude to resort thither and settle, whereby the abovementioned miseries are greatly restored and repaired.

Dureing the warrs with France, that Nation frequently landed and plundered the sea coasts, to prevent which they the said Inhabitants were absolutely obliged to be at great expenses to guard for the preservation of their propertys by establishing a force to repell them, which must ever be their care in point of any hostilities commenced by the French (tho' not foreseen) or any other Nation.

This Province hath many Islands therein, of which few are inhabitable from their scituation, as seated in the Main Land and Sea which together with the illconvenience of the Sand Banks prevent all large mercantile Vessells to pass and that thro'out the Country (Cape Fear river excepted) from the shallow inletts to such said Rivers which causes all Merchandize to be brought in small vessells thither or by land, either from Virginia or other neighbouring Colonies, where there are open Ports, and this occasions all the European Commoditys thither brought to be at least 5^s in the pound dearer than in any such Ports and adjoyning Colonies, and for the same reason the produce of North Carolina in return is sold ₱ 5^s in the pound cheaper than in said Virginia and other adjoyning Colonies, by which manifestly appears the difference in profitt of ½ in trade.

As North Carolina followed the rule and method of the adjoyning Colony of Virginia by setteing ye Quit Rents of Lands therein to be paid at 2^s for each hundred acres (which does not exceed 4^d English money) it's reasonable to believe that if such Quitt Rents are advanced so as to exceed the rates paid in Virginia, the Inhabitants must of course judge themselves rather oppressed than relieved, which will deterr them from cultivating an increase of Lands, when they must be more expensively obteyned than by their Neighbours, which will certainly prevent them from engaging as they flattered themselves to doe, on the Province becomeing the property of the British Crown

Which should certainly be avoyded for that North Carolina has vast tracts of Land not improveable by the Power of man some part thereof being Pine barren Land which can never redound to the least advantage of the Owners (except once in 20 or 30 years) when they gather there from a small quantity of light wood to make pitch and tarr, and many vast tracts there are very low and exceeding wett, in soe much that noe place thereon can be found to raise the least structure to dwell in, and attended with the great illconvenience of the overflux of the Rivers almost thro' out the Country, which terryfy all from any attempt of seetleing there which occasions a just fear of perishing by water and that in some places even for 30 miles together, as particularly on Roanoak River and soe in generall tho' in different degrees.

His Majesty's Subjects in North Carolina have in every sigular occasion (many of which have offered) evidently demonstrated their zealous loyalty unto His Majesty and His glorious Ancestor (particulars of which would be too tedious to enumerate) attended with a constant singular bravery, for which reasons and considerations it's humbly suggested that without regard to the previous reasons They are justly entituled to clayme His Majesty's protection and that with the indulgence of shareing his Royal Favour by being placed on the same Basis of payment of Quitt Rents as are the other of His Majestie's Subjects in North America

Which with due regard to your Lord^{pps} is submitted to your well experienced wisdome & Judgment by

Your Lord^{pps} most obedient

Most humble Servant

GEO. BURRINGTON

[B. P. R. O. NORTH CAROLINA B. T VOL. 21 P 26]

LORDS OF TRADE TO THE KING. 25 MARCH 1730

To the King's most Excellent Maj^v

MAY IT PLEASE YOUR MAJ^v

In obedience to yor Maj^tys commands signified to us by yor Order in Council of the 21st of ye last month directing us to cause the draught of a seal to be prepared for yor Maj Province of North Carolina & to lay the same before yor Maj^v for your Royal approbation We humbly take leave to annex a draught accordingly whereon Liberty is represented introducing plenty to your Maj with this Motto Quæ sera tamen respexit and this inscription round the circumference Sigillum Provinciæ nostræ Carolinæ Septentrionalis

In the reverse of this seal we would humbly propose Your Maj arms Crown, Garter, Supporters & Motto with this inscription round the circumference Geo II Dei Gratia Magnæ Britaniæ Franciæ et Hiberniæ Rex Fidei Defensor Brunsvici et Lunenbergi Dux Sacri Romani Imperii Archi Thesaurarius et Elector

All which is humbly submitted

WESTMORELAND

P DOCMINIQUE

T PELHAM

Whitehall   M. BLADEN

March 25th 1730   ED ASHE

[B P R. O NORTH CAROLINA B. T VOL. 8. A 7]

At the Court at St James's the 10th day of Aprill 1730.

Present

The King's most excellent Majesty in Councill

Upon reading this day at the Board a Report from the Lords Commissioners for Trade & Plantations dated the 25th of March last with the Draught of a seal for the Province of North Carolina, whereon Liberty is represented introducing Plenty to His Majesty with this Motto Quæ sera tamen respexit, and this inscription round the Circumference,

Sigillum Provinciæ nostræ Carolinæ Septentrionalis And the said Lords
Commissioners humbly propose that on the Reverse may be His Majesty's
arms, Crown, Garter Supporters and Motto with this inscription round
the Circumference, Georgius Secundus, Dei Gratia, Magnæ Britanniæ,
Franciæ et Hiberniæ, Rex Fidei Defensor Brunsvici et Lunebergi Dux;
Sacri Romani Imperii Archi-Thesaurarius Elector· His Majesty in
Councill this day took the same into consideration and was pleased to
approve thereof, and to order as it is hereby ordered that His Chief
engraver of Seals do forthwith engrave a silver Seal according to the
said Draught which is hereunto annexed and to what is above proposed
by the said Lords Commis" for the reverse of the said Seal , & his Grace
the Duke of Newcastle one of His Majesty's principall Secretarys of
State is to cause a Warrant to be prepared for His Majesty's Royall Signature to the said Engraver as usual upon the like occasions.

                    A true Copy
                                        JA· VERNON

———

[B. P. R. O. Am. & W. Ind. Vol. 22. p. 7]

———

PLACES IN THE PROVINCE OF NORTH CAROLINA IN THE GIFT OF HIS GRACE THE DUKE OF NEWCASTLE.

Chief Justice
Secretary
Attorney General
Provost Marshall

When I was Governour for the Proprietors the Bill mony was under
ten Thousand Pounds, att that time English Commodities sold for ten
times the prime cost in Bills In the last Assembly held in that Province in November Past an addition was made of thirty thousand pounds
new Bills, which consequently makes them of very little value, the Officers employments will be very inconsiderable if they are not allowed to
take their fees in Proclamation mony, or according to that value

[B P R O Am & W Ind Vol. 22 p 8]

Sir

I have known the Bearer Mr Smith for some years and can truly affirm that he hath had a Regular Education both at the University and the Middle Temple, and that he hath been a Barrister at Law for two years I believe him Qualified for the Imployment he is seeking after, and that he is well affected to his Majestys Person and Government

I am Sr your most humble servant

ELDE

April the 25th 1730.

[B. P R O North Carolina B T Vol. 8 A 4]

LETTER FROM THE DUKE OF NEWCASTLE TO THE LORDS COMMISSIONERS FOR TRADE
28 APRIL 1730

Whitehall April 28th 1730.

My Lords,

I send your Lordships herewith, by His Majesty's Command a Copy of a Letter wch I have received from Mr Porter Judge of the Admiralty at North Carolina, containing an account of the unwarrantable proceedings of Sir Richard Everard late Governor of that Province, in giving Grants of Land there, to the great prejudice of His Majesty's Right to the same, and I am to signify to you His Majesty's pleasure, that you examine into this matter, and report the state of the case as it shall appear to you, with your opinion what may be proper for His Majesty to order upon it

HOLLES. NEWCASTLE

[B P R O North Carolina B. T Vol. 21 p 27]

LORDS OF TRADE TO THE KING 28 APRIL 1730

To the King's most Excellent Majty

May it please Your Majty

In our Representation to the Lords Justices of the 30th Aug. 1720 accompanying a Draught of Instructions for Francis Nicholson Esqr to

11

be Governor of South Carolina We did propose that Commissions should forthwith be prepared to be used in the two Provinces of South & North Carolina for trying of Pirates in both y° s⁴ Provinces

Their Excellencies in Council on 20ᵗʰ Sept. following taking the same into consideration did order such Commission to be prepared for the Province of South Carolina & by their second Order in Council of the 11ᵗʰ Oct 1720 directed this Board to lay before them y° names of persons proper to be inserted in y° s⁴ Commiſſon which we did by our report dated the 27ᵗʰ of y° same month

But that Order not extending to North Carolina which was then under the Govern' of the late Lords Prop'ʳ no such Commiſſon hath ever yet been directed for the trying of Pirates in that Province and Your Maj having been graciously pleased to appoint Capt Burrington Gov' thereof We humbly propose to Your Maj that the like Commission may be sent thither for the trying of Pirates as has usually been sent to other Plantations under Your Maj. immediate Governm' And We humbly offer to Your Majesty the names of such persons as we conceave fit to be inserted in the said Commission, Viz'

George Burrington Esqʳ Your Majᵗʸˢ Capt Gen' & Governor in Chief of Your Maj Province of North Carolina in America or the Gov' or Command' in Chief of y° s⁴ Province for the time being

The Vice Admiral or Vice Admirals of y° s⁴ Province for the time being

The Members of Your Maj Council in y° said Province for the time being

The Judge of y° Vice Admiralty in North Carolina or y° Judge or Judges of the Vice Admiralty in y° s⁴ Province for y° time being

The Capt' & Command'ⁿ of Yor Maj ships of war within the Admiralty jurisdiction of North Carolina for y° time being

The Secretary of the Province of North Carolina for the time being.

The Treasurer or Receiver Gen'ˡ of y° s⁴ Province for the time being

The Survevor Gen'ˡ of Yoʳ Maj Customs in Yoʳ Maj. Southern Provinces on the Continent of America for the time being

The First or Chief Justice of the Provincial or Supream Court of North Carolina for the time being

All which is most humbly submitted

	WESTMORELAND	T PELHAM
Whitehall	O BRIDGEMAN	W CARY
April 28ᵗʰ 1730		

[B. P R O Am & W Ind No. 592.]

COUNCIL OF TRADE TO DUKE OF NEWCASTLE
MAY 1ᵗʰ 1730

My Lord

We have had under our consideration your Grace's Letters to us of the 12ᵗʰ of November last and of the 28ᵗʰ of last month and the Papers therein referred to in relation to the conduct of Sʳ Richard Everard late Governor of North Carolina with respect to his unwarrantable proceedings in giving Grants of Land in that Province, and as we conceive that all such Grants of Land as have been made since his Majesty has purchased that Province to be void Sir Richard Everard having had no Authority that we know of for granting the same, we shall insert an article in the Instructions which we are now preparing for Captain Burrington to declare them so, We shall likewise insert several other articles directing the manner of Granting of Lands for the future and for the collecting his Majesty's Quit Rents thereon and shall more fully explain the same in our Representation thereupon to his Majesty which we shall enclose to your Grace

My Lord Your Graces
most obedient and most humble Servants

WESTMORELAND
DOCMINIQUE
T PELHAM
THO FRANKLAND
OLIVʳ BRIDGEMAN

Whitehall
May 1ˢᵗ 1730

[B P R. O. North Carolina B. T Vol. 21 p 31]

A POPPLE TO FRANCIS TANE 4 JUNE 1730

To Francis Tane Esqʳ

Sir,

My Lords Commissioners for Trade and Plantations command me to send you the inclosed copy of the Carolina Charter and to desire your opinion in point of law whether according to the said Charter any Grant from the Lords Proprietors of that Province be valid unless signed by them all and under their common seal

I am Sir Your most humble Servᵗ

ALURED POPPLE

[B P R. O B. T South Carolina Vol 4 C 90]

MEM FROM COLL JOHNSON RELATING TO SOME CLAUSES IN THE DRAᵗ OF HIS ISTRUCTIONS FOR THE GOV. OF SOUTH CAROLINA.

*   *   *   *   *   *   *   *

I aprehend the running the boundary line between South and North Carolina would admitt of the following way of expresing it to answer the same intent vid That a line shall be run (by Commissioners appointed by each province) beginning at the Sea 30 miles distant from the mouth of Cape Fear River on the South West side thereof keeping the same distance from the said River as the Course thereof runs to the main sourse or head thereof and from thence the said boundary line shall be continued due west as far as the South Seas. But if Waccama River lyes within 30 miles of Cape Fear River then that River to be the boundary from the sea to the head thereof, and from thence to keep the distance of 30 miles Paralel from Cape Fear River to the head thereof and from thence a due West Course to the South Sea

(Endorsed)
Recᵈ June 8ᵗʰ
Read June 9ᵗʰ 1730.

[B. P R. O Am & W Ind Vol 22 p 9]

WHITEHALL August the 4ᵗʰ 1730.

SIR

I am directed by the Lords Commissioners for Trade and Plantations to acquaint you that they have signed their Representation to his Majesty in Council upon your Instructions so long ago as the 10ᵗʰ of June last, and have waited ever since for your List of Councillors, But if you do not bring them the names of Twelve persons proper to be inserted upon that occasion by Monday next Their Lordships will either send away your Instructions without Councillors, or name them without waiting any longer for your advice upon that subject

I am Sir your most humble servant

B. WHEELOCK

Honᵇˡᵉ George Burrington Esqʳ

[B. P R. O Am & W Ind Vol. 22 p 9]

LONDON the 8th of August 1730

SIR

Receiving the inclosed I waited upon the Lords Commissioners of Trade and shewed them my old list of Councellors without any names against Chief Justice, and Secretary, Coll Bladen filled them up with his own hand before Mr Pelham and Mr Brudenell; I hope his Grace the Duke of Newcastle (my noble patron) will not be offended, Mr Brudenell has promised to inform his Grace how cautious I behaved in this affair.

There is nothing done yet with Mr Germain tuesday next is appointed for meeting Mr Bowen

I am (Sr)

your most humble

and most obedient servant

GEO BURRINGTON

[B. P R. O North Carolina B. T Vol. 8 A 8]

LIST OF 12 PERSONS RECOMMENDED BY CAPTAIN BURRINGTON TO BE OF THE COUNCIL OF N CAROLINA

Smith. Chief Justice
Nathaniel Rice Secretary
James Jenoure Surveyor
Robert Halton Esqr
Edmund Porter Esqr
John Baptiste Ashe Esqr
James Stallard Esqr
Eliezer Allen Esqr
Mathew Rowan Esqr
Richard Eyans Esqr
Cornelius Harnett Esqr
John Porter senior Esqr

Smythe Esqⁿ Chief Justice
Nathanⁿ Rice Esqⁿ Secretary Esqʳ
James Genour Surveyor Esqʳ
Robert Halton Provost Marshall &c Esqʳ
Edmund Porter
John Baptiste Ashe
James Stollard
Eliezer Allen
Mathew Rowan
Cornelius Harnett
Richard Evans
The Surveyor Generall of our Customs for the South District of
America for the time being

Recᵈ
Read } 6ᵗʰ August 1730.

[B P R O North Carolina B. T Vol 21 p 32]

LORDS OF TRADE TO DUKE OF NEWCASTLE
13 AUGUST 1730

To his Grace the Duke of Newcastle

My Lord,

Your Grace will receive inclosed the Draught of General Instructions
and of those which relate to the Acts of Trade for Capt. Burrington His
Majesty's Governor of North Carolina with our Representation thereupon And we desire Your Grace will please to lay them before His
Majesty

We are
My Lord
Your Grace's
most obedient &
most humble Servᵗˢ

P. DOCMINIQUE
T PELHAM
M BLADEN
OR BRIDGEMAN
JA BRUDENELL

Whitehall
13ᵗʰ August 1730

[B. P R O North Carolina B T Vol. 21 p 33]

REPRESENTATION OF LORDS OF TRADE TO THE KING 13 AUGUST 1730.

To the King's most Excellent Majesty.

MAY IT PLEASE YOUR MAJESTY,

In obedience to Your Maj commands signified to us by a letter from his Grace the Duke of Newcastle one of his Maj principal Secretaries of State dated the 7ᵗʰ of Janᵧ last We have prepared the Draught of General Instructions and of those which particularly relate to the Acts of Trade & Navigation for George Burrington Esqᵣ whom Your Maj has been pleased to appoint Governor of the Province of North Carolina which Instructions we have made agreeable to those given to Your Maj other Governors in America and more particularly to those lately prepared for Col. Johnson Your Maj Govᵣ of South Carolina so far as they are applicable to the circumstances of this Province taking notice in this Report of such alterations as have been made therein

In the 1ˢᵗ Article we have inserted the names of twelve persons who have been recommended to us as fitly qualified to serve Your Maj. in the Council of this Province and have added to them the Surveyor General of Your Maj customs in the south part of America for the time being Your Maj by your Order in Council of 26 March 1729 having been pleased to approve of a proposal made by this Board for appointing him a Member of every Council in those Governments within his district which the Board conceived to be for Your Maj service

We have inserted the 19ᵗʰ Article to the same purpose as that in Col Johnson's Instructions for remitting Your Maj share of the arrears of quit rents and as they are for the future to be paid in Proclamačon money We take leave humbly to propose that all salaries and fees payable in the several offices there be likewise paid in Proclamačon money and we have added some words to the end of this article to that purpose

We have inserted the 41ˢᵗ Article directing the Governor to examine into several complaints of a very high nature made against Sir Richard Everard late Deputy Governor of this Province by the Council as likewise into the complaints made by the said Sir Richard Everard against the Council and others and to report his proceedings thereupon

We have added the following words to the 42ⁿᵈ Instruction Viz· You are likewise to enquire whether any Grants of land have been made in

No. Carolina and to whom without authority from us since we purchased the interest of seven of the Proprietors of that Province which was on the second day of July 1729 that we may give such orders therein as shall be thought convenient for our service being informed that Sir Richard Everard Deputy Governor for the late Lords Proprietors in North Carolina hath taken upon him to make several large Grants of land in that Province since Your Maj purchased seven eighth parts thereof

At the end of the 59th Instruction we have added the words unless by the laws of the Province there are other fees for the like services already establish'd having reason to believe there may be fees already settled there by law

All the other Articles in these Instructions are the same with those proposed by this Board for Col Johnson Your Maj. Governor of South Carolina

All which is most humbly submitted

> P DOCMINIQUE
> M BLADEN
> T PELHAM
> JA BRUDENELL
> OR BRIDGEMAN

Whitehall
   13th Aug' 1730

[B. P R O Am & W Ind Vol. 22. p 10.]

September the 3rd 1730

May it please your Grace

In North Carolina there are att this time ten Precincts, when the Country is all over peopled there may be as many more, att present there is a Register in every Precinct, but if his Majesty gives a Commission or Patent to any Gentleman to keep a General Register for the whole Country the Precinct Registers must drop.

> I am
>   my Lord Duke
>   your Graces
>   most humble
>   and most devoted servant
>   GEO. BURRINGTON

[B. P. R. O B. T VIRGINIA. VOL. 19. R. 127]

LIEUT. GOV. GOOCH'S ANSWER TO QUERIES.

*   *   *   *   *   *

What number of Indians &c—14th

The Indians tributary to this Government are reduced to a small number the remains of the Maherin and Nansemond Indians are by running the Boundary fallen within the limits of North Carolina. The Saponies and the other petty Nations associated with them being disturbed by the Tuscaruroes are retired out of Virginia to the Cattawbaws. So that there remain only the Pamunkeys on York River and they not above tenn Familys, and the Nottoways on the South side of James River whose strength exceeds not fifty fighting men. Both these Nations are seated in the midst of the English settlements, and hitherto have maintained a friendly correspondence with them

What is the strength &c 15th

We have no Indian Nation of any Strength nearer than the five Nations under the Government of New York on the North, and the Cattawbaws and Cherokees within the limits of Carolina to the South, and both of them near 400 miles from the Inhabitants of Virginia.

(Endorsed)
Rec⁴ 14th Sep¹ 1730.

[B P R. O. NORTH CAROLINA B T VOL. 8. A 9]

GOVʳ BURRINGTON TO ALLURED POPPLE ESQʳˢ SECRETARY TO THE BOARD OF TRADE.

LONDON December 8th 1730

SIR,

I desire the Lords of Trade &c will be pleased to giver other direction and opinion, Whether I may give new Patents to Old Land holders in North Carolina, paying the same Quit Rents they formerly paid for the same Lands Whether I may allow the House of Burgesses to nominate the Receivers of the Country Taxes or ought (myself) to appoint them

    I am (Sir)

      Your most humble servant

12   GEO BURRINGTON.

[B P R. O. North Carolina B T Vol. 21 p. 100]

ALURED POPPLE TO GOV BURRINGTON
10 DEC 1730

To Capt Burrington

    SIR,

In answer to the two questions in your letter to me of the 8th inst

1st Whether you may give new Patents to old Landholders in North Carolina paying the same Quit rent they formerly paid for the same land?

2dly Whether you may allow the House of Burgesses to nominate the Receivers of the Country Taxes or ought yourself to appoint them?

I am directed by the Lords Commiss'rs for Trade & Plantations to acquaint you that as to the first their Lordships think that you ought to make no Grant of land whatsoever without reserving the Quit Rents directed by your 43rd Instruction

As to the 2nd their Lordships being informed that His Majesty has appointed a Receiver General for North Carolina they are of opinion that no other Receiver of Public Taxes ought to be allowed there

          I am

            Your most humble Serv't

                    ALURED POPPLE

Whitehall
    December 10th 1730

[B P R. O North Carolina B T Vol 21 p 37]

INSTRUCTIONS FOR OUR TRUSTY AND WELBELOVED GEORGE BURRINGTON ESQr OUR CAPTAIN GENERAL AND GOVERNOR IN CHIEF IN & OVER OUR PROVINCE OF NORTH CAROLINA IN AMERICA. GIVEN AT OUR COURT AT ST JAMES'S THE FOURTEENTH DAY OF DECEMBER 1730 IN THE FOURTH YEAR OF OUR REIGN

G REX

With these our Instructions you will receive our Commission under our Great Seal of Great Britain constituting you our Capt General and Governor in Chief in & over our Province & Territory of North Carolina in America You are therefore to fit yourself with all convenient speed & to repair to our said Province of North Carolina and being arrived there you are to take upon you the execution & place of trust we have reposed in you and forthwith to call together the Members of our Council in that Province Viz:—William Smith, Nathaniel Rice, Jas Jenoure Robt. Halton, Edm⁴ Porter, John Baptiste Ashe, James Stallard, Eliezer Allen, Mathew Rowan Richard Eyans Cornelius Harnet John Porter Serᵗ Esqᵐˢ and the Surveyor General of our Customs for the South distⁱ.ct of America for the time being

2. You are with all due and usuall solemnity to cause our said Commission constituting you Captain General & Governor in chief as aforesaid to be read and published at the said Meeting of our Council which being done you shall yourself take & also administer unto each of the Members of our said Council the Oaths mentioned in an Act passed in the first year of his late Maj reign, our Royal father entitled an Act for the further security of his Maj person & Government and the succession of the Crown in the heirs of the late Princess Sophia being Protestants for extinguishing the hopes of yᵉ pretended Prince of Wales & his open & secret abettors As—also make & subscribe & cause the Members of our sᵈ Council to make & subscribe yᵉ declaration mentioned in an Act of Parliament made in yᵉ 25ᵗʰ year of the Reign of King Charles the 2ⁿᵈ entituled An Act for preventing dangers which may happen from Popish Recusants And you & every of them are likewise to take an Oath for the due execution of your & their places & trusts as well as with regard to your & their equal & impartial administration of justice And you are also to take the Oath required to be taken by Governors of Plantations to do their utmost that the Law relating to the Plantations be observed

3. You are forthwith to communicate unto our said Council such & so many of these our Instructions wherein their advice & consent are mentioned to be requisite as likewise all such others from time to time as you shall find convenient for our service to be imparted to them.

4. You are to permit the Members of our said Council to have & enjoy freedom of debate and vote in all affairs of public concern that may be debated in Council

5 And altho' by our Commission aforesᵈ We have thought fit to direct that any three of our Council make a quorum It is nevertheless our Will and Pleasure that you do not act with a Quorum of less than five members unless upon emergencies when a greater number cannot conveniently be had

6   And that we may be allways informed of the names & characters
of persons fit to supply the Vacancies which shall happen in our said
Council You are to transmit unto us by one of our Principal Secretaries
of State and to our Commissioners for Trade & Plantations with all convenient speed the names & characters of twelve persons inhabitants of
our s⁴ Province whom you shall esteem the best qualified for that trust
And so from time to time when any of them shall die depart out of our
s⁴ Province or become otherwise unfit You are to nominate so many
other persons in their stead that the list of twelve persons fit to supply
the s⁴ Vacancies may be always complete

7   Whereas by our Commission to you You are empowered in case of
the death or absence of any of our Council of our said Province to fill
up the Vacancies in the said Council to the number of seven and no more
You are from time to time to send to us as aforesaid and to our Comᵐ for
Trade & Plantations the name and qualities of any Members by you put
into the said Council by the first convenience after your so doing

8   And in the choice and nomination of the Members of our said Council as also of the chief officers Judges Assistants, Justices and Sheriffs
You are always to take care that they be men of good life and well affected
to our Government and of good estates and abilities and not necessitous
persons.

9   You are neither to augment nor diminish the number of our s⁴
Council as it is hereby established nor to suspend any of the Members
thereof without good and sufficient cause nor without the consent of the
majority of the s⁴ Council   And in case of the suspension of any of them
you are to cause your reasons for so doing together with the charges &
proofs against the said persons and their answers thereunto to be duly
entered upon the Council Books and forthwith to transmit copies thereof
to us as aforesaid and to our Commissⁿ for Trade & Plantations   Nevertheless if it should happen that you should have reason for suspending of
any Councillor not fit to be communicated to the Council You may in
that case suspend such person without their consent But you are thereupon immediately to send to us by one of our Principal Secretaries of
State and to our Commissⁿ for Trade & Plantations an account thereof
with your reasons for such suspension as also for not communicating the
same to the Council and duplicates thereof by the next opportunity

10.   You are to signify our pleasure unto the Members of our said
Council that if any of them shall hereafter absent themselves from our
said Province and continue absent above the space of twelve months
without leave from you or from the Commander in Chief of the said

Province for the time being first obtained under his or your hand & seal, or shall remain absent for the space of two years successively without our leave given them under our Royal Signature, their place or places in the said Council shall immediately become void and that we will forthwith appoint others in their stead.

11 And whereas, we are sensible that effectual care ought to be taken to oblige the Members of our said Council to a due attendance therein in order to prevent the many inconveniences that may happen for want of a quorum of the Council to transact business as occasion may require It is our Will & Pleasure that if any of the Members of our said Council residing in the Province shall wilfully absent themselves from the Council Board when duly summoned without a just & lawful cause and shall persist therein after admonition you suspend the said Councillors so absenting themselves till our further pleasure be known giving us timely notice thereof And we do hereby will & require you that this our Royal pleasure be signified to the several Members of our said Council and that it be entered in the Council Books of our said Province as a standing rule

12. You shall take care that the Members of the Assembly be elected only by freeholders as being more agreeable to the custom of this Kingdom to which you are as near as may be to conform yourself in all particulars.

13. In case you find the usual Salaries or pay of the Members of the Assembly too high you shall take care that they be reduced to such a moderate proportion as may be no grievance to the country wherein nevertheless you are to use your discretion so as no inconvenience may arise thereby.

14. And whereas the Members of several Assemblies in the Plantations have frequently assumed to themselves privileges no way belonging to them especially of being protected from suits at law during the term they remain of the Assembly to the great prejudice of their Creditors and the obstruction of justice and some have presumed to adjourn themselves at pleasure without leave from our Gov' first obtained and others have taken upon them the sole framing of money bills refusing to let the Council alter or amend the same all which are very detrimental to our Prerogative If upon your calling an Assembly in North Carolina you find them insist upon any of the abovesaid privileges you are to signify to them that it is our Will and Pleasure you do not allow any protection to any Member of the Council or Assembly further than in their persons and that only in the sitting of the Assembly and that you are not

to allow them to adjourn themselves otherwise than de die in diem except Sundays & Holidays without leave from you or the Commander in Chief for the time being first obtained and that the Council have the like power of framing Money Bills as the Assembly And you are hereby expressly enjoined not to allow the said Assembly or any of the Members thereof any power or privilege whatsoever which is not allowed by us to the House of Commons or the Members thereof in Great Britain

15 You are to observe in the passing of all laws that the style of enacting the same be by the Governor, Council & Assembly You are also as much as possible to observe in the passing of all Laws that whatever may be requisite upon each different matter be accordingly provided for by a different law without intermixing in one and the same Act such things as have no proper relation to each other And you are more especially to take care that no clause or clauses be inserted or annexed to any Act which shall be foreign to what the title of such respective Act imports And that no perpetual clause be made part of any temporary law And that no Act whatever be altered suspended revived confirmed or repealed by general words but that the title and date of such Act so suspended altered revived confirmed or repealed be particularly mentioned & expressed

16 You are to take care that in all Acts or Orders to be passed within that our Province in any case for levying money or imposing fines or penalties express mention be made that the same is granted or reserved to us our Heirs and Successors for the public uses of that our Province and the support of the Govern't thereof as by the said Act or Order shall be directed And you are particularly not to pass any law or do any Act by Grant Settlement or otherwise whereby our Revenue may be lessened or impaired without our special leave or command therein.

17. You are not to permit any clause whatsoever to be inserted in any law for levying Money or the value of money whereby the same shall not be made liable to be accounted for unto us and to our Comm'rs of our Treasury or to our High Treasurer for the time being and audited by our Auditor General of our Plantations or his Deputy for the time being.

18 And it is our express will & pleasure that no Law for raising any imposition on wine or other strong liquors be made to continue for less than one whole year as also that all other Laws made for the supply & support of the Government shall be indefinite and without limitation except the same be for a temporary service and which shall expire and have their full effect within the time prefixt

19 Whereas we have been at very considerable charge in purchasing the Sovereignty of the Provinces of South & North Carolina together with seven eighths parts of the land thereof from the late Lords Proprietors and have actually paid them in consideration of seven eighths parts of Quit rent only alleged to be due and in arrear to them from the inhabitants of our said Province the sum of £5,000 Now as a further mark of our Royal Bounty & fatherly indulgence to our people under your government We do hereby empower you to give your assent to a law if not already done for remitting the said arrears Provided that by the same law all possessors of land in our Province under your government do forthwith register their respective grants by which they claim such lands in the office of our Auditor General or his Deputy a copy of which Register and of all Grants to be made for the future you are to send to us as aforesaid & to our Comm^{rs} for Trade & Plantations and that every person possessing land in the Province by virtue of any Grant from the late Lords Proprietors do for the future pay to us our Heirs and Successors the annual Quit rents reserved upon such Grants respectively in Proclamation money and that the salaries and fees payable to all Officers under your govern^t be for the future likewise be paid in proclamation money.

20 Whereas Acts have been passed in some of our Plantations in America for striking bills of credit & issuing out the same in lieu of money in order to discharge their public debts and for other purposes from whence several inconveniencies have arisen It is therefore Our Will & Pleasure that you do not give your assent to or pass any Act in our Province in your government whereby bills of credit may be struck or issued in lieu of money without a clause being inserted in such Act declaring that the same shall not take effect until the said Act shall have been approved & confirmed by us our heirs and successors and It is our Will and pleasure that you do immediately send an account to us & to our Comm^{rs} for Trade & Plantations whether any paper bills be now current in North Carolina and if any to the amount of what sum and what fund is provided for striking of them as likewise whether the same be at any and what discount and for what time they are current

21 And whereas great mischiefs may arise by passing bills of an unusual and extraordinary nature & importance in the Plantations which Bills remain in force there from the time of enacting until our pleasure be signified to the contrary We do hereby will and require you not to pass or give your assent to any Bill or Bills in the Assembly of our said Province of unusual and extraordinary nature and importance

wherein our prerogative or the property of our subjects may be prejudiced or the trade & shipping of this Kingdom be any ways affected until you shall first have transmitted unto us the draught of such a Bill or Bills and shall have received our Royal pleasure thereupon unless you take care in the passing of any Bill of such nature as aforementioned that there be likewise a clause inserted therein suspending & deferring the execution thereof until our pleasure shall be known concerning the same

22 And whereas several laws have formerly been enacted in some of our Plantations in America for so short a time that our assent or refusal thereof could not be had thereupon before the time for which such laws were enacted did expire You shall not therefore give your assent to any law that shall be enacted for a less time than two years except in the cases mentioned in the foregoing 18th Article

23. And our further will and pleasure is that you do not re-enact any law to which the assent of us or our Royal Predecessors has once been refused without express leave for that purpose first obtained from us upon a full representation by you to be made to us and to our Comm[r] for Trade and Plantations of the reason and necessity for passing such law nor give your assent to any law for repealing any other law passed in your government whether the same has or has not received our royal approbation unless you take care that there be a clause therein suspending & deferring the execution thereof until our pleasure shall be known concerning the same

24 You are also to take care that no private Act whereby the property of any private person may be affected be passed in which there is not a saving of the rights of us our heirs & successors all Bodies politic and corporate and of all other persons except such as are mentioned in the same Act and those claiming by from or under them And further you shall take care that no such private act be passed without a clause suspending the execution thereof until the same shall have received our royal approbation It is likewise our will and pleasure that you do not give your assent to any private act until proof be made before you in Council (and entered in the Council Book) that public notification was made of parties intention to apply for such Act in the several parish churches where the premises in question lye for three Sundays at least successively before such Act was brought into the Assembly

25 And that we may the better understand what Acts & Laws are in force in our said Province of North Carolina You are with the assistance of the Council to take care that all Laws now in force there be revived & considered and if there be anything either in the matter or style of

them which may be fit to be retrenched or altered You are to represent the same to us with your opinion touching the said laws now in force (whereof you are to send a complete body unto us and to our Comm^{rs} for Trade & Plantations at the end of the first Session of Assembly after your arrival there as they now are together with such proposals for alterations as you shall think requisite to the end our approbation or disallowance may be signified thereupon

26. And we do hereby particularly require and enjoyn you upon pain of our highest displeasure to take care that fair books of accounts of all receipts and payments of all public monies be duly kept and the truth thereof be attested upon oath and that all such accounts be audited & attested by our Auditor General of our Plantations or his Deputy who is to transmit copies thereof to our Comm^{rs} of our Treasury & to our High Treasurer for the time being and that you do every half year or oftener send another copy thereof attested by yourself to our Comm^{rs} for Trade and Plantations and duplicates thereof by the next convenience in which Book shall be specified every particular sum raised or disposed of together with the names of the persons to whom any payments shall be made to the end We may be satisfied of the right and due application of the revenue of our said Province with the probability of the increase or diminution of it under every head or article thereof

27 And you are likewise to transmit authentic copies of all laws statutes and ordinances which at any time hereafter shall be made or enacted within our said Province each of them separately under the public seal unto us as aforesaid and to our Comm^{rs} for Trade & Plantations within three months or sooner after their being enacted together with duplicates thereof by the next conveyance upon pain of our highest displeasure and of the forfeiture of that year's salary wherein you shall at any time or upon any pretence whatsoever omit to send over the said Laws Statutes & Ordinances aforesaid within the time above limited and also of such other penalty as we shall please to inflict And you are hereby directed that the copies and duplicates of the said Acts be fairly abstracted in the Margins But if it shall happen that no shipping shall come from our said Province within three months after the making such laws statutes and ordinances whereby the same may be transmitted as aforesaid then the said Laws Statutes & Ordinances are to be transmitted by the next convenience after the making thereof whenever it may happen for our approbation or disallowance of the same

28. And our further Will and Pleasure is that every Act which shall be transmitted the several dates or respective times when the same passed

13

the Assembly, the Council and received your Assent be particularly expressed And you are to be as explicit as may be in your observations (to be sent to Our Comm^{rs} for Trade & Plantations) upon every Act that is to say whether the same is introductive of a new Law declaratory of a former Law or does repeal a Law then before in being And you are likewise to send to our said Comm^{rs} the reasons for the passing of such Law unless the same do fully appear in the preamble of the said Act

29 You are to require the Secretary of our said Province or his Deputy for the time being to furnish you with transcripts of all such Acts and public Orders as shall be made from time to time together with a copy of the Journals of the Council and that all such transcripts and copies be fairly abstracted in the margins to the end the same may be transmitted unto us and to our Comm^{rs} for Trade & Plantations as above directed which he is duly to perform upon pain of incurring the forfeiture of his place

30 You are also to require from the Clerk of the Assembly or other proper Officer transcripts of all Journals & other proceedings of the said Assembly abstracted in the margins to the end the same may be in like manner transmitted as aforesaid

31 Whereas several inconveniencies have arisen in our Governments in the Plantations by gifts and presents made to the Governors by the General Assemblies You are therefore to propose unto the said General Assembly and to use your best endeavour that an Act be passed for raising and settling a public revenue for defraying the necessary charge of the government of the said Province and that therein provision be particularly made for a competent salary to yourself as Capt General and Governor in chief of our said Province and to any other succeeding Capt General and Governor in chief for supporting the dignity of the said Office as likewise due provision for the contingent charges of our Council & Assembly and for the salaries of the respective Clerks and other Officers thereunto belonging as likewise for all other Officers necessary for the administration of that government and where such revenue shall have been settled & provision made as aforesaid It is our express will and pleasure that neither you the Govr nor any Governor Lieut Govr or Commander in Chief or President of the Council of our said Province of North Carolina for the time do give your or their consent to the passing any law or act for any gift or present to be made to you or them by the Assembly and that neither you nor they do receive any gift or present from the Assembly or others on any account or in any manner whatsoever upon pain of our highest displeasure and of being recalled from that Government

32 And We do further direct and require that this Declaration of our Royal Will and Pleasure contained in the foregoing article be communicated to the Assembly at their first Meeting after your arrival in that Province and entered in the Journals of the Council and Assembly that all persons whom it may concern may govern themselves accordingly

33. And whereas for some years past the Governors of some of our Plantations have seized and appropriated to their own use the produce of whales of several kinds taken upon those coasts upon pretence that whales are royal fishes which tends greatly to discourage this branch of fishery in our Plantations and prevent persons from setling there It is therefore Our Will & Pleasure that you do not pretend to any such claim nor give any manner of discouragem^t to the fishery of our subjects upon the coasts of the Province of North Carolina under your government but on the contrary that you give all possible encouragem^t thereto

34 And whereas great prejudice may happen to our service and to the security of our said Province by your absence from those parts you are not upon any pretence whatsoever to come to Europe without having first obtained leave for so doing from us under our Sign Manual & Signet or by our Order in our Privy Council Yet nevertheless in case of sickness you may go to New York or any other of our Northern Plantations and there stay for such a space as the recovery of your health may absolutely require.

35. And whereas we have thought fit by our Commission to direct that in case of your death or absence from our said Province and in case there be at that time no person upon the place commissioned or appointed by us to be our Lieut Govr or Commander in chief the eldest Councillor whose name is first placed in these our Instructions to you and who shall be at the time of your death or absence residing within our said Province of North Carolina shall take upon him the administration of the Government & execute our Commission & Instructions and the several powers and authorities therein contained in the manner therein directed It is nevertheless our express will and pleasure that in such case the said President shall forbear to pass any Acts but what are immediately necessary for the peace and welfare of our said Colony without our particular orders for that purpose And that he shall not take upon him to dissolve the Assembly then in being nor to remove or suspend any of the Members of our said Council nor any Judges Justices of the Peace or other Officers Civil or Military without the consent of at least seven of the Council And the said President is to transmit to us and to our said Commiss^m for Trade and Plantations by the first opportunity the reasons for such alterations signed by himself and by our Council

36 And whereas we are willing in the best manner to provide for the support of the government of our said Province by setting apart a sufficient allowance to such as shall be our Lieut. Governor Commander in Chief or President of our Council for the time being within the same Our Will and Pleasure therefore is that when it shall happen that you shall be absent from our said Province one full moiety of the Salary and of all perquisites and emoluments whatsoever which would otherwise become due unto you shall during the time of your absence from our said Province be paid & satisfied unto such Lieut Governor Commander in Chief or President of the Council who shall be resident upon the place for the time being which we do hereby order and allot unto him towards his maintenance and for the better support of the dignity of that our Government

37 You are not to suffer any public money whatsoever to be issued or disposed of otherwise than by warrant under your hand by the advice and consent of our Council but the Assembly may nevertheless be permitted from time to time to view and examine all accounts of money or value of money disposed of by virtue of laws made by them which you are to signify to them as there shall be occasion

38 Whenever it is necessary that our rights and dues be preserved & recovered and that speedy and effectual justice be administred in all cases relating to our Revenue You are to take care that a Court of Exchequer be called and do meet at all such times as shall be needful And you are upon your arrival to inform us and our Comm[rs] for Trade and Plantations whether our service may require that a constant Court of Exchequer be settled & established there

39 You shall not remit any fines or forfeitures whatsoever above the sum of ten pounds nor dispose of any forfeitures whatsoever until upon signifying unto our Comm[rs] of the Treasury or our High Commiss[r] for the time being and to our Comm[rs] for Trade & Plantations the nature of the offence and the occasion for such fines & forfeitures with the particular sums or value thereof (which you are to do with all speed) you shall have received our directions therein But you may in the meantime suspend the payment of the said fines & forfeitures.

40. It is our Will and Pleasure that you do not dispose of any forfeitures or escheats to any person until the Sheriff or other proper officer has made enquiry by a jury upon their oaths into the true value thereof And you are to take care that the produce be duly paid to our Receiver General of our said Province and a full account thereof transmitted to our Comm[rs] of our Treasury or our High Treasurer for the time being

and to our Comm⁸ for Trade & Plantations with the names of the persons to whom disposed And provided that in the Grants of all forfeited & escheated lands there be a clause obliging the Grantee to cultivate three acres for every fifty acres within three years after the passing of such Grant in case the same was not so cultivated & planted before And that there be proper savings and reservations of quit rents to us our Heirs & Successors.

41 Having received an Address from the Members of our Council of North Carolina and other papers containing several complaints of a very high nature against Sir Richard Everard Bart, late Deputy Governor of that Province and the said Sir Richard Everard having written a letter to the Duke of Newcastle one of our principal Secretaries of State whereunto are annexed the copies of such Orders & Resolutions as he the said Sir Richard Everard delivered to our said Council of North Carolina relating to the Grants of land there and the filling up vacant places in that government We have thought fit for our service that the said papers or true copies thereof should be delivered to you and you will receive them from our Comm⁸ for Trade & Plantations Whereupon it is our Will and pleasure that at your arrival in your government you do make diligent enquiry into the several matters contained in those papers copies whereof you are to communicate to the parties concerned allowing them free liberty to examine witnesses in support of their respective allegations And if upon enquiry you shall find them or any of them to be guilty of the crimes laid to their charge you shall give directions for their being prosecuted according to law sending a full account of your proceedings therein to us by one of our principal Secretaries of State and to our Comm⁸ for Trade and Plantations.

42 Whereas great inconveniencies have arisen in many of our Colonies in America from the granting of excessive quantities of land to particular persons which they have never cultivated and have thereby prevented others more industrious from improving the same more particularly in North Carolina where several persons claim a right to many thousand acres which they have not yet taken up and many other persons a right to many more acres of land than are expressed in their said Grants It is therefore our Will and Pleasure that you do not suffer any person to possess more acres of uncultivated land than are mentioned in their respective grants And you are hereby directed to recommend to the Assembly of our said Province to pass an Act or Acts whereby the owners of all lands already granted by the late Lords Proprietors shall be obliged within a reasonable time to take possession of and cultivate the lands by

them claimed on penalty of forfeiture of such right of claim   And to prevent the like inconveniencies for the future in all Grants of land to be made by you by and with the advice and consent of our Council You are to take especial care that no Grant be made to any person but in proportion to his ability to cultivate the same And that proper clauses be inserted for vacating the said Grants on failure of cultivation or payment of the Quit rents reserved thereon   And as the most probable measure for your judgment in this particular will be to proportion the quantity of land to the number persons and slaves in each Grantees family You are hereby directed not to grant to any person more than fifty acres for every white or black man woman or child of which the Grantees family shall consist at the time the grant shall be made   But in the laying out of all lands for the future where such lands shall be contiguous to rivers You are to take care that not above one fourth part of the land granted shall border upon the river that is to say there shall be four chains in depth backwards to every chain in front upon the said river respectively and so in proportion for any larger quantity and that a free passage to and from the said river be reserved for the use of all His Majesty's subjects.

43 And Whereas by our Commission you are empowered to settle and agree by and with the advice of our said Council with the inhabitants of our said Province for such lands tenements & hereditaments as now are or hereafter shall be in our power to dispose of and them to grant to any person or persons upon such terms and under such moderate quit rents services & acknowledgements to be thereupon reserved unto us as you by advice aforesaid shall think fit It is nevertheless our Will and Pleasure that you do not make any grant of land to any person whatsoever under a less Quit rent than four shillings Proclamation money for every hundred acres.

44 You shall not displace any of the Judges Justices Sheriffs or other Officers or Ministers in our said Province without good and sufficient cause to be signified unto us and to our Comm^rs for Trade & Plantations And to prevent arbitrary removals of the Judges & Justices of the Peace you are not to express any limitation of time in the Commissions which you are to grant with the advice and consent of our Council of our said Province to persons fit for those employments nor shall you execute by yourself or your Deputy any of the said Offices nor suffer any person to execute more Offices than one by Deputy

45 You are shall not erect any Court or Office of Judicature not before erected or established nor dissolve any Court or Office already erected or established without our special order

46. You are to transmit unto us and to our Commissioners for Trade and Plantations with all convenient speed a particular account of all establishments of Jurisdictions Courts Offices & Officers Powers Authorities, fees and privileges granted and settled within our said Province as likewise an account of all public charges relating to the said Courts and of such funds as are settled & appropriated to discharge the same together with exact and authentic copies of all proceedings in such causes where appeals shall be made to us in our Privy Council

47 And Whereas by an Act entitled an Act for establishing an Agreement with seven of the Lords Proprietors of Carolina for the surrender of their title and interest in that Province to His Majesty passed in the second year of our reign there is a saving to all persons claiming any office or place under any Grant made before Jan⁷ 1ˢᵗ 172¼ under the Lords Proprietors common seal of all rights to such offices or places as they had at the time of passing that Act or might have been entitled to in case the said Act had not been made You are immediately upon your arrival in North Carolina to make diligent enquiry what those Offices are, their several values how their profits arise in what manner executed for what term they are granted and whether they or any of them are useful or hurtful to the Province And that we may be the better apprized thereof you are to send to us and to our Commᵐ of Trade and Plantations as aforesaid authentic copies of all such Grants together with your explanations and remarks thereon in which you are to be very explicit to the end you may receive our further directions therein But in the mean time you are to take especial care that no Office or Place whatsoever in our said Province be executed but by Commission to be granted by us or by you our Governor under the seal of our said Province.

48 And you are with the advice and consent of our Council to take special care to regulate all salaries and fees belonging to places or paid upon emergencies that they be within the bounds of moderation and that no exactions be made on any occasion whatsoever As also that tables of all fees be publicly hung up in all places where such fees are to be paid And you are to transmit copies of all such tables of fees to us and to our Commᵐ for Trade and Plantations as aforesaid.

49 And whereas frequent complaints have been made of great delays and undue proceedings in the Courts of Justice of several of our Plantations whereby many of our good subjects have very much suffered, and it being of the greatest importance to our service and to the welfare of our Plantations that justice be everywhere speedily and duly administered and that all disorders delays and other undue practises in the administra-

tion thereof be effectually prevented We do particularly require you to take especial care that in all Courts where you are authorized to reside justice be impartially administered and that in all other Courts established within our said Province all Judges & other persons therein concerned do likewise perform their several duties without delay or partiality

50 You are to take care no Court of Judicature be adjourned but upon good grounds as also that no orders of any Court of Judicature be entered and allowed which shall not be first read and approved of by the Magistrates in open Court which rule you are in like manner to see observed with relation to the proceedings of our Council of North Carolina And that all Orders there made be first read and approved in Council before they are entered on the Council Books.

51 Whereas We are above all things desirous that our subjects may enjoy their legal rights and privileges you are to take especial care that if any person be committed for any criminal matters unless for treason or felony plainly and especially expressed in the warrant of commitment he have free liberty to petition by himself or otherwise the Chief Baron or any one of the Judges of the Common Pleas for a Writ of Habeas Corpus which upon such application shall be granted & served on the Provost Marshal Gaoler or other officer having the custody of such prisoner or shall be left at the gaol or place where the prisoner is confined   And the said Provost Marshal or other officer shall within three days after such service on the petitioner's paying the fees and charges and giving security that he will not escape by the way make return of the Writ and Prisoner before the Judge who granted out the said Writ and there certify the true cause of the imprisonment And the said Baron or Judge shall discharge such prisoner taking his recognizance & sureties for his appearance at the Court where his offence is cognizable & certify the said Writ & Recognizance into the Court unless such offences appear to the said Baron or Judge not bailable by the laws of England

52 And in case the said Baron or Judge shall refuse to grant a Writ of Habeas Corpus on view of the copy of commitment or upon oath made of such copy having been denyed the prisoner or any person requiring the same in his behalf or shall delay to discharge the prisoner after the granting of such Writ the said Baron or Judge shall incur the forfeiture of his place

53 You are likewise to declare our pleasure that in case the Provost Marshal or other officer shall imprison any person above twelve hours except by a Mittimus setting forth the cause thereof he be removed from his said office

54 And upon the application of any person wrongfully committed the Baron or Judge shall issue his warrant to the Provost Marshal or other officer to bring the prisoner before him who shall be discharged without bail or paying fees And the Provost Marshal or other officer refusing obedience to such Warrant shall be thereupon removed And if the said Baron or Judge denies his Warrant he shall likewise incur the forfeiture of his place

55. You shall give directions that no prisoner being set at large by an Habeas Corpus be recommitted for the same offence but by the Court where he is bound to appear And if any Baron Judge Provost Marshal or other officer contrary hereunto shall recommit such person so bailed or delivered You are to remove him from his place And if the Provost Marshal or other officer having the custody of the prisoner returns the Habeas Corpus or refuses a copy of the commitment within six hours after demand made by the prisoner or any other in his behalf he shall likewise incur the forfeiture of his place.

56 And for the better prevention of long imprisonment You are to appoint two Courts of Oyer and Terminer to be held yearly Viz On the 2ᵈ Tuesday in December and the 2ᵈ Tuesday in June the charge whereof to be paid by the public treasury of our said Province not exceeding one hundred pounds each sessions.

57 You are to take care that all prisoners in case of treason or felony have free liberty to petition in open Court for their tryals That they be indicted at the first Court of Oyer & Terminer unless it appear upon oath that the Witnesses against them could not be produced and that they be tryed the second Court or discharged And the Baron or Judge upon motion made the last day of the Sessions in open Court shall discharge the prisoner accordingly And upon the refusal of the said Baron or Judge or Provost Marshal or other Officer to do their respective duties herein they shall be removed from their places

58. Provided always that no person be discharged out of prison who stands committed for debt by any decree of Chancery or any legal proceedings of any Court of Record.

59 And for the preventing of any exactions that be made upon prisoners You are to declare our pleasure that no Baron or Judge shall receive for himself or clerks for granting a Writ of Habeas Corpus more than 2ˢ 6ᵈ and the like sum for taking a recognizance And that the Provost Marshal or other officer shall not receive more than 5ˢ for every commitment For the Bond the prisoner is to sign 1ˢ 3ᵈ For every copy of a Mittimus 1ˢ 3ᵈ And every Mile he brings back the prisoner 1ˢ

3ª Unless by the laws of that Province there are other fees already established

60. And further You are to cause this our Royal pleasure signified unto you by the ten articles of instruction immediately preceding this to be made public and registered in the Council Books of our said Province

61 You are for the better administration of justice to endeavour to get a law passed (if not already done) wherein shall be set the value of men's estates either in goods or lands under which they shall not be capable of serving as jurors

62. You are to take care that no Man's Life Member Freehold or Goods be taken away or harmed in our said Province otherwise than by established and known laws not repugnant to but as near as may be agreeable to the laws of this Kingdom And that no persons be sent prisoners to this Kingdom from our said Province without sufficient proof of their crimes and that proof transmitted along with the said prisoners

63 You shall endeavour to get a Law passed (if not already done) for the restraining of any inhuman severity which by ill masters or their overseers may be used towards their Christian servants and their slaves and that provision be made therein that the wilful killing of Indians & Negroes may be punished with death and that a fit penalty be imposed for the maiming of them

64 You are to take care that all Writs within our Province be issued in our name

65 You shall take care with the advice & assistance of our Council that all Court Houses & other public buildings & especially prisons that want reparation be forthwith repaired and be put into & kept in such a condition as is proper & necessary for the holding of Courts keeping offices and securing the prisoners that are or shall be there in proper custody

66 Our Will and Pleasure is that appeals be permitted to be made in cases of error from the Courts in our said Province unto you and the Council there in Civil causes Provided the value appealed for do exceed the sum of One Hundred Pounds sterling and security be first given by the Appellant to answer such charges as shall be awarded in case the first sentence shall be affirmed Provided also that if any of the said Council shall at that time be Judges of the Court from whence such appeal shall be made to you our Governor & Council or to the Commander in chief for the time being and Council such Councillor or Councillors shall not be permitted to vote upon the said Appeal But he or they may neverthe-

less be present at the hearing thereof to give the reasons of the judgment given by him or them in the cause wherein such appeal shall be made

67 And if either party shall not rest satisfyed with the judgment of you or the Commander in Chief for the time being and Council as aforesaid Our Will & Pleasure is that they may then appeal unto us in our Privy Council provided the sum or value so appealed for unto us do exceed the real value and sum of three hundred pounds sterling And that such appeal be made within fourteen days after sentence & good security given by the Appellant that he will effectually prosecute the same and answer the condemnation and also pay such costs and damages as shall be awarded by us in case the sentence of you or the Commander in chief for the time being and Council be affirmed And it is Our further Will and Pleasure that in all cases whereby your Instructions you are to admit Appeals unto us in our Privy Council execution be suspended until the final determination of such Appeal unless good and sufficient security be given by the Appellee to make ample restitution of all that the Appellant shall have lost by means of such judgment or decree in case upon the determination of such Appeal such judgment or decree should be reversed and restitution awarded to the Appellant And you shall cause this declaration of Our Will and Pleasure to be forthwith entred upon the Council Books of our said Province that all parties may govern themselves accordingly

68 You are also to permit Appeals unto us in Council in all cases of fines imposed for Misdemeanors Provided the fines so imposed amount to or exceed the sum of one hundred pounds sterling the Appellant first giving good security that he will effectually prosecute the same and answer the condemnation if the sentence by which such fine was imposed in North Carolina shall be confirmed

69 Whereas there are or may be several offices within our said Province granted under the great seal of Great Britain and that our service may be very much prejudiced by reason of the absence of the patentees and by their appointing Deputies not fit to officiate in their stead You are therefore to inspect the said offices and to enquire into the capacity and behaviour of the persons exercising them & to report thereupon to us and to our Commiss" for Trade & Plantations what you think fit to be done or altered in relation thereunto And you are upon the misbehaviour of any of the said Patentees or their Deputies to suspend them from the execution of their places till you shall have represented the whole matter unto us and received our direc̃ons therein And in case of the suspension of any such officer it is Our express Will and Pleasure

that you take care that the person appointed to execute the place during
such suspension do give sufficient security to the person suspended to be
answerable to him for the profits accruing during such suspension in case
We shall think fit to restore him to his place again   It is nevertheless Our
Will and Pleasure that the person executing the place during such suspension shall for his encouragement receive the same profits as the person suspended (if a Deputy) did or a moiety of the profits in case of suspension of the Patentee But you shall not by colour of any power or
authority hereby or otherwise granted or mentioned to be granted unto
you take upon you to give grant or dispose of any place or office within
the said Province which now is or shall be granted under the Great Seal
of this kingdom any further than that you may upon the vacancy of any
such office or place or upon the suspension of any such Officer by you
as aforesaid put in any fit person to officiate in the interval till you have
represented the matter unto us and to our Comm^{rs} for Trade & Plantations as aforesaid which you are to do by the first opportunity and till
the said Office or place be disposed of by us our Heirs and Successors
under the Great Seal of this Kingdom or that our further directions be
given therein   And it is Our express Will and Pleasure that you do countenance and give all due encouragement to our Patent Officers in the
enjoyment of their accustomed fees and rights privileges & emoluments
according to the true intent & meaning of their patents.

70   And whereas Orders have been given for commissionating fit persons to be Officers of our Admiralty and Customs in our several Plantations in America And whereas it is of great importance to the trade of
this Kingdom and to the welfare of our Plantations that all illegal trade
be prevented and suppressed You are therefore to take especial care that
the Acts of Trade and Navigation be duly put in execution & in order
thereunto you are to give constant protection and all due encouragement
to the said officers of our Admiralty and Customs in a due execution of
their respective offices and trusts in our said Province under your Government.

71   And whereas several complaints have been made by the Surveyor
General and other officers of our Customs in our Plantations in America
that they are frequently obliged to serve on Juries and personally to
appear in arms whenever the Militia is drawn out and thereby are much
hindered in the execution of their employments Our Will and Pleasure is
that you take effectual care and give the necessary directions that the several Officers of our Customs be excused and exempted from serving on any
Juries or personally appearing in arms in the Militia unless in case of

absolute necessity or serving any parochial offices which may hinder them in the execution of their duties,

72 And whereas the Surveyors General of our Customs in the Plantations are impowered in case of the vacancy of any of the Officers of the Customs by death removal or otherwise to appoint other persons to execute such offices until they receive further directions from our Commⁿ of our Treasury or our High Treasurer or Comⁿ of our Customs for the time being But in regard the districts of the said Surveyors General are very extensive and that they are required at proper times to visit the Officers in the several Govⁿ under their inspection and that it might happen that some of the Officers of our Customs in the Province of North Carolina may die at the time when the Surveyor General is absent in some distant part of his district so that he cannot receive advice of such Officer's death within a reasonable time and thereby make provision for carrying on the service by appointing some other person in the room of such Officer who may happen to die therefore that there be no delay given on such occasions to the Masters of ships or Merchants in their dispatches It is Our further Will and Pleasure in case of such absence of the Surveyor General and if he should happen to die and in such cases only that upon the death of any Collector of our Customs within that our Province You shall make choice of a person of known loyalty experience diligence & fidelity to be employed in such Collector's room for the purposes aforesaid until the Surveyor General of our Customs shall be advised thereof and appoint another to succeed in their places or that further directions be given therein by our Comⁿ of our Treasury or our High Treasurer or by the Commⁿ of our Customs for the time being which shall be first signifyed taking care that you do not under pretence of this instruction interfere with the powers & authorities given by the Commⁿ of our Customs to the Surveyor General when he is able to put the same in execution

73. You shall administer or cause to be administred the Oaths appointed to be administred in the Act entituled An Act for the further security of His Majesty's person & Government and the Succession of the Crown in the Heirs of the late Princess Sophia being Protestants and for extinguishing the hopes of the pretended Prince of Wales and his open & secret abettors to the Members & Officers of our Council and Assembly and to all Judges Justices and other persons that hold any office or place of trust or profit in our said Province whether by virtue of any patent under our Great Seal of Great Britain or the public seal of our said Province of North Carolina or otherwise   And You shall also

cause them to make and subscribe the aforesaid Declaration without the doing of all which you are not to admit any person whatsoever into any public office nor suffer those that have been formerly admitted to continue therein

74 You are to permit a liberty of conscience to all persons (except papists) so as they be contented with a quiet and peaceable enjoyment of the same not giving offence or scandal to the Govern'

75 You shall take especial care that God Almighty be devoutly & duly served throughout your Govern' the Book of Common Prayer as by law established read each Sunday & Holiday and the blessed Sacrament administred according to the rites of the Church of England

76 You shall take care that the Churches already built there be well and orderly kept and that more be built as the Province shall by God's blessing be improved and that besides a competent maintenance be assigned to the Minister of each Orthodox Church a convenient House be built at the common charge for each minister and a competent proportion of land assigned him for a glebe & exercise of his industry

77 And you are to take care that the parishes be so limited & settled as you shall find most convenient for accomplishing this good work

78 You are not prefer any Minister to any Ecclesiastical Benefice in that Province without a Certificate from the Right Reverend Father in God the Lord Bishop of London of his being conformable to the doctrine and discipline of the Church of England and of good life and conversation And if any person already preferred to a Benefice shall appear to you to give scandal either by his doctrine or his manners You are to use the proper and usual means for the removal of him and to supply the vacancy in such manner as we have directed

79 You are to give orders forthwith (if the same be not already done) that every Orthodox Minister within your government be one of the vestry in his respective parish and that no vestry be held without him in case of sickness or that after notice of a vestry summoned he omit to come

80 You are to enquire whether there be any Minister within your Government who preaches and administers the Sacrament in any Orthodox Church or Chappel without being in due orders and to give an account thereof to the Lord Bishop of London

81 And to the end the Ecclesiastical Jurisdiction of the Lord Bishop of London may take place in that our Province so far as may be We do think fit that you give all countenance & encouragement to the exercise of the same excepting only the collating the Benefices Granting licenses

for marriages and probate of Wills which we have reserved to you our Governor and to the Commander in Chief of our said Province for the time being as far as by law we may.

82 And We do further direct that no Schoolmaster be henceforth permitted to come from this Kingdom and to keep school in that our said Province without the license of the Lord Bishop of London and that no other person now there or that shall come from other parts shall be admitted to keep school in North Carolina without your license first obtained.

83 And you are to take especial care that a table of Marriages established by the Canons of the Church of England be hung up in every Orthodox Church & duly observed And you are to endeavour to get a Law passed in the Assembly of that Province (if not already done) for the strict observation of the said table

84 Having been graciously pleased to grant unto the Right Reverend Father in God Edmund Lord Bishop of London a Commission under our Great Seal of Great Britain whereby he is empowered to exercise Ecclesiastical Jurisdiction by himself or by such Commissaries as he shall appoint in our several Plantations in America. It is Our Will and Pleasure that you give all countenance and due encouragement to the said Bishop of London or his Commissaries in the legal exercise of such Ecclesiastical jurisdiction according to the laws of the Province under your government and to the tenor of the said Commission a copy whereof is hereunto annexed and that you do cause the said Commission to be forthwith registered in the public records of that our Province

85. The Right Reverend Father in God Edmund Lord Bishop of London having presented a petition to his said late Majesty humbly beseeching him to send instructions to the Governors of all the several Plantations in America that they cause all laws already made against Blasphemy Prophaneness Adultery Fornication, Polygamy Incest Prophanation of the Lord's Day Swearing & Drunkenness in their respective Governments to be vigorously executed and we thinking it highly just that all persons who shall offend in any of the particulars aforesaid should be prosecuted and punished for the said offences It is therefore our Will and Pleasure that you take due care for the punishment of the forementioned vices and that you earnestly recommend to the Assembly of North Carolina to provide effectual laws for the restraint and punishment of all such of the forementioned vices against which no laws are as yet provided And also you are to use your endeavours to render the laws in being more effectual by providing for the punishment of the aforementioned vices by present-

ment upon oath to be made to the temporal Courts by the Churchwardens of the several parishes at proper times of the year to be appointed for that purpose. And for the further discouragement of vice & encouragement of virtue and good living that by such example the Infidels may be invited and persuaded to embrace the Christian religion. You are not to admit any person to public trusts or employments in the Province under your Government whose ill fame & conversation may occasion scandal. And it is our further Will and Pleasure that you recommend to the Assembly to enter into proper methods for the erecting and maintaining of schools in order to the training of youth to reading and to a necessary knowledge of the principles of religion. And you are also with the assistance of the Council and Assembly to find out the best means to facilitate & encourage the conversion of Negroes and Indians to the Christian religion.

86 And whereas it is highly necessary for the welfare of Carolina that a good understanding should be maintained by the Indian Nations as well for the promoting of trade as for the security of the frontiers of your Government you are hereby particularly enjoined to use all possible means for the regaining the affections of the said Indians and to preserve a good correspondence with such of them as remain faithful to our interest. And you are hereby likewise directed to recommend in the strongest terms to the Indian traders to be just and reasonable in their dealings with the Native Indians and likewise to propose to the Assembly there if you and our Council shall judge it necessary to pass one or more laws for the better regulation of the said Indian Trade & for the encouragement and protection of such Indians as shall adhere to our interest

87 You shall send to us and to our Commiss^rs for Trade & Plantations by the first conveyance an account of the present number of planters and inhabitants Men Women and children as well Masters as Servants free and unfree and of the Slaves in our said Province as also a yearly account of the increase or decrease of them and how many of them are fit to bear arms in the Militia of our said Province

88 You shall also cause an exact account to be kept of all persons born christened & buried and send yearly fair abstracts thereof to us and to our Com^rs for Trade & Plantations as aforesaid

89 You shall take care that all Planters Inhabitants and Christian Servants be well and fitly provided with arms and that they be listed under good officers and when and as often thought fit mustered and trained whereby they may be in a better readiness for the defence of the

said Province And for the greater security thereof You are to appoint fit Officers and Commanders in the several parts of that Province bordering upon the Indians who upon any invasion raise men and arms to oppose them until they shall receive your directions therein

90 You are to take especial care that neither the frequency nor unreasonableness of remote marches musterings & trainings be an unnecessary impediment to the affairs of the inhabitants.

91 And you shall not upon any occasion whatsoever establish or put in execution any Articles of War or other Law Martial upon any of our Subjects Inhabitants of our said Province without the advice of our said Council there

92 And whereas you will receive from our Commiss" for executing the office of High Admiral of Great Britain and of the Plantations a Commission constituting you Vice Admiral of our said Province You are hereby required and directed carefully to put in execution the several powers thereby granted you.

93. Whereas great inconveniencies have happened by Merchant ships and other Vessels in the Plantations wearing the colours borne by our ships of war under pretence of Commissions granted to them by the Governors of the said Plantations and by trading under those colours not only among our own subjects but also those of other Princes & States. And committing divers irregularities they did very much dishonor our service for prevention whereof you are to oblige the Commanders of all ships to whom you shall grant Commissions to wear no other Jack than according to the sample here described that is to say such as are worn by our ships of war with the distinction of a white escutcheon in the middle thereof And that the said Mark of Distinction may extend itself to one half of the depth of the Jack and one third of the fly thereof

94 And whereas there have been great irregularities in the manner of granting Commissions in the Plantations to private Ships of War You are to govern yourself whenever there shall be occasion according to the Commiss' & Instructions granted in this Kingdom copies whereof will be delivered to you

95. But you are not to grant Commissions of Marque or Reprisal against any Prince or State or their subjects in amity with us to any person whatsoever without our especial command

96 You are to demand an account of the persons concerned of the arms ammunition & stores sent to our said Province from hence as likewise what other Arms Ammunition & stores have been bought with the public money for the service of our sd Province and how the same have

15

been employed and whether any of them & how many of them have
been sold spent lost decayed or disposed of and to whom and to what
uses which account is to commence from the time of the date of the Act
of Surrender of the Proprietors of that Province to us And you are to
transmit the said Account to us and to our Comm^n for Trade & Plantations

97 You shall take an Inventory of all such arms ammunition &
stores as are remaining in any of our magazines or garrisons in our said
Province under your Goverm^t and transmit the same to us and to our
Comm^n for Trade & Plantations with all convenient speed And the like
inventory afterwards half yearly as also a duplicate thereof to our Master General or Principal Officer of our Ordnance which accounts are to
express the particulars of ordnance carriage ball powder and all other
sorts of arms and ammunition in our public stores and so from time to
time of what shall be sent to you or bought with the public money and
to specify the time of the disposal and the occasion thereof

98 You are to take special care that fit store house be settled in the
said Province for receiving and keeping of arms ammunition and other
public stores.

99 And whereas it is absolutely necessary that we be exactly informed
of the state and defence of all our Plantations in America in every respect and more especially in relation to the forts and fortifications that
are in each Plantation and what more may be necessary to be built for
the defence and security of the same You are so soon as possible after
your arrival in North Carolina to prepare an account thereof in respect
to our said Province in the most particular manner and to transmit the
same to us and to our Commiss^n for Trade & Plantations and the like
accounts yearly

100 You shall cause a survey of all the considerable landing places
and harbours in our said Province and with the advice of our Council
there erect in any of them such fortifications as shall be necessary for
the security and advantage of the said Province which shall be done at
the public charge And you are accordingly to move the General Assembly to the passing of such Acts as may be requisite for the carrying on
of that work in which we doubt not of their cheerful concurrence from
the common security & benefit they will receive thereby

101 You are from time to time as before directed to give an account
what strength your Neighbours have (be they Indians or others) by sea
and land and of the condition of their plantations and what correspondence you do keep with them

102. And in case of distress of any other of our Plantations You shall upon application of the respective Governors thereof to you assist them with that aid the condition and safety of our Province under your government can spare

103 You shall transmit unto us and to our Comm⁰ for Trade & Plantations by the first opportunity a Map with the exact description of the whole Province under your government with the several Plantations upon it and of the fortifications as also of the bordering Indian settlements

104 And in order to prevent any disputes that may arise about the Southern Boundaries of the Province under your Government We are graciously pleased to signify our pleasure that a line shall be run (by Commiss⁰ appointed by each Province) beginning at the sea thirty miles distant from the mouth Cape Fear River on the South West thereof keeping the same distance from the said River as the course thereof runs to the main source or Head thereof and from thence the said Boundary line shall be continued due West as far as the South Seas But if Waggamaw river runs within fifty miles of Cape Fear River then that river to be the Boundary from the sea to the Head thereof and from thence to keep the distance of 30 miles parallel from Cape Fear River to the head thereof and from thence a due West course to the South Seas.

105. You are to examine what rates and duties are charged & payable on any goods exported or imported within our said Province whether of the growth & manufacture of our Province or otherwise And you are to suppress the engrossing of Commodities as tending to the prejudice of that freedom which Trade and commerce ought to have and to use your best endeavours in the improving the trade of those parts by settling such Orders & Regulations therein with the advice of our said Council as may be most acceptable to the generality of the inhabitants

106 You are to give all due encouragement & invitation to Merchants & others who shall bring trade into our said Province or anywise contribute to the advantage and in particular to the Royal African Company & others our Subjects trading to Africa   And as we are willing to recommend unto the said Company & others our subjects that the said Province may have a constant & sufficient supply of Merchantable Negroes at moderate rates in money or commodities so you are to take special care that payment be duly made and within a competent time according to their respective agreements

107. And whereas the said Company and other Traders having frequently great sums of money owing to them in our Plantations in Amer-

ica have been much hindered in the recovery of their just debts there and discouraged in their trade by the too frequent adjournment of Courts and it being absolutely necessary that all Obstructions in the Courts of Justice be effectually removed You are to take care that Courts of Justice be duly and frequently held in our Province under your Govern' so that all our subjects in the said Province and particularly the Royal African Comp. and others trading to Africa may enjoy the benefit thereof and not receive any undue hindrance in the recovery of their just debts

108 And we do hereby expressly command and require you to give unto us and to our Comm" for Trade & Plantations an account every half year of what number of Negroes our said Province is supplied with that is what number by the African Company and what by the separate traders & at what rates sold

109 Whereas We have been informed that during the time of War our Enemies have frequently got intelligence of the State of our Plantations by letters from private persons to their Correspondents in Great Britain taken on board ships coming from the Plantations which has been of dangerous consequence Our Will and Pleasure is that you signify to all Merchants Planters and others that they be very cautious in time of war whenever that shall happen in giving any account by letters of the public state and condition of our Province of North Carolina And you are further to give direction to all Masters of ships or other persons to whom you may entrust your letters that they put such letters into a bag with a sufficient weight to sink the same immediately in case of imminent danger from the enemy And you are always to let the Merchants and Planters know how greatly it is for their interest that their letters shall not fall into the hands of the enemy and therefore that they should give the like orders to Masters of ships in relation to their letters And you are further to advise all Masters of ships that they do sink all letters in case of danger in the manner beforement'

110 And whereas in the late Wars the Merchants and Planters in America did correspond & trade with our enemies and carry intelligence to them to the great prejudice & hazard of the British Plantations You are therefore by all possible methods to endeavour to hinder all such trade and correspondence in time of war

111, Whereas by the 5th & 6th Articles of the Treaty of Peace & Neutrality in America concluded between England and France the 16 November 1686 the subjects & inhabitants in each Kingdom are prohibited to trade and fish in all places possessed or which shall be possessed by the other in America And that if any ships shall be found trading contrary to the said Treaty upon due proof the said ship shall be confiscated But in case the subjects of either King shall be forced by stress of weather enemies or other necessities into the ports of the other in America they shall be treated with humanity and kindness and may provides themselves with victuals and other things necessary for their subsistence & reparation of their ships at reasonable rates Provided they do not break bulk nor carry any goods out of their ships exposing them to sale nor receive any Merchandize on board on penalty of confiscation of ship & goods   It is therefore our Will and Pleasure that you signify to our subjects under your government the purport & intent of the above said two Articles and that you take particular care that none of the French subjects be allowed to trade from their settlements to North Carolina or to fish upon the coast thereof

112   Whereas Commissions have been granted unto several persons in our respective Plantations in America for the trying of Pirates in those parts pursuant to the several Acts for the more effectual suppressing of pirates And by a Commission to be given you, you as Captain General and Governor in Chief of our said Province are empowered together with others therein mentioned to proceed accordingly in reference to the said Province of North Carolina Our Will and Pleasure is that in all matters relating to Pirates you govern yourself according to the intent of the said Acts & Commission beforementioned

113 Whereas We have thought it necessary for our service by our Commission bearing date the 9th day of August 1727 to constitute author- ize & appoint Robt Byng Esqr to be our Receiver General of the rights and perquisites of the Admiralty We do direct and appoint that you be aiding and assisting to the said Robt. Byng his Deputy or Deputies in the execution of the said Office of Receiver General and do hereby enjoin & require you to make up your accounts with him his Deputy or Deputies of all rights of Admiralty (effects of Pirates included) as you or your Officers may or shall at any time receive and to pay over to the said Receiver General his Deputy or Deputies for our use all such sums of money as as shall appear on the foot of such accounts to be and remain in your hands or in the hands of any of your Officers And whereas the said Robt Byng is directed in case the parties chargeable with any part of our Revenue refuse neglect or delay payment thereof by himself or sufficient Deputy to apply in our name to our Governors Judges Attornies General or any other our Officers or Magistrates to be aiding or assisting to him in recovering the same Now you our Gov- ernor our Judges our Attornies General and all other Officers whom the

same may concern are hereby required to use all lawful authority for the recovering and levying thereof

114 You are to propose an Act to be passed in the Assembly whereby the Creditors of persons becoming Bankrupts in this Kingdom and having estates in North Carolina may be relieved and satisfied for the debts owing to them

115 You are likewise from time to time to give unto us and to Our Comm⁺ for Trade and Plantations as afores⁺ an account of the wants and defects of our said Province what are the chief products of what are the new improvements made therein by the industry of the inhabitants & planters and what further improvements you conceive may be made or advantages gained by trade and which way We may contribute thereunto

116 If anything shall happen which may be of advantage or security to our said Province which is not herein or by our Commission provided for We hereby allow unto you with the advice and consent of our said Council to take order for the present therein giving unto us by one of our principal Secretaries of State and to our Commiss⁺ for Trade & Plantations speedy notice thereof that so you may receive our ratification thereof if we shall approve the the same Provided always that you do not by colour of any power or authority hereby given you commence or declare war without our knowledge or particular commands therein except it be against Indians upon emergencies wherein the consent of our Council shall be had and speedy notice thereof given to us as aforesaid.

117 And you are upon all occasions to send unto us by one of our Principal Secretaries of State and to our Commiss⁺ for Trade & Plantations a particular account of all your proceedings & of the condition of affairs within your Government.

Ex⁺ ℣
T. G
G. B

[B P R O North Carolina B. T Vol. 8 A 12]

At the Court at St James's the 14ᵗʰ day of December 1730
Present
The Kings most Excellent Majesty
in Council
Upon reading at the Board a Report from the Right Honourable the Lords of the Committee of Council upon Considering two Draughts of

Instructions prepared by the Lords Commissioners for Trade and Plantations for George Burrington Esq' Captain Generall and Governor in Chief of His Majestys Province of North Carolina—And their Lordships Offering it as their Opinion that the said Draughts were proper for His Majestys Royall Approbation—His Majesty in Councill was this day pleased to Approve thereof and to order as it is hereby ordered that One of His Majestys Principall Secretarys of State Do Cause the said Draughts of Instructions (which are hereunto annexed) to be prepared for His Majestys Royall Signatures

A True Copy

JA VERNON

[B P R O Am & W Ind. No. 592]

WARRANT TRANSMITTING NEW SEAL FOR NORTH CAROLINA 1730

To our Trusty and welbeloved George Burrington Esq" Our Captain General and Governor in Chief of our Province of North Carolina in America, Or to the Commander in Chief of our said Province for the time being Greeting   With this you will receive a Seal prepared by our order for the use of our said Province the Same being engraven on the one side with our Arms, Garter, Crown, Supporters and Motto and this Inscription round the Circumference Georgius II D G Mag Bri· Fr et Hib. Rex F D Brun et Lan Dux S R Y Arc Th et Pr El. on the other Side our Royal Effigies and Liberty represented introducing Plenty to us with this Motto Quæ Sera Flamen Respexit and this Inscription round the Circumference Sigillum Provinciæ Nostræ Carolinæ Septentrionalis. Our Will and Pleasure is, and we do hereby authorize and direct that the said Seal be used in the Sealing all Patents and Grants of Lands and all Publick Instruments which shall be made and passed in our name and for our Service within our said Province and that the Same be to all intents and Purposes of the Same Force and Validity as any other Seal heretofore used within the said Province. And we do further command and require you upon the Receipt of the Said Seal to return the former Seal to our commissioners of Trade and Plantations to be laid before us as usual in order to its being defaced in like manner with other Seals by us in our Privy Council   Given at our Court at St James the Day of   1730, in the fourth year of Our Reign

[B P R O North Carolina B T Vol. 8 A 10]

At the Court at St James' the 14th day of December 1730
Present
The King's Most Excellent Majesty
in Councill

A new Seale for his Majestys Province of North Carolina having been this day laid before His Majesty in Councill for His Royall Approbation His Majesty was pleased to approve thereof and to order as it is hereby ordered that the Lords Commissioners for Trade and Plantations Do Prepare a draught of a Warrant for transmitting the said seale to the Governor of the said Province and Empowering him to make use thereof And the said Lords Commissioners are to lay the said Draught before His Grace the Duke of Newcastle One of His Majestys Principall Secretarys of State in Order to Obtain His Majestys Sign Manuall thereto And afterwards to transmitt the said Warrant with the said Seale to the Governor of the said Province accordingly

          JAS VERNON

[B P R O Am & W Ind No. 592]

LORDS OF TRADE TO THE DUKE OF NEWCASTLE
DECEMBER 31th 1730

My Lord,

Having in obedience to his Majestie's order in Council of the 14th Instant prepared the Draught of a Warrant for transmitting a new Seal for his Majesty's Province of North Carolina to the Governor of the Said Province impowering him to make use thereof and requiring him to transmit the old Seal in order to its being defaced in like manner with other Seals by his Majesty in Council, we here inclose the Said Draught of a Warrant which we desire your Grace will please to lay before his Majesty for his Royal Signature. We are

    My Lords Your Graces
      most obedient and
       most humble Servants

         P DOCMINIQUE
         T PELHAM
         JA BRUDENELL
Whitehall   CH CROFT
 December 31th 1730
His Grace the Duke of Newcastle

[B. P R. O. Am & W. Ind. No. 592.]

(*Indorsed*)

Mr RICE SECRETARY & CLERK OF THE CROWN OF NORTH CAROLINA
1730.

Our Will and Pleasure is, that you prepare a Bill for our Royal signature to pass our great Seal, containing our Grant of the Offices or Places of Secretary and Clerk of the Crown of our Province of North Carolina in America unto our Trusty and Wellbeloved Rice Esqr, to have, hold exercise and enjoy the Same by himself or his Sufficient Deputy or Deputys (for whom he shall be answerable) during our Pleasure, and his residence within our said Province, with all Fees, Rights, Profits, Priviledges and advantages whatsoever thereunto belonging, in as full and ample manner as any other Person or Persons have held, or of right ought to have held and enjoyed the same. And for So doing this Shall be your Warrant. Given at our Court at St James the   Day of 1730 in the third year of our Reign

By His Majesty's Command

To our Attorney or
Solicitor General

[B P R. O Am & W Ind Vol. 22 p 127]

THE CASE OF Y^e INHABITANTS OF NORTH CAROLINA IN RESPECT TO Mr GEORGE BURRINGTON'S BEING REAPPOINTED THEIR GOVERNOR.

Mr Burrington was formerly appointed Governor of North Carolina by the late Lords Proprietors but afterwards for his ill conduct removed by them, his mal-practices were such that complaint was forced to be made against him, & a petition was presented supported by a number of Affidavits, a short Abstract of some of which we beg leave to set forth

Affidavit of Mary Badham of Carolina, That 14th of May 1724 Mr Burrington at that time Governor came to Depon^ts about 12 at night & threatened to ruin her husband, swore he would have ye Secretary &

Judge of ye Province in Goal, would lay them in irons & tye on neck and heels, would kill the Secretary whom he damned, and the lowsy Acts of the Assembly, did they pretend to bind him by Laws, did they think he would mind 'em, no, he swore he would not, he was Governor and he would do as he pleased, Depon^t says, she never heard of any reason for this, only their supporting Mr Dunstan's Commission & maintaining ye Acts of ye Assembly

NOTE.—Mr Dunstan was Naval Officer, & the Governor pretended he could turn him out, & would put one Goffe in his place, tho' a person disabled by a particular Act of Assembly

Affidavit of Wm Badham Clerk of ye Royal Court That Govr Burrington in presence of depon^t and several others called the Chief Justice a *Rogue* & a *Villain* (tho' deponent & he believes every one else present thought him a very honest man) said he hated the Chief Justice tho' he had never seen him, would slitt his nose and cropp his ears, That about May 1724, Mr Dunstan applied to Depon^t for a Writt to arrest Mr Goffe, Depon^t asked the Chief Justice if he should grant one, who said it was a thing of course & could not be denied, that in a few days after Mr Burrington asked depon^t by what authority he granted writts, depon^t told him as Clerk of the Court & told him the Chief Justice said he could not refuse it, upon which he fell into a great passion, doubled his fist, held it up, depon^t expected he would have struck him, and swore with many asseverations, he said the Secretary wanted to be Governor, but he would have him in iron before to-morrow night & depon^t too, and then how like Doggs they would look upon one another, as for the Chief Justice he said he had frighted him out of Town already and would put him in Prison

Affidavit of Mrs. Sara Gale, wife of the Chief Justice That on Sunday morning 25th of August 1724, hearing a great noise at the door as if somebody were breaking in, got up & looking out found it was Govr Burrington, he broke the windows and swore he would burn the house, he would have the dogg her husband by the throat and threatened to fetch a Barrell of Gunpowder and blow up the house, swore he would do her husbands business.

Affidavit of Wm Little Esqr that Governor Burrington threatening the Chief Justice with Irons and abusing him very much, one of the Company a relation of the Chief Justices with great modesty begged the Governor to forbear upon which the Governor threw a glass at him called for his sword & some disorder happened

Affidavit of Robt Forster Gen^t That 18th April 1724, deponent being in the room where the Council satt, Governor Burrington called deponent out and asked him to go in and take Co[n] West by the nose and he would bring him off but deponent told him he would not take a member of the Council by the Nose in Council for the world.

Upon these affidavits and several others then lodged with the Lords Proprietors now in their hands, M[r] Burrington was removed, and he has now lately been heard to declare that if he gets over them Governor again he will be the destruction of all those that had any hand in the removing him who were all the principal people of the Country, notwithstanding they did it upon so just an occasion, and the better to enable him to accomplish such his intentions has, as we are informed represented the present Members of the Council who are Rich[d] Fitz Williams, Christopher Gale, J[no] Lovick, Edw[d] Moseley, Francis Forster, Rich[d] Sanderson, Rob[t] West, Tho[s] Pollock J[no] Palis, Edm[d] Gale, J[no] Waley & Roger Moore Esq[rs] as unworthy and unfitt Persons, tho' they are really the most considerable inhabitants of the Province & for that reason chose by the late Proprietors to be the Council of that Country, who with the Governor compose the Court of Equity, determine matters of property, and have otherwise considerable power and therefore ought to be men of the best Estates & understanding, but M[r] Burrington instead of these has recommended some others to be Members who may better suit his purposes, for we are told that all the Persons at present named by M[r] Burrington and through his false suggestions recommended by y[e] board of Trade to His Majesty to be the Council of Carolina are of so mean circumstances that put them all together their Estates in that Country won't amount to £1500, and those whose names have come to our knowledge are of such vile Characters and poor understandings, that it is the greatest abuse imaginable upon the ministry to recommend such to them, Edm[d] Porter we are told is one, he was formerly sent over to England from Virginia to be tried for his life for some notorious facts committed by him, and after he got off from this, was concerned in the Scotch Rebellion, for which he fled to Carolina, another of them is Mathew Rowan no inhabitant of the Country, but only sent over thither to build a ship or two for some persons in Dublin & is now run away with one of them loaded with ennumerated goods contrary to the Acts of Trade Cornelius Hart is another, he keeps a little punch house, and if the names of the others were known it is to be presumed they would be found to be all of this kind, his whole aim being to gett a sett of Persons that will go into any measures he shall propose and M[r] Burrington not forgetting his old grudge against the Chief Justice and some other officers, has as we are informed very much misrepresented them and made as if their posts were of considerable value, tho' in fact not any one of them has ever been worth £100 a year, nor has near so much been made of them as can easily be shewn

For these and many other reasons too tedious to mention, and the daily Instances Mr Burrington gives of his mad extravagant behaviour, it is humbly hoped that his Majesty in tender regard to so many of his poor Subjects in that remote part of his Dominions, who have proposed to themselves great felicity by their being more imediately under his Royal Protection than heretofore will be pleased to enquire into the former conduct of this Gentleman when he was Governor, before he be permitted to go over thither in that quality again

[B P R O JOURNALS. B. T VOL. 40]

WHITEHALL Wednesday Jan^{ry} 7th 17$\frac{29}{30}$

At a Meeting of His Maj Comm^{rs} for Trade and Plantations
Present

Mr Docminique   Mr Ashe
Mr Pelham   Sir O Bridgeman
Mr Bladen   Mr Cary
Sir Tho Frankland

A letter from the Duke of Newcastle dated this day signifying His Majesty's having appointed George Burrington Esqre Governor of North Carolina & directing the Draught of Commission & Instructions to be prepared for him was read and directions were given for preparing the same accordingly

[Page 5]

WHITEHALL Thursday Jan^{ry} 8th 17$\frac{29}{30}$

Col Johnson Govr of South Carolina and Capt Burrington Govr of North Carolina attending with some other gentlemen belonging to those Provinces acquainted the Board that they had agreed upon a division line between those Provinces and their Lordships desired they would mark the line upon a Map and lay the same before the Board which they promised accordingly.

[Page 12.]

WHITEHALL Thursday Jan^{ry} 15. 17$\frac{29}{30}$

The Draught of a Commission for appointing Capt Burrington Govr of North Carolina ordered to be prepared the 7th inst. being agreed a Representation thereupon to His Majesty and a letter for inclosing the same to his Grace the Duke of Newcastle were sign'd

[Page 16.]
WHITEHALL Thursday Jan⁷ 22. 17¾⁰

Col. Johnson Gov' of South Carolina and Capt. Burrington Gov' of North Carolina attending as they had been desired in relation to the Boundaries between those two Provinces mentioned in the minutes of the 8ᵗʰ inst. Their Lordships after some discourse with them thereupon agreed upon the following divisional line Viz' the line to begin at 30 miles south westward of Cape Fear River and to be run at that parallel distance the whole course of the said river

These Gentlemen being withdrawn Ordered that an Article be for this purpose inserted in the Draᵗ of their Instructions.

[Page 24]
WHITEHALL. Thursday Jan⁷ 29 17¾⁰

Ordered that the Draught of a Representation be prepared for proposing a Great seal for North Carolina.

Agreed to & sign'd 3 February

[Page 64.]
WHITEHALL Wednesday March 18. 17¾⁰

An Order in Council of the 21ˢᵗ of February last approving a Representation of this Board of the third of the same month and directing a public seal to be prepared for North Carolina was read and their Lordships gave directions that Mʳ Rollos his Maj. Engraver should prepare a Draft thereof—(signed on 25 March 1730) Col Johnson's proposals for better improving and settling South Carolina with reasons against reserving a quit rent of one penny per acre were read as also

The Representation of Capt. Burrington with his reasons against advancing the Quit Rents in North Carolina

Ordered that copies of so much of the said papers as relate to Quit rents be given to Mʳ Walpole Auditor of the Plantations.

[Page 79.]
WHITEHALL Wednesday April 8ᵗʰ 1730.

Their Lordships then took into consideration the several papers from Sir Richard Everard & the Council of North Carolina in answer to complaints against the Governor and to Grants of land mentioned in the Minutes of the 16ᵗʰ Dec. 1729 and gave directions that copies thereof should be made for Capt. Burrington the present Gov' of that Province and that an Article should be inserted in his Instructions directing him upon his arrival there to examine into the truth of the several facts and lay an account thereof before His Majesty and this Board.

[Page 97.]

WHITEHALL Wednesday April 22 1730

Ordered that the Draught of a Representation be prepared for proposing a Commission for trying Pirates to be passed for North Carolina

[Page 106.]

WHITEHALL Wednesday April 29 1730

A Letter from the Duke of Newcastle inclosing copy of a letter from Mr Porter Judge of the Admiralty at North Carolina giving an account of the unwarrantable proceedings of Sir Richard Everard late Governor of that Province in the granting of lands there was read And their Lordps agreed to insert an Article in the Instructions preparing for Capt. Burrington the present Govr in relation thereto as also to the Disputes between him & the Council referred to the Board by the Duke of Newcastle's letter and Ordered that an Answer be prepared to the Duke of Newcastle's said letters to acquaint him with these resolutions of this Board

(Signed May 1st)

[Page 140.]

WHITEHALL Wednesday June 3. 1730

The Draught of Instructions for Capt. Burrington Governor of North Carolina directed to be prepared the 7th Janry last was agreed & ordered to be transcribed

WHITEHALL Thursday June 4 1730.

Ordered that a letter be wrote to Mr Fane for his opinion in point of law whether according to the Charter of Carolina any Grants made by the Lords Proprietors be valid unless signed by them all and be under the common Seal

The undermentioned copies of Orders in Council were severally read Vizt

Order in Council of 22 Janry 17¾⅜ approving the Draft of a Commission to Capt Burrington to be Governor of North Carolina.

Order in Council of 22d Janry last requiring copies of the papers of complaint from the Members of the Council of North Carolina against Sir Richard Everard Deputy Governor of that Province under the Lords Proprietors as likewise of the complaint made by Sir Richard against the said Council to put into the hands of Capt. Burrington now appointed Governor for his examination into and report of the Facts.

Order in Council of the 10th of April last approving a Representation for a new seal for the Province of North Carolina

[Page 150.]

WHITEHALL Tuesday June 9 1730

M[r] Fane's Report in relation to the validity of such Grants of Offices from the late Lords Proprietors as are not signed by them all was read and Ordered that copies thereof be given to Col Johnson and to Capt. Burrington Gov[rs] of South and North Carolina

[Page 194.]

WHITEHALL, Tuesday July 28 1730.

An Order of the Lords of the Committee of Council dated 21st inst. upon a Representation of the 23rd May foregoing relating to Lord Carteret's eighth part of the Province of Carolina and requiring this Board to send to his Lordship to know the value he sets upon the said eighth in order to treat for the surrender of it to the Crown was read And directions given for preparing a letter to the Lord Carteret thereupon—signed August 4th

[Page 199.]

WHITEHALL Tuesday August 4 1730.

Ordered that a letter be writ to Capt. Burrington appointed Gov[r] of North Carolina to acquaint him that the Board have signed their Representation upon his Instructions so long ago as the 10th of June last and have waited ever since for his list of Councillors but that if he does not bring the names of twelve persons proper to be inserted upon that occasion by Monday next their Lordships will either send away his Instructions without Councillors or name them without waiting any longer for his advice upon that subject

[Page 202]

WHITEHALL Thursday Aug[t] 6th 1730

A letter from the Lord Carteret dated this day in answer to their Lordships of the 4th inst relating to his eighth part of the Province of Carolina and the value his Lordship sets upon it was read Whereupon directions were given for preparing the Draught of a Report to the Lords of the Committee of Council mentioned in the Minutes of the 28th of the last month upon that subject—agreed to & signed on 11th August.

[Page 206.]

WHITEHALL Wednesday Aug[t] 12th 1730.

The Draughts of Instructions for Capt Burrington Gov[r] of North Carolina which were agreed the 3rd June last having remained in this Office for want of a List of persons expected from him to fill up his

Maj Council for that Province and some alterations having in the interim been found proper to be made in the said Instructions conformable to what has since been approved for South Carolina Their Lordships agreed the said alterations as likewise the usual instructions which particularly relate to the Acts of Trade and Navigation Whereupon the Draughts of a Representation for laying the same before His Majesty and of a letter to enclose them to His Grace the Duke of Newcastle were agreed and ordered to be transcribed and were signed Augt 13th

[Page 207]

WHITEHALL Thursday August 13 1730.

Mr Attorney and Mr Solicitor General's Report relating to the validity of certain Grants made by the Lords Proprietors of Carolina particularly one to Sir Nathaniel Johnson in 1686 was read Whereupon Ordered that copies of the said Report be prepared for Col Johnson & Capt Burrington Governors of South & North Carolina.

[Page 213]

WHITEHALL Wednesday August 19 1730

Sir William Keith attending as desired their Lordships had some discourse with him concerning the several nations of Indians bordering upon His Maj Plantations on the continent of America and the manner of conferring and treating with them Whereupon Sir William was desired to let their Lord^{ps} have in writing agreeable to the Indian style the form of a Declaration or Agreement properly to be mutually made by the Chiefs of the Cheroquee Indians now here & by such as his Maj shall appoint on his part for that purpose upon the said Indians having submitted their dominion and territories to his Maj which Sir William Keith promised according

Thursday August 20 1730

Sir William Keith attending presented to their Lordships as desired the form of a Declaration or Agreement proper to be mutually made by the Chiefs of the Cheroquee Indians now here and by such as his Maj shall appoint on his part which was read And the Draught of a letter to the Duke of Newcastle to Know his Majesty's pleasure on this subject was agreed & sign'd

[Page 215.]

Tuesday August 25 1730

Sir William Keith & Col Johnson attending with the Interpreter of the Indian Chiefs the Board had some discourse with them concerning the manner of treating with the said Chiefs

Wednesday August 26 1730

A letter from Mr Lowndes with some Sesamum seeds which grow in Carolina and some of the Oyl produc'd from them was read

[Page 218.]

Tuesday September 1. 1730

A letter from the Duke of Newcastle dated the 31st in answer to one from this Board of the 20th of the last month signifying His Maj having approved of their making some Treaty or Agreement with the Indian Chiefs of the Cherokee Nation who lately came from Carolina and directing the Board to make such Agreement and in such manner with the said Indian Chiefs as they should think for His Maj service was read Whereupon Order'd that Col Johnson Governor of South Carolina and Sir William Keith be desired to attend the Board on Monday morning next as likewise the said Indians and their Interpreter

Order'd that the Secretary do apply at the Secretary at War's Office that Two Sergeants with twelve Grenadiers may attend at the same time upon the said Indians.

Their Lordships then agreed the form of a Treaty with the Indians.

[Page 226.]

WHITEHALL Monday Sept. 7 1730
Present
Mr Pelham. Mr Bladen Mr Brudenell

The seven Indian Chiefs of the Cherokee Nation attending as they had been desir'd with their Interpreter, Col Johnson, Govr of South Carolina Sir William Keith and several other gentlemen Their Lords explained to them by their Interpreter (who was sworn) the Form of a Treaty with them agreed at the last meeting in the words following

Whereas you Scay-agusta Oukah Chief of the Town of Tassetsa You Scalilasken Ket-agusta, You Tethtowe, You Clogoittah, You Colannah, You Unnaconoy, You Oucounacon have been deputed by the whole nation of the Cherokee Indians to come to Great Britain where you have seen the great King George and in token of your obedience have laid the Crown of your Nation with the scalps of your enemies and feathers of peace at his Maj feet Now the King of Great Britain bearing love in his heart to the powerful and great nation of the Cherokee Indians His good friends and allies His Maj has empowered us to treat with you here and accordingly we now speak to you as if the whole Nation of the Cherokees their old men, young men wives and children were all present And you are to understand the words we speak as the words of the Great King our Master whom you have seen And we shall understand the words which you speak to us as the words of all your people with open and true hearts to the Great King And thereupon we give four pieces of striped duffles.

Hear then the words of the Great King whom you have seen and who has commanded us to tell you

That the English everywhere on all sides of the Great Mountains and Lakes are his people and his children whom he loves That their Friends are his Friends and their Enemies are his Enemies That he takes it kindly that the Great Nation of Cherokees have you sent you hither a great way to brighten the chain of friendship between him and them & between your people and his people That the chain of friendship between him & the Cherokee Indians is like the sun which both shines here and also upon the great Mountains where they live and equally warms the hearts of the Indians and of the English That as there are no spots or blackness in the sun so is there not any rust or foulness in this chain and as the Great King has fastened one end of it to his own breast he desires you will carry the other end of the chain and fasten it well to the breast of your Nation and to the breasts of your old wise men your Captains and all your people never more to be broken or made loose And hereupon we give four pieces of white cloth to be dyed blue

The Great King and the Cherokee Indians being thus fastened together by the chain of friendship he has ordered his people and children the English in Carolina to trade with the Indians and to furnish them with all manner of goods that they want and to make haste to build houses and to plant corn from Charles Town towards the Town of the Cherokees behind the great Mountains for he desires that the English and the Indians may live together as the children of one Family whereof the Great King is a kind & loving Father And as the King has given his land on both sides of the Great Mountains to his own children the English so he now gives to the Cherokee Indians the privilege of living where they please and he has order'd his Governor to forbid the English from building houses or planting corn near any Indian Town for fear that your young people should kill the cattle and young lambs and so quarrel with the English and hurt them And hereupon we give two other pieces of white cloth to be dyed red

The Great Nation of the Cherokees being now the children of the Great King of Great Britain and he their Father the Cherokees must treat the English as brethren of the same family and must be always ready at the Governor's command to fight against any Nation whether they be white men or Indians who shall dare to molest or hurt the English and hereupon we give Twenty guns

The Nation of The Cherokees shall on their part take care to keep the trading path clean and that there be no blood in the path where the English white men tread even though they should be accompanied by any other people with whom the Cherokees are at war Whereupon we give four hundred pounds weight of gunpowder

That the Cherokees shall not suffer their people to trade with the white men of any other Nation but the English nor permit white men of any other Nation to build any Forts Cabins or plant corn amongst them or near to any of the Indian Towns or upon the land which belong to the Great King and if any such attempt should be made you must acquaint the English Governor therewith and do whatever he directs in order to maintain & defend the Great King's right to the Country of Carolina Whereupon we give five hundred pounds weight of swan shot and five hundred pounds weight of bullets.

That if any Negro slaves shall run away into the woods from their English masters the Cherokee Indians shall endeavour to apprehend them and either bring them back to the Plantation from whence they run away or to the Governor and for every Negro so apprehended and brought back the Indian who brings him shall receive a gun and a match coat Whereupon we give a box of vermillion ten thousand of gun flints and six dozen of hatchets.

That if by any accidental misfortune it should happen that an Englishman should kill an Indian The King or Great Man of the Cherokees shall first complain to the English Governor and the man who did it shall be punished by the English laws as if he had killed an Englishman and in like manner if an Indian kills an Englishman the Indian who did it shall be delivered up to the Governor & be punished by the same English law as if he was an Englishman Whereupon we give twelve dozen of spring knives four dozen of brass kettles and ten dozen of belts.

You are to understand all we have now said to be the words of the Great King whom you have seen and as a token that his heart is open and true to his children and friends the Cherokees & to all their people he gives his hand in this Belt which he desires may be kept and shown to all your people and to their children and children's children to confirm what is now spoken and to bind this Treaty of Peace and Friendship betwixt the English and the Cherokees as long as the Mountains and Rivers shall last or the sun shine Whereupon we give this Belt of Wampum

And their Lordships desired they would give their Answers thereto on Wednesday morning next

Their Lordships then showed them the samples of the above-mentioned presents and the chief of the Indians said to the Board by his

Interpreter that they were not come hither as enemies but as friends
That altho' they did not expect to see the King yet they had seen him
And that they would give their Answer to the said Treaty on Wednesday
morning next

[Page 237]

Wednesday Sept. 9. 1730.

The seven Indian Chiefs of the Cherokee Nation attending as they
had been desired with their Interpreter as likewise Col Johnson & Sir
William Keith Their Lordships told them they were ready to hear what
the said Indian Chiefs had to say in answer to the propositions made to
them in behalf of his Majesty on Monday last

Whereupon Scahlosken Ket-agusta being directed by Sky-agusta
Oukah and the rest of the said Indians to speak in their behalf deliver'd
himself in the following terms—

We are come hither from a dark mountainous place where nothing but
darkness is to be found but are now in a place where there is light
There was a person in our Country with us he gave us a yellow token of
warlike Honour that is left with Moytehoy of Telloqua And as War-
riors we received it   He came to us like a Warrior from you a Man he
was his talk was upright and the token he left preserves his memory
amongst us

We look upon you as if the Great King George was present and we
love you as representing the Great King and shall dye in the same way
of thinking

The Crown of our Nation is different from that which the Great King
George wears and from that which we saw in the Tower But to us it is
all one and the chain of friendship shall be carried to our people

We look upon the Great King George as the Sun and as our Father
and upon ourselves as his children For tho' we are red and you white
yet our hands and hearts are join'd together.

When we shall have acquainted our people with what we have seen
our children from generation to generation will always remember it

In war we shall always be as one with you   The Great King George's
enemies shall be our enemies his people and ours shall be always one and
dye together

We came hither naked and poor as the worm out of the earth but you
have everything and we that have nothing must love you and can never
break the chain of friendship that is between us

Here stands the Gov' of Carolina whom we know   This small rope
which we show you is all we have to bind our slaves with and may be
broken but you have iron chains for yours   However if we catch your

slaves we shall bind them as well as we can and deliver them to our friends again and have no pay for it

We have look'd round for the person that was in our Country he is not here however we must say that he talk'd uprightly to us & we shall never forget him

Your white people may very safely build houses near us We shall hurt nothing that belongs to them for we are the children of one Father the Great King and shall live and dye together

Then laying down his Feathers upon the table he added This is our way of talking which is the same to us as your letters in the Book are to you And to you Beloved Men we deliver these feathers in confirmation of all we have said and of our Agreement to your Articles.

After which their Lordships told them they were well pleased with the consent they had expressed to the articles proposed to them in his Majesty's behalf

[Page 251]

Tuesday Sept. 29 1730.

A Memorial from Sir Alex Cuming Bart in relation to the Cherokee Indians was read And their Lordships resolved to consider further thereof at another opportunity

[Page 252.]

Wednesday Sept 30 1730

A letter from Sir Alex Cuming dated this day relating to the desire of one of the Indian Chiefs to continue in England with him was read And an Answer thereto was agreed & order'd to be sent

A letter to the Duke of Newcastle for inclosing a copy of the Articles proposed to the Indian Chiefs of the Cherokee Nation the 7th inst. as also of the Answer they gave the Board the 9th was agreed and signed.

[Page 327]

Thursday December 10. 1730

A letter from Gov Burrington, Gov. of North Carolina desiring the Board's directions in relation to the making out of New Grants to old landowners and to the appointment of Receivers for the Country taxes was read and an Answer agreed thereto.

[Page 339]

Thursday December 31. 1730

An Order in Council dated the 14th inst directing this Board to prepare a Draft of a Warrant for transmitting a new seal to the Gov' of North Carolina and empowering him to use the same was read And the Draft of a Warrant being accordingly prepared their Lordships signed a letter for inclosing the same to the Duke of Newcastle.

1731.

[B. P R. O. Am & W Ind. Vol. 22. p 108.]

To the Kings most Excellent Majesty

The Humble address of the Grand Jury for the whole Province of North
  Carolina now met at Edenton April the first 1731

This being the first Grand Jury called since the Publishing your Royal
Commission for the Government of this Province We with the greatest
Pleasure Embrace the occasion to assure your Majesty that we are a People devoted to your Royal Person and Illustrious Family and that nothing could be more joyfully received than the certain news of our being
immediately under the Government & direction of so mild, so just, & so
indulgent a Prince, whose Glory is the Ease & Happiness of his People,
whose remotest Regions feel the Influence & are made happy under it
and whom no Distance can seperate from the Good & Welfare of His
Subjects

We beg leave with hearts full of gratitude and Duty to acknowledge
your Majesties most Transcendant Goodness in that Tenderness & Care
shewn for the Ease & benefit of the People and preserving our Rights
& Liberties in those Instructions the Governor has been pleased to Declare   You have made the rule of his Government here, and we cannot
but look upon it a very great instance of your Favour, the sending us a
Gentleman for our Governor, so thoroughly acquainted with the State
and Condition of this your Majesties Province which will Enable him to
surmount many Difficulties that upon so great a Change of the Government must have been Insuperable to a Stranger   And we have the com-
fort & Pleasure to say we have already seen such instances of his mildness
and Generous Treatment and even of his humanity and Tenderness to all
sorts of People that we are persuaded he makes your Majestys exalted
virtues his Pattern in Government, than which we cannot have a greater
Blessing

His Excellencys great Impartiality in the Administration of Justice
gives us the firmest Assurance of enjoying the benefit of our Laws and
seeing Peace & order revive amongst us, and the generous Example he
has sett in forgetting all Private differances we doubt not will have that
happy Effect as to put an end to all heats & animositys amongst ourselves
that we may have no other strife but who shall be most Loyall & obedient and the truest friends to their poor Country almost worn out with
its own Disorders and the weakness of the Proprietory Government, but

we now please ourselves with the thoughts that our Country will again Flourish, our Trade increase and your Majesties Dominions will be enlarged by a Growing Colony

The New Settlement which our Governor at a very great Expence and Personal trouble some years since laid the Foundation of at Cape Fear will we hope encrease & become a great benefit to the whole Province There are several matters we should have presumed to have represented to your Majesty in whose favour we rest for granting whatever may contribute to the prosperity of this your Colony, but our General Assembly being to meet very suddenly we shall leave it to them to lay such things before your Majesty as may be wanting for our Country We have only to Repeat our Assurance of our most Profound Duty and Loyalty to your Majesty and of our utmost Care in our Stations of suppressing all Vice & Irregularity amongst us, which we think is the best means of obtaining the Blessing of Almighty God to whom we shall always pray that our most glorious King and Queen may long Reign over us. We are

Sacred Sir
    Your Majesties most Dutiful
        most Loyall & most Obedient Servants
          and Subjects

                JOHN LOVICK, foreman
                HENRY BONNER
                WILLIAM MORTON.
                THOMAS KEARNY.
                HENRY GUSTON
                WILL. GRAY
                EDW⁴ GALE.
                THOS. LOVICK
                Wᵐ HARDING JONES.
                CHAS: DENMAN
                RICH⁴ SKINNER.
                RICHARD WHEEBE.
                WILLIAM WILLIS
                JAMES MILLIKIN
                HENRY BAKER.
                Jⁿᵒ ISMAY
                JOSHUA LONG
                WILL ARKIL.
                JOHN BRICKELL

The Grand Jury's Address to His Majesty, April 1ˢᵗ 1731

[B P R. O. North Carolina B. T. Vol. 9 A 40.]

GEORGE THE SECOND BY THE GRACE OF GOD KING OF GREAT BRITAIN FRANCE AND IRELAND &c DEFENDER OF THE FAITH &c

To our Trusty and well beloved William Smith Esqr Greeting

Wee reposing special Trust and Confidence in the care prudence fidelity loyalty and integrity of you the said William Smith and out of our meer motion, certain knowledge and special Grace have ordained constituted and appointed and by these presents do ordain constitute and appoint you the said William Smith by the name and style of Chief Justice or Judge of this our said Province of North Carolina To have and to hold and determine all Pleas as well as civil as criminal and all other Pleas whatsoever arising and happening within our said Province of North Carolina giving and hereby granting unto you the said William Smith full power and authority to do perform and execute all acts matters and things whatsoever which in our said Province to the Office of a Chief Justice in any wise belong or appertain and in as large and ample manner to all intents and purposes as any Justice of any of the Courts of Westminster or any of the English Plantations in America may or ought to perform and execute To have and to hold the said office of Chief Justice in this our Province of North Carolina (During our Royall Will and Pleasure) Together will all Fees perquisites Priviledges Liberties Immunities and Casualties belonging unto the said Office and we do hereby revoke and make null and void all former Commissions granted for the said Office In Testimony whereof we have caused these our letters to be made Patent. Witness our Trusty and well beloved George Burrington Esqr Captain General and Governour in Chief in and over this our said Province of North Carolina

GEO BURRINGTON

Given under my hand and Seal of the Colony the first day of April in the fourth year of his Majesties reign Anno Dom . 1731

By order of the Governor and Council

Jos Anderson

P. Secretary

[B. P R. O Am & W Ind Vol. 22 p 11]

NORTH CAROLINA May 22ⁿᵈ 1731

MAY IT PLEASE YOUR GRACE

The General Assembly of this Province having voted an Address to be sent unto His Majesty, I put it under this cover, as in my opinion the most direct way of its coming to the Royal Presence, If I Err in the manner I humbly ask your Grace's Pardon

So soon as the committee shall have prepared the Representation of the state of this Country I shall transmit it unto your Grace and to the Lords Commissioners of Trade and Plantations pursuant to the Directions of the Assembly. In the mean time I ask Liberty to assure your Grace, that I find in the people of this Province a most hearty zeal and affection for his Majesty's person and Government, and a readiness to comply with all His Majesty's Instructions to the utmost of their Power, which I trust will be very evident to your Grace when you shall see the Journal of the Assembly.

I am preparing a large Map of this Province for his Majestys view, drawn from several Observations I collected when I was Surveyor General of this Province and many helps I have received from several Gentlemen of this and the neighbouring Governments, the particulars whereof I shall communicate to your Grace when I send the Map

I beg leave to subscribe myself, your Grace's most obedient
and most humble servant

E. MOSELEY

[B P R. O Am & W Ind Vol. 22. p 12.]

To the Kings Most Excellent Majesty

The Humble Address of the General Assembly of Your Majesty's Province of North Carolina.

MOST GRACIOUS SOVEREIGN

We your Majesty's most Dutiful and Loyal Subjects the Representatives of the People of this your Province now met in General Assembly with Chearfulness lay hold of this Opportunity on our first meeting after the Publication of your Majesty's purchase of the Sovereignty of this Province, to acknowledge with the Profoundest Gratitude the many

Blessings we enjoy under your Auspicious and Happy Reign   It is with
the greatest Pleasure we observe your Majesty and our Gracious Queen
Caroline always Intent on Promoting the Happiness of all your People,
and although we are so remote from your Royal Presence, we find ourselves Nevertheless the subject of your Fatherly Care and Concern

We are in Duty bound to acknowledge as a particular mark of your
Indulgence the placing over us His Excellency George Burrington Esqr
Captain General and Commander in Chief of this your Province, a
Person who by his Behaviour during the time he governed this Pro-
vince for the Lords Proprietors rendred himself very agreable to the
People by the Great Care he then shewed in his due Administration of
Justice and in promoting the wellfare of this Province, on which occa-
sion his Indefatigable Industry and the Hardships he underwent in car-
rying on the Settlement at Cape Fear deserves our thankful Remembrance

The Governour having laid before us several of your Majesty's Instructions relating to this Province, we think it our Duty thankfully to
acknowledge your Majesty's great clemency and Goodness expressed in
those Instructions toward the people of this your Province, and as some
of them do necessarily require that your Majesty should be informed of
the State and Condition of this Country, we have directed a Committee
to transmit a true State thereof unto his Grace the Duke of Newcastle
one of your Majesty's principal Secretarys of State, and to the Right
Honorable the Lords Commissioners of Trade and Plantations.

That the Life of your Majesty our Gracious Queen may be Long, Your
Reign Happy, and the Succession of your Throne Perpetuated in the Most
Illustrious House of Hanover to the latest Ages are the Prayers of your
Majesty's

   Most Dutiful
    Most Loyal and
     Most Obed^t Subjects
      E. MOSELEY. Speaker

By Order of the General Assembly

     (Endorsed)
    Address of the General Assembly
     of North Carolina.
    in the Speaker of the Assembly's
     Letter of May 22^d 1731

[B. P. R. O Am & W Ind Vol. 22. p 13]

NORTH CAROLINA 1st of July 1731.

MAY IT PLEASE YOUR GRACE

By his Majesty's Instructions I am commanded to transmit to one of the principal Secretarys of State Copies of the Proceedings of the Governor's Council, and Assembly with my report and remarks which haveing done, with care and diligence, I now do myself the honour to address them to your Grace

MY LORD

I have used my endeavours to settle this Government as commanded by the King's Instructions, if the Council would have assisted me much might have been effected, Mr Smith the Chief Justice, Mr Ashe and Mr Porter Councellors violently opposed me, the Assembly by their instigation instead of observeing his Majesty's Instructions, and makeing Laws for the good of their Country, in concert with the before named Councellors imployed themselves in promoting private Agencys and Complaints, Smith resigned his seat in Council, it is beliv'd here he is gone to England to complain against me, I treated him with great kindness and gave him very good advice, he might have lived very happily in this Country if he had either understanding or honesty I have reason to think this ungratefull youth was seduced by Mr Rice Secretary of this Province Coll: Bladen's Brother in Law, before his comeing everything looked well, he stayed but a short time then returned to his Family in South Carolina, I have heard from London and it is commonly reported here that upon any Complaint I shall be dismissed and Rice promoted to the Government by Mr Bladen's Interest, Mr Montgomery the Attorney General is very intent to prejudice me on all occasions, he came with Recommendations from Coll Bladen

The Province notwithstanding the Artifices that have been used is in a peaceable and quiet condition, I hope to keep it so, till such time as I am honoured with your Grace's commands, no good can be expected from an Assembly before

MY LORD

The Inhabitants of North Carolina expect they shall have Liberty to take up Land on smaller Quit Rents than are now sett for new surveys, being double to what is paid in Virginia and twelve time more then the Proprietors received, this circumstance is very prejudicial to all the

Officers more particulaly the Secretary two thirds of his perquisites accrued by Warrants and Patents for Land, when affairs are rightly settled the incomes of the several Officers will be the full value I named them to your Grace   I cannot flatter myself so much to think your Grace will looke upon my Report, or the Journals   The Favour I desire of My Lord Duke is to allow the Liberty of defending myself against my base enemys if attackt and that he will not pass Judgment upon me before my defence is seen, after that if your Grace finds me upon the strictest examination in fault, I will never complain punish me ever so severely, haveing acted with great care and precaution am certain my conduct will prove blameless (I hope commendable) therefore am fully satisfied your Grace will not permit Mr Bladen to ruine me if he attempts it

Your Grace was infinitely good in generously promoting me to this Government, I will allways act in the best manner for his Majesty's service, and take care never to give my Lord Duke cause to be displeased

I fear writing more would make this letter too long, therefore have instructed Mr Fury to inform your Grace, when commanded

   I am
     Your Grace's
       most humble
        and most devoted servant
          GEO BURRINGTON

[B. P R. O North Carolina B. T Vol 8 A 13.]

GOVr BURRINGTON TO LDS OF TRADE.
[1 July, 1731]

To the Right Honourable the Lords of Trade and Plantations

MY LORDS.

Having finished my Report of the State and Condition of this Province as I am commanded by His Majesty's Instructions, herewith I transmit the same to Your Lordships Board, and shall be Extremely pleased if it has the Good luck to meet with Your Lordships Approbation,   the accounts I give are Just and true according to the best of my Knowledge and Informations I could get   what Relates to my Own Behaviour is Submitted to Your Lordships Judgement I can truly say I have acted in everything to the best of my Capacity, and have not knowingly Deviated a Tittle from the Powers and directions I brought with me, when I have His Majesty's interest in View and pursue his Instructions, I think I cannot Err

I have been entirely left to myself since I entered upon the Country's Business and instead of help and Assistance from His Majesty's Council and Officers here as I might reasonably have Expected (and surely it was their Duty to have given me) I have had and still have them a weight upon me, There has been no foolery or Villany sett on foot that they are not Concerned Inn which has increased since John Mongomery the Attorney General arrived at once he struck in with this Party, I have the whole force of his Wisdom and the three following Gentlemens to Guard against.

If I am wanting in my Report or have Omitted any thing that might have been done for His Majesty's service it must be attributed to the conduct of these Gentlemen, I have been so farr from Disobligeing or doing any thing to make them Uneasy, that on the Contrary I have used all my Endeavours to serve them and cannot account for their behaviour to me (when I mention the Council I doe not mean all there being but three principally that I complain against) Mr Ashe a Gentleman (when I had the Charge of this Government under the Proprietors) I conceived so good an Opinion off that I intrusted him with all my Concerns during my stay in England The second is Mr Edmond Porter, who has to say of me that I Refused to make myself a party in his unjustifyable quarrels and would not screen him from several Prosecutions against him for his Violent and unlawfull proceedings in the Court of Admiralty of which he is Judge. The third is Mr Smith the Chief Justice a Weak Rash Young Man, Drunk from Morning till Night, set on work by the Other two and some of the Managers in the Assembly. when anything was to be said or done that the Others were ashamed off, he was their Mouth and Tool he has Resigned his seat at the Council Board sometime Past, it is now reported he is going home with Complaints Against me, this for anything I know may be true, Tho' upon the Strictest Examination into my Own Conduct I am no way Conscious, that I have given the least Pretence to these Gentlemen to Complain, but every thing may be Expected from the Folly and Madness they have shewn, and the heats of Nonsense that is for Ever among them.

MY LORDS.

I am convinced my Actions will speak for themselves and that I shall have no Occasion to bespeak your favour Your Justice I have a Right to

Demand and am sure it will not be Denyed me (which is) that if any complaints are Lay'd before you, I may not be censured unheard, I desire only an Oportunity of Answering whatever may be Objected against me

   I am

     With due Respect

      Your Lordships

       Most humble

        And Most obedient Servant

         GEO BURRINGTON

[B P R. O. Am & W Ind Vol. 22. p 14.]

       NORTH CAROLINA July the 2ᵈ 1731.

To the Duke of Newcastle One of His Majesty's Principal Secretarys of State

   MAY IT PLEASE YOUR GRACE

The 25ᵗʰ of February last I came to this Country found the Province in the greatest Confusion the Government sunk so low that neither Peace or Order subsisted, the General Court suppressed, the Council set aside a year and half, some of the Precinct Courts fallen, the admiralty Court haveing no restraint began to draw all manner of Business there and proceeded in such an Extraordinary Manner as occasioned a General Discontent and Ferment among People, who from all Parts on my arrival complained against that Court, the Gentleman that is Judge of it boasted of his success in putting down the supream Court, and is known to have been the Chief Actor in running the Country into Disorders The late Governor Sir Richard Everard being a very weak man was too easily put upon such rash and unadviced Measures that have since caused so many heats and divisions, I fear it will be some time before I shall be able to allay them though I have done my utmost Endeavour to effect it and to sett a good Example I freely passed by all Differences I had with any persons for their past Actions, which was gratefully received The first Grand Jury (which was for the whole Country) made a thankfull acknowledgement in their Address to me at the same time they signed a very Loyal and Dutifull Address to his Majesty That will be transmitted home with these Papers

  Soon after my arrival agreeable to my Instructions with the Advice of the Council I issued Writs for calling an Assembly which met on the

13th day of April I opened it with a kind speech recommending Peace unanimity and due regard to his Majesty's Instructions which I ordered to be laid before them, kept them sitting Five weeks when I was obliged to part with them finding the longer they sat the more their heats increased and less Inclination in them to observe his Majesty's Instructions as shall be further taken notice of in its Place, and proceed to make remarks upon what was done on the several Instructions.

As directed by the 19th Instruction a Bill was formed for an Act about the Fees and Quit Rents to that Part of the Instruction for remitting the arrears of Rents, it was readily enough accepted but instead of complying with his Majesty's Instructions about the payment of Fees and Quit Rents in Proclamation Money they pretended to allow the payment in that Money or Bills at Four for one Discount but then they would New Modell the Fees which accordingly they undertook, and ingeniously reduced them down four times as Low as they were before but this was so palpable, it was not long insisted on, but begat a good deal of Warmth in the Council to see such Prevarication several hot Debates and Messages insued, but I being desirous to enter more calmly on reasoning this affair in my message to the Lower House on the third of May and in the Amendments I made to the Bill on the first, I put the Matter in so clear and strong a light and with so much Temper that they never attempted any Reply but seemed as if they intended to proceed and allow the Fees already established, to be paid in proclamation money or rated Commoditys of the Country or Province Bills at an equivalent.

About this time I discovered there began to be Divisions in the Council and that the Lower House finding the argument bear to hard upon them they were resolved to make a Division (as they called it) in the Council, but I endeavoured all I could to prevent this madness, but I cannot answer for the Follys and Passions of Men, all my Endeavours failed, the Chief Justice who hitherto appeared the warmest against the Lower House and by his extravagant unwary way of Talking had irratated them, was at once by some means or other (to me unknown) made to alter his conduct and act quite a different part, and from that time I had as many Disputes with him and two more of the Council as with the Assembly who after this went but sloly on in complying with his Majesty's Instructions, which I can attribute to nothing but the Behaviour of some of the Council who seemed to be admitted into the Assemblys Secrets   This obstructed everything and obliged me at last to prorogue them, I could never get them to allow more than 150 per cent discount on the Bills to make the Equivalent to Proclamation Money, which was not half the real difference as the Bill pass   Though at the same time I offered if they would comply with his Majesty's Instructions in other things to submit my own Fees to their Discretion   And for that part of the Instruction that required the registring of Lands which I look upon to be very Material toward getting his Majesty a Rent Role, they only evaded it by answers that shewed plainly they designed to doe nothing therein, I look upon this Point to be the more Material because of the great difficultys hitherto in the collecting for want of power in the Lords Proprietors and a compleat Rent Role, and there being no Receiver General here the collection of the Revenue is like to be more perplexed and difficult, in my opinion will require an Officer immediately commissioned and not to be Transacted by a Deputy as is now designed—In respect to the payment of Quit Rents they had ingeniously contrived (under pretence of not being able to pay this year) that it would be near two years before Rents should be paid, and then the Bill added they might be paid in Tobacco or Rice at Eleven shillings per Hundred as an Equivalent for Proclamation Money, thō it is well known that neither of them are worth near so much   I desired the opinion of the Council as may be seen in the Council Journals whither any Equivalent at all could be taken instead of Money and if there might whither what was proposed in the Bill was sufficient, but I could obtain no answer or advice of the Council thereon while the Assembly was sitting, they being then gone to farr into that Spirit of Opposition before complained of

I must humbly beg to know his Majesty's Pleasure if the Receiver may take any Equivalent instead of money which is hardly to be raised in the Government it being affirmed that there has not been cash enough at one time here to pay a years rents   And the people have another Plea that the Grand Deed to the Inhabitants of Albemarle the Name this Government was then called in 1668 under which most part of the Lands are held—Grants the Lands to them on the same Terms as in Virginia where the Rents are paid in Tobacco or Money at the choice of the Partys, and it is submitted whither it would not be a means of putting People on raising Tobacco, and thereby increase our European Trade that so much wants encouragement

The 20th Instruction directs me to send an Account to the Lords Commissioners of Trade and Plantations whither any Paper Bills be Current in North Carolina and how many, on what Fund and at what discount they are current

To put this affair in a clear light it may not be amiss to take notice of the first Emission of Bills here, which was occasioned by the expence of a Bloody Warr with the Indians nere 20 years past. The Lords Proprietors complained of this as a Hardship upon them, that these Bills were made to pay their Rents and Fees to the Officers, but it was answered that they were to defray the Expence of the Warr to save their Lordships Country from a great danger, and which they had nothing contributed to defend, therefore it was reasonable the Lords should so far partake as to suffer their Rents and Dues to be paid in these Bills, which were made Current in all payments, and which by the Taxes laid as a sinking Fund in a Few years would call them all in, and put an end to them, to perform this the Publick Faith was pawn'd, However that Faith was afterwards broke in upon, The Taxes for sinking them were lessened and afterwards more Bills emitted, which all the while paying the Lords Rents and Dues was an apparent Injury to their Revenue. This the Lords ordered to be redressed but without any effect. However these old Bills are since called in and all the Bills of Credit now subsisting are by a pretended Law made in November 1729, After the King had purchased a Copy of the Act is herewith transmitted by which it appears the sum of Forty Thousand pounds was made of which Tenn Thousand Pounds were allotted to exchange the old Bills then current, the other Thirty Thousand Pounds were distributed into the several Precincts and Precinct Treasurers appointed to lett them out at Loan on Land Security, every year part of the principal with the Interest to be paid inn by such payments as in fifteen years to sink the whole whereby the Country is to gain 50 per cent upon the Emission, thõ there was Liberty for the Borrowers at the end of any year, to pay in all the Principal which was to be let out again in the same Manner, By this method the money being to be lett out as fast as paid in would make them perpetual, most of these Bills have according been let out at Interest and are now dispersed through the Country, thõ for want of care in the valuation of the Lands Mortgaged it is said there has been a great deal of fraud These are the Bills now current, and this the Fund they are upon The Act it self made an Estimate of them at Four for one with respect to Virginia Currency which is something better than Proclamation Money, Thõ not so much better as the Assembly seemed to deem it. For Proclamation Money makes the chief part of Forreign Coyns current at 6ˢ 10ᵈ per Ounce, and Spanish Money passes in England at about 5ˢ 6ᵈ per Ounce Sterling. The pretended Act says if the Bills in this Currency should sink from that estimate an allowance should by

19

the Assembly be afterwards ascertained on them, this was Intricately
enough expressed in the Act, and at the same time in Lieu of these Bills
when to be paid inn If they were paid in Silver it should be taken at 25ˢ
per Ounce which was stateing of it at four for one in Silver according
to the old Virginia Currency which till lately was at 6ˢ 3ᵈ per Ounce
This seems the Statement made by the Act but instead of Four for one
in Sterling Silver they will not pass so, nor purchase Silver under seven
or eight for one and their Credit seems more declineing from the Breaking up of this Assembly without settling things and its held by many
that the Act itself is Void not only as made and ratified in the name of
the Lords when they had surrendered to the Crown, and were no longer
a Corporation, but that if it had been otherwise the Government here
were not impowered to make such an Act without a Clause therein not
to be Force till their Assent was had For by the Charter the Lords had
power by themselves or Deputys with the Freemen to make Laws. They
impowered the Governour and Council in their name and behalf to ratify
Laws excepting such as affected their own particular Interest or Property
which was to have their own assent   And its undeniable that this Act
most materially affected them in their Right and Interest, and their
Attorney General for that reason on their Behalf protested against it,
which was entered on the Journal of that Assembly

This present Assembly in their message April the 28ᵗʰ as may be seen
in their Journal herewith sent are of Opinion that the Laws made in
1729 are not Void or at least ought to remain in force till his Majesty's
Pleasure be known thereon—Bills have been found so necessary in facilitating payments for defraying the contingent charges of the Government
as well as a medium of Trade that the destroying them wholly would
(I think) be a great loss and damage to the Country   And if his
Majesty's pleasure should be to declare the present set of Bills Void it
is humbly hoped an Instruction may be sent for issuing others on a
better foundation, and more agreeble to his Majesty's Royal Will and
Pleasure

In Observance to the 25ᵗʰ Instruction I have caused all the Laws in
force to be sent home with this Report and made Observations as directed
on the Margins   I intended to have had a Revisal of them by our Assembly had they agreed on doing any Business, some of them want explaining, some are obsolete, others need alterations, but in general they seem
to me a body of Laws well adapted to the place

The 31ˢᵗ Instruction (as directed in the 32ⁿᵈ) I laid before the Assembly and what they did will be seen marked in the Margin of the Journal of the Lower House

The Court of Exchequer mentioned in the 38th Instruction I have not yet erected this being left by the Instruction as I understand it discretionary in me to commissionate, when his Majesty's service may require, and nothing haveing yet been laid before me concerning his Majesty's revenue I forbear erecting the same till I see a necessity for such a Court there (wholly new) and how far his Majesty's service may require a constant Court of Exchequer to be held, I shall be better able in time to judge I am very certain there is no man at present in this Government capable of trying a cause in a Court of Exchequer therefore pray one may be sent from England to execute the office of Chief Justice Baron when the Court is set up.

Being directed by the 41st Instruction to inquire into the Complaint of Sir Richard Everard Barronet late Governour against some of the Members of the late Council and some of the Lords Proprietors Officers And of the late Council against Sir Richard Everard, I accordingly gave notice to the partys and ordered them respectively to be served with Copys and on the day appointed for the Inquirey Debates arose in Council upon some points wherein I desired their opinion I was not candidly dealt with by them as may be seen in the Journals of the Council at length the Board gave it me as their opinion that there was nothing Material in the complaint against Sir Richard that deserved to be proceeded upon only the words spoken against his Majesty which the Gentlemen alledged were to have been proved by Collector Gale who is now in England and Coll. Thomas Harvey who has some time been dead And as to the complaint of Sir Richard Everard against Secretary Surveyor General and Members of the late Council as soon as Sir Richard was called upon to make it good he declared he had nothing to say against the Surveyor General or any of the Members of the late Council, but only against the late secretary Sir Richard called several people who were admitted to give Depositions, but all they swore being Facts, long after the complaint was made, upon the motion of the said Secretary the Board gave their opinion that such Evidence could no ways support Complaint and Sir Richard failing to produce any other Evidence the said Secretary was by the unanimous opinion of the Board discharged from the said Complaint. and the said Secretary haveing put in an Answer to the said Complaint of Sir Richard to clear his character from any Imputation that might be drawn from the Depositions taken against him, the same was judged satisfactory and will be sent home with the Council Journal.

Complaint was made to me allso by Edmond Porter Esq.r Judge of the Admiralty against several persons for an intended Riot and combination of a great number of persons intending to assasinate him, or obstruct him in the Execution of Office upon which I promised him if he would draw up the Complaint in Form that the persons concerned might be served with Copys I would appoint a day for hearing, but the Judge having offered nothing further upon this complaint I conclude he has droped it   By what I can learn there was no Riot intended no any designe to do him hurt

Complaint was allso made to me against the Judge of the Admiralty for many illegal and arbitrary proceedings in that Court against all Law and common right, praying a suspension of the said Judge or other course to be taken with him which I ordered to be lay'd before the Council to be proceeded upon   To this the said Judge has not hitherto replyed as will be seen in the Council Journal

42.d Instruction   This I laid before the Assembly and recommended in my speech but nothing was done by them—To that part which relates to persons holding greater Quantitys of Land than their Grants express It was urged that they had a Law already about Resurveys in such cases which will be seen in the Body of Laws with my remarks.   As to the condition in this Instruction directed to be put into the patent it has allways been usual to add a clause in the Patent it has allways to render it void if not seated and planted in three years, But no condition hath been in the Patents to make them void for not paying the Quit Rents unless the words yielding and paying be thought a condition as the usual form of the Patents run, which have formerly been prescribed by a Law as may be seen in the Body of Laws, But now as the stile and form of Patents must vary I desire a Draft from the Board of Trade. It is directed in this Instruction that no more than Fifty Acres is to be granted for each person in the Family of the Taker of Lands,   If this is not altered there can be but little Pitch and Tarr made Because a Thousand Acres of Pine Land (of which nineteen parts in Twenty of this consists) will hardly employ one slave and will be very detrimental to the Revenue In some Places there are large Plains called Savannas, these are Boggy and as bad Lands as the Moors in the North and West of England so consequently unfitt for Agriculture.   The Pine Lands are chiefly sandy Barrens as improper for Tillage as the Savannas.   Another observation on this Instruction, that if people have so little Land it will be a very long time before all the Country is settled, and if Men are obliged to live so near one another they must make their own Apparell and Household

Goods because they cannot raise stock to purchase them brought from England, it is by breeding Horses, Hoggs, and Cattle that people without slaves gain substance here at first, not by their Labour If but one half of this Province is inhabited by consequence the produce of Cattle &c ll be but half what it might be were the whole taken up

I am commanded by this Instruction also to give an Account whither any Grants of Land have been made in North Carolina without his Majesty's authority since the purchase from the 25ᵗʰ of July 1729 That his Majesty may give such Orders as may be thought convenient for his service.

I have on this head been moved by the Assembly to joyn with them in an address to his Majesty to have all those Grants confirmed to the people My answer was I did not think proper to joyn in such an address but I would truly represent the matter to the Lords of Trade. Which is as follows.—

The Quit Rents as they have been collected did annually fall short of paying the Salarys and other payments to be made for the Lords Proprietors to supply the Deficiency, Lands were sold by order of the Governour and Council to such as could produce Grants or Warrants formerly obtained for them and on running the Line in 1728 Betwixt this Government and Virginia which was done by his Majesty's command and the Proprietors order There being no money in the Receivers hands to defray that charge an order was made by the Governour and Council that Lands should be sold at the usual rates to defray that necessary expence, it was undertaken and the Receiver General with the assistance of the late Secretary and others, on the credit of that order advanced the money needfull which amounted to £2000 in Bills (as appears by the accounts I have perused) which I think very moderate and declared so in one of my messages to the Assembly Certificates were accordingly taken out but before the Lands could be surveyed and Patents obtained and pass the seal, the purchase was perfected by the Crown, and the Government still continuing in the same Form and having no orders to the contrary went on as before to sign the Patents and compleat the sales—The late Receiver General was ordered to produce the accounts to me in Council the same were laid before a Committee who have not yet made their Report—This is the truth of the affair by the best Information I could get concerning the purchase of Lands since his Majesty has bought the Government which haveing now justly represented I shall suffer to remain till his Majesty's pleasure be further known.

43rd Instruction requires that in all Grants to be made for the future, the Quit Rents to be Four shillings, but the people urge that they have an undoubted Right by the Grand Deed from the Lords Proprietors (a copy of which will be found in the Assembly Journal) to hold their Lands on the same Tenure as in Virginia which is at two shillings per hundred So that if this Instruction be continued while the people imagine they ought to have the benefit of the Grand Deed, it will prevent them from taking up Land and hinder the increase of the revenue, prevent the perquisites of the Officers, and obstruct the growth and increase of the Country.

The 44th and 45th Instructions concerning the Jurisdiction of Courts will make due observance of

I am directed by the 46th to transmit an Account of the several Courts and Jurisdictions here established   The Court of Chancery by the former constitutions has allways been in the Governour and Council

The supream Court of common Law which is for the whole Province is called the General Court and hath consisted of a Chief Justice and two or more assistants which by the Lords Proprietors commission had the power of the King's Bench, Common Pleas and Exchequer. And the General Court by another Commission as a General Sessions of the Peace Court of Over and Goal Delivery consisted besides the aforesaid Members, of all Members of Council the principal Officers by name which before the late disorders was constantly held by act of Assembly three times a year at Edenton   Besides this General Court there is allso in every Precinct a Court established, called the Precinct Court with power to try all personal actions under Fifty pounds & is also an Orphans Court, appoints Guardians, takes security &c   Before I leave this head I begg leave to mention a great Debate I have lately had with the Chief Justice and his two allies in the Council, about the power of assistant Judges in the General Court as may be seen at large in the Council Journal herewith transmitted therefore say the less here   But I am very sure if the assistant Judges have no Judicial Power as they express it, and set only as supporters, being useless, No Gentleman will accompany the Chief Justice on the Bench   besides in my Opinion it will be erecting a single Judge of the Court of Common Pleas unknown here before, and I believe as little consistent with the Law, but since the Chief Justice is pleased to declare himself my enemy and so much argument has been upon this head I shall be glad to be favoured with an Instruction or advice hereon

The 47th Instruction   I never heard that any Officers in North Carolina had places under the Proprietors for life but only during their Pleasure which are all now superceeded

The Assembly of this Province have allways usurped more power than they ought to be allowed, one instance I now give in that of chuseing a publick Treasurer (the person now in possession of the office is Edward Moseley speaker and Manager of the Assembly) in the last Session there was some Debate on this subject as may be seen in the Journals—By the Assembly here in 1729 a pretended Act was passed that constituted eleven Precinct Treasurers who were all in the Assembly and as they have the Disposition of the Publick Money will be constantly chosen, which forms so great a Party that they can lead the Assembly as they please.   I am sure it will be for his Majesty's service and quiet of the Province that a Treasurer for this Government be appointed by the Lords of the Treasury

48th Instruction   Directing me with the Council to regulate Fees, and the 19th Instruction—Directing me with the Council to regulate Fees, and the 19th Instruction—Directing all Fees to be paid in Proclamation Money I ordered with the Assent of the Council, that the Fees as they then stood should be received till further regulation, But they should not be compelled to receive them in Province Bills unless at Four for one According to the Estimate made of them with respect to Silver in the pretended Act   This the Lower House at their Meeting with much Ill manners and a great deal of heat complained of (I have never heard that any man in this Country has complained out of the Assembly an well know how it was there managed) as Illegal and Oppressive an Injury to Trade and that they could hardly find a more general Evil which occasioned some writeings between the two Houses as will be seen in the Journals of either House—The Council declared what had been done was agreeable to the King's Instructions and therefore the complaint in effect made the King's Instructions Illegal and Oppressive to this the Assembly answered that they did not declare the Instruction was against Law, but the Officers takeing larger Fees than the Law appointed was illegal and arbitrary and a great oppression, whereas in Truth they took no other Fees than those already by Law established only refused to take them in Bills unless at a Paper discount this subject being carried on with great heat in my message the third of May (already mentioned) I expostulated the matter calmly with them and shewed how manifestly unjust it was that the Fees should be paid in those Bills at Parr, and let them see withall that the Bill Money stood on a precarious Foundation,

to this no reply was made, but the House began to come into Measures
to allow a discount on Bills to make them equivalent to Proclamation
Money on the rated Commodities, but there being afterwards heats and
divisions in the Council as observed before under the 19ᵗʰ Instruction the
Lower House fell off and could not be brought to exceed 150 ⅌ cent
discount on the Bills for an equivalent Thô in Reality its not half the
real difference so that Matter ended and the Assembly was prorogued to
the sixth day of September next when by a Law here the Election for
a Biennial Assembly comes on   I heartily wish I may then find a Temper in both Houses more disposed to his Majesty's service and a complyance with his Instructions

56ᵗʰ Being commanded by this Instruction to appoint two Courts of
Oyer and Terminer to be held yearly the charge whereof to be paid by
the Publick Treasury of this Province not exceeding one hundred
pounds each Session, If this Money is to be paid in Bills will not be
sufficient therefore pray I may be further instructed

61ˢᵗ Instruction directs a Law concerning Jurys if none already
This is settled here by a Law which the people are fond of   The Assembly has formed Lists of Jurors in each Precinct, and their names are all
put into a Box to be drawn at the ending of the Court by a Child
against the next Court but there seems two inconveniencys in this, that
the Assembly admit into those Lists persons not qualifved according to
the Intent of this Instruction, and the Jury drawn being known so long
before may give Opertunity for the Partys to be tampering with them
in the mean time

63ʳᵈ Instruction, I laid before the Assembly and recommended among
others in my Speech, to no purpose

I am commanded by the 69ᵗʰ Instruction to countenance and give all
due encouragement to his Majesty's Officers in this Province which I
have strictly obeyed and shall continue notwithstanding it has made several of my former Friends in this Government to become my illwishers.

75ᵗʰ & 76ᵗʰ Instructions I laid before the Assembly concerning Churches
and the Publick Worship but I could not observe much sence of Religion among them or that any notice was taken   This Country has no
Orthordox Minister legally settled those that formerly have been here
generally proved so very bad that they gave people Offence by their
vicious Lives   The Country is divided into Parishes and there are in
each Parish Church Wardens and a Vestry who have power to raise
money by Poll Tax not exceeding 5ˢʰ in Bill Money on Tythable
Persons which now the Bills are so Low amounts to a small sum this

is put to maintain the poor if any or paying some neighbouring Minister for comeing out of Virginia and to pay Readers there being one or generally more at a small stipend hired annually to read the common service of the Church on Sundays and some printed sermon at a Chapple House where there is any or in some Publick Place several Parishes haveing by contribution or otherwise built Chapples at convenient places

85th Instruction mentions the Indians here, Of late years they are much diminished, there are six Nations amongst us, they all live within the English Settlements having Land assigned them, and chuseing the Places most secure from the attacks of Forreign Indians that delight in slaughtering one another, the names of our Indian People are the Hatteras, the Maremuskeets, the Pottaskites, the Chowans, the Tuscarora, and the Meherrins not one of these Nations exceed 20 Familys excepting the Tuscarora Indians who were formerly very powerfull most of these were destroyed and drove away in the late Warr, only this Tribe under King Blunt made Peace and have ever since lived in amity with us consisting now of about 200 fighting men   There was lately a messenger from the Government of South Carolina complaining of Injurys done the White people of that Government by those Indians.   But they denying the Facts charged on them and refuseing Restitution are threatened by that Government with a Warr from the Cherokees and Catauba's.   On this affair their King is now with me to make some Proposalls, that the White people of South Carolina may not come against him, because he says it may bring on a Warr with the English in General, and may be a matter of consequence to the Country   I have but one Councellor left here to advise with on this affair, the others being out of this Province, or at a very great distance, therefore shall be obliged to fill up some of the Vacancies that I may have a Council to consult on Emergencys, my residence in this part of the Government for some time being absolutely necessary for his Majesty's service

87th Instruction requires me to report the number of Inhabitants in this Government· I have had no time to go upon this Inquiry, but shall obey the Instruction as soon as possible

According to the 85th Instruction there is allready a Law of the Country for registering all Births and Burials in each Parish, thõ little taken notice of it.

And as there are no Forts, Garisons or Magazines, or any Publick Arms or Amunition in this Province; No further answer is needfull to the 96th, 97th, 98th, & 99th Instructions only on the 99th If there should be a Warr or Rupture with the Indians then there will be a Necessity for Forts and Magazines of which an immediate account if it so happen shall be given

103rd Instruction—A Map of this Province I am procuring to be done very accurately and when effected shall transmit as commanded

104th When the Lords of Trade were settling my Instructions I gave them an Account how intricate and difficult it would prove to run a line as directed in this Instruction, moreover it will be an Expence of two thousand pounds sterling to the King   Whereas were all the Lands on the North side Peede River in this Government there would be no occasion for any line (Water bounds being certain) Nor his Majesty put to the Expence of running a Line,   I must further say that if the District between the Division intended by this Instruction and that River was to be sold it would not prove sufficient to pay commissioners, chain, carriers, labourers &c   This Instruction has not yet come under consideration in Council, but shall be duly observed   If I am not otherwise commanded, and if any difficulty arises thereon it shall be carefully represented   The River Santee which is further South formerly divided the two Governments as will appear by many books of Geography and other accounts

105th In answer to this Instruction I can find no rates or dutys charged on any goods exported or imported, nor any Imposition except Powder money which is paid in Bills at ⅜ ℔ Tunn and which was at first intended for Pilotage and buoying out the Inlets and Channels, and some small attempts were made but of late years shamefully neglected And the Chief use the money has been applyed too has been in paving the Assembly Men who have received Tenn shillings a day Travelling Expences to and from the place where the Assembly is held and during the sitting thereof   There is no Law for their being paid, therefore I refused to sign a Warrant at the late Prorogation   I hope for the Future the Assembly Men, may bear their own charges in North as they do in South Carolina   Here are no dutys on anything, nor any Taxes of any sort but a Poll Tax of 5ˢ Bill Money each Tythable (and that by the pretended act in 1729 abolished) and a Parish Tax to be issued by the Vestry not exceeding 5ˢ ℔ Poll for rateable Persons in Bill Money not exceeding 1ˢ 6ᵈ Sterling, and thô the people are thus free from Taxes or Impositions beyond any people in all his Majesty's Dominions they seem uneasy that the Kings Rents should be demanded in Proclamation Money or any thing else but Bills

As to the African Company mentioned in the 106th & 107th Instructions their Trade here hitherto hath been small, but as this Province is now in a way to increase all due encouragement shall be given by the most speedy and impartial Administration of Justice and all other ways that may be and due observance made of their Trade according to the 108th Instruction, as allso all the assistance required to the admiralty and custom Officers, and to the Receiver of the Admiralty Rights, agreeable to the several Instructions thereon   I shall take care when the next Assembly meets, to propose to them an act about Bankrupts as directed in the 104th Instruction.

The 115th and 116th Instructions concludes the remarks required The Instruction about the General state of the Country is near fully answered by what has been already observed,   I shall only further add that I found the Government in a very disorderly condition through the weakness of the late administration that suffered things to run into all manner of Licentiousness   I shall find it no easy matter to reclaim them but as I have a through knowledge of the Country I hope they will soon be in a better disposition and shall endeavour in the calmest and mildest manner to bring them to a sence of their Duty to his Majesty and his Government without which peace and good order cannot be maintained The Country is capable of being made a growing and flourishing Colony and yearly will increase by the coming of people from the Northern Settlements   The Lands to be taken up for the future by the Instructions are at Four Shillings every hundred acres, this is twice as much as in Virginia to a Trifle, the good lands lying commodiously are long since Patented, the remainder the greatest part of the Country are far from navigable waters—For the increase of his Majesty's revenue and good of this Province, hope I shall receive an order to grant lands at two shillings,   I have signed but one Warrant for takeing up land since my arrival   The Trade of this Government is now miserable except at Cape Fear River, the merchants on James river in Virginia supply most of the Inhabitants living on the North side Albemarle Sound and Roanoke river with Brittish Commodities at unreasonable rates being brought in by land or in little Canoos in small quantities.   The people of New England send in sorry sloops which sale from river to river   they furnish our people with West Indian goods and salt and carry away such things as cannot conveniently be transported into Virginia   the only method to put the Traffick in a right way and make the Trade of this country advantagious to Great Brittain is to settle a Custom house on Ocacock Island, where there is a good harbour and water sufficient for a ship that carrys 300 Tunns.   From this place the goods brought in may by small vessels be carried within Land to all places in this Country that doe not depend on Cape Fear River for their trade and be a Port for the three districts of Roanoke, Currituck and Bath Town.   Permit me to say that if lands may be granted at 2ˢ for every hundred acres, and a Port settled upon Ocacock Island this Province will soon be in good repute, I have made it my Business for several years past to study and promote the welfare of this Country and if I am so happy as to obtain what I have desired in relation to the takeing up lands and settling a Port on Ocacock Island I shall in a few years be able to give a good account of the Province his Majesty has honoured me with the care of Governing

I am, my Lord Duke

with all Duty and submission, your Grace's

most humble, most obedient and most devoted servant

GEO· BURRINGTON.

[B. P R. O North Carolina B T Vol. 8 A 14]

A SCHEDULE OF THE PAPERS TO BE DELIVERED TO THE LORDS OF TRADE AND PLANTATION

Drafts of a Bill to ascertain Fees and Quit Rents
Part of a controversy in writing to be read after The Council Journal
The Journal of the Council
Journal of the Upper House
Journal of the Lower House
Pretend Laws of 29
Laws of North Carolina.
A list of the Pattents granted by Sir Richard Everard after the King's Purchase
My Report and letter to the Board of Trade.

[B. P R. O North Carolina B. T Vol. 8. p 1]

North Carolina

These may certifye that Robert Foster Gent who hath attested the copys of the Council Journals, and the Journals of the Upper House of Assembly, is Deputy Secretary of this Province and Clerk of the Upper House of Assembly   That Ayliffe Williams Gent who hath attested the Journals of the House of Burgesses, and the several Papers relating to the proceedings of that House is Clerk of the said House of Burgesses, and that full faith and credit is and ought to be given to such their Attestations.

I do also hereby certifye that the several copies of the Laws hereunto annexed with the aforesaid Journals and proceedings are true Copys from the Originals carefully examined by me.

In Testimony whereof I have hereunto set my hand and caused the Seal of Colony to be affixed, this second day of July in the fifth year of His Majesty's reign Annoque Domini 1731

GEO BURRINGTON

[B. P R. O North Carolina. B T Vol. 8 p 23]

A BILL FOR AN ACT ENTITULED AN ACT TO REGU-LATE AND ASCERTAIN THE PAYMENT OF QUIT RENTS & FEES OF THE OFFICERS OF THIS GOVERN-MENT

This was the second Draft of the Bill about the Fees and Quit Rents which the House declared was the furtherst they would go in the matter & the Council declared they would not consent to it. Bills at 150 ℔ cent being not near the value in Proclamation money, and to this New Draft I objected that the Lower House in their last Amendments to the first Draft engaged to allow the table of Fees as they formerly stood but instead of that they now make a new regulation of them that reduces several of the Fees from what by law they had been establish'd at as may be seen by comparing this with the Tables of Fees in the Acts of Assembly, & I further declared that the statem' in this last draft of the Bill of Tobacco and rice for the payment of His Majesty's Quit Rents, and the suspending the payment of the Quit Rent so long was what I could not presume to allow off as will be seen more at large in the Journal. Had they valued the tobacco & rice at an equivalent & I had been per-mitted by the Instructions I should not have been induced to allow the payment of Quit Rents in those Comoditys because we have yet no Acts to regulate the makeing of them good and merchantable and till then any Trash might have been put upon the Receiver without remedy

The King's Most excellent Majesty as a Mark of His Royal Bounty and Fatherly indulgence to the Inhabitants of this Province having been graciously pleas'd to signify his pleasure to remit all arrears of Quit

Rents due from such Persons holding lands in this Province as had not paid the same on or before His Majesty's purchasing the sovereignty of this Province which was the 25ᵗʰ day of July 1729, and His Majesty having allso signified His pleasure that in the same Act to be pass'd for remitting the said Arrears all Persons should be obliged to register their Grants whereby they claim lands in the Office of His Auditor General or Deputy, and that the Quit Rents reserved upon such Grants respectively shall hereafter be paid in Proclamation Money and Fees payable to all Officers in this Government likewise to be paid in Proclamation Money.

Be it Enacted by His Excellency the Governor Council and General Assembly of North Carolina

That all and every His Majesty's subjects of this His Province of North Carolina shall be and are hereby acquitted, released and discharged against the King's Majesty His Heirs and Successors and every of them of and from all rents and arrears of rents which were due & owing to His Majesty the 25ᵗʰ day of July in the year of Our Lord 1729

And for the better ascertaining the Quit Rents due and payable hereafter to His Majesty His Heirs & Successors Be it Enacted by the authority aforesaid that all and every person and persons whatsoever hereafter taking up Lands in this Province shall within   after his receiving any Grant for Lands out of the Secretary's Office tender the same Grant to the Auditor of this Province or his Deputy that it may be registered in the Auditor's Office under the penalty of   and that the said Auditor be oblig'd to keep a Deputy in every Precinct in this Province

And Be it further enacted by the Authority aforesaid that for the future the Quit Rents that shall become due to His Majesty his heirs and successors by virtue of any Grant from the late Lords Proprietors, or by virtue of any Grant to be issued in this Province by His Majesty's Governor in Chief or Lieutenant Govʳ the same shall be paid in Proclamation Money as mentioned in an act of Parliament made in the sixth year of the Reign of Queen Anne Entituled an Act for ascertaining the rates of foreign Coins in Her Majesty's Plantations in America, or in such equivalent as is hereafter in this Act mentioned

And be it Enacted by the Authority aforesaid that none of the Officers or other persons that now do or hereafter shall belong to or officiate in any of the Offices or Imployments in this Act mentioned and expressed either by themselves, Deputys, Clerks or servants shall after Publication hereof neglect, refuse or delay to give due dispatch to the business of their respective Office for want of immediate payment when required by any

Freeholder or receive or take directly or indirectly any other Fee or larger summ than in this Act directed for dispatch of business in their respective Offices or any other pretence whatsoever under penalty of forfeiting and paying the summ of fifety Pounds Proclamation money or Commoditys or Bills of this Province to the value thereof according to the rates or allowance in this Act ascertain'd, the one Moyety thereof to be paid to the Publick Treasurer for the time being and for the use of this Province and the other moiety to him or them that shall inform or sue for the same in any Court of Common Pleas in this Province and the Party grieved left to his Action at Common Law to recover his Damage on such Officer or Officers for such his Offence.   And the said Officer shall further losse his or their Office or Offices, Imployment or Imployments.

And Be it further Enacted by the authority aforesaid that every publick Officer in this Government that shall have, take or demand any Fees in this Government from any Person or Persons whatsoever such Officer so taking or demanding shall be oblig'd immediately (if ask'd) or thereto required) to make out a ticket of the several Articles of such his Fees so taken, received or demanded and subscribe his name thereto and deliver the same to any person or persons from whom such Fees shall be taken, received or demanded under the penalty of   Pounds one half to the Church Wardens & Vestry for the use of the Parish where such Officer shall reside, the other half to him that shall sue for the same, to be recovered by Action of Debt, Bill, Plaint or Information in any Court of Record in this Government wherein no essoign, Protection or Wager of Law shall be allowed or admitted of

Provided that if the Person injured doth not complain or prosecute within one month after such offence shall be committed any other Person may complain or prosecute the Offendor—Provided it be done within eighteen months.

And be it enacted by the authority aforesaid that the respective Officers belonging to the Offices hereafter mentioned do forthwith after Publication hereof cause their Fees with the prises thereof according as they are in this Act sett down to be fairly ingrossed and set up in a Publick Place where their Offices are kept & the business belonging to the said Office is done and not to be from thence at any time under the penalty of forfeiting and paying the summ of ten pounds Proclamation Money or Commoditys or Current Bills of this Province to the value thereof according to the Rates or Allowances in this Act ascertained the one Moiety to be paid to the Treasurer for the time being for the use of the Province and the other moiety to him or them that shall informe or sue for the same in any Court of Common Pleas in this Government.

Provided Information be made within six months after such Offence shall be committed, and also the Clerks of the several Courts of this Government are hereby directed and required to keep a list of all Fees contained in this Act respecting their several Courts set up in some Publick Place in their respective Court Houses, and there constantly kept during the sitting of the Courts, under the like penalty.

And Be it Enacted by the authority aforesaid that every Officer hereafter mentioned who shall make out an exact account or list of his Fees and shall attest the same upon Oath before some Magistrate to be justly due and agreable to the following table and shall deliver the same to the Provost Marshall or His Deputy where such Fees shall become due on or before the 14th day of December yearly, that then and in such case the Provost Marshall or his Deputy shall and they are hereby obliged to collect, receive and pay the same at the rate of Tenn ⅌ cent And Be it Enacted by the authority aforesaid that if any person or persons shall refuse to pay the said Marshall or his Deputy all such Fees as are or shall become due to the several and respective Officers so attested & delivered as aforesaid, that then and in such case it shall and may be lawfull for the said Marshall or his Deputy at any time betwixt the 15th day of December and the last day of March yearly to levy the same by way of Distress and sale of the Goods of every Person so refusing

GOVERNORS FEES.

	£	s.	d
For a Marriage Licence		10	
For every Testimonial—Coll Seal		10.	
For ordinary keepers licence	1		
For the Master's report of every forreign Vessell		15	6
For signing Probats of Wills		10	
For signing letter of Administration		10	
For signing a Register of an open Vessell		5	
For Do deckt Vessell		10	
For Letters Patents of Denization		10	
For signing Writ of Escheat		10	
For a Pass People going out of the Country		5.	
For Every elaps'd and Escheat Patent		10.	
For Injunction in Chancery		5.	
For Difinitive Decree thereof		5	

COLLECTORS FEES

For entring and clearing forreign Vessells all Fees included except such as are hereafter mentioned	12.	6

	£.	s.	d
For entring & clearing open Vessells of the Country		2	6
For entring and clearing dockt Vessells of the Country.		5	
For granting and recording a Register		7	6
For Certificate on exchange of a Master	"	2.	6.
For Certific t of enumerated goods.	"	2	6
For Certificate for the Bounty & Oath	"	4	
For recording a Certificate for cancelling enumerated Bonds	"	2.	6.
For Permit from one District to another Open Vessells and			
Periag"	"	2.	
Deckt Vessells	"	4	

NAVAL OFFICERS FEES

	£.	s.	d
For entring & clearing forreign Vessells	"	7.	6.
For every Vessell belonging to the Country if open	"	2.	6
if deckt	"	5	
For Bond not to carry People out without Licence	"	2.	6.
For Certificate for the Bounty	"	2	6
For every other Certificate	"	1.	3
For filing the Certificate to discharge the enumerated & can-			
celling the same	"	2	6
For enumerated Bond	"	2	6

COMPTROLER'S FEES.

	£.	s.	d
	"	3.	

CHIEF JUSTICES FEES

	£.	s.	d
For a Writ	"	3	
For Filing a Declaration, Plea or Warrant of Attorney	"	2	6
For Copy of a Plea attested	"	1	
For a subpena	"	1	
For a Retraxit	"	1	3
For a Scire Facias	"	2	6
For entring Judgment in respite	"	1	
For entring every rule of Court	"	"	9
For the Venire for every action that goes to the jury	"	1	6
For swearing every evidence	"	"	6
For writeing every deposition in any Criminal Cause to be			
paid by the party convict	"	1	
For administring the oath & signing & endorsing the Certifi-			
cate to the deposition	"	"	6
For reading a Bond or other Paper	"	1	
For a writ of Enquiry	"	2	6
For entring an Action in the Judges book that goes to the Jury	"	3.	

21

	£	s.	d.
For Execution		" 2	6
For every special Court and attendance thereon	1		
For searching every Record of the Court		" 1	
For entring satisfaction		" 1.	
For Copy of a Record attested		" 1	
For the allowance of a writ of Error		" 5.	
For Bail taken before the Judge		" 5	
For confessing Judgment		" 1	3.
For admission of any Person to practice as an Attorney in Court	1.		
For filing the writ return'd by the Marshall		" 1	
For filing a Bail Bond or other writeing		" 1	
For a Bond from him who sueth by Letter of Attorney to pay Cost and Damages if Cast		" 2	6.
For a Replevin Bond		" 3	6
For giving Judgment on a special pleading if the Action be above 50£		" 10.	
For giving Judgment under		" 5	
For receiving & entring an Injunction		" 7	10
For the Judges book for every cause entred to be try'd that Court if above tenn pounds		" 5	
If under tenn pounds		" 2	6
For return of a certiorary		" 4	9
For every acknowledgm' or proof of a Deed, Lease or other Conveyance and for endorsing the acknowledgm' & proof thereof		" 3	4
For signing a Testimonial of a woman's examination and renouncing her right of Dower		" 10	
For acknowledging and proving a letter of Attorney & for all Fees incident thereto		" 3	4
For docketing every Appeal from the Precinct Court		" 1	
For a Dedimus to examine witnesses		" 2	6
For every recognizance taken in open Court for the Chief Justice & Clerk of the General Court		" 2	
For taxing Bill of Cost		" 2	4

SECRETARY'S FEES

	£	s.	d.
For making out and recording a Patent for 640 acres and under		" 9	2
For making out & recording a Patent above 640 ac		" 15	

	£	s.	d
For making out a warrant to the Surveyor General for run-ing out of Land		" 5.	
For recording the Surveyors return		" 1	
For recording the assignment of a warrant		" 1	
For a Copy of a single Patent		" 2	6.
For a Copy of a Dubble Patent		" 3.	
For Probate of a Will recording the same		" 5	
For Commission of Administration		" 5	
For return of every Invetory & recording		" 2	6
For every search		" 1	
For Commission of the Peace and Dedimus to be paid by the Publick		" 5	
For a Writ for election of Burgesses		" 2.	
For filing and recording every Inquisition of Escheat to be paid out of the fine		" 1.	
For recording every Coroners inquest to be paid out of the deceas'd Estate or out of the Publick Treasury		" 2.	
For a Copy of a Will if required		" 2	6.
For writeing a Testimonial		" 2	6
For a Copy of a Law		" 1	3.
For a Supersedeas to be paid by the Person granting		" 2	
For drawing a Bill of Indictment to be paid to the Clerk of the Crown		" 2	6.
For Copy of an Information to be paid to the Clerk of the Crown		" 2	6
For filing an Injunction		" 1.	
For Arreignment of Criminals to be paid to the Clerk of the Arreignment		" 1.	
For Letters of Demigation		" 10	
For a Copy of a Bill of Indictment to be paid to the Clerk of the Crown		" 2	6

SURVEYOR GENERALS FEES

For surveying one thousand acres & under	1	13	4
For every hundred above one thousand		" 2	

PROVOST MARSHALLS FEES

For an arrest and return thereof		" 2	4
For serving subpena or summons and return thereof		" 2	

For serving an Attachment, the same as for an Arrest and if further trouble to be taxed by the Court.

	£.	s	d.
For serving execution for 5£	"	5	
For every pound above 5	"	"	6
For summoning every Appraiser and Auditor or evidence to any Deed, Will or other matter	"	"	10.
For summoning and impanelling a Jury in every Cause	"	1	
For serving a Declaration	"	"	8
For putting into the stocks	"	1.	
For Pillorying any person	"	1	
For executing a condemn'd person	2	10	
For Whiping	"	1	
For Committment of a Criminal	"	1	
For discharge of the same	"	5	
For a Bail Bond	"	2	
For summoning a Jury of Escheat, Survey, Writ of Dower Partition, Writ of Enquiry for Damages in the Country or Jury for view	"	10	
For every day attendance on such Jury	"	3.	
For return of such Jury's verdict if taken abroad	"	2	
For every Proclamation for Outlawry	"	2	6
For executing every writ of Possession and Habeus Corpus on Prohibition	"	2	6
For all Public services viz.t for summoning His Majesty's Council, Publication of Writs for Burgesses, Impanelling Grand Jurys, Publishing all Proclamations and causing them to be publish'd in every Precinct for serving all publick orders of Court and other publick services to be paid annually by the Publick Treasury	on a claim to be allow'd		
For serving every Subpeana to answer in Chancery	"	2.	
For serving a Copy of a Bill in Chancery	"	2.	
For maintaining Debtors ⅌ day	"	1	
For maintaining every Criminal or Runaway Negroes and servants.	"	"	6.

CLERK OF THE CHANCERY'S FEES.

	£.	s	d.
For drawing a Bill in Chancery if drawn by the Clerk	"	5	
For filing the same	"	1	
For a Copy of the same	"	2	6
For a Subpena for the Deffendant	"	2	
For drawing an Answer if drawn by the Clerk	"	5	
For filing the same	"	1	

	£.	s.	d
For a Copy of the same	"	2	6
For every subpena for evidence	"	1	
For Injunction or supersedeas in Chancery	"	2	6.
For Copy of the Proceedings	"	2	6
For entring up the Decree	"	3	
For Calling and Dismission	"	1.	
For drawing an affidavit	"	1.	
For entring & recording interogatories	"	1.	6
For a Copy of the same	"	1.	6
For drawing, filing & recording Replication	"	1	
For Rejoinder Surrejoynder & Record	"	1.	

CLERKS FEES IN THE GENERAL AND PRECINCT COURTS.

	£.	s.	d
For Every Action	"	1.	
For Every Writ and Returne	"	2.	
For drawing every Declaration filing and Copy	"	3	
For Demurer or Plea & filing the same	"	1.	
For every Didamus Deposition & filing	"	1	
For subpaena for evidence and filing the same	"	1	
For Venire Facias and Recording	"	"	4
For recording the Pannel of the Jury and entring the Jury's Verdict	"	1	
For filing every Bill and Account	"	"	6.
For administring an Oath	"	"	4
For calling every action	"	"	6
For every original Order of Court	"	1	
For every Copy	"	1	
For every Petition if drawn by the Clerk	"	1	
For entring up every Judgment.	"	1.	
For searching the Records.	"	1	
For every Summons.	"	1.	
For every Attachment and Return	"	2	
For every Bond and recording	"	2.	
For proving & recording every power of Attorney	"	4	
For Copy if required	"	1	
For proving and acknowledging every Deed including the Chief Justices Fees	"	2	6.
For Copy of an Act of Assembly	"	1.	
For Scire Facias and Returne	"	2	6
For every execution and Returne	"	3	

	£	s	d.
For entring satisfaction on the record and every Retraxit	"	1	
For every Discontinuance and Dismission of suit.	"	1	
For every Continuance	"	"	6.
For a Referrence or Imparlancy	"	"	6
For every Certificate for proving of Right	"	"	4
For Writ of Possession, Writ of Enquiry or Writ of seizin for Dower	"	3	
For proving a Will and Certificate thereof to the Secretary's Office	"	2	6
For Order of Administration & Certificate thereof to the Secretary's Office	"	2	6
For Administration Bonds.	"	2.	
For entring every appeal and returning the Proceedings to the General Court	"	5	
For filing every warrant of Attorney	"	"	6
For ordinary Keepers rates	"	1	
For recording every Mark or Brand	"	1	

ESCHEATOR'S FEES

	£	s	d.
For Inquisition and Returne	2.	"	"

ATTORNEY GENERAL'S FEES.

	£	s	d.
For every Indictment, Information Bill found in the General Court.	2. 10		"
For the same in the Precinct Court.	"	5.	

ATTORNEY'S FEES

	£	s	d.
For every Cause in the General Court	"	10.	
For The Precinct Court	"	5.	

PUBLICK REGISTER'S FEES

	£	s	d.
For registring Birth, Burial or Marriage	"	1	
For registring Conveyance	"	2	6.
For Copy thereof	"	2	6

CONSTABLE'S FEES

	£	s	d.
For serving a warrant and Returne	"	2.	
For Every summons	"	1	
For every execution	"	2	
For an Attachment if served by the Constable	"	2	

ADMIRALTY FEES.

In Case of seizure and Condemnation of Vessells for unlawfull trade or as prize 10£ to be divided among the officers
as follows. vizt.

	£.	s.	d
$\frac{4}{15}$ To the Judge	4	3	4
$\frac{4}{15}$ to the Register	2	13	4
$\frac{1}{4}$ to the Advocate	2.	10.	"
$\frac{1}{15}$ to the Marshall	"	13	4

In case of open Vessells seamens Wages not exceeding 20£
to the Judge the first day .... 2 " "
For every other day .... 1 " "

REGISTER'S FEES IN THE LIKE CASE

For drawing the Lybel to be p^d to the Advocate	" 5	
For registring the same	" 5	
For answer & register	" 2	6

For affidavit, Deposition and Oath the same as in the Court
of Chancery.

For a Decree	" 2	6.
For a Copy	" 2	6.
For Dismissing	" 1.	
For Continuance	" 1	
For Citation	" 2.	
For summons for each evidence	" 4	

MARSHALL'S FEES IN THE LIKE CASE

Serving a Citation, seizing and return	" 5
Serving a Decree & return under 5 pounds.	" 10.
For every pound above 5	" 1

And whereas there is not in this Province Gold and Silver Coin sufficient to answer one twentyeth part of the Quit Rents and Fees as mentioned in this Act Wherefore that a just equivalent may be settled Be it
Enacted by the authority aforesaid that the Quit rents that shall hereafter become due shall be payable either in Proclamation money as aforesaid or in tobacco at 11 shillings ℔ hundred weight or rice at 12ˢ 6ᵈ ℔
hundred weight at the choice of the party owing the same and all Fees
which shall hereafter become due and payable by virtue of this Act, the
same shall be payable either in Proclamation Money or in such Commoditys according to the Rates mentioned in this Act vizt

	£	s	d
Tobacco ℔ hundred	"	11.	
Indian Corn ℔ bushell	"	2	
Wheat ℔ bushell	"	4	
Tallow Try'd ℔ pound	"	"	6.
Leather tann'd & uncur'd ℔ pound	"	"	8
Beaver & Otter skins ℔ pound	"	2	6
Buck and Doe skins ℔ pound	"	2	6.
Feathers ℔ pound	"	1.	4
Tarr ℔ barrell full gage	"	7	6
Pitch ℔ barrell	"	12	6
Whale Oyl ℔ barrell	2	5	"
Pork ℔ barrell	2	5	"
Beef ℔ barrell	1.	10.	"
Rice ℔ hundred weight	"	12	6.
Turpentine ℔ barrell	"	12	6

And for want thereof in Paper currency at 150 ℔ cent as the partys obliged to pay the same shall think fitt   Provided that no Officer hereafter shall oblige payment of the said Commoditys to be made but at convenient landings within the Precinct where they reside, and at such times as are by the laws appointed

And that such persons who have not or cannot procure silver or gold to pay the quit rents due to His Majesty may have convenient time to make tobacco for such payments the season for making the same for this present year being too far gone

Be it Enacted by the authority aforesaid that no Quit Rents shall be demanded of any Person untill after the 10th day of October which shall be in the year of our Lord 1732

This is a true copy

WILLIAMS Clk. G Assembly

[B. P. R. O NORTH CAROLINA B T VOL. 8. P 39]

These Papers that appear as an appendix to the Journals or proceedings of the Council were occasioned to be placed in this manner because they were never read in Council, therefore could not be regularly entred being contrary to an Instruction   Mr Ashe did not come to the Council that day tho' duly summoned, nor Mr Smith the Chief Justice, nor Mr Porter Judge of Admiralty, Mr Ashe entred the Council room in the evening when I was considering the Chancery Bills in the Office with these two Papers that I have answered and gave them to me, I read them over and told him that the next morning I hoped the Members of Council would meet and very civily desired his Company he absolutely refused to come and desired his Papers might be entered in the Council Journal I told him that could not be done without the Council met, I then told him he should have an answer to his Papers in an hour, he very rudely told me he would go out of town directly since which time I have never seen nor heard anything from Mr Ashe neither did he take any other leave of me than is above related

To His Excellency the Governor &c.

MAY IT PLEASE YOUR EXCELLENCY

Having read your Excellency's reply relating to the affairs of the Assistants, occasioned by a Message from the Assembly we beg leave to observe to you that you not only not opposed but concurr'd in the answer to the Message of the Assembly. However if your Excellency (having sufficient reasons) has altered your opinion we are so far from reflecting on you therefore that we readyly jovn with you in thinking it better to retract than obstinately to persist in error and we should with alacrity we assure you (were we once convinced) follow your example.

As to your Excellency's remark on our running into niceties and distinctions we say we think we made none but what were necessary As to the Question we asked relating to the Authority given to the Chief Justice by the King's warrant we still say that if the Chief Justice power is not a sufficient Power without that of Assistants to hold a Court, we cannot see how that Power can (as in His Majestie's said Warrant) be called a full Power and Authority to hold such Court as to what your Excellency is pleased to say that we wisely observe; we believe you mistake us what we observed was that all the inference which could be made from His Majestie's 8th Instruction was, that Assistants were or might be, not saying what Assistants that perhaps they might not be intended Assistants to the Chief Justice, but supposing they were, we argued that no inference could be made from thence of their power so as to define it neither can we think our doubt, whether by Assistants, there is meant Assistants to the Chief Justice is so extraordinary as you represent it. And indeed we do not perfectly understand your Excellency when you say the Instructions couple Judges, Assistants Justices

22

&c. the word Assistants stand severed from the rest by commas as do the titles of the other Officers one from the other and by it are intended distinct Officers for had it been only as an epithet or adjective to be affixed either to Judge or Justices then in the Instruction would have been used the word Assistant, not Assistants, and it would not by the Comma have been severed from its proper substantive We cannot see how the 45 Instruction affects your Excellency in the present case for allowing (which we do not) that the investing the Chief Justice with this Power was erecting a new Court or dissolving one already established yet the investing him with such Power is not an Act of your Excellency's but of His Majesty, for it is from the King's Warrant he derives it and by virtue thereof claims it

That there have been Assistants in the General Court we deny not but we cannot grant that Assistants have a Judicial Power equal to associate Judges, the very word seems to imply the contrary. We cannot here help thinking that your Excellency mistakes our words when telling us that we seem to recede from what we had said, we allow that there should be assistants to informe and advise the Chief Justice as Master in Chancery, whereas we said no such thing speaking indeed of the sence in which the word Assistant was generally taken when apply'd to an Officer of a Court we said it was to inform and advise, without having any judicial Power of which we gave an Instance Vizt. of the Masters of Chancery who were wont to be styled Assistants to the Chancelor, but we never said or meant that Assistants were to advise the Chief Justice as Masters in Chancery

We might ask your Excellency several Questions which according to your Secret of the Assistants Power would be attended (as we think) with difficulties as allowing an Assistant a Judicial Power how great it was? how to be distinguished from that of the Chief Justice so as not to equall it? if two Assistants were of the same opinion whither their united judgments would not be superior to, and over rule that of the Chief Justice? but as we have given our thoughts we are unwilling to proceed any further or raise new matter We shall only add as seeming to support our opinion the practice formerly in South Carolina where (we are well informed) the Chief Justice was wont to have the sole Judicial power in the supream Court how it is now we cannot say but if this is not thought a sufficient authority we beg leave to referr your Excellency to the thirty fourth & fifth of Henry VIII Cap xxvi by which statute it was provided that one Person should not only be Judge of one Court but of several by Turns and those too in the Common Law so that we cannot conceive that such Establishment is contrary to the nature of such Court nor to the Constitution of the Laws of England, but since your Excellency by your Reply seems fully resolved we shall desist without adding anything further on this subject

JN BAP^{ts} ASHE
CORN° HARNETT

To His Excellency the Governor &c

MAY IT PLEASE YOUR EXCELLENCY

I declare that for my part I could have wished (had not your Excellency insisted on the contrary) to have avoided this method of debating matter of Council in writing because it generally tends rather to prolong debates than to shorten or bring them to a final Issue

I believe if your Excellency will be pleased to recollect you may remember you not only gave your opinion in the affair relating to the evidence of the late Council against Sir Richard Everard but also your Resolution as to my evasive answers your Excellency only accuses me only in general Terms without pointing out any particulars so that I shall decline saying anything farther thereon, only than that if I used too many words it was to shew the reasons induceing me, or to state the matter in a clear light I shall pass over the reflection your Excellency is pleased to make of my want of Candour and Plainness, Indeed I should now (without at all rejoyning) have acquiesced had not your Excellency in this your reply as to the Bill of Rents &c. given the affair such a turn, as might perhaps tend to my disadvantage As your Excellency has recommended to me plainness I hope you will not be displeased with me if I now make use of it, when I say the reason or cause of my Papers coming out of time was that your Excellency after having given the Council a day to consider of & answer your Quæry relating to the Bill concerning Rents and Fees on that very day in the morning without informing the Council of your design to prorogue the Assembly (unless at the instant you sent for them) you sent for the Lower House to Prorogue them on which desiring only a few minutes time to transcribe my answer from the rough minutes, I offered to put it in, but that you should not stay the Prorogation. what indeed made me so solicitous to put in that answer, was the great desire I had of promoting His Majesty's service and the Country's interest, and the reason why I preferr'd it afterwards was (as your Quæry was entered on the Journal of the Council) to shew that I had not been backward or negligent in giving my answer (which I looked on as my Duty) in due time, or at least at the given time These my reasons for acting in this affair as I have done being (I think) very just, I am surprized that you are pleased to accuse me of being very particular, and of not the fairest dealing herein: As my proposalls (tho' made some of them by word of mouth before the last reading of the Bill) will be now of no use, the matter being over, I shall forbear (tho' I could) to expatiate in their vindication Let them who read them judge of their reasonableness.

If in this or any other of my Papers any indecent or misbecoming expression may have escaped my pen, I must beg you'l not impute it to design for I assure you I shall always strive to behave myself to your Excellency with great respect & good manners

JOHN BAP^{ta} ASHE.

———

To Mr Ashe & Mr Harnett Members of Council

GENTLEMEN,

I have your Paper of yesterday, I never intended this tedious debate when I put three short Quærys fairly stated in writing that I might obtain as plain an answer to them, but you ran into a long dispute upon it, which I complained of to you and now to mend the matter you have run it into further niceties that only perplex it the more, as to the Assistant Judges you say the 8th Instruction does inferr there should be Assistants, but then you seem at a strange loss what they should be, and go on to observe what perhaps it might not intend, and you add that their Power is not defined and from thence you are making out your argument that they have no Power, for that is what you are contending for and at last you are drove to the refuge of a comma in the writing and an adjective that might have been, and raise such distinctions upon it as the Common sence of the matter seems quite lost, for my part I think it sufficient to take the plain sence of things If the Instructions do do not define the Power of Assistants it no ways restrains them, and then it must be taken according to their usual Power and as the Chief Justice is usually called (by way of Eminence) the Judge so the other Justices of the General Court are usually called Assistants or Assistant Judges, and there are no other persons in the Government but they who are so called so that I cannot imagine why all this cloud of Difficulties is raised to find out who, or what is meant by Assistants, or to what purpose it is unless purely to perplex the matter to argue what the word might or could mean, and their Power might be easily known from the constant usage here, if the enquiry was fairly made instead of running divisions and multiplying arguments upon it. And as the General Court here hath constantly consisted of the Chief

Justice and Assistants, I am persuaded the allowing the Chief Justice to be sole Judge of the Court now would be establishing a new sort of a General Court and destroying the old form and so is directly against my 45th Instruction and it's but a weak shifting it off to say it would not be my breaking the Instruction since it's owing to the King's own Warrant that grants the Chief Justice full Power &c but as that mentions nothing of the Assistants, and my instructions from the King do not define their Power as you say I think my allowing that they have no judicial Power as you hold would be to make it a new sort of a Court, and plainly against the 45th Instruction as well as against the Nature of a settled supream Court of Common Pleas. And I am really at a loss to what purpose you referr me to the 34 or 35th of Henry the 8th that appoints an Itinerant Judge for the Sessions in several Counties in Wales unless you could produce some Act for a single Judge of the General Court here, or usage, or custom for it. Indeed you give me one example from South Carolina but you would have done well to have remembred that the complaint against that Judge unregarded by the Proprietors was one of the principal reasons the People gave to justify their taking up armes and throwing off the Lords Government. As to the King's Warrant which not withstanding what has been said you still insist on, that grants the Chief Justice full power of holding the Courts and you say if the Chief Justice's power is not sufficient without the Assistants how can it be called a full Power?

I think when you were in this way of disputing you might have gone a step further and said since the Chief Justice has full Power to hear and determine all causes and no mention is made of Juries, therefore he may hear and determine them without Juries for to use your own argument, if his Power to hear and determine causes is not sufficient without a Jury, how can it be called a full Power to hear and determine causes?

And here I shall leave it having I think said sufficient to convince you that your Paper is very triffling and only a Quibble upon words

GEO BURRINGTON

N. Carolina
   The 22[d] May 1731

Mr ASHE,

I have your single Paper of the 21st of May in which you say in the affair of Sir Richard Everard I not only gave my opinion but my resolution I remember I told you that upon His Majesty's Instruction requiring me to examine into the Complaint against him, I should act in it as my own Conscience and Judgment directed, but at the same time desired the opinion of the Council which had it been candidly given would have had great weight with me

As to what you say about you giving me your paper concerning the Bill for Fees and Quit Rents after the Assembly was prorogued, I am at a loss to know what you mean by a given time, and it's being ready against the day appointed for receiving it, but that on that very day in the morning I proroged the Assembly insinuating that I prorogued the Assembly on a sudden and by surprise which is a very false suggestion because Mʳ Ashe knows very well the contrary, nor do I remember I fixt any day or time for the Council to give me their advice about the Quit Rents when I demanded in writing their opinion upon it, but I expected at least on the Conference with the Lower House a day or two after upon that Subject that the Council would have assisted me with their advice being obliged by their oath so to do, I several times put it to the Board at the conference, if they had anything to offer upon it, but the whole debate was left to me Some in the Council indeed declared they would not concurr with the Bill in allowing the Fees should be paid in Bill money at 150 ⅌ cent which the Lower House after the Conference was over came to a final resolution to advance no further upon, and when I found that was their ulltimate and observing the secret Practiseing and Designs set on foot by yourself and others, I found it necessary to put an end to the Session, which Mʳ Ashe knew was expected on the Saturday before, but I continued them till noonday, and in all that time Mʳ Ashe who was several times with me in private and Publick especially the morning before the Prorogation, might if he had been so pleased, have acquainted me with this Paper he had or was about, but that was not the only Instance of shyness and reservedness Mʳ Ashe used on this and other Occasions However since you say your Proposals in the Paper were for His Majestie's service and the good of the Country, which if really so can never be out of time with me

I shall only desire Mʳ Ashe to consider whither it be for His Majesties Service that the Quit Rents should be received in Rice and Tobacco at 11 shillings ⅌ hundred that we all know is farr above their real worth in Proclamation money which His Majesty has graciously condescended they should be received in the place of sterling which is due to him, thereby giving away to the People one fourth of His Rents, and whither it be for the Good of the Country to run into Parties, beget misunderstandings and secretly to disaffect People to the Government and so keep things in suspense and confusion instead of concurring openly and heartily with me, who have always been your sincere friend, in settling things in the best manner for the Country and most agreable to His Majestie's Instructions, which I shall still go on to pursue tho' I have not the Pleasure of that Assistance I thought I had reason to expect from you, especially, tho' I find myself deceived For the designs against me are not unseen & I perceive I am to have all the difficulties that can be thrown in my way, but as I have acted steadily for His Majestie's service and the Good of the Country which are my constant Aims, I am sure those who with such Artifices oppose me whatever popular or specious pretences they may make will in the end be found far from being good Subjects to the King, or True Friends to this their Country which I can truly say no one man in it has done more for or wishes it better than

GEO BURRINGTON

N Carolina.

The 22ᵈ of May 1731

The within is true Copies from the Originalls lodged in the Secretary's Office & examined by

ROBT FORSTER Deputy Secretary

[B R R. O NORTH CAROLINA B T VOL. 8 P 189]

These following are the Acts that were past in November 1729 after the King had purchased the Government of the Lords Proprietors, about the Validity of which Laws there has been such debates viz' Whither they had then any Power of making Laws in the Name of the Palatine & Lords Proprietors of Carolina where there was none such they having before surrendered   And whither such Acts as affected the Publick Rights and Dues of the Proprietors could be of any force without being approved at home, the Government here having been restrained in such Cases by the Powers granted them for making Laws by the Late Lords Proprietors but this hath been fully set forth in the Journalls & my Report.

An Act for the making and emitting the Summ of forty thousand pounds Publick Bills of Credit of North Carolina

An Act for the more quiet settling the Bounds of the Mehorin Indians Lands.

An Act to make Hyde Precinct separate from Beaufort Precinct with power of erecting a Court house and holding Courts

An Act to appoint that part of Albemarle County lyeing on the south side of Albemarle Sound & Mooratuck River as high as the Rain bow banks to be a Precinct by the name of Tyrrell precinct

An Additional Act of explanation to an Act for appointing Tole Books and for preventing People from driving Horses, Cattle or Hoggs to other Persons Lands.

An Act for the more effectual and speedy putting in execution the Act for settling the Title and Bounds of Peoples Lands

An Act to confirm Bath Town Common

An Act to repeal the Act entituled an Act for encouragement of Tanning Leather in this Province.

An Additional Act to the Act for the Tryall of small and mean Causes.

An Act for regulating Vestrys in this Government and for the better inspecting the Vestrymen and Church Wardens Accounts of each and every Parish within this Government

An Act to regulate the Act for appointing indifferent Jurymen, and to repeal that Part thereof that referrs to Precinct Courts.

THE SIX CONFIRMED LAWS.

These Laws following called the Confirmed Laws had been out of use and lost for above 20 years when upon a revival of the whole body of Laws in 1715 an old copy was produced and transcribed into the Law Book the original of them are entirely lost and they are become quite obsolete

An Act concerning Marriages.

An Act transferring of Rights

An Act concerning the defraying the charge of the Governor & Councill

An Act prohibiting Strangers trading with the Indians

An Act for the speedy settlement of Lands

An Act concerning Escheat Lands and Escheators

This is a very old Law and not altered at the revival in 1715 I am told that there are laws of this kind in most of His Maj$^{ty's}$ Colonies But whither two pence ⅌ acre will be thought for the future a Compsation sufficient is submitted The Law otherwise being very fittfor the Purpose

An act for the more effectual preserving the Queen's Peace and establishing a good and lasting foundation of Government in North Carolina.

This was a Law after there had been Comotions in the Country and People in Armes which was called Cary's Rebellion and after the Government was settled this Act was made for securing the same and by the manner of wording of it referring to the then present Government establish'd, hath been held by some to be a Law made for that time only but by being confirmed in 1715, And having been put in practice several times since It should seem to be the better received Opinion that it is sitll in force and in so turbulent a Place is a Law not ill suited for the purpose, and that part of it declaratory of the Laws of England being in force here seems well Provided

An Act to regulate divers abuses in the taking up of Lands and to ascertain the method to be observed from henceforward in taking up & surveying of Lands.

This Law was generally called the Lapse Act, and indeed that part of the Law wch directs how Lands to be lapsed for want of the Lords Proprietors purchase being paid is the only material part of it But is since His Majesty's Purchase entirely out of use The other Part of this Law which directs the manner of takeing up and surveying Lands was the Antient custom & manner of doing it, & was found so good a method that about the year 1713. it was establish'd by this Law

An Act for raising the summ of twenty four thousand Pounds in Publick Bills of Credit for paying the remaining Debts of the Government and for sinking the remaining part of the sum of Twelve thousand Pounds publick Bills of Credit with two years Interest.

Be it enacted &c

And it is hereby enacted by the authority of the same that Collo: Cristopher Gale, Collo Edward Moseley, Tobias Knight and Daniel Richardson Esq^{rs} are hereby appointed and impowered to make out Publick Bills of Credit to the value of twenty four thousand Pounds in manner following That is to say three hundred of twenty pounds, three hundred of fifteen pounds, four hundred and eighty of ten pounds, four hundred and fifty of five pounds, three hundred of three pounds, three thousand of twenty shillings, three thousand three hundred of ten shillings, one hundred and fifty of eight shillings, three thousand of five shillings and seven hundred and twenty of two shillings and sixpence which said publick Publick Bills shall be made without Interest on them or

23

time of payment mentioned therein for which they shall be allowed, and paid out of the Publick Treasure the sum of two hundred pounds which Bills when made shall be signed by Christopher Gale, Edward Mosely, Tobias Knight and Daniel Richardson who are hereby commissionated thereto, and sealed with the Collony seal and then delivered into the hands of Edward Mosely on or before the 25ᵗʰ day of March next in order that the said Edward Moseley may pay unto the Treasurer of each Precinct the balance due to the Persons who have had claims allowed on the same Precinct which he is hereby required and impowered to do

And be it further Enacted by the authority aforesaid that all such publick Bills of Credit as are now outstanding shall not receive or have from the Publick or any other Person or Persons whatsoever any further Interest than two years which will be compleat and ended the 25ᵗʰ of March next within six months after which time all Persons whatsoever are required and commanded to exchange the same with the said Edward Mosely for such Bills as are to be made by virtue of this Act The said Edward Moseley or his Deputy being hereby empowered & required to exchange the same and to allow two years Interest thereon

And be it further Enacted by the authority aforesaid that all such Persons who shall refuse or neglect to bring their Bills to be exchanged before the 25ᵗʰ of August next shall not have nor receive any Interest on the said Bills, and such as shall refuse or neglect to change the same Bills before the 25ᵗʰ of March 1716 the same shall adjudged, held & taken to be of no value

And be it further Enacted by the authority aforesaid that as often as the said Edward Moseley or his Deputy shall have exchanged so many of the said Bills of Credit as shall amount unto the sum of three hundred pounds, the said Christopher Gale, Tobias Knight and Daniel Richardson or any two of them are hereby required to examine the same and having compared the same with the Counter part & taken an account of them and entered them in a fair List to pass a receipt for the same and publickly to burn them, for all which charge and trouble the said Edward Moseley shall be allowed one ⅌ cent for changing the said Bills

And be it further Enacted by the authority aforesaid that the said Bills shall be reckoned and taken to be a good payment and Tender in Law for any of the rated Commodities of the Country or other Money allowing 50 ⅌ cent between the same and sterling, he or they so refusing shall forfeit double the value of such Bills so refused, one half toward defraying the contingent Charges of the Government and the other to him or them who shall sue for the same to be recovered by action of Debt Bill Plaint or Informacōn in any Court of Record in this Government wherein no Essoin Protection Wager of Law or Injunction shall be allowed or received.

And be it further Enacted by the Authority aforesaid that if any Person or Persons shall counterfeit any of the said Bills or knowing any of the said Bills to be false or counterfeit or any other aiding & assisting him as well as the Utterer or Disposer of the Bill or Bills being thereof duly convicted shall be punished as guilty of Felony without the benefit of Clergie

And be it further Enacted by the authority aforesaid that in case any member of either house of Assembly shall hereafter make any mocōn which shall be judged by the House to which he belongs to be derogatory and prejudicial to the publick Credit of the said Bills, such Member of the Upper House shall be represented to the Proprietors as an enemy to their Lordships Interest & Country and unworthy of their Service and be suspended the Councill till their Ld⁰ pleasure be known and fined the sum of twenty pounds for such his mocōn and if a Member of the Lower House he shall be expelled the house and fined the like summ of twenty pounds and be forever after uncapable as serving as a Member of the House the fines to be appropriated for the payment of the Publick Charge.

And be it further Enacted by the authority aforesaid that for the faithfull discharging of the Office of Treasurer the Treasurer of each Precinct shall on or before the first day of February next give bond with good and sufficient security in the sum of two thousand pounds, the said Edward Moseley in the sum of twenty four thousand pounds to the honᵇˡᵉ Charles Eden Esqʳ Governor his Heirs & Successors with the condition for the faithfull performance of their severall Offices under the penalty of one hundred pounds, for every month he or they shall continue to officiate without giving such Bond with Security to be levyed by a Warrant from the Governor on the Goods and Chattels of such Person or Persons neglecting to give such bond & security, to be appropriated for and towards the defraying the Contingent Charges of the Government

And be it further Enacted by the authority aforesaid That the Treasurer of each Precinct shall depute such Person to be Deputy Treasurer in there Precinct as shall be nominated by the Justices of that Court so as that the Number do not exceed Two.

[B. P R. O North Carolina B T Vol. 8, A 15, p 231]

TITLES OF (THE 57) ACTS PASSED AT LITTLE RIVER 171⅘ WITH GOV⸲ BURRINGTON'S REMARKS

1 An Act for the better observing of the Lords Day called Sunday the 30ᵗʰ of January the 29ᵗʰ of May and the 22ᵈ of September And also for the suppressing profaneness Immorality and divers other vitious & enormous sins.

This Law is very well intended for the suppressing Vice and Immorality but it is like most laws of this kind too little regarded

2 An Act for establishing the Church and appointing Select Vestrys.

This Act not only confirms the Church of England here but divides the Country into Parishes according to the Scituation & Conveniency Appoints Church Wardens and a Vestry in each Parish and investeth them with Power, but as they allow them to raise a levy of but 5ᵗʰ ℔ Poll on the Parish since Bills are come into Payment it amounts to so little as will scarce do more (after maintaining the Poor if any) than to pay a Reader for reading the Common Prayer and a Printed Sermon on Sundays to the People but as to Gleebs & Collection of Parsons there is so little of it that there is not a settled Parson in the Country His Majesty's Instruction on this head I laid before the Assembly but nothing was done upon it.

3 An Act for Liberty of Conscience And that the solemn Affirmation of the People called Quakers shall be accepted instead of an Oath in the usual forme

This was an old Law and little altered on the Revisal—And as to the Affirmation of the Quakers they refuse taking it since the Act of Parliament in Great Britain that gives them further liberty they have usually taken the benefit of that Act here and in all the Plantations

4 An Act relating to the Bienniall and other Assemblys and regulating Elections and Members

This was an old Law taken from one of the Lords Proprietors Original Constitutions and hath undergone little alteration

This Act provides that the Burgesses chosen shall meet and sit at a certain day after the choice Whence they have sometimes been of Opinion that they could not be Prorogued or Disolved or Adjourned before they had mett and sate But there being a Clause in the Act that the Lords Proprietors Power of calling Proroguing and Disolving Assemblys shall no ways by this Act be Invaded Limited or Restrained it seems plainly to leave the Power of Progrogueing and Desolving as before

By this Act all Freemen are quallifyed to vote as well as Freeholders which is Contrary to my Instructions from his Majesty on that Head

The People also by this Law assemble and chuse Burgesses on the Day by the Act appointed without any writ for it which occasions a great deal of Mobbing and tumults, and returns so often that upon the whole I think it would be more for His Majesty's Service if this Act was repealed & Assemblys called only by writs as in all other His Maj⁷ⁱˢ Colonys.

5. Coroners Appointed

This is an antient Law and seems taken from one of the Lords Proprietors Constitutions.

6 An Act for the qualification of such Officers

This Act seems well provided to prevent any Persons disaffected to His Majesty from being put into Offices here and is made agreable to the Laws of Great Britain

7. An Act to appoint Constables.

This has been an antient Law and the method found satisfactory & agreable to the Purpose.

8 An Act relating to the Justices of the Court of Common Pleas and to prevent the Commissioners and other inferior Officers of the said Court pleading as Attorneys.

This has been an old Law and prohibits not only the Justices or Commissioners as they are called from Pleading or expounding the Causes, but also all Officers of the Court, to prevent the occasion of mall practise.

9. An Act for ascerting the time and method for the executing and return of Originall Writts and for the better regulating divers priviledges in the Court of Pleas.

This Act in general seems well adapted to shorten the practice of the Law, by preventing the necessity of several mean Processes that may delay justice, but is not so clearly worded as it might have been, and is in some Causes supply'd by Constructions and Practise accordingly and some other additional Acts have been made especially as to original Attachments, which in this Country where there are so many loose transient People is found very necessary This Act seems to require special Bayl in all Cases which the Laws of England in many Cases does not.

10 An Act to direct the method to be observed in the examination and Committment of Criminalls

This Act is intended in favour of the liberty of the Subject in criminall Processes & seems well approved of by the People.

11 An Act concerning Evidences

This is an antient Law and the Country well enough satisfyed with the method—But there seems wanting a sufficient Provision for takeing Depositions of People leaving the Country which often happens suddenly to the Detriment of the Partys.

12 An Act for the relief of such Creditors whose Debtors having land in this Government, depart without leaving personal Estate sufficient to pay the Debt

This Act subjecting the Lands of fugitive Debtors to the payment of their Debts, seems contrary to the Laws and useages of England, but is agreable to the Customs of the Plantations where real Estates are everywere more or less subject to different useages from what they are in England, and in this case one principal reason seems to be that Lands in England being improved to a great yearly value may by the annual income on an extent pay the Debt but Lands here are generally of little yearly rent and the Benifit of them is the accruing Improvements of the Occupyer which on extent in the end he must loose the Benifit off would be too hard

13 An Act concerning escapes of Persons under Execution

This Law was made before Goals was built in this Country but now that Part relateing to the Marshalls House since Goals are built is become obsolete.

14 An Act to direct the disposal of Goods upon execution and for the better regulation of Distresses hereafter to be made for Levys and Quit Rents.

This Law though the partiallity of the Appraisors often occasioned great frauds, they had formerly the same Law in the neighbouring Government of Virginia but finding the corrupt practices upon it had brought the method nearer to the Laws of England, and exposed the Goods seized, to be under certain regulations exposed to sale

15 An Act concerning Attorneys from forraign Parts and for giving priority to Country Debts

This Act obliges all Forreigners suing here to give security for the Cost & if cast and gives the Priority of Debts contracted in the Country to be paid before foreign debts.

16. An Act concerning Appeals and Writts of Error

This Law seems well provided for redressing errors which are often much sooner and better stop'd by appealing than could be by writ of Error at a distance and it would have been iconvenient to have set aside the Remedy by Writ of Error because the Appeal being always made instantly boath Partys being present without further notice, and if that were slip'd there would be no further remedy to the Law hath very well admitted remedy either way

And now there is liberty of appealing by the King's Instructions from the General Court to Me and Council, and in cases of Moment to the King and Council that Point seems thoroughly provided for

17 An Act to prevent the Inhabitants of Bath County bringing Actions in the General Court against one another for less than tenn Pounds.

This is an Act for the Ease of the People living at distance from the General Court and I have no Complaint against it

18. An Act for the Tryall of small & mean Causes

This is a Law People are generally fond of being an expedicious way of obtaining justice, and they have by subsequent Laws increased the Power of the Justices to determine for above double the sum here stated.

19 An Act for the better regulating the Militia of this Government.

This Act was made during the Warr & seems well enough to Provide for the Ends intended

20. A Form of a Patent.

This Act was made to confirme the tenure of Lands here according to the Grand Deed on the same footing as in Virginia the Rent at 2^s $\clubsuit$ hundred acres and ascertains what shall be deem'd seating and planting according to the Condition of the Grant and tho' in strictness imediately on faylure of the condition should revert, yet by this Act it is saved seven years after if the land be seated before it's granted to another by an elaps'd Patent as they are called which by the Formallitys in elapsing hitherto used renders it often fruitless and greatly frustrates the Condition of the Patent.

21 An Act concerning old Titles of Lands and for the Limitation of Actions and for avoiding Suite in Law

By this Act Titles are confirmed by Possession 7 years and the time for bringing Actions is limited to a shorter time than by the Statutes of Limitation in England they were reduced to

22 Feme Coverts how to pass Lands

23. An Act for Preventing Disputes concerning Lands already Surveved

The allowance of Tenn in the hundred on a Resurvey does not seem extravagant and as I am told is the same in Virginia but that the Patentee should have the surplusage Land prevents all discoverys of such frauds But could the Petitioner in such Case have the surplusage it would discover many Concealments that way

24 An Act for settling and maintaining Pillotts at Roanoke and Oacock Inletts

This Act was well design'd for the Encouragement of Trade but of late years has been wholly neglected and tho' all Vessells pay such a sum for powder money which ought to have been for Pilotage, the Publick of late have taken no Care about it I design to settle Pilots at OcaCock which is one of the best Inletts in the Country into a safe harbour, but shoally afterwards, but large ships may come in there and unlade and lade if such a Regulation could be made

25 An Act for Entering of Vessells and to prevent the Exportation of Debtors

This Act is to prevent the exporting Debtors till they give security for Payment of their Debts

26 An Act for raising a Publick Magazine of Ammunition upon the Tonnage of all Vessells trading to this Government

This Act is for raising an Impost Duty on Tonage of Vessells which is commonly called the Powder money and tho' the Title of the Act is for raising a Magazine there is nothing further mentioned about it in the Act nor is the money appropriated by the Act, it is provided to be paid in Ammunition, But as liberty is given in the Act to pay it in Bills little else but Bills has been paid which the Receivers have constantly accounted for to the Assembly Formerly some part of it was appropriated to Buoying out the Channels but that has been lately wholly neglected and the money has generally been appropriated to pay the Assembly Men and other Publick Charges.

27 An Act concerning Roads and Ferrys

This Act is well adapted to the Purpose and suitable to the circumstances of the Place and People but wants to be more effectually put in execution

28 An Act to encourage the building of Mills

This was made to encourage People to build Mills and settle the toll to be taken

29 An Act to appoint Publick Registers and to direct the method to be observed in conveying Lands, Goods and Chattels and for preventing fraudulent Deeds and Mortgages

By this Act the People by votes chuse three Persons out of which the Governor nominates one for Register in each Precinct, who is to register all Deeds and Conveyances of Land &c. and feofment of Lands so recorded having first been proved before the Chief Justice or Precinct Court are Good in Law to pass the Possession and Estate without Livery and Seizen Provided such Deed be recorded in a Year after date else to be void This Register is to record all Births, Burialls and Mariages.

30. An Act concerning Weights and Measures

By this Act every Parish is to Provide sealed Weights and Measures to be kept by the Church Wardens as a Standard.

31 Staple Comodities Rated

This Act seems to have been well intended at first for the Ease of the People to make a medium of Trade and means of Payment in the Produce of the Country, Silver being so scarce as not to be had; But there was two defects in it—One was that whatever Justness or equality was at first in settling the Price or Rates a few years necessary in the course of Trade varying the Price of Goods it must become unequal, as for instance Dear skins are to this day worth in Silver the Price rated while Pitch and Tarr have been scarce worth a quarter part what they are rated at in Silver, to prevent this the rates should have been regulated every Assembly at least. Another inconveniency in it is the rateing so many goods some of them being scarcely to be had, others too trifling to be called staple Comoditys as the Title of the Act is and had much better been confined to some few of the Commoditys, such as Tobacco, Rice, Pitch and Tarr, Beef, Pork, Wheat and Corn, those might justly be called Staple and are the chief Produce of the Country Always vendable and the greatest Merchandize While the Rates are so unequal People generally take advantage to pay in the worst Commodity which often occasions unfairness in Trade and Dealings; and the Fees and Publick Revenues were sure to be be constantly paid in the worst kinde, had not People a greater advantage still in paying in Bills that are worse than any of the Comoditys. Indeed I am of opinion that if His Majesty is pleased to allow their Publick Bills of Credit to subsist any rated Comoditys are entirely useless and only serves to perplex strangers tradeing and gives great opportunity for Frauds & Tricks in their Dealings

24

32 An Act to ascertain the time for Payment of Pork, Wheat and Indian Corn

33 An Act ascertaining the Gauge of Barrels and to prevent frauds in Pork, Beef, Pitch or Tarr

This Act was intended to prevent frauds & abuses in Trade and the Comoditys raised among us but hath in great Measure proved ineffectual through the shortness of time allowed and that Traders seldom care for the trouble and inconveniency if the Comodity be barely tolerable, and the Act itself hath been very dificult in the Construction of the dubble damages to the party, and the value to be forfeited or what to be done with the Comodity, some of which ought to be condemned and burnt others are of value though short perhaps in Quantity so that by one means or other there is little care taken in it, and great discredit & damage our Trade suffers by it which I think will not be sufficiently remedy'd till searchers are appointed to seal & mark the goods and none to pass without in Payment. But I doubt a due regulation in this or the last Act about Staple Comoditys would not be easily obtained to pass an Assembly here according to the present disposition I see in them

34 An Act to appoint the marking of Horses, Cattle & Hogs, and to prevent Injuries being done by killing mismarking driving away or destroying Peoples Stocks.

This Act is for the benifit of the Inhabitants that let their stock run at large in the Woods to prevent mistakes mismarking or taking from one another and in such Case gives a Penalty instead of the bare damage to be recovered, and on the other hand makes it but a Penal offence instead of a criminal Prosecution for Fellony or otherwise which might be to severe where stock run so promis-cuously and mistakes so easily made

35 An Act appointing toll Books to be kept at or near Khatharine's Creek in Chowan Precinct at the head of Pequimins Precinct and at the mouth of the N° West River in Currituck Precinct and to prevent persons from transporting or driving Horses, Cattle or Hogs to other Persons Lands

This Act is to regulate Abuses by the borderers and Traders of Virginia but hath not been effectually put in execution and some further Regulation therein seems necessary both in tradeing from Virginia and to it but must be left to time

36 What Fences are sufficient.

An Act concerning Fences.

37 An Act concerning Servants & Slaves.

This law is found very benificial to People that have Servants and Slaves, and is agreable to the Customs and Useages of other Places in America.

38 Private Burials Prohibited

This is an old Act made when People were thinly inhabited but now seems grown out of use

39. An Act concerning proving Wills and granting Letters of Administration and to prevent frauds in the management of Intestates Estates

The Substance of this Act seems to be taken from the Statutes of England but there hath been found a necessity of additional Acts twice as will be seen in their place.

40 An Act concerning Orphans

The occasion of this Act was the Injustice used to Orphans that often fell into hands that would obscurely bind them out or convey them away and destroy what they had which was by this prevented

41 An Act to encourage the destroying of Vermin
    Repealed.

42 An Act to ascertain what Persons are tithables and to direct the method to be observed in taking the Lists of them

This is an antient Law and the usual method for taking Lists for a Pole tax in Publick or Parish Leveys and hath been found no ways ill-convenient.

43 An Act for appointing a town in the County of Bath and for securing the Publick Library belonging to S't Thomas's Parish in Pamptico.

This tho' a long Act only concerns a Town where little Improvements have been made, and for securing a small Library that was too much embezelled before the Act was made.

44 An Act concerning Ordinary Keepers & Tipling Houses.

This is a very old Law, but that part of it which says that the Ordinary Keeper is to take Cent per Cent advance upon what Liquor he sels is altered and the Precinct Courts have Power from time to time to settle their Rents upon all sorts of Liquor and Dyet.

45. An Act ascertaining the currency of Dollars.

The intent of this Law was to bring Dollars into the Country and to make them current here, but it never had the effect

46. An Act ascertaining the Damage upon protested Bills of Exchange.

This is a Law copied from Virginia, & I think the Damage Given is no ways unreasonable

47 Public Letters how to be conveyed.

This Law was made during the Indian Warr when it was necessary Publick Letters should have dispatch but never answered the end and is now entirely useless

48 An Act to prevent the taking Boats, Cannoes and Pereanges from Landings without leave

This Law considering our scituation upon Rivers and Creeks and the Disapointment People meet withall in having their Boats and Cannoes taken away is no way amiss.

49 An Act to ascertain Officers Fees

This is the old Law for Fees (except in some few Articles that were altered in the year 1715) when the Country was without Bills of Credit and the rated Species was so low that it was full as good as Proclamation Money and ought allways to have been kept to this Standard which is fully observed upon in the Report

50 An Act for restraining the Indians from molesting or injuring the Inhabitants of this Government and for securing to the Indians the Right and Property of their own Lands.

This Law has proved very convenient to prevent any irregularities and misunderstandings with the Tributary Indians that live among us who have ever since behaved peaceably and are now excepting the Tuscaroras decayed and grown very inconsiderable

51 Public Treasurers to give Account

By this Act the Treasurers &c are obliged to account to the Assembly for all Moneys received by authority of Assembly

52 An Act for a Town on Roanoak Island   ·

This Project failed and the Act hath hitherto taken no effect, nor any Prospect at present of it

53 An Act for raising Corn to satisfy the Debt due from this Government to the Honble Charles Craven Esqr Governor of South Carolina And for the Subsistance of such Forces as shall be raised for the necessary Defence of the Frontiers of this Government.

This was a temporary Act to discharge a large Debt occasioned by the Indian Warr for Assistants given this Country from South Carolina.

54 An Act for raising the sum of two thousand Pounds annually 'till the Publick Debts are answered and paid, and for the better encouraging the Currency of the Public Bills of Credit

By this Act a tax was layd of 15ˢ ⅌ Poll for tithable and rateable Persons and a land Tax of 2ˢ 6ᵈ ⅌ hundred acres and a Method taken for a Rent Role at that time, tho' now the Assembly is so backward in doing anything of the like Nature for a Rent Role to collect the Quit Rents by which is so much wanted for His Majesty's Service And it's well provided by this Act if Lands were concealed three years unpaid and nothing to be found on the Land to levy, the Justices of the Precinct Courts where the Land lay had Power to sell so much of it as should pay the dues thereon and charges This tax being intended as a sinking Fund to call in the Bills & to lessen them 2000 ⅌ annum the publick Faith was pledged not only for encouragement of Merchants & other Traders to establish their Currency but to assure the Lords Proprietors that they should in a few years be sunk & it was enacted that no new Bills should afterwards be made nor this Tax lessened till all the Bills were called in but this was afterward broke in upon & the taxes lessened & new Bills emitted to the Apparent & continual loss of the Lords Proprietors in their Revenue & their Officers who were pay'd in the Paper Currency

55 An Act impowering Johanna Peterson Widow of Thomas Peterson late of Albemarle County Esqʳ to make sale of certain Lands late belonging to the said Thomas Peterson and to make other Provision for Anna the daughter of the said Thomas Peterson to whom the said Lands do descend

A private Act for sale of Land

56 An Act confirming the Titles of sundry Persons who have already or hereafter may purchase Lands of Col Thomas Cary in Bath County

This Act to confirm some doubtful Titles of Land purchased by Collonel Cary

57 An Act for the confirmation of the Laws passed this Session of Assembly and for repealing all former Laws not herein particularly excepted

This Act finishes the Revisal of the Laws in 1715 and having taken out of the former Laws what was thought necessary or convenient they made this to be the Body of Laws for the Government and repealed all former Laws excepting some few by name expressed and all private Acts &c. and a Method is prescribed for dispersing the Laws, and encouragement given for printing of them but it was never effected.

[B P R. R O North Carolina B. T Vol. 8 p 365.]

TITLES OF ACTS WITH GOV' BURRINGTON'S REMARKS

1 An Act for the lessening the Pole and Land Tax and preventing of Concealments

This was the first publick breach of the Funds laid for sinking the Bills but was soon repealed by another that made a greater Step

2 An Act to confirm a Decree made in the Court of Chancery of this Province upon a Bill of Compl' exhibited by William Duckenfield Esq"

A Private Act

3 An Additional Act to the Act intituled an Act for establishing the Chuch and appointing select Vestrys.

An additional Act to the Vestry Act

4 An Act in addition to the Act of making a Town at Queens Anns ,Creek

An additional Act for the Town of Edenton

5 An additional Act to an Act intituled an Act concerning Ordinary Keepers and Tipling Houses

An additional Act concerning Ordinary Keepers.

6 An Act in explanation of an Act concerning Servants and Slaves

An additional Act to the former about Servants and Slaves.

7 An act for a Road from Coare Pint in Pamplico to Newbern on Neuse River

Never comply'd with

8 An Act for making the sum of Twelve Thousand Pounds Publick Bills of Credit for exchanging such of the Publick Bills of Credit as are now current thereby to render them the more usefull to the Government And for regulating the Taxes.

This Act lessened the Taxes so as little or nothing was after brought in clear to sink the remainder of the Bills for when the Law in 1729 was made, that repealed this Law and called in those Bills tho' seven years after there was computed to be 10000£ out to be changed and it appears that was something short of the computation

9 An Additional Act, to an Act entituled An Act appointing Tole Books.

An addition to Toll Act.

10 An Act for enlargeing and encouragement of the Town called Edenton in Chowan Precinct.

Another additional Act about Edenton.

11. An Act for incorporating the sea Port of Beaufort in Carteret Precinct into a Township by the name of Beaufort.

This Act is for making a Town at Beauford in Core Sound which tho' a good Inlett and convenient yet the Town hath had but little success & scarce any inhabitants

12 An Act appointing that part of Albemarle County lying on the west side of Chowan river to be a Precinct by the name of Bartie Precinct

An Act appointing Bertie Precinct. This is a very thriveing Place which is so much increased that there is talk already of a new division in it

13 An Act concerning Fees and Officers.

This was an additional Act to the former about Fees and was the first Establishment of Fees for a Chief Justice, which being done when Bills were current is stated the highest of any Officer

14 An Act appointing that part of the S W parish of Chowan that lyes on the South Shore and Aligater to be a distinct Parish by the name of the south Parish of Chowan and for appointing Vestry men for the same Parish

An Act for dividing a Parish

15. An Act for settling the Precinct Court and Court Houses

Before this Act the Precinct Courts were held at divers Places which was found illconvenient and now reduced to a stated Place and Court Houses erected

16 An Act to provide indifferent Jurymen in all Causes Civill and Criminall

This is observed upon in my Report.

17 An Act entituled An additional Act relating to Biennial and other Assemblys and regulating Elections and divers other things relating to Towns.

An additional Act about Town Elections and Burgesses.

18. An Act for appropriating part of the Impost duty on Vessells or powder money to beacon or buy out the Channells from Roanoake and Ococock Inlets and severall other things to facilitate the Trade and Navigation in this Government.

19. An Act being an additional Act to an Act entituled Staple Commodity's rated

This was an advancement of the rates of Commoditys many years after the Fees and Quit Rents had been stated and allowed to be paid in Commoditys There was also other Commoditys added at a high valuation, which was an apparent Injury to the Lords Officers & their Revenue

20. An Act for settling the Titles and bounds of Land

This Act is called the Processioning Act and the substance of it is taken from a Law in Virginia but it hath never been duly put in execution

21. An Act for an additionall Tax on all free Negroes Mullattoes Mustees, and such Persons male & female as now are or hereafter shall be intermarried, with any such Persons resident in this Government

An Act about a Tax on free Negroes & Mullattoes.

22. An act for the better ascertaining Navall Officers and Collectors Fees.

This Act seems to make a better Provision than had been for the naval Officer and Collector who were obliged hereby to take their Fees in Bills about which there had been some Disputes. But at the same time it was taking from the Governor a Fee of 22ˢ 6ᵈ silver on every Vessell that was before allowed and by this Act repealed, which was farr more than what they added now to the naval Officers and was an apparent Injury to succeeding Governors, and could hardly have pass'd but under a President that did not expect to hold it It being the only Fee a Governor had worth any thing

23 An Additionall Act to an Act intituled an Act for quallification of Publick Officers

This Act was made under a President, just before the arrivall of a Governor and seems calculated purely to exclude any Persons from Office he might bring with him

24. An Act for destroying Squarrells

This Act is now repealed with all the Laws against Vermin

25 An Act for regulating Proceedings on Originall Attachments.

This is an addition and amendment on the former Law about originall Attachments and is a good regulation

26 An Additionall Act to an Act entituled An Act concerning proving
      Wills and granting Letters of Administration, and to prevent
      frauds in management of Intestates Estates.

This was a Provision much wanted before, when Orphans Estates and
Creditors by undue apprasement had been much injured and great
Frauds and abuses about them That are well remedyed hereby

27 An Act to restrain the keeping too great a number of Horses, and
      Mares and for amending the Breeds

An Act for mending the breed of Horses which are generally very
small in this Country.

28. An Act for enlargeing and Encouragement of the Town at the Island
      of Roanoake now called Carteret.

This Act was to promote a settlement on Roanoake Island at the
mouth of Roanoake Inlett but never took effect so I can say but little to
it only if due care was taken for Pilotage and making good the Channel there it would encourage our Trade.

29 An Act for the better settling of the Town of Newbern in the
      Precinct of Craven.

An Act for making a Town in Bath County on Neuse River, which
hath made but little Progress.

30 An Act to encourage the tanning of Leather in this Province since
      repealed.

31 An Act for regulating Towns and Election of Burgesses

This Act was made for regulating the Town Elections of Burgesses
there being three Towns in this Government that hath the priviledge of
sending Burgesses and this Act was to adjust the manner of chuseing
them

32. An Act to regulate Trade in Bath County, a Temporary Law Ex-
      pired.
    Expired

33. An Act for encouraging and facilitating Navigation in this Province

This Act was intended to make some Provision for a settlement at
Ocacock Inlett where large Vessells may safely come into good anchor-
ing and harbour but hath not taken effect for want of better encouragement and further measures taken about it.

34 An Act to encourage destroying Vermin a Temporary Law expired.
    Expired

35   An Act for enlargeing and confirming the Power of the Precinct
       Court and to prevent Actions and Indictments of small value being
       brought in the General Cour^t, a Temporary Law expired
   Expired

36   An Act to appoint the North West part of Bartie Precinct a District
       Parish by the name of the North West parish of Bartie Precinct
       And for appointing Vestrymen for the said Parish, & to appoint
       Commissioners in every Parish in this Government to call the
       Churchwardens and Vestry to account for the Parish money by
       them received

   This Act was to make a new Parish of the upper parts of Bertie Precinct which increases so fast that they begin to talk of another Division
and by this Act there was particular Commission" to be appointed in
each Parish for inspecting the Parish accounts on a pretence that there
had been some irregularities, but some Parishes not thinking it worth
while and where they were chosen none of the Commissioners having
detected any irregularities little came of it

[B P R. O North Carolina B T. Vol. 9 A 19]

COPY OF A LETTER FROM Mr BYRD TO CAP BUR-
RINGTON

VIRGINIA. the 20th of July 1731.

SIR,

   I had the honour to receive your Excellency's letter for which I return
you my humble thanks,   I think by some samples I have known of that
Country it will cost a pretty deal of trouble to bring it into order and a
less spirit than yours will never be able to affect it,   people accustomed to
live without law or gosple will with great Reluctance Submit to either.

   It must be owned North Carolina is a very happy Country where
people may live with the least labour that they can in any part of the
world, and if the lower parts are moist and consequently a little unwhole-
some every where above Chowan, as far as I have seen, people may live
both in health and plenty   T'is the same I doubt not in all the uplands
in that Province but no place has so great a character for fertility and
beauty of scituation, as the Haw old field which lye on the North branch
of Cape Fear River and I fancy that is the very spot your Excellency
has chosen because it answers both in distance and quantity to what you
say you have purchased

I should be very glad to follow so good a pattern as yours to make such distant Lands profitable in my time, it is true the soil is good and capable of bringing anything that the Climate will allow, but the labour of transporting the fruits of our labour to a market or to navigation makes all the difficulty however as our habitants come to multiply which to me is a distant prospect such remote Estates will be valuable. In the mean time if I could receive Instruction from your Excellency how to make an immediate advantage of a high-land territory I should be prodigiously obliged to you

I am sorry your late assembly was so resty as to oppose the matters you was pleased to recomend to them I make no doubt but that the proposals you made to them were very just and consequently the Fault lay on their side for not complying with them.

I should be glad to know upon what terms his Majesties lands are now to be taken up in that Province, how great the Quit Rent and in what specie to be paid, your Excellency will be pleased to forgive those questions because they proceed not from curiosity but from an Inclination to increase my terra firma there if the expence be not too great and the obligation for seating too troublesome

In the mean time I wish you all the success in the world in bringing the chaos into form and reducing that Anarchy into a regular Government in so doing you well deserve to your statue erected, or which perhaps is better to have your sallary doubled. I suppose if my Lord Carteret should not part with his share of Carolina it will be laid out for him in South Carolina as being commonly fancyed to be the finer clymate I'm informed there is a subscription in England for setling an hundred familys of poor Debtors on Savana River which I fear will prove a grave for them, they had better send them to North Carolina

I am Sir
your Excellencys
most obedient humble servant

W BYRD

This is the copy of
a letter I received from Mr Byrd
of Virginia I sent the Original to the
Speaker of the House of Commons
GEO BURRINGTON

[B P R. O North Carolina B T Vol. 8 A 11]

The case of the Inhabitants of the County of Albemarle in North Carolina bordering upon his Majestys Colony of Virginia humbly submitted to the Right Honorable the Lords Com⁰ of Trade and Plantation

Sheweth

That they haveing for many years been planters of Tob⁰ and by that
produce subsisted and provided their family with all kinds of European
Good &c they are now by a Law made in Virginia A° Dom 1726 prohibited the benefit of carrying the same to Virginia in order to be shipt
of for Great Brittain as formerly accustomed to the Great Impoverishing
of the s⁴ familys and now particularly of such who by the late running
of the line betwixt the two Governments have been taken out of the
province of Virginia into North Carolina and whose lands are scarce
capable by reason of their situation of any other Improvemt   That the
Inletts to that part of North Carolina are not capable of receiving vessels
of Burthen fitt for the Transporting of Tobacco from thence to Great
Brittain so that unless relieved by the favourable Representation of ye
Lordships to his most sacred Majesty for Repeal of that Law (w⁰⁰ is
humbly conceived to be not only Detrimental to his Majestys Revenue
but directly contrary to the acts of Trade) Many of the s⁴ Inhabitants
(being chiefly very poor people) are in danger of being reduced to the
Extremest poverty and must either be obliged to quit their plantations
or fall upon such usefull Manufactorys for their necessary Cloathing &c
as will prevent the sale of considerable quantitys of European Goods
and consequently be prejudicial to the Trade of Great Britain

[B. P R. O North Carolina Vol 9 A 22.]

Mr PORTER'S OPINION ABOUT THE APPOINTING OF ANY NEW COUNCILLOR BY THE GOVERNOR WHILST THERE ARE SEVEN MEMBERS OF COUNCIL IN THE PROVINCE 27 JULY 1731

[Rec⁴ with Mr Porter's Rep⁰ to the Board dated 19 Feb⁷ 173¼]

The Opinion of E. Porter in humble answer to His Excellency

1ˢᵗ That upon the greatest Emergencys His Majesty hath not allowed
a less number than three to make a Quorum in Council and there being

but two present I conceive I cannot give an opinion as a member in Council tho (to oblige Your Excellency) I may as Member of Council

2ndly A Member of Council is a Judicial Officer because as such he is also a Member of the Court of Chancery and therefore agreeable to his Maj Instruction ought to be chose by consent & advice of Council

3rdly That there is at this present time seven Members of Council in this Province viz Mr Secry Rice Mr Halton Mr Jenoure Mr Ashe, Mr Allen, Mr Harnett & myself which is the number limited by His Maj Royal Instruction until his pleasure be further known Wherefore these my several reasons why any persons cannot be chose or inducted at present a Member of Council I pray may be entred by the Depty Secry

    Signed E PORTER at the Council

      Board this 27th day of July 1731

[B P R. O Am & W Ind Vol. 22 p. 119]

Mr BADHAM'S VALUATION OF THE CHIEF JUSTICES PLACE IN NORTH CAROLINA

To His Excellency George Burrington Esqr Governor of North Carolina

        August 2nd 1731

SIR,

Pursuant to your Excellencys Directions I have Endeavoured to make a Computation of the Profits arising to the Chief Justice of North Carolina by Virtue of his Commission which I had the honour to serve him as Clerk of the General Court into which office I entered at March Genl Court Anno Domini 1722 His Salary from the Lords Proprietors was sixty pounds per annum, and fees due and paid for Deeds of Land acknowledged & proved before him were then about fifty pounds Yearly, besides proving Letters of Attorney & other Instruments of writing and warrants issued heard and determined by him and bayle taken before him which in all probability amounted to fifty pounds per annum more And the Fees due in all Actions before him as Chief Justice in the General Court I formed of him which brought me in near or quite five hundred pounds per annum for some years after our Agreement. But when Publick Differences & Divisions happened amongst us the perquisites & Profits of that office were wonderfully hurt and diminished and the writts & process thence issuing were very seldom executed as they ought to have been especially in the southern part of the Province, and in the Northern County, viz⁴ Albemarle County very badly, partly owing to the Defect of the Provost Marshall and his Deputys and the Disputes that arose about appointing that Officer, besides which our late Governor Sir Richard Everard in the year 1729 issued a Proclamation for suspending the Chief Justice and afterwards t'was very rare if any writt or other process by him sign'd were obeyed, which caused a great defect of Justice & delay in business so that many suffered thereby besides the Officers of the Court amongst whom one of the greatest sufferers was

Your Excellency's
most obedient humble servant

Wᵐ BADHAM

To His Excellency, the Governor

[B P R O Am & W Ind Vol. 22. p 120]

Mʳ LOVICKS VALUATION OF THE SECRETARY'S OFFICE OF NORTH CAROLINA AT £582.10. PER AN

To His Excellency George Burrington, Governor of His Majesty's Province of North Carolina

EDENTON August 3ʳᵈ 1731

SIR,

In obedience to your Excellencys directions I here send you an Estimate of the Value of the Secretary's office upon a Medium for seven years last past, I believe at present it is not of the value it was which is wholly owing to the High Quit rent that is put upon the Land; for it was a great Inducement to the settlement of this little Colony, that Land was to be taken up at a Quarter the Value that it was in our Neighbouring Province of Virginia, and the Quit rent being the same as in Virginia all new comers into that Province chose to come in here but now that the taking up of Land is made more difficult than it is in Virginia & the rent is double to what it is there, it will rather drive People from hence thither than Encourage any of them to settle here, And I believe your Excellency is very sensible that this is the true ground for the stop that is put to all business, not one survey or Patent having been made or issued that I hear of since your Excellencys arrival, and I am afraid few will be made unless the Quit rent is altered for People will always settle where they can live with most Ease, and are least Burthened   I could not help saying this much because perhaps when the Estimate is seen, it might be asked why the office is not so good now as it was.

ESTIMATE OF THE SECRETARY'S OFFICE OF NO CAROLINA

200 Patents one year with another .	£122	"	10⁵	"	—
200 Warrants for taking up of Lands . .	50	"	—	"	—
Lapse & Escheat Patents about 80 one year with another .	100	"	—	"	—
Clerks office .	100	"	—	"	—
To Wills, Probates & Afficons yearly .	80	"	—	"	—
To Council Business yearly .	50	"	—	"	—
Writts of Escheat & Testimonials .	40	"	—	"	—
Sallery per annum . . .	40	"	—	"	—
	£582	"	10	"	—

I have formerly made much more of it, but the Distractions heretofore in the Government prevented many from coming in that otherwise would have settled here.   And your Excellency may perceive by the Estimate that the principal Fees in the office is what arises from the Settling Lands.

      I am Sir
        Your Excellencys
          most Dutifull & most obliged
          humble Servant.

                    J LOVICK

[B. P. R. O. Am & W Ind Vol. 22. p 121.]

Mʳ FORSTERS VALUATION OF THE SECRETARY'S POST TO NORTH CAROLINA

To His Excellency George Burrington Esqʳ His Majestys Cap. Genˡ & Governor in Chief of North Carolina.

                 EDENTON, August the 8ᵗʰ 1731

SIR,

Your Excellency was pleased to ask me some time ago what the Fees of the Secretary's Office of this Province might amount to Annually, which I could not at once resolve before I had looked over that office

wherein I have acted for these eight or nine years past, & find for the
last three or four years from the great Distractions in the Government,
occasioned by the weakness of Sir Richard Everard late Gov' here it has
not exceeded £400 per annum, but before that time it could not amount
to less than £600, and I am confident that if the Quit rent of Lands were
no more than Two shillings per hundred which is the same rent as in
Virginia, that the Secretary's office for some years to come would be
worth considerably more than ever from the vast number of Surveys
made at Cape Fear which is not yet Patented, and the great quantities
that would be every day taken up there, as well as in many other parts
of the Governm' if the Quit rent was lessened, for till that is done I am
persuaded there will not One Patent be taken out, Everybody choosing
rather to loose their Land than pay so high a Quit Rent, and your Excellency very well knows there has not One Patent issued since your
arrival so that indeed the Secretary's office at present for want of Patents
issuing is now scarce worth One hundred Pounds per annum Clerk-
ships excepted

> I am
>   (with great respect)
>   Your Excellencys
>   most Dutiful & most obedient
>   humble servant
>
>   ROB' FORSTER

[B P R. O Am & W Ind Vol. 22 p 118.]

M' LITTLE'S VALUATION OF THE CHIEF JUSTICE'S PLACE AT £600 PER AN
[August, 1731]

MAY IT PLEASE YOUR EXCELLENCY,

In obedience to you I am to give your Excellency an Account of the
Profitts of the Attorney General's place of this Province which I cannot
pretend to do exactly, because the Incomes are more or less just as the business happens of late years the Authority of Government has been suffered to sink so low & the Courts so much obstructed that Law & Justice
seemed at a stand & but little business done

But since your Excellency has settled the Government & the Law has
its free course & Justice duly administered, the business of that office

will be considerable   I believe there will be 12 or fifteen Indictments a Court one with another which is held 3 times a year,   the Fee of each Indictment is 50ª, besides the incidental fees of it, & often a Fee from the Prosecutor too, & there is another business besides Bills of Indictment which will Augment the Fees so that by a moderate Computª without the Salary which is £40 per annum & besides his practice as a Lawyer in Civil Actions which that station recommends him to a full share if not always the Choice of I think the incomes of the office cannot come to less than £100 per. annum which is to be received in Proclamation Money   As to the Chief Justices place which you are pleased to mention too, it is not Easy for the reasons I before gave to make an Exact Estimate of it, the business being uncertain, the Clerk of the General Court is under his Appointment whose Fees are very valuable And according as that point is managed it makes the value of the other more or less,   there are also severall Fees out of Court such as probates & acknowledgements of Deeds & other writings that may be there or in the Precinct Courts, & so is more or less as People are brought into the way of it.

I am of opinion that with good Application, & if the most is made of the Clerkship the Chief Justices Place may one way or other Comunibis Annix be worth 5 or six hundred Pounds per Annum besides the Salary which has been Sixty Pounds per Ann but its supposed will now be raised to £100 per. Annum:

And if the Circuits come to be settled the Value of the Place will be considerably the greater for it   This may it please your Excellency is the best Account I am able to give, but you'l please to give me leave to add that in all offices as well as other business it depends much on the Person & his knowledge of the Place.

I am Your Excellencys most Dutifull
& devoted humble Servant.
WILLIAM LITTLE.

[B. P. R. O. AM & W IND No 592.]

EXTRACT OF A LETTER FROM CAPTAIN BURRINGTON GOVERNOR OF NORTH CAROLINA TO THE LORDS COMMISSIONERS FOR TRADE AND PLANTATIONS DATED 4ᵗʰ SEPTEMBER 1731

We expect our Indians will be attackt by those of South Carolina The Northern Indians called the five Nations are in Alliance and Amity with ours and have promised to assist them with a Thousand Men part of which are already come into this Province

[B. P. R. O. NORTH CAROLINA. B. T VOL. 9. A. 17]

GOVᵗ BURRINGTON TO LORDS OF TRADE.

NORTH CAROLINA September 4ᵗʰ 1731

MAY IT PLEASE YOUR LORDSHIPS

A After the Prorogation of the Assembly which I called pursuant to the Kings Instructions, I wrote a full State of the affairs of this Province and of my own Proceedings with that Assembly dated the first of July which I had the honour to address to your Board. Your Lordships must perceive the many difficulties I have had to encounter by the Artifices of some and folly of others in the Council which rendred the house of Burgesses obstinate I can truly Say I met with more Obstructions in my Endeavours for his Majesties Service and the good and Welfare of the Province from part of the Council than from all the heat and Rashness of the Lower house who were encouraged by some of the Council and spirited up in their undutifull behaviour and small regard they shew'd to his Majesties Instructions, notwithstanding all the mean Acts and little Tricks that have been used to cause Tumults among the People and render my Administration uneasy I can with great Truth and Satisfaction acquaint your Lordships that I keep all People in perfect Peace and Quietness and have entirely put a stop to those frequent Tumults and Riots which were frequent when I first came into this Country and were grown to that height that men were not a Security even in their own houses.

B. These disorders were generally sett on foot and the Rioters headed by Mr Edmund Porter Judge of the Admiralty and one of the Council of whom I have made mention in my Report to your Lordships this man bears so infamous a character that I think it would be for his Majesties Service and the Reputation of the Council and Country if he was removed

C. In my last dispatches to your Lordships I gave you an Account that Smith late Chief Justice here was reported to be gone out of this Country and designed for England I could then only Say it might be true because I had no better Information than common Rumour this man after travelling through Some parts of the Government Spreading many false and Scandalous storys to draw people into a Subscription for defraying the Expences of his voyage and maintenance in England (wherein he had Slender Success) Secretly went out of the Government after giving out many Boasts of his great Interest in England he has promised to procure the removal of myself and Several other of his Majesties Officers and has already nominated our Successors. Mr Smith by reason of his rashness and folly was much dreaded in this Country Sitting as chief Justice I aver upon my own knowledge that there was not a man among the Factions here that he did not threaten and personally affront however after they had deluded him they gave him Some money and Sent him home with a Prospect that if he had the Interest he brag'd of possibly he might create mischief against me but if not they were Sure of ridding the Province of a busy Shallow wretch on whom there was no dependance and who might in a little time be very hurtfull to them in the post he had the honour to be placed in and to which he was no ways equall, this fellow is now the Jest and Scorn of the very men that perverted him has left the Country with the Character of a Silly, rash boy, a busy fool, and engregious Sot to which I must add that I know him to be an ungratefull perfidious scoundrel and as much wanting in Truth as Understanding, after all the ill behaviour of this Creature to me, I never spoke an uncivil word to him nor did him one ill Office while he was here, but on the contrary gave him the best advice I was capable of, he never informed me of his intention of going home, neither did he write me any letter from Virginia where he Staid Some time.

D. I think it was the latter end of June when Smith quitted this Province, before I was certain of it July was far advanced, the General Court by Act of Assembly sit on the last Tuesdays in the months of October March and July yearly but had been prevented by Porters man-

agement almost two years before my coming in so much that no legall
course could be taken for suppressing the Tumults before mentioned which
caused great complaints against Porter throughout the Province, long
before my arrival, to this State and Condition my enemys desired to
bring the Country again, and by means of the Same Porter when I had
appointed a Council for the Nomination of a New Chief Justice which
I put off to the day before the General Court was to sit there only
appeared Coll Jounoure his Majesties Surveyor of this Province and
Porter the other Councillors being dead, out of the Government or at
Cape Fear (two hundred miles from this Place) I postponed the meeting
of this Council to the very last in hopes the Gentlemen of the Council
who were at Cape Fear would have come to me and I might have seen a
full Board on this occasion as I had all reason to expect because the Court
of Chancery constantly sits at the same time the General Court is held
and consists by the Rules of the Court of the Governour and four Members of the Council at least The Gentlemen from Cape Fear not attending and there being but two of the Council in this part of the Country
and no more than four in the other, two of which I then thought to have
been out of the Province viz' Mr Ashe who was reported to be gone to
England to joyn with the Chief Justice in the design of procuring my
removal, and Mr Rice the Secretary who had been in South Carolina to
fetch his Family but was then returned as I have been since informed
also Mr Ashe who after the most diligent enquiries throughout this
Country not being able to raise Materials for a charge against me would
not put his Reputation and sence so much at stake to go to England as
I am informed he had promised several men here who now curse him for
Nonperformance and [by which failure of his Baby Smith will be quite
lost haveing nothing but a few lies to Support his Cause unless he can
obtain an Instructor from a Gentleman in Hannover Square] there
appearing but two Members at the aforesaid Council I desired their
Opinion whether they did not judge it absolutely requisite for his Majesties Service the Peace and Wellfare of the Government that two Councellours should be appointed, otherwise the General Court would be
again stopped and the Court of Chancery the same by reason it could
not subsist without four Councellours being present Coll Jenoure very
readily declared he thought the Country would suffer extreamly and the
Government be disgraced if the Courts were not supported, on the contrary Porter gave in his objections in writing and declared that I had no
Power to nominate Members of the Council without a Majority of the
Council agreed to the appointment and asserted that there were Seven

Members of the Council then in the Government and that by my Instructions I was not permitted to make more, his first allegation had no foundation the Kings Commission and Instructions giving me full power to fill up Vacancies to the number of Seven, the Second was notoriously false, there not being so many then in the Province I have required him to prove the Persons he mentioned in his Paper were then in this Government, but as he knew it was not True he excused himself

E. Coll Jenoure recomended Mr Lovick late Secretary of this Province for one of the Council this Gentleman was first in the late Council and when I came here with his Majesties Commission and is perfectly well aquainted with the affairs of this Government Sir Richard Everad and Mr Porter had wrote complaints against him to the Duke of Newcastle when I examined into it neither Sir Richard nor Porter (though I called upon the last very particularly) had not the least proof to make good any thing against him, indeed there were some affidavits concerning Patents for land after the Date of their accusations which Mr Lovick answered these were sent your Lordships in the Council and Journal Mr Lovick has proved to me that after the certainty of the Kings purchase was known he advised Sir Richard to grant no more Patents but by the Artifice and management of Mr Moseley then Surveyor Sir Richard did continue to issue Patents on which the Said Moseley and his Kindred were the most considerable gainers as appeared to me by the relations of persons unconcerned the affidavits sent your Lordships are all that is laid to Mr Lovicks charge there having been no complaint of any sort but one by Mr Porter against him and many others for obstructing the Said Porter in exercising his office of Admiralty Judge which Porter delivered to me in Council and after some reasoning and debates upon the Subject he withdrew it before it could be entered on the Council Book and has continued Silent ever Since I am obliged to do Mr Lovick the Justice to Say he has comported himself very handsomely upon all occassions since the Change of Government here especially during the Sitting of the late Assembly of which he was a Member besides his capacity in Government affairs, another inducement for making him one of the Council was his knowledge in Indian business (we expect our Indians will be attackt by those of South Carolina, the Northern Indians called the five Nations are in alliance and amity with ours and have promised to assist them with a thousand Men part of which are already come into this Province) I assure your Lordships there is no man in this Colony more capable of serving the King than Mr Lovick for these reasons I swore him a Councellour and Mr Edmund Gale a relation of

Mr Gale a Commissioner of the Excise a Gentleman in very good circumstances and unblemisht Character

F. When this was done with the advice and consent of the Council I appointed Mr John Palin Chief Justice who has given a general Satisfaction by his wise and prudent behaviour

G I cannot doubt but that your Lordships will approve of these appointments made in So critical a time and will esteam them as I intended a real Service done this Government and the best means could be thought on for preserving peace and good order in North Carolina notwithstanding Mr Porter was of another opinion

H The knowledge I have of this man since I came last here (I knew little of him before) induces me to believe he will have the assurance to trouble your Lordships with a Paper delivered as reasons against my appointing any Councellours Mr Allen mentioned in his Paper to be in North Carolina was not then in this Government neither has he been here since I came myself that Mr Rice or Mr Ashe were either of them here at that time was what he did not know any more than myself thõ it really proved they were in the Government The Original I Send your Lordships weak and Silly as it Seems to me I am assured it was the result of the party I have against me and that Mr John Montgomery his Majesties Attorney General here drew it up which I believe it being much like the way of reasoning he uses and calculated to perplex me and disorder the course of Bussiness in this Government

I Give me leave to add what has been already said of Porter that he is a man of a most infamous Character, has been guilty of many vile Frauds and is now under many Prosecutions and Actions for Debt which will reduce him to great Poverty I am Sorry I am obliged to Say much of such a contemptible fellow

K In my remarks upon the Laws of this Country which were sent to your Board I made some observations upon the Law for holding Biennial Assemblys which I hope your Lordships have considered. In a few days the People (by Nature of that Act) are to choose Representatives will meet in Assembly (if not prorogued) the first Monday in November next, I am fully convinced no good can be done with an Assembly before his Majesties pleasure is known in relation to the pretended Laws in 1729 after his Majesties purchase was completed whether any Equivalent is to be taken in Lieu of cash for his Majesties Quit Rents, whether his Majestie will be graciously pleased to moderate Quit Rents for Lands to be taken up to the Same that is paid in Virginia which is insisted on by the people here as their undoubted Right, whether the Officers are not to take their Fees in Proclamation or Bills as they are rated by the Assembly to that value   Before I have an answer to these Material Points I know it will be to no purpose to hold an Assembly therefore Shall propose to the Council the Progueing them till I am further instructed

L In the Body of Laws sent home is an Act relating to Escheat and Lands and Escheators which I have already remarked upon and have refused to grant Patents for any Escheat Lands till I hear from your Lordships, the composition being very small in that act and the Quit Rents but two shillings for every hundred acres.   It is insisted upon here that I ought to grant Such lands agreeable to the Law but as I find this Law not to be consistent with the latter part of the 43rd Instruction I have obeyed the Instruction in not complying with the Law.

M I gave some reasons in my remarkes on the Act for Biennial Assemblies to which I beg leave to add the following to Shew the Act ought to be repealed   the time of an Assemblies continuance being So Short causes Several well meaning Members to be Timorous fearing they should not be chosen again   that by the Said Act a Small part of the Province have Twenty Six Representatives all the Remainder but ten   I judge it necessary to reduce the four Precincts called Chowan, Perquimmons, Pasquetank and Curratuck into Two because in the second and fourth there are neither Persons fit for Magistrates nor Burgesses   I am also of Opinion that two representatives are Sufficient for a Precinct   the Counties in Virginia send no more,   the number of Burgesses and Precincts are Settled by this Act.   This Act also allows all freemen to vote for Burgesses, but his Majesty's 12th Instruction to me is very particular that none but Freeholders be admitted to vote which being against that Law has occasioned a great deal of heat among the people and much heightened by those who love to raise a Clamour against me.   I cant help thinking we shall have more orderly Elections and more substantial men chosen if none but Freeholders vote as the Instruction directs so I hope the Law will be repealed that I may not be under the necessity of acting against a plain Instruction or against a Law of the Country and which may furnish my enemies with a handle for complaints against me.

N. By the 26th Instruction I am directed to take care that Just accounts of Receipts and payments of all publick monies being first attested by the Auditor be transmitted to the Lords of the Treasury but as there is yet no Auditor nor Receiver General nor the appointment of a Publick Treasurer yet Settled and as there has been very little money either received or paid I Shall not Send the Account before the Arrival of an Auditor or further Order from England.

O I have not yet been able to obey the 100 Instruction in Surveying the harbours being hitherto prevented by a Multiplicity of business and a dangerous Sickness of which I am not yet perfectly recovered   this will be a work of Some difficulty and expence which I Shall readily undertake as Soon as I am capable of travelling   the Inhabitants of this Country declare very much against Fortifications but as we have three harbours capable of receiving large Ships there will be a necessity of erecting Some at each of the Said harbours of which I will give your Lordships a further account before Christmas.

P The late Receiver General of this Province whose accounts lye before a Committee of the Council having given Sufficient Security to answer to the King for what money is in his hand I design not to pass the Said accounts before the Receiver and Auditor are appointed and present.

Q I am now able to give your Lordships an exact account of the value Bills are of in this Country,   A Pistole is not to be purchased under eight pounds in Bills   I have offered all people that have paid me Fees to take an eighth in Proclamation money in Lieu of four for one in Bills if they would let me have Silver,   only one man would comply of all those I have received any Fees from   English goods Sell from fifteen to twenty in Bills above the price they cost in England, but if the Bills are allowed by His Majesty to be current my opinion is they will Soon come to the value they are rated which is four for one in Proclamation money

R Your Lordships may think there was not enough said in my report of Sir Richard Everard, being commanded by an Instruction to enquire into the complaints made against him by the late Council   I have further to observe that Mr Moseley was in great Friendship with Sir Richard and his Family and they had been much concerned in taking up lands as appears by the List of Patents granted by Sir Richard   when the enquiry was made Mr Smith Mr Porter and Mr Ashe violently insisted nothing more ought to be enquired into than the words he had spoken against the King &c   there were but two Councellours present at that time   besides, for this good office they did him, I am informed Sir Richard his Lady and Son have promised to make some affidavits they judge will prove serviceable to their cause

S I must informe your Lordships that I have had Information of Mall practices by Mr Moseley and his Deputies in returning to the Secretaries office Immaginary Surveys by which his relations hold great quantities of land more than are specified in their patents   it is very certain

Moseley and his Relations have in four or five years time strangely enriched themselves

T I am assured by several people that my enemys have or will complain against me for buying some lands, the real truth I now declare to your Lordships which is that a few days after I came into this Province I heard M[r] Lovick and M[r] Moseley offer to sell some lands to Smith then Chief Justice and M[r] Halton one of the Council they offered me some also which I then declined, sometime after I was told the Indians took up oar upon those Lands of which they made Bullets with, upon this Intelligence I bought the lands and gave more for them than they are judged to be worth, if I cannot find the oar I have made a very bad bargain having no manner of occasion for the lands which are by water one hundred miles above the Falls of Cape Fear River if my enemies have impudence and villany enough to charge me with any clandestine or unfair practices upon this score I am ready to joyn issue with them and take upon me to prove the purchase was just, and that any other person might bought them as well as myself, the major part I bought of Moseley the great Land Jobber of this Country who has still twenty thousand acres to sell when he can find purchasers.

V Of the Council appointed by his Majesty M[r] Smith has resigned and left the Province M[r] Porter for several reasons already given I hope your Lordships will think ought to be left out M[r] Eleazer Allen was recommended unto me by several gentlemen in London to be put into the Council but he is not an Inhabitant in North Carolina lives in South Carolina where he is Clerk to the Assembly therefore ought not in my opinion to be in the Council here M[r] James Hallard and M[r] Richard Evans never came neither do I think they design it, M[r] John Porter is dead M[r] Matthew Rowan is not at this time in the Province but expected soon

As directed by my Instructions I send your Lordships a list of Names to fill up the Council I put M[r] Lovick first because I think he is the only person in this Government capable and fit to be intrusted with the care of this Province if his Majesties service or death takes me away John Lovick Chief Justice when appointed, Nathaniel Rice Secretary, Joseph Jenoure Surveyor General, Robert Halton John Ashe Thomas Pollock, Edmund Gale, Matthew Rowan Cornelius Harnet, George Martin and Mackrora Scarborough This is the best list I am able to make which I leave to your Lordships consideration

W By the running a Division line between Virginia and this Province many Plantations were gained from Virginia Some of the owners

27

have taken out Patents here but the Major part refuse. I desire your Lordships directions whether they that have not Patented their Lands here, ought not to do so

X I shall do myself the honour to send your Lordships before next Xmas an Account of the Militia and the Improvements that may be made in this country which I think entirely depends on the Quit Rents that are to be paid for Lands to be taken up and opening a Port on Ocacock Island the Pilots I have appointed assure me that at Ocacock they can bring in vessels that draw Sixteen or eighteen foot water, at Port Beaufort that draw twenty and at Cape Fear two and Twenty this account the Pilots offered to Swear too, Curratuck Inlett is shut up and Roanock is so dangerous that few people care to use it but go round to Ocacock

Y A great number of people have come into this Country to Settle lately I hear of more that are coming from the Neighbouring Colonies nothwithstanding there is but one Entry for taking up land neither has the person who made the Entry gone on with the Survey by reason of the Quit Rent I acquainted your Lordships how great a Prejudice this was to the Officers therefore shall omitt writing any more at this time on the Subject

Z When I undertook the Settlement of the Southern part of this Province (with consent of the Proprietors Council) warrants were given to people that were disposed to Settle there, by which inducement a great many people did then Seat lands in that uninhabited Country and have not since had Patents, I think it will be hard upon these people to be removed, many of them would be ruined I pray your Lordships directions in this tender affair

I am (with all respect)
your Lordships most humble
and most obedient servant
G BURRINGTON

[B P R O North Carolina B T Vol. 41 p 193]

BOARD OF TRADE JOURNALS

WHITEHALL Tuesday July 27 1731
Present
Mr Pelham Mr Brudenell Mr Bladen
Mr Fitzwilliams Surveyor Genl of the Customs in the Southern part of America and Mr Gale Collector of the Customs in North Carolina

attending presented to the Board a Memorial from the inhabitants of the County of Albemarle in North Carolina setting forth the great hardships they labour under from being denied the liberty of exporting their tobacco to Great Britain from the ports in Virginia occasioned by virtue of two Acts passed there the one in 1705 Entituled an Act against importing tobacco from Carolina and other parts without the Capes of Virginia and the other passed in 1726 entituled an Act for the more effectual preventing the bringing tobacco from North Carolina and the bounds in controversy And their Lordships taking the said Memorial into consideration as also both the Acts gave directions for preparing the Draught of a Report for repealing the said Acts.

[Page 198.]

Which Report was agreed and signed July 29th

[Page 242.]

Wednesday September 2 1731.

M[r] Thomas Lowndes having brought to the Office three Certificates one from James Bertie Esq[re] another from Henry Bertie Esq[re] Two of the late Lords Proprietors of Carolina and the third Certificate under the hand of M[r] Shelton their late Secretary relating to certain Grants of Lands made by the said Proprietors to M[r] Lowndes before the Treaty of Surrender of Carolina to the Crown the said Certificates were read and ordered to be kept with the papers which relate to the Province of South Carolina

----

[FROM MSS RECORDS OF NORTH CAROLINA COUNCIL JOURNALS.]

COUNCIL JOURNALS.

NORTH CAROLINA—ss.

EDENTON Feb[ry] 25th 173$\frac{4}{}$

Pursuant to his Majestys Royall Comission and instructions Constituting & appointing his Excellency George Burrington Esq[r] Gov[r] Cap[t] Generall and Comander in Chief of the Province and Territory of North Carolina the same was read and published and His Excellency thereon in Council took & subscribed the severall Oaths by law appointed for Qualification of Publick officers as Also the the oath for the due Execution of Justice Reposed in him Equall administration of Justice and due observance of the Laws of Trade and thereupon his Excellency took his Place at the board accordingly

William Smith Joseph Jenoure & Robert Halton Esq^{rs} appointed by his Majesties Royall instructions Members of Council for this Province appeared and took & subscribed the several oaths by Law appointed for Qualification of Publick officers and their places at the board accordingly

At a council held at the council Chamber in Edenton ye 25th day of Febry Anno Domini 1731

Present

His Excellency George Burrington Esqr His Majesties Governor &c

The Honoble { William Smith, Joseph Jenoure, Robert Halton } Esq^{rs} Members of His Majesties Council

His Excellency the Governor was pleased to order that a Proclamation Issue for continuing officers and magistrates both military and Civill within the Province till his Excellencys Pleasure be further known therein

Hiss Excell^y the Govr produced to this Board a Commission from the right Honble the Lords of the Admiralty Constituting and appointing him vice Admiral of his Majesties Province of North Carolina

Adjourned till tomorrow morning Eight of ye Clock

At a Council held at the Council Chamber in Edenton the 26th day of Febry Anno Domini 17 3¼

Present

His Excellency George Burrington Esqr Governour &c

The Honobles { William Smith, Joseph Jenoure, Robert Halton } Esq^{rs} Members of His Majesties Councill

His Excellency the Governour Representing to this board the necessity of calling together the Genl Assembly of this Province to Enact and make such Laws as shall as shall be for his Majesties Service and the good of the people within the same thereupon his Excell^y the Govr by and with the advice and Consent of his Majesties council doth order that Writs forthwith Issue requiring the ffreeholders in the several and respective precincts and Towns within this Province to Choose their Representatives on Tuesday the 23^d day of March Order^d that Proclamation Issue requiring the General Assembly of this Province to meet at Edenton on Tuesday the 13th day of April next an all persons concerned are to take notice thereof accordingly

NORTH CAROLINA—ss.

At a council held at the Council house at Edenton y⁰ 27 day of Febry Anno 173¾

Present

His Excell⁷ George Burrington Esq⁷ Gov⁷ &c

The Honble { William Smith / Joseph Jenoure / Robert Halton } Esq⁽ˢ⁾ Members of his Majesties Council

Ordered that Mr Joseph Anderson do act for Nathaniel Rice Esq⁷ Secretary of this Province till his arrival here or some person Lawfully Deputed by him and in all cases till farther orders.

Ordered That John Lovick Esq⁷ Late Secretary of This Province do forthwith deliver up all papers and records relating to the Secretarys office unto Joseph Anderson appointed by the Gov⁷ and Council to recieve the same

By order of his Excell⁷ the Gov⁷ & Councill

JOSEPH ANDERSON ⅌ Secty

NORTH CAROLINA—ss.

At a Council held at the Council Chamber in Edenton the 4 day of March Anno 1731

Present

His Excellency Geo Burrington Esq⁷ Gov⁷ &c

The Honble { William Smith / Joseph Jenoure / Robert Halton } Esq⁽ˢ⁾ Members of his Majesties Council

Sir Richard Everard Bart Late Gov⁷ having Exhibited a Complaint against the late Rec⁷ General that he has refused paying him his Salary as Governour & that there are Sev¹ years in arrears due to the said S⁷ Rich⁴ upon which both parties were called and appeared accordingly, And the late Rec⁷ producing his acco⁽ᵗˢ⁾ with Sir Richard and his vouchers for the same and Sir Richard examined and there appeared To have been paid Sir Richard the sum of £1658.7 6 which amounted to very near the whole sum due to him from the time of his coming into this Province to the day of the present Governours arrival But this Board having no direction for the allowance of any sallary since his Majesties Purchase of the said Province do forbear at present the allowing any further payment than from the 17ᵗʰ day of July 1725 to the 19ᵗʰ Day of July 1729 being the date His Majesties purchase which in the whole is £1200 at 300£ ⅌ annum which is allow to be paid and the Reciever General discharged for the sum of 1200 in his Acco⁽ᵗ⁾

This Board having taken into consideration the affair of the Tenth of Wheal Oyle and Bone taken on the sea coast of this Province which has been lately claimed by the Judge of the admiralty of this Province as a Dims of Admiralty and the said Judge and others having rec'd percells of the said Oyle and Bone without accounting for the same to the Gov'r for the time being which being the undoubted right and purquisitt of the Gov'rn of the several Provinces of his Majesties Dominion in America where wheals were taken till his Majesty pleased to alter y'e Contrary It is ordered that all Tenths of the oyle & bone rec'd by any Person whatsoever before his Majesties Royall Instructions relating to that affair were published be paid to the Honoble Sir Richard Everard Bar't Governor of this Province

By order of His Excell'y y'e Gov'r and Councill

JOSEPH ANDERSON ♃ Secty

NORTH CAROLINA—ss.

At a Council held at y'e Councill Chamber in Edenton y'e 9th day of March Anno Dom 1730

Present

His Excellency George Burrington Esq'r Gov'r &c

The Honble { William Smith / Joseph Jenoure / Robert Halton } Esq'rs Members of his Majesties Council

Edmond Porter Esq'r appointed by his Majesties Royall instructions a Member of Councill for this Province appeared and took and subscribed several oaths, by law appointed for Qualification of Publick officers and his place at the board accordingly

Present y'e Hon'ble Edmond Porter Esq'r

William Smith Esq'r producing to this Board Majesties Warrant under his sign manuel directing That Letters patents Issue under the Great Seal of this Province constituting and appointing him the s'd William Smith Chief Justice therein

Ordered that Letters patents issue for the same

Ordered that a Commission issue under the seal of y'e Province constituting and appointing Robert Halton Esq'r Provost Marshall & Commissary of the musters within This Province

Ordered that the said Provost Marshall be and he is hereby Impowered to take and recieve Two Shillings and six pence for signing a Messu Process By order of y'e Gov'r & Councill

JOSEPH ANDERSON ♃ Secty

NORTH CAROLINA—ss.

At a Council held at the Council Chamber in Edenton the 30ᵗʰ day of March 1731

Present

His Excellʸ Geo Burrington Esqʳ Govʳ &c

The Honᵇˡᵉ { William Smith, Joseph Jenoure, Robert Halton } Esqⁿ Members of his Majesties Council

Ordered that the old seal of the Colony be used till the new seal arrives

Ordered that Cullen Pollock George Martin Isaac Hill be assistant Judges to the Chief Justice.

Ordered that John Conner Esqʳ be and he is appointed Attorney General of this Province and that a Commission be prepared for the same

By order of the Governʳ and Councill

JOSEPH ANDERSON ℔ Secʸ

NORTH CAROLINA—ss

At a Council held at the Councill Chamber in Edenton Apˡ 3ᵈ Anno Dom 1731

Present

His Excellency Geo Burrington Govʳ &c

Yᵉ Honᵇˡᵉ { William Smith, Joseph Jenoure } Esqⁿ Members of his Majesties Councill

His Majesty having by his Royall Instructions been pleased to appoint Nathaniel Rice and John Bapᵗ Ashe Esqⁿ Members of Councill for this Province—and There upon yᵉ said Nathˡ Rice and John Bapᵗ Ashe appearing took and subscribed the several oaths by law appointed for Their Qualification of Publick officers and their places at The Board accordingly

Present

the Honᵇˡᵉ { Nathaniel Rice, Jno Bapᵗ Ashe } Esqⁿ Members of his Majesties Council

Nathˣ Rice Esqʳ producing to this Board His Majesties Warrant under his sign Manuel directing that Letters patents Issue under the Great Seal of this Province Constituting and appointing him the said Nathaniel Rice Secretary and Clerk of the Crown of North Carolina

Ordered that Lˣˣˣ Patents Issue for the same

By order of the Govʳ & Council

JOSEPH ANDERSON ℔ Secty

NORTH CAROLINA—ss

At a Council held at the Councill Chamber in Edenton the 13ᵗʰ day of Apᶦ Anno Doɱ 1731

Present

His Excellency Geo Burrington Esq Gov &c

The Honᵇˡᵉ { William Smith / Nathaniel Rice / Joseph Jenoure / John Bapᵗ Ashe } Esqⁿ Members of his Majestys Councill

Cornelius Harnett Esqʳ being appointed by his Majestys Royall Instructions a member of Councill for this Province appeared and took and subscribed the several oaths by law appointed for Qualification of publick officers and his place at yᵉ board accordingly

By order of the Gov & Council

ROBᵗ FORSTER Dep Secty

NORTH CAROLINA—ss

At a Council held at the council Chamber in Edenton yᵉ 19ᵗʰ day of April 1731

Present

His Excellency the Governour

The Honᵇˡᵉ { William Smith / Edmond Porter / Jos Jenoure / Jnᵒ Bapᵗ Ashe / Cornelius Harnett } Esqⁿ Members of his Majesties Council

His Excellency the Governʳ was pleased to be read his Majesties Royall Instructions requiring him to Examine into the Complaints of Sir Richard Everard Barᵗ late Govʳ of sᵈ Province against sevˡ members of the Late Council as also their Complaints against the sᵈ Sir Richard Everard and his Excellʸ acquainting this Board that the said Sir Richard Everard had prayed a Certᵃ day To be appointed for hearing the said Compᵗˢ Therefore the Govʳ was pleased to appoint Tuesday the 20ᵗʰ Instant for hearing the said Complaint

And whereas there being some of the Gentlemen who were of the late council now in the lower house of Assembly (who is now setting) His Excellency the Governour by and with the advice and Consent of Council doth Comand that the members of the lower house of Assembly be adjourned till Wednesday the 21ˢᵗ Instant and they are they by adjourned accordingly

By order of the Governʳ & Council

ROBERT FORSTER D Secty

NORTH CAROLINA—ss

At a Council held at the Council Chamber in Edenton the 21ᵗʰ of April Anno Dom 1731

Present

His Excellency Geo Burrington Esqʳ Govʳ &c

Yᵉ Honᵇˡᵉ { William Smith Edmond Porter }
{ Nathaniel Rice Jnᵒ Bapᵗ Ashe } Esqᵐ Members of
{ Joseph Jenoure Corn Harnett } his Majesties Council

Upon Petition of Elizabeth Moore Relict of Thomas Moore deceased setting forth that her husband dying in the begining of October last and that William Little in conjunction with John Pratt under pretence as greatest Creditor to the said Deceased obtained admᵐ thereon wᶜʰ she concieves to be Illegal praying the said admᵐ may be annulled and made void a Copy of which petition the said Little was served with and day assigned him to answer the same At which day yᵉ sᵈ Elizᵃ appᵈ at this Board by Mʳ Thomas Swann her attorney where the said Little was presᵗ and the matter on both side publickly debated

Thereupon His Excellʸ (as Ordinary) with the advice of the Council declares the Administration by Mʳ Little obtained to be Illegal annulled and Void and that administration be granted to the said Elizᵃ as relect widow to yᵉ said pursuant to Law

By order of yᵉ Govʳ and council

ROBERT FORSTER D Secty

NORTH CAROLINA—ss

At a Council held at the Council Chamber in Edenton on the 22d of April Anno Dom 1731

Present

His Excellency Geo Burrington Esqʳ Govʳ &c

The Honble { William Smith John Bapᵗ Ashe } Esqᵐ Members of
{ Nathaniel Rice Edmond Porter } his Majesties
{ Robert Halton Corn Harnett } Council

Joseph Jenoure Esqʳ his Majesties Surveyʳ Genˡˡ of this Province representing to this Board that he has Sundry times demanded from Edwᵈ Moseley Esqʳ Late Surveyor Genˡ all papers relating to the said Office and that the said Moseley had not as yet delivered the same to him Praying the oppinion of this Board thereon which being considered of his Excellency the Govʳ with the advice of his Majesties Council doth order and direct that the said Edward Moseley Deliver up to yᵉ said Joseph Jenoure all papers and platts to the said surveyor Genˡ Office

28

belonging by to morrow morning by Ten of the Clock   His Excellency the Governour Cause his Majesties 47 Instruction to read wherein his Majesty is pleased to direct the Governour that he take Especial care that no Office or place whatsoever be Executed within this province but by Commission from his Majesty or by comission from his Excellency the Governour under the seal of yᵉ Colony Therefore the Governour with the advice & Consent of the Council was pleased to appoint the Honourable William Smith Esqʳ Treasurer of this Province in the room of Edward Mosely Esqʳ and that a Comission be prepared for the same accordingly

By order

ROBERT FORSTER Dep Secty

NORTH CAROLINA—ss.

At a Council held at the Council Chamber in Edenton the 23ᵈ day of Apˡ Anno Dom 1731

Present

His Excellency Geo Burrington Esqʳ Govʳ &c

Willᵐ Smith Robert Halton	
Nathaniel Rice Edmond Porter	Esqʳˢ Members of his
Joseph Jenoure Jnᵒ Dapᵗ Ashe	Majesties Council
Cornˢ Harnett	

Read the Petition of Isaac Hill Esqʳ setting forth that he having an Indian slave named George amongst the Tuskaroore Indians who (as he is Informed) detains ye said Indian slave from his service praying and ordeʳ may Issue from this Board Directed to Blount King of the sᵈ Tuskaroornes, requiring him to deliver up the sᵈ Indian slave to the sᵈ Hill which being Considered of his Excellency the Govʳ was pleased to order and direct that Mʳ Charlton the Indian Interpreter should as soon as posible repair to King Blounts Town and there demand the sᵈ slave from Blount & on the sᵈ King refusal of delivering up the said slave that then the sᵈ Interpreter is hereby directed to summons the said King Blount immediately to answer the same before his Excellency in Council

By order

ROBERT FORSTER D Secty

NORTH CAROLINA—ss

At a Council held at the Council Chamber in Edenton the 24 Day of April Anno Dom 1731

Present

His Excellency Geo Burrington Esqr Govr &c

the Honble { William Smith   Robert Halton } Esq^{rs} Members of
             Natha Rice   Edmond Porter   his Majesties
             Corn^s Harnett   Council.

Sir Richard Everard Bar^t Late Govr of this Province appeared and
prayed to have some Depositions agst John Lovick Esqr Late Secretary
and Edward Moseley Esqr Late Surveyor Genl in Suport of the Complaint made by the s^d Sir Richard Everard against the said Lovick and
Moseley to his Majesty. And the said Lovick and Moseley having Notice
to be present the said Moseley appeared but Mr Lovick came not thereupon Colonel William Harding Jones being called appeared and gave the
following Dep^o vizt

The Deposition of Colonel William Harding Jones being sworn on the
Holly Evangilist sayeth that about a Twelve month agoe being at the
house of Mr George Pollocks the said Pollock produced a blank patent
without number of acres mentioned nor sum in the purchase reciept mentioned which reciept to ye best of his remembrance was signed by M^r
Lovick Late Secty which patent was sealed and the said Deponant upon
veiwing the patent told M^r——that he might put what Quantity of Acres
he pleased into that patent wth ye s^d Pollock made no answer but smiled and
the s^d Depon^t further saith that he has paid Mr Little the Late Rec^r General the sum of £14 10 for the purchase of 475 acres of Land and that
in reciept given from the said rec^d General he mentioned only ye reciept
£9.10 and without mention of Quit Rent

Sworn to April 24th 1731   WILLIAM HARDG JONES.

The Deposition of Mr James Castellaw who being Sworn on the
Holly Evangelist saith that about a Twelve month agoe and since he
hath seen in the hands of Mr George Pollock four or five Blank Pattents
without any mention of the number of acres & Sealed with a seal which
he believed was the seal of the Colony and that on the back of which
patents reciept signed by John Lovick Esqr Late Secretary without any
sum Mentioned and that this Deponant was concerned with Mr Eubank
in the purchase of Two of them the Title of which Patents he believed
not to be good he perswaded Mr Eubanks to return the same to M^r
Pollock again accordingly took one of them Mr Eubanks paying the
said Pollock a pistole for the same as the said Eubanks told me who likewise said that he sold the other Pattent to John Green for sixty pounds
and further this Deponant saith not

JAMES CASTELLAW

The Deposition of Cullen Pollock Esq' who being sworn on the Holly Evangelist saith that he hath a blank pattent in his hands signed by most of the late Councellors & sealed with the seal of the Colony on the back of which pattent is a reciept for the purchase mony   And further this Deponant saith not

    Sworn to Ap' 24ᵗʰ 1731   CULLEN POLLOCK

The Blank pattent which I had from my Brother George Pollock and made oath concerning had 1,000 marked on the back of it and for that sume or Quantity of Land I had it of him   I Declare this on oath
                                    CULLEN POLLOCK

The Deposition of Thomas Jones Gent who being Sworn on the Holly Evangelists saith that he having an Imaginary survey in the month of June Last he produced the same to Mr Lovick who filled up a Patent for the said Land in August or September Last Dated in the year 1728 And further this Deponant saith not

                              THOMAS JONES

The Deposition of Doctor George Allynn who being sworn on the holly Evangelists saith that being in Company with a man Living in Rappahannock river in Verginia and Richard Everard who on some Discourse about Pattents, the said Vergiman produced a pattent for Lands in Bath County and the purchase money mentioned in said Pattent appeared to be but Eight pounds Currency of North Carolina tho he declared he had paid Eight pound odd in Verginia and that he together with Mr Vail was Evidence to his paving Two Guineas in part of said sum to Mr Little and this Deponant further saith that about six or seven months agoe being at Mr George Pollocks with Mr Thomas Jones who having Discourse with Mr Pollock on an Exchange of Lands the said Jones agreed to part with Two Thousand on Marrattock river valued at £200. for a Patent for Lands in haw oldfield which was Blank and a reciept on the back of said pattent for yᵉ Purchase money but by whome signed this Deponant remembers not & further that he has seen a great many blank patents without any number of acres mentioned therein with reciept on the backs of said pattent for the purchase money paid but the sum not expressed

    And further this Deponant saith not
    Sworn to april 24ᵗʰ 1731   GEORGE ALLYNN

The Deposition of Mr John Nairn who being sworn saith that about two years agoe he ran out some Land at wch time he saw the said Whitmal produce a pattent wch he took to be blank and that to ye best of His remembrance the number of acres was not incerted in said Pattent

And farther this Deponant saith not

Sworn to April 24th 1731   JOHN NAIRN

Sir Richard Everard appeared before his Excellency the Govr and Declared he had nothing to Charge Mr Moseley with

By order

ROBERT FORSTER D Secty

N̄ŏ CAROLINA—ss.

At a Council Chamber Held at the Council Chamber in Edenton the 26th day of April Anno Dom 1731

Present

His Excellency George Burrington Esqr Gov &c

The Honble { William Smith   Edward Porter   Esq^m Members
Joseph Jenoure   John Bap^t Ashe   of his
Robert Halton   Corn^l Harnett } Majesties Council

Ordered that Edward Moseley Esqr Late Surveyor General Do imediately give in a list of the names of the several dep^t Surveyors who acted under him while Surveyor General to ye Governour and Council and that he Do not presume to take any returns from the said Deputys from the Date hereof   By order

ROBERT FORSTER D Secty

NORTH CAROLINA—ss.

At a Council held at the Council Chamber in Edenton the first day of May Anno Dom 1731

Present

His Excellency George Burrington Esqr Govr &c

The Honble { William Smith   Edmond Porter   Esq^m Members
Nathaniel Rice   John Bap^t Ashe   of his
Robert Halton   Corn^l Harnett } Majesties Council

William Little Esqr Late rec^r General appeared and produced his accompts to the 29 of September 1729 & and prayed time for the Exhibiting his accounts from that time till his Excellency arrival it being objected that the acco^{ts} ought to have Extended no further than the 29th July 1729 when the King purchased of the Lords and thereon it being debated if the rents that year should be allowed & and accounted for by the said reciever General The matter was put to a vote and passed in the affirmative being the opinion of the Gov' and Council that the Rents accrewing that year should be allowed an accounted for by the said Rec' Gen' and his accompts stand accordingly to the 29th of September 1729 And thereupon William Smith Robert Halton and John Bap' Ashe were appointed a Committee to Examine the s' accompts

By order

ROBERT FORSTER D Secty

North Carolina—ss

At a Council held at the Council Chamber in Edenton the 4th day of May Anno Dom 1731

Present

His Excellency George Burrington Esq' Gov' &c

The Honble { William Smith　Edmond Porter } Esq'' Members
{ Nathaniel Rice　John Bap' Ashe } of his
{ Robert Halton　Corn' Harnett } Majesties Council

Sir Richard Everard Bar' late Gov' of this Province appeared again at this Board & Prayed to have forthwith Depositions taken for the support of his Complaints against John Lovick Esq' Late Secretary which was granted and accordingly Capt William Downing being first called appeared and disposed as followeth Viz'

The Deposition of Capt William Downing being first sworn on the Holly Evangelist Saith that he had seen a blank patent at M' Cullen Pollock without any Number of Acres incerted and a receipt on the back of the pattent for the purchase money without mention of the sum which receipt was signed by M' Little or Lovick & has heard of several blank pattents in the hands of people but does not know in whose possession they were or who told him of it the same being a General report

Sworn to y' 4th May 1731　　　　W DOWNING

The Deposition of M' Richard Russell being first sworn on the Holly Evangelist saith that some time agoe M' John Galland Brother in Law to M' Lovick Brought a blank Pattent down to Core sound (as he remembers) without mention of number of acres inserted and a reciept inserted on the back of said Pattent signed by M' Lovick and the Deponant not approving to have y' s' Pattent filled up but at y' Secretarys office he sent y' same up to y' said office & had the patent perfected

And further this Deponant saith not

RICHARD RUSSELL

Doctor George Allynn sworn on y* Holly Evangelist saith that a Messenger Came from Coll. William Read y* 12ᵗʰ of December 1728 who informed him that the said Read was Dangerously ill in so much that his life was dispaired of and that he had been two dayes in coming to him and that he the Deponant sat off from Edenton the 13ᵗʰ of the same month to visitt the said Read and arrived at the said Reeds Plantation the same night when Mrs Reed (wife of the said Colonel Reed) told this Deponant that her husband Dyed the day before he arrived & was put in the Ground & she the said Mrs Reed and one Banks then present further told this Deponant that the said Deᶜᵉᵈ was taken Speeckles and continued so till he dyed

And further this Deponent saith not
Sworn to May the 4ᵗʰ 1731   GEORGE ALLYNN

The Deposition of Colonel Thomas Swann being first sworn on the Holly Evangelist saith that to y* best of his knowledge Col William Reed one of the members of the late Council dyed in the night between the Eleventh and Twelfth of December 1728, as he was Informed

And further this Deponent saith not
Sworn May the 6ᵗʰ 1731   THOMAS SWANN
           By order
           ROBERT FORSTER D Secty

NORTH CAROLINA—ss

At a Council held at the Council Chamber in Edenton the 8ᵗʰ Day of May Anno Dom 1731

Present

His Excellency Geo Burrington Esqʳ Govʳ &c

Y* honble { William Smith   Edward Porter } Esqʳ Members
       { Nathaniel Rice   John Bapᵗ Ashe }   of his
       { Cornˢ Harnett   Robert Halton } Majesties Council.

Ordered that a Comission of the Peace Issue directed to Henry Guston James Millekin William Kinchen William Latimer George Winn Arthur Williams John Holbrook John Speir Phillip Walston Needham Bryant Doctor John Bryan John Soan John Dew John Harrord Johnn John Edward of Roanoke & John Hardy Gent Constituting and appointing them Justice of the peace for y* precinct of Bertie

           By order
           ROBERT FORSTER D Secty

NORTH CAROLINA—ss.

At a Council held at the Council Chamber in Edenton the 12th day of May Anno Domini 1731

Present

His Excellency Geo Burrington Esqr Govr &c

the Honble { William Smith   Edmond Porter   Esqrs Members
 Robert Halton   John Bapt Ashe   of his
 Conr Harnett   Majesties Council }

To his Excellency George Burrington Esqr Capt General Governor Comander in Chief & Admiral of ye said Province

The Complaint of William Little in behalf of himself and other Executors of Colonel Harvey and for divers other persons Late sufferers of the Court of Admiralty here

Your Excellency having been pleased in Council to signify and instruction from his Majesty to have the complaint of any person injured here lately by the oppression of those in the Aministration of Justice the said Complaints beg Leave to lay before you the proceedings of Edmond Porter Esqr Judge of the admiralty and others under him who refusing and disregarding Prohibitions the usual remedy in such cases hath divested the Subjects of the Benifit of the common Law which is Every Englishmans birth right & an Incroachment on the rights & Libertys of the subject in subversion of Justice and in Violation of ye Laws of the Realm for barely suggesting of which some have been others severely and censured in a very high manner contrary to the Equitable proceedings of all Courts of Justice where every man without fear dread ought to have free Liberty to make his Defence the sd Judge pretending such prohibitions to have been a Contempt to his court as hath been pleased to stile it not Considering the necessity there was for some stop to have been put to such violent & Illegall proceedings & indeed as it hath been ruled at Law prohibitions are not discretionary or ad Libitum but ex Merito Justina and the denying them is said to be denying the benefitt of the Common Law Every Englishmans birth right & the reason is Manifestly Given in the books where its said

If there be but probable cause it must be granted ex Debite Justicca for if granted where it ought Not the other party Remedy by consultation but if denyed whereto be granted the party is without remedy And the Statutes of Richd the Second and other doth most fully restrain the Admiralty from Intermedling with any thing Done or Riseing within the bodies Counties by Land or water Indeed Disputes have arisen on the Construction of those Statutes and the Extent of the admiralty Juris-

diction but your Comp[s] concieve when the Late proceedings & Decrees
of this Court are fully represented they will appear without y[e] Least
colour of excuse and they bare re   of them they think without any
reflection made will sufficiently the oppressions & Grievous injuries people have sustained thereby A plain narrative of which they now Humbly begg Leave to offer

1 The first case in that Court after Judge Porters arrival was Trotter
V Northy for 1516 bill money not of the Value of three shillings sterling & was for a Tavern Score at an ordinary in Edenton and tho a
prohibition was obtained thereon it was not regarded by the s[d] Judge
who proceeded to decree the Debt and costs and taxed the costs to about
Twelve pounds or upward & the poor man was put into Gaol upon it in
Execution while a small Vessell he was Master of lay Exposed all the
while the voyage and Business hindred and Chiefly by means of this and
the next suit the said Northy suffered so much that at last he broake and
went of Laving a poor family in a very helpless condition

2 The next suit was Allyn v Northy Layd for Damages aledged in
the Libil it self to be an agreement at York river in Verginia & so infra
corpus comilatus and the Def[t] too tendered his oath which if admitted
must have discharged him but all did not avail he was Condemned &
Exorbitant fees Taxed on him and he was Committed to Close prison in
Execution tho there was a prohibition granted

3 Another affair in the said Court was concerning a Ship from Guina
cast away at Curratuck belonging to some Merchants in Bristol the Master was Drowned but some of the men saved & Goods & effects to a very
great Value which were seized and Confiscated by the said Judge &
officers Except a small matter allowed one or two of the sailors was
kept by the said Judge and his officers and tho the act of Parliament
requires in such cases that the Collectors take care of such Wrecked
Goods which no way belong to the Admiralty Judge yet the Collector
was not permitted to Intermedle therewith

4 Another case was between Sir Richard Everard And Christopher
Gale Esq[r] the Cheif Justice who indeed by the priviledge of his ought to
have been exempt from said Court the suit was for money lent at Land
as the very Libell aledged only was said to be borrowed to Pay a passage
from New Yorke which was all that had any Colour of Marine Neature
in it .a prohibition was thereon obtained but disregarded & decree past
for the Debt and Excesive costs taxed thereon and notwithstanding an
appeal made yet Execution was granted and your Compl[s] further alledge
that the said Christo[r] Gale which Chief Justice notwithstanding the

priviolidge of his office was by an admiralty Warrant from said Porter made a prisoner and held in Custody in a most Violent and Illegal manner

5 Another case in that court was Brought By a poor mariner belonging to a Vessell cast away that sued for his wages but the Master being advise that the wages were due there being effects saved & that the master was cognizable in Admiarlty Comply'd with matter but the sailor first went to the Register to know the Charges who told him it was matter these having no court held on it upon which was Compromised & the Sailor discharged the Master and told the Register to dismiss the suit but afterwards Judge Porter refused to permitt it to be so dismissed Saying his Court should not be made a   of and held his court notwithstanding & Condemned y°   for not prosecuting his suit in excessive fees & charges & the the sailor being poor and unable to pay it to save himself from being thrown into Goal thereon was forced to sell himself into servitude to discharge the matter

6 Another affair in Admiralty was at Port Beaufort where the proceeding were so Violent and Arbitratory that it hath been so deservedly Exclaimed against in other countrys three Vessells and their Cargoes were seized & prosecuted tho not the Fraud or Coulor of it appeared the Matter was there was Some Dispute between two persons about the Naval office the old Officer refuseing on some pretention to deliver up the office till further orders from the Governour Still Continued to act and the new Officer Claimed it the Masters who as it appeared too were Ignorant of the matter on their Arrival Entered with the old officer who still continued acting in the office upon a consultation with the then Governour Sir Richard Everard & Judge Porter the said Vessells and Cargoes were seized and Libelled on the statute 15th Charles IId that forfeits Vessells and Cargoes if the master does not Enter a Report or Manifest of his Cargoe with the Naval Officer on Tryall notwithstanding all the disadwenture the master were under the proceeding appeared so Barefaced & not the Least colour of Fraud in them that the Judge acquitted the Vessells that were seized which if the act was broak ought to have been Condemned & an Injuries was done to the King in acquitting them & if the act was not broake there was no offence Committed and the Libell should have been dismissed & the parties acquitted from any costs but the masters were Condemned in the most excessive costs and Charges amounting to several hundred pounds to satisfye which their cargoes nay their sail and rigging were siezed & exposed to sale which wholey disposed their Voyages and utterly ruined some of them

to the exceeding great discouragement of Trade & Great Complaints was made thereof from the owners of New England to the Government here and the matter in the General Assembly was voted a great Geivance & remonstrated In an adress to the Governour as such for some redress but thro the Indolence or favour of Sir Richard Everard then Gov' the matter was husht and no remedy cou'd ever be obtained

7 Another affair in Admiralty was at Bath Town on as frivilous pretence on West for Entering as was pretended with the wrong officer on which the man was condemned and thrown in Goal & obliged to pay seventy pounds to be released & coming to Edenton thereon for redress was unfortunately drowned.

8 Another Case before the Judge was between Cook and Phelpson on agreement at Core sound to pilot a Shallop to an Inlett some little distance in the same precinct and the vessell was Lost (tho no fault appeared in the Dep' nether) and on suggesting that the contract made at Land a prohibition was granted but disregard and the Defendant condemned in Damages & Great cost Committed to Goal in Execution

9 Another affair in said Court was concering a Boat belonging to James Trotter of Edenton the Judge under some slight pretence that she belong' to the Bristol man cast away mentioned in the third Article foregoing tho in truth it was not so) ordered his Marshall to seize her which he did & sold her without any contestation of Title permitted to the said Trotte' no Claim was made by him who wholey Lost the vessel thereby

10 The next case before the said Judge was the Famous case against Judge Harvey Exec'' who was formerly Judge of the Court of Admiralty here It would be too tedious to repeat y' whole proceeding here which were carryed on in unparelled manner there was three distinct suits made of it for what Reason is very obvious when it is considered what y' fees amounted to in every case according to the method in that Court used tho it is plain no new suit at all ought to have been Instituted therein if there had been occasion for any Inquiry in affair The matter was the collector at Bath some years ago had seized some goods of one Capt Phippen for w'' he cou' pro' no Cocketts (tho the collector as was then offered to be made appear told the master he would pass the matter by for a peice of Calico) a suite was brought for the affair before Judge Harvey & on hearing the master alledged some accident and prayed time to produce some fresh certificates whereupon the Judge ordered the goods to be appraised and delivered the owner on his Giving security in a limited time to return cocketts on Deposit the money to be forfeited in case of failure of the Goods appraised at Fifty pounds which was Called starling and the money was allowed

by the Judge to be deposited at 50 $\mathcal{P}$ cent in Bills agreeable to y^e Laws of the Country as in all Bills Bonds &c   Sterling were to be paid & the master finding it would be a great Charge to send for fresh Cirtificates or thro neglect failed in the time Limitted to produce them and the money deposited was according to the decree of the court forfeited & Distributed as the Law Directs so the matter rested for some years till stirred by Judge Porter who writt to Mr Ottvall to forward the matter which at first was pretended to be only concerning the Informers part there being some private dispute about it between the colector and the attorney that prosecuted it who by agreement with the collector was made Informer and prosecutor in the original suite by the thing grew upon hand till at length three found suites were made of it against the Executors of Judge Harvey $dec\overline{e}d$ & against William Little Agent therein pretending Judge Harvey had done amiss in suffering the money to be paid at 50 $\mathcal{P}$ cent & that the said agent had done amiss in recieving and paying it so tho by order of the court & tho it was subjected that if Judge Harvey had carryed in his Decree any person Grieved might have appealed & that Judge Porter the present Judge was not supreme Judge to reverse the Decrees of the former Judge much Less could he subject his Estate to Damages about it   Especially since it was appearent Judge Harvey recieved nothing of it nor any gainer by but on acted Judicially therein and the affair properly cognizable before him and in behalf of said Little it was objected that he $rec\overline{e}d$ and payed by order of court and cou'd be Lyable for no more that he $rec\overline{e}d$ and it was farther objected too that regularly no new seuts should have been brought upon it only the former parties cited in an examination & Enquiry duly made if the former decree had been done and Executed if not then to have complyd with and so was Judge Porter from home on his   of the affair Directed to have proceeded upon it but notwithstanding all this Judge Porter proceeded upon several Extraordinary decrees to condemn Judge Harvey Estate in Damages and costs amounting to several hundred pounds to make good out of his Estate what Judge Porter was pleased to Imagine Judge Harvey ought to have decreed   and the said Little was condemned great sums to make good what Judge Porter was pleased to Imagine s^d Little ought to have $rec\overline{e}d$ tho he both rec'd & p^d according to Judge Harveys order whose estate too at the same time is Condemned for making the order so & tho nothing is Plainer than that the said Little could be accountable for no more than he recieved by the courts order that appointed him Agent therein

From these decrees an appeal was made to his Majestys Councill &
Security offered but it was denyed by the s⁴ Judge tho in such cases
appeal from the plantations can   to his Majesty because they are not
cognizable before yᵉ Judge of the high court of admiralty in England
Seizure & forfeitures on the acts of Trade being Tryable at Common
Law only & are there brought in the Exchequer but in the plantations by
a special act of parliament are made Triable in the courts of Admiralty in
the plantations but that give the court of Admiralty in England no jurisdiction of it & Therefore it is that all appeals in such cases from the
courts of admiralty in the plantations are to the King in Councill also
and on suggesting all these Extrajudicial proceedings prohibition was
obtained but wholey disregarded & Execution made out against the said
Littles Estate, & his Estate seized thereon which was afterwards Replu-
reict & on Tryal at Common Law discharged) the Execution in Admiralty after such appeal interposed and prohibition to yᵉ Judge being
Deemed Null and void, whereupon the said Judge Porter afterwards
Granted another Execution for the very same matter matter against The
said Little Body who was violently taken into custody & his House
attempted to be broak open and he to save himself from Goal was compelled to pay the very great sum of money which the Porter recieved
himself as can be proved and as farter instance of the said Judges unjust
and partial proceedings the complainants Alledge that said William Little haveing in the suit aforesaid Excepted against the said Porters being
Judge in his coure for the open and known Enmity the said Judge bore
him and accordingly put in his plea Recusation & tho it was drawn in
the very form and manner Directed in the civill Law books which in
such cases allways allow it a sufficient   Yet the said Little was by
the said Judge very harshly Treated for it & fined the sum of one hundred pounds & some time after notwithstanding there was prohibition &
an appeal two for the decrees yet the said Judge before any Admonition
given which the course of those courts require made out Execution
against the said Littles Body upon it who was taken unto custody by the
Marshall who by the Judges Express orders attempted to Dragg the said
Little out of his sick Bed where to appear and he Lay dying not able to
get out of his Bed but as helpt which in human action was lookt only
all as a Shocking instance of the Judges Malice and Barbarity proceedings tho it sufficiently showed what reason the said Little had to make
his accusation against him.

And further the said Complainants alledge that in the said suite they
applyed to the Register for copies of the said Decrees they were told by

him he had them not but that the Judge had Carryed them not but that the Judge had Carryed them out of Town to correct & amend & some days after the said Judge having returned them to the Register he then refused to sign copies of them alledging they had been altered & he could not on oath cirtify them for Copies of the Decrees passed in Court so the Def' could get no copy of them

And the said Complainant alledgist complaint they have great Reason to bel've and Give Sufficient grounds for it that the said Judge hath often promoted and forwarded suits brought before him and hath been assisting in Drawing Libels if not Wholly Drawn by him who some time agoe gave out that he had Elleven Libels ready on proper Occation which were Understood to be Chiefly against such as he had known hatred and Enmity too and the said Judge having tho without any foundation as the Compl⁸ believe Informed the Hon¹¹ the Commission of his Majesties Customs that there was in this Country great frauds and concealments of the Kings monies he was more Upon by them Impowered to Recover the same at his own court on and agreement an agreement as the Com¹ᵗᵉ has been informed to have part of what should be Recovered and there upon the said Porter hath Caused suits to be brought against persons before himselfe and so was Judge Impropera Causa being therein both Judge and party which is Manifestly Unjust

11 Accordingly suit was brought before him in the Kings name against Christo' Gale Esq' about a Bark Cast away at Core sound many years agoe and tho suit were brought in Admiralty in the time of it to condemn her for the King and the Decree was against it and the said Gale appointed one the agents to Keep the Effects saved for the owners after Salvadge and wadges paid which Effects fell much short of Yet now without the least real reason suits is brought in the Kings name and great Vexations and trouble Given the Def' for which it being Craftily Done in the Kings name no Cost Could be obtained for time

The next suit in the said Court was brought by Sir Richard Everard against David Osheal and Bond entered into at Edenton as security for the faithfull Discharge of a Naval office which being so Clearly out of the Admiraltys Jurisdiction a prohibition was granted which was not only Disregarded as Usuall but it was deemed a Contempt to the Court to offer and the said David was fined £50 and Imediately by the Judges Order Draged away to the Common Goale in a verry rough manner which was broke open on the occation And with the Judges assistance the said David was thrust in and another Lock put on and he Lock up and kept till weary of so Noisome a place the Gent was compelled to pay the money to be Discharged which the Judge also recieved himself

Another suit in Admiralty was brought in the name of the King on the forementioned pretext of Monies Due to the crown Concealed against William Little for the Kings third of a small Seizure made at Bath Eight or Ten Years agoe when the said Little was appointed agent and the Condemnation money came into his hands and tho it appeared by Accounts that the Kings third amounted to but £39:7 bill money and the said Little offered the Judge a full Discharge from the collector for the Kings part and tho no prosecute appeared yet the said Judge would retain the suite and compelld the Def' to give Baile to the sum of £600 this Currency and tho it was Urged that no Baile Shoold be required nor no new suite Indeed Instituted only the partie Cited to shew and that such Excessive Bail was againts Magna Charta and the Laws and Liberties of an English Subject it did not availe the Judge replyd if the Def' was Cleare the Baile Could not be no harme not Considering how unjust it is to be Deemed Exorbitant Baile and how Difficult it might be for the Deffendant to find such Lardge Security which if he did not he must have gone to Goale

12 Another Suite also was brought against the said Little who being reciever of the Tenth of the fishery had recieved a small Quantity of Oyle in Certain Contracts made at Land with the Whalers but being so Notoriously wrong in the matter and since the present settlement and support of the Lawes finding a prohibition Coming he thought fit to Dismiss the suite himself

13 the Last prosecution in his Court was against the saide Little and William Mackie Esq'' provost Marshall and Robert Foster Gent the Court, the said Little finding prohibition being Disregarded and no stop to be put to the said Judges Arbitrary proceedings for the Injurys done them and for the monnies so Unjustly Extorted from them brought action at Common Law against the said and his Marshall upon which these prosecutions were brought in Admiralty Viz' against the saide Little for Ofering to comence seuites and against the Clerk of the Common Law Court for Granting process and the Marshall for serving them In high Contempt of his court as the Judge was pleased to Call it which Suites has been Drapt to such Unheard of proceeding while the reignes of Govem' were so loose in the late times caused an uncomon ferment among the people now knowing where these Violencies would end one thing more Your Comp''' beg leave to observe that altho the admiralty fees are here stated by Law and verry high too Yet the said Judge without any regard to them or having any Instructions or Lawfull warrants

232 COLONIAL RECORDS.

Arbitrarily assumed to Impose what costs he pleases and hath Constantly
Done it in a very Exhorbitant manner and as appears by aforegoing
Case above It is Teen time more than the Debt

May it please your Excelly Your compl^ts having now gone there with
the Narrative of the Cases into ye Court that they avoid making any
Reflections on them or giving those terms the proceeding really deserve
& would be natural on such occasions being satisfied they must appear so
Monstose that they rely upon Representing the bare facts but beg leave
only to make this observation that these are all the cases that have ever
been before the said Judge and Unhappily for the Judge it is remarkable that in Every one of them he hath most apparently proceeded with
partiality and Prejudice or Extrajudicialty in an arbitrary and unlawfull manner in oppression of the subject and manifest Preversion of the
Justice whereby your complt and divers others have been greviously
Injured which hath Induced them to lay the Complaint before your
Excelly to whom the matter in most humble manner is submitted humbly
praying that the said Judge may thereon be suspended or the matter be
represented & and such course taken as your Excelly in Great Wisdom
shall thereon think Just and proper   Wm LITTLE as Sup

NORTH CAROLINA—ss

At a council held at the Council Chamber in Edenton the 14th day of
May Anno Domini 1731
                        Present
            His Excelly George Burrington Esqr Govr &c
              ⎧ William Smith   Edm^d Porter ⎫ Esq^rs Members
the Honoble ⎨ Robt Halton   Jno Bap^t Ashe ⎬   of His
              ⎩   Corn^s Harnett   ⎭ Majestie Council

His Exce^lly the Governor was pleased to deliver a paper directed to
this Board in the ffollowing words Viz^t

GENT OF THE COUNCIL

Some debates arising yesterday at the Board upon Enquiry of the
affair of the late councils Complaint against Sir Richard Everard Bar^t
late Govr pursuant to his Majesties Instructions which I think were
fully clear^d up and being willing to have those matter then debated aper-
tained in such manner as I may before I proceed further know you sentiments therein I desire your oppinion and answer in writting to the
following Question if his Majesty Commands one by an Instruction to Enquire into any affair or if any thing comes before me to be

Enquired into for his majesties service & for my better direction therein
I lay the same before the Council Whether as it is their Duty to advise
me in all affair of Governm' the Council is not oblidged in such Cases
to give me their Oppinion & altho the affair be directed to me only and
the council not mentioned   2ᵈ— this affair of Sir Richard Everard
being only an Enquiry in order to form a prosecution thereon if it shall
be found Necessary I desire Your oppinion Wheither any Persons being
Complᵗ is a Sufficient objection against their Evidence being taken to
prove any matters they have Informed on their own knowledge

GEORGE BURRINGTON

NORTH CAROLINA—ss

At a council held at the Council Chamber in Edenton yᵉ 15ᵗʰ day of
May Anno Domini 1731

Present

His Excellency Geo Burrington Esqʳ Govʳ &c

the Honoble { Will Smith   Edmᵈ Porter } Esqⁿ Members
            { Robt Halton   Joⁿ Bap Ashe } of his Majesties
            { Cornˢ Harnett   } Council

His Exceˡˡʸ the Govʳ delivered the following paper to the Board Viz'

GENT OF THE COUNCIL

Upon a Message from the Lower house Last Tuesday Concerning
assistant Judges Seemed the oppinion of the upper House on perusing
the Cheif Justices Warrent that he had by it the sole power of holding
the General Court but upon Reading my Commission and the Eight
Instruction I see his Majesty has directed me to appoint Assistant Judges
which Instruction I now lay before you and your opinion upon the following Queries · 1 Whether assistant Judges appointed pursuant to
that Instruction have not power as such to give Judgment in all Cases
as Judges in Great Brittian do? 2. Whether the allowing the Chief Justice to be Sole Judge would not Establishing a common Law Court contrary to the Constitution of the English Law and against the meaning
of his Majesties Eight Instructions to me and in the Choice and Nomination of the Members of our said Council as also the Chief officers
Judges Assistants Justices and Sherriffs you are always to take Care that
they be men of good life and well effected to our Government & of good
Estates and abilities and not necessitous persons   the Eight Instructions
near the Meddle of my Comission are these word following

And we do hereby Impower and authorize you to constitute and
appoint Judges and in Cases Requisite Comisioners of Oyer & Terminer

30   GEORGE BURRINGTON

NORTH CAROLINA—ss.

At a Council held at the Council Chamber in Edenton the 18ᵗʰ Day of May Anno Domini 1731

Present

His Excell⁷ George Burrington Esq' Gov' &c

the Honble { William Smith   Edmᵈ Porter   }   Esq' Members
{ Rob' Halton   Joⁿ Bap' Ashe   }   of his
{   Corn' Harnett   }   Majesties Council

Ordered that a comission of the Peace Issue for the the Precinct of Curratuck Directed to Tho' Taylor Sen' John Etheridge John Woodhouse John Mann Moses Linton Henry White Francis Morse Ralf Mathan Tho' Robbs John Martin Richard Hodges and Tho' Davis Gent Constituting and appointing them Justices of the Peace for and within the said Precinct

Ordered that a New Commission of the Peace issue for the Prᶜinct of Perquimons Directed to Machrora Scarborough Richard Sanderson Jun Ezeakiel Maudlin John Wiat Samuel Swann Zebulon Clayton Jacob Perry James Sumner James Norfleet Thos Docton Thomas Norcom Thomas Sprieght and Moses Sprieght Gen' Constituting and appointing them Justices of them Justices of the Peace for and within said Prᶜinct

Ordered that a New Commission of the Peace Issue for the Prᶜinct of Pasquetank Directed to John Palin Esq' John Solley David Bailey Charles West George Linnington Simon Bryan Thomas Palin John Boyd Nath' Hall Gabreal Burnham John Relph Abell Ross Joseph Reading James Pritchard Gent Constituting and appointing them Justices of the Peace for and within said precinct

The Council desiring the Gov' they may be paid as usual Ten shilling a day paper money of this Province Each for their attendance During the time the Assembly were sitting pursuant to the Resolves of Both Houses the same being usual and Customary and also that their Demands may be Entred upon the Council Journal to which Request the Gov' answered that he agreed the Request or Demand afore Said should be Entred in the Council Book but would sign no Warrent for the payments of either the Council or house of Burgesses until he had Recieved Orders from the Lord of Trade and plantations.

John Bap' Ashe Esq' delivered in the two following Papers to His Excell⁷ the Gov' and pray'd the same might be Entered in the Council Journal which papers are these words Viz'

To His Excelly the Govr

MAY IT PEASE YOUR EXCELLY

In answer to the Query put by you relating to the bill of Ascertaining officers Fees and payments of Quit rents I say

As it is known and Confesed by all people that there is not Gold or silver Coin Enough in the Country to answer ye above one Tenth part of the payments of Rents

I am of oppinion that the Assembly have Endeavoured to answer his Majesties Intention as near as may be in proposing something as are Equivolent & if I am rightly Informed that Tobacco in Verginia at ten shillings ℔ Hundred Equivolent to there Currency of their Tobacco here & I take Eleven shillings ℔ Hundred will appear to be an equivolent to proclamation Money being nearest as ten to Eleven and if and if a Clause be incerted in such act declaring that it shall not take Effect as to the Rents His Majesty be pleased to confirm or approve the same   I think the King can recieve no prejudice thereby and what makes me propose such a Method is that provission might be immediately made for officers Fees & registering of Rents His Majesty having in his nineteenth Instruction directed that all those Matters should be Included in one and the same act

JOHN BAP^t ASHE

MAY IT PLEASE YOUR EXCELLY

Having this prepared at the Day appointed for the Consideration of your Excellys Query to which it is an answer & your Excelly before putting it in prorogued the Assembly I not withstanding prefer it to shew your Excelly I would in the least be backward in Complying with any of your Excellys Comand

JOHN BAP^t ASHE

To His Excelly the Govr &c

In answer to the paper put into the Council by your Excelly relating to debates which had arisen at the council Board on the Enquiry of the affair of the Late Councils Complaint against Sir Richard Everard Bar^t Govr which you say were not fully Cleared I beg leave in order to put that matter in a Clear light to recite it just as it happened some of the Council observing His Majesty in his Instruction to your Excelly relating to that affair had stiled both sides parties and (as it were) seems to have Directed that their Respective allegations should have been supported by Witnesses ordering that they should have free Liberty to

Examine Witnesses Observing Likewise that Sir Richard Everard Bart
had not Offered his own Evidence to support his charge against any of
the council observing moreover the great heat and Animosity which
seemed to be between both parties doubted Whether they mought be
admitted as Evidences to support their own Charge upon this your
Excelly was pleased in very Express & Emphatical Terms to declare
you are resolved to admit them and immediately thereon Demanded the
oppinion of the Council wither these should be admitted as Evidence this
with due submission be it spoken I did not look as a becoming Treatment
of his Majesties Council from the Govr and therefore as you had in so
positive a manner given your Resolution I then forbore giving my oppinion in which I hope I transgressed not the Rules of good manners and
all was out of my Duty and now in answer to your first Question without presuming to Determine what his Majestys Council is obliged to do
I assure your Excelly that for my part in all affair of Government
wherein I ought and shall be consulted I shall out of the great Loyalty
I bear to his Majesty's Shew a great Readiness in giving my oppinion or
Indeed of doing whatever else in me lyes which may conduce to His
Majesties Service

As to your second Question I beg leave to refer your Excelly to what I
have said before in Relation to the observation on his Majesty's Instructions which If it be not thought of sufficient weight as the Question
Seems as stated by your Excelly to be a point of Law and Indeed the
Gent of the late Council having desired Council to be heard on it I beg
leave to suspend my Judgement till (by hearing what their Council shall
offer to maintain That their own Evidence will be sufficient to support
their allegation) I shall be better Informed I beleive indeed on a Criminal prosecution an Informer may be admitted as an Evidence for the
King but then in such the Crime & it nature ought (as I take it) to be
precisly and Expresly alledged and set forth

                                        JNO BAPt ASHE

William Smith Edmond Porter Jno Bapt Ashe and Cornelius Harnett
Esqrs delivered the following paper To His Excelly & prayed the same
might be entered in the Council Journal which was in these words Vizt

To His Excelly the Governour &c

We are surprised that Instead of the usual method of openly debating
by word of mouth in Council and after debate of entering resolutions
your Excelly is fallen only into this of only stating Questions in writing

and Demanding answers thereon   What lead us to take notice of this is that your Excell[y] having been of the same oppinion with us in this case relating to the Message from the Lower House of Assembly Concerning the assistance as will appear by the answer to the said message as you now have   if you have altered you oppinion perhaps on hearing argument used by you which may have moved you we might be convinced and Retract with your Excell[y] But since it is your pleasure we submit to this Method

And in answer to your first Question after premising that in his Majesties Eight Instruction there is no mention made of Assistant Judges but only of assistants (not saying what Assistants) and that we think it with submission improperly said assistants Judges Appointed pursuant to that Instruction because that Instruction directs not nor Comands the appointment of Assitants but only supposing it prescribes realy to be observed in Choosing fitt persons for that among other offices So that no Inferrence Can be made from thence but of those being (and that only by Implication) none of their power therefore till we are better Informed what is their Power   we Think we cannot pretend to Determine whither it is Equal in all cases to that of Judges (not saying what Judges) in Great Brittain.

But perhaps your Excelly may Object to us that we (by Implication at least) acknowledge their being or that they may be & may ask what then is their power or use to obiate which we answer to Inform & advise if in the Chief Justices or the Supream Courts) as we conceive and not to adjudge and in this sence we believe the word assistant to be taken so the masters in chancery are styled assistants to the Chancellor

As to your Excellys Second Question we say that we find that his majesty in his Warrant for that purpose Orders and Directs that Letters pattants be passed Constituting and appointing W[illia]m Smith Esq[r] Chief Justice of this Province with full power & authority to hold the Supream Courts of Jyndicator &c   Now we beg your Exce[lly] to give us leave to ask Whither there is a power greater than a full power & Authority requisite to hold Such Courts   No to this whole Query we answer therfore negatively because we are of Oppinion such Establishment is not Contrary to the Constitution to the Constitution of the English Laws nor Indeed to his Majesties 8th Instruction

But had our Oppinion been otherwise we ought Rather Modestly & Cautiously to have represented it to his Majesty than to have reflected on his Justice by asserting it in such a manner as an affirmative answer to this Queery (it should seem) would lead us to   As to the paragraph recited out of your Excellys Comission We beg leave to say that we Cannot See how that is applicable to the present case because there may be Other courts and Judges whose Authorities Interfere not with that of the Chief Justice & his Or the Supream Courts & that such may be appointed I beleive none has Denyed nor Indeed do we deny but Assistants may be in his or the Supream Courts with their proper power but we think we have hitherto found no Sufficient Reason to Remove us recede from the answer we gave to the Message of the Assembly Viz.ᵗ

That the assistants had not a Judicial power

> WILLIAM SMITH
> EDM⁴ PORTER
> JNO BAPᵗ ASHE
> CORNELIUS HARNETT

Mr Chief Justice Smith deliv⁴ to His Excelly at the Council Board the following paper which he Desired might be Entered on the Council Journal which was in these word Viz.ᵗ

To His Excelly the Govʳ

Since your Excelly has been pleased to demand an answer in writing to two Queeries preposed to us by your Excelly I with great Chearfullness Embrace the oppertunity to Declare my Sentiments which hitherto I have been forced to conceal being Deterr⁴ therefrom by the Displeasure of your Excelly whenever I was so unhappy as to Differ in oppinion from you I cannot but think yᵉ Qeeries proposed by you Excelly to be very Extraordinary at this time seeing that after the whole Council very much Doubted whither the evidence of the Gent of the Late Council ought to be taken in their Own behalf your Excelly was pleased to declare that you was Bound in Honour and Consience to take their Evidence so that with due submission this Queery seems to be unnecessary

In answer to your second Queery I humbly conceive that His Majesty by his Instruction Calls both Sides parties & by his Directing Each partie to Examine Witnesses it may easly be Imagined that his Majesty expected that they should support their charge by other Evidence than their own It is very unaccountable that the Gent. of the Late Council should have nobody but themselves to make out a Charge in there are several things that one would think must have been known to many Others and by their praying that it might be put off till the return of Mʳ Gale when it is very much to be doubted whither he will ever return & when it is well known that Sir Richard Everard pretends to leave this Province within a few days Seems to make the Charge without any foundation & to be only the Effect of personal resentment without any View to the service of his Majesty or the Interest of this Province

These may it please your Excelly are my humble Sentiments and I have no Other End than to do my Duty in my Station So I never shall be lead into arbitrary and Illegal measures through any Temptations of Fear or Interest

WILLIAM SMITH

Adjourned till tomorrow morning 9 of the Clock

NORTH CAROLINA—ss.

At a Council held at the Council Chamber in Edenton the 20ᵗʰ Day of May Anno Domini 1731

Present

His Excelly George Burrington Esqʳ Govʳ &c

the Honble { William Smith Robᵗ Halton } Esqˢ Members of His { Jos Jenoure Cornˢ Harnett } Majesties Council

John Montgomery Esqʳ produced to this Board His Majesties Warrant under his sign manuel directing that Letters pattents Issue under the seal of this Province Constituting & appointing him the said John Montgomery Attorney General therein

Ordered that Lˢ pattent Issue for the same

Mʳ Chief Justice Smith declaring that there was not a Council Sufficient to do business the Govʳ in answer thereto Acquainted the Board that he yesterday morning directed the Marshall to summons all the members of Council and the Marshall being called acquainted the Board that he Summoned Mʳ Smith Mʳ Jenoure Mʳ Halton Mʳ Porter Mʳ Ashe and Mʳ Harnett which (Except Mʳ Secty Ric⁰ who was gone to South Carolina) are all the members as yet Qualified to attend the Govʳ in council this day at nine of the Clock in the forenoon

Mʳ Chief Justice Smith resum'd his place as a member of his Majesties Council for this Province

His Excelly the Govʳ Returned and answer to the paper given in at this Board the 18ᵗʰ Instance by Mʳ Chief Justice Smith in these words Vizᵗ

Mʳ CHIEF JUSTICE

the King having Comanded me to Enquire in to the Complaints made to his Majesty by the late Council against Sir Richard Everard late Govʳ

and by Sir Richard to the Duke of Newcastle against several members of
the then Council I was to proceed therein with the utmost care & Caution and having and having had your Cheerfull assistance in taking
Depositions on Sir Richard Complaint against the members of the
former Council I expected the same readiness upon Enquiring into the
Complaint against Sir Richard in which are some things that concern his
Majesty's Person & Dignity & for my better Guidence in so nice an
affair I was desirous in several matters to have the advice of the Council
but found so much warmth in some and so much backwardness In others
that Induced me to put two short and plain Queeries to the Council that
required only as short plain & Direct an answer   but Instead of Mr Cheif
Justice has in a long paper flew of from the plain Matter Stating it Different from the Questions I put & wide of the purpose you maketh doubt
to be as you word it whither the Evidence of the late Council ought to
be taken in their own behalf tho it is manifest the enquiry is in behalf of
the King   & having once got out of the path you go on further in the
same way and say his Majesty nameth both sides Parties and would inferr
from thence that these Genˡ in their Information are parties in it as tho
the Enquiry is to be carr'd on by order of the King in their behalf   is
the Cheif Justice in earnest in this   His Majestys Instruction is to make
Enquiry into the Complˢ and if found needfull to make a prosecution on
it & I dare say the Chief Justice will not deny to admitt those Genˡ that
Informed or Complained against Sir Richard to be Evidences for the
King in Case prosecution is Ordered   pray then Mr Chief Justice how
can I fully Enquire If there be sufficient grounds or not for a Prosecution if I may not have the same Evidence that may be given on the prosecution & as the prosecution if Ordered would be in the King behalf also
& I shall think the Chief Justice ought to be the Last man to debarr the
King from the Evidence that may any wise appear in his behalf   I cannot tell what Turn might be given to such slighting over the Kings Evidence   you go on in the same strain that it is unacountable that the Genˡ
of the Late Council have no Evidence but themselves   & do you really
think it unaccountable that men may Inform the King of their own
Knowledge or would that at all Invalidate their Evidence tho the Questions I put was neither   their Evidence might not be taken in any thing
they had informed the King of their own Knowledge   but what is more
surprizing Still is that the Chief Justice should prejudge the matter before
one Evidence is heard on it and allow the charge to be without any foundation & only the effect of Personal Resentment without any View of
serving his Majesty & this under your hand & in a matter to that may
come Judicially before you

I leave you sir, to reflect what may be said on it and how farr this would be thought obeying his Majestys Instructions but before I Conclude I must take notice of the Indecent manner you begin your paper intermating that you have been forced to conceal your oppinion if Contrary to mine being deterr'd by me   this would be a Hevy Charge against me if true but it happens to be so well known with what remarkable temper and Deliberation I have Proceeded in this and all other Matters and Causes that have been transacted or brought before me in Council that it gives me very Little Concern as to my self   I only look upon as an Effect of that Rash Inconsiderate way you are so apt to be led into & which I have so often in the mildest and friendlyest manner Cautioned you Against

GEORGE BURRINGTON

His Excelly the Gov' Delivered the following paper in answer to the paper giving in at this Board the 18th Instant signed by Mr Chief Justice Smith Mr Porter Mr Ashe Mr Harnett and ordered that the same be entered in the Council Journal & a copy thereof delivered to them forthwith which was accordingly Done which was in these Word Viz'

To William Smith Edmond Porter John Bap' Ashe and Cornelius Harnett Esqm Members of the Council

GEN'

I have read your Joynt paper about assistant Judges   I must own the paper came from the Lower house to Know the power of Assistant Judges I did not oppose the answer Sent by the Upper house to it Neither Did I declare my Oppinion upon it afterwards   Reflecting further upon it & Operning my Comission & Instructions & Considering Indeed the Nature of the thing I could not think it Right and for my own part Whenever I am Wrong I shall always think it better to Retract as you call it than Obstinately to Persist in an Error   I was willing to have the debate Resumed & in order thereto put in two plain Questions the Council for their Oppinion which might Easily been as plainly answer   But your paper upon it Runn into Niceties and distinctions forreign to that purpose   you ask me if the warrant for the Chief Justices Pattent Doth not Call it a full power & authority to hold the Court but then Certainly it must be understood in a Legall way it doth doth not say by himself only & therefore must Intend as the Usage Ever has been with assistants Which assistants my Comission and Instructions directs and impowers me to appoint tho you wisely observe upon it that it doth not so much

31

direct me to appoint them as Supposeing of them it directs the Rules to be Observed in Choosing them This I think make the matter much Stronger for it takes it for granted that they ought to be appointed but then you say the Instruction doth not say assistant Judges this is a pritty Extraordinary Construction of one of his Majesties plain Instructions when the Instructions Couple Judges Assistants Justices &c Besides the   Instruction which you had before you forbids me Establishing any new Courts or desolving any already Established and it is well Known the General Courts here hath Constantly been with Assistant Judges that have had a Judicial power & I cannot help beleiving that the allowing the Chief Justice to be sole Judge of that Court would be erecting a new Court but you seem to recede from all that & allow there should be Assistants but of what power or Use should they be why truly to Inform and advise the Chief Justice as Masters in Chancery For my part Gent I was not bred a Lawyer but I never heard of a Common Law Court where the business of any of the Judges was to advise only and Indeed the Establishing of a single Judge of the Supream Court of Comon pleas Seems Contrary to the very nature of it & I am sure would be Establishing a New Court of Judicature here Contrary to my Instructions & no way for his Majesties Service or the good administration of Justice & should I allow it it might be Just matter of Complaint against me as I am perswaded the Increasing of it would be against the Gent It he should Assume it

GEORGE BURRINGTON

Then His Excelly the Govt delivered the following Paper in answer to the paper delivered by Mr Ashe at the Council Board the 18th instant & directed to the same to be Entered in the Council Journal & a Copy thereof delivered to Mr Ashe forthwith which was accordingly done which paper was in these words Vizt

To John Bapt Ashe Esqr

In the late debate about the Complaints against Sir Richard Everard I put two short Queeries to the Council for their Oppinion I plainly told in the debate my oppinion was that those Gent who has complained against Sir Richard Everard might give their Evidence of any facts of their own knowledge but desired ye oppinion of the Council that if I was wrong I might be better advised which I never think myself above Recieving but Instead of a plain Categorical answer Mr Ashe has branched out into a long discourse upon it while I cannot help thinking quite evades the matter and I shall only say I expected more Candor

and plainness from you   there is another paper you offer too about the
late Bill Concerning fees and Quit Rents but comes quite out of tame
Being after the Assembly was prorogued   you make some adjustment
about tobacco in it which is not satisfactory neither but you mention
nothing of Rice that was Icerted for the payment of Quit rents   you
propose too now it is over a Clause of referring it to his Majesty but I
Observed it not so in the Bill   I shall only say I several time demanded if any person in the Council had anthing further to advance
upon it   you say your paper was prepared y° day of the debate   it
would certainly looked much fairer had you then offered it but being done
when the affair was all over seems very particular   Your paper about
Assistant Judges which you have joyned with three more of the Council
I answer bv itself

GEORGE BURRINGTON

His Excell⁷ the Gov' was pleased to desire the oppinion of the Board
Whither the officer attending both Houses of Assembly should be paid
for their service and attendance on the last session & y° Hono^bles   the Council was of oppinion that his Excell⁷ the Gov' Issue Warrants to the publick Treasurer to pay the same which was done accordingly

His Excell⁷ the Gov' was pleased to Direct that the first paragraph of
M' Chief Justice Smiths paper which he gave in at the Council Board
the 18th Instant might be read which was accordingly read in these
words Viz'

To His Excell⁷ the Gov'

Since your Excell⁷ has been pleased to Demand an answer in Writing
to two Queeries proposed to us by your Excell⁷ I with great Cheerfullness Embrace the Opertunity to Declare my sentiments which hitherto I
have been forced to conceal being Deterr⁴ therefrom by the Displeasure
of vour Excell⁷ whenever I was so Unhappy as to Differ in Opinion
from you   And the Gov' Desired this Board that they would Declare
whither or no there has not been all the freedom of debate imaginable
used at this Board and whither he ever Deterr⁴ M' Cheif Justice or any
other member from openly debating every matter and thing that came
before them at this Board and the Council thereupon Declared that they
have not at any time since His Excellys arrival observed that any member of this Board has been deterred or otherwise Hindred or obstructed
from debating openly and freely every matter any thing that has layn
before this Board

Ordered that a comission of the Peace Issue for Chowan p'cint directed to Col⁰ Henry Bonner William Badham Henry Baker Tho⁸ Luten Samuel Paget John Ismay Jacob Blount Samuel Spruell Francis Pough Aaron Blanchard William Roods Thomas Garrett Richard Parker John Sumner John Blount and Francis Branch Constituting & appointing them Justices of the peace within the said Precinct.

Ordered that a Comission of the Peace Issue for the P'cinct of Beauford & Hyde & Directed to Eward Salter Jno Snoad Simon Aderson Robert Turner Samuel Slade Robert Peyton Thos Worsley Jun' Churchill Reading Tho⁸ Smith William Barrows & W⁰ Cordant Constituting and appointing them Justices of the peac within the said p'cincts

Ordered that a Comission of the peace Issue for the p'cinct of Craven Directed to Capt W⁰ Handcock Cap⁸ Daniel Shine Tho⁸ Martin John Powell Capt Tho⁸ Masters Jacob Miller Jacob Sheets Martin Frank John Formyeil Jun' W⁰ Brice Simon Bright George Whittaker and Walter Lane Constituting & appointing them Justices of Peace Within the said P'cinct,

Ordered that a Comission of the peace Issue for the p'cinct of Carteret directed to John Nelson Rich⁴ Russell Enoch Ward Richard Whitehurst Joseph Bell   Taylor Capt Arthur Mabson Francis Brice Elenzer Harker and   Chaddock Constituting and appointing them Justices of Peace Within the said p'cinct

The Complaint of the members of the Late Council against Sir Richard Everard which was to have been Argued this Day and the Members of the Late Council Appearing Sir Richard was sent for & the messenger Returned & acquainted the Board that he was told Sir Richard Everard was not at Home but that M' Everard (Sir Richard's son) would appear & answer in his fathers behalf to morrow morning which was objected to by the said upon which His Excelly the Gov' & Council taken the same into Consideration it was consented to that M' Everard should appear in his fathers behalf

Ordered that y' Marshall do Sumons His Majestys Council to attend his Excelly the Gov' in Councill to Morrow Morning nine of the Clock

To which time the Board adjourned

_____

NORTH CAROLINA—ss

At a Council held at the Council Chamber in Edenton the 21ˢᵗ day of May Anno Domini 1731

Present

His Excelly George Burrington Esqʳ Govʳ &c

The Honble { Joseph Jenoure   Edmᵈ Porter } Esqᵗ Members
           { Robt Halton   Jno Bapᵗ Ashe } of His
           {   Cornˢ Harnett   } Majesties Council

Mʳ Everard in behalf of his Father Sir Richard Everard appeared this day at the Board as also the Genᵗ of the Late Council Whereupon reading their Charge against Sʳ Richard Everard the Govʳ & Council were unanimously of opinion that none of the articles of their Charge were sufficient Grounds of prosecution of the suit save the two last to which the Genᵗ of the Late Council faild to produce Any Evidence to support them alledgeing that Colˢ Harvey who was one of their Evidences was Dead and Coll Gale the other was out of the Country

CAROLINA—ss.

At a Council held at the Council Chamber in Edenton the 22ᵈ Day of May Anno Dom 1731

Present

His Excelly George Burrington Esqʳ Govʳ &c

The Honᵇˡᵉ { Jos Jenoure } Esqⁿ Members of His
           { Robt Halton } Majesties Council
           { Cornˢ Harnett }

John Lovick Esqʳ late Secty came before this Board & gave in the following paper in answer to the Several Depositions on the Complaint of Sʳ Richard Everard against him which was read in these words Vizᵗ

NORTH CAROLINA

To His Excellency George Burrington Esqʳ Govʳ Capᵗ General & Comander in Chief of His Majesties Province of North Carolina

The Remonstrance of John Lovick upon the Complaint of Sir Richard Everard against the Sᵈ Lovick & Edward Mosely Esqʳ

Humbly Showeth

that a Complaint being made by Sir Richard Everard to his Majesty against your Remonstrant and Edwᵈ Moseley Esqʳ which your Excelly by his Majestys Directions has been pleased to Enquire into & Several Depositions has been taken but they being all Matters sebsequent to that Complaint & your Excelly and the Council yesterday Declaring your Oppinion that such Evidence Could not be recieved to support that Complaint and Sir Richard failing to produce any other Evidence the said John Lovick Concieves the Charge must of Course drop and that it would be needful for him to answer thereto and that Regularly as he humbly Concieves they ought not to have been recieved as he had then been p'sent he could easily have shown and fully have obviated then but least those Depositions might seem to Reflect on the Conduct & Character of your Remonstrant which he is desirous to set Clear before your Excelly he begs leave to make his observations on the several Depositions taken & to shew how much they fall short of proving anything unjustifiable against him   the sum of them (for they all seem to tend to one thing tho Variously Modell'd) is about some blank patents that Mr George Pollock had your Remonstrant need not Observe the Constant method of signing pattents has been to sign them blank but the occassion of putting those patents into M' Pollocks hands upon which the Clamour was Endeavoured to be raised was as followeth) when the line was for to be run betwixt this Government and Verginia their being no money belonging to the Lords proprietors in their Rec'' hand to defray the Charge the Gov' & Council passed an order for the sale of Lands to Reimburse it & thereupon the line was runn to General Satisfaction & at a Charge that has been thought no way immoderate your Remonstrance being one of the Comissioners the Creditt of that Order of the Board advanced great sums of money towards the defraying the Charges and had lands afterwards assigned to him to Reimburse the same and upon it sold out to M' George Pollock Seventeen thousand acres but the said Pollock for his greater Conveyance in taking up the Lands desired patents might be left Blank in His hands not knowing in what Quantities he might take it up which patent he was to fill up when the surveys were made in such parcells as the whole should not Exceed that Quantity and the all to be returned into the Office to be Compleated on Record   to all this Col Tho' Pollock was Evidence then a member of Council who is ready to declare (if called upon) the whole affair was in this manner & no otherwise Neither is it pretended that your Remonstrant had any fee Rewarded Gratuity for so Doing   that if Mr. Pollock had Committed any fraud about it Must easily have been Detected   but that Gents Character is two good to be suspected of such Vile practice nor indeed is it so much as pretended that there has been the the least fraud or Design of it and your remonstrant averrs that he had no fee Reward or Gratuity Directly or Indirectly for his so doing or was any penny Gainer by it

This May it please your Excelly is the whole of that affair that there was so much pains taken by the Noise & Number of the Evidence to swell it up to a Charge

Having now giving this plain account of the affair it Self the said
John Lovick begs leave to Observe the amount of the several Depositions
taken   the first is Mr Harding Jones who swears he saw a blank pattent
in Mr George Pollocks hands about twelve months since & that he said
something that made Mr Pollock smile which is all that concerned the
said Lovick & may probably be true   the next is Mr James Castellaw
who Swears he saw four or five Blank pattents in Mr George Pollocks
hands & that Mr Pollock would have sold two of them but Mr Castellaw perswaded him against it   this is the whole of this Deposition   only
on hear Say and not to the purpose which being only hear say & is no
Evidence nor worth answering

Mr Cullen Pollock swears that he had a Blank Pattent in his Hands
of his Brother George Pollocks for one Thousand acres of Land and
that it is so Endorsed on the back by his brother which confirms what
your Remonstrant before related about it & there was no design of fraud
in it which the Gent Intrusted with them was above being Guilty of
Mr Thomas Jones Swears he had an Imaginary Survey (as he calls it)
wch he gave the said Lovick in August or September Last and got a pattent Dated in the year 1728   all the said Lovick remembers of this matter is that Mr Jones brought him one of the pattents Mr George Pollock
had with a Letter from the said Pollock to fill it up for Mr Jones but
there being some name or something in that pattent which made it im-
practiable the same was Destroyed and another pattent made of the same
date filled up which was what had been frequently done to other and if
the survey was not as it ought to be the said Lovick declares he was not
privy to it nor had he any fee or Reward for it nor in any manner one
farthing gainer so that all the account of that is that Mr Jones he Imposed a Sham Survey upon the Secretary which the present Surveyor
Gen^{ll} will Enquire into & see that no Damage Accrue to his Majesty
therefrom

The Next is Doctor Allyn who swear he saw blank pattent in M^r
Pollocks hands & heard a bargain between the s^d Pollock & Mr Jones for
two Thousand acres   all is but Consistant with all that is already said
he Swears too that he has Seen a great number of Blank pattents with a
Reciept on the back for the purchase Money but the not Express^d which
Seldom is but say^e the Consideration money within mentioned & Excepting about five of which mention is made he knew any to go out Blank
nor beleives it & is satisfied If Doctor Allyn saw any it must be as they
Lay in the Secty Office or Rec^r office and he dare to put the whole Cause
upon & is very sure where so much pains are taken if one single Instance

more could have been found it would by no means have bee Omitted M' Nairn swears only to his beleif which if true the remonstrant averrs was one of those pattents Left with M' Pollock and all but amounts that he beleives he saw a blank pattent as is very likely & and agree with what the Said Lovick has before observed

M' Downing Swears he saw a blank pattent in Cullen Pollocks hands & has heard of several others by report but can say nothing about it himself

As to M' Pollock pattent it has been mentioned already as to what heard by report its two uncertain to answer and therefore concieves it ought not to have been Incerted

The Last is M' Russell who swears that M' John Galland brought a pattent down to Core sound to be filled up but that it was sent back again & filled up in the office the truth of this Matter was there being a pattent to be made out for Mr Russell the Survey Could not be found in the Office & to save the man Coming one hundred and fifty miles the Secty gave the pattant blank to Mr Galland his Clerk to get the survey from the Surveyor and to fill it up and to return it to the Office & that Mr Galland geting the survey returned that and the pattent to the Secty to Copleat which was done in the offices as he Swears. Having now gone there with the Evidence the said Lovick cannot help taking notice how many were produced to the same thing Viz' that they had seen blank pattents which plainly with a Design to have it beleived they were Different and if it had been an offence it might have swelled the bulk of the charge and looked the greater when in truth there was never only the aforementioned and that done in the manner aforesaid which is humbly Submitted to your Excell'y if there was fraud or ill intention in the said Lovick there in but the said Lovick now beg leave to give his Reason why he Conceives the Evidences ought not to have been on the Enquiry that was ordered to be made on the Complaint of Sir Richard Everard for—

First they were all of matters since the Complaint and so ought not to have been admitted to have made it good as your Excelly and the Council have allowed 2' because is not one one Evidence that Evidence that pretends to prove the least corruption or foul practice in the said Lovick unless the bare signing of pattents blank be an offence & if it shall be thought a Crime Sir Richard Everard who was then Gov' and without whose name no pattent could have Issued was not capable and ought to have been the principal person in the Complaint Instead of Complainer & one thing further as to Sir Richard the said Lovick begs leave to remark upon the Complaint the Order from Sir Richard to the said Lovick about warrents and pattents bears date in Janry 1728 and his Letter to His Grace the Duke of New Castle soon followed & both seem'd founded on a double Mistake the first was that His Majesty was then in possession of the Goverment which did not happen till July following the Other was that the said Lovick had great numbers of old warrents in the Office which had been forbid by the proprietors to pass all which is without the least foundation the said Lovick never being possessed with such warrents in his office nor was there ever such an order from the Prop^r about them as he knows of nor any grounds for any & upon such mistakes it was that Sir Richard refused to sign pattent the apparent Injury of such as had Lands due to them but at the Assembly in November 1729 after the Surrender to the Crown by the Lords Prop^r at the Instance of the Assembly in hopes of the five Hundred pound they gave him he again Signed pattents Contrary to the oppinion of some Members of the Council and particularly of the said Lovick who then told him he Conceived the stopping of the pattents when they were Stopped was irregular and erect Injury but the granting of them after we were assured of the Sale were irregular but wither Sir Richard did it for his Majesties Service or for private gain will be Easily Judged Especially when it is known that besides the aforesaid Five Hundred Pounds the Extraordinary fees he took upon pattents beyond Law brought him in very great sums but the said Lovick would now Conclude begging pardon for being so Tedious and with great Gratitude acknowledging your Excellys patience Cander & Exemplary Impartiallity in this and indeed in all others debates before you the said Lovick thinks himself happy the Enquiry was made it being no small Satisfaction to him that having been so many years Secty of this province on such a   this was all that Could be produced against him and he was the more desirous that his Charecter might be Cleared Seeing he has for near a Dozen years been a member of Council & had the head of the Board & by his Enemies said to be at the head of most affairs here till your Excelly arived to take the Goverment for his Majesty

All which is humbly Submitted

S^r your Excell^ry most faithfull most Obed^t Huble Servt

J LOVICK

And the Complainant producing no Evidence to support the Complaint agreeable to the Determination of the Board yesterday it is the oppinion of His Excellys the Govr & Council that the Complaint of Sir Richard

Everard hath not been Supported & that the said Lovick be Discharged from that Enquiry

Ordered that the several Depositions and Complaint of Sir Richard Everard against John Lovick Esqʳ late Secty with his answer thereon be delivered in the hands of his Magesties attorney General of this Province for his Report to be made thereon to His Excellʸ the Governor

Then this Board adjourned by order

ROBERT FORSTER Dep Secʳ

NORTH CAROLINA—ss.

A Council being Sumoned to be held at the Council Chamber in Edenton on the 26 Day of July Anno Dom 1731 there appearing but two members of Council His Excellʸ Declared he would attend the next day to see if any more members would appear and on the 27 day of July met

His Excellʸ George Burrington Esqʳ Gov

The Honᵇˡᵉ { Jos Jenoure   } Esqʳˢ Members of
            { Edmund Porter } his Majesties Council

His Excellency the Govʳ was pleased to declare that William Smith Esqʳ Chief Justice having withdrawn himself out of this Government without any due Notice given or leave obtained for the same & said place thereby being become Vacant there was an absolute Necessity for appointing a Chief Justice in his room which could not be done without a Council

And his Excelly having Sumoned the Council to meet yesterday there appeared only the two members before mentioned (this day present) the rest being out of the Government or at Cape Fear a great distance from this place where the Council and Courts are Held & this day being the day for the General Court to be begun and held for the said Province which must unavoidable fall and the Business of the Country delayed and great failure of Justice thereby unless the same was prevented by appointing a Chief Justice and assistant for which it was absolutely necessary to have a Council and his Excelly declare that there being such urgent necessity he should appoint members to supply the place of those out of the Country that there might be a fuller Board and thereupon His Excelly the Govʳ was pleased to nominate and appoint John Lovick Esqʳ to be a member of his Majestys Council for and within this province and his Excelly was also pleased to nominate and appoint Edmund Gale Esqʳ to be a member of His Majesties Council for and within this province and accordingly the said John Lovick and Edmond Gale Esqʳˢ appeared and took and subscribed the several oaths by Law appointed for Qualification of publick Officers as also the Oaths of a councellor & took their places at the Board accordingly

Then Present as before

The Hono^ble { John Lovick / Edmond Gale } Esq^rs Members of his Majesties Council

His Excell^y Informing this Board the Necessity of Imediately appointing a Chief Justice in the room of William Smith Esqr who had secretly left this Government And having the Concurrence of the Council therein His Excell^y was pleased to nominate John Palin Esqr who was approved of by the Council Thereupon it is ordered that a Commission pass the seal Constituting and appointing the said John Palin Esqr Chief Justice of this Province till his Majesties pleasure be known therein His Excell^y the Govern^r named George Martin Henry Bonner Isaac Hill and Thos Lovick Esq^rs to be assistant Justices of the General Court of this Province who were appointed by the Council

Ordered that a Comission pass the seal Constituting and appointing George Martin Henry Bonner Isaac Hill & Thomas Lovick Esq^rs assistant Justices of the General Court of this Province

Ordered that a General Comission of the Peace pass the seal Constituting and appointing the present members of his Majesties Council and the members of the Council for the time being Nathaniel Rice Esqr Secretary and the Secretary of the said Province for the time being John Montgomery Esqr Attorney General and the Attorney General of the said province for the time being the assistant Justices for the time being The Chairmen of Each and Every precinct Court within this Province for the time being Justices for the Concervation of the Peace within and Justices of the General Sessions of the Peace & General Goal Deliverye

By order

R M FORSTER Cler Con^l

NORTH CAROLINA—ss.

At a Council held at the Council Chamber in Edenton the 31st day of August Anno Dom 1731

Present

His Excell^y George Burrington Esqr Govr

The Hono^ble { Joseph Jenoure / Edmond Porter / Edmond Gale } Esq^rs Members of His Majesties Council

His Excelly the Governor was pleased to name Robert Turner Samuel Slade Benjamin Sanders Thomas Bonner Thomas Worsley Junr

Benjamin Payton Seth Pilkington William Larner William Willis Churchil Reading John Tripp Cornelius Fowler John Coldham Samuel Sinclare Richard William Sylvester Henry Crafton John Pregg Roger Henyon and William Carruther Constituting and appointing them Justices for the precincts of Beaufort & Hyde who were approved of by the Council

Ordered that a Comission pass the seal Constituting and appointing the said Robert Turner Samuel Slade Benjamin Sanders Thomas Bonner Tho' Worsley Jun' Benjamin Peyton Seth Pilkington William Larner William Willis Churchill Tripp Cornelius Fowler John Coldham Samuel Sinclare Richard William Silvester Henry Crafton John Gregg Roger Henyon and William Carruther Gent Justices of the Peace for the precinct of Beaufort and Hyde in the County of Bath

Ordered that a Dedimus pass the seal Directed to Major Stephen Golde Impowering him to qualify the Justices in the Comission of the Peace for the precincts of Beaufort and Hyde

By order

R M FORSTER

NORTH CAROLINA—ss.

At a Council held in the Council Chamber in Edenton the 2d day of November Anno Dom 1731

Present

His Excelly George Burrington Esq' Gov' &c

the Honble { Joseph Jenoure   Edmond Porter } Esqs Members of his
          { Robt Halton   John Lovick   } Majesties Council

His Excelly the Governor informing the Board that he was delayed on his journey from Cape Fear by illness & bad Weather so that he could not be hear yesterday to hold a Court of Chancery yesterday being the usual time for holding the Same Required the Oppinion of the Council Whether he Should hold the said Court this day who were of oppinion that the said Court regurlarly sit this day Provided no advantage was taken any Person gone or not now attending

By order

R FORSTER

NORTH CAROLINA—ss.

At a Council held at the Council Chamber in Edenton on the 3d Day of November Anno Dom 1731

Present

His Excelly George Burrington Esq' Gov'

The Honoble ⎰ Joseph Jenoure   John Lovick ⎱ Esq' Members of his
⎱ Robt Halton   Edm⁴ Gale ⎰ Majesties Council
    Edm⁴ Porter

Monday last being the Day by Law appointed for the Assembly to meet and the Governor having been detained by illness and Bad Weather on his Journey from Cape Fear Could not arrive at Edenton on the said Day neither were five members of the council attending the Assembly and the Governor being informed that Number of Burgesses met on the day and still waited His Excelly thereupon sent for the Burgesses to attend him in Council and made the following Speack to them to Vir'

GENTLEMEN

His Majestices Service made it Necessary for me to visit the Southern Parts of this Government I took that journey so soon after a Violent Feavor was render by some Indispositions Uncapable of Returning by Land therefore was under a Necessity of Coming by sea the winds proving very Contrary and Tempestious my voyage took up much more time than I expected and altho I left the Vessel at the Barr and Used the Greatest Expedition I Could not arive at this Metropolis before yesterday

How farr my being Absent the first day of the Assemblys Meeting may Effect the being of the I will not enter into the arguments at this time the reason why I offer Nothing to your Consideration that the last Assembly would not Obey the Kings Instructions that I laid before them Nither did they do any thing for the good of the Province Notwithstanding I mentioned several affairs in My Speech to them very Necessary for the well fair of this Government and ease of the people their Ill conduct is the occassion I could not do Business with you at this time The Misbehaviour of the Late Assembly I have represented and have desired further Instructions how I am to act in Relation to the Revenue Officers Fees Registring Lands in the Auditors Office and other matter Contained in the Eight Instructions laid before that Assembly I hope to be Honoured with his Majesties Commands next March in Relation to them Instructions before I am fully Instructed I Judge it will not be proper for me to proceed any further upon them Instructions In the mean time I will take all Imaginable Care that the Business of this Province be Carefully transacted and that good order you now see so well Established Shall Continue between this and the Next Session

I Prorogue this Assembly to the first Tuesday in April Next Ensueing and it is hereby prorogued

By order

R FORSTER Cler Con^d

NORTH CAROLINA—ss.

At a Council held at the Council Chamber in Edenton on the 4th day of Novr Anno Dom 1731

Present

His Excell^y George Burrington Esqr Govr &c

The Hon^{bles} { Joseph Jenoure   John Lovick   Esq^{rs} Members of his
                     Robt Halton   Edm^d Gale   Majesties Council
                     Edm^d Porter }

His Excell^y the Governor was pleased to acquaint this Board that he was Informed by several persons at Cape Fear that Col Edward Mosely Maurice Moore and Mr John Porter Claim Such great quantities of Land on Cape Fear River that new Comers Cannot find Lands to take up but what is said to belong to one of those Gentlemen this Board doth thereupon order that the said Col Moseley Col More and Mr John Porter do attend this Board on the 17th day of Jan^{ry} next and that each of the said Gentlemen do then give particular account of Every Tract they hold on the said River and by what Title they Claim the same

His Excelly the Governor further acquainted that he had several Complaints made to him by the Inhabitant of Cape Fear that the several Deputy Surveyors appointed by Edward Moselev Esqr late Surveyor General have made and returned most of the survey at and about Cape Fear with only running the Front line so that ye People are uncertain as to the Bounds of their Lands.

It is Thereupon ordered that the Deputy surveyors at and about Cape Fear appointed by the Late surveyor General do attend this Board at their next sitting in January and that the Clerk of this Board do Issue Sumons's to Each of the said Dep^{ties} to appear before the Governor and Council on the 17th Day of January next

His Excelly the Governor Informed this Board that Cornelious Harnett Esqr one of his Majesties Council and another person did Contract with Capt Tate of Bristol for a large Cargoe of English Goods to the Amount of near £3000 Currency of this Province to be paid to him the said Tate in six weeks time about Eighteen months past at Cape Fear River The said Tate on his Complaint to his Excelly said that he had not recieved any thing for the said Goods but is still put of by Mr Harnett and the said Tates ship still lying in Cape Fear River to the Great Loss and

Detriment of his owners and his Ruin It is Ordered that Sumons's do Issue to every member of Council to attend His Excelly in Council the 17th Day of January next and that the said Cornelious Harnett be Served with a Copy of this Entry and that Capt Tate be then Likewise Sumonded to appear to make Good his said Complaint against Mr Harnett that this Complaint be not Entred in the Council Book

His Excelly acquainting this Board that His Majesties Instructions require him to transmitt to the Board of Trade attested accounts of the Receipts and Payments of all publick moneys in this Province

It ordered that several Treasurers and all others having any publick moneys in their Hands be Sumoned to appear before this Board on the 17th Day of Jany next at which time they are to give their Attendance and make up their accounts of all publick moneys in their Hands

Ordered that sumons's do Issue to every member of His Majesties Council within this Province to attend His Excelly in Council at the Council Chamber in Edenton on the 17th day of Janry next on pain of suspension there being a Complaint against a member of Council to be then heard

Ordered that a Dedymus be directed to the precinct Court of Beaufort & Hyde to Recieve and Qualify Mr Richard Harvey Capt John Tremble & Oliver Blackburn as Members of that Court

Ordered that a Dedimus be directed to the Court of Pasquotank to Recieve and qualify Mr John Turry and Terrence Swinney as Members of that Court.

His Excelly the Governor Read a paper sign by E Porter Esqr a member of this Board on the 27th day of July last past which being Read His Excelly Declared that the said Mr Porter had aserted a falsehood with a design to impeed and hinder His Excelly from His Majesties Service at that time in appointing a sufficient Number of Council to make a Court of Chancery and to appoint a Chief Justice

Ordered that the said Edmond Porter be Sumoned to appear and answer the same at the Council to be held at the 17th day January next

Mr Little moved this Board that Edmond Porter Esqr might answer to the Complaint that said Little and other Entered at this Board in May Last

Ordered that the said Edmond Porter be sumoned to appear at a Council to be held the 17th day of January next and that he file his answer by the 1st day of said month and have his proofs ready at the Council the 17th of the said Month

By order

R FORSTER Cler Concl

NORTH CAROLINA—ss.

At a Council held at the Council Chamber in Edenton the 23ᵈ day of Nov' Anno Domini 1731

Present

His Excelly George Burrington Esq' &c

The Honoble { Joseph Jenoure   Edmᵈ Porter   } Esqⁿ Members
{ Robert Halton   John Lovick   } of his
{ Edmond Gale   } Majesties Council

His Excelly the Governor having laid Before this Board his Majesties 56 Instruction for appointing two Courts of Oyer and Terminer yearly which having been duly Considered This Board are of Oppinion that a Special Comission Issue pursuant to his Majesties Said Instructions directed to John Palin Esq' Chief Justice the present members of his Majesties Council and the Assistant Justices for holding the said Court on the Second Teusday in December next and that a Clause in the said Comission be added to Impower the Chief Justice or any three of the members to be a Quoram to hold the said Court

Ordered that a Comission pass the seal accordingly

Upon Petition of the Inhabitants of White Oak new River and Topsail along the Sea Shore Praying to have a New precinct Erected from new Topsail to Batranis point on the East Side of White Oak River and this Board thereon taking into consideration the great hardship and expences The Inhabitants within the limitts above mention⁴ are at in going to Craterett Precinct Court

His Excelly by and with the advice and consent of his Majesties Council doth make the following Bounds in to a precinct Viz' Beginning at Bogue Inlett from Batranis point on Bogue sound including or taking it two miles on the North East side of White Oak River for the East and North East Bounds and from New Topsail Inlett Including all the Lands on the Creeks and Branches that run into New River to be the South & West Bounds of the said precinct is hereby Called and Distinguished by the name of Onslow Precinct and that a Comission issue for the same with such priviledges as other precincts have or Enjoy And it is further ordered that the said precinct shall be and Continue according to the above bounds untill there shall be a further Division of other Precinct and Counties

Ordered that a Comission of the Peace Issue for Onslow precinct Directed to James Tunis Edward Marshburn Joseph Mumford James Murry James Taylor Lazarus Thomas Thomas Johnson Capt Francis Brice Christopher Dudley Nocholas Hunter Abraham Mitchell Richard

Nickson and John Frederrick Constituting and appointing them Justices of the peace for and within the said precinct which Court to sit on the first Tuesday in January April July and October yearly

By order

[B. P R. O. North Carolina B. T Vol. 8. p 101]

LEGISLATIVE JOURNALS

NORTH CAROLINA—ss.

At a General Assembly begun and held for his Majesties Province of North Carolina at Edenton the 13th day of April Anno Domini 1731.

Present

His Excell'' George Burrington Esq''' His Maj''' Gover' & Capt. General of s'' Province

The Honō^{ble} { William Smith { Edmond Porter } Esq''
{ Nath' Rice { Jn° Bapt' Ashe }
{ Jos' Jenoure { Corn' Harnett }

Members of His Ma^{tys} Council being the Upper House of Assembly

The House met & adjourned till to-morrow morning Eight of the Clock.

Wednesday Aprill 14th The House met again

A Message came from the Lower House acquainting this Board that they were ready to present their Speaker and thereupon His Excell'' the Governor (by the Messenger of this House) Commanded their immediate Attendance. And the House in a full body came and presented Coll. Edward Moseley their Speaker who was thereupon approved of by His Excell'' the Governor

Then the Governor was pleased to deliver His Speech to the House of Burgesses in the following way Viz'

GEN' OF THE COUNCIL & GEN' OF Y' HOUSE OF BURGESSES

His Majesty the King our most gracious Lord & Master having Honoured me by His Commission to be Governor of this Province, on my arrival here by and with the Consent of Council I issued Writts for the several Precincts and Towns to Choose Burgesses to meet on the 13th of this Month   I assure you Gen'' it is a great satisfaction to me that we are now Assembled   I cannot doubt of your ready Complyance in passing such Acts as are Required by his Majesty in the 19th, 31st, 42nd, 61st, 63rd, 75th, 76th, & the 114th Articles of my Instructions, Transcripts of which I have ordered to be said before you

GENTLEMEN,

I assure you I have as much inclination to promote the Welfare of this Country now as formerly, I expect each Member of this Assembly comes here with an Intent to do everything that may be to the Kings Honour, & the Good of North Carolina I hope we shall behave our- selves with so much Duty that his Majesty will have pleasure in grant- ing us his Royall favours when we approach his Throne with our Hum- ble Petitions.

GENTLEMEN,

There are several matters absolutely necessary to be settled in this Assembly particularly how to keep the Bills to the Value they ought to pass for

The Settlements being so much Extended I think it Needfull that the Chief Justice with his Assistants should for the Ease of the People hold Courts in three different parts of the Province twice a year

That Wills should be proved & Lycences given by a proper Officer in every Precinct.

That Effectual methods be taken to procure a direct Trade to Europe and the West Indies without which this Country will always continue Poor.

To pass an Act for building a Town on Cape Fear River and appoint- ing Commissioners for that purpose.

To appoint an Agent & settle a Salary for Transacting the Affairs of this Province in England

GENTLEMEN OF THE HOUSE OF BURGESSES

I am fully Senseble how necessary your presence is at this time of the year on your Respective Plantations, therefore will do all in my power to make this a short session If you Judge it Necessary Depute some of your House to advise with me on any matters you have occasion to Debate which may Expedite Business and prevent Misunderstandings.

I recommend to you Unanimity and Agreement and that your Debates be carryed on with Modesty and good Manners.

GENTLEMEN OF THE COUNCIL

I return you my Sincere thanks for the readiness you have shown in dispatching all Business that has come before us. Your Demeanour to me has been so full of respect that I am at a loss for Words to Express the Esteem and due Regard I have for Persons of so Great Worth & excellent Qualifications.

GENTLEMEN OF THE ASSEMBLY

My diligence & industry in Promoting New Settlements in this Country when Governor for the Prop* you remember, and the happy effects thereof are known to every man in this Province, That on Cape Fear River begun by me six years past, is now the Place of the greatest Trade in the whole Province All the reward I ever received for the charges Necessary & unavoidably occasioned by that undertaking, the Losses I suffered and the great hardships I endured was the thanks of a house of Burgesses

GENTLEMEN OF THE ASSEMBLY.

Your behaviour at this time is of the utmost Consequence to North Carolina, it is in your Power to make it very happy by cheerfully and willingly performing what is required of you by the greatest and best King that ever sway'd the British Sceptre. Consider you have at this time a Governor that is entirely your Friend and wellwisher, that will joyne his own Interest to obtain for this Country all that is now or has any appearance of being for your Good, I sincerely desire your Proceedings may accomplish & perfect all that is wanting to make this Country Populous Happy and Rich

GEO BURRINGTON.

Then the House Adjourned till to morrow morning at Eight of the Clock

Thursday April 15th The House met again and adjourned to-morrow morning Eight of the Clock.

Frvday April 16th The House met again and adjourn'd till to-morrow morning Eight of the Clock

Saturday April 17th The House met again and adjourn'd till Monday morning Eight of the Clock

Monday April 19th The House met again and adjourn'd till to-morrow morning Eight of the Clock.

Tuesdav April 20th The House met again

Received the following Messages from the Lower House Viz'. The Publick Treasurer delivered in at the Table Sixteen Bundles of old Bills of Credit Exchanged by him, say'd to contain the Sum of £7343 10.6

Ordered that the Committee appointed to Settle the Publick Accounts do Exchange the same parcells & of Bills and make report thereof to the House that the same Bills may be destroy'd sent to His Exce^ly the Governor and Councill for Concurrence by Mr Arthur Williams & Mr Geo. Winn

By Order of ye Gen^ll Assembly

AYLIFFE WILLIAMS. Clk

Edward Moseley Esqre Publick Treasurer delivered in at the Table the Publick Accounts

Ordered that John Lovick Esqre Mr Charles Denman, Mr Gabrill Burnham, Mr George Powers, Mr Arthur Williams, Mr William Willson, Mr William Barrow & Mr William Williams be a Committee of this House to be joined by such Members of the Council as shall be appointed to Inspect & Settle the same and the Accounts of all others concerned with the Publick Money & report the same to this House. Sent to His Exce^ly the Governor & Council for Concurrence by Mr Arthur Williams & Mr George Winn

By Order of the General Assembly

AYLIFFE WILLIAMS. C^lk.

Ordered that the following Message be sent to the Lower House. Viz^t.

Mr SPEAKER & GENT OF THE LOWER HOUSE

This House has appointed William Smith, Edmond Porter and Cornelius Harnett Esqre to be joined with the Members by you appointed to Inspect & Settle the Publick Accounts.

By order

ROB^t FORSTER C^lk of ye Upper House

Then the House adjourned till to morrow morning Eight of the Clock.

Wednesday April 21st The House met again

Mr Speaker & Gent. of the Lower House came in a full body and gave in the following Paper in answer to His Exce^ly the Gov^rs Speech. Viz^t

To His Exce^ly George Burrington Esqre His Majesties Capt General & Governor in Chief of North Carolina.

We the Kings most Dutifull & Loyall Subjects the Representatives of the People of North Carolina with great pleasure congratulate your arrival in this Province with that Command which His most gracious

Majesty has been pleased to confer on you   We have formerly experienced your Care for the Welfare of this Country and we rest fully assured that we shall not want your best Endeavours to promote the lasting happiness of the People of this Province. We sincerely promise for ourselves that we will not be wanting to do everything that we think may contribute thereto, and the Honour & Interest of His Majesties Service.

The several Articles of His Majesties Instructions which you have laid before this House shall be duely considered by us, & as we propose to Address His Royall Majesty concerning some of the matter contained therein we doubt not but our Dutifull Behaviour to you & what we shall propose for His Majesties Service and the Welfare of this Province will procure our Addresses a Favourable Reception.

We observe how particularly you Recommend to us the Settling a Method to keep the Bills Currant in this Country to their Value. We imagine the same is already sufficiently provided for by the Act passed in the Biennial Assembly in November 1729   Nor do we find but that the Credit given them by that Act is preserved by the Currency they have obtained all over this Government, but if any better method can be proposed for Establishing their value we shall very readily take the same into our Consideration.

As everything your Excell[y] recomends shall have its due weight with us we are of opinion with you that the remote Scituation of divers parts of this Province from Edenton the Metropolis of this Government will make it necessary that some Provision be made for the more Easy administration of Justice in those remote parts. A Bill for which purpose we shall order to be prepared Accordingly.

We heartily thank you for the Ease you propose to the Inhabitants relating to Wills & Lycences, a Bill for which purpose we have ordered to be prepared, And as your Excell[y] has indulged us thus far we make no doubt but when we propose other matters of equal concern for the good of this Province we shall have your cheerful concurrence.

We understand there is a Town already Established on Cape Fear River called Brunswick in New Hanover Precinct in respect to one of the Titles of the illustrious House of Hanover and we are informed it is like to be a flourishing place by Reason of its Excellent Situation for the Trade of those Parts, to promote which or any other Place on that River that shall be judged more proper we will readily give such assistance as is in our Power

The services done to this Province by the Settlement begun by you at Cape Fear, we have a grateful sense of which we shall make Evident on proper occasions and in a particular manner we purpose to be mindfull thereof in our Address to His Majesty   All the other parts of your Excell'' kind Speech we will take into our serious Consideration, & we hope the behaviour of the Assembly of this Province at this Juncture & at all times hereafter will Demonstrate that the Inhabitants of this Province have the greatest Duty & Loyalty to his most Excellent Majesty, Zeal & Affection for your Excell' & the Welfare of this Province

By Order of the Gen' Assembly

E. MOSELEY Speaker

His Excell' the Governor thereupon commanded the Lower House to attend him at this Board to-morrow morning at Eleven of the Clock

Then the House Adjourned 'till three of the Clock in the Afternoon

The House met again and Read the following Paper from the Lower House in these words Viz'

Whereas by the Royall Charter granted by King Charles the second to the Lords Proprietors and the Inhabitants of Carolina it is granted that the Inhabitants of this Province shall have possess & enjoy all Liberties Franchises & Priviledges as are held possessed & enjoyed in the Kingdom of England   And whereas it is the undoubted Right & Priviledge of the People of England that they shall not be taxed or made Lyable to pay any Sum or Sums of Money or Fees, other than such as are by Law established Notwithstanding which it appears by Complaints made in most parts of this Province that the officers in General do demand take & receive from the Inhab'' and Masters of Vessells Trading to this Province Four times more than the Fees appointed by the Laws of this Province to the great Discouragement of the Trade of this Province & the oppression of the People

Resolved that this House do wait on the Gov' with this Complaint and that the Council be desired to join with this House in requesting his Excell' to issue a Proclamation declaring such Practices contrary to Law and the oppression of the Subject, and strictly forbidding all officers to take larger Fees than is by Law appointed under pretence of difference of money untill such time as the officers Fees shall be Regulated by Authority of Assembly This House now having the same under their Consideration pursuant to His Majesties Instructions

By Order of the Gen' Assembly

AYLIFFE WILLIAMS. C''

Sent by M' Scarborough & M' Denman

Then the House adjourned 'till to-morrow morning Eight of the Clock.

Thursday April 22ᵈ The House mett again
Present Robert Halton Esqʳ
The Lower House came in a full body and His Exceˡˡʸ the Governor spoke to them in these words Vizᵗ

Mʳ SPEAKER AND GENT OF THE HOUSE OF BURGESSES

I think it necessary to cause Two Articles of my Instructions to be read to you that no Person in your House may pretend ignorance in a Matter where the Kings Comands to me are Positive (Vizᵗ) the 37ᵗʰ & 47ᵗʰ you may apply to me when and as often as you desire to Inspect any Publick Accounts, and they shall be laid before you. I think it absolutely necessary for his Majesties Service and the good of this Country that a Treasurer be appointed, Therefore I shall with advice of the Council speedily appoint a fit Person to execute that Important office until His Majesty Commissionates one

GEORGE BURRINGTON

Received the following Message from the Lower House Vizᵗ

To His Exceˡˡʸ THE GOVERNOR

This House requests His Exceˡˡʸ the Governor that he will be pleased to lay before this House a Copy of the Two Instructions which he read to them and that what he shall think proper to say to this House on those Instructions may be put into writing

By order of the Genˡ Assembly

AYLIFFE WILLIAMS. Clk.

Sent to yᵉ Upper House by Mʳ Skinner & Mʳ Burnham
Then the House adjourned 'till to-morrow morning Eight of the Clock

Fryday April 23ʳᵈ The House mett again
Received the following Message from the Lower House Vizᵗ Fryday April 23ʳᵈ.

To His EXCELLʸ THE GOVERNOR.

Voted the Reverend Mʳ Nicholas Jones be paid the sum of Ten Pounds for officiating Divine Service this day before the Governor

Council and Assembly, and His Excell⁷ the Governor is requested to issue his Warrant to the Publick Treasurer for the Payment of the Same.

Sent to the Council for Concurrence

AYLIFFE WILLIAMS Cᵗᵏ

By Messʳˢ Symons & Burnham.

Which being read in the Upper House the same was concurred with

Then the House adjourned 'till to-morrow morning Eight of the Clock

Saturday April 24ᵗʰ

The House met again & adjourned 'till Monday morning Eight of the Clock.

Monday April 26ᵗʰ

The House met again and sent the following Resolve to the Lower House. Viz'

Mʳ SPEAKER & GENT. OF THE HOUSE OF BURGESSES

Whereas His Majesty in his Instructions to His Excell⁷ the Governor hath ordered & Directed that all Fees shall be paid to His officers in Proclamation Money and the said Instructions having been Laid before the Council and House of Burgesses the said Burgesses immediately came to a Resolution which they soon delivered to His Excell⁷ in Effect Declaring that the said Instructions were contrary to Law and tended to the oppression of his Majesties Subjects and the said Burgesses having in their said Resolution arrogated and assumed to themselves the sole Power of establishing Fees exclusive of the Governor & Council

Resolved that the said Resolution of the House of Burgesses is a great invasion of his Maᵗʸˢ Prerogative and does highly reflect on the Honour and Dignity of His Crown

Resolved that the said Resolution of the House of Burgesses openly sends to divest the Governor & Council of their share of the legislative authority vested in them by his Majesties Commission & Instructions founded on the Laws of the English Constitution and that they seem therein to sett up and Erect some other form of Government than is allowed by the Laws of Great Britain   By order

ROBᵗ FORSTER. Cᵗᵏ Up Hō

At the same time His Excell⁷ the Governor was pleased to send the following Paper to the Lower House Viz'

Mʳ Speaker and Gent of the House of Burgesses

In answer to your unreasonable Complaint concerning Fees I must inform you that I have proposed to the Speaker and most of the Members of your House that myself and all the Kings officers in this Province were very willing to have their Fees settled in the same manner as in Virginia Inspecting the Laws of that Country I perceive the Lawfull Perquisites of officers there are more beneficial than here, having also read the answer drawn up by the Council to the aforesaid Complaint desire you Gent. sedately to Consider of it. For my own part I cannot refrain from telling you that whoever the Person was who formed the said Paper of Complaint I compare him to a thief that hides himself in a House to rob it and fearing to be discovered Fires the House and makes his Escape in the Smoke

GEORGE BURRINGTON

Received the following Message from the Lower House Vizᵗ

To His Excellʸ yᵉ Governor

In answer to what your Excellʸ was pleased to deliver in writing with the 37ᵗʰ & 47ᵗʰ Articles of His Majesties Instructions, We are of opinion that no Publick money ought to be issued but by the Govʳ Council and Genˡ Assembly And this House is of Opinion that by the Act of Assembly passed in November 1715 Entituled an Act Publick Treasurers to Account this House in Conjunction with the Governor & Council hath a larger Right than only to view and Examine the Publick Accounts.

This House is of Opinion that the 47ᵗʰ Instruction doth not extend to officers appointed by Act of Assembly as are the Publick and Precinct Treasurers and sundry other officers.

And as to the office of Publick Treasurer which you are pleased to mention in particular This House declares they are very well satisfied with the Ability & Integrity of the present Publick Treasurer Edᵈ Moseley Esqʳ who was appointed to that office in an Act of Assembly by the Governor Council and Assembly and we Conceive that such an officer so appointed is not to be removed but by the like Power And further this House is of Opinion that the Publick Treasurers of our Neighbouring Governments are appointed in like manner by the Governor Council and Assembly

By Order of the Genˡˡ Assembly

AYLIFFE WILLIAMS Clk

Sent by Mʳ Powers & Mʳ Sayer

Then the House Adjourned 'till to morrow morning Eight of the Clock

34

Tuesday April 27ᵗʰ The House met again and sent the following Answer to the foregoing Message Viz'

Mʀ Speaker & Gent of the House of Burgesses

In answer to your Message yesterday we must observe that we find greater inclinations in you to Cavil & raise Difficulties than to do anything that may tend to His Majesties Honour and the good of the Province Gentlemen, we mistrust it is the intent of some Persons to create Animosities and Foment Divisions a Method too frequently Practised formerly as well as now in order to Skreen and Secure themselves from an Enquiry into their Conduct which we believe has not been the most upright and regular, Nothing can be more clear or Express than the latter part of the 47ᵗʰ Instruction wherein His Majesty declares that no officer whatever shall be appointed but by himself or his Governor which surely excludes the House of Burgesses from any share in the nomination of a Treasurer unless you can prove that the Treasurer is not a Publick officer As to your present Treasurer we agree with you that he is a Person of sufficient ability, and we heartily wish that his Integrity was Equall to it, we must likewise inform you that he was not appointed by any Lawfull Authority and as to your pretended Law of 1729 it is very obvious to any man who suffers not his Reason to be guided by a spirit of Faction that they are Void and was passed with no other intent than to deprive his Majesty of his just Rights settled upon him by the Laws & Constitutions of Great Britain

By order of the Upper House

ROBᵗ FORSTER Clk

Then the House Adjourned till to-morrow morning Eight of the Clock

Wednesday April 28ᵗʰ
The House met again and adjourned 'till to-morrow morning Eight of the Clock

Thursday April 29ᵗʰ
The House met again and adjourned 'till to-morrow morning Eight of the Clock

Friday April 30ᵗʰ
The House met again
Read a Bill for an Act Entituled an Act to Regulate & Ascertain the Payment of Quit Rents and Fees of the Officers of this Government the first time and passed with Amendments
Adjourned 'till to-morrow morning Eight of the Clock

Saturday May 1st
The House met again
Received from the Lower House the three following Papers Viz't

To His Excell'y George Burrington Esq'r Governor and Commander in Chief etc

It was the greatest surprise imaginable to this House when they received your Paper in answer to Complaints concerning Fees.

It is the undoubted right of your Representatives and nothing more properly their Business than to complain when they find the Subjects oppressed and the Trade of the Province injured And we can hardly find a more general Evil than what we have complained of As our Laws have stood for near Twenty Years the Officers Fees have been paid in Paper Currency at the Rates mentioned in the Acts of Assembly And now when we find the Officers taking four times as much altho' the same Laws remain in force Our complaints are called unreasonable, nor doth what you say of your proposal to some of the Members out of this House of having the Fees settled as in Virginia in our Opinion put that affair in any better, but rather a worse light, that proposal being contrary to the Kings Instructions which Recommended the Fees to be Established in Proclamation Money. But what this House is most astonished at is the Close of your Paper where you tell the House you cannot refrain from telling them that whoever the person was that formed the said Paper of Complaint you compare him to a Thief that hides himself in the House to Rob it & fearing to be discovered fires the House to make his Escape in the Smoke.

We assure you we have sedately considered your Paper and the answer of the Council sent therewith and as we think we have given them a Sufficient Answer so we trust we shall your Excell'y when we declare that the Complaint we sent was the unanimous voice of the whole House no one Member dissenting therefrom

And we are of Opinion that such Treatment of any Member of this House in Particular (which seems to be the intent of your Excell'y harsh simile) is a great Indignity and Contempt put on the whole House a Breach of Priviledge & Tends to the deterring the Members from doing their Duty which we are well assured will be as Disagreeable to the Known Justice of His Sacred Majesty to hear as it is Grievous & Hurt-ful to the Just Freedom of the Subjects.

By order of the Gen'll Assembly

A. WILLIAMS, Clk

April y'e 28th 1731
Sent by Messrs Russell & Bell

To the Honoble the Council

It is the opinion of this House that the 47 Instruction was never designed by His Majesty to Vacate such Authorities as are granted by Act of Assembly but only to prevent all Persons whatever acting by any Commission from the late Lords Proprietors even such whose Right to offices by grant from the Proprietors were preserved by the Act of Parliament are (as we understand the Instruction) obliged to have their Comissions renewed by His Majesty or the Governor   But we do not understand that Instruction in such sense as that those Persons who are Authorized by Act of Assembly must nevertheless have his Majesties or the Governors Comision And we hope we may retain this sense of that Instruction until His Majestys Pleasure be signified thereon without those severe Expressions mentioned in your Paper being flung on this House or any of its Members for whatsover you may say we are resolved by our Conduct & Behaviour to shew our Duty and Loyalty to His Majesty and to do everything we think may tend to His Honour and the good of this his Province, and we hope when we forbear to return such injurious Language as is given to this House, we shall shew we do not mean to Cavil and Raise Difficulties,   Nevertheless we think it our Duty to declare this House is of Opinion that the several Expressions contained therein reflecting in general Terms on some Members of this House and on the Publick Treasurer in particular are very unprecedented & a great violation and breach of the Priviledges of this House and as to the Character of the Publick Treasurer the present Speaker of this House The Members of this House declare they are very well satisfied as well with his Integrity as his Ability, his accounts always appearing to be just and True and have this present session been examined by a Committee of both Houses   and further we believe it to be our Duty to represent unto His Majesty the ill usuage this House in general and some Members in particular have received

As to your opinion declared in your Message that the Laws made in 1729 are Void we hope we may without offence declare our different opinion, which is that they ought to Remain in Force untill the Royall Pleasure is signified thereon, and where those Laws to be otherwise dealt with, we imagine it would cause great Confusion in this Province in that it would obstruct the Currency of Bills therein Established and be hurtfull in many other Cases, on which occasion we propose to Address His Majesty and to shew that the Assembly of this Province never meant to deprive His Majesty of any of his Rights.   What you say of the Publick Treasurers not being appointed by Lawfull Authority we doubt not but you will alter your opinion because were it to be admitted that the Laws passed in 1729 were isso facto Void as being made since His Majesties Purchase which yet we do not grant yet nevertheless his appointment to that office has been by several Acts of Assembly ever since the year 1715.

By Order of the Gen^{ll} Assembly

A WILLIAMS C^{lk}

April 28th 1731
Sent by Messrs Russell & Bell

To THE HONO^{ble} THE MEMBERS OF Y^e COUNCIL.

This House finding the Two Resolves sent from you founded on three particular Assertions mentioned in the preamble to the said Resolves, Viz^t

1st Concerning His Majesties Instructions.

2dly The Resolutions of this House thereon as you say.

3^{rdly} The Power which you pretend this House hath assumed

The House conceiving that you have not only put a wrong sense on the Kings Instructions, but also on the Proceedings of this House. We think ourselves bound to clear up such reflections as are cast on us by your Paper.

Wherefore we say to the first we are of Opinion you mistake the Royall Instruction it appearing to us to be only proposed by His Majesty that the Fees shall be regulated and Established by Act, yett untill that is done for which in Obedience to His Majesties Instructions this House directed ye 21st day of the instant April a Bill to be prepared for that purpose, Officers ought not to have Enacted what Fees they thought proper but to have observed our Laws provided therefore.

2dly This House never declared that the said Instruction was contrary to Law or tended to the Oppression of His Majesties Subjects but that the Officers their taking larger Fees than is by Law appointed was an oppression of the Subjects nor did this House immediately come to that Resolution altho' the nature of the offence could not but be most highly moving nor was it so soon delivered after the Instructions were laid before us as is suggested, for the Instructions came before the House the 19th and the Resolution pass'd the 21st day of that Instant, & then on reading the Complaints of the Masters of Vessells Merchants & Traders, not supposing that His Majesties Instructions had the least Tendancy to Countenance the oppression Complain'd of, and in truth nothing could have been more amazing unto to us than to see our Complaint against so illegall practice put off with so unjust a Construction

3^{rdly} This House never arrogated or assumed to themselves such Power as is represented in the last part of ye preamble, nor does the House conceive that their Complaint can be so construed, because in your Paper it is declared that they had the business of the Fees under their Consideration pursuant unto His Majesties Instructions, and as that Instruction proposed it to be done by an Act it ought not to be imagined it would have been proceeded on otherwise, indeed had this House published anything towards regulating the Fees otherwise than with the consent of Governor & Council such an attempt would have been highly blameable.

As this House hath thus given just Satisfaction to the Council in those particulars and Vindicated themselves from the aspersions cast on them as Invaders of the Royall Perogative or reflecting on the Honour & Dignity of the Crown, Endeavouring to divest the Govr & Council of their parts of the Legislature or arrogating any other part of Government than is consistant with the Laws of Great Britain and the Charter granted by King Charles the second to the Inhabitants of this Province, so we hope you will join with us in our Request to the Governor that he may issue a Proclamation declaring such practices to be contrary to Law and an Oppression of the Subject, & strictly forbidding all officers to take larger Fees than are by Law appointed under pretence of difference of Money untill such time as they are Regulated by authority of Govr Council and General Assembly, this House now having the same under their Consideration persuant to His Maj^{ties} Instruction.

By Order of the Gen^{ll} Assembly

A WILLIAMS C^{lk}

April 28th 1731

Sent by Messrs Russell and Bell

The House adjourned 'till Monday Morning Eight o'Clock

Monday May 3rd   The House met again & His Excell^y the Govr sent the following Paper to the Lower House Viz^t

Mr SPEAKER & GENT OF THE ASSEMBLY

As there are certainly several things in your last Message very Exceptionable I suppose it will be no breech of Priviledge in me calmly to point them out to you nor can it be any Injustice to say that the Language of your last Message as well as the former about Fees was very Coarse & Rough and certainly wanted the Respect that is due to a Person in my station which you will in time be Convinced of and obliged to alter your Method.

It is allowed you that the House of Representatives have a Right to Complain when Injured but it ought always to be done with Decency and Good Manners which I think is very much wanting in that part of your last Message which tells me I have put the Affair in a Worse Light and accuses me of having made a Proposal contrary to His Majesties Instructions in relation to the Offices in Virginia which I only Recommended as a Guide or Rule to regulate the Fees hereby in Proclamation Money, as His Majesty has positively directed they shall be taken for the Future And you will find Gent. if you will give yourselves time to peruse the Kings Instructions that one of them gives the Governor & Council Power to Regulate and settle Fees and Tables of such Fees to be hung up in the Respective Offices they belong to, I desire to know how you understand this Instruction? It appears to me that the Gov' & Council are impowered to Regulate and Establish Fees and whither there was not Occasion for it at this Juncture must be left to further Enquiry His Majesty has positively declared in His Instructions that for the future all Fees shall be paid in Proclamation Money which is in Effect Repealing all Laws that declare Fees shall be received otherwise. Before the Assembly met, myself and the Council pursuant to the above Instruction declared what was the Value of Proclamation Money in Bills as they now pass This is what you call Oppression, Arbitrary and Illegal Proceedings, General Evil and a hindrance to Trade, Charges that are very Extraordinary in their Nature and ought to have been well supported, but in the manner they are used are really very Surprising and Astonishing.

The Council have already in their Amendments to the Bill for Fees made it Evidently appear that the officers in their Fees by your late Emission of Bills of Credit in the year 1729 were very much injured, a Crown Sterling being rated before that time at seven shillings and six pence by Law, in the Regulation on the late Emission of Bills was valued at Twenty five shillings, And it is very manifest that most of the Fees now subsisting were stated before the Emission of any Bills at all, and that the Bills by this time had it not been for the Emission in 1729 would or ought to have been sunk, so that it is an apparent Loss and Damage to the officers if they are obliged to take the same Fees in Bills of the late Emission or anything near it, and what inducement it will be to His Majesty to tolerate the late Bills I leave you to judge when I tell you it must be Represented to the King that these Bills now Currant are hurt to no one but his officers only who must abandon their Employments and Depart this Province or starve here if they take their Fees in the kind manner you prescribe or desire

Gentlemen the disrespect shewn me I was informed by some Members of your House was occasioned by one Person who pulled the said Paper out of his Pocket that he might divert the House and take them off from another Subject then under Consideration It was my good opinion of the House induced me to think they were surprised into such Indescent Expressions, but you now Convince me Gentlemen that whoever was the Author thereof it is sufficiently supported by your Patronage

Since you sent that Gallant Paper there have been two Gent of the Council have moved to have Proclamations issued which I refused for the same reason you were denyed (there being no Occasion) I am Concerned that any Gent either in your House or in the Upper, will suffer their thoughts to run so much on Proclamations I judge it will Redound more to your Credit and the good of this Province if you diligently apply yourselves in perfecting what the King has recommend to you in the Eight Instructions delivered to your House.

GEO BURRINGTON

Then the House adjourned till to-morrow morning Eight of the Clock.

Tuesday May 4th The House met again & received the following Message from the Lower House. Viz:

To His Excellency Governor & Council.

This House desires to know whither the Power of the Assistant Justices in this Province is Equall to the Associate Justices in England or what is their Power, For we have now under our Consideration the Bill relating to Circular Courts.

By order of the Genll Assembly

A WILLIAMS. Clk.

Sent by Mr Kenyon and Mr Barrow.
Then the House adjourned 'till to-morrow morning Eight of the Clock

Wednesday May 5th The House met again and sent the following Answer to yesterdays Message

Mr SPEAKER & GENT OF THE HOUSE OF BURGESSES

This House having considered your Message and Perused the Warrant from His Majesty appointing William Smith Esqr Chief Justice Are of Opinion that the full & sole Power of holding the supream Courts of Judicature is in the sd William Smith and that the Assistants have not an Equall Power with the Associate Justices in England nor any Judicial Power.

By Order of the Governor & Council

ROB^t FORSTER C^k.

Received the following Message from the Lower House. Viz^t

To His Excell^y the Governor & Council.

This House being senseble that sundry Grants for Lands have been issued since His Majesties purchasing the Province, some of them on old Warrants & some for raising Money towards defraying the Charge of running the Dividing Line between this Province & Virginia, the purchase money for which has been paid to William Little Esqre late Rec^r Genl

It is the request of this House to his Excell^y the Governor and the Hono^ble the Council that they will joyn this House in an Address to His Majesty to Confirm all such Titles, thereby to prevent any Disputes that might otherwise arise.

And further this House requests that the said William Little may be obliged to give secu^ty to repay to all such Persons the purchase Money received by him for such Grants as shall be made Void by His Majesty if any such shall be in case the said William Little hath not paid away the same by order of the Government.

By Order of the Genl Assembly

A WILLIAMS C^k

Sent by Mr Russell & Mr Bell

Then the House adjourned till to-morrow morning Eight of the Clock.

Thursday May 6th   The House met again

Resolved that the Consideration of the Answers to His Excell^ys Speech be adjourned till next Wednesday.

Edmond Porter Esqre his Majesties Judge of Vice Admiralty and a Member of this House, made the following Protest

£10 Sterl Money to be divided amongst the officers of Vice Admiralty.

$\frac{5}{12}$ To the Judge	.. ... .	£ 4	3. 4
$\frac{4}{15}$ To the Register	..	2	13. 4
$\frac{1}{4}$ To the Advocate	.	2.10	–
$\frac{1}{15}$ To the Marshall	. .	– 13.	4

£10.— -

Or an Equivalent in Proclamation Money

35

Any Act made to the contrary of the above List of Fees, I do hereby dissent from and Protest against

Signed   E PORTER

at the Council Board this 6th day of May 1731

Then the House adjourned 'till to-morrow morning Eight of the Clock

Fryday May 7th

The House met again and His Exce^{lly} the Governor sent the following Paper in answer to the last Message from the Lower House Viz^t

Mr SPEAKER & GENT OF THE ASSEMBLY

In answer to your Message of Wednesday I must inform you that I am Commanded by His Majesty to send an account to the Lords of Trade & Plantation of all Patents for Land granted by Sir Richard Everard Bart. and the late Council since the time His Majesty compleated His purchase of this Province   I am Convinced the Charge given in by the Commissioners appointed to run the dividing Line between this Government and Virginia is very modest,   I believe the Lords of Trade will not deem it otherwise   I cannot think it proper for me to Joyn in the Address you desire   I will represent a true state of the Affair to the Lords of Trade, as to the last Paragraph I think the persons who signed those Patents, having no authority to dispose of the Lands may be as Lyable as Mr Little who acted only under them & by their immediate appointment

GEO BURRINGTON

Adjourned 'till to-morrow morning Eight of the Clock

Saturday May 8th

The House met againe

Read a Bill for an Act entituled An Act for Establishing & fixing the Supream Courts in this Province and enlarging the Power of the Precinct Courts the first time and past with amendments.

Resolved that Nathaniel Rice Robert Halton & J^{no} Bap^t Ashe Esq^{rs} be and they are hereby appointed a Committee to joyn with such Members as shall be appointed in the Lower house to confer on the subject matter of the Bill now before this House Entituled an Act to Regulate & ascertain the payment of Quit Rent & Fees of the officers of this Government

By order

ROB^t FORSTER C^{lk} of ye Upp House

And the Lower House thereon sent the following Resolve in Answer Viz^t

To the Hono^ble the Council

Resolved that Mr Callen Pollock, Mr William Downing, Mr Chas Denman, Col: Thomas Swann, Mr John Etheridge, Mr Edward Salter, Mr Thomas Pollock, Mr Richd Russell, Mr Thomas Smith, Mr William Willson, Mr Walter Lane, & Mr William Williams be a Committee to joyn with the Committee of the Upper House to confer on the Bill for an Act Entituled an Act to Regulate and Ascertain the Payment of Quit Rents & Fees of the officers of this Government.

By order of the Genl Assembly

A. WILLIAMS C^lk

Sent by Mr Wm Williams & Mr Geo Winn
Then the House adjourned 'till Monday morning Eight of the Clock.

Monday May 10th
The House met againe
Read a Bill for an Act Entituled an Act to Regulate and Ascertain the payment of Quit Rents & Fees of the officers of this Government the second time so passed with Amendments.

Then the House Adjourned 'till to-morrow morning Eight of the Clock

Tuesday May 11th
The House met again & Adjourned 'till to-morrow morning Eight of the Clock.

Wednesday May 12th
The House met again.
Received the following Message from the Lower House

To the Hono^ble the Council

Resolved that Major Henry Bonner Mr Charles Denman, Mr Gabriel Burnham, Mr John Etheridge, Mr James Castellaw, Mr Thomas Smith, Mr Richard Rustull, Mr William Williams and Mr Walter Lane be a Committee of this House to joyn such Members of the Council as shall be appointed to Examine and Settle the acco^ts of all such Persons as have any Claims on the Publick, and they Report their Proceedings to this House for Approbation

Sent to the Council for Concurrance

A WILLIAMS C^lk of ye Genl Assembly

By Mr Thomas Pollock
Mr Isaac Hill

Then the House adjourned 'till to-morrow morning Eight of the Clock

Thursday May 13th
The House met again and sent the following Resolve to the Lower House Viz'

Mr SPEAKER & GENT OF THE HOUSE OF BURGESSES

Resolved that John Bapt Ashe, Edmond Porter, and Cornelius Harnet Esqrs be and they are hereby appointed a Comittee to Joyn such members as is appointed in the Lower House to Confer on, Examine, and Settle the accots of all such Persons as have any Claims on the Publick

By order of the Governor & Council
            JOS ANDERSON Clk of the Upper House.

Read a Bill for an Act Entituled an Act for Establishing & fixing the supream Courts in this Province & enlarging the Power of the Precinct Court the Second time & passed with amendment

Adjourned 'till to-morrow morning Eight of the Clock

Fryday May 14th   The House met again

His Excelly the Governor delivered in the following Paper to this House Viz'

GENTLEMEN OF THE COUNCIL

The Bill for ascertaining officers Fees and Payment of Quit Rents being now before you and having been thrice Read in the House of Burgesses I think it proper before it goes further to ask your opinion upon His Majesties Instructions about Quit Rents wither (by the Instructions) I may safely pass an Act whereby an Equivolent is to be taken instead of Proclamation Money, and if you shall be of the opinion of may, whether what is offered for payment of Quit Rents in the Bill before us is a sufficient Equivolent to Proclamation money
            GEO BURRINGTON.

Received the following Message from the Lower House Viz'

To HIS EXCELLY THE GOVERNOR

This House having now prepared such Bills as are thought necessary to be offered (pursuant to His Majties Instructions laid before us) this Session and the present Season of the year being proper for our Residence in our Plantations. We request that the Session may be ended in a few Days, & if any other matters may be thought necessary to be laid before the Assembly, it may be done at the next Biennial the Election whereof is now within a few months

By order of the Gen¹ Assembly

AYLIFFE WILLIAMS Cᵏ

By Mʳ Wᵐ Williams &
   Mʳ Geo: Powers

Adjourned 'till to-morrow morning Eight of the Clock

Saturday May 15ᵗʰ
The House met again
Received the following Message from the Lower House

To His Excelly yᵉ Govʳ & Council.

This House taking into Consideration the several Resolutions touching His Majesties Instructions and other matters proposed to be laid before the Lords Commissⁿ of Trade & plantations Representing the true state of this Province and as the same will make the address to His Majesty very large if the same were to be incerted therein

Resolved that Col. Edward Moseley, Thomas Pollock and Cullen Pollock Esqⁿ Col. Thomas Swann, Capt William Downing, Mʳ Charles Denman, Mʳ John Etheridge, Mʳ Walter Lane or any four of them to be a Committee to draw up the said Address, representing the true state and Condition of this Province with respect to its Laws Currancy Trade Lands Rents and Tenures & other Affairs pursuant to the several Laws of this Government and the Notes & Resolves of the House relating to His Majesties Instructions and that the same be signed by the Speaker in the name and by the Appointment of the General Assembly of this Province and Transmitted to His Grace the Duke of Newcastle principal secretary of state, and the Right Honᵇᵇᵉ the Lords Comissⁿˢ of Trade & Plantations by such Agent or Agents as the said Committee shall appoint and that the said Committee shall be empowered to draw out of the Publick Treasury to defray the Charge of that Agency such sums of money as they shall think proper not exceeding £500 Paper Currancy

Sent to the Governor & Council for Concurrance

A WILLIAMS Cᵏ Gen¹ Ass

By Mʳ Kenyon &
   Mʳ Islands

Received the following Message from the Lower House

To His Exce^{lly} the Governor & Council

This House taking into Consideration the charge that Mr Chief Justice Smith must be at in fitting himself for going the Circuites pursuant to the Bill now proposed to be Enacted

Voted that he be paid the sum of One Hundred Pounds paper Currency the better to enable him to proceed on that service This House being willing to Express their good will and Esteem they have conceived of the said Mr Chief Justices conduct & behaviour in his Station

Sent to the Upper House for Concurrance

AYLIFFE WILLIAMS C^{lk} Genl Assembly

By Mr Burnham &
    Mr Thos Swann

Received the following Resolve from the Lower House, Viz^t

To His Excell^y the Govr & Council

Resolved that the Comiss^{rs} of Edenton be and they are hereby invested with Power to make Rules for the better ordering and Regulation of the said Town Affairs and that they have power to make & levy any Equall assm^{ts} on the Inhabitants towards fencing in the said town or clearing what shall be needfull or for defraying any Petty Charges for the good & benefit of said Towne

Sent to the Govr & Council for Concurrance

By order

AYLIFFE WILLIAMS C^{lk} Gen Ass

Concurr'd with so as such assessment be legally made

By order

JOS ANDERSON C^{lk} Upper House.

Received the following Message from the Lower House

To His Excell^y the Governor & Council

This House has appointed Mr Thomas Pollock, Col Cullen Pollock, Mr Mackrora Scarborough, Col· Thos Swann, Mr Wm Wilson, Mr William Barrow, and Mr Evan Jones to be a Committee of this House to joyn such Members of the Councill as shall be appointed to examine the old Paper Currency and see the same destroyed

By order

A WILLIAMS C^{lk} Gen Ass·

Resolved that the former Committee William Smith Edmund Porter and Cornelius Harnett Esq.ʳ be a Comittee now to joyn such Members as is appointed in the Lower House to Examin the old Paper Currancy and make their Report to both Houses.

By order

JOS ANDERSON Cˡᵏ Upp House

His Excellʸ the Governor proposed to have a Conference with the Lower House about the Bills for ascertaining the payment of Quit Rents and officers Fees and for Establishing and fixing Supream Courts

Whereupon the following Message was sent to the Lower House Viz.ᵗ

Mʳ Speaker & Gent of the House of Burgesses

This House demands a Conference of your House at four of the Clock this afternoon upon the subject matter of the two Bills Viz.ᵗ a Bill ascertaining officers Fees and paym.ᵗ of Quit Rents and a Bill for an Act Entituled an Act for Establishing and fixing supream Courts in this Province and enlarging the Power of the Precinct Courts.

By order

JOS ANDERSON Cˡᵏ Upp House

The Governor laid on the Boards some heads for the Conference on the subject matter of the Debate concerning the the Bills with their last Amendments Viz.ᵗ

In the beginning of the second page

It is Expressed only Lands taken for the future shall be registered with the Kings auditor or His Deputy   It is the King's intention that all Lands already taken up should be Registered (19 Instruction) a Proviso that the Auditor shall keep a Deputy in every Precinct, I think we have no authority to compell him, and he may keep his office & appoint Deputies as he pleases.

In the third Page

In the Sixteenth Instruction, It is writte that all Fines Penalties etc must be reserved to His Majesty his heirs and Success.ᵗ for Publick use & support of Government

In the 4ᵗʰ—It is my Opinion that Officers acting by Patent in this Government can only be turned out of their Places by the King upon some occasions a Suspension may be Lawfull

Last Article—We cannot by any means postpone the Payment of the Kings Quit Rents a Recᵈ Genˡ is appointed 'tis supposed he is not without Instructions how he is to Proceed having Comission under the Kings Great Seal or Warrant

And the Lower House attending accordingly a Conference was had and His Excelly the Governor delivered in his sentiments according to the above heads After which the Lower House withdrew and desired a Copy of the Heads spoke to by His Excell' the Governor which was accordingly delivered them.

His Excell' the Governor sent the following Message to the Lower House Viz'

M' SPEAKER & GENT OF THE HOUSE OF BURGESSES

As an answer to your Message this day delivered to me by M' Kenyon & M' Islands I again repeat what I have formerly said, that the business of this Country absolutely require an Agent in London for which reason I recommended to you in my Speech at the opening this session for the appointing one with a proper salary   I now consent that an Agent shall be appointed by myself, Council and Assembly

GEO BURRINGTON

May 15ᵗʰ 1731

Received from the Lower House the following Message Viz'

To HIS EXCELL' THE GOV' & COUNCIL.

In answer to the Conference this day

To the 1ˢᵗ Paragraph we say that as all Grants already passed are or ought to be Registred in the Secretaries Office, from thence the Auditor or his Deputy may have Transcripts, but if any Grants should not be Registred there, we will consent to have some method provided compelling People holding Lands to enter the same on the Rent Roll as yᵉ Recʳ of the Rents shall make his Collections or to enter the same with the Auditor or his Deputy so as Offices for that purpose be kept in each precinct or after any other manner so it be not done at the Expence of the People

To the 2ⁿᵈ—We will use the style proposed by His Maᵗʸ

To the 3ʳᵈ—We shall be content that in the Cases of Officers holding by Patent making a Breach of the Law they may be only suspended or otherwise Punished

To the last—As the King proposes to receive Proclamaċon money we are willing for want thereof to make the best Equivolent we can to His Majesty, and therefore offer Tobacco according to the Practice of Virginia and as People are not provided to make sufficient for that purpose this year, we propose the payment thereof to be postponed untill it can be made, but if ready payment is expected we shall consent that it

be made in other Comodities that may be made this present year according to a just valuation.

This House doth not consent to alter the £150 per cent on Bill currency.

Concerning the Court of Chancery.

That Court has always used to be held at the times and places when and
where the General Courts have been, and all process returnable thereto
to the third day of the General Courts but as that day was generally taken
up with the Crown business it was Ruled that the doing the business in
Chancery should be putt off untill the Monday following, and a Court
so Established we Conceive ought not to be removed but by the Authority of Assembly, nevertheless as it has been proposed to give Ease to
the Inhabitants by appointing General Courts in each of the three Counties proposed to be erected, so we think it may be as necessary to Ease
them with respect to the Court of Chancery, and if his Exce^lly shall
be willing we propose that the power of the Court of Chancery may be
lodged in the Justices of the Countys as it is in Virginia or in the Chief
Justice or other proper Commissioners appointed for that purpose.

By order of the Genl Assembly

A. WILLIAMS C^lk

Received the following List of Claims from the Lower House Viz^t

To THE HONO^ble THE GOV^r & COUNCIL

THE REPORT OF THE COMMITTEE OF CLAIMS ALLOWED.

To Thomas Murphy for a horse lost in the Countries Service, if found to be returned to the Provost Mar-sh^ll or Deputy for the use of the Publick and imme-diately disposed of by him at Vandue for that Pur-pose & the money lodged with the Precinct Treas^r unless Mr Murphey chooses to keep his horse.	£ 22 12. 6
To D° for his trouble and horse hire to White Oak	2 " 7 " 6
To Mr Wm Willson for horse hire in ye Countrys Service	8 " 10 " -
To Mr Roger Kenyon for a pair of hand cuffs to Con-fine a Criminal.	— 15 —
To Major Bonner for Expenses on His Excell^ry ar-rivall	35 " 10 " -
To 4 Grand Jurymen for Chowan Viz^t Major Bonner Mr Thomas Lovick Mr Will: Arkill & Col. Wil-liam Harding Jones, 6 days each	6 " — —

36

To 4 Grand Jurymen for Perquimons Vizt Mr Charles Denman Mr Richard Skinner Mr Joshua Long, Mr Richard Whitbee, 8 days each   £ 8 " — -

To 2 Grand Jurymen for Bertie Vizt Mr Gray & Thos Kearney 10 days each   5 " — -

To 3 Petit Jurymen for Bertie prec{t} Vizt Edward Moor, Wm Charleton & Robert Warren 7 days each   5 " 5 " -

To 4 Petit Jurymen for Chowan Thomas Matthews, John Duning, William Egerton & John Robertson   7 " — " -

To James Potter for work done about the Court House   2 " 10 " -

To Edmond Gale for hiring workmen about the Court House   2 " — -

To Peter Young for two Journeys to Cape Fear on publick business including Ferrys & all other charges (horse hire excepted) £40, whereof £20 is already paid   20 " — -

To Major Bonner going to the Chowan Indians   3 " 10 " -

To viewing the body of a negro as Coroner & paid the Jury as by Law   2 " 5 " -

To sundry claims allowed William Mackey late Provost Marshall   48 " 5 " -

To Jno. Rogers Deputy Marshall for Craven Prec{t} for executing two writts for Election of Burgesses & hiring a man to go to Core sound   4 " 6 " 8

To Sr Richd Everard for going over the sound upon Complaint made against the Tuskarooro Indians Serv{ts} Boats & Hands for 10 days   25 " — -

To Attendance on 2 Assemblies who could not meet to do business for want of an Upper House   10 " — -

To Jno Saunders for apprehending & bringing up to Goal one Soloman Smith a condemned Criminal from Core sound   10 " — -

To Mr Wm Williams for Victualls for the Tuskarooro, pr Governors Order   1 " — -

To D{o} for the Committees Expenses this Session   7 " — -

To Ayliffe Williams for a Journal Book & a Lock & Key for the office   2 " 12 " 6

                   £259 " 8 " 2

Sent to His Excell{y} the Govr & Council for Concurrance

         AYLIFFE WILLIAMS. C. G A

Sent by Mr Smith &
     Mr Barrow

Adjourned 'till to-morrow morning Eight of the Clock

Monday May 17th

The House met again.

His Excell^y the Governor sent the following Paper to the Lower House Viz^t

Mr SPEAKER & GENT OF THE HOUSE OF BURGESSES.

I cannot think you sufficiently expressed your Good Will & Esteam to the Chief Justice of this Province by your voting him so trifling a sum as one Hundred Pounds Paper Currency, I think a Gent who possesses so high a post as Chief Justice of North Carolina & so Eminent a station as the first in His Majesties Council here, ought to be better regarded Therefore let you know it is my opinion you cannot make him a less present than Eight Hundred Pounds Currancy (in Value) is but one hundred Pounds Sterling which I will forthwith issue out a Warrant for if you desire me

GEO BURRINGTON

Received the following Message from the Lower House in Answer to the Above Paper. Viz^t

To HIS EXCELL^y THE GOVERNOR.

As we are very well satisfied with the Abilities, Conduct & Behaviour of Mr Chief Justice Smith in his station We thought ourselves obliged to offer him a sum as might purchase horses for the service he shall undergo & we look on ourselves the more obliged to do so in regard the first Quarterly paym^t of his Salary is not to Coffience untill September next & the reason of our offering no larger a sum was owing to the poverty of the Country which at present is encumbered with a large Debt

We cannot be of the same opinion with your Excell^y to think there can be such a vast discount on our paper Currancy, Bills of Exchange being lately sold at five for one, so hope his honor will rest satisfied with what the House has voted on that head.

By order

A. WILLIAMS C G A

By Mr Smith
    Mr White

His Excell^y the Governor requiring the Attendance of the Lower House they came in a full Body & the Govr delivered his Speech to them in these Words. Viz^t

GENTLEMEN,

It is now five weaks since I conveen'd you together and within a few days after your Meeting I laid before you such of His Majesties Instructions as I was Commanded in order to have Laws framed upon them, in all which time nothing of that Nature has been offered from the House of Assembly but one Bill for the regulating Fees and Payments of Quit Rents, which Bill being thought in the Upper house in many things to Deviate from His Majesties Instructions particularly about the Quit Rents it could not be passed and you signifying in your late Message you had gone your furthest in it, having passed your last Amendments and that you had nothing now to offer, though there are several of His Majesties Instructions no ways yet considered of by you. I fear it will be to little purpose to keep you longer together, and indeed the Divisions, the Heats, and the Indecencies of your Debates growing daily among you gives me but a little room to hope that His Majesties Instructions and the true Interest of the Country will have their due weight with you. There was another Bill sent from the Upper House for the Ease of the Country by Circular Courts but was Clogg'd with such Amendments in your house as put a stop to it, and finding you are not now inclined to proceed upon anything further, but have in your Message desired a Recess I shall comply with your Message hoping time will compose you to better thoughts

GENTLEMEN

After the many instances I have given of my affection for this Country I need not take pains to Convince you how much I have at heart the welfare and prosperity of it, that cannot be obtained by Private and narrow Views which I wish I had not occasion to say I find prevails more than a publick spirit, for my part nothing shall be wanting in my power for the benefit of this Province and I only ask in return your Dutifull Behaviour to His Majesties Commands the only way to recommend you to the best of Kings who never did, nor will impose anything unreasonable on his subjects.

GENTLEMEN OF THE ASSEMBLY

I do now prorogue this General Assembly unto the sixth day of September next and it is hereby Prorogued accordingly

                                        GEO BURRINGTON

A Copy Exm'd by

                                        ROB⁵ FORSTER Cᵏ
                                          of the Upper House

NORTH CAROLINA—ss.

A Journal of the Proceedings of the General Assembly of North Carolina began and held at Edenton on Tuesday the 13th Day of April 1731.

MEMBERS RETURNED

Chowan Prec^t
Coll Edward Mosele̤y
Maj^r Henry Bonner
Collen Pollock ⎫
Willm Downing ⎬ Esq^rs
John Lovick ⎭

Pasquitank
Coll Thos Swann
Mr Gabr^l Burnham.
Mr Griffin Jones
Mr Jerem^h Symons.
Mr Charles Sayer

Bertie
Mr Auth^r Williams
Mr Jam^s Castlaw
Coll: Tho: Pollock
Mr Isaac Hill
Capt, Geo: Winns

Hide
Mr Tho Smith.
Mr Willm Barrow

Carteret.
Mr Richd Russell
Mr Jos^h Bell

Bath Town.
Mr Rog^r Kennion

Pequimans
Mr Mackrora Scarborough
Mr Sam^ll Swann
Mr Richd Skinner
Mr Char^s Denman
Mr Marma^k Norfleet.

Currituck
Mr John Etheridge
Mr Henry White
Mr Geo. Powers.
Mr Richd Islands.

Beauford.
Mr Edwd Salter
Mr Sym: Alderson

Craven
Mr Willie Willson
Mr Evan Jones.

Eaden Town
Mr Willm Williams

Newbourn Town
Mr Walter Lane

The Members attended on His Excellency the Gover. in the Council Chamber, and were directed by him to chuse their Speaker, and said he would be ready to receive him in the Council Chamber at 9 'oth clock tomorrow morning

The Members returned to their house and chose Edw⁴ Mosely Esq⁽ʳ⁾ to be their Speaker

John Baptista Ashe Esq⁽ʳ⁾ one of the members of the Council came to the Table of this House to administer the Oaths for the Qualification of the Members, and imediately Edw⁴ Moseley, Esq⁽ʳ⁾ Speaker Maj⁽ʳ⁾ Henry Bonner John Lovick Esq⁽ʳ⁾ Cullen Pollock Esq⁽ʳ⁾ Will⁽ᵐ⁾ Downing Esq⁽ʳ⁾ M⁽ʳ⁾ William Williams M⁽ʳ⁾ Mackrora Scarborough, M⁽ʳ⁾ Sam⁽ˡˡ⁾ Swann M⁽ʳ⁾ Rich⁴ Skinner M⁽ʳ⁾ Char Denman M⁽ʳ⁾ Marmaduke Norflect Coll Tho Swann M⁽ʳ⁾ Gabrill Burnham M⁽ʳ⁾ Griffin Jones M⁽ʳ⁾ Jeremiah Symons M⁽ʳ⁾ Charles Sayer M⁽ʳ⁾ John Etheridge Capt Tho Lowther M⁽ʳ⁾ George Powers M⁽ʳ⁾ Rich⁴ Islands M⁽ʳ⁾ Tho Smith M⁽ʳ⁾ Will⁽ᵐ⁾ Barrow, M⁽ʳ⁾ Edward Salter M⁽ʳ⁾ Roger Kennion M⁽ʳ⁾ Will⁽ᵐ⁾ Wilson M⁽ʳ⁾ Joseph Hannis M⁽ʳ⁾ Arthur Williams M⁽ʳ⁾ James Castelaw Coll Tho Pollock M⁽ʳ⁾ Isaac Hill Capt Jno Wims, took and subscribed the Oaths, made and Subscribed the Declaration by Law appointed for their Qualification in the presence of the said M⁽ʳ⁾ Ashe

Adjourned to 8 'oth Clock Tomorrow Morning

Wednesday April 14ᵗʰ
Mett according to adjournment
The House attended the Governor and presented Edw⁴ Moseley Esq⁽ʳ⁾ their Speaker, and then the Governor made the following Speech

GENTLEMEN OF THE COUNCIL AND GENTLEMEN OF THE HOUSE OF BURGESSES

His Majesty the King our most Gracious Lord and Master having honoured me by his commission to be Governor of this Province on my arrival here by and with the consent of Council Issued writts for the several precincts and Towns to chuse Burgesses to meet on the 13th of this month I assure you Gentlemen it is a great satisfaction to me that we are now assembled   I cannot doubt of your ready complyance in passing such Acts as are required by his Majesty in the 19ᵗʰ 31ᵗʰ 42ᵗʰ 61ᵗʰ 63⁴ 75ᵗʰ 76ᵗʰ & the 114ᵗʰ Articles of my Instructions

GENTLEMEN

I assure you that I have as much inclination to promote the Welfare of this country now as formerly   I expect every member of this Assembly comes here with an Intent to doe everything that may be to the Kings Honour and the Good of North Carolina   I hope we shall behave ourselves with so much duty that his Majesty will have pleasure in granting us his Royall Favours when we approach his throne with our Humble Petitions

GENTLEMEN

There are Several matters absolutely necessary to be settled in this Assembly Particularly how to keep the Bills to the value they ought to pass for, The settlements being so far attended I think it needfull that the Chief Justice with his Assistants should for the ease of the people hold Courts in three different parts of the Province twice a year

That Wills should be proved and Licences given by a proper Officer in every Precinct.

That effectual methods be taken to procure a direct Trade to Europe and the West Indies without which this Country will always continue poor

To pass an Act for building a Town on Cape Fear River and appointing Commissioners for that purpose.

To appoint an Agent and settle a Salary for transacting the affairs of this Province in England

GENTLEMEN OF THE HOUSE OF BURGESSES.

I am fully sensible how necessary your presence is at this time of the Year on your Respective Plantations therefore will do all in my power to make this a short Session If you judge it necessary depute some of your House to advise with me on any matters you have occasion to debate which may expedite business and prevent Misunderstandings, I recommend to you Unanimity and agreement and that your Debates be carried on with Modesty and good manners

GENTLEMEN OF THE COUNCIL

I return you my sincere thanks for the readiness you have shown in dispatching all Business that has come before us, Your Demeanour to me has been so full of respect that I am at a loss for words to express the esteem and due regard I have for persons of so great worth and excellent Qualifications.

GENTLEMEN

My diligence and industry in promoting new Settlements in this Country when Governor for the Proprietors you remember and the happy Effects thereof are known to every man in this Province, that on Cape Fear River began by me Six years past is now the place of the greatest Trade in the whole Province   All the Reward I ever received for the Charges necessarily and unavoidably occasioned by that undertaking the losses I suffered and the great Hardships I endured was the thanks of a House of Burgesses

GENTLEMEN

Your behaviour at this time is of the utmost Consequence to North Carolina   it is in your power to make it very happy by cheerfully and willingly performing what is required of you by the Greatest and best King that ever Swaid the British Scepter,   Consider you have at this time a Governor that is intirely your Friend and Well Wisher that will joyn his own Interest to Obtain for this Country all that is now, or has any appearance of being for your good,   I sincerely desire that your Proceedings may accomplish and perfect all that is wanting to make this Country populous, happy and rich

The Members returned to their House where the Governors Speech was read, also the articles of the Governors Instructions referred to in his Speech

Ordered   That the Consideration of the Governor's Speech be referred untill tomorrow morning

Mr   Williams delivered to the House his Majesties Commission to the Governor for the perusal of the members and the Satisfaction of the House   the Same was publickly read, and a Copy thereof that was Delivered by Mr Williams being examined and corrected

Ordered   That the Same be Kept among the Papers belonging to the House and an Entry thereof in the Journal book and that the Original Commission be delivered to the Governor by the Members of Chowan Precinct with the thanks of the House

The House made choice of Christr Becket to be dore keeper and John Nairne to be messenger of this House

Ordered   That Mr John Lacky late Clerk of this House, do forthwith deliver at the Table of this House, all the Journals and Papers belonging to the General Assembly

The House proceeded to enquire into controverted Elections and Returns, and resolved that any Member of the House as is a Magistrate may give an Oath if thought necessary for the better discovering the Truth concerning such elections

On examining the Several returns for Newbern it appeared to the House that Mr Walter Lane was elected for that town

Ordered   That the name of Joseph Hannis inserted in the return of the writ be erased and the name of Walter Lane inserted

Ordered That Mr Benjamin Peyton the Marshall of Bath County do cause John Rogers his Deputy to attend this House on the 26th day of this month or sooner if it may be

Read the Petition of Mr Patrick Complaining of an undue return of a member for Bath Town

Ordered. That Mr Benjamin Peyton do cause his Deputy Jno Collisson to attend this House the 26th day of this month or sooner if it may be

Adjourn'd to 3 'oth Clock afternoon

Met according to adjournment

The Members of Clowan precinct reported to the House that they waited on the Governor at his House and delivered him the Commission.

The House made choice of Mr Williams to be Clerk of the General Assembly

Ordered That the said Mr Williams do give sufficient security in the sum of 2000^l Currancy of this Province for the faithfull Discharge of his Office the preserving and safe keeping the Journals and papers belonging to the house and his delivering them to the Table of the house when required

Ordered. That the Original Deed of Grant from the true and absolute Lords Proprietors of Carolina, to the inhabitants of the County of Albemarle dated in the year 1668 which was lodged by a former Order of Assembly in the hands of George Sanderson Esqre be laid before the house a Monday next

Read the Petition of Mr Thomas Lowther as Burgess for Currituck Precinct, on which the House Examined Otho Holland the Marshall of Currituck and after the matter had been fully debated

Resolved That Mr Lowther was not duly elected.

Ordered. That a Writt do issue for electing a Member for Currituck Precinct in the room of Mr Lowther

It appearing to this House that Otho Holland hath misbehaved himself in the Said Election it is Ordered That the Messenger do take the Said Holland into Custody so as he have him before this House tomorrow

Read the petition of Joseph Hannis complaining of an undue Election and return of Mr Walter Lane as Burgesse for Newbern

Ordered that the said Petition be referred untill the Deputy Marshall of Cravan Precinct do attend the House

Mr White, Mr Jones, Mr Alderson, Mr Lane, Mr Rustall and Mr Bell, Members of this House Mr Ayliffe Williams Clerk Christopher Becket

37

Dore Keeper and John Nairne Messenger, took the Oaths made and subscribed the Declaration by Law appointed at the Table of this House before Cornelius Harnett Esq a member of the Council

Adjourn'd to 8 'oth clock tomorrow morning

Thursday April 15th
Met according to adjournment.

Mr Ayliffe Williams Clerk of this House produced His Excellency the Governors Certificate in these Words vizt I do hereby certify that Ayliffe Williams Gentleman Clerk of the Assembly within this Province, hath this day given security in the Sum of five hundred Pound sterling for his Said Office which Bond is lodged with me

GEO BURRINGTON

Which was endorsed by Nath^a Rice Esqre Secretary of the Province in these Words   I do hereby certify that the within mentioned Bond is lodged in the Secretarys office of this Province April 15th 1731

NATH RICE Secretary

Ordered That the same Certificate do remain with the Speaker.

The House directed the Governors Speech to be read   Whereupon it was Resolved that an address to his Excellency the Governor be prepared, giving him the thanks of this House for his kind Speech to this Assembly and to acquaint him that this House will Proceed to consider the several paragraphs thereof as soon as the same can conveniently be done

Ordered That Mr William Downing, Mr Charles Denman, Coll Thomas Swann, Mr John Etheridge Coll Thomas Pollock, Mr Thomas Smith, Mr William Williams and Mr Walter Lane be a Committe for preparing the said address and that the Same be laid before the House tomorrow

Sundry Books and papers belonging to the House were delivered at the table by John Leaky said to be the Same as was lodged at Mr Westbeer's.

Ordered That the same members who were present at their being removed from Mr Westbeer's do Examine the same, and report to the House whither the same are all that were lodged there

Adjourned to 8 'oth clock tomorrow morning

Friday April 16th
Met according to adjournment
Ordered That John Lovick Esqre Coll. Cullen Pollock and Mr James Castelaw be a Committe for preparing a Bill for the Ease of the People

of this Province—relating to the Probat of Wills granting marriage Licences and other things.

Read The humble Petition of Esua Albertson, and other Petitions of Merchants and Owners of Vessels in Beauford and Hide in reguard to their Hardships in paying such large Fees to the Officers of the Ports in this Province

Resolved That this House will resolve itself into a Committe of the whole House on Monday Morning next to consider of those and all other Grievances as shall come before this House

Read The Petition of Grievances of the upper Inhabitants of Chowan Precinct   also the Petition of Watkin Price

Ordered. That the said Petitions be referred to the Comitte a Munday next

Adjourned to 3 'oth Clock in the afternoon

Met according to Adjournment

Otho Holland appeared at the Barr of this House according to order and made an humble acknowledgement of his Fault, humbly prayeth to be discharged.

Ordered That he be discharged paying his Fees

Mr Dawning reported from the Committe for drawing up an address to his Excellency the Governor which was read and after several amendments made

Ordered That the same be engrossed and that this House will wait on his Excellency with the same Tomorrow

Adjourned to 8 'oth Clock Tomorrow Morning.

Saturday April 17th
Met according to Adjournment

Ordered That the Publick Treasurer accounts and all others concerned with Publick moneys be laid before this House a Wednesday next

Ordered That a Bill be prepared for the more easy Administration of Justice to the Inhabitants in the Remote parts of this Government.

The Address to the Governor in Answer to his Speech was read in the House and consented to

Ordered That Mr Isaac Hill, and Mr Arthur Wilhams do wait on the Governour and acquaint him that this House is ready to attend with their address in answer to his Speech,   they waited on the Governor and reported to this House that the Governor informed them their House was adjourned till Monday Morning

Adjourned to 9 'oth clock Monday Morning

Monday April 18th

Met according to adjournment

Ordered That the address of this House in answer to the Governors Speech be referred to further time for the Delivery

Ordered. That the Articles of the Governors Instructions laid before this House be referred to the Committe appointed to draw up an address to the Governor

Mr Swann delivered at this Table the Original Deed of Grant from the Lords Proprietors to the Inhabitants of the County of Albemarle dated May 1th 1668

Ordered That a Coppy Thereof be inserted in the Journal Book of this House and the Original kept by the Speaker for the time being

George Duke of Albemarle Master of his Majesty's Horse, Edward Earl of Clarendon, William, Earl of Craven, John Lord Berkeley, Anthony Lord Ashley, Chancellor of the Exchequer, Sir George Carteret Vice Chamberlain of his Majesty's Household, Sir William Berkeley Knight and Sir Peter Colleton Barronet The true and absolute Lords Proprietors of all the Province of Carolina.

To our Trusty and wellbeloved Samuell Stephen Esqr Governor of our County of Albemarle and the Isles and Isletts within tenn Leagues thereof, and to our Trusty and Wellbeloved our Councellors and Assistants to our said Governor Greeting.

Whereas We have received a Petition from the Grand Assembly of the County of Albemarle praying that the Inhabitants of the said County may hold their Lands upon the same terms and conditions that the Inhabitants of Virginia hold theirs, and forasmuch as the said County doth border upon Virginia and is much of the same nature Wee are content and do grant that the Inhabitants of the said County do hold their lands of us the Lords Proprietors upon the same Terms and Conditions that the Inhabitants of Virginia hold theirs

Wherefore Be it known unto all men by these presents that Wee the said Lords and Absolute Proprietors of the County with the Province aforesaid Have given granted and by these presents do give and grant full Power and Authority unto our said Governor by and with the Consent of our Council or the Major part thereof, or to any Governor for the time being or that shall hereafter be by us appointed full Power and Authority by and with the Consent of our Council then being or the Major part thereof to convey and grant such Proportions of Land as by our Instructions and Concessions Anexed to our Commission bearing Date in October 1667 Wee have appointed to such persons as shall come into our said County to plant or inhabit, to be held of us and our Heirs and Assignes upon the same terms and conditions that land is at this time present usually granted in Virginia anything in our Instructions and Concessions aforesaid to the Contrary Notwithstanding And we do hereby declare and consent that the Warrant to the Surveyor for the laying out of said land and the and the return thereon being registered and also the Grant of you our said Governor and Council, or Governor and Council that shall that shall be when such land is due having the Seal of the County affixed to it and signed by yourself and major part of the Council for the time being, being registered shall be good and effectual in Law for the enjoyment of the said Land or Plantation and all the Benefits and proffits of and in the same Except one half of all Gold and Silver mines to the party to whome it is granted his heirs and assigns for ever he or they performing the Conditions aforesaid Given under our hands and great Seal of our Province this first of May Anno Domino 1668

Registered y⁰ 13 day of July 1693

℔ Edwᵈ Mayo Clerk Council

ALBEMARLE, JO: BERKLEY, G CARTERET
CRAVEN, ASHLEY, P. COLLETON

```
++++++
: THE :
: SEAL :
++++++
```

That as this day was appointed to examine into Several Grievances it be referred till tomorrow

Adjourned to 9 'oth clock tomorrow morning

Tuesday April 20ᵗʰ

Met according to adjournment

Edwᵈ Moseley Esqʳ Publick Treasurer delivered in at the table the Publick Accounts

Ordered. That John Lovick Esqʳˢ Mʳ Chaˢ Denman, Mʳ Gabrill Burnham, Mʳ Geo Powers, Mʳ Arthur Williams Mʳ William Wilson, Mʳ Willᵐ Barrow, Mʳ William Williams be a Committe of this House to be joyn'd with such members of the Council as shall be appointed to inspect and settle the same and the Accounts of all others concerned with the Publick money and report the Same to this house

Sent to the Governor & Council for Concurrance

By order

AYLIFFE WILLIAMS Cᵏ Genˡˡ Ass:

Bᵥ { Mʳ Williams
     & Mʳ Winns }

The Publick Treasurer also delivered in at the table Sixteen Bundles of Old Bills of Credit Exchang'd by him Said to contain £7343 10 6

Ordered That the Committe appointed to settle the Publick Accounts, do exchange the Same parcels of Bills and make report thereof to the House that the Same Bills may be destroyed

Received the following message from the Upper House

M' Speak' & Gent' of the Lower House.

This house has appointed Will'm Smith Edm'd Porter & Cornel Harnet Esq'r to be joyn'd by the Members by you appointed to inspect and settle the Publick Accounts

By order

ROB FORSTER for C'lk of the upper house

Adjourn'd to 9 'oth clock Tomorrow Morning

Wednesday April the 21th

Met according to adjournment

The Articles of His Majestys Instructions referred to in the Governor Speech were read and debated

Whereupon the house came to the Following Resolutions: viz'

On the 19th Article—Resolved in the Address to be prepared to his Majesty the thanks of the General Assembly be dutifully given to his Majesty for his Fatherly indulgence in remitting the Arrears of Quit Rents due from Sundry persons in this Province

At the same time it may be mentioned that the Arrears in this Province were very small in comparison with South Carolina.

That the General Assembly accepts of his Majestys Gracious offer of receiving the Rents for lands in Proclamation money

That this house will proceed to regulate and ascertain the Fees of all Officers in Proclamation Money and as this House is of Opinion there is not a sufficient Currancy of Silver and Gold for a Twentieth part of what shall be necessary for the several payments to be made to the Officers and for Rents This house will propose that all such payments be made in some valuable commoditys or in the Bills Now currant in this Province at proper Rates. And that a Bill for that Purpose be prepared accordingly

On the 31—The Resolution of the House was

That as the Inhabitants of this Province pay so large Quit Rents which we are of Opinion amounts to the sum of 1200' ⅌ Annum which sum will increase as the Province becomes more fully settled it is conceived we are not obliged to pay the Salaries of any Officers but that

Salaries were established by the Lords Proprietors and by their orders paid out of their Revenue arising by the Quit Rents and the sale of Land

The charge of the Govʳ Council and assembly during their Session has been allways defrayed by the Publick

On the 42ᵈ—The Resolutions of the House was

That this will be ready to give such assistance as shall be necessary to cause a due cultivation of the Lands hereafter to be taken up but as to the Method of cultivating 3 Acres on every 50 which is said to be the Rule layd down by his Majesty, it is the Opinion of this House that so strict a rule will very much impeed the settlement of this Province, and thereby lessen his Majesty's Revenue, and that his Majesty be humbly address'd to permit Lands to be taken upon more easy terms and that in the said address to his Majesty mention be made of the Deed of Grant to the Inhabitants of the County of Albemarle As also to confirm the Titles of such as have purchased Lands and paid their money for the same before the arrival of his Excellency the Governor

On the 61ᵗʰ—The Opinion of the House was

That the Law relating to Jurors do stand, in regard none are to be on Jurys but such as are in the Lists formed by the Assembly

On the 63ʳᵈ—The House resolved that it Should be further considered and that Some proper Method be Provided for the better Government of Slaves.

On the 75ᵗʰ & 76ᵗʰ—They are already provided for in the Acts relating to Vesterys.

On the 114ᵗʰ—That it be further considered

Ordered That the Committee appointed to draw the address to the Governor be a Committe for drawing up an address to his Majesty, and to prepare Such Bills as are necessary & agreeable to his Majesty's Instructions, Referred to in the Governor's Speech

The House waited on His Excellency the Governor with the following addres.

To his Excell.ʸ Geo· Burrington Esqʳ His Majᵗᵉˢ Capᵗ Genˡˡ & Govʳ in Chief of North Carolina

The humble Address of the General Assembly of North Carolina

We the Kings most Dutifull and Loyall Subjects the Representatives of the People of North Carolina With great pleasure congratulate your Arrival in this Province, with that command which his most gracious Majesty has been pleased to confer on you, We have formerly Experianced your care for the Welfare of this country and we rest fully assured that We Shall not want your best Endeavours to promote the lasting Happiness of the People of this Province We Sincerely promise for ourselves that we will not be wanting to do everything that we think may contribute thereto and the Honour and Interest of Majesty's Service

The several Articles of His Majesty's Instructions which you have laid before this House shall be Duly considered to us, and as we propose to address his Royall Majesty concerning some of the matters contained therein, we doubt not but our dutifull behaviour to you, and what we shall propose for his Majesty's service and the Welfare of this Province will procure our Addresses a favourable Reception

We observe how particularly you recommend to us the settling a method to keep the Bills currant in this Country to their Value, We imagine the same is already sufficiently provided for by the Act passed in the Biennial Assembly 1729 nor do we find but the Credit given them by that Act is preserved by the Currancy they have obtained all over this Government but if any better Method can be proposed for establishing their value we shall very readily take the same into our Consideration

As Every thing your Excellency recommends shall have its due weight with us we are of opinion with you that the remote Scituation of Divers parts of this Province from Edenton the metropolis of this Government will make it necessary that some Provision be made for the more easy Administration of Justice in those remote parts A bill for which Purpose wee shall order to be prepared accordingly

We heartily thank you for the ease you propose to the Inhabitants relating to Wills and Licences a Bill for which Purpose Wee have ordered to be prepared and as your Excellency has indulged us thus farr We make no doubt that when we propose other matters of equal concern for the good of this Province we shall have your Cheartull Concurrance

We understand there is a Town already established on Cape Fear River called Brunswick in New Hanover Precinct in Respect to one of the Titles of the Illustrious House of Hanover and we are informed it is like to be a flourishing place by reason of its excellent scituation for the Trade of those parts, to promote which or any other place on that River that shall be judged more proper We will readily give such assistance as is in our Power

The Services don this Province by the settlement began by you at Cape Fear we have a gratefull sence of which we shall make evident on proper Occasions and in a particular manner we propose to be mindfull thereof in our Address to His Majesty

All the other parts of your Excellency's Kind Speech we will take into our serious consideration We hope the Behaviour of the Assembly of this Province at this Juncture and at all times hereafter will demonstrate that the Inhabitants of this Province have the greatest Duty and Loyalty to his Majesty, Zeal and affection for your Excellency and the Welfare of this Province

By order of the General Assembly

E. MOSELEY Speaker

The House returned and Mr Speaker reported that the Governor ordered this House do attend him at Eleven a Clock to morrow morning

Read the Petition of Merchants and Masters of Vessells &c

Complaining of Exorbitant Fees taken by the Collector and Naval Officer of Port Bath

Ordered that the following Resolution be sent to the Governor an Council

Whereas By the Royal Charter granted by King Charles the Second to the Lords Proprietors of Carolina it is granted that the Inhabitants of this Province shall have, posses enjoy all Liberty's Franchises and Privileges as are held possest and enjoyed in the kingdom of England

And Whereas it is the undoubted Right and Priviledge of the People of England that they shall not be taxed or made lyable to pay any sum or sums of money or Fees other than such as are by Law established Notwithstanding which it appears by Complaint made in most parts of this Province that the Officers in General, do demand, take and receive from the Inhabitants and Masters of Vessells trading to this Province, four times more than the Fees appointed by the Laws of this Province to the great Discouragement of the Trade of this Province and the Oppression of the People

Resolved, That this House do wait on the Governor with this Complaint and that the Council be desired to joyn with this House in requesting His Excellency to issue a Proclamation, declaring such Practices to be contrary to Law and an Oppression of the subjects, and strictly forbidding all Officers to take larger Fees than is by Law appointed, under Pretence of difference of money untill such time as the Officers Fees shall be regulated by Authority of Assembly, this House now having the same under consideration pursuant to His Majesty's Instructions

By Order
WILLIAMS ℗ C^{lk} Gen^{ll} Assem^{bly}

By { Mr Scarborough
     & Mr Denman

Adjourned to 8 'oth clock Tomorrow morning

Thursday April 22^d

Met according to adjournment

The House waited on His Excellency the Governor pursuant to yesterday Order

The House returned and Mr Speaker Reported that the Governor caused two of his Instructions to be read before them vizt 37th & 47th

Resolved That this House Send the following Request to His Excellency the Governour

The House Request his Excellency the Governor that he will be pleased to lay before this House a Copy of the Two Instructions which he read to them and that what his Excellency shall think proper to Say to this House on those Instructions may be put into writeing

By order
WILLIAMS C^{lk} Gen^{ll} Assem^{bly}

By Mr Skinner
   & Mr Burnham

Adjourned to 9 'oth clock tomorrow morning

Friday April 23^d

Met according to adjournment

To His Excellency the Governor

Voted That the Rever^d Mr Nicholas Jones be paid the sum of tenn Pounds for officiating Divine Service this Day before the Governor Council & Assembly and his Excellency the Governor is requested to issue this Warrant to the Publick Treasurer for payment of the Same

Sent to the upper house for Concurrence

By order
WILLIAMS C^{lk} Gen^{ll} Assem^{bly}

{ Mr Symons
{ & Mr Burnham

Received the following message and the Copy of the 37th & 47th Instructions from the upper House

Mr SPEAKER AND GENTLEMEN OF THE HOUSE OF BURGESSES

I think it necessary to cause Two Articles of my Instructions to be read to you that no Person in your House may pretend ignorance in a Matter where the Kings Commands to me are positive vizt 37th & 47th you may apply to me when and as often as you desire to Inspect the Publick Accounts, and they shall be laid before you. I think it absolutely necessary for his Majesty's Service and the good of the Country that a Treasurer be appointed, Therefore I shall with advice of the Council speedily appoint a fitt Person to execute that Important office untill His Majesty Commissionates one

CH FORSTER for the Clk of the upper house

Adjourned to 9 'oth clock Tomorrow morning

Saturday April 24th
Met according to adjournment
This House takeing again into consideration that Article of the Governor's Instructions relating to purchase of land whereupon it was proposed by some Members of this House that this House should address the Governor and Council to compel the late Receiver to give Security to repay the severall sums received by him for lands in case his Majesty shall declare those Grants to be void, with which William Little Esqr the late Receiver was acquainted by the House and was heard.

Ordered. That the Governor and Council be addressed and that Coll. Tho. Swann, Coll. Cullen Pollock and Mr James Castlaw be a Committee and do prepare an address by Monday Morning Next.

The opinion of this house on the 37th & 47th of his Majesty's Instructions was sent to his Excellency the Governor but he not being in Council the delivery thereof was deferred till Monday

Adjourned to 9 'oth clock Monday Morning

Monday April 26th
Met according to adjournment.
Received the following message from the Council

Mr SPEAKER & GENTl OF THE HOUSE OF BURGESSES

Whereas His Majesty in his Instructions to His Excellency the Governor hath ordered & directed that all Fees shall be paid to the officers in Proclamation Money and the said Instructions having been laid by his

Excellency's orders before the Council and House of Burgesses the said Burgesses immediately came to a resolution which they soon delivered to His Excellency in effect declaring that the said Instructions were contrary to Law and tended to the Oppression of his Majesty's subjects and the said Burgesses having in their said Resolution Arrogated and assumed to themselves the sole power of Establishing Fees Exclusive of the Governor and Council—

Resolved That the said Resolution of the House of Burgesses is a great invasion of his Majesties Prerogative and do highly reflect on the Honour and Dignity of His Crown

Resolved That the said Resolution of the House of Burgesses openly tends to divest the Governor & Council of their share of the legislative authority vested in them by his Majestys Commission and Instructions founded on the Lawes of the English Constitution, and that they seem therein to set up and erect some other form of Government than is allowed by the Laws of Great Britain

By order

CH FORSTER for the C^k of the upper House

MR SPEAKER AND GENN OF THE HOUSE OF BURGESSES

In answer to your unreasonable complaint concerning Fees I must inform you that I have proposed to the Speaker and most of the Members of your House that myself and all the Kings Officers there are more beneficial than here Having also read the answer Drawn up by the Council to the aforesaid complaint, desire you Gentlemen Sedately to consider of it, for my own part I cannot refrain from telling you that whoever the person was that formed the said Paper of Complaint, I compare him to a Thief that hides himself in a house to rob it & fearing to be discovered, fires the house to make his escape in the smoak

GEO BURRINGTON.

This House immediately declared that the same complaint was the Unanimous Voice of the whole house no one member dissenting thereto

That this House never intended to assume to themselves alone the Power of establishing or altering Fees, this house having ordered a Bill for an Act to be brought in for regulating and establishing Fees.

That this House will give a more full answer to the two Instructions which was to have gon a Saturday

To HIS EXCELLENCY THE GOVERNOR

In answer to what your Excellency was pleased to deliver in writing to us with the 37th and 47th Articles of his Majesty's Instructions, we are of Opinion that no public money ought to be issued but as directed by the Governor Council and General Assembly, and this House is of Opinion that by the Act of the Assembly passed in November 1715 Entituled an Act Publick Treasurer to Account This House in conjunction with the Governor and Council hath a larger Right than only to view and examine the Publick Accounts

This House is of Opinion that the 47th instruction doth not extend to Officers appointed by Act of Assembly as are the Publick and Precinct Treasurers and sundry other Officers

And as the office of Publick Treasurer which you are pleased to mention in particular, this House declares they are very well satisfyed with the Ability and Integrity of the Present Publick Treasurer Edward Mosley Esqr who was appointed to that Office in an Act of Assembly by the Governor Council and Assembly, and we conceive that such an Officer so appointed is not to be removed but by the like Power, and further this House is of opinion that the Publick Treasurers of our neighbouring Governments are appointed in like manner by the Governor Council and Assembly

> By Order
> WILLIAMS ⅌ Clk of the Genl Assembly

Mr Powers
& Mr Saver

The Elections of Newbern and Bath were disputed
Ordered That the same be further considered Tomorrow Adjourned to 9 'oth clock Tomorrow Morns

Thursday April 27th
Met according to adjournment
On Debate this day concerning the Election for Bath Bath Town, it appeared to this House that Mr Roger Kennion was duly elected and returned
On Debate it appeared concerning the Election for Newbern Town that Mr Walter Lane is duly elected and returned
Ordered That leave be given to bring in a Bill for the better regulating the Elections of Burgesses for the Town
Ordered That Coll Cullen Pollock, Mr Cha Denman Coll Tho Swann, Mr John Etheridge, Coll Tho. Pollock Mr Walter Lane and Mr Tho Smith be a Committe to draw up a more full answer to the two papers received from the Governor and from the Council

Received the following Message from the upper House

Mr SPEAKER AND GENT^t OF THE HOUSE OF BURGESSES

In answer to your message yesterday we must observe that we find greater inclination in you to Cavill and Raise difficultyes than to do any thing that may tend to his Majesty's Honour and the good of this Province

Gentlemen—We insist it is the intent of some persons to create animosity and ferment Divisions a method too frequently practiced formerly as well as now in order to screen and secure themselves from an enquirey into their conduct which we believe has not been the most upright and regular

Nothing can be more clear or more express than the latter part of his Majesty's 47th instruction wherein his Majesty declares that no Officer whatever shall be appointed but by himself or his Governor which surely excludes the House of Burgesses from any share in the nomination of a Treasurer unless you can prove that the Treasurer is not a publick Officer   And as to your present Treasurer we agree with you that he is a person of sufficient ability and we heartily wish his Integrity was equal to it,   we must likewise informe you that he was not appointed by any lawfull authority, and as to your pretended Laws of 1729 it is very obvious to any man who suffers not his reason to be guided by a spirrit of Faction that they are void and were passed with no other intent than to deprive his Majesty of his just rights settled upon him by the Laws and Constitutions of Great Britain

By Order

R FORSTER C^{lk} upper house

This house is of opinion that the Several Expressions contained in the foregoing paper reflecting in general terms on some of the members of this House and on the publick Treasurer in particular are very unpresidented and a great Violation and Breech of the Priviledges of this House, and as to the caracter of the Publick Treasurer the present Speaker of this House who is particularly named therein The members of this House declare they are very well satisfyed as well with his Integrity as his Ability His Accounts allways appearing to be just and true, and have now this Session been examined by a Committee of Both Houses

Ordered That the Committe appointed to answer the other papers, Do draw up an answer to this

Read the Petition of Jn° Gilbert, Cha' Jones Chris Zehn praying they may be levy Free—Granted

Ordered That Josiah Montgomery of Hide prec' be Levy free.

Ordered That Willm Hooker of Bertie prec' be clear of duty and working on the high ways

Adjourned to 9 'oth clock Tomorrow Morning

Wednesday April 28th
Met according to adjournment

To His Excellency the Governor

Voted. The Messenger that went to Cape Fear to Summons the Council on the first arrival of his Excellency the Governor in this Province be paid the Sum of tenn pounds for his Journey, and his Excellency the Governor is requested to issue his Warrant to the Publick Treasurer for the payment of the Same

Sent to the Council for Concurrance

By Order

WILLIAMS C^lk Gen^ll Assem^bly

To His Excellency the Governor

Voted The Messenger that went to Cape Fear to fetch the Publick Seal of this Province be paid the Sum of tenn Pound for his journey And his Excellency the Governor is requested to grant His Warrant to the Publick Treasurer for the payment of the Same

Sent to the Council for Concurrance

By Order

WILLIAMS C^lk Gen^ll Assemby

Ordered That Rich^d & Willm Islands of Currrtuck precinct be Levy Free

Read the Petition of Willm Killingsworth Praying that a Ferry be established on Roanoke River

Ordered That leave is granted, and that Mr James Castelaw & Mr Arthur Williams do prepare a Bill accordingly

The Committe reported to the House that they had prepared a Draft of an Answer to the Governors as also an Answer to the two resolves of the Council, as also to the message delivered yesterday from the Council which were all read and consented to by the House nevertheless this House will defer the Delivery of the Same untill further order

Ordered That Cornelius Daniel Jn° Brock and David Perkins and Jn° Proctor of Beauford be Levy Free

Adjourned to 9 'oth clock Tomorrow Morning

Thursday April 29th

Met according to adjournment

Read The first time a Bill for an Act Entituled An Act To regulate an ascertaine the Payment of Quitt Rents & Fees of the Officers of this Government and passed

Read The first time a Bill for an Act appointing a Ferry on Roanoke River and passed

Adjourned to 9 'oth clock Tomorrow Morning

Friday April 30th

Met according to adjournment

Sent to the Upper House a Bill for An Act Entituled An Act to regulate and ascertaine the payment of Quit Rents and Fees of the officers of this Government Also a Bill for appointing Killingsworth Ferry on Roanoke River both having been read the first time

Adjourned to 9 'oth clock Tomorrow morning

Saturday May 1st

Met according to adjournment

To His Excellency Geo Burrington Esqr Governor & Commander in Chief &c

It was the greatest surprise imaginable to this House when they received your Paper in Answer to complaints concerning Fees

It is the undoubted Right of the Representatives and nothing more properly their Business then to complain when they find the subjects oppressed and the trade of the Province injured and we can hardly find a more generall Evil then what we have complained of.

And as our Laws have stood for near twenty years the Officers Fees have been paid in Paper currancy at the Rates mentioned in the Acts of Assembly, and now when we find the Officers taking four times as much altho' the same Laws remain in Force our Complaints are called unreasonable—Nor doth what you say of your proposal to some of the members out of this House of having the Fees settled as in Virginia in our opinion put that affair in any better but rather in a worse Light, that proposal being contrary to the Kings Instructions which recommended the Fees to be established in Proclamation Money

But what this House is most astonished at is the close of your Paper when you tell the House you cannot refrain from telling them that whatsoever the person was that formed the said paper of complaint, you compare him to a Thief that hides himself in a House to rob it and fearing to be discovered fires the house to make his escape in the smoak.

We assure you we have sedately considered your paper and the answer of the Council sent therewith and we think we have given them a sufficient answer so we trust we shall your Excellency when we declare that the Complaint we sent was the unanimous Voice of the whole House no one member dissenting therefrom

And we are of Opinion that such Treatment of any member of this House in particular (which seems to be the Intent of your Excellencys harsh Simily) is a great indignity and contempt put on the whole House, a Breach of Priviidge and tends to the deterring the members from doing their Duty which we are well assured will be as disagreable to the Known Justice of his Sacred Majesty to hear as it is grievous and hurtfull to the just Freedom of the Subjects.

By Order

WILLIAMS ℈ Cⁱᵏ Genˡˡ Assembly

Mʳ Rustell
& Mʳ Bell

To the Honᵇˡᵉ The Members of the Council.

This House findeing the two Resolves sent from you founded on three particular assertions mentioned in the Preamble to the said Resolves, viz⁴

1ˢᵗ Concerning his Majestys Instructions

2ⁿᵈ The Resolutions of this House thereon, as you say

3ʳᵈ The Power which you pretend this House hath assumed.

This House conceiving that you have not only put a wrong sense on the Kings Instructions but allso on the Proceedings of this House, we think ourselves bound to clear up such reflections as are cast on us by your paper Wherefore we say to the first, we are of opinion that you mistake the Royall Instruction it appearing to us to be only proposed by his Majesty that the Fees shall be regulated and established by by Act, yett untill that is done for which in obedience to his Majestys Instructions this House directed the 21ˢᵗ day of the instant Aprill a Bill to be prepared for that purpose Officers ought not to have exacted what Fees they thought proper but to have observed our Laws provided therefore.

2ˡʸ This House never declared that the said Instruction was contrary to Law or tended to the oppression of his Majesty's Subjects, but that the Officers there taking larger Fees than is by Law appointed was an oppression of the Subjects, nor did this House immediately come to that Resolution Altho' the Nature of the offence could not but be most highly moveing, nor was it so soon delivered after the Instructions were laid before as is suggested, for the Instructions came before the House the 19ᵗʰ and the Resolution the 21st day of the Instant and then on reading the Complaint of the Masters of Vessells, Merchants and Traders, not supposing that his Majesty's Instructions had the least tendancy to countenance the Oppression complained of, and in truth nothing could have been more amazing unto us that to see our complaint against so Illegal Practice put of with so unjust a construction

3dly This House never arrogated or assumed to themselves such Power as is represented in the last part of the Preamble Nor does the House conceive that their complaint can be so construed because in your paper it is declared that they had the business of the Fees under their consideration pursuant to his Majesty's Instructions, and as the Instruction proposed it to be done by an Act it ought not to be imagined it would have been proceeded on otherwise indeed had this House published any thing towards regulating the Fees otherwise then with the consent of Governor and Council such an attempt would have been highly blameable And as this House hath thus given just satisfaction to the Council in those particulars and vindicated themselves from the Aspersions cast on them as invaders of the Royall Prorogative or Reflecting on the Honour and Dignity on the Crown endeavouring to divest the Governor and Council of their part of the legislature or arrogating any other part of Government than is consistant with the Laws of Great Britain and the Charter granted by King Charles the Second to the Inhabitants of this Province So we hope you will join with us in our request to the Governor that he may issue a Proclamation declaring such practices to be contrary to Law and an Oppression of the Subjects and Strictly forbiding all Officers to take larger Fees than are by Law appointed under Pretence of difference of money untill such time as they are regulated by authority of Governor Council and Assembly this House now haveing the same under their consideration pursuant to his Majestys Instructions

By Order

WILLIAMS ⅌ Cth Genl Assembly

Mr Russell
& Mr Bell

TO THE HONORe the COUNCIL

It is the Opinion of this house that the 47 Instruction was never designed by his Majesty to vacate Such authorities as are granted by Act of Assembly but only to prevent all persons whatever acting by any commission from the late Lords Proprietors even such whose right to offices by grant from the Proprietors were preserved by the Act of Parliament are (as we understand that Instruction obliged to have their

Commissions renued by his Majesty or the Governor, but we do not understand that Instruction in such sence as that those persons who are authorized by Act of Assembly must nevertheless have his Majesty's or the Governor's commission, and we hope we may retain this sence of that Instruction until his Majesty's Pleasure be signifyed thereon without those Severe Expressions mentioned in your paper being flung on this house or any of its members for whatever you may say we are resolved by our conduct and behaviour to Show our Duty and Loyalty to his Majesty and to do everything we think may tend to his honour and the good of this his Province, and we hope when we forbeare to return such injurious language as is given to this House, we shall show we do not intend to cavil & raise Dificulties Nevertheless we think it our duty to declare this House is of opinion that the severall Expressions contained therein, reflecting in general terms on some Members of this House and on the Publick Treasurer in particular are very unpresidented and a great violation and breach of the Privileges of this House And as to the Character of the Publick Treasurer the Present Speaker of this House the members of this House declare they are very well satisfyed as well with his Integrity as Ability His Accounts always appearing to be just and true, and have this present Session been examined by a Committy of both Houses, and further we believe it to be our Duty to represent unto his Majesty the ill usuage this House in generall and some Members in particular have received, as to your opinion declared in your message the Laws made in 1729 are void We hope we may without Offence declare Our Different Opinion Which is that they ought to Remain in Force until the Royal Pleasure is Signifyed thereon, and were those Laws to be otherwise Dealt with we imagine it would cause great confusion, in this Province in that it would obstruct the Currancy of Bills therein established and be Hurtfull in many other cases, on which Occasion we propose to address His Majesty, and to shew that the Assembly of this Province never meant to deprive his Majesty of any of His Rights.

What you say of the Publick Treasurer's not being appointed by lawfull authority, we doubt not but you will alter your opinion because were it to be admitted that the Laws passed in 1729 were Ipso Facto, void as being made since His Majesty's purchase, which yet we do not grant yet nevertheless His appointment to that Office has been by severall Acts of Assembly ever Since the year 1715.

By Order

Mr Russell   WILLIAMS ȹ Cⁱᵏ Genᵗ Assemᵇˡʸ

& Mr Bell

Received a Bill for an Act Entitled an Act to regulate and ascertain the payment of quit rents and Fees of the Officers of this Government, endorsed from the upper house Passed with amendments

R FORSTER C^th of the upper House

Adjourned to 9 'oth clock a Monday morning

Monday May 3^d
Met according to adjournment
Received the following message from His Excell^y the Govr

Mr SPEAKER & GOV^r OF THE ASSEMBLY

As there are certainly several things in your last message very exceptionable I suppose it will be no Breach of Priviledge in me calmly to point them out to you nor can it be any injustice to say that the language of your last message as well as the former about Fees is very coarse and rough and certainly wanted the respect that is due to persons in my station which you will in time be convinced of and oblidged to alter your method

It is allowed you that the House of Representatives have a right to complain when injured but it ought always to be done with Decency and good manners which I think is very much wanting in that part of your last message which tells me I have put the affair in a worse Light and accuses me with having made a proposall contrary to his Majesty's Instructions in relation to the Fees in Virginia which I only recommended as a guide or rule to regulate the Fees here by in Proclamation money as his Majesty has positively directed they shall be taken for the future And you will find Gentlemen if you give yourselves the Time to Peruse the Kings Instructions that one of them gives the Governor and Council Power to regulate and Settle Fees, and Tables of such Fees to be Hung up in the Respective Offices they belong too, I desire to know how you understand this Instruction it appears to me that the Governor and Council are impowered to regulate and Establish Fees and whither there was not Occasion for it at this Juncture must be left to further Enquiry

His Majesty has positively declared in his Instructions that for the future all Fees shall be paid in Proclamation money which is in Effect Repealing all Laws that declare Fees shall be received otherways

Before the Assembly met myself and the Council pursuant to the above Instructions declared what was the Value of Proclamation money in Bills as they now pass This is what you call Oppression Arbitrary and Illegal Proceedings, General Evil and a Hindrance to Trade, charges that are very extraordinary in their Nature and ought to have been well Supported, but in the manner they are used, are really very surprising and astonishing

The Council have already in their Amendments to the Bill for Fees made it evidently appear that the Officers in their Fees by your Late Emission of Bills of Credit in the Year 1729 were very much injured a Crown Sterling being rated before that time at seven shillings and six pence by Law, and in the regulation on the late Emission of Bills was valued at five and twenty shillings, and it is very manifest that most of the Fees now Subsisting were stated before the Emission of any Bills at all and that the Bills by this time had it not been for the Emission 1729 would or ought to have been sunk so that it is an apparent loss and damage to the Officers if they are obliged to take the Same Fees in Bill of the late Emission or anything near it and what Inducement it will be to his Majesty to tolerate the late Bills I leave you to judge when I tell you it must be represented to the King that these Bills now currant are a Hurt to no one but his Officers only, who must Abondon their Employments and depart this Province or starve here if they take their Fees in the kind manner you prescribe or desire

Gentlemen   The disrespect shown me I was informed by some Members of your House was occasioned by one person who pulled the said paper out of pocket that he might divert the House and take them of from another Subject then under consideration   It was my good opinion of the House induced me to think they were surprised into such indecent expressions but you now convince me Gentlemen that whoever was the Author thereof, it is sufficiently supported by your Patronage

Since you sent that gallant paper there have been two Gentlemen of the Council have moved to have Proclamation issued which I refused for the Same reason you were denyed (there being no occasion)   I am concerned that any Gentlemen either in your House or in the Upper will suffer their thoughts to run so much on Proclamations   I judge it will redound more to your Credit and the good of this Province if you diligently apply yourselves in perfecting what the King has recommended to you in the eight Instructions delivered to your House

GEO BURRINGTON

Read the Bill for an Act Entituled An Act to regulate and ascertain the payment of Quit Rents and Fees of the officers of this Government and after Debate t'was referred untill Tomorrow

Adjourned to 9 'oth clock tomorrow morning

Tuesday May 4ᵗʰ

Met according to adjournment

The Debate was resumed on the Bill for an Act Entituled An Act to regulate and ascertaine the payment of Quit Rents and Fees to the officers of this Government and passed this House the second time without amendments

Sent to the uper House

WILLIAMS Cᵏ Genˡˡ Assemᵇˡʸ

Mʳ Etheridge
& Mʳ Powers

Received from the Upper House

A Bill for an Act Entituled An Act appointing Circular Courts in this Province uppon debate sent the following message to the upper House

To His Excellency the Governor and Council

This House desires to know whether the Power of the Assisting Justices in this Province is equal to the Assotiate Justices in England or what their Power is, For we have now under our Consideration the Bill relating to Circular Courts

By order

WILLIAMS Cᵏ Genˡˡ Assemᵇˡʸ

Ordered. That the consideration of the Bill be referred
Adjourned to 9 'oth Tomorrow Morning

Wednesday May 5ᵗʰ

Met according to adjournment

Received the following message from the upper house

Mʳ Speaker and Gentlemen of the House of Burgesses

This House having considered your Message and perused the Warrant from his Majesty appointing Willᵐ Smith Esqʳ Chief Justice are of opinion that the full and sole power of holding the Supream Courts of Judicature is in the said Wᵐ Smith and that the Assistants have not an equal Power with the Associate Justices in England nor any Judicial Power

By order of the Gov · & Council

R FORSTER Cᵏ Councˡ

The Chief Justice sent down his Warrant which was read in the House and returned again

Sent the following Message.

To his Excell^y the Govr & Council

This House being Sensible that Sundry grants for Land have been issued since his Majestys purchasing the Province Some of them on old Warrants and Some for raising money towards defraying the charge of running the divideing line between this Province and Virginia The purchase money for which was paid to William Little Esqre late Receiver General

It is the Request of this House to his Excellency the Governor and the Honorable the Council that they will joyn this house in an address to His Majesty to confirm all such titles thereby to prevent any disputes that might otherwise arise

And further this House requests that the said Willm Little may be obliged to give Security to repay to all such persons the purchase money received by him for Such Grants as Shall be made Void by his Majesty if any such shall be, in case the said William Little hath not paid away the Same by order of the Government

By Order
WILLIAMS C^{lk} Gen^{ll} Assem^{bly}

Adjourned to 9 'oth clock tomorrow morning

Thursday May 6th
Met according to adjournment

Ordered that Willm Jones of Bertie be Levy Free.

This House resumed the Debate on the Bill for an Act Entituled An Act appointing Circular Courts in this Province.

Ordered the Same be referred to a Committee and that Coll. Tho: Swann, Mr Cha Denman and Mr James Castelaw be the Committee to consider thereon

Adjourned to 9 'oth clock Tomorrow morning

Friday May 7th
Met according to adjournment

Received the following Message from his Excell^y the Govr

Mr Speaker and Gent^l of the Assembly

In answer to your message of Wednesday I must inform you that I am commanded by his Majesty to Send an Account to the Lords of-

Trade & Plantations of all Pattents of Land granted by Sir Richard Everard Baronet and the late Councel Since the time his Majesty compleated his Purchase of this Province

I am convinced the charge given in by the Commissioners appointed to run the dividing line betweene this Government and Virginia is very modest, I believe the Lords of Trade will not deem it otherwise I cannot think it proper for me to joyn in the address you desire I will represent a true state of the affair to the Lords of Trade, as to the last Paragraph I think the Persons who signed those Pattents having no Authority to dispose of the land may be as lyable as Mr Little who acted only under them and by their immediate appointment.

GEO BURRINGTON

The Committee appointed to consider on the Bill for an Act Entituled An Act appointing Circular Courts in this Province Informed this House that they had prepared a Bill for an Act Entituled an Act for establishing and fixing the Supream Courts in this Province and for enlarging the Power of the Precinct Courts in this Province, which was read in this house for the first time and passed with amendments.

Sent to the upper House

WILLIAMS Cth Genll Assembly

Adjourned to 9 'oth clock Tomorrow morning

Saturday May 8th
Met according to adjournment
Received the following message from the upper House

Mr Speaker and Gent of the Assembly

Resolved That Nathl Rice Robt Halton and John Baptista Ashe Esqr be and they are hereby appointed a Committee to joyn with Such Members as shall be appointed in the Lower House to confer on the subject Matter of the Bill now before this House Entituled An Act to regulate and ascertain the payment of Quit Rents and Fees of the Officers of this Government

By order
ROB FORSTER for Cth of the uper house

Ordered That Mr Willm Downing, Mr Cullen Pollock, Mr Cha Denman, Coll Tho Swann, Mr John Etheridge Mr Edw Salter, Mr Tho Pollock, Mr Rich Russell, Mr Thom Smith, Mr Willson, Mr Walter Lane, Mr Willm Williams be a Committe to joyn with the Committe of the

Upper House to confer on the Bill for an Act Entituled An Act to regulate & ascertain the payment of Quit Rents and Fees of the Officers of this Government.

Sent—By Mr Winn and Mr Williams of the upper house

Received from the upper house a Bill for An Act Entituled An Act for establishing and fixing the Supream Courts in this Province and for enlargeing the Power of the Precinct Courts.

Endorsed Read in the upper house and passed with amendments
By Order
ROB FORSTER 劣 Cth of the upper house
Adjourned to 9 'oth clock a Munday morning

Monday May 10th

The Committe of Both Houses met in this House to debate and Settle the Bill for Act Entituled An Act to regulate and ascertain the payment of Quit Rents and Fees of the Officers of this Government and proceeded on the amendments

Adjourned to 9 'oth clock Tomorrow Morning.

Tuesday May 11th

Met according to adjournment

The Committe reported to this House the Severall proceedings on the Bill for An Act Entituled An Act to regulate and ascertain the payment of Quit Rents and Fees to the Officers of this Government the House proceeded to Debate the Same then referred it untill to-morrow

Adjourned to 9 'oth clock to morrow morning

Wednesday May 12th

Met according to adjournment

This House took into their further consideration the Bill for an Act Entituled An Act to regulate and ascertain the payment of Quit Rents and Fees of the Officers of this Government to which they made Several Amendments.

Resolved That Major Henry Bonner, Mr Charles Denman, Mr Gabriel Burnham, Mr Jno Etheridge, Mr James Castlaw, Mr Tho Smith, Mr Rich. Russell, Mr Will. Williams & Mr Walter Lane be a Committe of this House to joyn Such members of the Council as Shall be appointed to examine and Settle the accounts of all Such persons as have any claims on the Publick and that they report their Proceedings to this House for approbation

Sent to the Council for concurrance

40   WILLIAMS Cth Genll Assembly

Read in this House the second time and passed a Bill for An Act
Entituled An Act establishing and fixing the Supream Courts in this
Province and for enlargeing the Power of the Precinct Courts
    Sent to the Upper House

                    WILLIAMS Cᵗᵏ Genˡˡ Assemᵇˡʸ

    Mʳ Pollock
    & Mʳ Downing
Adjourned to 9 'oth clock Tomorrow morning

Thursday May 13ᵗʰ
Met according to adjournment
Ordered That Cha Kerby of Bertie be Levy Free.

To Mʳ SPEAKER & GENT: OF THE HOUSE OF BURGESSES.

    Resolved That John Baptiste Ashe Edmᵈ Porter & Cornelˢ Harnet
Esqʳˢ Be, and hereby appointed a Committe to joyn such Members as is
appointed in the Lower House to confer on, Examine, and Settle the
Accounts of all such persons as have any claims on the publick
    By Order of the Gov and Council

                JOS ANDERSON ℔ Cᵗᵏ of the upper house

Received from the upper house a Bill for an Act Entituled An Act
for establishing and fixing the Supream Courts in this Province and for
enlargeing the power of the Precinct Courts   Endorsed Read the Second
time and passed with amendments

                JOS ANDERSON Clk of yᵉ Counˡ

Read for the third time a Bill for an Act Entituled An Act to regulate and ascertain the payment of Quit Rents and Fees to the Officers of
this Government, and passed this House with amendments   Sent to the
upper house

                    By order
                WILLIAMS. Cᵗᵏ Genˡˡ Assembly

    Mʳ Norfleet
    & Mʳ Scarborough
Adjourned to 9 'oth clock tomorrow morning

May 14ᵗʰ
Met according to adjournment
    Read the third time a Bill for an Act Entituled An Act for establish-
ing and fixing the Supream Courts in this Province and for enlargeing
the power of the Precinct Courts and passed with amendments
    Sent to the upper house

                WILLIAMS Cᵗᵏ Genˡˡ Assembly

To His Excellency the Govr & Council.

This House taking into Consideration the Charge that Mr Chief Justice Smith must be at in fitting himself for going the Circuits pursuant to the Bill now proposed to be enacted

Voted That he be paid the sum of one hundred pounds paper currency the better to enable him to proceed in that service, this House being willing to express their good will and esteem they have conceived of the said Chief Justices conduct and Behaviour in his Station

Sent to the upper house for Concurrance

By order

WILLIAMS ⅌ C^{lk} Gen^{ll} Assembly

Resolved That the Commissioners of Edenton be and they hereby are invested with Power to make Rules for the better ordering and regulation of the said Town affairs and that they have power to make and levy any equal assessments on the Inhabitants towards fencing in the said town or clearing what shall be needfull, or for defraying any petty charges for the good and Benefit of the said town

Sent to the Govr & Council for Concurrance

By order

WILLIAMS C^{lk} Gen^{ll} Assem^{bly}

Sent the following message to the upper house

To the Governor and Council

This house having now prepared such Bills as are thought necessary to be offered (pursuant to his Majesty's Instructions lay'd before us) this session and the present season of the year being proper for our Residence on our Plantations, we request that the session may be ended in a few days and if any other matters may be thought necessary to be laid before the Assembly it may be done at the next Biennial the election whereof is now within a few months

By order

WILLIAMS ⅌ C^{lk} Gen^{ll} Assem^{bly}

Adjourned to 9 'oth clock To Morrow Morning

Saturday May 15th

Met according to adjournment

This House takeing into consideration the several resolutions touching his Majestys Instructions and other matters proposed to be laid before the Lords Commissioners of Trade and Plantations representing the true state of this Province and as the same will make the address to his Majesty very large if the same were to be inserted therein Resolved—That Coll Edw. Moseley, Thom. Pollock and Cullen Pollock Esq[rs] Coll: Tho Swann Cap William Downing, M[r] Cha Denman, M[r] John Etheridge & M[r] Walter Lane or any Four of them be a Committe to draw up the said address representing the true state and Condition of this Province with respect to its Laws, Currency, Trade, Lands Rents and Tennours and other affairs pursuant to the severall Laws of this Government and the votes and Resolves of this House relateing to his Majesty's Instructions, and that the same be signed by the Speaker in the name and by the appointment of the General Assembly of this Province and transmitted to his Grace the Duke of Newcastle Principal Secretary of State and the Right Honorable the Lords Commissioners of Trade and Plantations by such Agent or Agents as the said Committe shall appoint. And the said Committe shall be empowered to draw out of the Publick Treasury to defray the charges of that agency such sums of money as they shall think proper not exceeding the sum of £500 Currancy   Sent to the Gov & Coun[l] for Concurrence

     By order
     WILLIAMS ⅌ C[lk] Gen[ll] Assembly

M[r] Kennion
& M[r] Islands

To the Kings most Excellent Majesty

The humble Address of the Gen[ll] Assembly to your Majestys Province of North Carolina

  Most Gracious Sovereign

We your Majestys most dutifull and Loyall Subjects the Representatives of this your Province now met in General Assembly, with cheerfullness lay hold of this opportunity on our first meeting after the Publication of your Majestys purchase of the Sovereignty of this Province to acknowledge with the profoundest Gratitude the many Blessings we enjoy under your Auspicious and happy reign, it is with the greatest Pleasure we observe your Majesty and our gracious Queen Caroline always intent on promoting the happiness of all your people, and altho' we are so remote from your Royall Presence we find ourselves Nevertheless the Subject of your Fatherly care and Concern

We are in duty bound to acknowledge as a particular mark of your Indulgence the placing over us his Excellency George Burrington Esq[r] Captain General and Comander in Chief of this your Province a person who by his behaviour during the time he governed this Province for the Lords Proprietors rendered himself very agreeable to the people by the great care he then showed in his due administration of Justice and in promoting the Wellfare of this Province, on which occasion his indefatigable industry and the hardships he underwent in carrying on the Settlemen at Cape Fair deserves our thankfull remembrance

The Governor having laid before us several of your Majestys Instructions relating to this Province we think it our duty thankfully to acknowledge your Majestys great Clemency and goodness expressed in those Instructions towards the people of this your Province and as some of them do necessarily require that your Majesty should be informed of the State and Condition of this Country, we have directed a Committe to transmit a true State thereof unto his Grace the Duke of Newcastle one of your Majestys principal Secretarys of State and to the Right Honorable the Lords Commissioners of Trade and Plantations

That the life of your Majesty and our gracious Queen may be long, your reign happy and the Succession of your throne perpetuated in the most Illustrious House of Hanover to the latest Ages are the Prayer of

Your Majesty's
most Dutifull
most loyall and
most obedient Subjects

To His Excellency the Gov' & Council.

This House hath appointed Coll Tho. Pollock, Coll Cullen Pollock, Mr Mac' Scarborough, Coll. Thom Swann, Mr William Williams, Mr Will Barrow & Mr Evan Jones to be a Committe of this House to joyn Such Members of the Council as shall be appointed to examine the old paper Currancy and see the same destroyed

By Order
WILLIAMS ℈ Cᵗ Genᵗ Assembly

Mr Kennion
& Mr Island

Several of the members of this House informing that Peter Young had uttered divers scandalous speeches reflecting generally on the Members of Assembly. The messenger was ordered to bring the said Peter to the Barr of this House were being informed of the Charge against him and particularly of his threatening Mr Walter Lane one of the members He acknowledged he spake the words in Passion and hoped the House would forgive him.

Ordered That he do in a submissive manner ask pardon on his knees at the Barr of this House and that he stand committed to close Prison during the Pleasure of this House

The Message from this House appointing a Committe was under writ from the Upper House, vizt Agreed to that the former Committe Willm Smith Edm^d Porter and Coll Harnet Esqre be a Committe now to joyn such members as are nominated in the Lower House to examine the said old paper currency and make their Report to Both Houses

By Order

JOS ANDERSON ⅌ C^ck of the upper house

The Resolve of this House concerning Edenton was under writ for the upper House (in these words) Concurred with so as such assesment may be legally made.

By order

JOS ANDERSON ⅌ C^ck Council.

Peter Young having asked pardon on His Knees at the bar of this house pursuant to order

Ordered That he be discharged paying his Fees

Received the following Message from the upper house

To Mr Speaker & Governor of the House of Burgesses.

Saturday May 15th

This house demands of conference of the Lower House at 4 of the clock this afternoon upon the Subject matter of two Bills vizt a bill ascertaining Officers Fees and payment of Quit Rents, and a Bill for an Act Entituled An Act for establishing and fixing Supream Courts in this Province and enlargeing the power of the Precinct Courts.

By Order

JOS ANDERSON C^ck of the upper house

CLAIMS ALLOWED BY THE COMMITTE OF BOATH HOUSES VIZT:

To Tho Murphey for a horse lost in the Country's Service if found to be returned to the Provost Marsh^l or Deputy for the use of the Publick & immediately disposed of by him at vandue for that purpose and the money lodged with the Precinct Treasurers unless Mr Murphey chuses to keep his horse	22 " 12 " —
To Do. for his trouble & horse hire to White Oke	2 " 7 " 6
To Mr Will Wilson for horse hire in the Country's Service	8 " 10 " —

To Mr Roger Kennion for a pair of handcuffs to confine a criminal.   0 " 15 " —

To Maj^r Bonner for Expence on his Excellency's arrival   35 " 10 " —

To 4 Grand Jurymen for Chowan vizt Maj^r Bonner. Mr Tho Lovick Mr Willm Arckhill Coll Wm Harding Jones 6 days each   6 " ⸺ " —

To 4 Grand Jurymen for Pequimens vizt Mr Chas Denman Mr Richd Kinner Mr Jos^s Long & Mr Richd Whitbee 8 days each   8 " — " —

To 2 Grand Jurymen for Bertie vizt Mr Tho Gray and Mr Tho Kerney 10 days each   5 " — " —

To 4 Petty Jurymen for Chowan vizt Tho Mathews Jno Dunning Wm Egerton & John Robertson   7 " — " ⸺

To 3 Petty Jurymen for Bertie vizt Edwd More William Charlton & Robt Warren 7 days each   5 " 5 " —

To James Potter for work done about the Court House.   2 " 10 " —

To Edm^d Gale for hiring workmen about the Court House.   2 " — " —

To Peter Young for two Journeys to Cape Fear on Publick business including Ferrys and all other charge (horse hire excepted) 40£ Twenty being paid already   20 " — " —

To Maj^r Bonner going to the Chowan Indians   3 " 10 " —

To D^o for viewing the body of a Negro as Corroner and paid the Jury as by Law.   2 " 5 " —

To Sundry Claims of Mr Mackey late Provost Marshall   48 " 5 " —

To John Rogers Deputy Marshall for Craven for executing 2 writs for Burgesses & horse hire to go to Core Sound   4 " 6 " 8

To Sr Richd Everade for going over the Sound upon complaint against the Tuscarra Indians, Servants boat and hands for tenn days   25 " — " —

To attendance 2 assemblys who could not meet to do business for want of an Upper House   10 " — " —

To John Sanders for apprehending & bringing up to Goal Soloman Smith a condemned criminal from Core Sound   10 " — " —

To Mr Willm Wilhams for Victualls to the Tuscarra Indians by order of the Governor   1 " — " —

To D' for the Committees Expences this Session   7 " — " —
To M' Ayliffe Williams for a book for the Journals of
   this House & a Clock for the Office Dore   2 " 12 " 7
                                               259 " 8 " 2

Sent to the Governor & Council for concurrance.

M' SPEAKER AND GOVERNOR OF THE GENERAL ASSEMBLY
   The Report of the Comm'' of Claims

Sheweth That upon Examination of Claims we find that the late Foreman of the Grand Jury M' John Lovick and eight others were not in
the list of Jurors by our Law and therefore not quallified as such and
moreover on further enquirey we do likewise find seven of the Petty
Jurymen not quallified to serve in the Generall Courts which being contrary to the Law of this Government, and in that it may tend much to
the prejudice of the Inhabitants therefore we conceive it our duty to represent the same to the House just as we find it having only allowed the
claims of such as we find duly and legally quallifyed
                      JAM CASTELAW Chairman

Upon reading the above Report of the Committe of Claims t'was
ordered that the list of Claims be Transcribed & sent to the Governor
and Council for Concurrance
   This house also considered the Report of the Committe concerning
Jurors at the last Generall Court, Whereupon the Provost Marshall and
his Deputy M' Makey were desired to attend the House where they were
told that it was the opinion of the House that no person ought to be
returned as Juror but such as is on the list agreed unto by the Assembly
   Received the following Message from the Governor

M' SPEAKER AND GOV' OF THE HOUSE OF BURGESSES.

As an answer to your Message this day by M' Kenmon and M' Islands
I again repeat what I have formerly said that the business of this Country absolutely requires an Agent in London for which reason I recommended to you in my Speech at the opening this Session, the appointing
one with a proper Salary, I now consent that an Agent shall be appointed by my self Council and Assembly
                    GEO BURRINGTON

This house waited on the Governor according to order   Heard what
the Governor & Council offered concerning the two Bills now before them.
   The house returned and M' Speaker reported to the house, that the
Governor as concerning the Bill for an Act Entituled An Act to regulate

and ascertain the payment of Quit Rents and Fees to the Officers of this Government as follows.

Vizt: In the beginning of the second page

It is expressed only Lands taken for the future Shall be registered with the Kings Auditor or his Deputy. It is the Kings Intention that all Lands already taken up should be Registered (19 Instruction) a Proviso that the Auditor shall keep a Deputy in every Precinct, I think we have no authority to compel him, and he may keep his office & appoint Deputys as he pleases.

In the 3ᵈ page.

I my Sixteenth Instruction, It is wrote that all Fines Penalties &ᶜ must be reserved to His Majesty his heirs and Successors for Publick use & support of Government.

In the 4ᵗʰ

It is my opinion that Officers acting by Patent in this Government can only be turned out of their places by the King upon some occasions a suspension may be lawfull

Last Article

We cannot by any means postpone the payment of the Kings Quit Rents, a Receiver General is appointed tis supposed he is not without Instructions how he is to proceed having commission under the Kings great seal or warrant.

And on the part of the Council it was offered that they did not look on a 150 ⅌ cent in paper currency to be an equivalent, and that Pitch and Tarr was raised since the Report of the Committe

And concerning the Bill for An Act Entituled an Act for establishing & fixing the supream courts in this Province and for enlargeing the power of the Precinct Courts, the Governor declared he would no more hold a Court of Chancery at Edenton and therefore he proposed that this House should withdraw the Clause relateing to the Court of Chancery

To His Excellency the Govʳ & Council.

In answer to the first Paragraph we say that as all Grants already passed are or ought to be registered in the Secretarys Office, from them the Auditor or his Deputy may have Transcrips, but if. any Grants should not be registered there, we will consent to have some Method provided compelling people holding Lands to enter the same on the Rent Role as the Receiver of the Rents shall make his Collections, or to enter the same with the Auditor or his Deputy so as offices for that purpose be kept in every Precinct, or after any other manner so it be not done at the expence of the People

41

To the 3ᵈ We will use the stile proposed by His Majesty   To the 1ᵗᵃ We shall be content that in the Cases of Officers holding by Pattent makeing a Breach of the Law they may be only suspended or otherwise Punished

To the last   As the King proposes to receive Proclamation Money we are willing for want thereof to make the best Equivalent we can to His Majesty and therefore offer Tobacco according to the Practice of Virginia and as people are not provided to make sufficient for that purpose this year we propose the payment thereof to be postponed until it can be made, but if ready payment is expected, we shall consent that it be made in other Commoditys that may be made this present year according to a just valuation

This House doth not consent to alter the 150 ⅌ cent on Bill currancy

Concerning the Court of Chancery—That Court has always used to be held at the times and places when and where the General Courts have been, & all Process thereto returnable to the third day of the General Court, but as that day was generally taken up with the Crown business it was ruled that the doing the business in Chancery should be put off until the Monday following And a Court so established we conceive ought not to be removed but by the Authority of Assembly. Nevertheless it has been proposed to give ease to the Inhabitants by appointing a general Court in each of the three Countys proposed to be erected, so we think it may be as necessary to ease them with respect to the Court of Chancery & if his Excellency shall be willing we propose that the Power of the Coʳʳt of Chancery may be lodged in the Justices of the Countys as it is in Virginia, or in the Chief Justice and other proper commissioners appointed for that purpose

By order

WILLIAMS ⅌ Cᵗʰ Genˡˡ Assembly

Adjourned to 9 'oth clock Monday Morning

Monday May 17ᵗʰ
Met according to adjournment.
Received the following Message from his Excelᵞ the Govʳ

Mʳ SPEAKER & GENˡ OF THE HOUSE OF BURGESSES.

I cannot think you Sufficiently expressed your good will and esteem for the Chief Justice of this Province by voteing him so trifeling a sum as one hundred pound paper Currency   I think a Gentlemen who possesses so high a post as Chief Justice of North Carolina and so eminent a Station as the first in his Majesty's Council here, ought to be better reguarded therefore let you know that it is my opinion that you cannot make him a less present than eight hundred pounds currency (in value is but one hundred pounds Sterling) which I will forthwith issue my warrant for if you desire it

GEO: BURRINGTON

The House sent the following answer

To His Excellency the Governor.

As we are very well satistyed with the abilityes conduct and behaviour of Mr Chief Justice Smith in his Statstation we thought ourselves obliged to offer such a sum as might purchase horses for the service he shall undergo, and we look on ourselves the more obliged to do so in regard the first quarterly payment of his Salary is not to commence until September and the reason of our offering no larger a sum was owing to the poverty of the Country which at present is incumbered with a large Debt.

We cannot be of the Same opinion with your Excellency to think there can be such large discount upon our paper currency bills of Exchange being lately sold at five for one, so we hope his honour will rest satisfyed with what the house has voted

By order

WILLIAMS

The proceedings of the Committe of Both Houses appointed to examine the publick Accounts and the old Bills that has been exchanged

Tuesday April 20th The Committe of Both houses met & examined the Publick Accounts of Edwd Moseley Esqr Treasurer and do find vouchers for the payment of £2582 0 6 also examined 16 bundles of old Bills amounting to £7343.10.6 Ordered the said Bills remain with the Clerk—Wednesday April the 21st John Baptista Ashe Treasurer of New Hanover Precinct exhibited his account of Bills of Credit emitted in the said Precinct amounting to the sum of £2748.15 0— Edwd Moseley Esqr Treasurer of Chowan Precinct exhibitted his account of Bills of Credit emitted in the said Precinct amounting to the sum of £4000.0 0 Edward Moseley Esqr as Publick Treasurer also delivered to the Committe several bundles of old bills endorsed said to amount to the sum of £1062 18 0, Ordered that the same be lodged with the former bills. Mr Jno Etheridge Treasurer of Currituck precinct made up his accounts for the year 1729 and paid the Publick Treasurer

£43 10 9   Saturday April 24ᵗʰ Edward Moseley Esqʳ Public Treasurer delivered to the Committe five bundles of old bills amounting to £788 15 0, which with the former parcels makes £9195 3 6, he also delivered a box containing the Counterparts of the old bills and the new Ordered those bills and counterparts remain with the Clerk—May 1ˢᵗ Edwᵈ Moseley Esqʳ Publick Treasurer delivered to the Committe six Bills containing £359 19 0 which with the former makes £9555 2 6, Ordered that those bills remain with the former

Monday May 17ᵗʰ continued

Ordered That all the old paper currency which hath been exchanged and delivered to the Committe of Both Houses amounting to the sum of £9555 2 6 and by the Direction of the Committe lodged with the Clerk of this House, be forthwith produced at the table

The same was accordingly produced and in the presence of the Members of the House put into a Box and locked and the Box corded and sealed and then delivered to the Publick Treasurer who was directed to keep the same and to produce it to the Next Assembly the key of the box was sealed up in paper and delivered to Cap Willᵐ Downing who was required to keep the same and to deliver it to the Speaker of the next Assembly at the Table, the charge of securing the old bills being Thirty five Shillings paid by the Publick Treasurer, to be allowed on his accounts

His Excellency the Governor sent for this House to attend him, which the House accordingly did and the Governor made the following Speech

GENTLEMEN,

It is now five weeks since I convened you together and within few days after your meeting I laid before you Such of his Majesty's Instructions as I was commanded, in order to have laws framed upon them in all which time nothing of that nature has been offered from the House of Assembly, but one Bill for the regulating Fees and the payment of Quit Rents which Bill being thought in the upper house in many things to deviate from his Majesty's Instructions, particularly about the Quit Rents it could not be passed and you had gon your farthest in it having past your last amendments, and that you had nothing now to offer though there are several of his Majesty's Instructions no ways yet considered of by you, I fear it will be to little purpose to keep you longer together, and indeed the Divisions the heads and the indecencies of your Debates growing Daily among you gives me butt little room to hope that his Majesty's Instructions and the true Interest of the Country will have

their Due weight with you, there was another Bill sent from the Upper
House for the ease of the Country by Circular Courts but was lodged
with such amendments in your House as put a stop to it & finding you
are not now inclined to proceed upon anything further but have in your
message desired a Recess I shall comply with your message hopeing
time will compose you to better thoughts

GENTLEMEN

After the many instances I have given of my affection for this Country I need not take pains to convince you, how much I have at heart the
wellfare and prosperity of it, that cannot be obtained by private and narrow views which I wish I had not occasion to say I find prevails more
than a publick Spirit, for my part nothing shall be wanting in my
power for the benifitt of this Province, and I only ask in Return your
Dutifull behaviour to his Majesty's commands, the only way to recommend you to the best of Kings who never did nor will impose anything
unreasonable on his Subjects

GENTLEMEN OF THE ASSEMBLY

I do now Prorogue this General Assembly unto the Sixth day of
Sep^br next, and it is hereby prorogued
A Copy   WILLIAMS C^k G. Assembly

1732.

[B. P R. O North Carolina B T Vol. 9. A 20, 21 and 23.]

PORTER VS. BURRINGTON

NORTH CAROLINA.

To the Honourable the Lords Commissioners of Trade & Plantation.

The humble Representation and address of Edmund Porter, late Member of his Majesties Council and Judge of the Vice Admiralty Court of
the said Province.

Sheweth

That his Excellency George Burrington Esqr by and with the consent
advice of Joseph Jenour and Rob Halton Esq^rs Members of Council

by his Majesties appointment and Mr John Lovick and Edmund Gale of the Governors appointment) hath thought fit to suspend me from the aforesaid offices with black and infamous caracters   In as much therefore as his Majesty is graciously pleased by the 9th article of his Royal Instruction to direct our Governor not to suspend any of the Members of Council without good and sufficient cause nor without the consent of the Majority of the said Council (unless in matters not fit to be communicated to the Council) and in case of suspention of any of them his Excellency is required to cause his reasons for so doing together with the charges & proofs against the said members and their answers thereunto to be duly entered upon the Council Books and forthwith to transmit Copys thereof to your Lordships &c   Least therefore the Clerk of the Council (from whom I can procure no Copy) should be induced to attest the proceedings relating to my suspention otherwise than in a genuine manner I humbly ask leave in my defence to inclose to yours Lordships his Excellencies original charge consisting of five general articles Signed under his own hand & given me the morning of the Same day I was suspended annexed to which is my answer and a certification under the hands of Mr Ashe and Mr Harnet Members of Council by which your Lordships will perceive that three Members of Council appointed by his Majesty did dissent from my Suspention (thõ I believe it will be represented otherwise and in what manner the Governor vaunted and sported with my misfortunes after he had Suspended me from the office of Judge of Admiralty the day before and the next day from the Council Board not giving me one hours time in the former office to defend myself and threw a paper which I told him relating to my defence into the fire without reading it or suffering any one member of the Council to peruse it During which Trials (if I may so call them) permit me to assure your Lordships that the lerned have not described Malice on the furies halfe so terrible to my apprehension as this Gentleman appeared, thõ he was at the Same time my Judge' In the two first General Articles the Governor accuses me with Obstructing all proceedings in Council by rusing unnecessary disputes and cavils &c   As his Excellency might not think it Policy to desend to the particulars of the first and second charge I beg leave to observe to your Lordships from whence I apprehend they are founded

1st In faithfullness to his Majesty and the Trust reposed in me whilst a Member of Council I was often under necessity to differ in Sentiments and opinion with the Governor more especially in matters which related to Lands wherein I did repeatedly advise him in private not to accept, purchase or otherwise be concerned in the Property of such Lands which in all probability was like to be controverted and of Right belonged to the King   here began the Governors resentments and my misfortune

2ᵈˡʸ I gave an opinion in Council that the best expedient to find the frauds that had been Transacted by means of Mr Lovicks emitting blank pattents &c was (if his Excellency thought fit) to issue forth Proclamation to call in all pattents that had been made out from a certain time, that thereby compareing the povity of hands, quantity of acres, Situation of Land and record of the Same &c the fraud and injury don his Majesty might be discovered

3ʳᵈˡʸ I gave an opinion in Council that it was improper for His Excellency (who negative power was distinct and Separate in the making Laws) to come into the Council Chamber and by himself alter such Bills that were by the Upper House preparing or amending for his assent

4ᵗʰˡʸ I gave an opinion in Council that Mr Wm Little receiver general under the Lords Proprietors for the Quit Rents and purchase money of lands ought to produce a regular Rent Role by which he and his Deputies did collect the Same that thereby it might appear obvious to the Council what the amount thereof was annually before his Accounts could be admitted or he discharged   Moreover the Said Little I observed (to a Committy of Council) that in one article of purchase money paid by Martin Franks he had given credit but thirty Shillings to his Majesty whereas in Truth the Sum paid by Mr Franks was above three hundred pounds, as appears by a Memorandum here inclosed

5ˡʸ I gave an opinion in Council that the Governor could not appoint Mr John Lovick and Edmund Gale Members of Council in Derrogᵃ to his Majesty's 7ᵗʰ and 9ᵗʰ Instruction when seven in the Province did subsist and finding these Royal directions were like to be no guide, I drew up the enclosed Dissent and prayed it might be entered in the Council Books, but it was refused me which I looked on as a breach of priviledge and of evil consequence for by that means the different opinion and reasoning of Governors and Council would be unknown to his Majesty the Secretary of State or your Lordships and such matters perhaps only inserted in the transmitted Records of Council which the Governor and a few members thought proper

6ˡʸ I often gave an opinion in Council that the Governor of himself is not sole Chancellor (as he hath repeatedly insisted) and this my opinion is founded from the 66 & 67 articles of His Majesty's Instruction whereby it appears that appeals in cases of Error from the Courts in this Province in Civil causes, are directed to be made to Governor and Council

7ly I gave an opinion in Council that his Excellency and a less number than five of the Council could not hold Courts of Chancery, that the Judicial proceeding of such corts were fixed to three certain Termes in the year, vizt March, July and October therefore could not be deemed an emergency, so as to tolerate a Quorum of three or four (thō his Excellency hath made a practice with that number) to proceed in matters of equity—I will not trouble your Lordships to insert any further particulars wherein my conscience or opinion led me to assent or dissent from the Governor I hope what I have said will be sufficient to convince you that I have behaved in Council as became my station, neither hath any man in this Government according to my capacity demonstrated a greater regard for his Majesty's service, for as soon as it was reported that this Province was a purchase to the Crown, I was the first person (let who will attribute to themselves) that did by three several Memorials advise my Lord Duke of Newcastle concerning such Frauds in Land which I apprehended were carried on as well before as since the said purchase all which I doubt not have been fully made appear 'ere now to his Grace and your Lordships by Sir Richard Everard Mr Smith and others

My Lords I was apprehensive when I attempted the several Informations and matters before mentioned that (considering the policy prejudice and strenth of those who such injuries did effect) it was a very hazadous and dangerous undertaking for one of my fortune and ability but my confidence and dependance lay in finding protection from his Majesty and those great officers who are intrusted with his affairs. Wherefore I do most earnestly beseech your Lordships to take my distressed case under your consideration that others hereafter in these distinguished Countreys may be encouraged for their faithfull endeavours to serve his Majesty

                    I am
                        your Lordships
                            most dutifull & obedient servant
        Albemarle   E. PORTER
            Feb 19th 173½

MEMor MADE BY E PORTER CONCERNING THE PURCHASE OF LANDS IN No CAROLINA

[Recd with Mr Porter's Repn to the Board dated 19th Febry 173½]

Memorandm

On the twentyth day of Jany 1731 at the House of Mrs Dunstons in Edenton before Col Moore and Edmond Porter, Mr Martin Franks of

Nuce expressed himselfe Viz' that he was ready to swere that M' W'
Little the late Receiver Gen' of the purchase money and quit rents of
Land under the late Lords Prop" had received of him £302 57 purchase
money for 10175 acres of land for which he had M' Little's receipts and
that at the time he paid it to M' Little he desired M' Franks not to
acquaint the then Gov' Sir Rich' Everard with the sum that he had so
paid   And he the said Franks further said that M' Little told him at
the same time that if he would not let him have half of some lands he
had on Nuce river it should be the worse for him   M' Franks soon after
meeting with M' Lovick the then Sec'' he told him what M' Little desired
about the pay'm' of the money afores' viz' not to discover the same to Sir
Rich Everard at which M' Lovick (he saith) smiled & walked off   So
far the conversation passed before Col Moore & Ed Porter

On the 22' Jan'' M' Franks I met in Edenton who further said to me
Viz   You thought I was afraid to let the rela* of y' money be known
least those people follow me to destroy me "but you are mistaken   I
acquainted Gov' Burrington therewith this morn* & he says it is very well
All which when called on I am ready to make oath to

Test   E PORTER.

[Indorsed]

EXTRACTS OF MIN OF COUNCIL & COPIES OF COMPLAINTS & ANSWERS RELATING TO CAPT. BURRINGTON'S SUSPENDING M' PORTER FROM THE COUNCIL & BEING JUDGE OF THE ADMIRALTY

NORTH CAROLINA.

To the Right Hon''' the Lords Commissioners of Trade and Plantation
Exceptions humbly offered by Edmund Porter Esq'' against the Legality
of his Excellency George Burrington Esq'' Governor &c   Suspending
me from the Council Board the 21'' day of Feb'' 173½

1'' Because on the 20'' of January aforesaid the Governor put the
question (before I was called on to answer any charge made against me)
immediately on his Declaration of my suspention as Judge of the Vice
admiralty, whether I ought not to be suspended from Council, thereupon
for of the Members viz' M' Jenoure, M' Halton, Deputy Provost Marsh'
M' Lovick and Edward Gale (to shew their willingness to oblige his
Excellency) voted me unfit to sit in Council and therein prejudged me

2ly Because three of those four assenting members vizt Mr Jenoure, Mr Lovick and Edmund Gale were at the same time themselves under an accusation of a Murther they intended on me the 7th of Janry 1730 and giving a Rout to the Court of Admiralty of this Province, whereupon my Lords of Admiralty on my representation of the same hath given directions to our present Governor (by a publick Letter wrote by Mr Secretary Burchett, bearing date the 17th of last May) to make strict inquiry therein &c which publick Letter Governor Burrington received about fifteen days before my suspension, and notwithstanding the said directions permitted those three Gentlemen before they were acquitted of the facts to sit as judicial members not only to give Judgement on me as a Member of Council but also to Judge of my proceedings in the Courts of Admiralty which Court and all the Officers thereof they had put to the Rout as aforesaid

3ly That the Governors nomination and appointment of Mr John Lovick and Edmund Gale was as I do apprehend in Derogation of his Majesties 7th & 9th Instructions when seven did subsist in the Province wherefore such votes Extrajudicial

4ly That the Governor by his general charge hath prejudged me himself and the next day brought on my Trial for a further Judgment.

5thly And lastly, because the Governors charge is a compound of ill nature containing nothing but general accusations without a proof of any one particular matter

MY LORDS,

From the severall foregoing recited Observations, I beg leave to make this conclusion

That admitting the reasons contained in my 2d & 3d Exceptions to be grounds sufficient for excluding Mr Jenoure, the Lovick and Ed. Gale as Legal Judges on these Trials, that then and in Such case the Members Dissenting (vizt Mr Ashe, Mr Rowan and Mr Harnet) was a Majority of two against my Suspension and therefore contrary to his Majesties 9th Instruction who is graciously pleased to direct our Governor not to suspend any of the Members of his Council without good and sufficient cause, nor without consent of the Majority of the said Council &c

All which is dutifully submitted to your Lordships consideration, beseaching you if you should be of opinion that I have not merited this suspention, to grant me your favourable Report or Recommendation to his Majesty so that I may be restored to my place in Council thereby to wipe off from me and my posterity, that undeserved Loade of infamous

Caracters and Epithets which are bestowed on me in the Records of Council through the prejudice (more than Justice) of my Enemies.

This mark of your Indulgence and goodness to me, will ever be Acknowledged as becomes

Your Lordships

most faithfull and

obedient servant

E. PORTER

Feb^{ry} 19th 1731 [1732.]

———

[B. P. R. O. B. T North Carolina Vol. 9, A 38.]

———

LETTER FROM CAP^t BURRINGTON, GOV^r OF NORTH CAROLINA, DATED 20th OF FEBRUARY 173¼

To The Right Honourable the Lords of Trade & Plantations

I humbly represent to your Lordships that being received with the Greatest Demonstrations of Joy by the People of the Province when I published His Majesty's Commission, it must appear very surprising that the late Assembly would not pass one of the Acts required, or recommended in the King's Instruction, nor of my proposeing, which were only designed for the Ease of the People, and their own good, I had been seven or eight weeks in this Country, and held several discourses with the leading Men, who seem'd very well satisfyed with all I said to them of my Instructions, except the paving their Quit Rents in cash, and the Great advance of Rents for the Lands to be taken up.

Immediately before the Assembly I had summoned met, Mr Rice the Secretary and Mr Ashe came together from Cape Fear to Edenton the seat of this Government, till then there was not an immagination of any difference or dispute, every time the Council met the business before them was transacted with harmony & decency, Mr Ashe when quallified, began immediately to oppose me in the Council, and endeavoured with false reasoning, and fallacious arguments to impose upon the Judgements of the Gentlemen in the Council, he was very unsuccessfull in the beginning, but in some time gained Mr Smith & Mr Porter to joyn him

Moseley Speaker of the last Assembly and one James Castellaw a very factious Assembly man, came to me the third day after the Assembly met, and desired me or rather required me, to Promise to give my Assent, to an Act of Assembly to confirm the pretended Laws made here in 1729 after the King's Purchase, this I absolutely refused, there being many things in them Acts contrary to His Majesties Service, and such as I am forbid by my Instructions to pass, I was also Publickly and Privately sollicited to use my Interest and Endeavours that possession of the Lands, sold & granted by Sir Richard Everard and the late Council, should be confirmed to the Purchases, this I denied, judging any more therein, then sending a true account, would have been great presumption, these denyals to the Representations occasioned the cool answer they returned in their address to my Speech, and their subsequent behaviour

I think the Journals of that Assembly make evident, how much I was in the right, and the advantages I obtained in every matter controverted, I am well assured the Assembly men would have carried themselves in another manner, if the Council had done their Duty

Upon Smith's defection Mr Rice the Secretary resolved to go to South Carolina, I used my endeavours to persuade him to stay with me till the session was ended, but all my arguments proved ineffectuall

The Surveyor General's Wife about this time landed in Virginia, coming from England dangerously sick, which caused him to go there, by this Ashe, Smith & Porter gained their end for then my own vote made but an equality in the Council, which obliged me to put an end to the Session, I have given the Characters of Smith & Porter in a Report and letter sent to England last Summer

Mr Ashe is altogether bent on Mischief, I have been a great friend to him, my benefits he has returned with ingratitude, his wicked management in Tate's Affair is an undeniable Demonstration that he is a Villain, and unworthy of sitting in the Council of this Province (this Tate's complaint etc is inserted in the Council Journal

Mr Cornelius Harnett another of the Council, was bred a Merchant in Dublin, and settled at Cape Fear in this Colony, I was assured by a Letter I received in England Harnett was worth Six Thousand Pounds Sterling, which induced me to place his name in the list of Persons to be Councellours, When I came into this Country he was reputed by many worth seven Thousand Pounds, but is now known to have traded with other men's goods, nor worth anything, and reduced to Keep a Publick House, How Harnett abused Capt Tate, and what he attempted against me in that busyness, may be seen in the Journals I am humbly of Opinion Harnett's sitting in Council is a disgrace to it.

It is a misfortune to this Province and to the Governor in particular that there are not a sufficient number of Gentlemen in it fitt to be Councellours, Neither to be Justices of the Peace, nor officers in the Militia, there is no difference to be perceived in Dress and Carriage, between the Justices, Constables and Planters that come to a Court, nor between the Officers and Private men, at a Muster which Parity is in no other Country but this

Sir Richard Everard the late Governour for the Proprietors had the meanest Capacity, and worst Principles of any Gentlemen I ever knew, his Administration was equally unjust and Simple, he was under the Direction sometimes of one sett, then of others who advised him for their own Interest, and being incapable of Judging, was led to do anything they put him upon, which brought infinite Confusion on the Country, every man did as he pleased, the Militia which was very good, became so neglected that very few men now have serviceable Arms The Roads so neglected that in my last Progress, I not only found them troublesome, but dangerous to pass.

I cannot refrain from astonishment when I consider that Sir Richard Everard complained against the late Secretary and Surveyor for Granting the King's Lands, when it was himself, that the Secretary advised him against it has been Proved, that the Surveyor Edward Moseley and Sir Richard were perfect Friends, is as well known, as Sir Richard and his Son having a large part of those Lands allotted to them

I was informed at Cape Fear that the late Surveyor Edward Moseley and his relations there (some of them his Deputy's when Surveyor) used very unfair methods in their surveying, and claiming Lands they had no right too, by which means they imposed upon strangers and induced many to pay them for Lands, that they ought to have had the liberty of taking up, and that they held great quantities more than the Patents mentioned, some of these were summonded, before the Council in last January, Moseley gave in an account I knew to be false, others delivered me in Council evasive Papers to prove why they ought to be excused from giving in any account of what Lands they claimed, the further Consideration of this Matter is referred to a Council in March

The Frauds and Concealments of Moseley and his Relations will constantly occasion them to oppose an Act required in my Instructions to oblige all People to Register their deeds for the Lands they hold in the Auditor's office, I judge such an Act, and such a Registry to be for the advantage of all honest men in the Country, without it the receipt of the Quit Rents Intricate and uncertain.

The Erecting a Court of Exchequeur has been deferred to the coming of a receiver, and Auditor, I humbly give my opinion (as Commanded)

that it is not only for his Majesty's service to have a constant Court of Excheq' in this Country, but absolutely Necessary The Chief Justice, the Secretary, Receiver and Auditor for time being, proper Persons to compose the Court, but much good cannot be expected from it without there was a real, not Nominal Lawyer to Preside Such a One I hope to see from England, there is not a man that professes the Law here knows the Proceedings of an Exchequeur Court

Before the Receiver and Auditor are present, I have thought the late Receiver's Accounts could not be Pass'd and if his Majesty declares the Grants void made by Sir Richard Everard after the Purchase, he cannot have any money in his hands, for this reason allso, am of opinion his Accounts should be deferr'd till the King's Pleasure be known

Sometime after Smith the late Chief Justice left his Province I thought there had been no more than four of the Council in the Government, but M' Rice was returned from So Carolina, and M' Ashe not gone to England as reported, which I know not till some weeks after, only two Members appearing at the Council Summoned in July, I swore two Councellours, otherwise I could not have held the Chancery Court, nor regularly appointed a Chief Justice, in September I sent a full account of this to your Lordships, I humbly hope this will not be judged a breach of my Instructions.

I desire leave to say a little about the Fees pay'd in this Govern' particularly of those to the Governor and Naval officers, After the death of M' Eden Governour of this Country, in an Assembly nine years since they altered the Fees of this office, which had been till then £1 2.6 to the Govern' and fifteen shillings to the Naval officer is Sterling money, or fresh pork at one penny halfpenny per pound for Entring and Clearing etc, every Vessel not belonging to the Country and half that money for those belonging to the Country, this the President and Assembly altered by a Clause in an Act then passed, and made it £3.11 0 in Province Bills to the Naval officer, but quite omitted the Governour's Fee which is now at four for one £14 14.0 but it is not near so good as the old Fees, for fresh pork now sells for a shilling a pound, and less than twenty shillings worth of goods bought in England will sell for more than £14 14 0 Neither will any Master of a Vessel pay the old Fee, some busy People of the Country complain of this, I have not heard any Masters of Vessels that think it unreasonable it is certain the Trade is not lessened thereby, for more Vessels have come this Year than I ever knew.

Before the Year viz' the Fees were usually paid in Commodities which as then Rated, were better than four for one in the Present Bills, these Species of Goods now selling from six to tenn more in Bills than Rated till that time

As the officers in this Province take their Fees, they are less in value than in any of the King's Governm* in these Parts, the Fees accrueing to the Chief Justice, Secretary and their Clarkes, are three times as much, as to the Governor & all the rest of the officers here

Bills will be of Great use to this Country, if His Majesty is pleased to allow them, but then, there ought to be no rated commodity's both will cause confusion in Trade, and the rated Goods depreciate the Bills, (as Remarked in the Laws.

Repealing the Biennial Act, would cause the elections to be more orderly and the Persons chose to behave more dencently in Assemblys than hitherto they have done, and if they serve at their own expense will be willing to do the busyness before them, and the best & most substantial men be Chose

The settling Treasurers by the Pretended Act in 1729 is taken from the Method in New England, if this were suffered here, these men would have such an influence in Elections, that scarce a man could be Chose but by their approbation, in the Assemblys they must inevitably carry every matter in Debate as they please, I hope the Lords of the Treasury will be pleased to appoint one Treasurer for the Province.

In June last I was so extreamly buisied in writing letters drawing up a Report, causing the Laws of this Country to be transcribed, remarkeing upon them, making up the Journals of the Council and Assembly and abstracts in the Margins, that I generally was confined to my pen twenty hours in every day and night, And as there was not one Person in Confinement at that time, and having no assistance in my business; I did not make out a Commission for a Court of Oyer Terminer, & Goal delivery, in December there was a Commission of Oyer etc and the Court sate, but found no busyness for them to do, the Prisons being empty throughout the whole Province

The dangerous sickness I was afflicted with last Autumn and tedious indisposition that followed, prevented me from finishing the Drafts and soundings of the Harbours, and completing the account of the Militia in the latter I have made some alterations for the Ease of the People, in April I design to put an end to both, and send them home as Commanded

I have held several Conferences with the Tuscaruro Indians some Complaints against them from the Governour of Virginia, I setled their business to the satisfaction of all Parties, they remain in perfect Ease and Quietness

I received a Letter in January from the Governour of South Carolina, to appoint Commissioners for running a Dividing Line between the two Provinces the Council then sitting, shew'd them the said Governour's letter, and a Paragraph in my Report of the first of July, they advised me not to appoint Commissioners, before I was honoured with an answer from England on that Subject

It is mentioned in my Report that there are no Fortifications in this Country At the South end of an Island called Ocacock there is a sufficient depth of water for any Merchantman to come in, & a secure Harbour, this Island is seperated from the main land by a Sound about fourteen leagues over, that cannot be passed by a Vessell, that draws tenn foot water, it has a Communication with many large Rivers that water so great a part of this Country, as contains four parts in five, of all the Inhabitants within the Province on this Island there is a Hill, whereon if a small fort was Erected Cannon would from thence Command the **Barr, Channell and Harbour**, there is no one thing would cause the trade of this Province to Flourish, like settling a Custom House on this Place, to serve the three districts of Roanoke, Currituck and Port Bath Town, this would procure a Trade from England, in a little time put an end to the Pedling carried on by the Virginians and People of New England, to this Place ships loads of Negros might be brought and sold well

Port Beaufort and the Harbour at Cape Fear, may be made secure by being Fortified, but the Cost prove more than the Country is able at present to Discharge, these three are all the Places in this Country fit for shiping to sail into, there are a great many Inletts that shift their Channels, frequently the old ones fill and new break out, but none of them are good

It has been a Policy of the Subtle People of North Carolina never to raise any money but what is appropriated, to pretend and insist that no Publick money can, or ought to be paid, but by a Claim given to, and allowed by the House of Burgesses, insomuch that upon the greatest emergency there is no coming at any money to fitt out Vessells against a Pirate, to buy Arms, Purchase Amunition, or on any other urgent occasion This I hope will be redressed. The whole amount of the Publick Levys, and Powder Money paid by shiping, little Exceeds two Hundred Pounds sterling a Year

It being hoped and believed here his Majesty will be pleased to let Lands be granted at two shillings per hundred, a few Warrants have been issued lately.   to prevent all injustice and Confusion, in this affair, I have altered the Method used heretofore in this Government, was was to leave sign'd Warrants in the Secretary's hands to fill up as any man came for them, and very often the Deputy Surveyors, kept numbers in their Possession, by which they made considerable advantages,   by their management some people were injured, and others benefitted,   to put an end to all unfair Practices, the warrants are now all filled up before my signing, and Directed only to the Surveyor General, Who afterwards gives Directions to his Deputy's,   All the Warrants made out are entred in a book at the Secretary's Office,   when I sign them they are entered in another I keep on purpose, and when they come to the Surveyor's hands he do's the same   I know not any method more fair and just than this.   Desire to be further instructed by the Lords of Trade, if they see Cause,   there are not any Returns made of the Surveys,   by the time they come into the Secretary's Office, I hope to receive a form from the Lords of Trade (as formerly desired) to make out the Patents by

There seems to be extraordinary care taken in the 47ᵗʰ Instruction that People should not hold much Land, but cannot answer the end Designed, a very little Money will purchase a vast Quantity of Land in North Carolina,   any one may buy old Patented Land at this time,   the Quit Rents at six pence per hundred Acres, under ten pounds Sterling the Thousand, the greatest price ever given in North Carolina for an Improved Plantation, Buildings and all included has not exceeded a Thousand Pound in Bills, which sixty pounds worth of Commoditys from England will sell for,   the reason is, the small Value the Planters receive for their Produce,   a Bushell of wheat is given for six penny worth of English Goods,   a Bushell of Indian Corn, peas, beans, and other Pulse, for what costs fourpence, and a barrell of Tarr will not fetch above eighteen penny worth, besides the trouble of making the barrel, gathering and splitting the lightwood,   the very bringing it out of the woods to a Landing in other Places would be worth the Money

It cannot be expected that this Province should increase in People, if the Quit Rents are higher here, than in Virginia, and other Governments that are more Commodious upon many Accounts and Healthier

Great Improvements may be made in North Carolina Here in Iron Oar enough to serve all the world, and I believe other sorts will be found when the upper Parts of the Province are Inhabited.

Great quantitys of Potash might annually be made, if the true Method was known

The soil in some Places produces wild Hemp, small Parcels are cultivated, some I have seen has excelled in strength, and colour any grown or brought into England

Flax and Cotton are very good and easily Produced Mulberry Trees that bear the thin leaf proper to feed silk worms grow naturally, this Country is certainly as proper and Convenient to produce silk as any in the world, the reason so little has been made, is that the very time required to look after the silkworms, is the season of Planting and Cultivating Rice, Tobacco, Indian Corn and Pulse

The soil and Climate is particularly adapted for producing seeds to make Oyl, I put several sorts into the ground when last in the Country, the increase was beyond Expectation

When this Province is better Peopled, and more Lands cleared of the Trees, it may reasonably be thought, these Improvements and many others may be undertaken to increase the Trade of Great Britain

The Inhabitants of North Carolina, are not Industrious but subtle and crafty to admiration, allways behaved insolently to their Governours, some they have Imprisoned, drove others out of the Country, at other times sett up two or three supported by Men under Arms, all the Governors that ever were in this Province lived in fear of the People (except myself) and Deaded their Assemblys.

The People are neither to be cajoled or outwitted, whenever a Governour attempts to affect anything by these means, he will loose his Labour and show his Ignorance They never gave a Governour any Present except Sir Rich⁴ Everard, with him they agreed for five hundred Pounds in Bills to pass the Pretended Laws in 1729, in the name of the Proprietors when he was showed the Act of Parliament of the King's Purchase, it must be allowed were those Acts Valid, the Assembly Men made a Good Bargain for the People they Represented

About twenty men are settled at Cape Fear from South Carolina, among them three brothers of a noted family whose name is Moore, they are all of the sett known there, by the name of the Goose Creek Faction, these People were always very troublesome in that Governm⁴ and will without doubt be so in this Already I have been told they will expend a great sum to get me turned out, Messengers are continually going and coming from Moseley and his crew too and from them Notwithstanding these Menaces, and the constant discourse that has passed here, allmost from my first Entrance upon the Government, that I should be superceeded by the Contrivances of a Gentleman in England, I have not been terrifyed, but Acted with such Resolution and

Firmness, that the Province was soon put in a quiet condition, and has so continued without any Imprisonments or Persecutions.

I have patiently expected to be Honoured with your Lordp's Commands, when I am so happy to receive them, and the hopes of my being Cashier'd extinguished, soon will the factious People here alter their Carriage, it is an insupportable grievance to them, they cannot invent, nor devise any stratagems to make me swerve from my Duty to the King, or inveigh me to favour some men to the Prejudice of others, by Acting Partialy in my Administration

    I am

      with great Respect
       (your Lordships)
        most humble
         and most obedient servant
          GEO BURRINGTON.

N Carolina. February 20th 173$\frac{1}{2}$

[FROM NORTH CAROLINA LETTER BOOK OF S. P G]

M' BURRINGTON TO THE BISHOP OF LONDON.

        N° CAROLINA Mar 15. 173$\frac{1}{4}$

MY LORD

I was not able to Prevail with the Last assembly to make necessary provision to subsist a convenient number of Clergymen but have a very good expectation, the ensuing one will come into the measures I proposed Dr Marsden continues in the South Part of this Province He sometimes Preaches Baptizeth children & marrieth when desired The Revd Mr Bevil Granville nephew to the Lord Lansdown is also here He was going to Maryland but we have hopes he will continue with us if your Lordship will procure the usual allowance from the Society

These are all the ministers of the Ch^b of Engl^d now in this Gov^t there is one Presbyterian Minister who has a Mixed audience, and there are 4 meeting houses of Quakers. Mr. Jn° Boyd, (the Gentleman who delivers this letter), was bred at the university of Glasgow, has practised Physic in the Colony of Virginia 7 years, is now desirous to take orders, several Gentleman of my acquaintance in this Country give him the Charack^t of a worthy, conscientious man, well qualified for the Ministry,

they are desirous of having him for their Pastor, and earnestly requested
me to recommend Mr Boyd to my Lord Bishop for orders, a certificate
and an allowance from the Society, the Better to support him, if your
Lordship thinks him deserving, as I believe Mr Boyd's designs are
purely to do good in takeing the Ministry upon him and not out of any
view of gain. I humbly recommend him to your Lordship for Orders
and a certificate

I am, my Lord, your most humble and most obd' servant,

GEO BURRINGTON

[FROM NORTH CAROLINA LETTER BOOK OF S. P G]

MR GALE TO THE BISHOP OF LONDON

EDENTON N° Carolina April 6, 1732

My Lord

Your Lordship having been so good as to permit me to address you,
on the account of the State of Religion, in N° Carolina, and not meeting
with any one in London, whilst I was there whom your Lordship
thought fit to send upon such a mission, I take leave to inform your
Lordship that here is now at Edenton one Mr Bevil Granville, who
seems to have the General approbation of the inhabitants, and who was
designed for Maryland at the request and by the direction of the Lord
Baltimore, but falling in here in his passage thither, the Gov' has prevailed with him to stay for one year, and he so well likes the place, that
he promises to continue with us, in case he has encouragement to support him   For this year the people have made very considerable subscriptions to his satisfaction, but as those methods of support are too
Precarious to be depended on for continuance, If your Lordship thinks
fit to approve of him for the mission upon the footing I laid down to the
Society, he says he shall very willingly accept of it, and make his abode
amongst us, but as he is under the misfortune of not being known to
your Lordship yet being sensible of your tender care in not approving
of any Missionaries but such as are well recommended, he beggs leave to
refer your Lordship for his charack' to the Lord Ducy & the Lord Lansdown, who (he says) know him very well,   as for myself I have but once
heard him perform divine service or preach, but I must say he did both,
in so devout and graceful a manner, that I cannot forbear mentioning of
it to your Lordship   But as I presume his Excellency the Gov' may

have writ to you on his acct., Nothing but the duty I owe to your Lordship and the concern I have for the yet unhappy state of religion in this Province, would have occasioned you this trouble from,

My Lord, your Lordship's most devoted humble servant

GALE.

(P S) My Lord, Since your Lordship was pleased to talk with me on Carolina affairs in general and being in Council when, the Petition of Mr. Smith, Ch Justice against our Gov' and others, was read, I hope your Lordship will not take amiss my informing you, that the facts in that Petition, now I am upon the Spot, appear to me more notoriously, not only to be false and Scandalous, as I said in London, but to be form'd only, by himself and one or 2 busy fellows, without any authority that I can learn from the several bodies of people he pretends to represent His accusation against the Gentleman he mentions, and his pretense of the Gov' Screening them, is equally groundless, and as little truth is there in his representation of the Gov's Conduct, who has acted with remarkable caution and temper

Your Lordship's &c.

C G

[FROM NORTH CAROLINA LETTER BOOK OF S P G]

MR. GRANVILLE TO THE BISHOP OF LONDON.

EDENTON, No. Carolina May 6—1732.

MY LORD

From Lord Baltimore's frequent solicitations to leave England and settle in Maryland & upon his promise to provide for me, in the best manner, that, that province would allow, I took shipping from Dublin in order to go there, landing in No. Carolina I accidentally met Mr Burrington, who earnestly entreated and persuaded me, to stay in this Province, there being so great occasion for Ministers as you Lordship will judge when I assure you that I baptized near 1000 children & persons in a very short time after my coming in. As Mr Burrington & Mr Gale are pleased to write in my behalf, I thought it my duty (tho' personally unknown to you) to acquaint your Lordship how willing I am to fix in a country where the clergy is so much wanted & where so few care to settle, hoping that (as unworthy a member as I am) I may be of some service to that church, whereto I belong, being well assured of one thing that let my abilities be never so poor, yet the name of a minister will hinder the growth of various dangerous sects, willing and ready to over run the whole Province Should your Lordship think me worthy of the mission, you shall always hear that I am industrious in the service of God & these people & that I shall act in such a manner I hope as to deserve your Lordships approbation & as becomes the Person indulged with the friendship of the afore mentioned Gentlemen

I am My Lord yours &c
BEVILLE GRANVILLE

[FROM NORTH CAROLINA LETTER BOOK OF S. P. G.]

MR BURRINGTON TO THE BISHOP OF LONDON

No CAROLINA, May 10, 1732

MY LORD,

I did myself the honor to address a letter to your Lordship sometime since by Mr Boyd, wherein the Rev'd Mr Granville is mentioned, this Gentleman I prevailed with to stay in this country one year A subscription has been made for him by particular persons, more adequate to the circumstances of the contributors, than to Mr Granville's merits, who is incessant and indefatigable in his endeavours to promote the service of the church of England Already has christened about a thousand children & is now on a progress in which he will baptize some hundreds we fear Mr Granville will leave us when this year is expired, unless your Lordship with the Society think proper to establish him a missionary in this Province

Mr La Pierre a French clergyman has an allowance from some people at Cape Fear in this Govm't which is renewed, when I wrote the former letter was told he had quitted that place, but after was certainly informed, he had agreed to stay another year Dr Marsden officiates Gratis, at a place called Onslow 40 miles from his own habitation & a clergyman beneficed in Virginia preaches once in a month in a precinct named Bertie on the Borders of this country, this is my Lord the condition we are at present in in respect to Ministers.

Mr Gale who came from Engl'd lately brought a copy of complaints against me to his Sacred Majesty by W'm Smith the S'd Mr Gale informed me, an order of council passed for the complainer to examine witnesses to make good his charge which I think, he will not attempt because he knows the chief part to be false, as those complaints lye in the council office, if my adversary doth not proceed in a little time I will send my ans' (almost finished) till it is seen I hope your Lordship nor any Lord of the council will entertain an ill opinion of me, being very wrongfully calumniated as I shall in due time make appear I beg your Lordships pardon for presuming to write the foregoing Paragraph, and leave to subscribe myself as really.

I am with all due respect My Lord
Your most humble &
most obd' Servant
GEO. BURRINGTON

[B. P R. O North Carolina B. T Vol. 9 A 39]

ABSTRACT OF A LETTER FROM CAPTAIN BURRINGTON GOVERNOR OF NORTH CAROLINA TO THE SECRETARY DATED THE 27ᵗʰ OF MAY 1732

A He received the Secretarys Letter of 10. June 1731—Reason of his not receiving it sooner.

B He refers to His Report sent last year alsoe an answer to this Letter—The Biennial Act must be repealed to bring the people into good Disposition

C. Many people came to settle there last winter, some of good American Fortunes—He may now make a creditable Council, and will write next month to the Board on that subject

D The best conveyance to him is by N England in Summer, Virginia in Winter

E This the first opportunity of sending

NORTH CAROLINA the 27ᵗʰ of May 1732.
SIR

A I received a letter from you by Captain Daniel Beckman on the 6ᵗʰ of April dated the 10ᵗʰ of June 1731 the reason it was so long kept undelivered was that the vessell went to several places before it came here

Upon peruseing my papers, I think as good an answer as I am able to give to this letter may be taken out of the Report I sent to the Lords of Trade last Year, upon the 25th & 115 Instructions,   the whole Laws have been sent to your Board already, which I believe have taken up some of their Lordships time to examine,   the Biennal Act must be repealed before the people of this Country can be brought into a good disposition

C A multitude of people have come into this Country to settle last Winter,   some have very great American fortunes, insomuch that I now think there are Men here to make up a creditable Council for which reason (Sir) I desire you will give my Duty to their Lordships, & let them know I design myself the honour of writing them a letter on that subject next month

D When the Lords of Trade honour me with their Commands the best conveyance is, by the way of N England in the Summer and Virginia in the Winter

E The Packet this letter goes in is the first I have had an opportunity of sending since the Receipt of yours

           I am

               (very truely Sir)

                  Your most humble

                     and most obedient servant

                        GEO BURRINGTON

To Allured Popple Esq

[B P R O North Carolina B T Vol 21 p 104]

LORDS OF TRADE TO GOV^r BURRINGTON
20 JUNE 1732

To Capt Burrington

   Sir,

We have received your letters of the 1st July and 4th Sept 1731 and shall receive His Maj pleasure on such parts of them wherein his service or the welfare of the Province are any way concerned   But as to those paragraphs which relate to yourself and those who have disagreed with your measures We cannot but take notice that they are couched in a very extraordinary particularly that where speaking of Mr Ashe's declining to come to England with the Chief Justice you write in the following words By which failure of his Baby Smith will be quite lost having nothing but a few lies to support his cause unless he can obtain an Instructor from a Gentleman in Hanover Square Of these words we expect an immediate and distinct explanation and are

Your most humble Serv⁺

WESTMORELAND
P DOCMINIQUE
T PELHAM
EDW ASHE
OR. BRIDGEMAN
M. BLADEN

Whitehall
June 20ᵗʰ 1732

[B. P R. O Am & W Ind No 592.]

BOARD OF TRADE TO THE DUKE OF NEWCASTLE
JUNE 21 1732

MY LORD,

We take leave to enclose to your Grace the Extract of a Letter we have received from Captain Burrington His Majesties Governour of North Carolina by which he seems to apprehend the Indians of South Carolina were preparing to fall upon those under his Government who hope to be supported by a Party of the five Nations.

As an Indian War may be of the most fatal consequence to both these Colonies, we have wrote both to Coll Johnson and to Cap⁺ Burrington to desire they will take the best Precautions to prevent the same We have likewise wrote to the Governour of New York to interpose his authority with the five Indian Nations who are said to be concerned in this affair. But as her Majesties Orders to these three Governours upon this subject will be much more effectual, We desire your Grace will please to lay this matter before Her for Her Majesty's Directions therein.

We are my Lord
Your Graces
most obedient & most humble ser⁺

P DOCMINIQUE
T PELHAM
EDW. ASHE
ORL⁺ BRIDGEMAN
M. BLADEN

Whitehall
June 21ˢᵗ 1732

44

[B P R O North Carolina B. T Vol. 21 p 106.]

Mr SECRETARY POPPLE TO GOV BURRINGTON
21 JUNE 1732

To Capt Burrington

SIR,

My Lords Commiss's for Trade & Plantations having under their consideration your letter to them of the 4th Sept last wherein you mention some apprehension you had that the Indians of South Carolina might make an attempt against those of your Government I am commanded to acquaint you that their Lordships think that it will be for His Maj service and the good of the Province under your command that you should use the most effectual means to prevent any misunderstanding among the Indians

My Lords Commiss's for Trade and Plantations have wrote by this occasion to Col Johnson and to Col Cosby to use their endeavours to put an end to these misunderstandings.

I am

Your most humble Servant

ALURED POPPLE

Whitehall
June 21st 1732

[B P R. O North Carolina B. T Vol. 21 p 107]

SECRETARY POPPLE TO ATTORN' & SOLIC' GEN'
30 JUNE 1732

To Mr Attorney & Mr Solicitor Gen'

GENTLEMEN,

My Lords Comm's for Trade & Plantations having under their consideration some papers relating to North Carolina upon which they are to make an immediate return command me to send you the inclosed Case and Queries thereon and to desire your opinion thereon as soon as possible

There may possibly be some Clause in the Act of Parliament passed in the 2d year of His Maj Reign for establishing an Agreement with seven of the Lords Proprietors of Carolina for the surrender of their title and interest of that Province to His Majesty that may affect the foregoing case of which my Lords do not take upon them to judge

I am

Gentlemen

Your most humble Servant

Whitehall   ALURED POPPLE
    June 30ᵗʰ 1732

THE CASE

The Lords Proprietors of Carolina having always appointed Governors of that Province before they made a sale thereof to the Crown those Governors with the consent of the Council & Assembly there passed Laws and have continued so to do ever since the purchase made by the Crown not having notice of the said Purchase.

Q' Whether any Laws passed after the said purchase by the Proprietors Governor in their names before notice of sale are valid?

Q' Whether the Laws passed in the Proprietors names after notice of such purchase and before the King appointed a Governor of his own be valid

[B. P R. O. B T NORTH CAROLINA VOL. 9 A 24.]

MEMORIAL OF WM SMITH ESQ' RELATING TO THE LAWS OF Nᵒ CAROLINA

[Recᵈ & Read 13 July 1732.]

To the Rt. Honᵇˡᵉ the Lords Comissʳˢ for Trade and Plantations

The Humble Representation of William Smith Esqʳ Chief Justice and Chief Baron of the Province of North Carolina in America concerning the present state of the Laws of the sᵈ Province

That the said William Smith being ready to depart for the said Province in order to take upon him the execution of his said respective offices has first thought it his duty to lay before your Lordships the present state of the laws of that Province to the end that your Lordships might be pleased to remove some of the difficulties (wᶜʰ in the sᵈ Smith's humble opinion) obstruct his putting the said Laws in execution for the reasons following Vizᵗ

That in the 76th Article of the Fundamental Constitutions of the late Lords Prop" of the s'd Province It is Ordain'd that no Act or Order of Parliament shall be of any force unless it be ratified in open Parliam' during the same Sessions by the Palatine or Deputy and three more the Lords Proprietors or their Deputies And then not to continue longer in force but until the next biennial Parliam' unless in the mean time it be ratifyed under the hands & seals of the Palatine himself & three more of the Lords Proprietors themselves and by their orders published at the next Biennial Parliament

That in the year 1707 there were further orders from the said Lords Proprietors corroborating the afores'd 76th Article that no law should be of force longer than two years unless confirmed by them

That by the 12th Article of their said Lordships Instructions to Sir Richard Everard their late and last Govern' dated the 17th of April 1725 they thought fit even to abridge that length of time and to make the continuation of the laws of that Province but for one year unless confirmed by the s'd Lords Prop"

That ever since the establishment of the said several Constitutions by the said Lords Proprietors as before mentioned they have been only six several Laws or Statutes of the said Province duely confirmed in pursuance of the said Constitutions Wherefore the said William Smith humbly submits himself to your Lordships for your directions how to act in relation to those Laws which have from time to time been made in the said Province but have not as yet received a due confirmation conformable to the several limitations of the afores'd articles And humbly prays Your Lords" to take the same into consideration & to give him instructions accordingly that so he may be enabled to administer justice to all parties with Honor to His Majesty & safety to himself

And your Memorialist shall ever pray &c

[B. P. R. O. North Carolina B. T Vol. 21. p 108.]

SECRETARY POPPLE TO ATTORN' & SOL' GEN'
20 JULY 1732.

To M' Attorney & Solicitor General

GENTLEMEN

M' Smith Chief Justice and Chief Baron of North Carolina having presented a Rep' to my Lords Commiss" for Trade & Plantations stating

some difficulties he labours under with respect to the Laws of that Province I am commanded to send you a copy of the said Rep[a] and to
acquaint you that my Lords have given directions to M[r] Smith to attend
you upon this occasion to explain more particularly the matters contained
in his said Memorial upon which my Lords desire your opinion as soon
as may be

                    I am
              Your most hum[ble] Serv[t]

                                        ALURED POPPLE

Whitehall
     July 20th 1732

[B P R O North Carolina B T Vol. 21 p 108.]

SECRETARY POPPLE TO SEC. BURCHETT 1732 JULY 22 (OF THE ADMIRALTY)

To Josiah Burchet Esq[r]

     SIR,

My Lords Commiss[rs] for Trade & Plantations having received from
Capt. Burrington His Maj Gov[r] of North Carolina and from M[r] Porter
late a Member of His Maj Council & Judge of the Vice Admiralty
Court there several complaints against each other their Lordships command me to send you for the information of the Rt. Hon the Lords Commiss[rs] of the Admiralty the enclosed copies of so much thereof as relates
to the said Court of Admiralty and to acquaint you that my Lords Commiss[rs] have transmitted to Capt. Burrington and M[r] Porter copies of the
said Complaints respectively in order to their taking and interchaning
upon that place such proofs as they may have to support their several
charges which my Lords have directed them to transmit hither without
loss of time

                    I am
              Your most hum[ble] Serv[t]

                                        ALURED POPPLE

Whitehall
     July 22[d] 1732

[B. P R. O South Carolina B T Vol. 5 D 41]

Mr ATTORNEY & Mr SOLICITOR'S GEN^l REPORT UPON QUERIES RELATING TO THE VALIDITY OF LAWS PASSED IN NORTH & SOUTH CAROLINA

The Lords Proprietors of Carolina having always appointed Governors of that Province before they made a sale thereof to the Crown those Governors with the consent of the Council & Assembly there passed Laws and have continued so to do even since the purchase made by the Crown not having notice of the said purchase.

Q^y Whether any Laws passed after the said purchase by the Propriety Governors in their names *before notice* of the sale are valid?

Whether Laws passed in the Proprietors names *after notice* of such purchase & before the King appointed a Governor of his own be valid?

We are of opinion that Laws passed by Governors appointed by the Lords Prop^{rs} & in their names after the sale and before notice arrived in the Province are of the same validity as such Laws would have been if they had been passed in like manner before such sale But that any Laws passed in the Prop^{rs} names after notice of their having conveyed their interest to the Crown are absolutely null and void

P YORKE
C TALBOT

11th August 1732

[B P R. O North Carolina B. T Vol 21 P 120]

M^r SEC POPPLE TO JUDGE PORTER 16 AUGUST 1732

To Edmund Porter Esqre late Judge of Vice Admiralty Court in No Carolina

SIR,

My Lords Commiss^{rs} for Trade and Plantations have received from you and considered a Representation and other papers containing complaints of the proceedings of Capt. Burrington Govr of His Maj Province of North Carolina against you as a Member of His Maj Council there and Judge of the Vice Admiralty Court and have transmitted copies thereof of so much as concerns you in the capacity of Judge of the Admiralty to M' Burchett for the information of the Lds Comm" of the Admiralty

I herewith send you by their Lordships Order an extract of what Capt. Burrington has writ to them by way of complaint against you at the same time I am likewise directed to transmit to him copies of your forement^d Representation and other papers and that my Lords may be enabled to make a judgment of the true state of this affair I have by their command acquainted him that their Lord" expect he should return to them such depositions and proofs in his own behalf as he should think convenient giving you at the same time full liberty or any other persons concerned to make affidavits before any Judge or other Magistrate of what they know concerning the subject matter of the said Complaints and such Judge or Magistrate be likewise enjoined to summon such persons as the complainants respectively shall name in order to give their testimony in this affair   M' Burrington is further directed to interchange with you true copies of the Proofs and Affidavits so soon as they shall be made which you are likewise to observe on your part and that twenty days be allowed to make his & your reply by affidavits or otherwise to be in like manner interchangeably communicated to each other and afterwards transmitted hither without loss of time

I am

Sir

Your most hum^ble Servt

ALURED POPPLE

Whitehall
Augt 16th 1732.

[B. P R. O North Carolina B T Vol. 21 p 109]

M' SECRETARY POPPLE TO GOV' BURRINGTON
16 AUGUST 1732.

To Capt Burrington Governor of North Carolina

Sir,

My Lords Commiss" for Trade & Plantations command me to acknowledge the receipt of your letters of the 1st July and 4th Sept. last with the several public papers you therein mention to be inclosed

My Lords observe the complaints you have made against Mssrs. Ashe, Porter & Smith for obstructing His Maj service and that you apprehend they may make some complaints against you

No such complaints have as yet been lodged in their Lordships Office but by Mr Porter which their Lordships having had under consideration command me to transmit to you the inclosed copies thereof And at the same time I am likewise directed to send Mr Porter a copy of what you have writ to my Lords Commiss^rs by way of complaint against him and that my Lords may be enabled to make a judgment of the true state of this affair they further command me to acquaint you that their Lordships expect you to return to them such depositions and proofs in your own behalf as you shall think convenient giving Mr Porter at the same time full liberty or any other persons concerned to make Affidavits before any Judge or other Magistrate concerning the subject matter of said complaints & that such Judge or Magistrate be likewise injoined to summon such persons as the Complainants respectively shall name in order to give their testimony in this affair That you interchange with Mr Porter true copies of the proofs and affidavits so soon as they shall be made which he is likewise directed to observe on his part And that twenty days be allowed to make your and his reply by Affidavits or otherwise to be in like manner interchangeably communicated & afterwards transmitted hither without loss of time

In this manner My Lords will have the whole matter properly laid before them and as you renounce any favor from their Lordships and demand at the same time their justice I am to acquaint you that you and every one else may be assured they will ever meet that from their Lordships in every affair that may come under their consideration

Until this affair shall in the manner proposed come before their Lordships my Lords do not take upon them to judge between Mr Porter and yourself yet they cant help observing that Mr Porter stands acquitted by het old Councillors and only condemned by those whom you have nominated for new ones.

Upon this occasion I am to remind you of that part of your Commission whereby you are empowered to appoint Councillors whenever the Council shall be reduced under the number of seven to which number and no further you have liberty to appoint As there is some doubt whether there were not seven Councillors in the Province under your government at the time you took upon yourself to nominate My Lords expect you will send an exact account thereof by which it will appear how far you have observed your instructions

I am further to acquaint you upon this subject that you have not the liberty of altering the rank in which His Maj^y has been pleased to place the several Councillors in the first Article of your Instructions as you acquaint my Lords you have done   You will therefore do well to restore every gentleman to the rank His Maj has been pleased to place them in of which I send you the inclosed List

My Lords have read & considered the several transactions between yourself the Council and Assembly and command me to acquaint you that they think it might have been advisable not to have recommended so many things as you did to their consideration at once especially as you represent the Assembly not so ready to dispatch the matters laid before them as you could have wished

My Lords observe that you proposed in one of your speeches that the Assembly might as they saw occasion send a Deputation from their Body to advise with you altho' you may have proposed this in order to facilitate the business of the Province yet as it is a very unusual practise you will do well for the future to avoid any such thing as well as the joining in any conference which the Council and Assembly may have together as you have the honor to represent His Maj person and as such are one of the three parts of the Legislature of the Province You have a negative on all their public proceedings and therefore cannot in the least intermeddle in debating or voting in either Council or Assembly or in any Conference between them

Upon this occasion my Lords cant avoid observing the great irregularities you have committed in your commerce with the Lower House but particularly where you compare one of their members to a thief who to prevent his being discovered sets the house on fire and escapes in the smoke   As every Member of the Assembly has an undoubted right to propose whatever he judges for the service of the Province this proceeding of yours looks too much like intimidating the Members of the Assembly and therefore my Lords are of opinion that a more cool behaviour in you may not only be a good example to both Houses but may prevent any complaint against yourself upon this head

My Lords having referred several questions upon the Acts of this Province to His Maj. Council for their opinion in point of law an answer to that part of your letters must yet be deferred for some time But I am now to acquaint you with respect to that part of your letter where you ask the opinion of the Board whether the Receivers of His Maj Quit rents may not accept of an equivalent for Proclamation money that you are steadily to adhere to your instructions upon all occasions and therefore whenever any Act shall be passed It must be enacted that His Maj Quit Rents be punctually paid in Proclamation money And if it shall appear that there is not money sufficient to answer the said pay-

45

ments His Maj may then upon a proper application agree to take an
equivalent in the products of the Province

I am likewise to inform you that the Grand Deed of 1668 from the
Lds. Propriet^{rs} which you mention as pleaded by the people against paying any higher Quit Rent than is paid in Virginia can only be understood as temporary letter of Attorney from the Lords Prop^{rs} revocable
at their pleasure as in effect it was many years ago when they directed
their Governor Mr Eden to grant no Land without reserving one penny
℔ Acre However as the paying 4 shill^{gs} Proclamation Money per hundred Acres as well as paying all Officers fees in the said Currency &
registring all Grants of Land are by your Instructions made the terms
upon which His Maj has been graciously pleased to declare he will
remit the payment of the Arrears of quit rents His Maj Officers may
soon have directions to collect the said arrears unless the people do
speedily think fit to comply with His Maj terms which are calculated
for their advantage and for quieting them in their possessions.

My Lords observe some disputes you have had with the Assembly
about the appointing a Clerk to that House and find by the Minutes of
Assembly that they have taken no notice of the Commission you gave
to Mr Williams and have appointed him their Clerk by their own
authority But I must remind you of your 14th Instruction by which
you are not to allow the Assembly any greater privilege than is enjoyed
by the House of Commons in this Kingdom where that Officer is appointed by His Majesty You therefore must take care not to give up
this point wherein His Maj prerogative is concerned

As to that part of your letter which relates to the dispute between the
Chief Justice and the Assistant Judges My Lords desire you will send
copies of the Commiss^{ns} you have given to the Chief Justice and the
Assistant Judges that they may judge of the several powers thereby
granted to them

My Lords likewise desire to know how the matter stands with respect
to the power claimed by the Assembly of chusing the public Treasurer of
the Province & what has been the constant practise and by what authority Mr Moseley was originally appointed for altho' he is styled Public
Treasurer by several of the Laws yet it dont appear to their Lordships
how or when he was made so.

In answer to what you say with respect to the allowance not being
sufficient for holding Courts of Oyer and Terminer I am commanded to
acquaint you that whenever your instructions mention money Proclamation money is always thereby intended unless any other currency is particularly mentioned

My Lords Commiss^{rs} having thoroughly considered the settlement of the Boundaries between your Province and South Carolina before your Instruction relating thereto was concluded are of opinion that you should put that instruction in execution and the rather because they cant think of advising any alteration therein upon hearing one party only.

When the Attorney and Solicitor Gen' shall have made their Report concerning the Laws of your Province my Lords will then be able to give an opinion upon the Act for Biennial Assemblies but so long as a doubt remains concerning the force of that Law you ought not to make any alteration in the Assembly And whenever any alteration shall be thought necessary it will be more proper to be done by an Instruction than by an Act of Assembly

In answer to that part of your letter wherein you desire the opinion of the Board whether the Proprietors of such plantations as are gained to your Province of Virginia are not to renew their Patents in North Carolina I am commanded to acquaint you that they are not obliged to renew their Patents but only register them

You acquaint my Lords in your last letter that Warrants have been given to several people in the time of the Lords Proprietors to take up land and settle to the Southward but no Patents have been issued in pursuance thereof upon which you desire the directions of the Board Upon this occasion my Lords desire you will send them a distinct account of that affair a list of the several Warrants with the dates of them to whom given upon what consideration what quantities of land are thereby intended to be granted what Quit Rents are thereby reserved whether any of those Lands have been taken up and whether the particular quantities of land and the situation thereof are specified in the said Warrants.

I am your most obed^t hum^{ble} Servt

ALURED POPPLE

Whitehall
   August 16th 1732.

[B. P. R. O North Carolina B T Vol. 9 A 29]

RICE, MONTGOMERY AND ASHE VS. BURRINGTON

NORTH CAROLINA

To His Grace the Duke of New Castle one of His Majesty's Principal Secretarys of State

The most humble Memorial and Remonstrance of Nathaniel Rice and John Baptista Ashe two of the Members of Council and John Montgomery Attorney General and Deputy Inspector and Controller General of his Majesty's Province of North Carolina.

MAY IT PLEASE YOUR GRACE

We beg your Grace to permit us (by way of Apology for thus addressing you) to shew the reasons inducing us to this Method of representing to your Grace the State of this Province George Burrington Esqr Governor being conscious that his proceedings in the administration of the Government have been most arbitrary and illegal has used his utmost endeavours to prevent a true State of this Colony being exhibited to his Majesty not only by refusing to call Assemblys whereby the people might be enabled to remonstrate in a Parliamentary way, but also by his arbitrary acting and artfull management in Council in concert with a few Members of his own apointment and by means of a Deputy Secretary a creature of his and by him imposed in a manner upon his principal, he has so mutilated altered perverted and misrepresented things in the Journals of the Council that scarce any affair transacted at the Board appears in a true light We therefore finding it improbable thrő these and many other artifices of the Governor that his most excellent Majesty will receive any true information of the affairs of this Province, think we cannot faithfully discharge a trust reposed in us by our most gracious King as officers of this Government unless we truly represent to your Grace the deplorable State of this Country, the many breaches of his Majesty's Royal Instructions and the greivances and oppressions Suffered by the people, humbly praying your Grace will represent them to his Majesty in Such manner as your Grace in your great wisdom Shall think fitt What we shall represent to your Grace will be contained under these General heads

   1. His arbitrary exercise of power respecting proceedings in Council

   2dly His Arbitrary exercise of power relating to the Courts of Justice

3dly His arbitrary proceedings relating to the disposition of the Kings Lands

4^{thly} His disrespect to and insulting and abusing the Kings officers and others.

5^{thly} His illigal and arbitrary actions relating to the Extorting moneys from the Kings Subjects.

We proceed on the first General head

1st During a Session of Assembly after his arrival (the only one he has suffered to be since he has been in the Province) he assumed to himself and affirmed he had a power of acting and of voting as a member of Council and of the upper House of Assembly distinct from his power of Governor or of his Negative willed and ordained him by the King, and he thereupon proceeded to alter and rase Bills on their readings in the upper house without consulting the Council particularly a Bill relating to the appointment of Circular General Courts and when some of the Council in the most humble manner objected to such a proceeding, he flew into a passion, particularly in this case with John Baptista Ashe, alledging that from him of all men he expected not to have heard such an objection or to have received such usuage, expressing himself in an angry tone Sufficiently denoting his displeasure, thô the objection was made of the said Ashe in the most mild and respectfull terms

2dly. When by an order in full Council several Gentlemen of the best fortune, ability and character in the Country were nominated and appointed Justices in the General Commission of the Peace, the Governor afterwards believeing those Gentlemen would not be obsequious to his arbitrary dictates, or subservient to his ends, the said order by his artifice was left out of and not entered in the Journal of the Council and a commission was by him ordered to be made out by assent of Council wherein three Members only were present (and those three Such as are always conformable to his pleasure be it what it will) in which those Gentlemen were omitted

3dly The Governor being desirous of introducing Mr Lovick and Mr Gale into the Council pretends a very great emergency vizt the appointment of a Chief Justice and assistants Mr Smith having withdrawn himself out of the Government without leave as is represented in the Journal of the Council the 27th of August 1731 when those Councellours were introduced. Now it is notorious and was publickly known that Mr Smith left the Province the beginning of the month of June so that there were six or seven weeks interveening his departure and this pretended Emergency Certainly this was time enough to summon the other

Members from Cape Fair or any other part of the Government and yet
none were summoned but he introduced them, two only of the Council
being present and one of them objecting against it as contrary to his
Majesty's Seventh Instruction which forbidds his filling up the Council
beyond the number Seven· It is plain his Intent in thus acting was to
introduce these Gentlemen into Council and by their means to appoint
the Chief Justice and assistants which he did being all men he was
assured would be subservient to his ends and it was done with design
Art and management whereas he would represent the matter as if he was
obliged to it by a sudden and unexpected Emergency.

4thly To cast a slurr on the characters of some particular Gentlemen
and to give them needless vexation and trouble He has exhibited charges
against them in Council causing them in the depth of Winter (not at the
usual times of Courts or meetings of Assemblys or Councils) at their very
great Expence and fatigue to travel two hundred miles to answer, and
when they have appeared and in writing made answer to such charges and
defended themselves and have prayed that as their charges were their
defences might be entered in the Journal also, he by his sole power has
refused and prevented the entry of such written defences and only enters
short inferences from them of his own making (made out of and after
such Councils are over) as their answers whereby things are misrepresented in the Council Journal and the true state of such cases disguised,
and several illegal and arbitrary proceedings of his, in such answers set
forth prevented from coming to the notice of our most Gracious King
and his Ministry Such were the cases of Maurice Moore John Porter
Edward Moseley John Baptista Ashe and several others whose answers
thō they humbly requested they might be entered he has forbidden to be
entered, the reason is plain, they contain matters which he would conceal, as reference being had to such answers will appear These two last
Articles out of a multitude of others which we could give (were we not
afraid of trespassing on your Graces patience) will serve as well as instances of his misrepresenting things in the Council Journal as for his
arbitrary exercise of power in it.

5thly On the receipt of a private copy (not attested by any officer) of
Mr Smith's complaint to his Majesty against him the Governor he has
proceeded to bring people before him in Council to declare whether they
imployed Mr Smith to complain against him In the choice of such to
be brought before him he has generally hitherto taken such as he was
pretty sure would either thrō fear or for other cause purge themselves for
a denial, on so doing such have been complimented and had his thanks

and some few who have refused to stand such an inquisition have highly
incurred his displeasure so as he has bestowed on some of them the Titles
of Rogue and Rascal in Council   In this affair he has without his Majesty's directions proceeded exparte (no persons being present to cross
examine) to examine Witnesses, one to take affidavits, depositions and
solemn Declarations on Oath, many of which are made by himself and
the partys concerned, at the contents of which we shall only at present
say we are amazed   as for Instance where in some of them it is set forth
that he bona fide for a full and valuable consideration purchased the lands
mentioned in Mr Smith's memorial to his Majesty to which we refer,
moved to it on the report of a lead mine being on them, The lands are
known to be some of the most fertile in America and the Governor has
(it seems) of them about forty thousand acres, but as to the report of the
lead mine being on them we are confident it was never heard of till these
solemn Declarations were thought necessary. and if true we cannot conceive that the mines should render those lands less valuable.   There are
many other (we forebear saying falsities) absurdities and irregularities in
these his proceedings which we could point out to your Grace but forebear
of being too tedious   we shall at present decline it.   If his Majesty shall
think fit to direct a full and impartial enquiry, they will then appear

We could give many other Instances under this General Head but least
we be too tiresome to your Grace we shall proceed to the second general
head respecting his arbitrary exercise of power relating to the Courts and
administration of Justice.

1st With respect to the Courts and his own administration of Justice, his proceedings are without example.   He has appointed a Man
Chief Justice of this Province whom he has often declared to be the
greatest rogue in this Country and we can truly say is unskilled in the
Law and in all respects unqualified to execute that post, and four assistant Justices of the Supreme Court, one of whom can neither read nor
write and all very weak persons and unskilled in the Law but Such as
he imagined fitt for his purpose and the event has to the grief of this
Province shewn that he was not mistaken

He frequently appears in the Courts either to influence them, in favour
of his friends or to the prejudice of those he is displeased with, and this
not by his bare presence only, but by openly speaking to and directing
the Courts according as he is inclined to the party.   So intent is he to
crush those he has conceived a prejudice against that he has forbidden
the General Court to admit any person to plead there but Such as Shall
obtain his licence, atho there is no law requireing Such licence.   By which

means he deprives persons formerly licenced and admitted as Attorney (being old Practioners) of their business unless by proper ways and application they can procure his favour And when Mr Moseley the oldest practioner of the Law in this Province (who was licenced and practiced near twenty year past) appeared and made a defence for some persons who were indicted by the Governors means for supposed facts said to be done before his arrival in this Government and which the party said to be injured in open Court declared was not of his promoting The Governor after the Jury were gone out on that Trial came down out of the Gallery (where he and his Lady appeared to influence the Court and Jury) to the Court table where Mr Moseley stood with his hand on the Bible being about to take the Oaths and notwithstanding the said Moseley prayed the protection of the Court he ordered the Marshall to take the said Moseley out of the Court and to bring him before him, and in Court commanded all his Majesty's subjects to assist the Marshall, and when Mr Moseley was brought before him he treated him with great scorn and contempt offering him many indignities, and commanded the Marshall verbally to commit him to prison At another time viz at the General Court held in July last some debate arising in Court about the granting time to the Def^t after over prayed of certain writings mentioned in a Declaration where the Governor was plaintiff and on which occasion the Governor and his Lawyers pressed for the Defendant to plead immediately, the Defendant having no Lawyer Mr Moseley told the Court that during the many years he formerly practiced as a Lawyer he never knew it refused The Governor went out of Court and immediately after commanded the Marshall to take the said Moseley into custody and carry him to Goal for what he had spoken in Court, altho the Court declared they were no ways offended at what he had spoken accordingly by the Governor's verbal order he was carryed to the common Goal and there confined, untill by motion to the General Court for a Habeas Corpus he was brought before the Court and discharged by the unanimous Judgment of the Court, consisting of the Chief Justice and three assistants, for which they have (as its said) fallen under the Governours high displeasure, who declares he has power to commit any person to prison without cause shewn for twelve hours, and indeed he has exercised this his assumed power in another case vizt in that of Doctor George Allen a Physician whom he committed and confined in the common Goal ten hours without shewing any cause, and before a Warrant or Mittimus was delivered to the Goaler The severe usuage of Mr Moseley is the more to be taken notice of in as much as for near twenty eight years past he has been an Inhabi-

tant of this Province having a very good Estate and for near half that
time has been an Eminent Member of the Lower House of Assembly
being 5 or 6 times chosen Speaker thereof; the other part of the time a
Member of the Lower House of Assembly Council and Surveyor General and has had the greatest Trust reposed in him by the Province, and
he is thought by most people to have received this usuage for his endeavours to hinder and prevent the Governours violent proceedings. Miserable must be the state of that Province where the Governor shall take
on him to hinder Lawyers who have been received as such by the Court
for near twenty years past, from pleading or speaking of those he intends
to crush and injure and indeed this is experimentally found to be a sure
means of such persons being left defenceless without any one dareing to
speake or plead for them

To these Instances may be added his eagre desire of Serveing his
favourites: So partially favourable is he to Mr William Little (a person
whom he consults on all occasions relating to the King's Business tho'
there are many notorious complaints against him for injustice and wrong
done to the King as well as to the Subject) that lately in a case vizt
Rowell against Jones at his the Said Littles Instance he granted a writ
as Chancellour (without any preceeding Suite or Bill brought or filled in
Chancery by the Plaintiff and without notice given the Defendant
whereby he enjoyned and commanded the Officer to oust or put the defendant who was bona fide a purchasor and actually in peaceable and quiet
possession out of possession, and this without any view or inquest of
forcible Entry; there being none indeed So much as pretended and to
put the Plaintiff (who was only Wife of the Vendor and had not the
least Title or interest in the Lands Sold) into possession which by the
Officer was accordingly done And of this when the Attorney General
complained to the Governor and Council Setting forth what a dangerous
precedent it might prove, and how grievous a practice it might introduce,
and praying relief in behalf of the defendant he was denied it or at
least he was delayed being put off as was pretended for want of a full
Councill (which for Several reasons he then prevented as tis thought its
being full) tho the Act was committed or done by himself Solely, and
the Attorney General was insulted and abused having much reproachful
language bestowed on him and the lye given him in Councill by his Excellency when he had asserted a Truth as was apparent, by the record in
the Court of Chancery Thus he acts in behalf of his favourites: but
when the case comes to be his own he Sticks at nothing to gain his purpose, as in the case of Mr Porter, who having obtained a Patent for Some

46

Lands, and built and Seated a family thereon consisting of a Man his wife and Six Small children, and the Wife big and ready to lay in with another; the Governour making Some trifling and frivolous pretensions (as on Examination we doubt not they will appear to be) to the land, he went to the Tenant told him the next day he designed to burn the house required him to move his family and goods or otherwise he would burn them in it   The poor people frightened with this threat, moved and took out as many as they could of their goods to Save them from being burned   The Governor was as good as his word, for the next day he burnt the house and Several things belonging to the poor Family, what and how fatal by this time had been the End of one under his displeasure who should have presumed to have perpetrated So wicked an action We think we may justly Say the Gallows had been his portion   Give us leave to deliver our opinions to your Grace, that it is impossible any Country Should long Subsist under the Administration of a Governour So extravagant (to give him no worse an Epithet) as this, and we doubt not but your Grace comiserating our Condition will justly represent these things and the State of this Province to our most gracious Sovereign from whose conspicious Justice and goodness we expect and hope for relief

Some months after the arrival of the Governour in this Province seven Negro Slaves were brought into Cape Fear River and sold to sundry persons   soon after it was reported that they were stolen from the Spaniards settled at St Augustin   As soon as the Governour had notice of that report he took those slaves from the persons who had purchased them and sett them to work upon his own Plantation with design as he then declared, that they might be secured for the Spaniards, but (as it plainly appeared afterwards) he sole design was to appropriate them to his own use, for not long after the Governor of St Augustin in conjunction with the owner of those Negroes appointed an Agent to demand and carry them to St Augustin who according to his Instructions, applyed to the Governour and demanded the same   but so was he from complying that he absolutely refused to deliver them, pretending they were the property of those persons who bought them upon their arrival in this Province   Thus when the Purchasors who bought them he insisted they were the property of the Spaniards· but when the Spaniards, his pretence was they were the property of the Purchasors, on such pretext he keep them a long time, till most of them have escaped and are lost to both partys   This proceeding of the Governor the Inhabitants upon Cape Fair River are apprehensive will be highly resented by the Spaniards,

and as there is no Fort to protect that young Settlement and being open
any every way easy to be invaded, they are in great fear the Spaniards
will make reprizals, by taking their Negroes, as they may without difficulty

3dly His arbitrary proceedings relating to the disposal of the Kings
Lands The Governour by his Majesty's commission is impowered to settle and agree with the Inhabitants for lands &c and to grant them by
and with the advise and consent of the Council, and that such their advise and consent is necessary, is also plainly implyed by his Majesties
42 & 43d Instructions to his Excellency · yet so arbitrary are his proceedings herein that he grants Warrants contrary to the Kings Instructions in undue proportion to whom and in what manner he pleases without consulting or requiring the advice and consent of the Council, whilst
he refuses others who want Lands and are ready to comply with the
Kings Instructions   Thus instead of impartially granting Lands according to the Kings Instructions to such as are capable of improving them
he uses his power partially and dispences Warrants for the Kings Lands
as acts of favour to such as by complying with the Terms and measures
render themselves well pleasing to him. This is not all he exacts two
shilling and sixpence for every fifty acres he signs a Warrant for, when
nothing like it is expressed or intended by the Kings Instructions and
this he requires in Silver or Gold, the scarcity of which is so very great
in this Province that many people are forced to procure it (with much
trouble too) at double and treble the real value in currency, while others
are not able to procure it at all. Thus what his Majesty is graciously
pleased freely to give unto the people he extorts and demands a consideration for, to his own use. The consequences of this Method are very
prejudicial as well to the Kings revenew as to the subject   To the Kings
Revenew in that, there are many Plantations of which people were put
into possession by and pursuant to an order of the Governor and Council
in the time of the Proprietors (Mr Burrington then being their Governour)
till the Proprietors pleasure should be known as to the granting such
lands in Fee   these persons as they have generally been at great expence at
cultivating improving and occupying such Lands, continue in possession,
and as Gold or Silver is by the Governor insisted on and is not possibly
to be had they cannot take up their lands on the tenure his Majesty proposes and graciously offers, and so the King has already been deprived
of near two years Rent of such Plantations; except for some for which as
the possessors could not possibly procure gold or silver, Warrants have
been granted to others (and those chiefly the Governors creatures) whereby

people have been thrown out of such possessions and in a manner ruined, Such is the case of one William Grey at Cape Fair, who after he had been at the Expence of above two hundred pounds currency for such a possession had it taken from him by Coll Robert Halton one of the Council and Provost Marshall of the Province by the Governors appointment, Such too are the cases of John Smith and William Bartram, who after being at a considerable Expence have had their lands taken by the said Halton, many more Tracts the said Halton hath and yet he has not six souls in his family for whom he can claim an allowance of land pursuant to the Kings Instructions In the same case are several Inhabitants of New River who lands have been taken up by one John Williams, who, thô having very few in his family had granted him by the Governor (what he calls) rights to lands as at his Rate of selling came (it is said) or amounted to more than twenty cows and calves delivered on the Governors Plantation at Cape Fair and accepted in lieu of silver We can give many more Instances of this nature. But these we suppose may suffice at present to shew the illegality of his proceedings in this case, which is like to be the case of many more so that we think we may justly say—such a method is injurious to the King, prejudicial to the subject and detrimental to the settlement of the Province for his thus embarassing and loading with difficulties (contrary to the Kings Instructions) the taking up of lands deters many poor strangers who come in quest of lands from settling, it makes many already here talk of removing and discourages others from coming who hear of these proceedings.

4ly We shall now proceed to the 4th General Head viz' his disrespect to and insulting the Kings officers and others.

In the first general Assembly after his arrival he frequently in Council, or the Upper House used menaceing speeches and insulted Mr Chief Justice Smith particularly on a complaint of contempt offered to Mr Porter then one of the Council, by one Mackey The Chief Justice Saving the said Mackey might be committed for the contempt The Governor asked him where he had learnt that law told him he knew nothing of the Law, explained in a contemptuous manner, Saving, a pretty Chief Justice' repeating the words several times, bade him give in Instance of any one committed for such contempt several Instances were given of commitments of contempts to persons of a Lower House of Assembly, a fortiori of an upper house Mr Smith much agitated and disturbed with such treatment rose from his Chair and was about to withdraw from Council the Governor obliged him to sit down again, again used reviling language and scoffed at him During the same sessions he very grossly abused several Members of the Lower House of Assembly   He would (with an intent to make differences it was thought) sometimes affirm that one Member had informed him of such and such a matter, or of such and such words spoken by another member, the member by him alledged to have made the information (and there happened to be no Witnesses) would deny and then the Governour would publickly call him Rogue, Rascall and villain,   this was the case of one Mr James Castlelaw to whom it is notorious he bears implacable malice   The Attorney General is the Subject of his repeated Scoffs and jests   he is frequently bestowing on him and that publickly Nick-names and terms of reproach   He forewarns people from keeping him company, and lets them know, if they are seen in it, they will incurr his displeasure, nay he will openly call to persons in the Street, in company with Mr Montgomery and tell them they are in badd company, and letts them know, if they are seen in it, they will incurr his displeasure nay so great is his hatred to him, that he never consults him in the Business of the Crown, no not even when he is the proper Officer to be consulted, but Mr Little (in his representation before mentioned) a person notoriously disaffected to the illustrious House of Hanover) is in all such cases applyed to and by that means executes a large share of the Office of Attorney General, and enjoys the greatest part of the perquisites

To Mr Harnet one of the Council (after having Signed a paper together with Mr Ashe in answer to one of the Governors put to them by the way of query) he writes a letter to let him know that he was no longer his friend but had conceived a resentment against him equal to the baseness and ingratitude (such are his expressions) of him and his conceited scribler   He, and Mr Harnets own House called him Fool, Blockhead, Puppy, Ashes, Tool, and this without any provocation or any thing then Said by Mr Harnet.   We could give you Instances of many most abusive and scurrilous letters written to Several gentlemen of the Province without any provocation but we shall not trouble your Grace with such Trifles but proceed to the 5th and last General head vizt

5thly His illegal and arbitrary Actions relating to the extorting moneys from the Kings subjects.

By the ancient laws of this Province, there was a fee of twenty two shilling and sixpence in silver money or 180 weight of Pork payable to to the Governour by every foreign Deckt vessell trading to this Province, on the revisal of the Laws in 1718 the same fee was again established, some of the Governours little regarding that Establishment (and fresh Pork or Silver not always to be had) took of the Masters of Vessells a

Barrel of Porke which was at least one third more in value   Thus was
very justly thought to be a hardship put on the Traders wherefore in the
year 1723 a Law was made Entituled an Act for the ascertaining Naval
Officers and Collectors fees, whereby the fees for such vessells were
established at about three pounds six shillings, as by the several Articles
in that Act mentioned will appear, and those fees were expressly declared
by that Law to be payable in the paper currency of this Province, that
sum of three pounds six shillings being, as near as could be estimated,
the value of the Porke or silver article, and those fees so ascertained
were from that time constantly paid in paper currency, no other being
demanded untill the arrival of the present Governour whose avaritious
temper not being content therewith he causes his private Secretary (who
acts as Naval Officer for him) to take the sum of thirteen pounds fifteen
shillings in paper currency pretending it his Majesties commands or
directions that all Officers fees shall be paid in silver money, thô the
contrary is very apparent from his Majestys Instructions to him   This
sum of thirteen pounds fifteen shillings is taken althô the Act aforesaid
is unrepealed, and were that Law repealed we conceive no more ought
to be taken than the value of twenty two shillings and sixpence the former silver fee, whereas now (as we have shewn) about four times the value
is taken   The badness of the Inletts is discouraging enough to the merchants trading hither, but the encrease of fees that are now taken (only
since this Governors arrival) upon such small vessells as generally come
hither more than used to be, or than the Laws allow being about eight
shillings ℔ Tonn on the vessells trading to this Province is so very
extravagant that divers Merchants of New England and other places
have foreborn trading hither   What makes it highly necessary for us
(who are actually in his Majesties service) to represent this to your Grace
is not only the great injury done thereby to Merchants and the People of
this Province but the abuse offered his Majesty, whose name and authority
he uses to counternance such his unlawfull doings

Another Instance of his Extortion is the case of a poor old Man, one
Lewis Johns, who before Mr Burrington's departure last out of this
Province had for a Bill of Exchange sold him twenty cows and calves
to be delivered in the fall and the cows to be big with calf again   The
Man after Mr Burrington was gone being given to understand the Bill
would be protested for that reason before forbore delivering the cows
and calves till the spring was twelve months after, then (the Bill being
paid) instead of twenty he brought and delivered to Mr Burringtons
overseer thirty cows & calves   by which (in the opinion of all indiffer-

ent people) he made ample amends for his former default sometime after this during Mr Sir Richard Everard's Government this Lewis John's being assaulted by a drunken man with a naked knife in his hand, Lewis John's unfortunately struck the man after which stroke, in a little time he dyed thō it was the opinion of most people present that his death was not occasioned by the stroke there being no mark or sign of hurt, and the man very sickly of a weak constitution and on opening of his body by a doctor found to be much disordered and decayed in his liver and other internal parts. However Lewis John's imediately surrendered himself to Justice and in order to his Tryal he was conveyed in from Cape Fair to Edenton to the General Court and so were the Evidences The Grand Jury found the Bill Ignoramous and he was discharged Since Governour Burrington's arrival he went to this poor mans house demanded of him forty or fifty cows and calves more: the man denyed paying him any more alledging he had made ample satisfaction, whereupon the Governour called him old Rogue, Rascall, Villain and many other hard names, threatened to ruine him, told him he would have him tryed by a Jury of honest men, alluding to his formal Tryal concerning the death of the Man, and at last by his threats (an attendant and creature of his at the same time coaxing and persuading) he extorted from the poor man his bill obligatory for the payment of twelve cows and calves more and then he no longer insisted to bring him to tryal

The Governour had formerly a fee of ten shillings in silver for marriage Licences, but such Governors exacting largely of persons seeking Licences (as silver was not to be had) that fee was established by Act of Assembly at twenty shillings in Bills For which the Governor extorts five pounds and such is his practice of disposing of such Licences that their end vizt (the preventing of clandestine marriages) is entirely defeated for without consulting who takes them or directing any security to be taken on delivering them out he makes Merchandizes of them, exposing them to sale to any purchasor at Ordinarys ale houses or Publick Taverns, employing people keeping such houses as his Brokers to dispose of them through the Province, by which means any young persons may and many actually are married without and even contrary to the consent of their Parents or Guardians

These of many more instances of the like nature which we could give, we have presumed to lay before your Grace that you may judge how consistent his Actions are with justice his duty to the King, regard to his Majesty's Interest, and the Liberty and Privileges of British subjects. We again most humbly intreat your Grace so to represent this Matters to

our most gracious sovereign as you shall judge meet   for from his con-
summate justice and clemency (thô your Graces intercession) his poor distressed subjects of this Province hope and pray for relief

    We are with the greatest respect & submission
        May it please your Grace
          Your Grace's most Faithfull and
            most obedient humble servants.

                  NATHANIEL RICE
                  BAPTISTA ASHE
                  JOHN MONTGOMERY

North Carolina the 16th of Sepr 1732

[B P R O Am & W Ind No 592]

LORD DELAWAR, OCTOBER 16th 1732

MY LORD,

    Mr Cole whose head of hair your Grace is perfectly acquainted with
is the occasion of my troubling you with this   He has been informed
that Captain Burrington Governor of North Carolina is to be recalled
and is very desirous that your Grace would be so kind as to recommend
him to be his successor   Indeed my Lord it would be an Act of great
good nature and charity, and I doubt not but he will behave himself
entirely to your Graces Satisfaction,   if my recommendation has any
weight with your Grace I shall esteem myself happy and own my obligation, there being nobody with greater truth and respect, My Lord
        Your Graces
          most humble
           and most obedient servant

                  DELAWAR

[B P R O North Carolina B T Vol 9 A 41]

LETTER FROM CAPTAIN BURRINGTON TO THE SECRETARY

                No Carolina the 2d of Novr 1732

SIR,

    I received two letters from you by the way of South Carolina last week,
one dated the 16th of June the other the 21st   That of the 16th is a Dupli-

cate of one you formerly sent me by Capt Beckman dated the 10th of June 1731. wch I answered in last May 10th The addition that for the future I must send to the Board of Trade yearly accounts of the Laws made Manufactures set up and Trade carryed on here which may in any manner affect the Trade, Navigation & Manufactures of Great Britain I will assuredly perform this.

I can at present only add to what I wrote in my Report on 25th and 115th Instructions, that abundance of Saw Mills are erecting here by which the Builders propose to carry on a Trade in boards and other saw'd Timber.

The Trade of this Country increases pretty fast and the Province flourishes, but I attend the orders of the Lords of Trade before I go about makeing or altering Laws, of which much is said in my Report, long letter of the 20th of February and Representation.

I gave their Lordships an account in the Representation that I had settled the Indian affairs to the satisfaction of all Partys and they continue in the same manner tho' there happens small acts of Hostility now and then in hunting on the upper parts of Cape Fear River between our Indians and the Cataubes of South Carolina, which we look upon to be for our advantage, thinking Indians love and will be doing a little mischief, therefore had rather they should act it upon their own tawny race then the English, in my opinion our affairs are in as good condition as can be desired in respect to the Indians in this and the neighbouring Governments.

I have been intollerably plagued with settling the Militia and altho' I was last year and this in every Precinct in the whole Government the work is not compleated, the death of two Colonels and my own terrible sickness were the hinderance but I shall soon sett out to finish the remaining part when returned shall send their Lordships the State and Condition of this Province, to them I desire you will give my humble Duty, it is in their Power to make this Country one of the best Colonys in North America

              I am
                Sir,
                   Your most obedient
                      humble servant
                          GEO BURRINGTON

[B. P R. O North Carolina B. T Vol. 9 A 42]

LETTER FROM CAPTAIN BURRINGTON GOVERNOR OF NORTH CAROLINA   14th NOVEMBER 1732

MAY IT PLEASE YOUR LORDSHIPS,

I am honoured with a letter signed by seven of your Lordships dated the 20th of June last by which I have the great satisfaction to understand I may in a short time expect His Majesty's Commands in such matters as relate to His service in this Province, or wellfare of the same, those commands I impatiently wait for and shall obey with duty and reverence when received

The extraordinary vile and unpresidented Behaviour of William Smith late Chief Justice, & some other Officers in this Government made it necessary for me to write to your Lordships some Paragraphs relateing to myself and them, which I wish there had been no occasion for, that they are couch'd (to use your Lordships words) in a very extraordinary stile I am at a loss to know what may be your Lordship's meaning Couching being not customary to me, but the few lines that require an immediate and distinct explanation, shall pursuant to your Lordships expectation be immediately and distinctly explained   The words as marked by a Black line in your Lorships letter are these following, by which failure of his, Baby Smith will be quite lost having nothing but a few lies to support his Cause, unless he can obtain an Instructor from a Gentleman in Hanover Square   These words upon due consideration I am sensible do require an explanation that your Lordships may know what is the real meaning of them, so proceed to inform your Lordships that the aforesaid William Smith was a very idle drunken young man that he would frequently weep over his cups and was horribly given to fibbing & boasting of his Family and Interest among the good People of North Carolina but to his great misfortune there came two men out of the north that knew Smith his Father and Mother the accounts these men gave of him and his Family was that his Father had been a smugling Trader but broke & had a statute of bankruptcy taken out by his creditors against him and that he had also been concerned in carrying on several trayterous correspondencys against the late King, and that Smiths Mother was a very mean poor family, both these Northern men that knew Smith's Family so well were pleased to say he (Smith) was a Baby and ought to be sent home and whipt att school for talking in a manner so false and foolish & ever sence that time he has had the name of Baby added to Smith when People have mentioned him in conversation

I now proceed to Ashe the other Person mentioned in the words now explaining When I first came into this Country to govern the same for the late Lords Proprietors Mr John Baptista Ashe was poor clerke to a very inconsiderable Precinct court, but being informed what family he was off, and haveing been acquainted with several Gentlemen of that name, I gave him a good Place for this Country, caused him to be chosen Speaker of the Assembly and promoted his interests upon all occasions that offer'd, when I returned to England I left the management of my Affairs in this Country to him, which he so managed that instead of improvements I found my Estate and chattells a thousand pound sterling worse then when committed to his care. And Mr Ashe from poor became rich, however I was most extreamly civil and obligeing to Mr Ashe till he endeavoured to fix a vile scandal upon me in an affair between Tate and Harnett in last January which Transaction is in the Councel Journals, Mr Ashe by himself and Partisans used many inducements to inveigle the men of North Carolina to advance money for defraying the charges of a voyage he designed to take for England and expences during the time he should solicit his own business and that of North Carolina under the denomination of Agent which he designed to confer upon himself and honour Baby Smith with the same Title, but all his endeavours and designs were frustrated by the stupidity of these People, who were not to be persuaded to part with their money, this unexpected denval was the reason Ashe did not keep his word in going to England to assist Baby Smith, or Chief Justice Smith in the wicked design he rashly and ungratefully undertook to ruin me that had been his friend and Benefactor, Ashe failing to raise money for the concerted usage remained here, but I am well informed did assist in composeing a sett of horrid crimes calculated to make me odious which were incerted in a Petition delivered by Smith to the Kings most Excellent Majesty I hope your Lordships have seen those complaints and my answer if not be pleased to send for them to Mr Delafay

I have had several controversys in writing with the said Ashe the last not being gone home I send by this conveyance to Coll Bladen (altho' his name is not subscribed to the letter I am now answering) a Gentleman all men that have the honour to know will allow to be an excellent judge of such compositions.

I thought Smith would be at a great loss how to proceed in his projected designs against me Upon Mr Ashe's breach of promise in not repairing to London, therefore judged he would want an Instructor, and for

Hanover Square I might very well think that a fitt place of Instruction, it was there I used to wait upon two Gentlemen for advise and assistance in my own affairs, The right honourable Mr Edgcombe allways generouse, wise and benificent is one of the persons I mean and the other Doctor Sayer dead to my great misfortune whose good sence and humanity was known and experienced by many his friendship to me will appear by many letters I still retain Other Gentlemen of great parts live in Hanover Square, But to be very plain I had strong intimations that Mr Smith would make application to a certain Gentleman liveing there, the reasons I had to beleive it as became a man of honour I wrote to the Gentleman himself and others and have had assurances from my friends that I need not in the least doubt his friendship, or think my Enemys could find any countenance from him which I have since acknowledged with great pleasure to myself and I hope entirely to his satisfaction

My Lords I know my conduct to be blameless and my Enemys vile and implacable in their designs to blast my honour and reputation, and if I know any person in Hanover Square or elsewhere should espouse them, I shall not be afraid to call him to an account but when I am assured to the contrary no person can more openly acknowledge his mistake

I hope your Lordships will receive this as a very sincere and satisfactory answer and will please to be assured that no Person can have a greater respect for your Lordships and every Member of your Board which I shall on all occasions demonstrate and doubt not of your esteem & favourable reception of everything I lay before You, and hope my Representation of the state of this Country and the account of things here formerly presented to your Lordships have had your approbation

I have now the honour to transmit your Lordships Drafts of Beaufort and Ocacock Harbours in this Province that of Cape Fear River sent some time past I hope you like

Next month I design to send your Lordships a further state of the Colony and the Council Journals to that time which I hope will give much satisfaction

I had agreed to give ten Guineas for a Map of the Country which was drawn for me but is sent as I am told a present to Coll Bladen which is better then if I had pay'd for it being at this time very Poor

     I am
        With due respect
          Your Lordships
           Most humble
             and most obedient servant
                GEO BURRINGTON

[B. P R. O. Am & W Ind No. 592.]

MEMORIAL OF GOV' BURRINGTON 15 NOV 1732.

To His Grace the Duke of New Castle Principal Secretary of State
The Memorial of George Burrington Governor of North Carolina.

Herein humbly begs to lay before your Grace, the great injuries done him by William Smith Esq'' late Chief Justice of this Province and his Confederates, who nefariously inverted several matters very false and scandalous against him with design to ruine and destroy his reputation and procure his Dismission from the post in which he has the Honour to serve his Majesty That to compleat their intended wicked projection the said Smith did deliver a Petition to the King consisting of several Articles containing heinous Crimes set forth to be committed by your Memorialist and many Omissions, and great neglects of his duty charged on him, an Office Copy of that Petition was brought into this Country in the month of May last, your Memorialist having read the same was induced in Vindication of his Character to draw up a hasty answer several Gentlemen Voluntarily (in Council) upon their Oaths proved the falseness of Smiths accusations which answer and depositions were sent to England in the same Month to be laid before your Grace

It is not supposed Smith and his Accomplices will attempt to prove their assertions, knowing the whole to be only invented, they expected those complaints would be credited and my ruine compleated by means of a great Interest they boasted to have in England it was industriously reported throughout this Country, and by many believed I should be turned out of my present Imployment when any complaints were lodged against me

Notwithstanding one year is past since M' Smith obtained an Order of Council for examining of Witnesses, in order to prove his allegations, yet nothing has been done in the matter on his side, for that reason your Grace is humbly prayed to prefix a time for him to make out and prove the Charge, or on failure thereof he may suffer according to his demerits

MAY IT PLEASE YOUR GRACE

With truth I aver it was oweing to the faults of some men that had the Kings Commissions, the Assembly I held in this Country would do no business, many of the then Members have since owned it and expressed their concern for suffering themselves to be misled I was unhappily deserted by the Persons His Majesty appointed to assist in the administration, had an uncommon task to perform in this Government, which from the beginning continued loose and disorderly under the faint rule of the Lords Proprietors, and came to nothing under Sir Richard Everard their last Governor, who was sunk to so low a degree as to be contemptible and the Government with him

Quit Rents Publick Levis and Officers Fees were paid in Province Bills at Par they are of so little Value that to be paid in such manner Men in Offices could not live by their places for which reason pursuant to His Majesties 19th Instruction that Fees should be paid in Proclamation money the Officers received their dues in Bills, four for one, which is the Rate they were issued at and to be received in payments, in respect to Silver Money except in discharge of Publick Levies and Officers Fees, but these Bills are little more than half the Value rated at, extraordinary endeavours were used with the People to persuade them this was a grievous imposition and burthen and is made by Smith a cause of Complaint tho himself and some others his Associates in this Clamour always took their Fees in Bills at four for one and encouraged the inferior Officers to do the Same—for my own part the little inconsiderable perquisites accrueing to me as Governour I offered to give up entirely to the Assembly all this is proved by some depositions in support of my answer to Smiths Calumnies

The said Smith, Mr Rice the Secretary and Montgomery the Attorney General have not assisted me as the duty of their places required but contrary thereunto, invent and foment all things they believe may prove prejudicial to the Authority of Government and cause uneasiness to myself

The Inhabitants have been greatly solicited to to raise money by subscription for Mr Ashe one of the Council to go home and manage against me but the People would not be drawn into so great a folly declaring throughout the whole Province their Satisfaction on my conduct and gratitude for the services I had done them, when formerly Governour for the Proprietors and since (by your Graces favour) honoured with the Kings Commission I cease enlarging on this Subject, designing in a future Paper to trouble your Grace with the exact state of this Province, and how much I have promoted the Welfare thereof at my own expence it is now in a quiet orderly State and flourishing condition

MAY IT PLEASE YOUR GRACE.

I have served the crown in every reign since the Abdication of King James, & always was allowed to behave as became a Man of Honour, and the Family whose name I bear, their Services at the Revolution and during the life of King William of glorious memory I hope are not yet in Oblivion

MY LORD DUKE

When my Proceedings have been considered I make no doubt but that your Grace will grant I have acted with Zeal and Diligence for his Majesties Service justly and honestly upon all occasions in the Administration of this troublesome unprofitable Government Therefore your Grace is most humbly requested to give such orders as may effectually set in a true light the actions of your Memorialist, and his Accusers

By

My Lord Duke

your Graces

most obedient

and most devoted servant

GEO BURRINGTON

North Carolina the 15th of November 1732

[B. P R. O. B T NORTH CAROLIN VOL 9 A 26, 27 AND 28]

RICE, MONTGOMERY AND ASHE vs BURRINGTON

To the Right Honourable the Lords Comissioners for Trade & Plantations

The Humble Memorial of Nathaniel Rice Secry & John Baptiste Ashe Esqr Two of His Majesty's Council and John Montgomery Esqr Attorney Genl and Deputy Inspector and Comptroller Genl of the aforsd Province.

MAY IT PLEASE YOr LORDSHIPS

We sometime since sent to your Lordships a Memorial, or Remonstrance against several illegal and unwarrantable Actions of George Burrington Esqr, Governor of this Province, which we thought it our duty to do, for that we plainly perceived the Governor used many Arts to

prevent a true state of the Case of the Province being exhibited to yo'
Lordships The same reasons still continueing, and the Governor proceeding on to still more extravagant Actions, we beg we may not offend
your Lordships, in presenting this Additional Memorial, & we hope we
shall be more readily excused, in that we are now forced to fly to your
Lordships for Protection, for so great is the wrath and malice, which he
has conceived against us, for opposing him in what we thought Arbitrary,
Illegal & destructive to the King's Interest, that he sticks at nothing to
crush & ruin Us, as well as others who submit not to his violent & arbitrary Acts & Measures

1ª In our last we observed to yo' Lordships that the then Chief Justice and the rest of the Judges of the General Court, had fallen under
the Governor's high displeasure for acting pursuant to the King's Instructions concerning the Habeas Corpus Act, as became them in relation
to his illegal Commitment of M' Moseley, (tho' they were scarce ever
before known to oppose his Will) the Consequence of which has been
the Chief Justice has been so threatened that he has resigned, and the
Assistants without any such Ceremony or indeed so much as a Charge or
Accusation being exhibited against them, have been Arbitrarily removed,
directly contrary to His Majesty's 44th Instruction to the Gov', which
expressly forbids the displacing or arbitrary removal of Justices without
cause and this he proceeded to do with only two of the Council, viz'
M' Lovick & M' Gale (one of which had been introduced into the Council contrary to His Majesty's 7th Instruction, there having been then
seven in the Governm',) except the Surveyor General of the Customs, a
Stranger and just arrived in the Province when a full Council was at
the same time summon'd, and did meet Time enough to have appointed a
Chief Justice & Assistant to have Transacted the Business of the Court
But the Gov' revolving in his mind what Designs he had to execute
found it necessary to displace them, to make room for Instruments more
proper for his purpose, as well as to be Examples of his Vengeance on
Judges not entirely subservient to his will Accordingly displacing them
he put others fitter for his Designs in their Places, viz' William Little
Esq'', Ch Justice Roger Moor, M' Owen Jn° Worley, M'roro, Scar-
boro', all these (except Rog Moor, who he was sure would never qualify
or attend, and M' Owen a very weak & ignorant man) of bad (not to
say infamous) Character. The Chief Justice is a Person against whom
the whole Province (as it were) has exclaimed for his unjust, illegal and
Fraudulent Practices He has been publickly accused by Assemblys of
this Province of Bribery, Extortion and other great Crimes, of which he

has never acquitted himself He is now under accusations of Fraud and Injuries done both to the King & Subject Many are the Compl⁸ of Multitudes of People against him for many illegal Acts and violent Oppressions both in his private Capacity, and when he has acted as an Officer It is no wonder that a Person so obnoxious to Justice in hopes of being sheltered by the Gov' therefrom (as indeed he is) should become entirely subservient to him, and obedient to his Dictates and Commands.

Of a Court consisting of Persons so entirely devoted to him, most People dread the Consequences; and the next Article (which is M' Ashe's Case) will be an instance how much reason they have so to do.

2ᵈˡʸ The Governor when he was last at Cape Fair, it being about the middle of Sept' last, sent his servants, & with a violent hand took up and drove away two Mares of M' Ashe's, branding them with his own Brand M' Ashe coming into Court the last of October (there being a great Concourse of People at the Court) declined moving in the Affair, till the last of the Court, when the Multitude were gone, that it might plainly appear he had not the least design to irritate the People, and then in the Council Chamber before the breaking up of the Council (none but the Governor and Council being present) he in the humblest manner addressed himself to the Gov' telling him that he was well informed his Excell'ˢ Servants had by his Orders taken up two of his Mares and branded them, that he thought it advisable to apply himself to his Excell' on the Occasion, and to pray him to restore them The Gov' flew into a violent passion, and using much scurrilous & reproachful Language to the s' Ashe, came up with his face close to M' Ashe's & shaking his head at him in a jeering taunting tone & manner called him (repeating the words often) pretty fellow, very pretty fellow ! threatening at the same time to take some of his Negro Slaves. M' Ashe mildly answered he was Gov' and might say what he pleased, that he would not be provoked to return his ill Language, but that he hoped his Excell' would not be offended (since he had refused to restore the Mares) if he sought his right by a Course of Law The Governor answered No he might go to Law & welcome. Whereupon M' Ashe the next day filed an Information in the General Court on an Act of Assembly of this Province giving Relief in such cases, and this methodly Information he the rather chose, because it would not touch or effect the Governor's Person, the original leading Process here otherwise being generally by Capias. Some time after this (M' Ashe being absent) the Governor came into Court and calling for the Information read it & used much reproachful Language to M' Ash's Council. The next

48

day Mr Ashe appeared again and the matter was debated in Court, Whereupon the Court gave it as their opinion that such suits could not be brought against a Govr in the Plantation but must be brought at home in England, agreable (as they alledged) to the Statute of XI and XII W III Cap XII for such was the Exposition of that statute We think we may be allowed to assert that this Judgment is most preposterous and extravagant, when we shall have shown how great absurdities attend it. It is plain that law was designed for relief of the Inhabitants of the Plantations against Govern^r comitting great Crimes & Offences, giving Power to try Causes in England which before with respect to locality or other Circumstances (it might be disputable) were not cognizable in the Courts there, or where it might be thought that a Govr in Consideration of the Great Power wherewith he was invested, should deter or prevent People from seeking their Right But does it from thence follow that Govern^r are exempt from answering for Torts or Injuries done in the Plantations, anywhere but in England Surely the Lawgivers by that Statute never designed to screen Govr from Persecutions, or to prevent suits for small Trespasses where the party injured would venture to try his cause in the Plantations To say so were to say Govr were to answer in England for great oppressions, but that if they would confine themselves to smaller trespasses or Injuries that Statute was a Dispensation for them, & as in this Case of Mr Ashe, the damages he sues for are not above £15 sterl it is not worth his while to sue in England to recover them, where he would be perhaps at the Expence of £200 sterl before he could recover he had better sit down with the first Loss, and so the Govr may go on to take by violence a horse from one, a cow from another, and as he shall think proper, whatever other small matters or things he wants from others, and this Statute instead of relieving the People would be a bar to it, and support such Governor in his oppressions should he proceed (being warranted by such a judgement) to lay the whole Country under (as it were) a Contribution

The obtaining such a Judgm^t in his favour one would have thought might have contented the Governor for that time, but matters were so concerted between him and his Justices that immediately on Mr Ashe's coming out of Court, he was apprehended by a Warrant (ready prepared) from Judge Owen, for publishing a scurrilous Libel, such was his information stiled, (tho' all manner of Scurrility or even Termes Aggravating the Offence, were carefully avoided therein) and was carryed before the Govr and Judge Owen (tho' Mr Ashe desired to be carryed before the Chief Justice who better understood the Law, but was denyed,) the Govr directing the Judge to demand of him One Thousand Pound sterl Bail for himself, and five hundred each of his securities, to appear at March Court then next following, to Answer   The Judge took the words from the Governor's mouth, and repeating them, demanded the same Bail, without ever examining into the Cause of Comĩtmᵗ Mʳ Ashe refused to comply with so unreasonable a Demand, whereupon he was ordered away, and imẽdiately carryed to the Comon stinking Goal, and thrust in among the comon Criminals, by virtue of a Mittimus (ready prepared too,) from the sᵈ Judge Owen, there to continue till he complyed with that Demand, it being a Condition in the Precept and what rendered it illegal   Mʳ Ashe petitioned the Chief Justice for a Habeas Corpus, and after lying sometime in Prison, (vizᵗ about four hours, during which time the Chief Justice had been with the Governor) he was brought before the Chief Justice, who refused to examine into the legality of the Cause of Comĩtment, (altho' the King by his Instructions, and the Habeas Corpus Act itself directed it,) for he well knew no person was punishable for seeking a Remedy by Law for any Injury he conceived done him, and indeed there is great reason to believe that it was purposely contrived, that Mʳ Owen should do this drudgery (which could not well have been done by one that knew better) with a view of engaging Comʳ Walker (whose nephew Mʳ Owen is) to use his Interest for his Nephew's sake to support so illegal and arbitrary an Act   Mʳ Little therefore denyed enquiring into the Cause of Comĩtmᵗ alledging it was already done by One of the Judges and only mitigated the Bail, taking the one half of what was before demanded   As it is plain (having Justice so devoted to him) he design's Mʳ Ashe's ruin, and as it is very notorious that Mʳ Ashe has incurr'd all this his hatred and Malice, for only opposing him in his many illegal Acts, More especially in his Breach and Contempt of the King's Instructions relating to his Arbitrary and undue disposal of the King's Lands, he begs leave to throw himself under yoʳ Lordships protection, desiring nevertheless no favour if it shall appear upon a due and impartial Examination, that he has acted otherwise than as he was, (being one of his Majesty's Council,) in duty bound, or than according to Law, or than as became an honest man   And what necessitates him in this manner to beg voʳ Lordships protection is, that the Governor, (notwithstanding the Judgmᵗ of Court refers him to Great Britain for relief) has taken an Effectual method by holding him so long a time (& no doubt it will be continued, if thought necessary,) under such Bail to prevent his prosecuting that Affair, as well as appearing as an Agent for the Country, most of the principal Inhabitants (for want of an Assembly,) having desired and Impowered him so to do, and to Represent their Grievances.

The Govr having Exhibited a Charge in Council, against Mr Montgomery Attorney Gen^{ll} of this Province, he was commanded to answer by the 31st day of October last, in obedience thereto he filed his answer upon the day appointed The Council thereupon proceeded to a hearing of that Affair, and the charge and answer thereto being read, a witness was examined, and an Affidavit read in support of the charge, and the next day appointed for Mr Montgomery to produce his witnesses, and for reading several Depositions, (sworn before the Governor,) in his Defence But his Excell^y perceiving his innocence upon every Article would plainly appear, and that the Council, (tho' that the Majority were his creatures,) would not be prevailed upon to do so manifest an Act of Injustice, as to suspend him, he drop'd the Prosecution and abruptly broke up the Council, by which means the Attorney Gen^{ll} had no opportunity of having his witnesses examined, or Proofs read in Council   And his Excell^y being resolved to make use of every method, he thinks may either ruin or injure Mr Montgomery, has caused the Charge with the Depositions taken against him to be inserted in the Council Journal to be sent home, (without inserting the Answer thereto,) in hopes that a Charge being seen therein by His Majesties Ministers, and no Answer thereto, they would believe he had submitted, or could make no Defence to the Charge

We are sorry to say this is his Method of proceeding in almost every Case that comes before the Council, & so far is he from being ashamed of such Practices, that he values himself upon them, as instances of his great abilities in Politicks, and the Arts of Governm^t

4^{thly} The Govern^r has, (on pretext of some former old Precedents in this Province, of the Governor & Council appointing Precincts, where no Precincts before were, (the legality of which, more especially of late years, has been by the Assemblys deny'd,) proceeded with the advice & consent of such of the Council as are of his own Appointment, & never oppose his schemes, be they ever so absurd, to divide old Precincts established by Law, & to enact new Ones in Places, whereby his Arts he has endeavoured to prepossess People in a future election according to his desire, his Designs herein being (as we verily believe) either to endeavour by his means to get a Majority of his creatures in the Lower House, to support him in his arbitrary measures, or if he should fail therein, (as it is more than probable he will) that this should be a stumbling Block, to prevent the Assembly's proceeding to busyness he being well assured from what has passed in former Assemblies, that the Assembly would object against such an invasion of their Priviledges, in so momentous a point as that of their Constitution, the first thing they should do after their meeting, and so perhaps break up without proceeding so far as to move in Matters which (it is to be thought) he is willing should not be heard of or represented elsewhere. For we are well assured that he has ernestly promoted such Petitions, (even forming and writing some of them himself,) where there was no Necessity for such Precincts on the contrary some have not above thirty families inhabiting them, and can scarce make out a sufficient number of People for Justices and Jury These Considerations moved Mr Rice & Mr Ashe to offer in Council Objections and Reasons against this Method, which (as we have much reason to suspect,) he will not suffer to be entered in the Council Journal, to be transmitted to your Lordships, We beg leave (having enclosed a Copy thereof,) to offer the same to your Lordships Consideration

5thly He takes occasion at Publick Meetings of People, as at Courts, or the like, before great Audiences, of reflecting on, abusing, reviling, detracting and defaming Gentlemen without any regard to Truth, sometimes when they are present, at others when they are absent and cannot speak in their own Vindication, on purpose to injure them in the opinion of the People Such is the Case of Mr Moseley, Mr Ashe, Mr Montgomery, Mr Swan etc Tho' this Matter otherwise than as it is inconsistant with good-manners, ill becoming the Governor of a Province, and very ungrateful and provoking to the Parties, is scarce worth the Representing For we assure your Lordships he is now so notoriously known to have no respect to Truth, that no man suffers in his character from any defamatory Report of his, let it relate either to Gentlemen in Great Britain, or in this Province

6thly Since our last Remonstrance to your Lordships, notwithstanding our frequent Applications to him, and objections against his arbitrary Disposal of the Kings Lands, he has solely proceeded to issue many hundred Warrants in undue Proportions, taking to himself two and sixpence in silver or gold Virginia Currency, for every 50 Acres. And this last Genll Court tho' the Council unanimously gave it as their opinion that Warrants ought to be issued pursuant to his Majts Instructions, & not otherwise, yet he declared his Resolution notwithstanding to pursue his usual Method which he perceiving Mr Rice and Mr Ashe designed to protest against, abruptly broke up the Council, not meeting them afterwards during that Court or Term, so that they were obliged to file the enclosed Protest by way of Caveat in the Secretary's office, to prevent (if possible) any more warrants issuing in such an arbitrary manner, and so the Consequences which would attend or ensue on such a Practice, vizt either the defeating the King's Intent of seating the uninhabited parts of this Province, or very great injuries to the Purchasers of such warrants, if His Majesty should not approve of them

This so highly provoked him that it is believed to be one of the Principal motives of his violent Proceedings against Mr Ashe, purposing it is to be feared, (if possible,) to crush and ruin him, before he can be relieved by, or shelter himself under yor Ldps (and by yor Ldps means His Maties) Protection As also of his grossly abusing Mr Rice, he having used to him very scurrilous Language A Copy of the aforesd Protest & Caveat, we send herewith to your Ldps, wch he would not receive when offered to be given him by the Dep Secy, who informed him of the contents but he proceeds still to issue warrants in the same manner to the Purchasers, let the quality be ever so large, or disproportionate to the Rule prescribed by His May He uses many Wiles & Artifices to asperse Gentlemen & to blacken their Characters, at the same time endeavouring to impose by his Misrepresentations on the Ministry, particularly by exhibiting charges agt them in the Council Journal, & when they answer, stifling their answers, or making answers for them, as best suits his purposes, as will be apparent from some inclosed Answers of Mr Montgomery, Col Moseley, & Col Moore, which are true & genuine answers by them made, tho' by him either wholly suppressed or altered, which will be evident by comparing them with the Council Journals, a very vile & wicked Practice We give those Instances which now occur, as a specimen, out of many of the same Nature which (but that it would be too tedious) might be added Now we have great room to believe (Nay in some cases we are assured) that he has used us in the same manner, and has endeavoured to blacken our Characters to the utmost of his Power. We therefore (after having assured yor Ldps that we have acted in our several stations as we were bound by the Ties of Duty to our Sovereign Lord the King, & the dictates of honour & conscience, beg your Lordships before you shall give ear to any false suggestions of his to our discredit or Prejudice, that we may be informed of them, so as to have an opportunity of vindicating ourselves from such aspersions, And we doubt not but your Lordships will pronounce us quite other men, than (it is highly probable) he has represented us to be

We are with the most profound respect,

> May it please Your Lordships,
> > Your Lordships most obedient
> > > humble servants

> > > > NATH RICE
> > > > JNo BAPT ASHE
> > > > JOHN MONTGOMERY

November the 17th 1732

To His Excellency the Govern^r in Council

Nathaniel Rice and John Bapt^a Ashe Esq^{rs} Two of His Majesty's Council humbly shew

That His Ex^{cy} the Governor hath issued out and given a very great Number of Warrants for Lands to sundry Persons, in undue and large Quantities, not observing the Rule of Proportion prescribed by His Majestys, of granting Lands by and with the Advice and Consent of the Council, vizt of fifty Acres only for every Person in the Grantee's Family   For all wch Lands mentioned in those Warrants the Govern^r hath taken for every fifty Acres the Sum of two shill^s and six Pence Virginia Currency in Silver or Gold   Wherefore We think Our Selves obliged, out of a due Sense of our Duty to his Most sacred Majesty to object against the same,   And We do hereby humbly pray his Excellency that he would be pleased strictly to pursue his Majesty's Instructions to him in that behalf given,   And that no Warrants may issue but to such Persons & in such Proportions as shall be agreeable to His Majestys said Instructions

We conceive Ourselves the more under a Necessity of thus humbly remonstrating this Matter to Your Ex^{cy} for that (if this Method should be disallowed by the King) it may hereafter very much injure such People as have paid their Moneys for such Lands, but more especially for that it is not agreeable, but contrary to his Majesty's Instruction to Your Ex^{cy} on that behalf which to his Majestys Council has by Yo^r Excell^y been exhibited and shown

Reasons and Objections made and humbly offer'd in Council by Nath Rice and Jno Bap^{ta} Ashe two of His Ma^{tys} Council to the Govern^r & Council against the dividing Precincts and erecting New Ones by the Govr & Council alone without the Concurrence and Assent of the Assembly

1st As every Precinct is to send a certain Number of Representatives to the lower House of Assembly, such a Method may be destructive of and subvert the present Constitution of the Legislature, which as it consists of an upper & lower House whose Powers and Privileges are separate & distinct they ought in such Points to be independent either of the other, more especially in so fundamental a one as is this of Representation For it stands to Reason that if a Power of altering the Form of Representation either by adding to, or diminishing the Number of Representatives, or by causing an unequal Representation be lodged in the Persons of whom the upper House consists, that then the Lower

House is dependent on and owes it's being, at least the form thereof (which is in effect the same) to the upper House, by which means the upper will be solely, (as it were) the whole Legislature   As for instance suppose the Gov'r and three of the Council on an Emergency to meet (We speak this by way of Supposition and for Argum't sake) and think it proper to divide a Precinct, whose Inhabitants for some particular Ends may be at such Governour's & Council Devotion) into ten Precincts, will not by this mean a Majority be obtained in the Lower House

2 It is absurd to suppose that a Power of the part should be greater than or indeed equal to that of the whole   Now as the Constitution of the Legislature must be antecedent to any Act thereof, it cannot be dependent on any such Act, much less on an Act of part, as indeed by this Method it would, in that the whole Legislature would owe its Being (at least the form thereof w'ch as We observ'd before is in effect the same) to the upper House, And this amongst others, We take to be the Reason, that the Legislature of Great Britain avoid (tho' many are there the Inconveniences ensuing from unequal Representation) endeavouring to remedy them, or touching on so tender and constitutional a Point.

3. Another Consequence of such a Method extremely absurd will be this   An Order of Gov'r & Council only will have force to supersede repeal and annull a Law   For if by Law a Precinct is limited & circumscribed by certain Bounds and by an Order of Gov'r and Council those Bounds are altered or taken away and new ones prescribed, is not this in effect repealing such Law?

4 We conceive such Busyness, as it relates to the Constitution of the Legislature, most properly to lie before the Governour Council and Representatives of the People in General Assembly, and as it is to be presumed they are the most competent Judges when such Precincts shall be necessary so it is that they will readily concur in erecting new ones, when they shall be so judged to be for the good of the public and Benefit of a competent number of Inhabitants

5 We are of opinion that this method of erecting Precincts, is not only illegal and may be attended with many evil consequences, but is also not warranted by his Majesty's Royal Instructions which forbids erecting new Judicatories without His Majestys Licence   Now by this Method new Judicatories will be erected   But it it were done by an Act of Assembly at the Prayer of the Representatives of the People the same would regularly come before His Majesty for His Allowance or Dissent

6. We are the more Confirmed in this Our Opinion of the Illegality of doing it without the Consent of the Representatives of the People in General Assembly, from the General Practice of the Neighbouring Governments more particularly Virginia where many Precedents appear in their printed Laws of such Busyness being done by their Gov' Council and Assembly And We are apt to believe our Gracious King (for we pretend not in the least to deny or even so much as to dispute the Royal Prerogative has given as full Powers to the Govern' and Council of Virginia as to the Govern' & Council of this Province Nor can We think it the pleasure of Our most gracious Sovereign (who on all Occasions has shown so tender a Regard to us his People that the Constitution of the Legislature of the Province should be on a more precarious establishm' than that of others

On Argument in the last Council His Excellency the Govern' seeming to have taken a Resolution to pass Warrants as before he had done which Method We humbly objected against in Council and prepared the foregoing Paper designing to have preferr'd it in Council, but the Council breaking up unexpectedly We were prevented putting it in But now finding that his Excell' still continues to issue Warrants for Lands in undue Proportions & contrary (as we conceive) to the Kings Instructions We think it our Duty to file this by way of Caution to the Secretary's Office, requiring and desireing the Deputy Secretary to prefer the same to his Excell' before he (the Dep Sec'y) subsign or make out any more Warrants Humbly praying his Excell' that if he shall think w' we object reasonable he would be pleased to have Respect thereunto.

(Endorsed)

North Carolina

Compl' of M' Rice and M' Ashe against the Gov' for granting too large Tracts of Land and dividing of Precincts

NORTH CAROLINA—Sc'

October Gen' Court or Term 1732

To the Chief Justice, and Assistant Justice of the Gen' Court of the said Province, Justice of our Lord the King of his Bench

Be it remembered that John Baptista Ashe comes here into Court y' 31" day of October the same Form in his proper person, and exhibits to the Justices here a certain information against George Burrington of

North Carolina Esq' Governor &° at present of the said Province   The tenour of which said Informacon follows in these words

To the Chief Justice, and Assistant Justices of the Gen' Court &° Justices of our Lord and King of his Bench &° North Carolina S˙   But it remembered that John Baptista Ashe who for himself as owner as well as Informer or he that sues in this behalf prosecutor comes here into Court y° 31ˢᵗ day of October the same Term in his proper person and for himself as owner as well as prosecutor, or he that sueth, gives the Court here to understand & be informed That George Burrington Esq™ of North Carolina present Governour of the s⁴ Province at the Precinct of New Hanover in the said Province on y° 15ᵗʰ day of Sep' in this instant & Year, Did take up, and drive, or did cause to be taken up, and driven to the s⁴ George Burrington Esq™ & his plantation in the afores⁴ precinct two large black mares, viz' one about the age of nine years of the price or value of fourty pounds, the other about two and a half years old of the price or value of fifty pounds, which said mares were not properly his own, but were properly the mares of the plaintiff, or Informant, and the aforesaid two mares he did also then & there misbrand, or did cause to be misbranded, by branding them with a brand not the brand of the Pᵗʰ against the Statute or act of Assembly of this Province in the like case published and provided   Whereupon the said John Baptista Ashe for himself as prosecutor or he that sueth, as well as owner prays the Advisement of the Court in the premises, And that the afores⁴ George Burrington Esq™ &° may be lawfully thereof Convicted, and for his offence may forfeit the value of the said mares & twenty pounds, that is to say ten pounds for each mare over and above the value of each of the said mares   And that the aforesaid John Baptista Ashe the forfiture aforesaid may have to himself being as well owner as he that sueth for the same, according to the form of the Statute or Act of Assembly of this province aforesd And that the aforesaid George Burrington Esq™ &° may come hereinto Court to answer in and upon the premises &°

                                   JN° ASHE Pᵗʰ or Inform'

Jno Doe   ⎫
Richᵈ Roe ⎬ pledges &°

Whereupon David Osheal Gen' Attorney in behalf of his Excellency George Burrington Esq' Governor Comes into Court & prays the Advisement of the Court upon the Informacon and prosecution of John Baptista Ashe against him, whether they will receive the same, for that he saveth the said George Burrington Esq™ then was and still is his Majestys Lieutenant of s⁴ province & Governour in Cheif Chancellor and

Supreme Magistrate within y' same and is not to be drawn or compelled
in this Court in manner aforesd to answer for any Crime or Offence, and
further the said Attorney in behalf of his Excellency George Burrington saith and avers that the said mares mentioned in s'd prosecution are
and then were bona fide the property of the said George Burrington
Esq'r and that as Attorney to him & by his immediate orders the s'd
David Osheal will Consent to a rule in behalf of the said Governor
Burrington, that he will receive a declaration from the said Ashe in
Trespass, Detinue Trover or otherwise, and plead thereto so or to try
the Title & property at Law But prays this prosecution being scandalous
& what this Court can not compell the Gov'r to answer to may be dismist

D O'SHEAL

Then Jno Bapta Ashe aforesd comes into Court and objecting against
a certain paper put or pretended to be put in & preferred to this Court
by David Osheal Gen'l Attorney in behalf of his Excell'cy George Burrington Esq'r Gov'r &c (against whom an information had been exhibited
by the said Ashe) prays that the same may not be received, for that it is
irregular illegal & contrary to the practice of this Court And he offereth
these reasons to shew why the said paper ought not to be received but to
be rejected

1st The said paper seems to be in the nature of a plea to the jurisdiction of the Court or of a plea of privilege in both which cases there
are certain direct and legal pleas, which ought to have been pleaded (if
such were the Case) according to the practise and rules of this Court and
not thus ambiguously uncertainly and Contrary to the practice of all
Courts of Law.

2d By way (as it were) of privilege he the said George Burrington
Esq'r &c by his Attorney aforesd assumes a title which I humbly conceive is not conferred on him by his Majesty Viz't that of his Majestys
Lieutenant of the s'd Province Neither does he shew how or in what
manner he is entituled to privilege or an exemption from Suite in this
his Majestys supreme Court of Comon Law in this Govern't in which if
the Pst cannot have relief, or exhibit this his Suite, he conceives himself
to be without remedy

3dly The Pst is surprised that his Excellency his learned Council should
trifle so egregiously with this Hon'ble Court and the Pst as to pretend to
offer to consent to a rule of receiving a declaration from the Pst in an
Action of a different nature of his own proposeing forreign to the purpose viz't to try the title and property at Law whereas the Pst sues not

for the mares, but for damages (accruing from a tort or injury done) given him by the Law, in which Case it behoved him to have shewn that the Govern' was excepted out of or exempt from the force of such Law and not bound by it, Or at least that the Informant had no remedy by means or force of the said Law against his Excellency in this Honble Court

{ The learned Gent might as well urge, should a Govern' think fit to cut off a persons earr or nose & such person should proceed to cause him to be prosecuted on the Statute against maiming &c y^t the prosecution was scandalous &c and what this Court could not compel such Govern^r to answer to, and offer to receive a declaration from the party injured in Trespass detinue Trevor &c to try the title & property at Law to his Ears and nose

This paragraph struck out by the Court

4^tly The P^et is humbly of opinion, that this action well lies in this Court in that it is by Informacon avoiding any scandalous or approbreious expressions and the penalty is pecuniary without any attack or Copies to be Executed or served on his Excellencys persons

Lastly The P^et is well aware that this way of giving in such argumentative papers is not agreeable to the ancient practice of this Court and thinks he ought to have demurred to the paper put in by Mr Osheal as to an insufficient pleas, but this Honble Court seeming yesterday to be of a different opinion having received and read the said paper but not at a plea He hopes and humbly prays that his answering in the same manner may not be offensive to this Honble Court; And that his Action may be received, and that he may have relief according to the advisement of this Hono^ble Court in this his Majestys Supreme Court of Comon Law in this Province But if this Honble Court shall be of a different opinion he humbly prays their further advisement

Thereupon the Court proceeded to ye following Judgement

NORTH CAROLINA—ss

At a Genl Court of Sessions of the peace Court of Assize and Genl Goal delivery begun and held at Edenton for the said Province on the last Tuesday in Oct 1732 & by adjournments continued to the 16th day of Nov^ber 1732

Before

William Little Esqr Chief Justice

William Owen
Macrora Scarborough } Esq^rs Justices s^d Court

David Osheal Esqr Genl Attorney for his Excell^y George Burrington Esqr Govr pray'd leave to amend exceptions he had put into the Informaçon of John Baptista Ashe exhibited to this Court against the said Govern' which was granted by the Court, and the same was amended and read, And thereupon John Baptista Ashe put in a replicaçon or exception thereunto, which was read and the matter being duly argued, and fully heard, and by the Court here considered upon and the advisement thereof desired, It is the unanimous opinion of the said Court that the said Information being a prosecution against the said George Burrington Esq' now Governor here for a Crime or offence alledged to be done by him whilst Governor which by Act or Parliament is ordained else where to be heard & determined, and for that the said Court cannot compell the said Governor here to appear or answer thereto they cannot hear & determine the same & will not proceed in Judgement thereon

---

NORTH CAROLINA—ss

George the Second by the Grace of God of Great Britain France & Ireland King Defender of the faith &c

To the provost Marshall or his Deputy Greeting

We command you that you have the body of John Bap'a Ashe Esq' in our Goal at Edenton unlawfully detained as he sayeth, before William Settle Esq' our Chief Justice together with the Cause of his Commitment to do & receive as our said Chief Justice together with the Cause of his Commitment to do and receive as our said Chief Justice shall in that part Consider and have you there this writ

Witness William Little Esq' Chief Justice at Edenton this 10th day of November 1732

A True Copy

WILLIAM LITTLE Ch Justice

℘ WILLIAM MACKY D M.

NORTH CAROLINA—ss

On Complaint of His Excellency George Burrington Esq' Govern' & Capt. General of this Province, that John Baptista Ashe Esq' on or about the tenth day of this Instant November in this present year of our Lord Christ one thousand seven hundred & thirty two did write & publish certain Scurrilous Libells to defame the said Governor against the peace of His Majesty that now is, and the Statutes or Acts of Assembly of this Province in that case made & provided these are therefore in His Majestys name to command you to apprehend and take into your safe Custody the said John Baptista Ashe and bring him before me or some other of the Assistant Justices of the Gen' Court to answer abide & perform what our said Justices in the premises aforesaid then and there shall Consider & make due returne hereof Given under my hand and seal this 10th day of November 1732

To the provost Marsh or his Depu'y these to execute & returne

A True Copy   ⅌ WILLIAM MACKY D M

NORTH CAROLINA—ss

To the Keeper of the Goal at Edenton

I send you herewith the body of John Baptista Ashe Esq'r this day brought before me and accused of writing and publishing certain false & scandalous Libels against His Excelly George Burrington Esq'r Gov'r Capt General &c of this province against the peace of our Lord the King that now is & the Act of Assembly of this Province

Therefore you are hereby strictly charged & commanded in his Majestys name to receive the said Jn° Baptista Ashe and him in Goal to keep untill he give bond with two suff't securities, the said Ashe as principal in one thousand pounds sterling and his securitys in five hundred pounds ster each personally to appear before the Justices of the Gen'll Court of this province at the next Gen'll Court to be held for the same at Edenton then and there to do & receive what the s'd Justices in this behalf shall order or be otherwise discharged by due Course of Law

Given under my hand and Seal at Edenton the 10th day Nov'r in the 6th yeare of his Majestys Reign Anno Dom 1732

W'm OWEN   [SEAL.]

True Copy Examined

⅌ WILLIAM MACKY D M

NORTH CAROLINA—ss

Att a General Court of Sessions of the Peace Court of Assize & General Goal delivery begun & held at Edenton for the said Province on the last Tuesday in October 1732 & by adjournments continued to the 10th Day of November 1732

Before

William Little Esq'r Chief Justice

William Owen
Macrora Scarborough } Esq'rs Justice of s'd Court

David Osheal Gentleman Attorney for his Excellency George Burrington Esq'r Governour prayed leave to amend the Exceptions he had

put into the Information of John Baptista Exhibited to this Court
against the said Governour which was granted by the Court & ye same
was amended and read & thereupon John Baptista Ashe put in a Repli-
cation or Exception thereto which was read & the matter being duly
argued & fully heard & by the Court here considered upon the advisement thereof desired it is the Unanimous opinion of the said Court that
the said Information being a prosecution against the said George Burrington Esq' now Governour here for a crime or offence Alledged to be
done by him whilst Governour which by Act of Parliament is ordained
Elsewhere to be heard & determined & for that the said Court cannot
compel the said Governour here to appear or Answer thereto they cannot
hear & determine the same & will not proceed in Judgment thereon

  Exam⁴ & Compared with the records

                                        Wᵐ LITTLE Ch Just°

[FROM NORTH CAROLINA LETTER BOOK OF S. P G]

MR LAPIERRE TO THE BISHOP OF LONDON

CAPE FEAR ALIAS NEW HANOVER Novʳ 29, 1732

MY LORD

  As I am one, who in Queen Anne's Reign 1708 was by your Lordship's most worthy predecessor, sent to South and North Carolina to
officiate in Both at several times as minister of the Church of England
under the Royal and Espiscopal Protections, having for the full space of
20 years, Shared my office between a French Parish named St. Dennis
& an English Parish called St. Thomas under the Rev⁴ Mr. Hazell the
Rector of the same, I was at last called from this former Province to the
next adjacent country named Cape Fear or New Hanover belonging to
North Carolina where I have been already 4 years following my functions & now I see myself under the sad necessity of superseding them,
for the reasons I shall acquaint your Lordship with, the people of my
charge did at the first carry a fair correspondence with me, till one
Mr. Rich⁴ Marsden came among us with a commission as he said
from the Bishop of London & from the Honorable Society for the pro-
pogation of the Gospel in Foreign Parts, to be an inspector over the clergy
in these parts of the North, tho' I could never hear that your Lordship
had any other commissary besides the Rev⁴ Mr Garden in South or
North Carolina, moreover the said Mr. Marsden since that time has for-

saken such Pretentions, having taken upon him to be a public Merchant & traffickant Since his late voyage to Lisbon in Portugal & follows it daily amongst us & thinks it no way inconsistent with the Sacred orders, for he it is who has set my hearers against me, with his proffers of serving them Gratis, which is the reason why my subscribers have not paid me according to their promise in writing & thereby have disabled me to wait upon them as their Minister & compell'd me, by the same means to work as a Slave, in the field for my living, after gratifying them with 8 months of my time & the same Mr Marsden himself who had made the people of Cape Fear such generous proffers, has left them since, having made interest with Gov' Burrington for the new Parish of Core Sound & New River tho' not as yet settled but he is contented with the private acknowledgements of the inhabitants of that place   I have already laid before your Lordship the first obstacle to my going forward in my office, but there is still another my Lord of no less consequence viz the great misunderstanding between the great men of the place & Gov' Burrington, for having at his first arrival applied to his excellency on the behalf of their church in order to recommend it, to the Societys bounty & your Lordships protection, his excellency returned them this answer from both, that this could not be done, till their church can be erected into a Parish & till they could allow to their Minister a parsonage & a Glebe, a thing they have not as yet thought upon but have endeavoured to shew in opposition to the Governors words that it was a Parish & their Vestry is gone so far that way as to assess the country for my last Payment which was before, consisting of Private subscriptions, but they altered it at their pleasure without the Governors consent, so that at this time I am the sufferer depending upon no manner of certainty & not daring to take the Bare word of those, who have already sufficiently imposed upon my simplicity, therefore my Lord as I account myself happy in following your commands, suffer me likewise to desire the favor of your paternal advice, tending to the preservation of,

          My Lord Your Lordships
               Most dutiful &
                    Most obedient Servant
                         JOHN LAPIERRE.

[B P R. O. America and West Indies. Vol. 19.]

GOVᵣ JOHNSON TO D OF NEWCASTLE

Charles Town Decᵣ the 15ᵗʰ 1732

My Lord,

In my last to your Grace I had the Honour to acquaint you, that I had appointed a Chief Baron of the Exchequer, and that I humbly prayed His Majᵗʸˢ further Instructions on that subject.

Every thing is very quiet upon the Borders of North and South Car-olina, Governor Burrington was indeed some time ago apprehensive that our Indians would have disturbed those under his Government, but it afterwards appear'd there was little room to suspect any commotion of that kind, and if anything material shall happen upon that on any other occasion, your Grace may be persuaded I shall always acquainte you with it, but shall ever be cautious how I take up any of your Graces time, which is so much better imploved, on more important matters.

It is with great satisfaction that I have the Honour to acquaint your Grace, that the Assembly have admitted Mᵣ Amy and to be their Clerk, by which admission one of his Majesties Prerogatives here, can suffer no further dispute.

The great sickness which raged in this Province last Summer and carried off many whites and blacks is now quite over, and the Province is now very healthy

Mᵣ Purry is lately arrived with about 120 Swish, 50 of which are men, and the rest women and children, they like the Country very well, and are very chearfull, I have taken care they should be provided with all necessarys, and doubt not but that the accᵗ they will send to their friends of the reception they have met with, will encourage many more to come and settle here, which will in time greatly redound to his Majᵗⁱᵉˢ Honour and service

I cannot forbear just hinting to your Grace the behavour of the Sur-veyor General Mᵣ Sᵗ John, who has a Head so unfortunately turned, that he has not only brought a great deal of uneasiness upon himself, but has also given his Majᵗⁱᵉˢ Council and me a great deal of unnecessary trouble, he has had the weakness to reject advice given him by myself Council and several other worthy Gentlemen and to pin his Faith intirely upon one Whitaker late Attorney Genˡˡ (and the Craftsman amongst us) who leads him into the most rediculous and absurd measures, enconrageing him to despise the authority of his Maj^{ties} Governor and Council who design to make a Representation of his conduct to the Ministry, which has been of manifest disservice to His Majesty, and disturbed the Peace and quiet of this Province, but the unthinking man beleives and brags that his Interest in England is so great that let him behave as he will all his Actions will pass muster

    I am with great respect, My Lord
      Your Graces most obedient
       and most humble servant
          ROB^t JOHNSON

[FROM NORTH CAROLINA LETTER BOOK OF S. P G]

The Petition & Representation of John Boyd to the Society for the propagation of the Gospel in Foreign Parts
Sheweth,

That your petitioner hath lived for some time in North Carolina & is well acquainted with the Country & there is no minister residing of the Church of England in any part of that Government, for want of which many of the people are drawn away by Presbyterian anabaptists or other Dissenting Teachers, many of their children unbaptised & the administration of the Sacrament of the Lords Supper wholly neglected

---

[B. P R O BOARD OF TRADE JOURNALS. VOL. 42. P 143]

BOARD OF TRADE JOURNALS

     WHITEHALL Wednesday June 7th 1732
       Present

Earl of Westmorland.	Mr Bladen
Mr Docminique	Sir O Bridgeman
Mr Pelham	Sir H Croft.

A letter from Capt Burrington Gov of North Carolina to the Board without date was read and the papers therein referr'd to were laid before the Board, Viz^t

A schedule of the papers transmitted

Attested Copies (under the Seal) of the Journals of the Council and of the Upper & Lower House of Assembly as likewise of the Acts in force in North Carolina.

Account of Patents for Land in North Carolina granted by Sir Richard Everard late Deputy Governor of that Province for the late Lords Proprietors.

[Page 151]

WHITEHALL Friday June 16 1732

A letter from Capt. Burrington Gov' of North Carolina dated 4th Sept. last was read and the papers therein referred to were laid before the Board Viz't

Mr Porter's reasons against Governor Burrington appointing Members of the Council in North Carolina whilst seven remain

Copy of a letter from Mr Byrd of Virginia to Capt. Burrington Gov' of North Carolina dated 20 July 1731 relating to the nature & fertility of the lands in North Carolina.

Their Lordships then gave directions for preparing the Draught of a letter to the Duke of Newcastle to desire he will move the Queen for orders to be sent to the Governors of North & South Carolina to use all possible precaution to prevent an Indian war as apprehended by Capt Burrington in his aforemention'd letter

Directions were also given for preparing the Draughts of Letters to Col. Johnson and Capt Burrington for the same purpose As also another Draught of a letter to Capt Burrington for a distinct explanation of that part of his letter of the 4th of Sept. last which relates to a Gentleman in Hanover Square.

The above Draughts of Letters were agreed and signed on June 20th & 21st

[Page 155]

WHITEHALL Wednesday June 21 1732

Their Lordships taking again into consideration the letter from Capt Burrington read the 16th inst made a progress therein

A Representation and Address of Edmond Porter late of the Council and Judge of the Vice Admiralty Court of North Carolina were read, as also the following papers referr'd to

Extracts of Minutes of Council and Copies of Complaints & Answers relating to Capt Burrington's suspending Mr Porter from the Council and being Judge of the Admiralty in North Carolina.

Mr Porter's opinion about the appointing of any new Councellor by the Governor whilst there are seven Members of Council in the Province

Memorandum made by Mr Porter concerning the purchase money of lands in North Carolina

And their Lordships gave Directions that copies thereof should be sent to Mr Burchet to be laid before the Lords of the Admiralty.

Ordered that a letter be wrote to Mr Porter with copies of such parts of Capt Burrington's letters as relate to him for his Answers thereto.

Ordered that in the next letters to Capt Burrington copies of the above-mentioned Representation and papers from Mr Porter be sent to him for his Answers thereto.

[Page 157]

WHITEHALL Thursday June 22 1732

Mr Shelton Secretary to the late Lords Proprietors of Carolina attend-ing he was desired to give the Board an account of the Grand Deed from the said Lords Proprietors in 1668 under which the inhabitants pretend a right of paying but 2 shs per hundred acres for land in North Caro-lina which he promised to do accordingly

The Board then took into consideration the letters from Capt Burring-ton mention'd in yesterday's Minutes and made a progress therein

[Page 147]

June 9th 1732

A Memorial from Mr Shelton setting forth his services concerning the sale of Carolina and the Bahams & praying the Board's recommendation of him to the Crown was read and their Lordps resolved to consider further thereof on Tuesday morning next.

[Page 158.]

June 23rd 1732

Their Lordships taking again into consideration the Memorial from Mr Shelton read the 9th inst praying the Board's recommendation of him to the Crown A certificate to the Lords of the Treasury was accordingly agreed and signed

[Page 160]

WHITEHALL Wednesday June 28 1732

The letter from Capt Burrington Govr of North Carolina and the papers therein referred to mentioned in the Minutes of the 16th inst being again considered directions were given for preparing the draught of a letter to him thereupon

Ordered that a letter be writ to Mr Attorney & Solr General for their opinion upon a case and queries relating to the validity of laws passed in North Carolina in the Lords Proprietors names after the purchase of that Province by the Crown

[Page 162.]

WHITEHALL Tuesday July 4th 1732

The Board then took into consideration the Draught of a letter to Capt. Burrington order'd to be prepared the 28th of last month and made a progress therein

July 5th 1732

The Board taking again into consideration the Draught of a letter to Capt Burrington mention'd in yesterday's Minutes made a progress therein

[Page 163.]

July 11th 1732

The Board taking again into consideration the Draught of a letter to Capt. Burrington mention'd in yesterday's Minutes made a progress therein

Mr Smith Chief Justice of North Carolina and Chief Baron of the Court of Exchequer there attending he presented to the Board the Warrants from his Majesty appointing him for those Offices which being read Ordered that copies be taken thereof And the Board asking his opinion with respect to the necessity of holding the Court of Exchequer He said he thought that Court the more necessary because the King was defrauded of much land and that that was a matter only cognizable in that Court

[Page 165.]

July 12th 1732

The Board taking into consideration the Draught of a letter to Capt Burrington mention'd in yesterday's Minutes made a progress therein

[Page 167]

July 13th 1732

Mr Smith Chief Justice & Chief Baron of North Carolina attending he presented to the Board a Memorial relating to such laws of the Province as have not been confirmed by the Lords Proprietors upon which he states some difficulties with respect to the duration of them which was read And directions were given for stating the said difficulties to the Attorney & Solicitor General

[Page 170]

July 19th 1732

The letter to the Attorny & Solr Genl order'd to be prepar'd the 13th inst relating to such laws of North Carolina as have not been confirmed by the Lords Proprietors was agreed and order'd to be sent

[Page 206]

WHITEHALL Tuesday Janu^{ry} 16, 173⅔

Present

The Secretary laid before the Board the forty four following copies of orders in Council and the same were read

*   *   *   *   *

Order in Council dated 25th Nov 1731 repealing an Act passed in Virginia for the more effectual preventing the bringing tobacco from North Carolina &c

[Page 247]

WHITEHALL, Wednesday Dec 6th 1732

Mr Attorney and Mr Solicitor General's Report upon Queries relating to the Validity of Laws passed by the Proprietors authority in Carolina before and after notice of the purchase by the Crown was read and directions were given for sending attested copies thereof to Col Johnson & Capt Burrington

---

[FROM THE MSS RECORDS OF NORTH CAROLINA COUNCIL JOURNALS]

COUNCIL JOURNALS

NORTH CAROLINA—ss

At a Council held at the Council Chamber in Edenton the 17th day of January Anno Dom 173½

Present

His Excell^y George Burrington Esqr Gov &c

The Honoble { Joseph Jenoure Cornelious Harnett } Esq^{rs} Members
           { Robert Halton   John Lovick   } of his
           { John Bap^t Ashe Edm^d Gale } Majesties Council

Mathew Rowan Esqr appointed by his Majesties Royal Instruction a member of Council within this Province appeared and took and subscribed the several oaths by Law appointed for Qualification of publick Officers as also the Oath of a Councellor and his place at the Board accordingly

Present Mathew Rowan Esqr

His Excell^y having laid before this Board a letter he lately Received from the Governor of South Carolina Dated 27th October last desiring that Commissioners might be appointed for speedy running out a line for Settling the Southern Bounds of this Government Pursuant to his Majesties Royall Instructions But his Excell^y Having some time before made a proposals to the R^t Honobles the Lords Comissioners of Trade and Plantations on that head which he ordered to be read   This Board having duly Considered of the same are of oppinion that the said proposals made by his Excelly will be of service to his Majesty and save him a Very great Expence Wherefore it is the further Oppinion and Advice of this Board to his Excelly that he Deferr the appointing Comissioners to run the said line till such time as he shall know his Majestie's further pleasure therein

Then the Council adjourned till to morrow Morning at Eleven of the Clock

Teusday January the 18th

Present

His Excelly George Burrington Esqr Govr &c

The Honoble { Joseph Jenoure   Mathew Rowan
Robert Halton   Cornehous Harnett
John Bap^t Ashe   John Lovick
Edm^d Gale } Es^{rrs} Members of his Majes^{ties} Council

Coll Edward Moseley Treasurer of Chowan precinct Mr Charles Denman Treasurer of Perquimons Precinct Mr Cullen Pollock Treasurer of the South Shore Mr Thomas Smith Treasurer of Hyde Precinct and Mr Simon Alderson Treasurer of Beaufort Precinct Exhibited to this Board (in obedience to an Order of Council Passed the 4th Day of November last) their accounts of all publick moneys in their Hands which is ordered to lye on the Table

Cornelius Harnett Esqr appeared here this day pursuant to an order of Council of the 4th of Novr last to answer the Complaint of Capt Tate an the said Tate appeared also and the said Harnett delivered to this board a paper which is as follows Viz^t

Cornelious Harnett of North Carolina humbly sheweth that in obediance to the Order of Governor and Council passed Novr 4th 1731 Concerning a Complaint said to be made to Governor against him and another person by Capt Tate of Bristol he appeareth and for answer thereunto Saith

That he doth not understand that by the Laws of Great Brittain or this Province Complaints touching matters of Debt or Contract are to be heard or tryed before Governor & Council

That if the same were Cognizable by Govr and Council he would have Expected that the Governor would have proceeded thereon when he was last at Cape Fear River in the month of October (at which time he supposes the said Complaint must have been made) The Major Part of his Majesties Council being then at Cape Fear River and not have drawn the said Pet by a writ of Supana under the penalty of one hundred pounds and the Debt by a Copy of the Order of Council only two hundred miles from the place of their residence in the Depth of Winter

If the Governor and Council shall be of Oppinion (as he thinks they will not) that they have power to hear such Complaint he then Offers herewith a Paper signed by the said Tate before substantial And Credible Witnesses wherein he Disclaims his having made any such Complaint to the Governor as seeking relief or justice at his hands or from him or that the said Tate ever asserted that he ye said Harnett and the other person owed him the sum of three Thousand pounds in which paper as the said Tate denys his ever having promoted any such suit or Complaint so he forbids any Prosecution of the same to which paper he the said Harnett Referrs himself

Prays that in as much is the said Cornelious Harnett hath been Slandered and under some Disrupute Concerning this matter by means of the said order of Council he humbly prays that this his said answer and the said paper signed by the said Tate may be entered for his justification

CORNELIUS HARNETT

And then the said Cornelius Harnett Delivered another paper signed by the said Tate Endorsed John Tate Retraxit which was in these words Vizt

NORTH CAROLINA

I the subscribed John Tate do hereby Solemnly declare before the persons who Subscribe as Witnesses here to that I never did Exhibitt or make any Complaint to his Excelly George Burrington Esqr Governor against Cornelius Harnett Esqr of his and another persons Owing the sum of three thousand pounds is Seeking relief at his hands or Justice from him it is true (at least I believe) that occasionally before before him as before others I may have alledged that the said Harnett and the Revd Doctr Richard Marsden had Injured me in not punctually Complying with their Contraction with me but I deny Ever to have Aserted that they owed me the Sum of £3000 for they never did owe me that sum and as I do hereby Deny my promoting any such suit or Complaint before the Govr and so I do as to my part forbid the prosecution of the same in Witness Whereof I have hereunto my hand this 24th of Novr Anno Dom 1731

JOHN TATE

Witnesses Johnathan Shrine John Cox Charles Burnham John Bapt Ashe Saml Swann

Which papers being read the said Tate was Sworn and on his Examination declared that he was an Unfortunate man and lost his ship upon the Middle Grounds of Cape Fear River and that he sold and Delivered his Cargoe to Docter Marsden and Mr Harnett for the Value of £2793 who were to have given him their Bond or Security and that he was to have been Paid as soon as he could get Vessels to Carry of the Effects and that he had been a great sufferer as well as his owners and expected he should be turned out of his Employ and Ruined if he had not those Effects paid him and that he made this Complaint to his Excelly the Governor about the 2ᵈ of October last who told him that he had his remedy at Law against Docter Marsden and Harnett for those Effects

Robt Halton one of his Majesties Council being sworn and Examined Saith that Capt John Tate spoke to him and told him he Came to complain to his Excelly the Govʳ against Mʳ Harnett and Docter Marsden at the time mentioned in the said Tates Examination and that he accordingly introduced him to the Govʳ

ROBERT HALTON

Coll Maurice Moore being summoned to appear this day before the Board to give an account of the Lands he held or Claimed at Cape Fear now appeared and Declared that he held about 15000 acres in those parts but for greater Certianty reffered himself to the Grants or records in the Secretary office and at the same time offered to this Board a paper by way of Exception & representation on the affair but his Excelly Conceiving the same to be a very untrue representation the Said paper was laid on the table for further consideration

Adjourned till to morrow morning

Wednesday January the 19ᵗʰ 173¼
Present
His Excelly George Burrington Esqʳ Govʳ &c

The Honoble	Joseph Jenoure	Mathew Rowan	Esqʳˢ Member
	Robert Halton	Cornelius Harnett	of his Majesties
	Joⁿ Bapᵗ Ashe	John Lovick	Council
		Edmᵈ Gale	

His Excelly delivered the following paper to the Board in relation to Mr Harnett affair Vizt Having perused the answer of Mr Harnett to the Complaint of Capt Tate now under Examination as well as the paper the said Tate signed before Substantial and Credible Witnesses (which I think since the Man appears was Needless to have been produced) and therefore I consented the same Should have been Withdrawn

51

and the Mans Examination fairly taken but it being insisted on that the
said paper Should lye as a Justification of the said Harnett I am
obliidged to make some remarks upon that paper as Mr Harnett answer
nether of which are writ with decency or truth as appears plainly by
the Said Tates Examination now before us upon Oath

The foul manner of obtaining the paper is very Evident from what
Tate swears Vizt that unless he signed it he should be kept out of his
money A year longer and the absolutely Denys that he asserted he had
not made a Complaint to me but now upon his Oath declares he did
make such a complaint and told me he should be quite Ruined and
udone if not Releved and I cannot help Observing how Disingenerous
it was in the Penner of the paper to make the man say he never aserted
that the sum of £3000 was owing to him When Mr Harnett is not
Charged with owing so much only near that sum and now the man tell
you the Debt is £2793 and to what end that strong denyal was made the
penman of the paper best knows   I will make no other remark upon
what the man swears of the unmannerly and slight speeches made by the
pretending Gentlemen made upon my self and the Council only that I
sure such misbehaviour will be no recommendation of those concerned

Mr Harnetts answer is Divided into four parts upon which I will
remark as they lay before me   first Mr Harnett says that he apprehends
that the Govr and Council have not power to hear and try Matters of
Debt or Contract which certianly true except as a Court of Chancery or
by appear Nor was Mr Harnett called her for that end   what Mr Harnett was called upon to answer was this Tate as you have now heard
upon his oath made very Grevious Complaint against Mr Harnett which
if true would greatly obstruct the trade of that young settlement which
as I have Ever Done will allways continue to promote & Mr Harnett
being a Member of his Majesties Council I thought as such it became
me to Enquire in the truth of it in Order to have represented the Matter
home and I shall allways take the same Method when I think any of his
Majesties Council Misbehave themselves being unwilling to lay Charge
to the prejudice of any person liveing till I am Satisfied of the truth
this as it acting with the greatest Tenderness mus have the Approbation
of all men who are not wiltully set against every thing I do.

The 2d Article Says that if the Matter had been Cognizable before the
Governor and Council he Expected to have been proceeded against at
Cape Fear where I was and a Majority of his Majesty's Council at the
same time

To this I say that I did not recieve the Complaint till Just as I was setting sail for these parts but if I had recieved it before I wonder with what Assurance Mr Harnett can assert that a Majority of his Majesties Council was then at Cape Fear when it is notoriously known there were at that time but four Member of which Mr Harnett was himself one tho had there really been a Majority there as is said I could not have proceeded by his Majesties Instructions upon this Enquiry till the whole council had been Sumoned which has now been done and the Council now attends where all other business is transacted And if the Governor and Council had been Impowered to try the Debt or Contract as suggested in the answer they must have been a Court of Record and form to have removed any Court of Record from Edenton the seat of this Government (would have been a great and heavy Oppression

The 3d Article only recites what is said in Tates paper and the 4th is only to request that the paper & answer may be Entred which I allow & order these Remarks to be entred with them which will be a lasting Testimony of the Candor of the Gentlemen Concerned and of the assistance I recieve from some member of his Majesties Council Then His Excelly desired that Capt Tate might be further Examined upon Oath how he Came to Sign that paper Endorsed his Retraxit put in yesterday by Mr Harnett and the said Tate being thereon sworn saith that Mr Ashe drew the first Draught of the paper put in at the Council Board yesterday by Mr Harnett which is signed by the said Tate and that the said Ashe declared that if he the said Tate did not Sign to an Instrument to stop the prosecution Mr Harnett not pay him in Twelve months and for fear he should not be paid his Debt he signed the said paper

Mr Porter late a Deputy surveyor at Cape Fear appeared at this Board pursuant to an Order of Council passed the 4th of Novr 1731 and his Excelly the Governor asking the said Porter whether upon the Surveys he made he runn all the the lines according to his returns made in the Secretary Office when he was Deputy Survevor the said Porter answered he did not

The Said Porter being further Sumoned to appear this day to give an account of the Lands he holds or Claims at Cape Fear appeared and declared he Could not Certainly tell what Quantity but that he believed they were all Recorded in the Secretary Office if they were not he would cause them to be recorded soon

John Baptista Ashe Esqr Treasurer of the New Settlements of Cape Fear in Obediance to an Order of Council passed the 4th of November last appeared at this Board and Exhibited his Accot of publick Moneys in his hand which is ordered to lye on ye Table The said John Bapt Ashe Esqr one of the late Deputy Surveyors at Cape Fear now appeared and gave in a paper which was laid on the Table for further Consideration

The Question being put by the Governor whether the Complaint against Edmond Porter Esqr Judge of the Court of Vice Admilty should be called and heard to morrow Morning altho he be absent or put off till a further Day It was the oppinion of the Councill that the matter be Called and heard to Morrow Morning Adjourned till to Morrow Morning 9 of the Clock

Thursday January the 20th 1731
Present

His Excelly George Barrington Esqr Govr &c

The Honoble { Joseph Jenoure Mathew Rowan
Robert Halton Cornelius Harnett
John Bapt Ashe John Lovick
Edmd Gale } Esqrs Members
of his
Majesties Council

Coll Thomas Pollock Treasurer of Bertie precinct in Obediance to an order passed at this Board the 4th Day of November last appeared this Day and Exhibited his accot of publick Moneys in his Hands which was ordered to lye on the Table

Read the petition of Thomas Pollock Esqr Shewing that at a very great Charge having Obtained patents for some Lands lying between Roquiss Swamp and Marattoke River in Bertie precinct said to be claimed by Tuskaroroe Indians for which Reason your petitioners has hitherto forborn to settle the said Lands tho he is altogether unknown in the right the said Indians have to these Lands but not knowing how much he may be injured by not settling the same according to the Tenour of his patents praying an order for settling the said Lands or otherwise that a minnute may be made in Council for him that the Lands may not be Lapsable Neither be charged with any Rents till Such time as the Indians shall remove or quit their pretended Claims

This Board is of Oppinion they cannot give up his Majesties Quit rents to any pattented Lands but if the said Lands lye within the Bounds Claimed by the Indians they are of Oppinion that the said lands Ought not to be Elapsed till such time as the Said petitioner is allowed quietly to possess the same

Ordered that no lapse pattents do issue for the Lands Set forth in Said petition

Mr Charles Harris one of the Late Deputy Surveyors at Cape Fear being sumoned to appear at this board to give an Acco[t] of the practice & manner of this Surveys lately made at Cape Fear being Sumoned to appear at this board to give an Acco[t] of the practice and manner of the Surveys lately made at Cape Fear did not appear having writ to the Governor and Council a Letter of Excuse the same was laid upon the Table for further Consideration

Read the petition of Mathew Machard against Isaac Ottiwell Collector of his Majesties Customs of port Bath which being Sworn to the Same is ordered to lye on the Table for further Consideration thereon

Present

Edmond Porter Esq[r] one of his Majesties Honoble Council Edmond Porter Esq[r] Judge of the Court of Vice Admiralty Appeared and Delivered in at the Board a paper which he desired to be Entered which are in the words Viz[t]

To His Excell[y] George Burrington Esq[r] Gov[r] Vice Admiral &c

SIR

I was in hopes to have returned timely from Cape Fear to put in my answer to the Complaints of Mr Little against me but in my return have been frozen up in Shallop at three several places which I am able to prove being but lately arrived for which reason I hope your Excelly will be so good as to grant me a reasonable time to put in my answer to the said Complaints they being of an Extraordinary Nature the granting this favour will be an Obligation on

S[r] Your Most Obedient Ser[t]

E PORTER

Edenton January 20th 1731

Edmond Porter Esq[r] being present His Excelly the Governor directed the Complaint filed by M[r] Little & others against the said Edmond Porter Judge of the Court of Vice Admiralty to be read which was accordingly done and then the Complaints proceeded on the first article of the Charge and a Copy of the Registry of the Court of Admiralty together with the Records of the General Court which were Read and the Oath of James Trotter taken

His Excelly the Governor thereupon desired the Oppinion of the Council whether the Complainants had made good the first Article of their Charge or Complaint against the said Porter who was of Oppinion that the Complainants had fully made good and proved the first Article in the Said Compl[t] the article being Read and a Copy of the Registry of the Court of Admiralty Sworn to by the present Register as also the records of the General Court on that affair and the oath of Mr John Leahy Deputy Register of the Court of Vice Admiralty at the time of the tryal mentioned in the second Article Thereupon the Governor Desired the oppinion of this Board whether the Complainants had made good their Second Article of Complaint who were of the Oppinion that the Complainants had made good and fully proved the second article of their Complaint

3d Article being read together with a Copy of the Registry of the Court of Admiralty sworn to by the present Register & Mr Leahy on his oath who was Deputy Register of the Court of Vice Admiralty at the time mentioned in the third article Thereupon the Governor desired the Oppinion of the Council whether the Complainants have made good and fully proved the third Article of their Complaint Oppinion the Complainants had fully proved and made good the Said Article

4th Article being read together with a Copy of the Registry of the Court of Admiralty sworn to by the present Register and the records of the General Court Concerning the same desired the Oppinion of the Board whether the Complainants had made out the fourth Article who were of Oppinion the Complainant had fully proved and made good the said article

5th Article was read and the Complainants declaring they had no Records to produce to make out this article and thereupon the present Register of the Court of Vice Admiralty being asked on his oath whither there is any Register of that Suit in the Office declared there was none delivered to him then the Complainant produced Mr John Leahy who at the time mentioned was Deputy register of the Court of Vice Admiralty who having heard the fifth article read declared it was true with this addition that he drew the Indenture and he believes Mr Porter had £30   or there abouts for the sale of the said Edward Moor and that he the said Leahy forgave Moor his own fees And Mr William Macky being Sworn Said that he heard Mr Rowelen Deced who bought the said Moor & Moor himself declare the same and that he knows the said Moor served his time out Thereupon the Council were of Oppinion the fifth article was fully proved

6th Article being read together with a Copy of the Registry produced by Richard Rastull Esqr the Register of the Court of Admiralty upon oath and the Complainant desireing Mr James Winright (who was sworn) might declare whether Judge Porter did not know of the Seizures & proceedings Mentioned in the said Pomplt before they went upon them answered that he the said Porter did know and sent a Deputation by him to Docter Patrick Maule to act as Deputy Judge in that affair and being asked if any part of the fees came into Judge Porters Hands answered that he understood that the Deputy Judge & all the Officers paid him one half of their fees   Richard Rustell Esq' late Regester of the said Court being Sworn and Asked whether any part of the Fees Came into Judge Porters hands answered that he paid to Judge Maule for the use of Judge Porter one half of all the Fees accruing to him as Regester on the Seizure & Tryal of the three Sloops and that he believes the Deputy Judge and Marshall likewise paid the Same   Thereupon it was the Oppinion of the Council that the Sixth article was fully proved and made good

7ᵗʰ Article the Evidence being gone the Complainant failed in their proof

8ᵗʰ Article being read together with Copy of the Registry produced as also the records of the General Court the Question being put it was voted by the Council the Same was fully proved

9ᵗʰ Article being read the Complainants produced their proof it was the Opinion of Board that the Said article was fully made out and proved

10ᵗʰ Article Read and the Registry produced and the Evidence of Mʳ Leahy the Late Deputy Register and others heard there upon Oath the Council were of Oppinion the Articles the Complainants had fully made good and proved

11ᵗʰ Article and the several Complaints mentioned therein read and Mr Osheal being sworn saith That after he was discharged from paying the Fine and that the Marshall of the admiralty had obstructed the Deputy Marshal from serving the Habeas Corpus he was again taken into custody for the very same thing he obtained his Majesties writ of Habeas Corpus for and held to £800 Bail and the Registry being produced and the Complainants heard on the several articles of this Complaint It was the oppinion of this Board the same were fully proved

12ᵗʰ Article Read and on hearing the Complainants thereon the Council were of oppinion the same was fully proved

13ᵗʰ Article Read and the Complainants Evidences heard thereon the Council were of Oppinion the same was fully proved and made good

Upon the several Articles of Complaint aforesaid Exhibited against Edmond Porter Esqʳ Judge of the Court of vice admiralty Mr Ashe refused to vote or give his oppinion but all other members of the Council present were unanimously of oppinion that all the several Articles of the Complaint were fully proved by the Complainant Except the 7th article wherein the Complainants alledge their witness to be gone and in the Eight article Mr Rowan doubted whether the same was fully proved

Edmond Porter Esqr being present and hear the first article Read & pleaded to it but then withdrew and afterwards Came in again several times during the hearing and behaved himself in a very Insolent manner to the Governor and Came in and went out of the Council Chamber several times and walkt and stood before the Door with his hatt on while this Examination was taken

Mr Ashe produced the following paper as his Reasons why he refused to vote praying the same may be Entred which was allowed by the Governor and is as follows

Upon the several articles of Complaint Exhibited against Edmond Porter Esqr Judge of the Court of Vice Admiralty the said Porter not withdrawing which Mr Ashe not appearing to answer the Charge the said Ashe gave it as his Oppinion that the Council Could not proceed to Examine the Evidences because it would be Exparte as it were but ought rather if he were guilty of a Contempt or made default to take the fact proconfesso and this he gave as his Reason why he could not proceed to give Oppinion to the Question on each Article as it was put Vizt Whether the Fact were fully proved or not

His Excell^y the Governor after the Complainants had gone through with their proofs and made good their Charge against the said Mr Porter Caused his Majesties 49th and 55th Instruction to be Read Thereupon His Excell^y Asked the Opinion of the Board whether the said Porter ought not to be suspended from his Office as Judge of the Court Vice Admiralty within this Province and thereupon it was the unanimous opinion and Advice of the Council that ye said Edmond Porter Esqr Judge of the Court of Vice Admiralty ought to be Suspended from the s^d office

The Governor thereupon having the unanimous Opinion of his Majesties Council and having heard the several Facts wherewith the said Porter was Charged made good and fully proved

His Excell^y thereupon by and with the advice and consent of the Council did sespend the said Edmond Porter Esqr from acting as Judge of the Court of Vice Amiralty within this Province untill his Majesty or the Lords of Admiralty their pleasure be known thereon

His Excell^y the Governor further asked the advice and Oppinion of the Council Whether so bad a man as Mr Porter was proved to be should be continued a member of Council within this province. Thereupon the Council were Unanimously of opinion that the said Edmond Porter was not fit to sit at this Board The Governor thereupon Gave Mr Porter time to the Last Tuesday in March next to Shew reason why he ought not to be suspended from the Council But at the Instance of Mr Porter it is ordered that the same be heard to morrow at four of the Clock in the afternoon the said Porter desiring His Excelly to give him this Night the Articles he should proceed upon therein which the Governor promised to do

Fryday January 21st 173$\frac{3}{4}$

Present

The Honoble $\left\{ \begin{array}{ll} \text{Joseph Jenoure} & \text{Mathew Rowan} \\ \text{Robert Halton} & \text{Cornelious Harnett} \\ \text{John Bapt Ashe} & \text{John Lovick} \\ & \text{Edmd Gale} \end{array} \right\}$ Esqr Members of his Majesties Council

His Excelly the Governor having last night filed in the Secretaries Office the Several articles against Edmd Porter Esqr as Reasons for suspending him from this Board the same were now read in the words Vizt

Thursday Eleven a Clock at night

I complain against Mr Porter as a Member of Council

First Because he has made it his whole Endeavour ever since my arrival to perplex and obstruct all proceeding in Council by Raising unnecessary disputes and Cavils

2dly That when his Oppinion has been asked upon affairs of the Greatest Consequence wherein the Peace and Quiet of this Province has Depended he hath asserted direct falsehoods with an Intention to Embarras and Perplex the Administration

3dly He hath behaved at the Council Board with So much Insolence to me that the Council have taken notice of his Rude behaviour in their Minutes and have Entered it as their Opinion that he is too bad a man to sit at the Council Board

4thly That the Council upon a very full Examination of his Vile behaviour as Judge of the Court of Admiralty given their oppinion that he deserve a Sespension from that Office and he being suspended accordingly I think it cannot be proper to Continue him a Member of Council when as such he must sit as a Judge in the Court of Chancery for this Province

52

5^{thly} That he being a Person of very Ill Fame and Character and now under many prosecutions & Indictments not only for his barbarous proceedings as a Judge but for Tumults Riots and other disorders I think it would be a Reflection on his Majesties Council here to have such a Profligate Person sit with them and therefore ask the opinion and advice of this Board whether the said Edmond Porter ought not to be Suspended from being a Member of his Majesties Council for North Carolina

There upon the said Edmond Porter gave in his answer to the same which was read in these words Viz^t

NORTH CAROLINA

Fryday following Thursday Eleven a Clock at Night

The answer of Edmond Porter to the Compl^t of His Excelly George Burrington Esqr Govr &c

His Excelly exhibiting a Charge against me Setting me forth a very heanous person and yet alleadging no particular fact Urged me (that I might acquit myself and Convince the world that I merited not such Titles as in the said Charge are given me) to an immediate answer which I shall make in as few words as I can hoping no advantage will be taken of any slips which may happen to a thing so hastily Conceieved and delivered

1st As to the first Charge I observe it is so General no particular Fact being alleadged against me that I know not how to answer to it otherwise than that it will serve to be applyed to any of the Council who Differing from the Governor in Oppinion shall Raise disputes thereon

2^d As to the second I observe that the Generalty of of the Charge admits no answer

3^d As to the third Charge I observe that it is also very General saving as to the Notice the Council have taken of my behaviour and the Oppinion they have already before my Charge Exhibited against me delivered thereon Entred in a Council which plainly shews that they Viz^t such of the Council as have so done have Prejudise me how far this Conduces to their Qualification of being my Judges in the present cases I shall leave to others to Judge

4^{thly} I must patiently bear the harsh Terms the Governor is pleased to bestow on me in this Article and to the proceedings of the Governor in my case as Judge of the Admiralty and the Oppinion of the Council as to my Meriting a Suspension from that office I shall only say that I thought it hard Considering how unavoidably I was delayed from appearing (being frozen up with my vessell far from Edenton and not posible to come to it any otherwise than by water which detained me till Wednesday last in the afternoon from my plantation) that I should so immediately on my very first appearance be pressed to a hearing and that after Examination of the Evidence of the Complaiants against me I was not allowed time to produce those in my defence this I expected because as I moved last night I remembered well it was the method observed in the Complaints between Sir Richard Everard and Mr Lovick against each other but this I shall take more particular notice of at another time and place. As to the reason given by His Excelly that because I am suspended as a Judge of the Admiralty it is not therefore proper I should be continued a member of Council I beg leave to observe that supposed I was fully convinced of the Charges against me as Judge yet these facts were all done before my being in the Council I would therefore beg leave to make this Query Whether after I am nominated by his Majesty of his Council in this province and Qualified according to the Law Facts done before no wise respecting that office may be Exhibited against me and allowed a Sufficient Reason for turning or throwing me out of the Council And if the Governor and Council Shall be of that Oppinion I hope it may a standing Rule and that others be also Examined as to past actions of their Life before their being in Council as well as me

5thly As to the fifth Article I must observe as before as to the Generalty of the Charge and the Language bestowed on me (as yet I hope one of his Majesties Council by his Excelly in the present case my Judge at least one of my Judges as to the prosecutions Indictments and so forth against me I beg leave to say that others have been Indicted before me and that every accused is not to be concluded Guilty and therefore this is no Reason for Suspension or for throwing on me such hard names if it were it would be an Easy matter to make the most Innocent person deserve it and to have bestowed on him the Titles of ill Fame and Character and a Profligate Person

To conclude as your Excelly hath been pleased to suspend me as Judge of Vice Admiralty I think it a most insurportable Grieviance that after I put in my first paper yesterday prayed reasonable time to make answer to the Complaints of Mr Little your Excelly not only overuled the same but my second paper produced on the Board your Excelly in great heat threw it into the fire tho I told you it related to my defence

Delivered at the Council Board this 21st day of January 1731 humbly praying that this my answer may be Entred in the Council Book

Signed   E PORTER

The Several Articles Exhibited by His Excelly as a Charge against Edmond Porter Esq' was again Read and the two first article pospon'd and on Reading the 3d Article and Mr Porter answer thereto the Question was put whether Mr Porter had not behaved in a very Insolent manner to his Excelly the Governor several times and more particularly yesterday at the Council Board The Council gave their Opinion that had behaved very Insolently to the Governor and Especially yesterday while sitting in Council

Then the 4th Article was read and Mr Porters answer thereto Thereupon the Governor asked the Opinion of the Council that as they had yesterday Unanimously consented to the suspending the said Porter from being Judge of the Admiralty for his Manifest Injustice and scandalous oppressions Wither for the same Reasons he ought not to be suspended from being a member of Council being as such one of the Judges of the Court of Chancery and the Council were of opinion that he ought also to be suspended from being a member of the Council

5th Article Read and Mr Porters answer thereto upon the Governor desired the opinion of the Whether so ill Fame and Character as Mr Porter is from his barbarous proceedings as Judge would not be a reflection on his Majesties Council here to sit at this Board and Whether the sd Ed Porter ought not to be Suspended from being a member of his Majesties Council for North Carolina for this Reason also the Council thereon were of opinion that it would be for His Majesties Service that he Should be suspended from being a member of his Majesties Council

The Governor having proceeded on the 3d 4th & 5th Articles in the Charge against Mr Porter and having the councils opinion waved the Article of Mr Alleyns being in or out of the Government he again desired the Opinion of the Board whether on the Whole the said Porter should be suspended from being a member of his Majesties Council or not which being put to the Vote the same past in the affirmative and the Council accordingly did advise and consent that the said Edmond Porter Should be suspended from being a member of his Majesties Council

Thereupon his Excelly the Governor by and with the advice of His Majesties Council Declared that the said Edmond Porter Esq' to be and stand suspended from being a member of His Majesties Council of this Province till his Majesties pleasure be known therein and he is hereby suspended accordingly

His Excelly orderers the latter Part of Mr Porters answers to the Governors Charge to be Read which was done and then desired Gent' of the Council to relate the truth of that affair who thereupon wrote and signed a paper in the words following Viz'

M' Porter Came into Council yesterday and gave the Governor an Open Letter which he begged he would Read for he had left it behind to be Delivered in Case he should not have been there upon which the Governor Declared he would Recieve no Letter from M' Porter and then took it up and threw it into the fire and as we think as the Letter was upon the toss M' Porter called out it related to the affair and then afterwards with heat Just at the Council house door said that it was his Defence and that he had a Copy to shew of it which paper was signed by

JOSEPH JENOURE
ROBERT HALTON
MATHEW ROWAN
CORN' HARNETT
EDM' GALE
JOHN LOVICK &
JOHN BAP' ASHE

who before he signed entred the following Viz'

Excepting as not hearing the following words and then afterward and following the End of the above writing and adding as hearing moreover the Governor say he would burn them if they were a Bushell of them for he would recieve no Letter from him

By order

RBT FORSTER Clerk Con'

NORTH CAROLINA—ss

At a Council held at the Council Chamber in Edenton the 22' day of January Anno Domini 173½

Present

His Excell' George Burrington Esq' &c

The Honoble ⎰ Joseph Jenoure   Matthew Rowan ⎱ Esq' Members
            ⎱ Robert Halton   Corn' Harnett ⎰ of his Majesties
              Jo' Bap' Ashe   John Lovick   Council
                    Edm' Gale

His Excelly the Gov' by and with the advise and Consent of his Majesties Council having Suspended Edmond Porter Esq' Comissioned from the Right Honoble the Lords of Admiralty for several Notorious Crimes fully proved against the said Porter as a Judge His Excelly thereupon desires the Council to Recomend a proper person to act as Judge of the Court of Vice Admiralty within this Province till His Majesty or the Rt Honobles the Lords of Admiralty their Pleasure be further known And they accordingly Recomended Edmund Gale Esq'

His Excelly thereupon with the advice and consent of His Majesties Council Doth Constitute and appoint Edmund Gale Judge of the Court of Vice Admiralty for and within this Province till his Majesty of the Right Honoble the Lords of Admiralty their Pleasure be further Known

Ordered that a Comission pass the seal Constituting and appointing Edmund Gale Esqr Judge of the Court of Vice Admiralty within this Province till His Majesty or the Right Honoble the Lords of Admiralty their pleasure be further known

Resolved that a Comission issue directed to Mr Coll Robert West Mr Francis Pugh Mr Thomas Bryant Mr John Spier and Mr Thomas Hearney appointing Comissioners for the Indian Trade for and within this Province

Ordered that the Marshall have Notice to Summon each Member of his Majesties Council within this Province to attend His Excelly in Council at the Council Chamber in Edenton the last Tuesday in March next

By order

ROBt FORSTER Cler Conc

GEORGE R

Trusty and well beloved We Greet you well   Whereas we have taken into Our Royal Consideration the Loyalty Integerity and ability of our Trusty and well beloved Nathaniel Rice Esqr We have thought fit hereby to authorize and Require you forthwith to cause Letters Pattents to be passed under Our Seal of that Our Province of North Carolina for Constituting and appointing him the said Nathaniel Rice Secretary and Clerk of the Crown of & in our said Province To have hold Execute and Enjoy the sd Offices during our Pleasure and his Residence within our said Province together with all and singular the Rights salaries Fees Profits Privilidges and Emoluments thereunto belonging or appertaining And for so doing this shall be your Warrant And so we bid you farewell Given at our Court at St James's the Thirtyeth day of November 1730 In the fourth year of Our Reign

By His Majesties Command

ROBERT NEWCASTLE

To Our Trusty and well beloved George Burrington Esqr our Capt General and Governor in Chief of our Province of North Carolina in America And in His absence to our Comander in Chief or to the President of our Council of our said Province for the time being

NORTH CAROLINA—ss

Att a Council held at the Council Chamber in Edenton the 28th day of March Anno Dom 1732

Present

His Excelly George Burrington Esqr Govr &c

The Honoble { Joseph Jenoure, John Lovick, Edmd Gale } Esqrs Members of His Majesties Council

The Council met and adjourned till Thursday Morning next at Ten of the Clock in Expectation of more members Coming to Council

Thursday March ye 30th

Present

His Excelly George Burrington Esqr Govr &c

The Honoble { Joseph Jenoure, John Lovick, Edmd Gale } Esqrs Members of His Maties Council

His Excelly the Governour desired this Board to give him their opinion whether it would be safe to proceed with the present Assembly since he was prevented from meeting them on the day appointed by Law for their Convention at first

The Council thereupon gave their Opinion unanimously in the Negative and it was their advice and Consent that the said Assembly should be Disolved To which his Excelly consented

Resolved that the present Assembly be Disolved and a Proclamation Issue accordingly

By order

RBT FORSTER Cler Conc

At a Council held in the Council Chamber in Edenton the 3d day of April Anno Dom 1732

Present

His Excelly George Burrington Esqr Govr &c

The Honoble { Joseph Jenoure, John Lovick, Edmd Gale } Esqrs Members of His Majesties Council

No more members of Council yet appearing His Excelly the Governour declared that Col Robert Halton a member of this Board has his Leave to be absent this Council

His Excelly the Governour delivered in at the Board the following paper which was Read and ordered to be Entered in these words Vizt

GENTs OF THE COUNCIL

You that are here must remember that the last day that the Council sat in January past I ordered the Deputy Marshall Mr Mackey to summon all the Members then present to attend the Council appointed to be held the last Tuesday in March following being the first day of this Court and as it was well known that much business lay before the Board the Treasurers for the several Precincts having filed their publick Accounts which I designed to have had Examined before the constant business of the Council and Chancery came on I have now waited from Tuesday last the Day named for their meeting to this when the Court of Chancery Should sit and there being no likelyhood of any other members attendance I am obligded to adjourn the Business of Chancery over and Do dismiss all the Suitors The rules of the Court requiring no less than five Members to be present,   What injury that must be to the People who have Travelled far and have attended at great Expence I must be forced to Represent home   I have received several Complaint against some of the officers and others for Male practices which I would have laid before the Council for their Enquiry if there had appeared a sufficient Number of Members but these & all other Matters must be Deferr'd to the next council which I will appoint to be on the third Tuesday in May

Ordered That the marshall have Notice to Summon every Member of His Majesties Council to appear at a Council to be held at the Council Chamber in Edenton on the Third Tuesday in May next

By order

———   RBT FORSTER Cler Con⁶

NORTH CAROLINA—ss

At a Council held at the Council Chamber in Edenton the 6th day of April Anno Dom 1732.

Present

His Excelly George Burrington Esq' Gov' &c.

The Honoble { Joseph Jenoure / John Lovick / Edm⁴ Gale } Esq⁷ Members of His Majesties Council

His Excelly the Governour by and with the advice of His Majesties Council and in pursuance of His Majesties 56 Instruction doth order that a Comission pass the seal of this Province constituting John Palin Esq' Chief Justice the present members of his Majesties Council and the assistants Justices Justices for holding a Court of Oyer and Terminer and General Goal Delivery for this Province on the second Tuesday in June next and that a Clause be added in the said Comission to Impower the Cheif Justice or any three of the members to be a Quorum to hold the s⁴ Court

By order

———   RBT FORSTER Cler Con⁹

At a Council held at the Council Chamber in Edenton the 16th day of May Anno Dom 1732

Present

His Excelly George Burrington Esqr Govr &c

The Honoble { Joseph Jenoure, Robt Halton, Matt Rowan, John Lovick, Edm Gale } Esqr Members of His Majesties Council

Read the Petition of the south side of Roanoke River Fishing Creek and places adjacent praying to have a New precinct Erected from the County line on the south side of Roanoke River and from thence down the South Side of Said River to the mouth of Conoconaro from thence in a Straight Line down to Blounts old Town on Tarr River observing the Courses of said Line to Neuse River and from thence to the North East Branch of Cape Fear River with such Powers and Privilidges as other precincts within this Province have and Enjoy.

His Excelly the Governour taking the said Petition into Consideration and from the several Reasons contained therein and by and with the advice and consent of His Majesties Council Doth hereby Ordain make and sett off the bounds above mentioned Vizt from the Country Line on the South side of Roanoke River and from thence down south side of said River to the mouth of Conoconaro from thence in a Streight line down to Blounts old Towne on Tarr River observing the Courses of said Line to Nuse River and from thence to the North East Branch of Cape Fear River into a precinct which is hereby Distinguished by the name of Edgecombe precinct & invested with all such Powers and Priviledges as other precincts have or enjoy untill a further Division of precincts or Counties be made

His Excelly the Governour by and with the advise & Consent of This Board doth order that a Comission pass the seal of this province Constituting and appointing Colo Henry Gaston, Major James Millikin, Docter James Thompson, Capt John Pratt, Joseph John Alston, Docter John Bryant, John Hardy, James Speir Francis Elleby, William Kane, John Pope and Edward Young Justices of the Peace for and within Edgecombe precinct with all such power and Priviledges as other Justices have and enjoy in any Precinct within this Province.

Ordered that the Justices of the Precinct Court of Edgecombe do sit and hold the said Precinct Court on the third Tuesday in the months of August November February and May yearly.

Several of the Members for Bertie Precinct being now in the Commission of the peace for Edgecombe precinct His Excell[y] the Governour thereupon with the advice of his Majesties Council Doth order that a Comission of the peace pass the seal of this Province Constituting and appointing Col[o] Robert West, Benjamin Hill, John Bonde Thomas Bryant John Speir John Holbrook William Lattermoor Thomas Kearney James Lockhart Francis Pugh Peter West Edmund Smithwick John Edwards John Harrell Needham Bryant and John Soan Justices of the Peace for and within the Prect of Bertie

His Excelly the Governour desired the Opinion of this Board Whether he should proceed to state the publick accounts Who are of the Opinion that the said Accounts should be left till the arrival of His Majesties Rec[r] General & Auditor of this Province

His Excelly the Governour with the advice of His Majesties Council doth order that a Comission and Ded[n] pass the seal of this Province constituting and appointing Roger Moore Richard Husbands James Tuness Edward Hern John Davis Job How   Hall Esq[rs] Roger Haynes John Marshall Hugh Blaning Joseph Clarke David Evans and Edward Smith Gent Justices of the Peace for New Hanover Precinct in the County of Bath within this Province.

The Petition of John Lovick Esq[r] late Secretary of this Province and William Little Esq[r] late Rec[r] General of the same was read in these words Viz[t]

NORTH CAROLINA—ss.

To His Excelly George Burrington Esq[r] Cap[t] General and Govern[r] in Chief and the Honoble the Council now sitting at Edenton May 16th 1732

The Petition of John Lovick late Secretary of said Province and William Little late Rec[r] General

Whereas Mr Smith late Chief Justice of this Province has Exhibited a Petition to the King against His Excelly the Governour therein also accusing us with several things very Grosly and falsely insinuated (a Copy of which Petition we having obtained) do lay the same before this Honoble Board, and humbly begg leave to declare Our innocence as to the several matters so falsely charged against us And Mr Smith in his Petition having accused the Gov[r] not only of having skreen'd and protected us from prosecutions at Law for Male practices in Our offices of Secretary and Rec[r] General, but for participating within our Unlawfull gains in the s[d] Offices

We do hereby solemnly declare that the same is utterly false and Groundless and that we have so behaved that we were under no apprehensions of Prosecutions, and further that if we had, we should not have dared to have made any such motion to him   And we also further Declare that we never made any present to the Governour upon that or any other account, other than small matters as Neighbours which the Gov' has returned in the like Civilitys And as to the Lands sold the Governour, which M' Smith seems to make such an Outcry about, the matter was truly thus, We having as Commissioners for running the Boundary Line betwixt this Government and Virginia pursuant to the order of Council for it, taken up about Eight Thousand acres of Lands near the mountains to Reimburse us for our Expences in that service, which sometime after the Gov" arrival we acquainted him with, who having heard there was Lead Oar upon those Lands, told us, that if we would part with them, he would purchase, them and give us such a price as any others would, and we being very willing to part with the same (they lying at a great Distance and out of the way) we agreed to let the Gov' have them at double the value they originally stood us in, and Deeds were made of the same to the Govern' accordingly and Publickly Executed, being acknowledged in Open Court and we further Declare that we are well satisfied it was the value of those Lands, and that were they again our we would part with them again for the same money   This we declare to be Truth and are ready to make Oath thereto in Vindication of His Excelly from so false a Charge, he having never threatned us about them, or used any force or compulsion to make us part with the s'd Lands, but it was done Voluntarily & freely & a fair Purchase   And We humbly pray the Gov' if His Excelly please to declare in Council upon Oath what he knows of us relating to those matters which M' Smith has represented in such a Scandalous & Malitious manner in his Petition afores'd

J LOVICK
W" LITTLE

Thereupon the said John Lovick and William Little were Sworn in Council to the Facts mentioned in said Petition

His Excelly the Gov' thereupon directed the Petition of M' Smith to the King to be Read which was in these words Viz'

To The Kings most Excellent Majesty, &

(This Pet" and y' Depoçons thereon is in a book marke A B)

NORTH CAROLINA—ss.

At a Council held at the Council Chamber in Edenton the 25th day of July Anno Dom 1732

Present

His Excelly George Burrington Esqr Govr &c

The Honoble { Joseph Jenoure   } Esqrs Members of His
            { John Lovick   }
            { Edmd Gale   } Majesties Council

The above members met in pursuance of the order of Council pass'd the 17th day of May Last and no more Members appearing His Excelly thereupon adjourned the Board to Thursday the 27th Instance

By order   R F C C

Thursday July 27th

His Excelly the Govr and the Three Members above mentioned Met and no more appearing His Excelly adjourned the Board to Monday the 31st Instant

By order   R F C C.

Monday July 31st

Present

His Excelly George Burrington Esqr Govr &c

the Honoble { Nathl Rice   John Lovick } Esqrs Members of His
            { John Bapt Ashe   Edmd Gale   } Majesties Council

Colo Thomas Swann Treasurer of Pasquotank precinct appeared at this Board and filed his Publick Accots which is ordered to lye on the table

Ordered that the Attorney General do prepare a Draught of a Commission for Erecting a Court of Exchequor to be Laid before this Board on the Last Tuesday in October next.

His Excelly desired Mr Secretary Rice and Mr Ashe to Declare whether they gave Mr Smith the Late Cheif Justice any authority to Complain against him to the King   Mr Ashe and Mr Rice thereupon Desired His Excelly to put the Question in writing which His Excelly did and is in these words Vizt Mr William Smith having presented a petition to the Kings most Excellent Majesty against me which he says in behalf of Assembly several Members of Council &c Mr Rice the Secty and Mr Ashe being two Members of the Council are desired by me to declare if they appointed the said Smith to appear against me and Complain to the King in the manner he the said Smith has done in his said Petition a Copy of which is now on the Table or in any other manner

Mr Secretary and Mr Ashe desired time to answer the above paper which is granted

Ordered that the several precinct Treasurers within this Government do attend this Board on the Last Tuesday in October next and Exhibit their publick Acco⁻

Adj⁴ till to morrow morning at Eleven of the Clock

Tuesday August 1ˢᵗ

Present

His Excelly George Burrington Esqʳ Govʳ &c

The Honoble { Nathˡ Rice, Jno Bapᵗ Ashe, John Lovick } Esqⁿ Members of His Majesties Council

Mr Secretary Rice delivered the following paper in at the Board Vizᵗ Nº 1

His Excelly the Govʳ Read a Paper directed to Mʳ Secretary Rice which he ordered to be Entered and is as follows Vizt Nº 2

His Excelly the Governour caused to be Read a Writing containing several Articles of Complaint concerning the Conduct and proceedings of Jno Montgomery Esqʳ His Majesties Attorney General of this province which is as follows Vizᵗ Nº 3

Ordered That the Attorney General be served with a Copy of this and that he make answer thereto at the Council to be held on the Last Tuesday in October next.

His Excelly the Governor directed Col Thomas Pollock (who was one of the Committee appointed by the Last Assembly to draw up the state of this Province to be represented in England &c to declare whether he gave Mʳ Smith Late Chief Justice of this province any orders to Complain to his Majesty against him who answered that he gave Mʳ Smith no Orders nor did not know that any of the sᵈ Committee did and being asked if he had notice to appear at the said Committee answered that he never had nor never knew they did meet

Adj⁴ till tomorrow morning at Ten of the Clock

Wednesday August 2ᵈ

Present

His Excelly George Burrington Esqʳ Govʳ &c

The Honoble { Nathˡ Rice, Jno Bapᵗ Ashe, John Lovick, Edmᵈ Gale } Esqⁿ Members of His Majesties Council

His Excelly the Governour delivered at the Board a Paper in answer to Mʳ Rice and Mʳ Ashe which was read in these words Vizᵗ Nº 4

By order   R F C C

NORTH CAROLINA—SS

At a Council held at the Council Chamber in Edenton the 7th day of October Anno Dom 1732

Present

His Excelly George Burrington Esq[r] Gov[r] &c

The Honoble { John Lovick } Esq[r] Members of His Majestics { Edm[d] Gale } Council

The Honoble George Rhenny Esq[r] Surveyor General of His Majesty's Customs of the Southern District of N[o] America being appointed by his Majesty's Royal Instructions a Member of Council within this Province appeared this day at the Board and took and subscribed the several Oaths by Law appointed for Qualification of Publick officers as also the Oath of a Councellor and took his place at this Board accordingly

Present

The Honoble George Rhenny Esq[r]

The other members of his Majestys Council not appearing this day according to sumons His Excelly adjourned the Board till to morrow morning at Ten of the Clock for a fuller Board

Wednesday October 18th
The Council met again

Present

His Excelly George Burrington Esq[r] Gov[r] &c

The Honoble { George Rhenny } { John Lovick } Esq[rs] Members &c { Edm[d] Gale }

His Excelly the Govern[r] ordered the Marshall to enquire whither any more of His Majestys Council were come to Towne who returned for answer there was not Upon which His Excelly declared he had Business of great consequence for his Majestys Service to lay before the Board which if delayed would prove injurious to the Province The Council thereon prayed His Excelly to proceed His Excelly the Governour acquainted this Board that Joseph Jenoure Esq[r] His Majestys Surveyor General of Lands for this Province was dead And His Majestys Service at this time requiring that a fit person be appointed to succeed him there being a great deal of Business in the Office to be done His Excelly thereupon Recommended John Lovick Esq[r] to be Survey[r] General in the Room of the s[d] Jenoure till His Majestys Pleasure should be known therein who the Council unanimously approved of

Thereupon His Excelly the Govern[r] by and with the advice and Consent of His Majestys Council doth order that a Commission pass the seal of this Province Constituting and appointing the said John Lovick Esq' Survey' General of Lands within this Province till his Majestys pleasure be known therein

Wm Little Esq' Rec' of the late Lords Prop^{rs} delivered a Petition with a Duplicate of Acco^{ts} to the Gov' and Council which was read and the same being Considered of the Board declared that they very well knew that M' Little had always been desirous to have his Acco^{ts} past and notwithstanding they had been so long with a Committee of Council to have a Report made on them yet there has hither to no Report been made and not the least Fraud appearing to us in these acco^{ts} It is the Oppinion of this Board that M' Littles Petition be Entred and his Acco^{ts} lodged in the Secretary Office to be Examined by the Members of His Majestys Council and refered to the farther Consideration of a fuller Board which Petition is in these words Viz^t N° 1

His Excelly the Governour having laid before this Board a Lett' from John Palin Esq' Ch Justice of this Province desiring Leave to resign his Office of the Justice he being very sick & infirm and not able to attend the Duty of his Office His Excelly thereupon Recomended Wm Little Esq' as a fit person to succeed the said John Palin as Chief Justice of this province who the Council unanimously approved of

Thereupon His Excelly the Governour by and with the advice and consent of His Majestys Council doth order that a Com^t pass the seal of this Province constituting and appointing the said Wm Little Chief Justice of this Province till His Majestys Pleasure be further known.

His Excelly the Gov' desiring of the Council their Opinion if they thought Wm Little Esq' a person proper to be C^k of the General Court declared their approbation of him and that he be impowered to appoint a C^k of the said Court during his acting as Chief Justice

His Excelly the Governour recomended Roger Moore John Worley William Owen, Mackrora Scarborough and William Badham Esq^{rs} Assistant Justices of the General Court of this Province who were approved of the Council.

His Excelly the Governour with the advice and Consent of the Council doth order that a Comission pass the seal of this Province constituting and appointing the s^d Roger Moore John Worley and Wm Owen Mack^a Scarborough & William Badham Esq' Assistant Justices of the General Court of this Province and that a Clause be added in the Comission that in Case the Justice should be sick or absent that any two or more of the assistants should be a Quorum to sit and do Business

His Excelly the Governour delivered a Paper to this Board wch was read in these words Viz^t No 2

To which the Honoble the Council delivered in the following paper in Answer thereto & is as follows Viz^t N° 4

John Lovick Esqr took and subscribed the several Oaths by Law appointed for Quallification of Publick Officers as Survey^r General of this Province

William Little Esqr took and Subscribed the Several Oaths by Law appointed for Quallification of Publick Officers as Chief Justices of this Province

By order   R F C C

NORTH CAROLINA—ss.

At a Council held at the Council Chamber in Edenton the 31st day of October Anno Domini 1732

Present

His Excelly George Burrington Esqr Govr &c

The Honoble { Nath Rice / Robt Halton / Jno Bap^t Ashe } Esq^{rs} Members of His Majestys Council

Adj^d till tomorrow morng at Ten of the Clock

Wednesday Novr 1st

Present

His Excelly George Burrington Esqr Govr &c

The Honoble { Nath Rice   Jno Bap^t Ashe / R Halton   John Lovick / Edm^d Gale } Esq^{rs} Members of His Majestys Council

His Excelly the Govr cause a Letter from Corn^s Harnett Esqr to be read which is in these words vizt N° 1

His Excelly the Govr produced a Letter from Corn^s Harnet Esqr a Member of his Majestys Council of this province desiring Leave of his Excelly to Resign his place in Council

John Montgomery Esqr His Majestys Attorney General in Obedience to the order of this Board the 31st of July last Exhibited a Draft of a Commissⁿ for Erecting a Court of Exchequer within this Province which is ordered to lye on the Table for consideration

His Excelly the Govern^r caused his Majestys 42^d Instruction to be read and desired the council Opinion thereon, who taking the same into Consideration are unanimously of Opinion that Every person has thereby a Claim to take 50 acres of Land for himself and for Every White and Black person in his family he making Oath before a Magistrate of the Number he Claims

Upon Petition the Inhabitants on the south side of Moratoke River that are not annexed to Edgecombe precinct praying that the Inhabitants from Hoskins Line at the Rainbow Banks upon a Straight line to Blounts old Town on Tarr River and so up Roa^k River to the Line of Edgecombe be added to Edgecombe prec^t the council taking the same into consideration do consent that the above Limits and bounds be added to Edgecombe precinct

His Excelly the Governour by and with the advice and consent of His Majestys Council doth Establich and Confirm the Limits before recited to be within Edgecombe precinct

Ordered that a Dedimus Issue constituting & appointing Capt John Speir and Capt William Whitehead Justices of the Peace for & within Edgecombe precinct

Upon Petition of the Inhabitants on both sides of the N^o W^t river of Cape Fear praying to have a New precinct Erected from Mr Epraim Vernons Plantation Exclusive thence to the midway between the N^o W^t & N E Rivers keeping a Line of equal Distance from both Rivers to the heads of them for the N^o & E bounds of the same and from the said Mr Ephraim Vernons to the nearest part of Wiccamaw River and so up the said River for the S^o & W^t bounds. His Excelly the Governor by and with the advice and consent of his Majestys Council doth Erect and make the before mentioned bounds into a precinct to be hereafter Distinguished & called Bladen precinct with all such rights and Privilidges as other precincts within this province have and Enjoy And it is further Ordered that the s^d precinct shall be & continue according to the above bounds untill there shall be a further Division of other precinct and Counties

Ordered that a Comission pass the seal appointing and Constituting Mat Rowan John Davis Nat Moore Corn^s Harnett, Hugh Blaning Joseph Clark John Clayton Epraim Vernon John Earle Richard Singletory James Camble & William Salter Justices of the Peace for and within Bladen precinct which s^d Justices shall sit & hold the Court for the s^d precinct on the third Tuesday in the Months of December March June and September Yearly

Read a paper directed to His Excelly the Govern^r sign by Nath Rice & John Bap^t Ashe Esq^rs which is in the words Viz^t No 2

To which paper His Excelly gave in the following Answer Viz^t N° 3

Then His Excelly adj^d the Board till tomorrow Morng Ten of the Clock

Thursday Nov' 2d

Present

His Excelly George Burrington Esq' Gov' &c

The Honoble { Nath Rice   Jno Bapt Ashe } Esqn Members
            { Robt Halton   John Lovick   } of His
            {   Edmd Gale   } Majestys Council

Read the Petⁿ of Edward Moseley Esq' praying a warrt be granted him to the Surv' Genl for three Thousand One hundred Acres of Land he having Sixty two white and Black persons in his Family

Granted the sd Moseley proving his Right on Oath

Read the Petition of Roger Moore Esq' praying a Warrant may be granted him for five Thousand acres of Land he having a Claim thereto from the Number of persons his Family consist of

Granted the said Moore proving his Right

Read the Petition of Mr John Porter praying a warrt may be granted him for three Thousand one hundred acres of Land he having a Claim thereto from the number of Persons his Family Consist of

Granted the sd Porter first proving his Rights

Read the Petition of John Lovick Esq' praying a Warrt may be granted him for Seventeen hundred and fifty Acres of Land he having a Claim thereto from the number of Person his Family consist of

Granted the sd Lovick first proving his Right

His Excelly the Gov' laid before this Board a Paper which was read in these words Vizt No 4

Accordingly Mr Martin Franks was called and declared on oath that Mr Ashe sometime last January told him he was going home this spring to England and if any of his Countrymen would contribute any thing to it he would represent their Grievances for that they would not be imposed upon which the said Franks said none of his Countrymen would give any thing to him upon that account but said if he would appear about the Pollocks Land that the Germans would give him One hundred and fifty pounds meaning money of this Country upon which the sd Ashe declared he would not be concerned in that affair

Read the Petition of the Inhabitants of Craven precinct in these words Vizt Nº 5

This Board thereon are of Opinion that the matter properly lyes before the Survey' General of the Customs and desire his Excelly to recommend the same to him since it appears it will be of so much interest to the Trade & settlement of that River

His Excelly the Govern' desired to know of Mr Rice and Mr Ashe whether they were summoned to appear at the Council held the 17th of

Last Month who answered they were, but were prevented by sickness from attending

Adj⁴ till to morrow morning at Ten of the Clock

Frvday Nov' 3

Present

His Excelly George Burrington Esq' Gov' &c

{ Mᵣ Rice   Mᵣ Ashe }
{ Mᵣ Halton   Mᵣ Lovick }
{   Mᵣ Gale }

It is the Opinion of this Board that if any person claiming Lands for the future shall have a Right to any Quantity of Land Exceeding 640 Acres as formerly or otherwise if it shall be more Beneficial or Convenient to the parties to take out their Warrants or Grants in one parcel that the fees accruing to the several Officers be the same as if taken out in seperate Tracts which may hereafter be at the Choice of the Parties Claiming Lands And it is the Opinion of this Board that Every person Claiming Lands on Rights proved and filed in the Sec⁷ Office shall be Exhibited to have a Warrant or Warrants for the said Lands Granted

Mr Ashe no answer to his Excelly Question yesterday put in the following answer thereto Viz' N° 6

Read the Petition of Cornelious Harnett and Hugh Blanning Esq" in behalf of themselves and other relating to pine Lands Lying near or adjacent to saw mills which Petitions are in these words Viz' 7 & 8.

It is the Opinion of this Board that their prayer to the Grant of a Larger Quantity of Lands than is proposed by the Kings Instructions cannot be allowed, but as they think the prayer in its self reasonable and would at Great service to promote the Trade of the Country. His Excelly is desired to recommend the matter to His Majesty praying an Instruction thereon and in the mean time it is ord⁴ that no Warrants shall be Issued nor pine Lands surveyed lying adjacent to or within Two miles of any saw mill now Erected or which is actually Erecting or hereafter within any that shall be Erected or actually be Erecting till His Majestys pleasure shall in favour of the purport matter of the s⁴ Petition then the Erectors of such saw mills have the Refusal of such Lands for the use of such saw Mills

Adj⁴ till to morrow morning Ten of the Clock

Saturday Nov 4

Present His Excelly &c

The General Court having sent to this Board a Copy of the Sentence this day pronounced against Joseph Haynes and Ann Pettifer having been capitally convicted of the Murther of John Pettifer

His Excelly thereupon by and with the advice and Consent of his Majestys Council doth order that a warrant Issue to the Provost marshall or his Deputy to cause the said Sentence against the said Joseph Haynes & Ann Pettifer to be put in Execution according to Law on Monday next between the Hours of Ten and Two

Mr Attorney General Having made a Motion for a Writt of Enquiry to discouver what goods and Chattles Anne Pettifer was Seized of at the time of the said Annes Conviction of Petty Treason for aiding and Encouraging Joseph Haynes in the Murther of John Pettifer her late Husband The Board Thereupon refers the matter to the consideration of the Ch Justice and his Assistants

His Excelly the Govern' delivered the following paper which was read & is in these words Vizt No 9

At a Council held at the Council Chamber in Edenton the 7th day of November Anno Dom 1732
Present

His Excelly George Burrington Esq' Gov' &c

The Honoble { Nath Rice   John Bapta Ashe } Esqrs Members
{ Robt Halton   John Lovick } of His
{ Edmd Gale } Majesties Council

The Draft drawn by Mr Atto General for Erecting a Court of Exchequer was this day read and referd to the Consideration of Mr Secry Rice & Mr Lovick Members of this Board and the Chief Justice for the time being who are to make their Report thereof at their next sitting on the Last Tuesday in December next

Ordd That a Comission pass the seal of this province (in pursuance of His Majestys Royal Instructions) Constituting and appointing the Chief Justice for the time being the Members of His Majestys Council and the Assistant Justices of the General Court Members of the Court of Oyer and Terminer to be held for this Province on the second Tuesday in December next

Read the Petition of John Bapta Ashe Esq' praying a Warrent may be granted him for Two Thousand of Land he having a Claim thereto from the Number of persons his Family consist of

Granted his proving his Rights.

John Montgomery Esq' produced to this Board a Deputation from James St John Esq' Appointing the said John Montgomery Deputy Inspector & Compr of His Majestys Quit Rents within this Province which was read and allowed of

Wednesday Nov' 8th

Present

His Excelly George Burrington Esq' Gov' &c

The Honoble { Nath Rice   Jn° Bap'' Ashe } Esq'' Members of His
{ Rob' Halton   John Lovich } Majastys Council
{ Edm⁴ Gale }

Read the Petition of the Inhabitants of the Town of Newbern & precinct of Craven Shewing &c N° 10

Refer⁴ to the next council

1733.

[B. P R. O North Carolina B. T Vol. 9 A 33.]

CAPTAIN BURRINGTON'S REPRESENTATION OF THE PRESENT STATE AND CONDITION OF NORTH CAROLINA JANUARY 1ˢ 173¾

To the Right Honourable the Lords of Trade and Plantations.

MAY IT PLEASE YOUR LORDSHIPS,

I do myself the honour to send the Lords of Trade, an account of the present state, and condition of North Carolina, which continues in perfect quietness, Peace, and good order subsist throughout the whole Province I beg leave to assure your Lordships, this is oweing to my industry, and care, in vissiting the several districts of the Government, by adviseing, and encourageing the Magistrates faithfullv to discharge the duty of their offices, countenanceing and assureing them by my own presence frequently, in the Precinct Courts; this Method, to me very troublesome and expensive, has proved effectual, in resetling the Authoritys of the Judicatures, and restraining Profligate, lawless men, from unruly Actions.

There is not one clergyman of the Church of England, regularly setled in this Government The former Missionarys were so little approved of, that the Inhabitants seem very indifferent, whither any more come to them

Some Presbyterian, or rather Independent Ministers from New England have got congregations, more may follow, many of them being unprovided with liveings in that Country; where a Preacher is seldom pay'd more than the value of twenty Pounds sterling a year by his Parishioners

The Quakers in this Government are considerable for their numbers, and substance, the regularity of their lives, hospitality to strangers, and kind offices to new settlers inducing many to be of their persuasion

Plantations continue to sell very cheap, those with Houses, Barns, Orchards, Gardens, Pasture, and Tillage grounds fenced yield about thirty or forty pistoles, Notwithstanding the work done upon them, oft' times has cost four times as much The reason why they yield no more is, that several People chuse to remove into fresh Places, for the Benefit of their Cattle, and Hogs, which is a great convenience to new Comers, who may always buy convenient settlements, for less mony then the buildings, and other improvements could be made

A few years past a Planter removed from Virginia into this Government, he bought eleven inhabited Plantations, adjoyning each other in the old settlements, on the said Plantations lived almost one hundred white People when I was here formerly, now all removed into new settlements, this Purchaser has no white Person in his family except a wife, and not more then ten Negroes, yet keeps all the Plantations in his own management, by this and many other instances I am able to give, it appears how easy a man that has a little mony may purchase much Land in North Carolina

The Trade of this Country is on so bad a footing, that it is thought, the People who traffick with the New England and Virginia Merchants, loose half the value of their goods, the way to remedy this, will be to open a Port on Ocacock Island, more fully shewn in former writeings.

It is by most Traders in London believed, that the Coast of this Country is very dangerous, but in reality not so There are no more than three shoals in about four hundred miles on the sea-side Cape Fear river, Beaufort & Ocacock are very good harbours, will admitt the largest Merchant ships, as may be seen by the Drafts of these places, made by my orders, and sent the Lords of Trade.

Great is the loss this Country has sustained in not being supply'd by vessells from Guinea with Negroes; in any part of the Province the People are able to pay for a ships load, but as none come directly from Affrica, we are under a necessity to buy, the refuse refractory and distemper'd Negroes, brought from other Governments, It is hoped some Merchants in England will speedily furnish this Colony with Negroes, to increase the Produce and its Trade to England

I had been almost a year in the Government, before People began to enter Land   Edward Moseley Surveyor General for the late Lords Proprietors, and his Deputys, more especially Mr John Ashe, one of them, (now in the Council) had been guilty of many vile frauds, and abuses in surveying,   one of their Practices was, to survey without Warrants for Gratifications,   to men that enquired into the validity of those Surveys the Deputys answered, they were right and good   Near upon a year since, Mr Rice the Secretary entered some Lands held in that manner and keeps them,   this put several men who had no other Titles than the Deputy Surveyors could give them, upon makeing proper entrys,   many others have them still to make, of Lands they have been in Possession of seven or eight years, without paying Quit rents.

The Method I take in signing Warrants (related in a former Paper) has effectually put an end to unfair Practises in takeing up of land, too much used formerly,   as the old Land Jobbers are now restrained from getting mony, by selling Warrants, and Entrys, they complain, but all the fair dealing honest men approve & commend what is done

Upon application from some men who imploy their slaves chiefly in makeing Tar and Pitch, that less quantitys would be made and their business cramped, if they were not permitted to take up more then fivety Acres, for each Person in their Familys. I was prevailed upon to sign Warrants, for a small quantity beyond that complement,   the land was barren and unfit for cultivation

In this Country is a Law called the Lapse Act, which seems to allow every man the liberty to take up 640 acres, and it was never refused any one, in the time the Proprietors held this Province,   I will be careful to observe the Instructions on on this head in signing warrants. Before I am honoured with an answer to the Report made last year and know what Laws will be continued and which repealed

A Gentleman liveing in Virginia, reputed rich, and owner of above one hundred slaves, desired to enter five thousand acres of land, part of a Savanna between Panticough and Nuse River,   I went to view this Place, and think I never did ride over worse land,   I granted the Gentleman's request,   am not able to judge what use he designs to put it to, in my opinion the whole is not worth one shilling   There are millions of acres of Savanna Land in this Country,   if they were taken up the King's rents would be much increased

The Instruction for takeing up land (if not alter'd) will greatly obstruct the Peopleing of this Province   Not an hundredth part of the grounds are Plantable, the barren Pine lands will never be cultivated, the several sorts of wet lands, called in these parts, Dismals, Pocosans, Swamps, Marishes and Savannas cannot be cleared and drained, without great charge, and labour, therefore not hitherto attempted

The sure way to increase the Quitt rents, will be to allow all men liberty to take up what quantitys, of these barren and wett lands they are willing to pay the rent off, without being tyed down, to obligations of cultivateing soils, that cannot recompense the charge of any labour. It is obvious to all men, how prejudicial it must prove to this Colony, should the Quitt rents be higher here, then in all other Governments, from this Place even to Nova Scotia Where only the good lands to be taken up, the Quitt rents will increase but slowly, but if all the poor lands were Patented the Revenue ariseing from them will amount to a considerable sum

I am able to demonstrate, that the two Provinces of North and South Carolina contain above one hundred Millions of Acres

It is computed at this time, not five millions are Patented in both Countrys.

Land is not wanting for men in Carolina, but men for land

Several Saw mills have been lately erected in the South Parts of this Government and others are now building   Two Petitions were delivered to me in Council, the third day of November last, on behalf of the subscribers and other Proprietors of Saw Mills, praying Grants of Pine Lands lyeing near their respective Mills, which is deferr'd to such time as I can receive orders about it

The granting five thousand acres or more, to each owner of a mill, cannot be a prejudice to any person, and may increase the quitt rents, one or two hundred pounds ℔ annum

The Petitions and resolve of Council in Answer are incerted in the Journals.

The Reputation this Government has lately acquired, appears by the number of People that have come from other Places to live in it Many of them possessed of good American Estates   I do not exceed in saying a thousand white men have already settled in North Carolina, since my arrival, and more are expected

This increase of Inhabitants, made it necessary to erect new Precincts On receiving Petitions from those that lived remote from Court Houses, setting forth the hardships they laboured under, in being at great expences, and loss of time in attending Courts from great distances, to ease these People, three new ones have been made,   the bounds are incerted in the Council Journals.

I have taken great care and gone thro' much fatigue in settling tho Militia, which had been totally neglected, dureing Sir Richard Everard's administration, two Colonels dyeing last summer prevented my receiving lists of their Regiments. In November last I sett out in hopes to have finished that affair but was prevented by a severe frost that came on after I had began my journey, the way I was to travell not being passable for Ice, that covered the brooks and low grounds. The Militia I am certain consists of five thousand men, and there are at least another thousand not enrolled. I compute the White men, women, and children, in North Carolina, to be full thirty thousand, and the Negroes about six thousand The Indians, men, women and children, less then eight hundred

The last Spring and Summer proved excessive hot and dry, which rendered this and neighbouring Provinces very sickly, Feavers and bloody fluxes made great havock among the People, violent heats and want of rain, damaged the crops so much that there is scarce sufficient grain made this year, to suffice the Inhabitants who usually exported great quantitys.

Mr Palin . . . succeeded Mr Smith as Chief Justice of this Province, upon the departure of the last for England, being incapacitated by sickness to attend the business of that Office, resigned, with the approbation and consent of the Council, I appointed Mr Little Chief Justice because there was no other Person in this Government capable of duely executeing that Imployment This Gentleman was Attorney General, and Receiver of the Quitt rents, to the Lords Proprietors, is heavily charged by Sir Richard Everard, and Mr Smith, with accusations of concealments and embezzlements, amounting to a great sum, but it is well known he never received by the sale of lands, and for Quitt rents in this Province, the value of one thousand pounds sterling I think the accounts he has delivered are fair and just, much is said in my answer to Mr Smiths complaints upon this subject, therefore will add no more, then that I think he is an honest man, and am sure he is a very good lawyer, and in all respects well qualified to discharge the Office of a Chief Justice, in North Carolina.

After the decease of Col Joseph Jenoure, Surveyor General of his Majesty's Lands, Mr Lovick was appointed to succeed him; this gentleman is also virulently attacked, by the Knight and Squire before named, not for that Mr Little and Mr Lovick had in particular done ill, but because they refused to joyn with them, and others (tho' much sollicited) in carrying on the Designs formed against me. Mr Lovick can be of singular use and service, in the next Assembly, by helping me to draw Bills, being on the conferences between the Council and Assembly, and many other ways. It is impossible for one man to do everything requisite during the sitting of an Assembly, as maintaining all the Debates and writing all Papers that pass on those occasions. If Mr Lovick does not assist, it will fall to my lot to have all that to do, the other Members of the Council are not inclined or not capable of giving me sufficient assistance on those occasions. Therefore hope Mr Lovick will be continued in his present imployment, or obtain some other when a vacancy happens, to reward the services he has and is able to do the King in this Province

The Act for resurveying Land in this Country is framed artfully and fraudulently, if the Law is repealed, and every man has liberty to resurvey, at his own expence, any Plantation, where he knows more Land is held, than specified in the Patent, & have liberty to take up the overplus, a multitude of frauds and concealments will be discovered, and the Quitt rents increased without putting the King to any charge.

I have been informed Mosely when Surveyor, did make Surveyes in his own House, & plotted out Land upon paper, with bounds by waters, trees, and other signs, and tokens, that he never saw, nor knew anything off, includeing much more than in the Returns set forth, for which Patents went out in Course By all I can hear, his deputys seldom measured, but contented themselves to mark two Trees in front for corners, and then guessed the other bounds, and so returned the Pretended Surveys into the Secretary's office

A Commission was drawn for the erecting a Court of Exchequer, and layd before the Council last November, several objections being made to it, the present Chief Justice, with two of the Council, we appointed to consider thereof, make alterations if they see cause, and lay them before the next Council to be considered, in the meantime, the Lawyers in Virginia, have been desired to give their opinions, upon several matters we are not clear in

It is thought by every man here, that this Country is not without a Court of Exchequer at this time, the General Court of this Province under the Proprietors, had the powers, of the King's Bench, Common Pleas, and Exchequer granted them, which Court is no ways altered, but invested with as full Powers as heretofore

All the time Sir Richard Everard governed this Province, the Publick Roads were in a manner unregarded, one markt by my order when Governor for the Proprietors, from Nuse to Cape Fear River, about one hundred miles in length remained unwrought upon The last summer

I prevailed upon the men liveing in that part of the Country, to take in hand that necessary work which was chearfully and effectually performed, Bridges lay'd, and Causeways made over all the Waters, and Morasses, it is the way men travel, that go from this, and the more Northern Governments into South Carolina

Having succeeded in that affair, I made a journey to the Inland parts, and proposed to those People makeing a Road from the Borders of Virginia, to Cape Fear River, through the middle of the Country, a considerable distance higher then the former, which they readily assented to, proper measures are taken for marking and laying out the said Road this winter, I hope to see it perfected before the next Christmas.

The old Highways that I found very much in decay are tolerably well repaired, what remains wanting to be done on them, will be easily compleated in the ensueing Spring

Nothing has been done in respect to the boundary between this Government and South Carolina, if a line is run, it must prove a great expence to the King, Pedee River will be a natural and proper division, that Water being made the Bounds of each Province, South Carolina will contain double the quantity of Land left to North Carolina, the elder settlement. What I formerly wrote upon this head, and now in some measure repeat, is purely to save His Majesty an unnecessary expence But if His Majesty gives order for a line to be run, Money must be provided before we can begin the work, the charges will not be less in my opinion then three thousand pounds sterling

There remain in the Government Mr Rice, Mr Halton, Mr Ashe and Mr Rowan appointed Councellours in the King's Instructions one more viz Mr Eleazar Allen, I have never seen, he was lately Clarke to the Assembly of South Carolina I hear he designs speedily to settle on his Estate in this Country, the former exception against his sitting in the Council here, by reason of the Imployment he held in South Carolina, ceased, by the appointment of another to that Place

Since my last account of the Council, Colonel Jenoure departed this life, and Mr Cornelius Harnett resigned, to make up the number of Councellours seven I swore Colonel William Forbes a Member, the chief Justice when appointed in England Mr James Tunes, Mr Thomas Pollock, Mr William Owen, and Mr Mackrora Scarborough are fit persons to fill up the Council I beleive Mr John Baptista Ashe will be thought unworthy to remain any longer therein, by every Person that reads the Council Journals now sent.

Mr Secretary Rice has openly placed himself at the head of my enemys, sets his name to Mr Ashe's compositions, as will be seen in the Council

Journals, I think he has made it his whole business to create mischief, and disturb the Administration, ever since he came into the Province, Mr Smith is able to unravel all this Mistery of iniquity having been a principal actor

The King's business in this Government will greatly suffer by the Attorney General's want of capacity, and knowledge in the law His Majesty's service requires in that office, a very industrious, skilfull lawyer, to assist and advise the Deputy Auditor and Receiver Generall in makeing a Rent Role, inspecting and examining the Titles of Lands (which will prove a tedious and very difficult work) and to transact the other business incident, and belonging to an Attorney General, In all these matters the present Attorney General Mr John Montgomery is without the requisite understanding So much concerning him the Duty of my Imployment demands.

Part of the King's business is delay'd by the absence of the Deputy Auditor and Receiver General No Quitt rents have been pay'd nor accounts audited in North Carolina since His Majesty purchased this Province

North Carolina was little known or mentioned before I was Governor for the Proprietors, when I came first, I found the Inhabitants few and poor, I took all methods I thought would induce People to come from other Countrys to settle themselves in this, and put myself to very great charges, in making new Settlements in several Parts of the Government, succeeded according to my expectation in all, Perfecting the Settlement on Cape Fear River cost me a great sum of money, and infinite trouble I endured the first winter I went there, all the hardships could happen to a man destitute of a house to live in, that was above a hundred miles from a Neighbour in a pathless Country and was obliged to have all Provisions brought by sea at great charges to support the number of men I caryed there, paid and maintained at my sole expence it can hardly be imagined what pains I took in sounding the Inlets, Barrs and Rivers in this Province, which I performed no less than four times, I discovered, and made known the Channells of Cape Fear river and Port Beaufort, or Topsail Inlett, before unused and unknown In attempting these and other discoverys by Land & Water often run the hazard of drowning & starving, and never obtained any other reward, or gratification, but the thanks of two Assemblys in this Country, For all the pains I took and money I expended in carrying on, and compleating those enterprises Horses and Cattle were of very little value in this Country before Cape Fear River was Inhabited As very few men came there provided with these creatures, they were obliged to come into the old settlements to purchase them, which doubled the Prices, they sold att formerly, this still continues and will last some years longer, to the great benefit of Persons who have large Stocks

As the foregoing Paragraph relates to myself in some measure, I have carefully avoided, couching the same in a very extraordinary stile, if your Lordships are of opinion it ought to be explained or proved, either, or both, shall be faithfully performed by

Your Lordships

Most humble

and most obedient Servant

GEO BURRINGTON.

N° Carolina
the 1ˢᵗ of January 173⅔

(Indorsed)

Rec⁴ 1ˢᵗ June } 1733
Read July 25ᵗʰ

[B P R O Aᴍ & W. Iɴᴅ Vᴏʟ. 22. ᴘ 148]

N Cᴀʀᴏʟɪɴᴀ the 1ˢᵗ of March 1732 [3.]

Mᴀʏ ɪᴛ ᴘʟᴇᴀsᴇ ʏᴏᴜʀ Gʀᴀᴄᴇ.

I have the honour with this letter to address a Representation on the affairs of N Carolina to your Grace, I am very sensible of my disability and incapacity of writing anything worth your Grace's reading, beg leave to assure my Lord Duke that if he is pleased to direct this province to be put upon the footing humbly recommended in the said Representation, it will soon be much altered for the better, and become a Country of Trade and Reputation.

Your Grace I hope has not forgot, that I made bold to mention a suspicion I had of Coll Bladens ill intentions to me, nor the generous answer you were pleased to give (viz) that if I faithfully performed my duty I need not fear any man; I presume to mention this because it was reported in London, I should very suddenly be turned out, the same has been constantly said here and declared particularly by Mongomery the Attorney General the first day he came

I think my self bound in duty to inform your Grace that Mʳ Rice the Secretary has neither attended the Councils nor his office I do all his business except receiving the fees.

The Chief Justice and Attorney General of this Province ought to be Men of understanding and Lawyers, neither of the persons your Grace bestow'd these places upon in this Government ever knew Law enough to be Clarke to a justice of the Peace That there are People will contrive Villanys in this Country and can procure others to swear them is notoriously apparent by an inquiry, I lately made by order of the Lords of Amiralty upon a complaint made by Edmund Porter to them against several Gentlemen, and Planters, for designing to murther him, this examination is sent to Mr Fury for delivery to their Lordships.

Part of my Adversarys in this Government are subtle and Artfull, others ignorant and hotheaded, the last I am certain will say, or swear anything the others direct therefore, I humbly desire your Grace not to credit the inventions, or accusations of ill designing Men against me, before I have an opertunity of justifyeing myself

                    I am
                (with the greast Duty)
                    Your Grace's
                        Most humble
                            and most devoted Servant
                                GEO BURRINGTON.

[B P R O North Carolina B T Vol 9 a 30.]

DUKE OF NEWCASTLE TO LORDS COMM" OF TRADE

WHITEHALL, March 27th 1733

MY LORDS,

His Majesty having been pleased to appoint Gabriel Johnston Esqr to be Governor of North Carolina in America in the room of George Burrington Esqr, I am to desire you will prepare draughts of a Commission and Instructions for him, in order to be laid before the King for His Majesty's approbation

                    I am
                        My Lords
                        Your Lordships
                            most obedient
                                humble servant
                                    HOLLES NEWCASTLE.

Lds Commn of Trade

[B. P R O North Carolina B T Vol. 21 p 122.]

LORDS OF TRADE TO DUKE OF NEWCASTLE
5 APRIL 1733.

To His Grace the Duke of Newcastle

My Lord,

Having in obedience to His Maj commands signified to us by Your Grace's letter of the 27ᵗʰ of the last month prepared a draft of a Commission for Gabriel Johnston Esqʳ to be Governor of North Carolina in America We herewith inclose the said Draft to your Grace with our Representation thereupon which you will be pleased to lay before His Majesty

    We are

        My Lord

            Your Grace's

                most obedient and

                    most humble servᵗ.

                       WESTMORELAND

                       T PELHAM

                       P DOCMINIQUE

                       ED. ASHE

                       M BLADEN

                       OR BRIDGEMAN

Whitehall

   April 5ᵗʰ 1733

[B P R O. North Carolina B. T Vol. 9 A 45.]

RICE AND ASHE VS. BURRINGTON—ERECTION OF
NEW PRECINCTS.

Mʳ Rice and Mʳ Ashe to Lords of Trade 20ᵗʰ April 1733.

May it please your Lordships,

His Excellency Governor Burrington proceeding to appoint (there being no apparent necessity) several new precincts, in most of which there were very few Inhabitants, This as it was making to the surprize of most People a very great and sudden alteration in the Constitution of the Legislature, as it would cause a very unequal Representation of the People, as His Majesty had not been advised or apply'd to therein, as it seemed to be directly contrary to one of His Majesty's Instructions, as there was a violent suspicion that there were secret and by-ends aimed at therein, his Excellency himself writing and forming some Petitions for such Precincts, and promoting them by much Art and persuasion, as we suspected one end or design in particular was, that it might be an obstruction or hindrance of the Assembly's proceeding to business when it should meet These considerations moved us to offer objections and reasons against such a practice which objections are hereunto annexed as also the Governor's Answer in which he has bestowed on us much reproachful language and endeavoured to misrepresent us as Persons opposeing His Majesty's Prerogatives, a censure we think very unjust in that we have and always shall carefully avoid the least opposition or even so much as touching on them, and to prevent his success in such his endeavours, we have put the matter in a just and true light, & submitting it to your L⁴ᵖˢ Judgements, are

      My Lords
         Your Lordships most obedient
         and most humble servants

                     NATH. RICE
                     J BAPTˢ ASHE

20ᵗʰ April 1733

Reasons and Objections made and humbly offer'd in Council by Nath Rice and John Baptˢ Ashe, two of his Majesty's Council, against the dividing Precincts, and erecting new one by the Governour and Council alone, with[out] the concurrence & assent of the Assembly

1 As every Precinct is to send a certain Number of Representatives to the Lower House of Assembly, such a method may be destructive of and subvert the present Constitution of the Legislature, which as it consists of an upper and Lower House, whose Powers and privileges are separate and distinct, they ought in such points to be independent either of the other, more especially in so fundamental a one as is this of Representation For it stands to reason, that if a Power of altering the form of Representation, either by adding to or diminishing the Number of Representatives be lodged in the Persons of whom the upper House consists, that then the Lower House, is dependent on and owes it's Being at least the form thereof (which is in effect the same) to the Upper House, by which means the Upper House will be solely (as it were) the whole Legislature

As for instance. suppose the Governor and three of the Council on an emergency to meet (we speak this by way of supposition and for argument sake,) and think it proper to divide a Precinct whose Inhabitants for some particular ends may be at such Governor and Council's devotion into ten Precincts; will not by this means a Majority be obtained in the Lower House?

2. It is absurd to suppose that a power of the part should be greater or indeed equal to that of the whole · Now as the Constitution of the Legislature must be antecedent to any Act thereof, it cannot be dependent on any such Act, much less on an Act of part, as indeed by this Method it would, in that the whole Legislature would owe its Being (at least the form thereof which as we observed before is in effect the same) to the Upper House And this among others we take to be the reason that the Legislature of Great Britain avoid (tho' many are these the inconveniences ensueing from unequal Representation) endeavouring to remedy them or touching on so tender and constitutional a Point

3. Another consequence of such a method extreamly absurd will be this An order of Governor and Council only will have force to supersede, repeal and annul a Law, For if By Law a Precinct is limited and circumscribed by certain Bounds, if by an Order of Governor and Council those Bounds are altered or taken away and new ones prescribed, is not this in effect repealing such Law?

4. We conceive such Business as it relates to the Constitution of the Legislature, most properly to lye before the Governor, Council and Representatives of the People in General Assembly, and as it is to be presumed, they are the most competent judges when such Precincts shall be necessary, so it is, that they will readily concur in erecting new ones, when they shall be so judged to be for the good of the Publick and the benefit of a competent Number of Inhabitants.

5 We are of opinion that this method of erecting Precincts is not only illegal and may be attended with many evil consequences but is also not warranted by His Majesty's Royal Instruction, which forbids the erecting new Judicatures, without his royal Licence, Now by this Method new Judicatures will be erected But if it were done by an Act of Assembly, at the Prayer of the Representatives of the People, the same would regularly come before His Majesty for his allowance or dissent

6. We are the more confirmed in this our opinion of the illegality of doing it without the consent of the Representatives of the People in General Assembly from the general Practice of the neighbouring Governments, more particularly Virginia where many precedents appear in

56

their printed Laws of such busyness being done by their Governor Council and Assembly, And we are apt to believe our gracious King (for we pretend not in the least to deny or even so much as to touch at the Royal Prerogative) has given as full Powers to the Governor & Council of Virginia, as to the Governor & Council of this Province, nor can we think it the pleasure of our most gracious sovereign (who on all occasions has shewn so tender a regard to us His People of this Province) that the Constitution of the Legislature should be on a more precarious Establishment than that of others

---

Governor Burrington's Paper in Relation to the Erecting of Precincts.

Mr Rice and Mr Ashe delivered a paper at the last Council containing reasons and objections &c against erecting new Precincts, by Governor & Council without the concurrence and assent of the Assembly in this my Answer I shall endeavour to refute their pretended reasons and objections But first it may be proper to give some account of the Precincts lately erected, and then to relate in what manner it has been customary, to make Precincts in this Government

Some time after I came into this Country with His Majesty's Commission, the People inhabiting on white Oak river and Onslow river and parts adjacent presented a Petition to me and the Council, praying they might be erected into, and made a new Precinct, the reasons the Petitioners sett forth appeared so fair and just that what they desired, was granted, vizt they were made a new Precinct by the name of Onslow, which Precinct contains a square of above fifty miles, and will soon be (in all likelihood) one of the most considerable in this Province

The people on the south side Roanoak River and those on Tar River petitioned about a year since to be erected into a new Precinct, which was also granted, and is known by the name of Edgecombe Precinct, and contains so much land that I hope in a few years to see two or three grow out of it

Another Precinct was established on the N W River above Cape Fear by the name of Bladen, on the Petition of the Inhabitants, this last in process of time will be divided

I omit setting down the reasons contained in the forementioned Petitions because they are in the Council Office, and may be read by any man

Mr Rice and Mr Ashe have by way of Discent given reasons and objections in writing, against making new Precincts, by a Governour and Council without the concurrence of the General Assembly as if it was a

new Practice of dangerous consequence, and tending to the destruction of
the Government Priviledges and Libertys of the People of this Province
&c. Notwithstanding Mr Rice and Mr Ashe present and insinuate that
the erecting new Precincts by a Governor & Council is an innovation and
a breach in the Constitution of this Government I shall prove the same
has been usual, and the constant custom from almost the first settlement
of this Province, and sure I am, that the Inhabitants have enjoyed the
fullness of Liberty, under this form of Government, without apprehension or suspicion of being deprived of so valuable a Blessing, but now
it seems, Mr Ashe has made a discovery and let Mr Rice into the secret
(viz') that the present Governor and Council have for the ease of the people in several parts of this Province acted in like manner, as former Governors and Councils did upon the very same occasions (I think to their
just praise) And it came to pass that a paper was wrote and signed by
Mr Rice and Mr Ashe, and by them produced at the last Council, to
which I promised an Answer, when we met again, and doubt not of giving full satisfaction to all unprejudiced Auditors, and Readers of the
justice and regularity of my proceedings, and the Councils also in relation to this affair

Nevertheless it is my opinion the motives that induced Mr Rice and
Mr Ashe to publish their paper, were to disquiet and amuse the People,
and to shew their zeal for the support and augmentation of the Power
and privileges of the House of Burgesses, nay further to carry them to a
[point] hitherto unknown and unthought of even in North Carolina, how
well it becomes them to behave in this manner I leave to the consideration of the other Members of His Majesty's Council of this Province,
and proceed to recount the methods used of erecting Precincts in this
Government as I find them in the Council Books.

After the Charter was obtained from King Charles the second by the
Lords Proprietors, their Lordships agreed upon a form of Government
which was called the Constitutions of Carolina, which every Officer in
their service, every Magistrate and every Member of Assembly was
sworn to maintain By these Constitutions made by the Proprietors,
without any Assembly, the Province was designed to be divided into
eight Countys, and each of these Countys was to contain four Precincts
and each of those Precincts was to send five Representatives to the General Assembly, accordingly the County of Albemarle was settled on this
plan, and twenty Members sent from the four Precincts (there being no
more at the first Appointment in that County) The twenty Representa-

tives together with the Lords Proprietors, or their Deputys made what was at that time called, the Grand Assembly of Carolina, this was the first Rise of the General Assembly, and this the first Establishment of Precincts.

Had these Constitutions contained, as Countys were settled and laid out (which the Proprietors were then the only appointers of) the same number of Precincts, must have been made in each County and the like number of Representatives, must have been sent to the Generall Assembly till all the Countys had been settled, and no disputes of this kind could have happened But the Lords Proprietors having thought fit to abrogate those Constitutions and no other Precincts being erected besides those in the County of Albemarle, the method from that time has been for the Governor and Council as the settlements increased to erect new Precincts, which has always been done upon the Petition of the Inhabitants, and by this Authority only, four Precincts were at different times formerly erected, in Bath County, and one more four years since, These continue by the same authority, Precincts to this day, nor was the validity or regularity of such appointment ever doubt'd till very lately In the year 1715 the Generall Assembly were so far from questioning the Power of the Governour and Council in that Affair, that by a Law then made they did allow those Precincts erected by the Governour and Council to be regularly appointed and in that Law took great care to prevent any unequal Representation It being then enacted that for the future every new Precinct which should be made after that time was to send but two Members to the Generall Assembly, which must certainly mean and intend Precincts made by the Governour and Council, as former Precincts had been made, otherwise it should have directed in what manner Precincts should be made for the future, as well as what number of Members should be sent from such Precincts. This makes it clearly appear that the Assembly allowed, nay did not dispute at that time the Power of the Governour and Council in erecting new Precincts without their concurrence otherwise they would certainly have made some Provision on the occasion, as they did to prevent five Members, going to each of the new Precincts But they well knew that the manner of appointing Precincts by the Governour and Council had always been the practice, and seemed satisfied with the Provision they made for lessening the number of Representatives, to be chosen in the new Precincts, and thought what was then done sufficient to prevent the consequences now charged upon myself and the Council and the absurdity of the method in making new Precincts by the Governour and Council

After the passing this Law to prevent the new Precincts from sending five members, as those appointed, by the Constitutions did The Governour & Council as the settlements enlarged appointed other Precincts which still remain by that appointment, nor did the Assembly ever interfere in this matter till it was referred to them by the Governour and Council for the following reasons About the year 1722 the settlements in the Precinct of Chowan, one of the four Precincts in Albemarle County, erected by the Lords Proprietors Constitutions were so much extended, that the Inhabitants settled on Morattuck River petitioned to be erected into a Precinct, separate from Chowan, with the same Preveledges as the other Precincts of Albemarle County enjoyed, to which many objections were made by reason of the Act of Assembly before mentioned, which it was thought the Petition was not conformable too, therefore it was laid before the Generall Assembly and a Law passed for making them a Precinct with the same Preveledges, as the other Precincts in Albemarle County had and enjoyed (viz') of sending five Representatives to the Generall Assembly This is the only instance, one of thirteen Precincts, now established in the Province, was erected by an Act of Assembly, all the rest were made either by the Lords Proprietors or their Deputys (the Governour & Council) or the Governour & Council appointed by the King After this will it not be thought strange that two Members of His Majesty's Council should make so many objections to the Governour and Councils using an authority always exercised by them, And as it has been the constant practice, they have a right to do, before His Majesty's royall commands forbid the same or a Law is made to the contrary

This plain account of the Precincts that are now in North Carolina, and the manner of their being erected, I have fairly and truly deduced & stated, am certain Mr Ashe knew the same, as well as any man in this Province Yet so it is that he and Mr Rice with their usual modesty and veracity term the proceedings of the Governour and Council, in making new Precincts at the request and on the humble Petitions of the Inhabitants, altering the form of the Representation destructive of the Government, illegal, unwarrantable, and subverting the Constitution These men ought to have strong reasons to support so weighty a charge those they assign will fall far short, as will be proved in the following part of this paper

Messrs Rice and Ashe make one thing very plain by their writing (viz') that they desire to be thought Advocates for the People and insinnate that the Governour and Council are doing things very illegal and subverting the Constitution, altho' they have done no more then former Governours and Councils were accustomed to do.   Mr Rice and Mr Ashe are sworn Members of His Majesty's Council in this Province & have read my Instructions, one of which is a Command not to suffer Assemblys exceed their due bounds, should the Assembly claim it as their sole right to erect Precincts, in the new settlements, and declare that it ought not to be done, by an Act or order of Government Mr Rice and Mr Ashe would ill comply with or observe the oath they took as Councellors, if they advised me to give up a right of Government, always made use of by the Governours & Councils in this Province

If there is any strength or validity in the Arguments urged on the subject now controverted by Mr Rice and Mr Ashe it may well be suspected there had been a design on foot in this Government of long continuance to subvert the Constitution, Laws and Libertys of the People liveing in Albemarle County, and that the former Governours and myself have been in a plott with the Inhabitants of eight Precincts to effect the said Design, there having been so many Precincts erected on the Petitions of the People in Bath County, without the concurrence of the Assemblys since the Proprietors Constitutions were laid aside

I come now to examine their reasons, and objections as they have sett them down

1st They say this method alters the form of Representation, makes the lower House dependent on, & it's being to the upper House by which means the upper House will be solely (as it were) the whole Legislature, with submission to these wise men, I deny that by this method the form of the Representation is altered, The number of the Representatives are indeed increased   It is strange there should be imminent danger of subverting the Constitution by a method always used and which has not hitherto made the Upper House *solely the whole Legislature* Nor (as it were) *the whole Legislature*   It is true there are many things that might be amiss, if all bounds were exceeded, which is not a sufficient argument against the matter treating off, regard the Instance they wisely bring to shew in what manner this destruction can be brought about, they alledge that for particular ends a Governour & Council may split a Precinct into tenn parts and so get a majority of Representatives chosen at the Governour & Council's devotion, this is put for arguments sake, Our Writers say they might as well have supposed that the Governour and all the Council of North Carolina were run mad (two Members excepted) who were only bedevil'd and therefore it would be better to have no Governour nor Council

2ᵈ They say it is absurd to think a power of part greater than the power of the whole. By this Argument Acts of Assembly could not make new Precincts. They add as the Constitution of the Legislature must be antecedent, to any part of it, it cannot be dependent on any Act thereof, much less on an Act of part. How this will enforce their Arguments I know not, therefore will let it rest until such a time as they think fit to explain themselves on this head And only observe that if these two men give themselves the Liberty to write and Publish anything that comes into their heads for Argument sake, and put what constructions they please thereon afterwards such proceedings may produce very ill consequences in this Government

3ᵈ They say another consequence extreamly absurd will be that an Order of Governour & Council should alter the limits, or bounds of a Precinct made by a Law, and infer it would be repealing the Law itself, but this is without Foundation for of all the Precincts in North Carolina, one only was made by Act of Assembly (as before observed) and that for particular Persons, When a Precinct extends its settlement so much that a new Division is necessary, and made, that doth not repeal the former Law, for example when Edgecombe was taken out of Bertie, the Law that made Bertie a Precinct subsists, and that Precinct is still very large and contains more Inhabitants than any other in the whole Government

4ᵗʰ As it relates to the Constitution of the Legislature it should lye before the Governour, Council and Assembly In their second reason they advanced, that the whole Assembly could or ought not to alter the Representation and mention the Parlement of Great Britain, which is not to the matter in hand, Great Britain is an ancient Kingdom but North Carolina a young Colony belonging to and dependent thereon I believe Mr Rice and Mr Ashe are the only Persons, that ever doubted of or questioned the Power the Governour & Council of this Province had of erecting Precincts by themselves, or in conjunction with the General Assembly When any real inconveniencys arise from the method and Practice hitherto followed in erecting new Precincts; and when it is found to be for the Interest, and Good of the People to have the same settled by a Law, no doubt but the same will be effected, before that time I think such matter may and ought to be transacted in the usual & accustomed manner

5ᵗʰ In this they suggest it is not warranted by His Majesty's Instructions, because they forbid the erecting any new Judicatures, but this is beside the matter, and nothing to the purpose, all men of common understanding may easily discover that by new Judicatures, is meant any new Courts of Judicature not usual in this Province, I believe no man (M' Rice and M' Ashe excepted) will say that when a new Precinct is erected the appointing a Precinct Court therein as in other Precincts, is erecting a new sort of Judicature, nor can I think it possible for any man but those two Members of Council to put so uncommon a construction upon one of His Majesty's Instructions or so lightly play with it

6th They are the more confirmed in their Opinion (as is wrote) of the illegality of making new Precincts, without the consent of the Representatives of the People in General Assembly from the Practice of the neighbouring Governments, more particularly of Virginia &c I own myself unacquainted with the Laws of Virginia and therefore will not pretend to write about them but having been several times in that Province, am sure that the Precincts in this Country are much larger than the Countys in Virginia more especially that made in the time Sir Richard Everard was Governour of this Province, and the three new ones, since erected, and I am the more confirmed by the weak arguments produced by M' Rice and M' Ashe that there is nothing illegal in making new Precincts by the Governour & Council of this Province, neither is it a new but an old Custom as I have proved out of the Council Books

I take this opportunity to join with Messrs Rice and Ashe in recommending some Precedents of Virginia, to be followed by the good People of this Province of which I will mention a few In Virginia there is a noble House for the Governour to live in, built at the publick expence, there are handsome Fees allowed by Acts of Assembly towards his maintenance, the Inhabitants pay a very great respect to their Governour, more especially those in the Council of which I have been a witness In Virginia there are also large taxes raised to keep up the honour, and support the Government, and the Clergy have competent allowances by Acts of Assembly annually paid them, as these precedents are laudable Messrs Rice & Ashe would do well to recommend them as Examples worthy to be followed by all the People of this Province on whom they have an influence

I never saw the King's Instructions to the Governor of Virginia, therefore should be guilty of a great absurdity, if I took upon me to write upon a subject I know nothing off, nor have nothing to do with, The instructions I receive I obey to the best of my knowledge, and understanding That our sovereign Lord the King has a most tender regard to the just priviledges (libertys also may be added) of his subjects, in the four parts of the world is acknowledged with due gratitude by them, neither can it be imagined that His Majesty would have the Priviledges of Mr Rice & Mr Ashe (if he ever heard of such men) to be on a more precarious establishment, than those of others As Mr Rice and Mr Ashe are well read in my Commission and Instructions they must do me the Justice to own, I have hitherto made a very moderate use of the Power therein given particularly in respect to them

If Mr Ashe continues his custom of writing from one Council to another, he ought to studdy the subject he takes in hand better than he has these about Precinct Courts, now answered, and reputed, and for Mr Rice I am of opinion it would be more to his advantage (being secretary) to learn the business belonging to his Imployment than to take upon him to censure or instruct me.

GEO BURRINGTON

Edenton the 26th of December 1732

North Carolina—ss.

To His Excellency the Governor and the Honble the Members of His Majesty's Council

His Excellency the Governor has by way of answer to some reasons and objections, which we put in against the dividing old Precincts and erecting new ones, by the Governor and Council only, without the concurrence and assent of Assembly, put in a long writing, wherein besides bestowing on us much opprobious language, he has made several invidious reflections & insinuations as if (it should seem) we affected to be thought Patriots & Advocates of the People, ill becoming His Majesty's Councillours His Excellency in the same Paper makes also a kind of historical narrative of the Constitution of the Legislature of this Province.

We shall pass over the language without other resentment than to say, we think we merit it not; that we ought as Members of His Majesty's Council to be exempt from such freedom as his Excellency often takes with us that way in Council, both in writing and by word of mouth And we humbly conceive such his treatment of us cannot be approved of by his and our superiors in Great Britain, when they shall be made sensible thereof His Excellency's unjust reflections and insinuations as to the motives induceing us to offer those objections, we shall obviate by shewing some true motives, we shall vindicate ourselves from such aspersions as we think designed to blemish our characters as Members of His Majesty's Council in this Province, And then we shall proceed to give a just history, as briefly as we can, of the Constitution of our Legislature, & of it's form from it's original to this day, in which (with due submission be it said) we doubt not of making His Excellency sensible of some mistakes in his

We shall now proceed to shew some of the reasons which moved us to object as we did

1 We observed that the Governor (notwithstanding former Assemblys had strenuously insisted on and asserted the People's right in this particular, and had had it allowed them, as we shall shew hereafter) proceeded to divide old and erect new Precincts with a very small number of the Council consenting thereunto, as at the dividing Hanover, erecting Bladen Precinct out of it, at the dividing Bertie adding part thereof to Edgecombe Precinct, there were only three Councellors consenting thereunto, viz' M' Halton M' Lovick and M' Gale one of which it is well known was introduced into Council contrary to His Majesty's Instructions to His Excellency there being seven others then in the Government

2. We observe that before the aforementioned Division, Bertie and Hanover Precincts had been divided by the Governor and Council in the same manner. We could not see any reason or necessity for such Divisions for (for instance,) in Bladen Precinct there are not (we think) above three Freeholders viz' M' Nal Moor, M' Tho. Jones and M' Rich⁴ Singletery inhabiting, and not above perhaps thirty Families, including the Freeholders, Now as his Excellency pursuant to His Majesty's Instructions, has directed the writs to issue for Freeholders only to elect, then of those three, two are to stand candidates and the third to elect them. The case is much the same as to Onslow Precinct in which (we are pretty confident) there are very few more Freeholders, (and those chiefly taken from Carteret Precinct,) inhabiting where then is the necessity of these divisions? these new appointments?

3 These Divisions and Subdivisions, as they would make a great alteration of the Representation in the House of Burgesses, and as there was not, (as we could perceive) any visible & apparent necessity for such new Precincts, We concluded the Assembly whenever they should meet (as these remarks are very obvious) would look upon them as an innovation and violation of the Privileges, and so might prove such a stumbling Block as might prevent their proceeding to busyness, which has been long desired, as is very requisite both for His Majesty's service and the publick Utility. We could give several other reasons which moved

us, but that we would contract this paper as much as may be and some of them might perhaps offend the Governor We shall therefore decline reciting them here, and content ourselves with representing them elsewhere

As to those insinuations His Excellency is pleased to make of our affecting popularity, they touch us not, nor give us any uneasyness, because we are conscious we have had no such view: what we have said in asserting the Privileges of our fellow subjects against what we esteemed incroachments of Governors and Councils on them, has been with great caution, we have a true sense of our duty & loyalty to His Majesty, and the strictest regard to his interest, not pretending in the least to deny or even dispute the royal Prerogative, which (totidem terbis) in our said Paper we have declared our most gracious King as He is tender of his Prerogatives (which tend always to his peoples good) so is he of the rights and privileges of his subjects, and of this we are made sensible by the Instructions to the Governor, wherein cautioning him against suffering Assemblies to assume uncommon Privileges, to which they are not entitled, the rule he gives or prescribes for their limitation, is that of the Priviledges of the Parliament of Great Brittain. And can we desire more? No Thus good & thus gracious is our most gracious King to us his subjects far remov'd from his royal Person, therefore we cannot think our asserting such rights as he admits us graciously, to enjoy, will be offensive to him or his Ministry, nor that the love of our Country, or the spirit of Patriotism, (if his Excellency is pleased so to call it,) is inconsistent with our places in Council, for we assure His Excellency we shall always consult His Majesty's interest and have the tenderest regard to his prerogatives, whether we are in or out of His Council, and indeed we cannot conceive how the contending for a just and equal representation of the People will interfere with them or obstruct his interest, or how an unequal one will advance it

We shall now endeavour to give an account of the Constitution of our Legislature & of it's Original.

It will (we believe) be acknowledged the birthright of British subjects, to be governed by no Laws but what are of their own making, that is, such as they have assented to on the first planting or settling of this Colony this right was confirmed to the Inhabitants by Charters from King Charles the Second, in which, such as should remove hither, and their Descendants or Posterity born in the Colony were declared free Denizens and liege People of the Crown of England, and as it was necessary (the Laws of England not being in all Cases and Circumstances suitable to so remote a Country) that there should be Laws enacted and made for the due Government thereof, that King of his royal authority granted to the Proprietors, together with the People (their advice, assent and approbation being requisite and necessary) a power of making Laws, reserving allegiance to the Crown, and a due subjection or subordination to our Mother Country   In this Grant the manner of the People's assenting to such Laws, or if it shall be requisite the appointment of Deputies or Delegates to represent them, is left entirely to the People, and not to the Direction of the Proprietors   The words, (after a recital of the words empowering the Proprietors) are these vizt "by and with the advice, assent and approbation of the Freemen of the said Province or Territory, or of the Freemen of the County, Barony or Colony for which such Law or Constitution shall be made, or the greatest part of them, or of their Delegates or Deputies, so that in the infancy of the Colony, when the People were few, the whole might have met, advised, assented to and approved such Laws as should be made, but that King foreseeing the Inconveniencies which in Process of Time, when the Colony should abound with People, might arise from such numerous Assemblies, seems to have provided against it, by inserting an Alternative in these words, vizt "or their Delegates or Deputies" impowering hereby the whole to choose a less number to represent them and this we think without any dependency on the Proprietors for Directions of Representation. and indeed it's absurd to think when the whole People, one part of the Legislature, have had a right of advising and assenting to Laws, that the Proprietors the other part, (much less their Deputies should have the power of transfering such right from the whole people to (we will say) one eigth or any less part, as by directing and altering at their pleasure the Representation, they might   Pursuant to the Charters aforesaid, Fundamental Constitutions were formed in the year 1669, which in the Province of North Carolina, (tho' not in South) the People received In these as his Excellency observes Albemarle County (then the whole of this Governm^t) was divided into four Precincts, which were to send twenty members, that the People's assent to the receiving these Constitutions was requisite, is evident   Why else were their delegates required to sign them? why were they not imposed on the People of South Carolina, who refused to receive them?   Again after these, in the year 1698, there was another set of Constitutions formed which were signed & sealed by the Proprietors.

These Constitutions are evidences of the Compact and agreement in those times as to the formation of the Legislature between the Proprietors and the People of North Carolina, (for as we have said the People of South Carolina would not agree to receive them, tho' they were equally designed for both Provinces) and that the Proprietors did not think themselves solely invested with a power of directing the Representation of the People, is evident from these Constitutions themselves.

The 10ᵗʰ section of the 2ᵈ sett are in these words viz' "The present "number of the Representatives of the Commons shall be
"who (as the County shall increase,) shall also proportionably be "increased, if the Commons do so desire, but shall in no future time be "increased beyond one hundred

The 19ᵗʰ Section are in these words, viz' "the whole Provinces shall "be divided into Counties by the Parliament

Give us leave to observe that in the time intervening these two setts of Constitutions the Assembly proceeded to direct elections, as for instance, in the year 169⅘ by a biennial Act in which they ordained that every Precinct in new Counties should send but one Member, accordingly in the next ensuing Assembly, viz' in the month of Novʳ 1697, there came but two Representatives from the whole County of Bath viz' Richᵈ Smith and Nicholas Daw In the year 1699 there was a Biennial Act passed, in the latter end of which there is a clause wherein are these words, viz' if this Bill be ratifyed and confirmed by the Lords Proprietors under their hands and seals, then the Constitutions shall be void, or otherwise that the section or sections relating to biennial Parliaments shall take place as formerly received amongst us.

This Clause plainly shews that the Delegates of the People thought themselves concerned in the form of Representation, and also that the aforementioned Constitutions were not imposed on them, but assented to and received by them

After this in Governor Cary's time, Bath County which sent at first but two Members, was by Govʳ and Council divided into Archdale and Wickham Precincts and sent four members, and again in the Governors Hyde and Eden's times were added Craven and Carteret Precincts by the Governor and Council, and the names of Archdale and Wickham Precincts were changed into those of Beaufort and Hyde In the year 1715 the Assembly proceeded to fix and establish this form of Representation by what is commonly called the Biennial Act.

We will now allow or suppose that that Assembly did not (perhaps) dispute the Power of the Governor and Council but we cannot therefore grant, that from their assenting to a Law to allow of and establish those Precincts, the inference is necessary that they approved of them as legally and regularly appointed the contrary we think may be more naturally inferred, for if they were legally and regularly appointed, what need was there of a Law to establish them? Nor can we be of the opinion that the not disputing the Govern' and Council's Power herein gave them any

We come now with his Excellency to the year 1722, or thereabouts, when this supposed Power of the Governor and Council was contested, and here we think his Excellency gives up the point for he allows that the Governor and Council thought they could not erect Bertie Precinct because it was against Law, therefore they concurred with the Assembly or Delegates of the People to erect that Precinct If the Power of erecting was in the Governor and Council solely, what need was there of the assent of the People?

If it be said it is by Law they have this Power, where is that Law? and how, in what words is the Power conveyed? how, by whom, and in what words have the People divested themselves of their natural right confirmed to them by a royal Charter and long enjoyed (viz' that of choosing their own Representatives) and resigned it to Governors & Councils solely? It is true some Governors and Councils may have construed these words in some Biennial Acts, (viz' " Precincts to be erected) to convey to them a Power of erecting Precincts for sending new Representatives of the People, and so (tho' the inference is in no wise just,) deeming themselves Trustees of the Legislature, or rather the People, in that point have proceeded to erect four Precincts, the validity of which appointments, (tho' perhaps not disputed) was so far doubted of, as afterwards to require the assent of the People, or their Deputies, by an Act to confirm them

That the Assembly in 1722 did not allow such Power to be in the Governor and Council, is plain, for being about to erect a Precinct their Power was controverted and given up, and the Precinct erected with the advice and consent of the People or their Delegates by Act of Assembly Again in the year 1729 there was an attempt by Governor and Council to erect new Hanover into a Precinct, Their Power was contested and denyed by that Assembly, and the new Representatives not admitted to sit and vote in the House till accepted & approv'd of by the Assembly, being confirmed and allowed of by a Clause in the Bill for emitting Money on Loan. The same Assembly erected a Precinct by the name of Tyrrel, which by Act of that Assembly was to send but three Representatives

By this Account the whole force of his Excell'n argument, will be this some (two or three) Governors and their Councils, fancying that

some words viz.ᵗ (Precincts to be erected) in a Biennial Act, gave the
Governor and Council the Power of erecting Precincts to send Representatives of the People, proceeded to appoint four Precincts, the validity
of which appointments (tho' perhaps not disputed, the Representation
being pretty equal & just) yet was so far doubted of as to require the
assent of the People or their Delegates by Act of Assembly to establish
them   The Precedents of the erecting these four Precinct are to be
opposed to the People's natural rights or privileges, the grant of Confirmation of them in the royal Charter, the Contract between the Proprietors & the People in the Constitution, the Precedents and Practice
before the time of erecting those four Precincts, the Precedents since, as
well as the denial of such Power by the People or their Deputies in
Assembly ever since   We leave His Excellency or any other reader to
judge whether they are of sufficient weight.

Our second Argument viz.ᵗ, that it is absurd to think or say that a
Power of part should be greater than that of the whole, and that as the
Constitution of the legislature must be antecedent to any Act thereof it
cannot be dependent on any such Act, much less on an Act of part, His
Excellency charges with absurdity, and leaves us to explain ourselves
For by this Argument says His Excellency, Acts of Assembly would
not erect new Precincts, we acknowledge there seems to be an absurdity,
but it proceeds from this   From giving the Title of Acts of Assembly
or of Laws to such as may more properly be stiled Fundamental Constitutions   When the several parts or persons out of which a legislative
Body is to be formed & consist, meet together and mutually agree on the
manner of Formation of such body, or of part, and cause such contract
as to such formation to be committed to writing, such instruments of
writing containing such contracts are properly the Fundamental Constitutions of such Legislature, (or evidence, or Records thereof,) but not
Acts of it, this is evident from this invincible reason, viz.ᵗ no corporation or body can act before it is formed, or has a being   To make this
more plain, We will suppose in the Infancy of this Colony the Proprietors and the People to have met, and to have mutually agreed that the
Proprietors should chuse a Governor and Council as their Deputies,
which should represent them, and that twenty persons in a certain manner to be chosen by the People should be delegates of and represent the
People, That these united should constitute or be the form of the Legislature of the Province, the Charters containing such mutual contracts
and agreements would be evidences of the Form or Constitution of the
Legislature and may properly be stiled Fundamental Constitutions.   Let

us now reduce these mutual contracts and agreements into the form of an Act or Law and use an enacting style, will it not run thus? *"Be it enacted by the Governor & Council & Representatives of the People in General Assembly the Legislature of this Province, and it is hereby enacted by the Governor & Council and Representatives of the People in General Assembly the Legislature of this Province, that the Governor and Council and Representatives of the People in General Assembly shall be the Legislature of this Province,* does not this seem absurd? In short such instruments tho' they may run in an enacting stile, are properly records or evidences of the Formation or Constitution of the Legislature and not Acts of it

Does it not savour of absurdity to say that the People have a part in making their Laws, for that their Representatives are to advise, assent and approve of them before they are made, but that the Governor and Council are entirely of themselves to say and direct what shall be the Representatives to give and declare such advice, assent and approbation, as if they may divide old & erect new Precincts at their pleasure, in effect they will do   Will such be the Delegates of the People? Will the People have any part in enacting such laws? Will they not be the Laws of the Governor and Council?

It is plain that our most gracious King is desirous that the form or Constitution of Governm^t of this his Province should as near as may be (allowing for some unavoidable differences wch must and will be between a Mother Country & it's subject infant Colony) resemble that of Great Britain   We cannot therefore think we greatly erred in instancing the caution used by the Parliament of Great Britain of avoiding to touch on what they thought a constitutional point   Neither can we think our instancing the practice & privileges of Virginia amiss, because we cannot believe that our most gracious Sovereign will be willing to deprive the poor People of North Carolina of Privileges allowed to and enjoyed by those of the neighbouring Colonies.

If we have mistaken the sense of His Majesty's Instruction forbidding the erecting new Courts, & that by the words in that Instruction vizt "Court of Judicature" are not intended a Court of Judicature as we construed it but a sort of judicature agreable to His Excellency's Construction, we can only say humanum est errare   our's as it was a liberal one, was to us most obvious

If by proposing to us to recommend to the Assembly some laudable examples of Virginia, His Excellency would insinuate that we have opposed such   we may truly say that we are not conscious of it, nor can

accuse ourselves on that score, particularly as to not encouraging the
Clergy, we believe we have not, and hope shall not, incur any censure,
especially as so good an example is set us by our Governor, whose zeal
for the church is on all occasions so conspicuous.   Let us conclude on the
point in hand, and expostulating with all due submission with his Excellency, let us have leave to ask, why, supposing the People of North Carolina in its infant state, had suffered their Privileges to be encroach'd on,
and had neglected to assert them, why we say should this be pleaded to
deprive them of them entirely?   Why should they only lose them, when
the neighbouring Colonies without any contest enjoy them?   But as we
have (we think shewn that they have always or for the most part, enjoyed
them, as they are privileges which have been granted and confirmed to
them by the Crown, as it does not appear that His Majesty has revoked
such Grants, or directed his Governor to alter the Constitution, as infring-
ing on his royal Prerogatives, which we shall never presume to deny, or
in any wise derogate from, we hope our most indulgent and gracious Sovereign will suffer his poor subjects of North Carolina to continue in the
enjoyment of them,

NATH RICE
JNO. BAPT. ASHE

[B. P R. O. B. T North Carolina Vol. 9 A 46.]

RICE AND ASHE VS BURRINGTON—SALE OF LANDS IN NORTH CAROLINA

LETTER FROM Mr RICE & Mr ASHE, TWO OF Ye COUNCIL OF N
CAROLINA, DATED APRIL 20th 1733.

To the Rgt Honble the Lds Comrs for Trade and Plantations

MAY IT PLEASE YOUR LORDSHIPS

Governour Burrington on his first issuing Warrants for Lands, proceeding Contrary to His Majesty's Comission and Instructions to him, in
selling the King's Lands without any Instruction impowering him so to
do, at the rate of two shill & sixpence Virginia or Proclamation Money
for every fifty Acres, and issuing Warrants for much larger quantities to
some than by the King's Instructions he was directed, Arbitrarily denying or refusing to others what was their Right or Proportion allowed

them by the King, not in the least consulting the Council in the Affair
We objected to the legality of such a Method, and some Petitions of
Persons claiming Rights, (wch had been denyed them by the Govern^r) to
Lands pursuant to the Kings Instructions being read, brought the mat-
ter into Debate in Council, whereupon the Council gave it as their opin-
ion unanimously on reading his Majesty's 42nd Instruction, that every
Person proving his Rights, or swearing to the number of Persons in his
Family, had a claim of fifty acres of Land for every such Person, and
on some Petitions relating to Saw Mills, praying a larger quantity of
Land might be granted, than directed by the King's Instructions, They
likewise unanimously were of the opinion that it could not be allowed

These Opinions of the Council, and the Debates on the Delivery of
them notwithstanding the Governour proceeded to sell and grant Lands
in very large undue Quantities, so that we (thinking ourselves obliged
as much as in us lay to prevent such an unwarrantable Practice, detrimental both to His Majesty's Interest and to the People,) drew up the
annexed Protest, which the Governor (as we believe) suspecting, or
having Intelligence of, broke up the Council unexpectedly, to prevent
its being offered   Thereupon we filed it in the Secretary's office together
with the Caution following the same   This has drawn on us his Excellency's highest displeasure, and being the Cause of many real Injuries
he has done us (of which we shall be obliged by the next Conveyance,
(there being now no time) to inform your Lordships) has brought on us
that load of unjust and groundless Reproaches he has bestowed on us in
his paper herewith sent to your Lordships   We hope and believe your
Lordships will readily pardon us for thus troubling you, when you shall
Consider that it is a Matter relating to the King's Interest, and that we
cannot but be solicitous of Vindicating ourselves and of preventing or
obviating any Misrepresentation of our Conduct and Characters to your
Lordships

      We are with the greatest Submission
        and Respect
          My Lords,
            Your Lordships
              most obedient humble Servants
                        NATH RICE.
                        BAP^s ASHE

20th April 1733

Mʳ Rice and Mʳ Ashe's Remonstrance to Govʳ Burrington   April 20ᵗʰ 1733

To His Excellency the Governour in Council

Nath Rice and John Baptista Ashe, two of the Members of his Majesty's Council, humbly shew, that his Excellency the Governour hath issued One and given a very great Number of Warrants for Lands to sundry Persons in undue and large quantities, not observing the Rule of Proportion prescribed by His Majesty of granting Lands by and with the Advice and Consent of the Council, vizᵗ of fifty Acres only for every Person in the Grantee's Family, For all which Lands mentioned in those Warrants the Governour hath taken for every fifty Acres the sum of two shill. And six pence Virginia Currency in Silver or Gold Wherefore we think ourselves obliged out of a due sense of our Duty to his most Sacred Majesty, to object against the same, & we do hereby humbly pray His Excellʸ that he would be pleased strictly to pursue His Majesty's Instructions to him in that behalf given, & that no Warrants may issue but to such Persons, & in such Proportions, as shall be agreable to His Majesty's said Instructions   We conceive ourselves the more under a Necessity of remonstrating this Matter to your Excellency, for that, if this Method should be disallow'd by the King, it may hereafter very much injure such People as have paid their Monies for such Lands, but more especially for that it is not agreable, but contrary to His Majesty's Instructions to your Excellency on that behalf, which to His Majesty's Council has by your Excellency been exhibited and shewn

NATH RICE.
Jᵒ BAPTᵃ ASHE.

On Argument in the last Council, His Excellency the Governour seeming to have taken a Resolution to pass Warrants as before he had done, which Method we humbly objected against in Council, and prepared the foregoing Paper, designing to have preferred it in Council, but the Council breaking up unexpectedly we were prevented putting it in But now finding that his Excellency still continues to issue Warrants for Land in undue Proportions, and contrary, (as we conceive) to the King's Instructions We think it our Duty to file this by way of Caution in the Secretary's Office, requiring and desiring the Deputy Secretary to prefer the same to His Excellency before he (the Deputy Secretary) subsign or make out any more Warrants; humbly praying His Excellency that if he shall think what we object reasonable, he would be pleased to have Respect thereunto.

NATH RICE
JOHN BAPTᵃ ASHE.

11ᵗʰ November 1733

Governour Burrington's Paper in Relation to Grant of Lands.

GENTLEMEN OF THE COUNCIL

Mr Rice and Mr Ashe sometime after the breaking up of the last Council signed a Paper and put the same into the Secretary's Office, Endorsed upon the outside, Filed in the Secretary's Office November the 11th 1732, which Paper was shewn to me the 13th of this Month   In this Paper I am taxed with not observing my Instructions in granting Lands, which is ridiculous, for there has not one patent passed the Seal since I came into this Province, neither will I sign a Patent for Land before I receive further orders from England

Great numbers of People had been imposed upon by Mr Ashe and others who were Deputy Surveyors before my coming with the King's Commission in the follow* manner   The said Mr Ashe surveyed without Warrants and took Exorbitant Fees from People for so doing and upon their inquiring whither that was sufficient, he told them it was the same thing if he surveyed with or without Warrants, nay that was not all, for Mr Ashe laid out and surveyed great Quantitys of Land for himself on Cape Fear river and parts adjacent, & then sold them to new comers   I have also been inform'd by sundry Persons that Mr Ashe did not regularly make the Surveys, but marked a Couple of Trees in front, and imagined the other bounds, and then drew a plot upon a piece of Paper, these Plots of Mr Ashe's making have been frequently sold and transferred from one man to another, by the craft and knaving of Edward Moseley Mr Ashe and some others in Confederacy

People that came from the adjacent Governments to settle on Cape Fear River were obliged to purchase Lands of them (for they could not obtain them without) by which they acquired great substance   Mr Roger Moore told me they had of him for Land twenty two Negroes, and Bill of Exchange for some Hundred Pound Sterling   When I was last at Cape Fear several men desired my opinion on the following Occasion, they bought Lands about the time and after His Majesty completed the purchase of Carolina of Edward Moseley and Confederates and paid money and Negroes for it, and afterwards had Patents made out in their own Names for the Lands, altho' the same were pretended to belong to Edward Moseley or some other in the Confederacy before their Purchase and as such sold by them,   these men desired me to tell them wither their Titles were good, to which I answered nothing could be said before the King's Pleasure was known, some of these men declared they shou⁴ be ruined if the Lands they had purchased in the manner related were taken from them   But to return to the Paper   a great many People who had no other titles to Lands they had settled and lived some years upon than plotts from Deputy surveyors, thought proper to make Entrys in a regular manner, and obtained Warrants which are constantly entered in three Books,   one is kept in my house, another in the Secretary's Office, and one in the Surveyors which are always shewn to such Persons as desire to inspect them without Fee or Reward   Mr Rice and Mr Ashe say that I have taken two shillings & sixpence is silver Virginia Currency for every fifty Acres which I say is false and will prove to be false in three Particulars

In the first place I have freely given my Fees for taking up Lands to a great many Persons.   2ᵈˡʸ, I have taken in lieu of money Provisions of all kinds and Grain without once refusing any offered me   Thirdly, when Money was paid it was Proclamation And not Virginia currency the Money I have received has scarcely paid the Expenses of Journeys I have taken for the King's service and promoting the good of the Country, And the Provision received for them Fees were but a small part of what have been expended in my House.

Mr Rice & Mr Ashe sent the Deputy secretary to me one day in last Court with a parcel of warrants drawn without my knowledge to be signed for them which I refused, and gave Mr Rice my reasons for it at the Council Table,   that refusal brought on their paper, tho' they say it is out of a sense of their Duty etc.   But I am sure they will gain no man's belief that knows them in this particular,   when the Patents are to be signed, that will be done in Council, and then objections may be made, and if any Person have warrants for more land than they have a right to take up, any man may enter Caveats against them in the mean time I have wrote very fully upon this subject to his Grace the Duke of Newcastle and the Lords of Trade,   am in daily Expectations of Answers upon this Subject,   one thing I will say which is that I have acted for the King in this Respect, as I would have done for myself

As it is known to every man in this Province how Mr Ashe acquired his Estate, I have no occasion to enlarge upon that matter, but as he has shewn in the latter part of his paper a great concern that People should not be injured by paying me the accustomary Fees for taking up Land I take the Liberty to advise and desire Mr Ashe to return to the defrauded men the money he has received for surveying Lands without Warrants, and for sales of Land he had no Right to, which I believe

amount- to a greater sum than ever I received for Fees from the first day
I was Governour of Carolina to this time

Whether I have Exceeded my Instructions or acted contrary to them,
I will advise upon with the Council, and conclude there must be some
design in writing this Paper by the strange manner it was left in the Secretary's Office, by the secretary himself without speaking one word to
me about it, nor proposing any part of what it Contains to the Council

GEO BURRINGTON

Messrs. Rice & Ashe to Gov Burrington   3 April 1733

NORTH CAROLINA—ss.

To His Excellency the Governor and the Honorable the Members of His
Maj'ts Council

To a Paper of ours touching the King's Interest in a part (viz' the disposal of Lands), wherein together with the Governor, the Council are
intrusted, We are surprized His Exce'lly should put in an Answer, consisting chiefly of invidious, personal Reflections for wch there are not the
least Grounds, and which indeed no ways relate to the matter

We beg leave to put this matter in a fair light, so as to remove some
reproaches, which his Exce'lly in his anger has cast on us, in order to
which we shall take notice of two Remarks of the Governor's, The first
is as to the motive, wch, (as he would have it thought) induced us to put
in this paper   He says Mr Rice & Mr Ashe sent the Deputy Secretary
to him one day in the last Court, with a parcel of Warrts drawn without
his knowledge, to be signed for them which he refused. It will be
remembered that on reading the Governor's paper in Council, we immediately deny'd this Assertion, & referred ourselves to the Testimony of
both the Deputy secretary & the Govrn Secy, who being both called before
the Council, the Deputy Secy denyed the matter of fact and the Governrn
Secy declared he knew not of the Dep Secy's bringing any such Warrants, so that that Assertion appears to be without Grounds His Exce'lly
has indeed on many Occasions declared that he would grant no warrants
to persons conveying their Petitions thro' our hands, tho' one of us be
the proper Officer for receiving & preferring the same

The next Remark of the Governor's is, that there was some Design
in writing the Paper, by the strange manner it was left in the Secretary's
Office That there was a Design in it is true, and we should be both
sorry and ashamed to have put in such a Publick paper without Design,

The Design is set forth in the Remonstrance itself, and the reason of its being put in the Secretary's Office is likewise shown in the Caveat, to both which we refer. That Design is the true design, and that Reason the true Reason. More over we beg leave to observe, that tho' the Governor says in this his Paper, that our Paper bearing date the 11ᵗʰ Novʳ 1732 was shown to him the 13ᵗʰ of this month (meaning we suppose March last past for his Excellʸˢ paper bears no date,) Yet the Deputy Secʳʸ being called declared that he gave or offered it to the Governor the day it was filed, *but I would not receive it*

This leads us to take notice of that little the Governor has said in this his paper concerning the subject matter of our said Remonstrance. His Excellʸˢ words are these vizᵗ "In this Paper I am taxed with not observ- "ing my Instructions in granting Lands, which is ridiculous, for there "has not one Patent passed the seal since I came into this Province, "neither will I sign a Patent for Land before I receive further Orders "from England" We can scarce believe our eyes when we see such a Paper as this under His Excellʸˢ own hand. What we objected to in our Paper was His Excellʸˢ receiving Right (or Consideration) Money, and issuing Warrants without advice & Consent of Council in undue Quan- tities, contrary to the King's Instructions, and this too after the unani- mous Opinion of the Council to the Contrary. To which His Excellʸ makes the foregoing Answer, from which if we infer anything to the purpose, it must be, That he may issue Warrants without the advice and consent of the Council, & that tho' he receives moneys (not directed to be received by the King) for Lands, and issues Warrants in undue Quantities putting the People to the Charge of making the Surveys & some to that of settling such Lands, yet he acts not contrary to the King's Instructions (the objection of the injury done the People passing without other notice than his Endeavour to Recriminate) because he signs no Patents. The contrary of which we shall now make evident.

It is plain not only from his Majesties Instructions but also from his Comission to His Excellʸ, that the Agreements with the People or Inhab- itants for Lands are to be made by & with the Advice & consent of the Council, as well as the Grants, before such Agreements the Warrant cannot legally issue, and inded it serves, (or ought to serve) as well for the Certificate in writing of the Contract as for an order to the Surveyor General for the Admeasuremᵗ, & tho' it is not an absolute Right to or Fee in the Lands, yet (where it is legally issued & according to the King's Instructions,) it is a virtuall & initial Right & ought to be obligatory on the Grantor to confirm & convey the Lands (in fee or according to the contract) to the Grantee.

It is certain and well known that all persons taking out Warr.ts expect to have Patents or Grants for as much Land as is expressed in the Warrant to the Survey.r Gen.ll & they have the greater reason to expect it where they pay Right money or a Consideration, but the Gov.r says, or rather the necessary Inference from what he says is, that they ought not to expect it, for that he may take monies for more Lands than he is empowered to grant, & issuing Warrants may cause an admeasurem.t to the Buyers or takers up in order to their obtaining Grants, but that he has not, nor will give out Grants or Patents for such Lands Supposing a Letter of Attorney to be given to a Person empowering him to agree with and to grant and convey Lands to John or to James, with an express Exception or Limitation that he shall not agree with grant or convey those lands to Thomas, might it not as justly as what is now said be said, It is true the Attorney could not, & should not grant Deed of Conveyance to Thomas for such Lands, but (the Exception notwithstanding) he might contract or agree with Thomas for such Lands, and receive a Consideration, provided he did not Execute Deeds of Conveyance

We shall leave his Exce.lly to account for the justice of such a Method of proceeding or acting

What the Governor says as to fixing falsities on Us will appear to have very little weight   It is plain that in our Paper when we say two shillings & sixpence for every fifty acres, we mean it for the rule of proportion by which his Excellency takes the Gold and Silver, if so, then the first particular of falsity vanishes, even tho' his Excellency should have bestowed this Right Money on many Persons, tho' we have been altogether ignorant of such his Bounty, till he himself has now informed Us.

2. It concerns not us, nor is it to the purpose, what his Excellency takes in lieu of Gold and Silver   We suppose his Excellency in taking Provisions or grain has had his pennyworth for his Penny, however we can truely say that till now, we have never heard or understood that he would take anything in lieu, except Cows & Calves to be delivered at Cape Fair, at the rate of 25 shillings for a Cow and Calf, which is esteemed there an exceeding small price, and as to the Currency of the Country, it has been refused, (we have heard) at 6, 7 & 8 for 1, tho' the Governor has taken a great many of his Fees in Currency

3 The disparity between Virginia and Proclamation Money is so small, that such a Mistake is not worth contending about and we believe still his Excellency for some time might have taken Virginia money, tho' he has since altered his practice, and takes Proclamaõon, this if we are guilty of a Mistake has lead us into it   If we have erred we acknowledge our

Error and pray that it may be rectifyed and called Proclamation Money Mr Ashe says that he is sorry that the doing what he thought his Duty, in an Affair wherein, with and among others, he is (as it were) a Trustee of His Majesty, should so provoke his Excellency, as to throw on him (tho' foreign to the purpose) so many groundless and unjust Calumnies, which were they calculated for this Province only where he is known, as they would have no effect, he should pass them over without any Notice, but as they seemed signed to asperse his Character with Gentlemen who are Strangers to him, he thinks himself obliged and begs leave to say that His Excellency has been very unsuccessful in all his attempts to fix a blemish on him Last January was twelve months Mr Ashe was brought 200 miles to answer a General Charge among others, wherein was no particular Person named as his accuser and in which he was not accused, he complained of the hardships he was laid under thereby, and made an Answer or Defence, (if it may be properly so called, where he was not named as accused,) to it. The General Charge was inserted into and remains on the Council Journal but his Excellency would not suffer that Answer, which set the matter in a clear Light to be inserted But his Excellency did Mr Ashe so much justice as at that time to declare he had never heard any Complaints of him as to what he is now charged with it would be too tedious to descend to every particular, he therefore in the General says, that he knows what small Estate he has to be so justly acquired that he will not only (as his Excellency advises and desires) restore, but if any person complains and makes it appear that he has injured him, he will restore him four fold If his Excellency of his great Justice had condescended to have particularized & named the persons complaining with the Matters complained of, he should have known how to have answered, till he so does, he can only say generally That he was formerly a Deputy Surveyor and laid out Lands pursuant to an order of Governor and Council, part which his Excellency was formerly Governor of which Lands as the Law and Custom always was, he gave the takers up Plots, which Plots they may have transferred to others (as he supposes they well might,) and in no way concerns him whether they did or did not, or whether they could so do As to the Governor's bringing Mr Moseley's name into his paper, he cannot imagine it was for any other purpose than to tack these two hard words, Craft and Knavery, to Mr Moseley's name and his with an etc, because Mr Moseley had no Concern, nor was any ways mentioned in the Matter in dispute, which was the Granting Warrants for Land contrary to the King's Instructions. He thinks he need say nothing concerning Mr Moseley's Character, because

59

he believes it to be so well Established as not to suffer anything by such attempts to blemish it, only this he is desired to say, that Mr Moseley never sold any Lands to Mr Roger Moor on Cape Fair River, he confesses he has sold him Rights which he had to take up Land from the Proprietors, with and by which he believes Mr Moor has himself taken up Lands very much to his profit and Advantage.

But Mr Ashe avers he never had a Negro, or one penny either stirling or other Money for Land or for Rights to hand from Mr Roger Moor, so that he knows not how to account for this Charge and accusation exhibited against him in the name of Mr Moor If Mr Moor has made any Complaint to his Excellency of any Injury of this nature which Mr Ashe has done him, he has done Mr Ashe much Injustice, if not the Governor has done Mr Moor much injustice in reporting him as the author of a scandal or Calumny, (if it may be so called) so groundless.

If Mr Moor will show that Mr Ashe ever had a Negro or one shilling stirling Money of him either for lands sold him or for his Rights to any Land, Mr Ashe will deliver to him not only the twenty two Negroes, but all the Sterling Money he has expended that way, if what small Estate he has, will raise it or amount to it

If Mr Moor shall deny his making any such Charge or Complaint of or against Mr Ashe, (as it is no doubt he will,) the Governor will certainly do Mr Ashe the justice to acknowledge, that tho' he has used much Art to calumniate him, yet he has not been able to fix any scandal on him

                                        NATH RICE.
3rd Aprill 1733.   Jno BAPT ASHE

The Case of Mr Moseley Concerning Warrants for Land in North Carolina

[Recd with Mr Rice & Mr Ashe's letter of 20 Apl 1733]

To the Right Honorable the Lords Commissioners for Trade and Plantations

The Petition or Memorial of Edward Moseley of North Carolina Gent Humbly sheweth

That your Petitioner having very often made application that he might have Warrants for Land agreable to His Majesty's Royal Instructions, and the same being denyed him, tho' granted to multitudes of other Persons at the Govern's will and Pleasure, For relief under such a hardship he Petitioned the Governour and Council July 31, 1732, which

Petition was granted by an Order of Council at the following October General Court

Your Petitioner thereupon requested Mr Forster the Deputy Secretary to make out a Warrant for Three Thousand one hundred Acres pursuant to the Order of Council, who did so, but told your Petitioner the Governor would not sign it until seven Pounds fifteen shillings Proclamation Money was paid for it, This your Petitioner looked on as a Hardship, there being no Law of this Province, or Royal Instruction requiring such a Payment to the Governour Nevertheless being in want of Land for his slaves to work on, he consented, and told Mr Williams the Governour's Secretary, that he would endorse so much as paid to your Petitioner on the back of an obligation the Governour passed for Fourty six Pounds sterling he owed your Petitioner, but this would not be allowed of as Mr Williams told your Petitioner

Thereupon he did again Petition the Governor and Council, the thirtieth day of March last past, setting forth the hard & severe usuage he met with from the Governour and pray'd Relief, which Petition he has been informed was that day read in Council and Debated, but the Governour would not suffer any Entry to be made thereof.

Your Petitioner being afterwards given to understand that he might have Land on the aforesaid Order of Council if he would pay the sum before demanded, and being much in want of Land for his Slaves at Cape Fear to work on he concluded to take it on those Terms, rather than suffer, altho' no Resolution was past by the Council that such sum ought to be paid, Thereupon your Petitioner gave Directions to the Deputy secretary to make out five Warrants for five hundred Acres each and one for six hundred, making in the whole Three Thousand one hundred, and paid unto him half a pistole being so much the Governor instructed him to receive as the Ballance the rest of the Money, as he understands, the Governour allow'd for Interest on his Obligation aforementioned past to your Petitioner, Interest being mentioned therein

But so it is, the Governour refused to sign those Warrants, and your Petitioner was again put off, and being given to understand that it was thought the Governour would alter his mind, and sign them, if that matter was again moved, Your Petitioner did write unto the Governour's Secretary the fifth of this present April, to which he received from Mr Williams An Answer the same day, together with a Warrant in the Governour's own hand writing for 3100 Acres all in one Tract, mentioned to be at a place exceeding far from the Place Your Petitioner designed or desired

Your Petitioner being informed that the Governour had been at an Entertainment, and imagining that this proceeded only from a gaiety of temper, and a willingness of the Governour to show his wit at your Petitioner's Expense, He wrote to Mr Williams the sixth of Aprill, and desired to have in lieu of the Warrant for 3100 those six warrants before mentioned, In Answer whereto Mr Williams wrote the same day a Letter to your Petitioner, wherein he return'd the Warrant for 3100 and informed your Petitioner that the Governor would not sign those Warrants, which he called in fact Blank Warrants, Whereas in truth those Warr contained the Number of Acres, and the Precinct where to be taken up with other Descriptions of Place than what the Governor has been pleased to insert in that Warrant he sent your Petitioner Nor did yr Petitioner ever desire to have those Warr other than to have the number of Acres, & in what Precinct to be survey'd Exprest therein, as in fact those Warrants were so shown to yr Petitioner by Mr Forster, but yr Petitioner hoped & expected that he should have the liberty of laying out those Warr on such vacant Lands in those Precincts as he pleased, & not where the Governor pleased, The Law of this Province, Entituled an Act to regulate divers Abuses in the taking up Lands etc, passed in the year 1715, directing that the Surv should Endorse on the back of the Warr the place where the taker up intends to have his Land survey'd by that Warr Your Petitioner humbly lays the hardship of this his Case before your Lrs, the truth of which will appear from the several attested Copies hereto annexed, And he humbly prays that your Lordships will duely consider thereof, so as he may be Relieved

And your Petitioner as in Duty bound shall ever pray etc

E MOSELEY

No CAROLINA—ss

On this seventh day of Aprill 1733 Before Us Nathaniel Rice & John Baptista Ashe Esqrs Members of His Majesty's Council of North Carolina, Personally appeared Moseley Vail of Chowan Precinct, who on his oath on the Holy Evangelists taken saith, That the Petition to the Govern and Council hereto annexed he verily believes to be a true Copy, he having examined it by one his Depont Copied from the Original before it was delivered the said Depont further saith that the several Letters between Mr Moseley and Mr Williams hereto annexed, to the best of his Judgement are true Copies, this Depont having carried and brought the originals to and from each other, that he hath Examined those from Mr Moseley to Mr Williams by the Copies of the Originals, which Copies he signed for his greater Certainty, and he hath now compared in presence of Us the Subscribers the Copies of Mr Williams's Letters by the Originals he brought   And we do hereby Certify, that the Original Warrant, now produced to be Examined, we do verily believe to be the Governor's own hand writing And that the Letters from Mr Williams now produced and examined were wrote by Mr Williams, we being well acquainted with the Governours handwriting and his Secretary's   And we do further Certify that we were present in Council when Mr Moseley's Petition was read the thirtieth of March last past, (which the annexed we think is a true Copy of) that Debates arose in Council thereon, One of us moved that the same might be Entred, But the Governour absolutely refused

Sworn before Us & certifyed the Day & Year first above written

NATH RICE
J^{no} BAPst ASHE.

N^o CAROLINA—ss.

To His Excellency George Burrington Esqr Govr & Comm^r in Chief of His Majesty's Province of North Carolina, & to the Hono^{ble} the Members of his Majesty's Council for the said Province.

The Petition of Edward Moseley Gent, Humbly sheweth

That yor Petitioner having a considerable number of Slaves, and no Lightwood land for his Slaves to make Tar, he applyed himself to the Secretary's office, & to the Governour's Secretary, sometime after His Excellency's arrival in order to obtain a Warrant for Six Hundred Acres of Land, but was told, (after repeated application) by Mr Forster the Deputy Secretary of this Province, and by Mr Williams his Excellency's Secretary; that the Governour would not on any Terms let your Petitioner have any Warrants for Land, altho' your Petitioner represented his great want of Lightwood Land, and was ready, & offered to pay what should be required for the same   Your Petition^r conceiving that he had a Right to take up lands according to the number of his family pursuant to His Majesty's Royal Instructions, and that he was very much injured by His Excellency's not granting him a Warrant, when he had issued divers hundreds Warrants to Persons who had not as he conceives such just a claim to take up Land as your Petitioner had, Thereupon he filed a Petition the 31 of July 1732 To His Excellency the Governor and Council (being the first of that kind since his Excellency's arrival) Praying that a Warrant might issue for your Petitioner to take up Lands pursuant to His Majesty's Royal Instructions, Which Petition was read

in Council the   day of   following, being the first Council held after
filing his Petition, and an order of Governor and Council passed, that
your Petitioner should have a Warr' for 3100 Acres on your Petitioners
proving his Rights, Accordingly your Petitioner pursuant thereto proved
Rights for 3100 acres and lodged the same proof in the Secretary's office
pursuant to order of Council past for that purpose   But from that time
your Petitioner cannot obtain Warr⁸ for Lands, altho' ready to pay the
Fees justly due for the same, a Demand being made that your Petitioner
should pay 2⁸ 6ᵈ silver money to His Excellency the Governours Use, as
due to him for Rights, altho' your Petitioner hath proved his Rights as
aforesaid

Your Petitioner therefore humbly prays, that the hardship of his Case
may be considered by this Board, inasmuch as he Conceives there is not
the least pretence, either by the Laws of this Province or by His Majesty's Royal Instructions for such a Damand, And that your Petitioner
may be heard by himself and Council Learned in the Law touching the
premises, And that Warrants may issue pursuant to the Royal Instructions for your Petitioner to have so much Land as he hath proved Rights,
Your Petitioner being ready to pay such Demands as this Board shall
declare he ought to pay agreable to the Laws of the Province or His
Majesty's Royal Instructions

And your Petitioner as in Duty bound shall ever pray etc.

                                        E MOSELEY

                                        CHOWAN April 5 1733
SIR

As I have now a passage to Cape Fear, I desire to have the Warrants
sent me, which yesterday you said would be ready for me   Mᶜ Forster
told me he delivered the Gold, I now send by Moseley Vail Paper
money to pay the Secretary's Fees and the Surveyor General's

            I am Sir
                Your most humble servant

                                        E. MOSELEY

To Mᶜ Ayliffe Williams
        at Edenton

N B Moseley Vail carryed 14th paper money, Mᶜ Williams took five
pounds for Surveyor Generals Fee for Entry of the Warrant

SIR

Upon your Letter the Governour imediately signed the enclosed Warrant for 3100 acres, and says, that if any of your Friends are inclined

to settle that part of the Province, He will always be as ready as now to show how much he has at heart the settling the said part of this Colony, And upon the whole he concluded that you (Sir) think a Governour nothing, But that in the end you will find him the first man in the Province

I am Sir

Your most humble servant

A WILLIAMS

Edenton, April 5 1733

I pray'd this Instant the half pistole to the Governors Account which with the Interest money on the note of hand and the Governor and Mr Littles pays his Fees

A W

For Col^o Edwd Moseley, then

To the Surveyor General Greeting

You are forthwith to lay out and admeasure unto Edwd Moseley of Chowan a Plantation containing Three thousand and one hundred acres of Land lying in Bladen Precinct on the North East side of the North West River beginning on the line of Sr Richd Everard Bart above the Haw old Fields Observing His Majesty's Instructions for running out of Lands and a Platt and Certificate thereof to return into the Secretary's Office, and for so doing this shall be your Warrant

GEO BURRINGTON

Given at Edenton under my hand the 6th day of April Anno Dom 1733 Rights proved.

R^d Forster Dep Secry

Entered a Certificate in the office the 6th day of Aprill 1733

A WILLIAMS Dep Surv^r

N B The Warrants, E. M desired were four for New Hanover, and but two for Bladen and were so filled up by Mr Forster, to complete the 3100 Acres, as I have set forth in my Petition to the Board of Trade.

CHOWAN April 6th 1733

SIR

My desire was not to have the Warrants for 3100 acres of Land so far up the Country, Nor did I expect His Excellency would have given himself the trouble to write the Warrant himself, the Warrants for the Land I desired being prepared by the Deputy Secretary, I therefore put under this cover the Warrant sent me yesterday, desiring to have in Exchange thereof those Warrants that were prepared by Mr Forster which he showed me

His Excellency makes a wrong Conclusion for me, if he imagines I think a Governour Nothing, I always thought and still do, with His Excellency, that every Governour of a Province, representing his Majesty, is the first Man in it.

I am sir
Your most humble servant

E MOSELEY

To Mr Ayliffe Williams at Edenton.

EDENTON, April 6th 1733.

SIR

I communicated yours to the Governour, who says them warrants you mention to be prepared by the Deputy Secretary, were in fact Blank Warrants, and such as he will not —— sign   I am order'd to let you know the Enclosed Warrant is entered in the Books, which cannot be altered

I am sir
Yr most humble servt

A WILLIAMS

To Colo Edwd Moseley, this

The Objections of Mr Rice & Mr Ashe, two of the Council of N. Carolina against Mr Owen's being admitted a member of ye sd Council, together with their Affidavit of Govr Burrington's refusing to suffer their Objections to be Entred

[Recd with Mr Rice & Mr Ashe's letter of 20 Apl. 1733]

His Excellency the Governour having been pleased to appoint William Owen Esqr a Member of His Majesty's Council within this Province, as it is a point which greatly affects his Majesty's Council, We think it our Duty to object thereunto

In as much as it is contrary, to His Majesty's Royal Instructions, which forbid his Excellency to add any more Members to His Majesty's Council, there being seven in the Province, And we beg leave to show that at the time the sd Mr Owen was sworn into the Council, there were eight Members in the Province, Viz: Nath Rice, Robt Halton, Jno Bapt Ashe, Matt Rowan, Eleazor Allen, Jno Lovick, Edmd Gale, Wm Forbes Esqr, and that there are now seven besides the said Owen

NATH RICE.
JOHN Ba ASHE.

The 7ᵗʰ of April 1733. This day came before me John Montgomery Esqʳ His Majesty's Attorney General of this Province, two of the Members of His Majesty's Council viz' Nath Rice Esqʳ Secʸ, & John Bapᵗ Ashe Esqʳ, who being duely sworn on the Holy Evangelists Declared,

That on the first day of the Council's meeting in March last, they offered the within Objection to the Governor in Council, desiring that it might be entred, which the Governor after reading the same absolutely refused, saying, I am Governour here, I will do as I think fit; You may Complain if you will, I will answer it.

NATH RICE.
BAPTᵃ ASHE.

Jurᵗ Coramm
 8° die April 1733

JOHN MONTGOMERY.

Deposition of Mʳ Montgomery, Attorney General of North Carolina, Relating to several abuses he has suffered from Capᵗ Burrington Governour of that Province.

[Recᵈ with Mʳ Rice & Mʳ Ashe's letter of 20 Apl. 1733.]

John Montgomery Esqʳ Attorney General of the said Province came before us Nathaniel Rice and John Baptista Ashe Esqʳˢ Members of His Majesty's Councill, and upon the Holy Evangelists deposeth That the greatest part of the time he has executed the said office Mʳ Burrington Governour of the said Province, has been so far from treating him with that Respect due to his Post or supporting him in the Execution of his office, that on the contrary he has even in Publick Courts of Justice treated him with Indignity and Contemptuous and abusive Language, and not content to use him in that manner, has taken great pains to deprive him of his said office and has carried his hatred and animosity to him to so great a height (as he verily thinks and has reason to believe) as to Design to take away his life or to do him some great Injury, and once did Endeavour to execute that Design in the manner herein sett forth   This Deponᵗ says that some time ago he had notice given him that the Governor's hatred to him was so great, that it was apprehended he would proceed to use violence against him, and that it would be prudent to avoid meeting him as much as possible. Whereupon this Deponᵗ did decline as much as his business would permit to meet him, but notwithstanding his Caution, the Governor one morning in January

last, went into the house of one Trotter in the town of Edenton, and came
into a room in the said house where this Depon[t] then was, and immediately without any sort of Provocation given by him this Deponent took
up a Chair and Damned this Deponent, then with all his force (as he
believes) attempted to strike him on the head therewith (this Deponent
being then unarmed) but this Deponent having raised his arm, saved his
head from the Stroak, and received it on his arm, which was thereby
bruised and wounded and so disabled that for some time after this Deponent was deprived of the use thereof Immediately after the said
assault the Governor attempting to strike him a second time, this Deponent opposed another Chair, and thereby prevented him, and then the
Governor closed with this Deponent and after some struggle got him
down and with his knee several times violently punched him on his Belly,
and verily believes if some persons had not interposed he the Governour
would have used his utmost Endeavour to deprive him of life or to do
him some great Injury Immediately after the said assault and violence
this Deponent did (in regard he could not have liberty to execute his
office in peace) require his Excellency to grant him a Licence to depart
out of the Province Whereupon His Excellency desired him to stay till
the next Council, and then he would grant him or he should have a
Licence to go to the Devill, and at the same time challenged this Deponent
to meet and fight him in Virginia This Deponent further says that his
Friends have advised him to forbear appearing in the Town of Edenton
(where His Excellency resides and where the Council and General Courts
are held) as dangerous for this Deponent, and this Deponent says he has
accordingly declined (as much as conviently he can) going into, or
appearing in the said Town, for that he verily believes it to be dangerous
for him to be often there.

                                        JOHN MONTGOMERY
Jurat coram Nobis 7[o] die Aprilis 1733.

                                        NATH RICE Sec
                                        J[no] BAP[t] ASHE.

                        ———

[B. P R. O. North Carolina B T Vol. 9 A 31]

                        ———

At the Court of S[t] James's the 10th day of May 1733
                        Present
        The Kings most Excellent Majesty in Councill
Upon reading this day at the Board a representation from the Lords
Commissioners for Trade and Plantation together with a draught of a

Commission prepared by the said Lords Commissioners for Gabriel Johnston Esq' to be Captain Generall and Governor in Chief in and over the Province of North Carolina in America, which draught of a Commission being in the usual form—His Majesty in Councill was pleased to approve thereof and to order, as it is hereby ordered, that His Grace the Duke of Newcastle one of His Majesty's principal Secretarys of State do cause a Warrant to be prepared for His Majesty's royal signature in order to pass the said draught of a Commission (which is hereunto annexed) under the Great Seal of Great Britain.

A true copy

W SHARPE.

[B. P R. O. NORTH CAROLINA B. T VOL. 9. A 40.]

LETTER FROM CAPTAIN BURRINGTON GOVERNOR OF NORTH CAROLINA, DATED MAY 19th 1733 IN ANSWER TO THE SECRETARY'S LETTER OF THE 16th OF AUGUST 1732. AND A FURTHER ACCOUNT OF THE STATE OF AFFAIRS IN THAT GOVERNMENT WITH SEVERAL COPIES OF PUBLICK PAPERS ANNEXED TO IT.

NORTH CAROLINA May 19th 1732 [1733.]

MY LORDS OF TRADE AND PLANTATION,

The 26th day of March past, I received a letter from your Secretary Mr Popple, dated August the 16th 1732 by the way of South Carolina, which obliges me to send your Lordships the following Answer.

I had much occasion to complain of Mess" Ashe Smith and Porter, for obstructing His Majesty's Service in this Province and had sufficient reason to Judge, they would endeavour to misrepresent my conduct as the sequel has demonstrated.

All that I have wrote to your Lordships concerning Mr Porter shall be proved by Witnesses of undoubted credit, and I will proceed, in the exact manner prescribed, in your Secretary's letter thō Mr Porter has once refused to do the Same (Publickly in the Council Chamber) he may perhaps alter his opinion in July at the Sitting of the General Court; I am necessitated to stay till that time because it is not possible to get my Witnesses together before.

I know not what Mr Popple intends, by inserting the following words, *And as you renounced any Favour from their Lordships.* I have made no such renunciation In my first letter to your Board I signified that I thought my conduct did not need any favour therefore only desired your Lordships would do me Justice Your Lordships know better than I can do at this Distance, what Justice you have done me

Mr Popple in the next Paragraph writes that your Lordships cannot help observing that Mr Porter stood acquitted by the Old Councellours, and only condemned, by those I had nominated for New ones. This Observation (that your Lordships could not help makeing) surely is not well grounded, for that Colo Jenoure, and Coll Halton who were the foremost in rank of Councellours when Mr Porter was suspended did both vote his Suspension those members of Council (vizt) Mr Ashe, Mr Rowan and Mr Harnet that voted against Porters being Suspended did not acquit Mr Porter of any one Article alleadged by me against him, but it may be worth observing that on the day before Porters Suspention (the 20th of January 173½) the Council unanimously gave their opinion that Porter was not fit to Sitt at the Council board and notwithstanding that Declaration Mr Ashe, Mr Rowan and Mr Harnet the next day voted against his being Suspended I pray your Lordships to let me know your thoughts of their behaviour on that occasion

I gave your Lordships so full and so true an account of the reasons that induced me to introduce Mr Lovick and Mr Gale into his Majesty's Council of this Province in a letter bearing date the 4th of September 1731 as I thought would have given your Lordships full satisfaction of my Proceedings in that Matter but as it is your Lordships pleasure to expect an exact Account, I now send the best I am able

It was publickly reported in this part of the Province and credited that Mr Ashe was gone for England when Mr Lovick and Mr Gale were Sworne Members of the Council and that Mr Rice the Secretary was at the same time in South Carolina but it appeared that Mr Ashe did not go for England and it Might be that Mr Rice was returned from South Carolina about the said time   there were besides these two Councellours, Coll Jenoure, Coll Halton Mr Porter and Mr Harnett within the Province and no more   Mr Allen appointed one of the Council in the Instructions, was not then in this Country neither has he yet been Sworn If Mr Rice was returned from South Carolina when Mr Lovick and Mr Gale were admitted it must be allowed that I exceeded my Instructions thō unknowingly and I can only aver, as I now do that I did then believe Mr Ashe was gone for England and that Mr Rice was not come back from South Carolina   Mr Rice is now far distant from me, therefore I am not able at this Instant to write possitively where he was when the aforesaid Gentlemen were made Councellours

I did never believe I had a liberty of altering the Rank in which His Majesty has been pleased to place the several Councellours, in the first Article of my Instructions, or at any time, acquainted your Lordships I had so done.   It may be possible your Lordships are led into this mistake, by a list inserted in my Letter of the 4th of September 1731 which was sent for your Lordships consideration and could be of no effect without being approved, and confirmed in England, in due form   Your Lordships may see by looking over the Council Journals that the Members are always placed according to their several Ranks except the times when Governour Phenney Surveyor General of His Majesty's Customs for the South District of America assisted in the Councils held dureing a Short Stay he made in this province the other Members then Present desired his name might be placed first, the Same compliment had been payed in former times to Mr Fitswilliam in this Country when that Gentleman enjoyed the Same post.   Your Secretary writes in the close of the Paragraph I am in this place answering *You will therefore do well to restore every Gentleman to the Rank His Majesty has been pleased to place them in of which I send you the enclosed list.* As the same list is in my first Instruction, Mr Popple might have spared himself the trouble of writeing or sending the same to me   Mr Popple does not intimate by any word in the whole Paragraph that your Lordships are of Opinion I shall do well to restore every Gentleman in the said list to his former Rank therefore I must suppose this Judgement proceeds from him only   I informed your Lordships that William Smith had resigned his place in Council that Cornelius Harnett had done the same thing (the Council Journals prove it) that John Porter was dead, that Eliezer Allen had never appeared at the Council, and does not reside in this Province, that James Stallard and Richard Evans (being disappointed in the Expectation) did not come to North Carolina Edmund Porter is the only person, that has been suspended I think he will be proved to be an unfitt Man to be a Member of the Council by the next Papers I have the honour to transmitt to your Lordships if any doubt remains with you about him   Upon due reflection your Lordships will discern that I have taken no Man's Rank from him (Porter excepted) when James Stallard Eliezer Allen or Richard Evans come to the Council Chamber, I will admit them Members and Give them their due Rank at the Council Board, but I begg to be excused from restoreing John Porter not thinking myself sufficiently authorized to raise the dead   the only meaning I can perceive to be contained in Mr Popple's opinion is, to induce me to readmit Edmund Porter to the Council Table but I assure your Lordships I should act extreamly ill in So doing and that I will not restore him without a proper Order.

From the time I came into this Government to the sitting of the Assembly there appeared no likelihood that any disputes or differences would happen between myself and the Assembly therefore I was in hopes the Assembly would have gone through what I proposed in my Speech to them and as I have already given your Lordships Just and full accounts of those matters, I think it unnecessary to trouble you with repetitions.

The Liberty I offered the Assembly to send some of their Members to me dureing their sitting, if they saw cause, had no other meaning than that mentioned in the same part of the Speech, but the like shall be avoided hereafter

1. It must be allowed, that Governours in some sort represent the King Yet the Plenary power of ratifying or nulling Acts, being still in the King, Governours do not stand in the legislature, alltogether as the King do's; and may and do interfere where his Majesty do's not. His Majesty's Council here sitt in a double capacity and represent the Privey Council as well as the House of Lords, without being ever yet distinguished into two Bodys; and it has been the constant practice in all Debates at the Council Board for the Governour to be present and assist therein, whenever he thought proper and is agreeable enough to the people, nor do they complain of any Illconveniency's in it   The Governour is looked upon as part of the Assembly and assists in the debates which is of Service on both sides for matters to be discussed before they come to the Governours hands to be passed, for the Royall Approbation or Repeal, the Governour's right of being Present at all debates at the Council Board whether about things Legislative or Executive I believe is allowed everywhere   I have heard that about 12 or 14 years ago, it was objected and by some men made a complaint against Governour Shute in New England but it was strenously maintained on behalf of the Crown as the Governours Right   for my own part its a matter I am indifferent in   I think it is my Duty to support the Rights of Government and faithfully state the Matter to your Lordships in order to be further instructed therein.

Your Lordships cannot avoid observing (Mr Popple writes) the great irregularitys I committed in my commerce with the Lower House, but as he has mentioned only one I have not an opportunity of answering the rest,   this one is that I compared one of their Members to a Thiefe &c Moseley in confederacy with some Members of the Council and others in the Lower House had formed designes to distract the Administration and prevent the Assembly from doing business (as I was informed and the

sequel evidenced)   in order to carry on this design, he wrote a Paper and
it was handed about in the House of Burgesses and in a thin House
resolved and sent up to me and the Council.   Moseley judged if he
could excite and stir up divisions in the Assembly, he should put off
any inquiries into the frauds and cheats he had been guilty of while Surveyor General, and escaped an Examination into his management of the
publick money   Therefore to prevent the House of Burgesses from being
deluded and led away by him I made that comparison which I know was
just and true and not improper on that occasion   it will not appear to an
unprejudiced reader, by the following part of the Journals of that House
that the Members were intimated by my answer to that Message or any
other I sent them   on the contrary I think it is manifest I behaved with
temper calmness,   neither can I find out those great Irregularitys I am
charged with but hope your Lordships will be induced to alter your opinions upon allowing that Journal a second reading att your Board

I answer the two following Paragraphs together and begin with the
second.

2. The Grand Deed from the Lords Proprietors to the County of Albemarle in 1668 your Lordships Secretary says *Can only be understood as*
a temporary Letter of Attorney revokeable at pleasure and that in effect it
was revoked in an Order to Mr Eden to grant no lands under one Penny
P Acre Quit Rent.   I cannot tell whether your Lordships considered, the
Copy of the Grand Deed, incerted in the Journals of the House of Burgesses, nor what information has been given you of the Supposed order
to Governor Eden   As it is an incumbent duty on me truely to represent
things I am under a necessity of stateing that affair in another light than
your Lordships seem to apprehend it.

The Great Deed of Grant from the Lords Proprietors to the County
of Albemarle still carefully preserved was dated May 1st 1668 and entered
in the Publick Records of the Government, being a Grant of so much
land, to any person settling therein according to the conditions and
Tennure of the Grant,   this hath from time to time been allways held as
firm a Grant as the Proprietors own Charter from the Crown and the
people have allways claimed it, as an undoubted Right by virtue of
that Grant from the Proprietors to the People of any part of the Country;   is as valid as their Grant or deed to any particular person
would be and no more revokeable and thô the Grand Deed is general, without nameing any particular person yet every particular person, fullfilling the Condition entitles himself then to a part of the Grant
and it becomes a particular Right and Title to him, and thô the Proprietors

Establishments in point of Government might be revokeable yet Grants of lands cannot be revoked and that the Grand Deed has allways been looked upon as a firm and absolute grant of the lands in Albemarle County (on conditions) they further evidence by any patent made out since to each particular person in the County for this Grant by the Grand Deed and people complying with it is made the consideration expressed in each private Grant   The form of the Patents in Albemarle County running thus *His Excellency &c—Know ye that we &c—According to our great Deed bearing Date the 1ˢᵗ day of May 1668 do give and grant— Acres &c—* and after the land is described and bounded it's added *Which is due for the Importation of one person for every fifty acres &c.* which importation was made a Right and being proved entituled People to so much land, under the General Grant of the Grand Deed, and upon it, a warrant from the Governour issued to the Surveyor General to measure out so much land where the claimant lay'd his Rights (that is) wherever he chose to have it layed out to him and on the Return of the Survey a Patent was made out—still referring to the Grand Deed (as I just now mentioned) so that the Patent is but a confirmation of their previous conditional Right by the Grand Deed and a concession of it, and the people further plead, that this Grand Deed is confirmed by a Law of the Country still unrepealed among the Body of their Laws that Establishes the forms of particular Grants or Patents under the Grand Deed and what Rent is to be reserved on it   So that by the Charter from the Crown to the Proprietors and their Heirs and assignes and by the Grant from the Proprietors to the County of Albemarle, by their Grand Deed on such conditions and Rents (vizt) the same as in Virginia which is two shillings for every hundred acres) and this confirmed and established by a Law still in force, which provides that Patents should issue under the Grand Deed to Albemarle County upon those Conditions and on that Rent reserved   The people still claim it as their undoubted Right in Albemarle County to take up Lands on those conditions and at that Rent   Upon the whole they conclude that although the Grand Deed from the Proprietors to Albemarle County was a Grant on condition to be fullfilled, yet it is an absolute Grant, and what was never in the power of the Lords Proprietors to revoke if they had been desirous so to do, but they never did attempt to revoke the said Grand Deed.   And as to the supposed order to Governour Eden mentioned by your Lordships Secretary I am pursuaded your Lordships have been misinformed in that particular for I can find no such order, nor can I learn that ever any such order came here but am in the most possitive manner assured there was not. Nor was there ever any grant made at the Rent of one penny ℔ Acre nor any Patents ever issued at a higher Rent than two shillings ℔ hundred acres which is the same as the Quit Rents of Virginia and being there paid in Tobacco or money at the Choice of the Tennants, the people here claim a right of paying in the same manner but this affair is not yet come in debate because the Kings Receiver has not been in this Government nor any Quit Rents collected since my arrival The Proprietors it is reported once denyed the deed nor could any Record be found in their Office at home but the Original being in this Country was by the Assembly ordered to be recorded in the Secretary's Office and in every precinct in the Government and then sent home a copy which convinced the Prop™ it was a firm Grant & they let the dispute drop & the Assembly have since chosen a person to keep it. Before I left London I informed your Lordships of this Grand Deed & carefully inspected the books belonging to the affairs of this Province delivered up by the Lords Proprietors but could find no Copy of this Deed.

3ᵈ As the People claim it as their Right to have lands surveyed and Patents made them on the Conditions of seating and planting and two shillings ℔ hundred Quit Rent I have granted Warrants after the usuall manner and some surveys have been made, yet I have not ventured to make out any Patents nor indeed will people take them at the Rent prescribed of 4 shillings ℔ hundred which has discouraged abundance of people and is not only a Detriment to the offices but a great hindrance to the settling and growth of the Country and here I must begg leave to observe that what is mentioned in my Instructions and now repeated in your Secretary's letter, as a great reason and inducement for the people to pass an Act for such a Rent and for Registring their Lands &c is upon a very different foot in this Government from what it is in South Carolina, there the Quit Rents were due, and in arrear allmost 20 years before the Kings purchase which His Majesty graciously offers to remitt on passing such an Act, but here the Quit Rents were annually collected and applyed towards supporting the Government, in paying the Governour's and other Salarys and charges so that what would be really a great Favour to the People of South Carolina from His Majesty would not be so here where the case is very different nor will the people ever be easily brought to register over their lands again indeed if that was done it would be a certain means to make a Rent Role by, that is so much wanted and which for that very reason the People will endeavour to avoid, I mean a register of every man's land that he now holds (whether by Patent or mean conveyance) and the same to be continued for the future which would effectually make and keep a compleat Rent Role.

As to what is mentioned in the Same Paragraph of your Secretarys letter that Officers Fees should be paid in Proclamation money I must acquaint your Lordships that even the Permitting them to be received in Bills at four for one, as an equivalent (which is much less than Proclamation money) has been made the greatest handle to raise Clamours against me among the people and has been artfully and maliciously, underhand heightned even by those that at the same time receive the Benefit of it I early foresaw those difficultys and fully stated them in my Report and Representation of the State of the Country and desired a full and speedy answer to them as allso about the Laws particularly those passed in the name and Authority of the Proprietors in 1729 after the Surrender to the Crown especially as to the Act for the Bills now current (that the Fees are so strenously endeavoured to be paid in at Parr) which was not only passed after the surrender, but contrary to the Powers, the Proprietors had given on their behalf to ratify Laws and perhaps beyond any power they possessed themselves had I been so happy as to have obtained proper answers to those points I could have made every thing very easy here as in other things I have the pleasure to say I have done particularly in Settling an Orderly and peaceable behaviour so much wanted among this distracted and disorderly people but for want of full Instructions in those matters of such importance to them, the people have been kept in suspence, waiting the event impatiently, and thus fluctuating they have been the more susceptible of Discontent and Ill impressions against me, and are informed that such means are used that no settlement should be made while I was Governour, and Rumours artfully spread through the whole Country that I shall soon be removed whither I have done anything amiss or not which is highly reflecting upon the honour and Justice of his Majesty's Government, and a great prejudice to me giveing encouragement to invertors of lyes framed to hurt me, by the sett of vile and base men I have to deal with lyes have been industriously propogated by wretches who stick at nothing and affect to have it believed that the heaping complaints thö false and pretending grievances thö without cause will work a change and I shall be removed but as I have acted with sufficient caution and given no real grounds of complaint I hope nothing will be received so much to my prejudice, as to be condemned unheard

Notwithstanding your Lordships observe some disputes I have had with the Assembly about the appointing a Clerke to that House yet there

never were any nay not one word about it ever passed when I had the
Journal of the Lower House before me to make notes on to be sett in
the Margin as commanded by an Instruction I saw in the Minutes, that
they had appointed Mʳ Williams their Clerk and therefore wrote the
following Remark which your Lordships will see upon the Margin of
that Journal *Mr Williams was appointed by a Commission from me which
was produced to the House and he acted by virtue of it but the House pretending a Right to appoint their own Clerke omitted takeing notice of the
Commission I had given.*

The 14ᵗʰ Instruction I will observe and obey to the best of my knowledge and understanding and will insist on my Right to nominate and
appoint the Clerke of the Lower House in the next Assembly and will
not give up that point It is my Opinion the Burgesses which are to
sett in July next will aim at much more power and Privileges then the
Members of Parliament in Great Britain. Copys of the Commissions
given to the Chief Justice and assistant Judges will accompany this
Letter to your Lordships.

Your Lordships desire to know how the matter stands with respect to
the Power claimed by the Assembly of chuseing the Publick Treasurer of
the Province, what has been the constant practice and by what authority
Mʳ Moseley was originally appointed.

I have formerly been very full in the Debates with the Assembly one
that Head in the Journals and Representations I sent your Lordships
which to avoid Repetition I referr too, but to obey your Lordships I
shall again state the arguments about the Treasurer in the strongest
lights.

The Assembly claim it as their Right to appoint the Province Treasurer who is the keeper of the Province Money, they say that the moneys
ariseing out Rents and such His Majesty's dues which are an inherent and
herditary Right, and like the Domains of the Crown His Majesty is to
appoint his Collectors and Receivers or Treasurers for, but where the
money is raised by the Assembly for particular Ends and Uses for the
Defence and service of the Country, as the same is to be applyed to such
uses, as the Assembly think proper to appropriate it, so they think they
ought to appoint the manner and persons for the directing and manageing
thereof, and insist that as they have the direction of the end they ought
to have the appointment of the means or the End may be frustrated, and
they further affirm that it has all along been the Practice of this Country
to appoint the Treasurers for receiving the money they raise and add
that it is so in other Colonys, On the other hand in the behalf of the

Crown it may be said that thō the Assembly as the legislative part of the
Country is to raise and appropriate the money for the Publick Service
yet the executive part of the Government being in the King and his
Ministers under him as he is the Head and intrusted with the Government for the Publick Good whatever is executed and done for the Publick Service is under His Direction and to be done by his Orders and
Officers.   And as the Treasury of Great Britain is under His Majesty's
immediate appointment thō the money is raised and appropriated by Act
of Parliament it would be very extraordinary for the Colonys to assert
or claim a higher right or Privilege then the People of England enjoy
and if the Colonys have assumed that Power in any place it may have
rather passed unobserved then allowed of or Established.   As to Mr
Moseley's appointment when I came first into this Country I found Mr
Moseley called Publick Treasurer and had some Bills of the Publick
Currency in his hands but by what Right he was made publick Treasurer of the Province I could not be satisfied and pursuant to my Commission and Instructions I nominated Mr Smith then Chief Justice to
be Treasurer of the Province but he privately withdrawing before the
Commission was made out the matter has rested waiting to be further
instructed from home   Upon receiving your Lordships Letter I writt
to Mr Moseley to know how he was appointed and received an invasive
answer which I thought proper to send herewith to your Lordships

Your Lordships observe that thō he is stiled Publick Treasurer by
several of the Laws yet it doth not appear how or when he was made
so   I have taken the pains to search the Laws and Publick Acts of the
Government but can no where find that he was expressly appointed
Treasurer of the Province   In antient times the Quit Rents and other
dues of the Proprietors were received by their Receiver General being
applyed to the Support of the Government.   I cannot learn there was
then any other Treasurer and what Small levys were raised by the
Assembly were collected by the Sheriffs or marshalls and accounted for
to the Assembly who paid what Small claims there were on the Publick
therewith but when the Indian War broke out in 1711 a great duty was
layed on all goods exported or imported by land or water and several
persons appointed to collect it that were called Treasurers who gave security for their Offices but because this could not be speedily raised they
were obliged by the Emergency of the War to make a paper currency
and enacted £4000 in Bills should be struck the Bills to be paid to the
Possessors, at times limited in the Bills with Interest, and were appointed
to be paid the possessors when due, by the Treasurers of the dutys, Mr

Moseley was one of the Commissioners for emitting these Bills, and others in the Service that had Certificates of their Claims being allowed by persons appointed to examine and grant them   I am the more particular in this because it was the first appointment of Bills and the first time I find Mr Moseley regularly concerned with the Publick Money indeed he in his letter Says it is from 1708 but from 1708 till near the time I mention was what they call to this day the troublesome times, or Cary's usurpation, when all things were in confusion   Afterwards more Bills were made much in the same manner, a Land Tax and a Pole Tax were lay'd to call in and sink the Bills and a Treasurer appointed in every Precinct who had collectors under them to gather in the Taxes,   these Precinct Treasurers were sometimes called Publick Treasurers to distinguish them from their under Treasurers   In 1715 £24000 in Bills were made without running on Interest or any determinate time of payment mentioned in them   Mr Moseley was of the Commissioners for makeing them and when compleated they were to be deposited in Mr Moseley's hands to exchange the old Bills that were called in and the rest were to be delivered by him to the Precinct Treasurers in order to be sunk   Afterwards Mr John Lovick and others were appointed Commissioners for takeing and stateing the Publick Accounts,   they were to adjust the Several Treasurers Accounts and receive what Bills they had collected in and burn them, which was accordingly done Till 1723 but then on pretence of the old Bills being torn and defaced a new Emission was made of £12000 to exchange them it being computed there were about that sum outstanding Christopher Gale Mr Lovick and Edward Moseley Esq^rs were appointed Commissioners for makeing them, and when made, they were ordered by the Act to be delivered to E Moseley (Publick Treasurer) in order to exchange the old Bills (which were to be burnt) and to pay the Marshall any County charges due, and at that time the Act for the land Tax and Pole Tax was repealed and a new Levy made of 5 shillings Pole Tax to be levyed in these Bills by the High Sheriffs, or Provost Marshalls and their Deputys Annually and to be paid to the Publick Treasurer who was to have the Bills so brought in before the Assembly who usually ordered them to be pay'd by Mr Moseley out again, for paying the Assemblys and other contingent charges of the Government which kept up the Sum of Bills circulateing   in the same Act it is provided, that Edward Moseley *Publick Treasurer give bonds of £15000 to the Governour for his faithfull discharge in his said Office and disposeing the Publick Money as directed in this Act*.   This was the first time Mr Moseley was called

Publick Treasurer and from this Act it is argued, that by being called
Publick Treasurer and haveing the Publick Treasury thus put in his
hands and being required to give Security for the Office, he in effect was
made Publick Treasurer And the Secret seems to be that Moseley who
had a considerable share in getting the Act passed, chose to be called
Publick Treasurer rather then formerly appointed Treasurer of the
Province least it might start difficultys   On the other hand against Mr
Moseley it may be argued that by the Act he is not even called Treasurer
of the Province but only a Publick Treasurer and the business he is
appointed to manage is only with respect to that sett of Bill money
For the disposal of the Publick Money as directed in the Act As it is
expressed in the last Clause of the Act and consequently when that sett
of Bills should expire his Treasurership should end so that he was publick Treasurer only to a particular purpose and not Province Treasurer,
nor by this Act could he be Treasurer of any other moneys, the Country
should raise and therefore not province Treasurer   Thus the matter stood
for some years the Bills as fast as they were drawn in by the Sheriffs, and
paid Mr Moseley were by order of Assembly paid out again by him for
contingent charges, and in their orders, on his makeing up the Accounts he
was usually called Publick Treasurer till 1729 When a new sett of
Bills were made and the old ones called in   That year an Act was
made for Emitting £40 000 Mr Lovick Mr Moseley and others appointed Commissioners for makeing them done £10 000 Pounds were
ordered to be delivered to Moseley to take in the Old Bills then
to be exchanged and the rest to be delivered to Precinct Treasurers,
appointed in each precinct to be delivered out on Interest or land security and thō the validity of this Act is questioned it being ratifyed by
the old Government after the Purchase and surrender to the Crown, yet
in fact it was done and the old Bills called in and the Bills now current
are of that New Sett Mr Moseley is in this Act several times termed
Publick Treasurer but then it is only in such places as mention the Ex-
changeing the Old Bills of which he was made Publick Treasurer by the
Law in 1723 But he is nowhere in this Act called Publick Treasurer,
in anything relateing to these Bills or Publick Money for the Future
on the contrary the Act looks on the Publick Treasury to be devolved
on the several Precinct Treasurers and provides that the Publick Treasury may have wherewith to answer contingent charges of the Government   A Pole Tax of three Shillings is layd to be received by the Precinct Treasurers and not by Mr Moseley and the paying the Interest
Money to the Precinct Treasurers is called paying into the Treasury and

they are ordered to dispose off £5000 of it to particular uses and contingent charges of the Government so that it doth not seem to be intended by this Act that there should be one Treasurer or the Publick Treasury in one Man's hands but in all the Treasurers of which Mr Moseley was one (viz't) for the Precinct of Chowan So upon the whole whether Mr Moseley by the Law of 1723 was made Treasurer of the Province or only to be looked upon as Treasurer for that sett of Bills which are now Extinct and how far the new revival of Precinct Treasurers and Mr Moseley's being appointed one of them for this New sett of Bills determines His authority derived by the law of 1723 I shall leave your Lordships to determine haveing done my duty in fairly stateing the Matter to your Lordships and shall be glad I may be favoured with full Instructions on an affair of so much consequence.

As all Publick Dues are paid in Bills only in North Carolina it is reasonable and just that they should be received for no more than they are rated att.   Yet I am very certain when Warrants are signed for paying Judges and other attendants on the two Courts of Oyer and Terminer, I am commanded to call every year the whole Country will be in an uproar and I am in doubt whither the Council will consent to my issueing of them in that manner   There has not been anything paid for the three Courts allready held

I did myself the honour some time past to acquaint your Lordships with the Motive that induced me to endeavour to perswade your Lordships to cause an Alteration in the Bounds sett down in the Instructions between the two Governments of Carolina (vizt) to save the Kings money, your Lordships well know how much was paid to the Commissioners and others imployed on the part of Virginia in running a line, and how much land was sold in this Province to defray the said charge. To mark out a divideing line between North and South Carolina will be a much greater Expence because that part of the Country, where the line will go is uninhabited   If a line is to be run, your Lordships will direct how mony sufficient to pay for it may be procured to enable me to Execute the Instruction to that end   without money it cannot be performed

Haveing before shown your Lordships what difficultys I labour under for want of directions about the Laws of this Country desire your Lordships after the Attorney and Soliciter General have given their opinions upon them you will be pleased to send your Instructions with the Dispatch necessary on this occasion

4 The Direction your Lordships give in respect to the Inhabitants that were taken from Virginia by running the line I think it is very just,

when I came first into this Country I was informed that about one third of them People had renewed their Patents in this Government and are upon the list I sent your Lordships from this place the first of July 1731   I informed some others who had not renewed, that it was my opinion they had no occasion to do so but that I would desire your Lordships opinion therein and they might be easy till I was honoured with your commands.

5 In the year 1724 an order of Council (hereunto annexed) was made at the request of the Assembly to encourage the settling the Southern Parts of this Province and many Warrants issued but no account was kept of the number   it was the custom for the Governor (while the Proprietors held this Country) to Sign Warrants for land,   these Warrants were not filled up when signed but a Blank remained to contain the names of the takers and the Warrants remained in the Secretary's hands who either filled them up himself or they were delivered by him to the Deputy Surveyors who did the Same for Such as imployed them, in Surveying but they have not made returns of those Surveys   Therefore it is impossible to send your Lordships a distinct account either of the Number of those Warrants, their Dates or to whom given   This Province being divided into two Countys named Albemarle & Bath, the people who took up lands in Albemarle did it under the Grand Deed, in Bath County the Proprietors sold the land att a small price and reserved a less rent then in Albemarle,   the consideration upon the Warrants I now write of was to be three shillings (in Bills) ⅌ hundred acres and seating and planting within two years   I am informed a great deal of land taken under that order of Council was purchased and patented dureing the time Sir Richard Everard was Governour   he superceded me in 1725 and I him in February 1734   not more than 640 acres were to be held by one of them Warrants, but people took that or any less Quantity as they judged proper att the signing the Warrants,   there was no other Scituation specifyed then lying and being in Bath County

Haveing given your Lordships in former Letters an Account of the frauds and roguerys practiced by Mr Moseley Mr Ashe and their confederates in surveying and selling lands I shall only add under this Head that my endeavouring to serve the King faithfully in this matter has made them and their friends and partakers my inveterate Enemys,   a dangerous Crew they are, and unhappy must be, every honest man that has anything to do with them

I beg leave to inform your Lordship that soon after the date of my last letter I sett out with Indian Guides and some white men to mark a

Road thō the middle of this Province from Virginia to Cape Fear Province River and to discover and view the lands lying in those Parts till then unknown to the English inhabitting this Government I spent seven weeks in that Expedition, believe the land sufficient to contain about three Thousand Plantations I remarked that Several Rivers began their courses much higher up the Country then delineated in the Map and some that I crossed are not taken notice of This part of North Carolina thō none of the Rivers are navigable so high for boats, and as yet uninhabited will hereafter be full of People The lands are very good and healthy and well supplyed with Springs and Brooks of Excellent water The road is layd out which will prove very serviceable to people that have occasion to go from the Northern Countrys to South Carolina by my computation allmost two hundred miles rideing will be saved them and the crossing many broard Rivers prevented Wackamaw Lake comes within five miles of the Northern branch of Cape River I expended a great deal of money on this occasion in Presents to the Indians and in paying the other men that went with me

I have taken Great care to transmit to your Lordships from time to time the state of affairs in this Province and sett forth to your Lordships the methods by which this country may be rendered flourishing & usefull to Great Britain As Mr Popple's letter touches but upon some few of the many particulars I have layd before your Lordships I hope speedily to be honored with your commands in relation to the Laws of this Country and other matters of great consequence to the Wellfare of the Province not taken notice of in your Secretary's letter

  I have the Honour to remain (with due respect)
   My Lords of Trade and Plantation
    Your Lordships
     Most Humble
      and most obedient servant
        GEO BURRINGTON

To His Excellency the Governour and Council of North Carolina

Copy of Mr Moseleys Letter when he was required to shew how he was made Treasurer

His Excellency the Governour haveing been pleased to send for me to the Council Chamber and causeing to be read unto me a Paragraph of a letter from the Right Honble the Lords Commissioners of Trade and Plantations concerning the Publick Treasurer of this Province and desiring my answer thereto I answer and say

1st As to the power claimed by the Assembly of choosing the Publick Treasurer I think it proper to be answered by the Assembly

2nd To the best of my Remembrance for upwards of Twenty eight years I have been concerned in the Publick affairs of this Province   The constant Practice has been for the Assembly to appoint the Treasurers and gatherers of money raised by the Assembly. And this was always the Practice before as far as I can learn by those Journals and Acts of Assembly which I have seen nor do I remember to have met with any Precedents to the contrary

3rd The first of my appointment to be Publick Treasurer was by that Assembly that first emitted Publick Bills of Credit, or near that time; For the Truth of which I refer myself to the Journals and Acts of Assembly and the several Bonds I have given for the faithfull discharge of that Office pursuant to divers Acts of Assembly.

E. MOSELEY.

April 3rd 1733

George the Second by the Grace of God King of Great Britain France and Ireland &c Defender of the Faith &c

To our Trusty and well beloved William Smith Esqr Greeting

NOTE BY GOV BURRINGTON.—Copy of Mr. Smith's Patent issued upon his producing in Council the Kings Warrant to be Chief Justice of No Carolina. [See page ante 136.—EDITOR]

No CAROLINA—ss

George the Second by the Grace of God of Great Britain France and Ireland King Defender of the Faith &c

To our Trusty and Well beloved John Palin Esqr Greeting

We reposing especial Trust and Confidence in the Loyalty and Fidelity and Ability of you the Said John Palin Esqr and out of our meer motion certain knowledge and Special Grace Have ordained constituted and appointed and by these Presents do constitute ordain and appoint you the Said John Palin Esqr by the name and Style of Chief Justice or Judge of our Said Province of North Carolina to hold and determine in our General Court of Said Province all Pleas as well Civil as Criminal and all other Pleas whatsoever arising and happening within our

Said Province of North Carolina Giving and hereby granting you the Said John Palin Esq full Power and authority to do perform and execute all Acts matters and things whatsoever which in our Said Province to the Office of a Chief Justice in anywise belong or appertain and in as large and ample manner to all intents and purposes as any Justice of any of our Courts of Westminster or any of the English Plantations in America may or ought to perform or Execute To have and to hold the Said Office of Chief Justice in our Said Province during our Pleasure Together with all Fees Perquisites Priviledges Liberties Immunities and Casualties belonging to the Said office In Testimony whereof we have caused these presents to be done under the Great Seal of our Said Province Witness our Trusty and Well beloved George Burrington Esq Captain General and Governor in Chief in and over our Said Province at the Council Chamber in England the 27th day of July in the fifth year of our reign Anno Dom 1731

GEORGE BURRINGTON

By command of his
   Excellency the Governor and
   Council
        RT FORSTER.
        Deputy Secretary

NOTE BY GOV. BURRINGTON —Copy of Mr Chief Justice Palin's Commission who was appointed when Chief Justice Smith withdrew and left his Post without leave the King's Warrant to Smith being only during his residence in the Province and so on his quitting it the post was vacant.

No CAROLINA—ss.

His Excellency George Burrington Esq Captain General and Governor in Chief in and over His Majesties Province of North Carolina.

To George Martin Henry Bonner
Isaac Hill and Thomas Lovick Esq   } Greeting

By virtue of his Majesties Commission appointing me Captain General and Governor in Chief of the said Province with full power and authority to commissionate and appoint all Officers Civil and military within the same and being commanded by his Majesties Royal Instructions to choose Persons of good abilitys for assistants Justices and Majistrates in the said Province. Out of the assurance I have of the Loyalty

Integrity Prudence and abilitys of you the said George Martin Henry Bonner Isaac Hill and Thomas Lovick I do by these presents by and with the advice and consent of his Majesties Council appoint commissionate and assign you the said George Martin Henry Bonner Isaac Hill and Thomas Lovick Esq during Pleasure to be assistant Justices of the General Court of the said Province which Court you or any two of you are hereby impowered together with the Chief Justice of the said Province to hold at such times and places as by Law are or shall be appointed for holding the same with full power and authority with the said Chief Justice to hold Plea hear and determine all causes real personal or mixt of what kind or nature soever arising or happening within said Province to be there heard and determined and generally to act and do whatsoever to the office and duty of assistant of said Court doth or may belong with as full and ample power as any assistant Justices or associates of said Court have had used and enjoyed in all things proceeding according to the Laws customs and usuages of this Government and as near as may be agreeable to the Laws and Customes of Great Britain In Testimony whereof I have hereunto Sett my hand and caused the Great Seal of the said Province to be hereunto affixed at the Council Chamber in Edenton the 27th day of July In the fifth year of the reign of our Sovereign Lord King George the Second Anno Dom 1731.

GEORGE BURRINGTON.

By command of his
 Excellency the Governor and Council
    RT FORSTER
       Deputy Secretary.

NOTE BY GOV BURRINGTON —Copy of the Assistant Justices Commission Note the first that was made out is not to be found and its supposed Mr Smith carryed it off with him as he clandestinely took away the King's Warrant to me to appoint him Chief Justice.

No CAROLINA—ss.

George the Second by the Grace of God of Great Britain France and Ireland King Defender of the Faith &c.

To all to whom these presents shall come   Greeting

Know yee that wee reposing special Trust and confidence in the Loyalty Integrity and great abilities of William Little Esq and out of our meer motion certain knowledge and special grace have assigned and ap-

pointed and by these presents do constitute ordain and appoint the said
William Little Esqr by the Name Authority an Style of Chief Justice of
our Province of North Carolina to hear hold and determine in our General Court of said Province all Pleas as well Civil as Criminal all Pleas
of the Crown or betwixt party and party Real personal or mixt or of
other kind arising or happening within our said Province to be there
heard and determined and of all Crimes and Offences done or perpetrated
capital or not capital after the due Form of Law in all cases to proceed
award and determine as to Justice shall appertain and of right is to be
done. Giving and hereby granting to the said William Little Esqr full
power and authority to award Process and do and perform all and every
act or thing whatsoever which to the compleating of Justice and due order
of the same in the said office of Chief Justice doth or may belong or hath
been held used and accustomed And Generally to act and do with as
full power and authority in our said Province as any Chief Justice or
Baron in any of our Courts at Westminster or any Chief Justice in any
of our Plantations in America hath or ought to have respectively To
have and to hold the said Office of Chief Justice of our Province of
North Carolina during our Royall Will and Pleasure together with all the
Jurisdictions Rights Priviledges and Immunities thereunto belonging
Incident or of Right appertaining with full power and authority to take
demand and receive all Fees Perquisites Profits and allowance to the said
Office belonging accrueing or that may be granted or assigned. In Testimony whereof we have caused these our Letters Patents to be done under
the Great Seal of our said Province Witness our Trusty and well be-
loved George Burrington Esqr Our Captain General and Governor in
Chief of our said Province. Given at Edenton the Eighteenth day of
October in the Sixth year of our reign Anno Dom 1732.

                                        GEO BURRINGTON.

By order of his Excellency
    the Governor and Council
                RT: FORSTER.
                        Dep^y Sec^y

NORTH CAROLINA—ss.

His Excellency George Burrington Esqr His Majesty's Captain Gen-
    eral and Governor in Chief of said Province

To Roger Moore John Worley William Owen Mackrora Scarborough
    & William Badham Esqr Greeting

By Virtue of his Majesties Commission appointing me Captain General and Governor in Chief of the said Province of North Carolina with

full Power and Authority to commissionate and appoint all Officers Civil and Military within the same and being comanded by his Majesties Royall Instructions to choose Persons of good abilities for Assistant Justices and Magistrates in the said Province.

Out of the assurance I have of the Loyalty Integrity and good abilities of you the said Roger Moore John Worley William Owen Mackrora Scarborough and William Badham I do by these Presents by and with the advice and consent of His Majesties Councel appoint commissionate and assign you the said Roger Moore John Worley William Owen Mackrora Scarborough and William Badham Esqr during pleasure to be assistant Justices of the General Court of said Province which Court you or any one of you together with the Chief Justice of said Province are hereby impowered to hold at such times and places as are or shall be appointed for the same with full power and authority to hold plea hear and determine after the due form of Law all causes Civil Real Personal and mixt or of other kind whatsoever whether Pleas of the Crown or betwixt Party and Party or any matter or thing whatsoever arising or happening within the said Province to be there heard done and determined And generally to act and do whatsoever to the Duty and Office of Assistant Justices of the Said Court doth or may belong with as full and ample Power as any Assistant Justices or associates of said court have held used and enjoyed in all things proceeding after the Laws customes and usuages of this Government and as near as may be according to the Laws and Customs of Great Britain. And if the said Chief Justice at any time by sickness or any other accident be absent or hindered from setting you or any Two of you are hereby impowered to hold said Court and to do and perform whatsoever is there to be heard done or determined with full power also to any one member of said Court from time to time to adjourn the same. In Testimony whereof I have hereunto set my hand and caused the Great Seal of the Province to be hereunto affixed at the Council Chamber in Edenton the Eighteenth day of October in the Sixth year of His Majesties reign Anno Dom 1732

GEORGE BURRINGTON

By order of the Governor and Council

R. FORSTER, Depy Secy

[B P R O North Carolina B. T Vol 9 A 32.]

REMARKS UPON THE INSTRUCTIONS TO THE GOVERNOR OF NORTH CAROLINA.

1ˢᵗ By the Papers I have seen in your Lordship's office it appears that in 1728 Sir Richard Everard then Deputy Governor in Council ordered John Lovick then Secretary to dispose of no more of the soil of North Carolina until His Majᵗʸˢ pleasure should be known But in the year 1729 the said Sir Richard being prevailed upon by the arts of the said Lovick and William Little the receiver and others issued a great many Pattents wherein the number of acres was left blank and the Receiver General Little's receipt likewise in blank for the purchase money so that the possessors of such Patents have it in their power to putt in as much land as they please.

It seems to have been Sir Richard's intention that every Patent he signed should contain only a Tract which is 640. acres, instead of which some People have filled up their Patents with 5000 some with more, some less.

Mr Burrington's Fourty first Instruction related to this affair and is as follows.

In consequence of this Instruction Mr Burrington called the Partys before him and after a superficial enquiry acquitted Messrs Lovick and Little but as Sir Richard Everard is now dead this Instruction cannot continue in the form that it now is and as these blank Patents are every day produced, and have been transferr'd from one Person to another, and valuable considerations have been paid for them by several persons It is humbly submitted to your Lordships whether in Place of the said Instruction it will not be proper to substitute one ordering the frauds of the blank Patents to be strictly enquired into & the Persons guilty to make good what money has been paid for their Patents to them, and that they should be prosecuted according to law

2ⁿᵈ Fourty seventh Instruction

The Beginning of this is already complied with and was in its own nature temporary the last Clause is—"But in the meantime you are to take especial care that no office or place whatever in our said Province be executed but by Commission to be granted by us or by you our Governor under the seal of our said Province"

Tho' this part of the Instruction is very full and strong yet when it was laid before the Assembly of North Carolina the lower house came to the following Resolution—"This House is of opinion that the fourty seventh Instruction doth not extend to officers appointed by act of assembly as are the publick and precinct Treasurers and several other officers It is therefore humbly proposed that at the end of the above mentioned Clause it may be added And this to extend to such officers as were formerly used to be appointed by act of Assembly particularly the publick and precinct Treasurers.

3 As Mr Burrington thought proper to give coppies of his Instructions to a great many people, which may give great handle for contention about the Governors Power and as the Instructions are the same in Number It is humbly proposed that your Lordships would alter their order so as that when the Instructions which are necessary to be laid before the Assembly shall be found to be of a different Number from what the same was in Mr Burrington's, they can never be certain that our Instructions are the same

4 Your Lordships please to let me have a Coppy of the Attorney General's opinion as to the validdity of the Laws particularly as to the emission of Bills of Credit in 1729 after His Majesty's purchase took place A point that deserves the utmost attention

5. I find Mr Burrington has represented at several times to your Lordships how proper it would be to reduce the quitt rents from three shillings to two sh ℔ 100 acres which is the quitt rent of Virginia the neighbouring Province I cant help informing your Lordships that all the People of that County whom I have seen have represented it to me as a great hardship that they should pay one shilling ℔ 100 acres more than Virginia which has so good a staple as Tobacco and such a number of good harbours for navigation but which they are deprived of

Quere If it be necessary to enquire into the complaints of the Province against Mr Burrington

---

[B P R O North Carolina B. T Vol 21 p 125]

LORDS OF TRADE TO THE KING 18 JULY 1733.

To the King's most excellent Majesty

MAY IT PLEASE YOUR MAJESTY,

In obedience to Your Maj commands signified to us by His Grace the Duke of Newcastle in his letter dated 27 March 1733 We have prepared Draughts of General Instructions and of those which relate particularly to the Acts of Trade & Navigation for Gabriel Johnston Esq whom Your Majesty has been pleased to appoint Governor of the Province of North Carolina wherein we have made no material alterations from the instructions which Your Maj was pleased to approve for Mr Burrington your late Governor of this Province except in the 41st Article whereby he was directed to examine into several complaints against Sir Richard Everard formerly Deputy Govr of this Province as also concerning his having issued several blank patents for land which the possessors were at liberty to fill up with as great a number of acres as they should think fit but Sir Richard Everard being since dead we have left out that part of the instruction which related personally to him and have prepared a new one for Mr Johnston by which he is directed to make a particular enquiry into the Grants of land which have been made in this Province since the Year 1728 and upon discovery of any fraudulent practises therein to order the necessary prosecutions for vacating the same of all which he is directed to transmit particular accounts to be laid before Your Majesty

We further beg leave to acquaint Your Majesty that James Jenoure and John Porter Esqrs lately Members of Your Maj Council in North Carolina being lately dead Cornelius Harnet Esq. some time Member of the same Council having resigned and Edward Moseley, Roger Moore and Cullen Pollock Esqrs having been recommended to us as persons every way qualified to serve Your Majesty in this station we have inserted their names instead of the said James Jenoure John Porter and Cornelius Harnet

All which is most humbly submitted

P DOCMINIQUE
T. PELHAM
Whitehall   M BLADEN
    July 18th 1733

[B. P R. O Am & W Ind No. 592.]

BOARD OF TRADE TO THE DUKE OF NEWCASTLE
. 18 JULY 1733.

My Lord,

We take leave to inclose to your Grace, the Draughts of General Instructions, and of those which particularly relate to the Acts of Trade and Navigation for Gabriel Johnston Esq[r] whom his Majesty has been pleased to appoint Governor of North Carolina and to desire your Grace will please to lay them before his Majesty.   We are

    My Lord
     Your Grace's
      most obedient &
       most humble Servants

            DOCMINIQUE
            T PELHAM
Whitehall   M BLADEN
 July 18th 1733

His Grace the Duke of Newcastle

[B. P R O North Carolina B. T Vol 21 pp 128–213]

INSTRUCTIONS FOR OUR TRUSTY AND WELBELOVED GABRIEL JOHNSTON ESQ[r] OUR CAPTAIN GENERAL AND GOVERNOR IN CHIEF IN AND OVER OUR PROVINCE OF NORTH CAROLINA IN AMERICA GIVEN AT OUR COURT AT ST JAMES THE 18th DAY OF JULY 1733 IN THE SEVENTH YEAR OF OUR REIGN

[N B. These Instructions are identical with the Instructions to Governor Burrington, dated 14 Dec 1730, as stated in the Representation to the King inclosing Draught of same for His Maj approval of 18 July 1733—except the 41st Article and the alteration of three Councillors' names.—W N. S]

[B P R O Am & W Ind No 592]

SAM WEBBER & OTHERS TO THE DUKE OF NEWCASTLE LONDON 21th JULY 1733

May it please your Grace,

We understand S[r] Phillip York's opinion is that his Majestie to grant us a Charter might cramp the Woolen factory &c (Wee are sorry his Honors business would never spare to hear us which can be made as clear

as noon day against all its enquiries that nothing yet don for Trade &
inriching England in any Kings reign or administration for the more
inlargeing it as by our scheme ready to be produced may appear Though
Sᵣ Phillip ordered me to print last May 300 Letters throughout England when some Members of the House of Commons and Merchants would
faine brake our Interest when their Agents offered to lay me 700ˡ if we
did not joyn them we should never obtain it for his son had an Interest
with Sir Phillip this could not move us or numerous Brethern from your
Graces Interest we are sorry lest Motives and Misrepresentations should
unhinge ours after being delayd soe long to our great loss of time and
expence without oppertunvty to clear us of such callumny of loading
trade with diffiquilty when a million recᵈ Petitions for it as if among
such Noᵐ Bred in trade they dont know whats most conducive to its
promotion better then the ingenvousest Lawyer living never informing
by us except by our enquiries we humbly begg lave to wait on your
Grace a Munday for to assist and favour us to be heard by Council before
his Majestie and Council where when heard can make it appear and
every well Wisher to his Majestie and Country will own in no Kings
Reign yet (or administrations was so much good don for Englands Trade
and Glory in inriching it begging your Grace to hear us and favour such
just and loud complaints and as we hold our Interest yet in the Hearts
of our numerous Brethern when cald too will make a Suteable return (if
Tradesmen free from falsehood or flattery of honest Character &c ·
(ware not kep at such distance Ministers of State would even live free
from envie and the Nation more eassie Humbly Begging your Graces
pardon for this in desiring to be heard ir trades defence and leave to
subscribe ourselves for ever ingadged on all oppertunytys to serve your
Graces Interest

EDWARD TOWNSEND	SAM WEBBER.
JOHN SOWDON	HUGH BILLING
HENRY OLAND	WILLIAM DAWE
ROBERT RUNDALL	JOHN GINGELT.

[B P R O North Carolina B T Vol. 9 A 36]

At the Court at Hampton Court, the 2ᵈ day of August 1733
Present
The Kings most Excellent Majesty in Councill
Upon reading this day at the Board a Report from the Right Honour-
able the Lords of the Committee of Councill upon considering a Draught

of Generall Instructions as also of those relating to Trade and Navigation prepared by the Lords Commissioners for Trade and Plantations for
Gabriel Johnston Esq' His Majesty's Governor of the Province of North
Carolina By which Report it appeared that there were no materiall alterations made in the said Draughts of Instructions from those which his
Majesty was pleased to approve of for M' Burrington late Governor of
this Province except in the 41 Article, whereby he was directed to examine into several complaints against Sir Richard Everard formerly Deputy
Governor of this Province as also concerning his having issued several
blank Patents for Land which the Possessors were at Liberty to fill up
with as great a number of acres as they should think fit but Sir Richard
Everard being since dead the said Lds Comm" for Trade and Plantations
have left out that part of the Instruction which related personally to him
and have prepared a new one for the present Governor by which he is
directed to make a particular enquiry into the Grants of Land which
have been made in the said Province since the year 1728 and upon discovery of any fraudulent practises therein to order the necessary Prosecutions for vacating the same of all which he is directed to transmitt
particular accounts to be laid before his Majesty and that therefore the
said Lords of the Committee were of opinion the said Draught were
proper for His Majesty's Royall Approbation And it likewise further
appeared by the said Report that in the list of Councellors named in the
Draught of General Instructions the three following persons have been
inserted by the said Lords Comm" for Trade viz' Edward Moseley,
Roger Moore and Cullen Pollock to supply the places of James Janoure
and John Porter Esq' deceased and of Cornelius Harnet Esq' who hath
resigned—which persons the Lords of the Committee were of opinion
might be proper to be appointed Councellors in the said Province   His
Maj'y this day took the said Report into consideration and was thereupon
pleased with the advice of His Privy Council to approve of the said
Draughts of Instructions together with the said three New Councellors,
and to order as it is hereby ordered that His Grace the Duke of Newcastle one of His Majesty's principal Secretarys of State do cause the
said Draughts (which are hereunto annexed) to be prepared for his Majesty's Royal Signature
    A true Copy

                          TEMPLE STANYAN.

[B. P. R. O. North Carolina B. T Vol. 9 A 50]

BURRINGTON VS PORTER

LETTER FROM Mr PORTER TO THE SECRETARY DATED IN NORTH
CAROLINA THE 15th OF AUGUST 1733.

SIR,

After waiting four months in Expectation that Governor Burrington would have proceeded agreable to the Directions of my Lords for Trade and Plantations (as you were pleased to signify to me by a letter bearing date the 16th of August last) I am at last constrained in my defence to send over the enclosed Depositions and papers without their being perfected in the manner I could wish all which several Papers, I pray of you to present with my most humble Duty to their Lordships

After the Depositions of four such creditable persons as Colonel Moseley Mr Chief Justice Smith Mr Ashe and Mr Montgomery it would be needless and impertinent in me to trouble their Lordships with any further Testimony relating to those allegations against Mr Burrington; who has since his arrival here last been guilty of almost every crime saving that of murther and in that he hath bid very fair on the person of the Kings Attorney General   After their Lordships are pleased to perceive the enclosed papers, and give their Judgment thereon I do beseech you Sir (with their permission) to cause the said papers and their Lordships sentiments on the whole to be layd before my Lords Commissioners of Admiralty because it may probably be of great service towards my restoration to the Office of Judge and the vice admiralty here, which Mr Burrington hath maliciously and undeservedly suspended me from, and all because I would not come into his measures relating to the Kings lands &c which if I had don it might have been a prejudice to the Crown of above five hundred thousand acres of land, about fifty thousand whereof Mr Burrington himself holds (as it is thought) by presents made him from Lovick Little and Foster besides ten thousand acres which he did unjustly acquire by a breach of the Lords Pproprietors Instructions about lands when he was Governour under them in the year 1725, those practices in general I did formerly by three several Memorials intimate to his Grace the Duke of Albemarle New Castle and I prevailed at the same time on Sir Richard Everard when Governor to do the like, as accordingly he did though afterwards Sir Richard himself fell roundly into the fraude by the instigation of his son R who filled up an old obsolute blank warrant for ten thousand acres of land which warrant had been given to his Father by a brother of mine and although this warrant which was but temperary and preparatory to a better Title) was procured by Sir Richard in 1730 above twenty years after it was issued on and had for many years lain about my brothers house as wast paper yet, so corrupt was those times that upon Sir Richards son filling the same up and giving a bribe of about three hundred pounds our C⁓ to Mʳ Little the receiver general there was a pattent procured out of the secretarys office for 10000 acres of the rich Saxapawhaw Lands on the Nor West Branch of Cape Fair River   If young Sir Richard Everard (who has succeeded his Father lately and now in London) be taxed home with this fraud before he hath any previous knowledge thereof I am persuaded notwithstanding his great Tallent of assurance he will not be able to conceal the Truth and if so it will be an argument to induce their Lordships to credit my writings.   Mʳ Burringtons Stagg-park and Burgar Ladds on the North East Branch of Cape Fair River, has also been procured much after the same manner, or rather worse because he was guilty of raceing out and fourgeing the warrant which procured part of those lands, that is to say, he altered an old Albemarle warrant of 640 acres at 2ˢ 6ᵈ ℔ hundred Quit rent into a Bath County purchase warrant of 5000 acres at 6ᵈ ℔ hundred Quit rent as can be made appear

How far I have deserved to be encouraged for endeavouring to detect and discover such fraudes by representing the same in an Early manner to the Secretary of State, is most humbly submitted to the consideration of his Grace the Duke of New Castle and to my Lords for Trade and Plantations.

I am with all difference and due regard

Sir, your most obedient humble servant

E PORTER

A List of the papers (in their proper order) herewith Inclosed. vizt

Nº 1 Is a deposition of Coll Moseley principal Treasurer of the Province and now Speaker of our General Assembly

2 Is the deposition of John Baptista Ashe Esqʳᵉ a Member of Council by his Majestie's appointment

3. Is the deposition of John Montgomery Esqʳᵉ Attorney General

4 Is a Narrative and deposition of E. Porters.

5 A paper proving that the Governor and four of the Council did prejudge me

6 A further proof and confirmation of that prejudging

7. My Letter to Governour Burrington, advertiseing him him that I did intend to proceed to the taking Deposition agreeable to the directions of the Lords for Trade and Plantation

8 A Paper shewing the great unwillingness of peoples giving Evidence in Matters relating to the Governor who they well know (according to his temper) would Seake revenge if they did

9. A parcell of Letters tacked together which I formerly received from Governor Burrington, beginning all with Dear Sir, thō he has pretended to the Board of Trade that he knew but little of me &c

10. The Deposition of Mr Chief Justice Smith

Signed   E PORTER

(Endorsed)

Recd 1st October } 1733.
Read

Depositions Recd with Mr Porter's Letter of 15 August 1733.

No CAROLINA—ss.

In obedience to the Directions given to the Right Honoble the Lords Commissioners for Trade and Plantations in their Letter dated August 16 1732 Edward Moseley of the Precinct of Chowan Gentleman was at the Instance of Edmund Porter Esqr summoned to appear before me Nathaniel Rice Esqr Secretary of North Carolina who on his Oath on the Holy Evangelists taken, saith

That he hath been for many years very well acquainted with the said Mr Porter, and his Estate in North Carolina, this Deponent living within six mile of him, That he knoweth but very few persons in this Province whose Estate and Fortune are superior to Mr Porter

Imediately after Mr Porter came into this Province from the West Indies (which was about April 1725) during the time Mr Burrington was Governour for the Lords Proprietors there appeared to this Deponent (who was very conversant with them both) a very Familiar and Friendly acquaintance and good understanding, They were frequently in each others company and this Deponent hath heard that after Governor Burrington was removed from the administration of the Government he hath been for divers week entertained at the said Mr Porters house

This Deponent further said that sometime after Mr Burrington's arrival as his Majesties Governour of this Province, there appeared to be no good understanding between the said Governour and Mr Porter, and

there being some Criminal Prosecutions raised against him (as was supposed chiefly by the Governours means) for some Riots supposed to be
done or committed before the Governours arrival All the Lawyers of
the greatest skill being against Mr Porter he applyed himself to this
Depon^t (who was licenced to practice the law in 1714 thô he has for some
years past declined it) to assist him in his defence   The Depon^t assisted
Mr Porter at March General Court 1732 and the Jury brought in their
Verdict, Not Guilty   But while the Jury were going out, the Governour
left the Gallery where he had been during the Trial, came within the Bar
and in great heat and passion commanded the Marshall attending the
Court to take this Deponent and bring him before him (althô he had his
hand on the Bible ready to take the Oaths) This Deponent moved the
Court for their Protection and that they would take notice of the Governour's usuage but this Deponents motion was not regarded the Court
being seemingly astonished   This Deponent was taken from the Court
Table carried before the Governour, afterwards held in Custody some
time, and not permitted to go home til late that Night   And this deponent further saith that by the Governours behaviour towards him, and
other circumstances he hath great reason to believe the Governour
intended to murder him or to do him some very great personal injury

   This Deponent further saith That he was afterwards at July Gen^{ll} Court
1732 —— by the Governour's express commands by word of mouth only
(as the Marshal declared) taken just after his coming out of Court, and
carried to the common Goal, and there detained some time, for speaking
to the Court (in a cause between the Governour, Plaintiff and Mr Porter
defendant) his knowledge of the practice used in this Province in case of
Over pleaded by the Defendant and &c   And with what this Deponent
said the Court declared they were not displeased or offended   Afterwards
on a Habeas Corpus brought and return thereof made to the Marshal to
the Court, this Deponent was discharged from that Imprisonment by the
unanimous Opinion of the Court

   This Deponent further saith, that he was at the Council Chamber when
the Governour was hearing some complaints against Mr Porter   Mr Porter offered divers times to speak, but was not allowed   He delivered to
the Governour at the Council Table a paper, the Governour reaching
out his hand, took the paper off the Table and by his action shewed he
was going to throw it behind him into the fire, Mr Porter spoke to the
Governor and told him it related to his Defence, but the Governour threw
it into the fire,   this Deponent was very near the Governour, so as he

very well observed the Paper was not out of the Governour's hands when Mr Porter spoke to him

E MOSELEY

Jurat coram me septimo
   die Aprilis 1733
               NATH RICE Sec^y

NORTH CAROLINA—ss.

Pursuant to an order of the right Honble the Lords Commissioners for Trade and Plantations dated August the 16th 1732 John Montgomery Esqr being summoned to appear before me Nath Rice Esq his Majesties secretary of the said Province to give his Testimony touching several Matters complained of by the Governour against Edmund Porter Esqr and by the said Porter against his Excellency thereupon appeared and being sworn on the Holy Evangelists deposeth and sayeth that he was present some time in January 1731, when the Governour and Council were hearing several articles of complaint exhibited against the said Porter by William Little Esqr on behalf of himself and others for several injurys alledged to be done by him in the Execution of his Office of Judge Admiral and during the time of the said hearing this Deponent saw Mr Porter deliver to the Governour a Paper which he declared he had directed should be delivered to him in case he the said Porter had been absent or not able to attend the Councill at that time or words to that purpose which Paper the Governour taking in his hand, moved his hand seeming to design to throw the same into the fire and declared he would receive not papers or letters from him and would serve them all in that manner or words (to the best of this Dep^{ts} remembrance) to that purpose. The said Deponent says that on the same day a Majority of the Councill having voted that Mr Porter ought to be suspended from the execution of the Office of Judge Admiral, the Governour immediately thereupon demanded the Opinion of the Councill whether Mr Porter should be suspended from his place in Councill in regard he was so bad a man and not fitt to sitt therefor to that effect) whereupon this deponent to the best of his remembrance, heard some of the Councill declare it was their opinion, that he ought to be suspended but it being objected to by some Member of Councill that it was irregular to suspend him from Council before a charge was exhibited against him for misbehaviour in that Office, his Excellency delayed the said suspension, and as this Deponent heard ex-

hibited a charge against him next morning upon which charge he has
heard and believes Mr Porter was on the same day the said charge was
exhibited suspended as a member of Councill.

                                       JOHN MONTGOMERY.

   Jurat coram me septimo
      die Aprilis 1733
            NATH RICE Sec

NORTH CAROLINA—ss

   Pursuant to the directions of the Right Honᵇˡᵉ the Lords Commission-
ers for Trade and Plantations in their Letter dated August 16 1732 I
Nathaniel Rice Esqʳ Secretary of North Carolina Do hereby certify that
at the Instance of Edmond Porter Esqʳ I summoned John Baptista
Ashe Gentleman to appear and give Testimony touching matters in some
Complaints made by his Excellency Governour Burrington and the said
Edmond Porter against each other, thereupon the said John Baptista
Ashe appeared and on his Oath on the Holy Evangelists saith That at
Edenton in the Council Chamber on or about the 20 day of January
173½ His Excellency Governour Burrington and the Council proceeding
to the Tryal of Edmond Porter Esqʳ then Judge of the Vice Admiralty
of this Province on a charge or complaints of Sundry persons exhibited
against him by Mr William Little for wrongs done or said to be done by
him in the Execution of his said office, both parties being called Mr
Porter came in and addressing himself to His Excellency told him that
on a voyage he had made to the Southern parts of the Province he had
been frozen up a long time in his vessel so that he could not possibly
reach home Sooner being as he said but a little before that arrived, that
he was unprovided with an answer to his charge wherefore he prayed a
little time to prepare one   The Governour answered he would allow him
no more time,   there passed several words between them, Mr Porter
urging and repeating his request, the Governour his refusal or denyal
Upon which Mr Porter went out of the Council Chamber and in a very
small time came in again with a paper which seemed to be a letter that
had been folded up and opened again and offering it to the Governour
laid it before him on the table, telling him it was what he had left to be
delivered to his Excellency in case by any accident he should have been
prevented being at Council (or words as near as may be to that effect)
The Governour replyed he would receive no letters from him and taking
the letter or paper into his hand, he lifted his hand being about to toss it

behind him into the fire, whereupon Mr Porter said Sir it relates to my
defence (or words to that effect) the Governour said he would serve them
so or burn them it there was a bushel of them or words as near as may
be to that effect to the best of the Deponents remembrance.   The Governour then ordered the Articles to be read   Mr Porter tarried in the
Chamber some time, then withdrew, afterwards came in again and made
some objections to the proceedings (which what they were in particular
the Deponent has forgot) And after this he went out of the Council
Chamber and came not again (as the Deponent saw or heard of) during
the Tryal   After Mr Porter was gone and the first Article had been
read and Evidences heard, the vote being put to the Council, whether
the facts in that Article were fully proved or not The Deponent refused
to give his Vote for that as Mr Porter had withdrawn and would not
appear to answer the charge, his opinion was the Council could not proceed to examine the Evidence because it would be ex parte (as it were)
but ought rather if he were guilty of a Contempt or had made default
to take the facts proconfesso and this the Deponent gave as his reason,
why he would not proceed to give his opinion to the question on each
article as it was put vizt   Whether the facts were fully proved or not
After sitting some time (the Council going on in the manner aforesaid)
the Deponent went out,   while he was out the Governour ordered his
peremptory refusal to vote (without reasons given) to be entered in the
Council Journal of which the Deponent having notice by a friend he
returned and complaining of the injustice of such an act prayed that his
foregoing reasons for refusal might be entered, which was allowed of
(and since by whose artifice the Deponent shall not say) the words he
finds have been purposely as he believes so perverted and entered in the
Council Journal as to be rendered unintelligible and made nonsence.
After the Governour and Council had gone through with most of the
Articles of the charge (as the Deponent was informed giving their opinions or votes to the question put as aforesaid) Mr Porter was suspended
The next day Mr Porter appeared before the Governor and Council to
answer a complaint of the Governours against him as a member of Council   The Governour shewed during the Tryal much heat and passion
argueing with great eagerness and warmth against Mr Porter and after
the Majority of the Council vizt Mr Jenoure Mr Halton Mr Lovick and
Mr Gale had voted for his suspension (Mr Ashe, Mr Rowan and Mr Harnet dissenting) the Governour told Mr Porter he doubted not but he
should have him sending some very humble messages quickly.   Mr Porter answered he would be cut to pieces first to which the Governour

replyed he might not perhaps come at first himself but he would be sending his wife

This Deponent further Sayeth, that he has been well acquainted with Mr Porter these seven or eight years that he knows but few persons in the Government whose Estates are greater than Mr Porters. That after Mr Porters arrival in this Province in being in the latter end of Governour Burrington's administration under the Proprietors he observed a very great intimacy and familiarity between the Governour and Mr Porter, as also after Sir Richard Everard was Governour of this Province, Mr Burrington Mr Porter and the Deponent being in the Lower house of Assembly together and very conversant with each other   And upon Proposals during that Assembly of sending home Agents for the Country, the Deponent remembers the said Governour Burrington his proposing Mr Porter and Mr Goffe as two very proper persons for such agency in his opinion, but seemed to dislike Mr Dukinfield who had been proposed by some others

JOHN BAPTISTA ASHE.

Jurat coram me Septimo
    Die Aprilis 1733
        MATH   RICE Sec.

Narrative upon oath of Edmond Porter Esqr relating to his Complaints against Captain Burrington Governour of North Carolina

[Rec^d with Mr Porter's letter of 15 Aug 1733.]

NORTH CAROLINA—ss

In pursuance of the Directions of the Right Honble the Lords Commissioners for Trade and Plantations in a Letter dated August the 16. 1732 directed to me Edmond Porter of the aforesaid Province and Signed by Secretary Popple touching complaints and Representations of Governour George Burrington against me and my Complaints and Representations against him wherein their Lordships are pleased to give me leave or any other person concerned to make affidavits before any Judge or other Magistrate concerning the subject matter of the said complaints. I have therefore examined Several papers and memorandums now by me, and to the best of my knowledge beliefe and observations have here under written given a True and genuine narrative respecting the said complaints Vizt   The Governor in his charge against me on my suspersion the 21ᵗʰ of January 1731 as member of Council intermixed matters which related to my suspension as Judge of the Vice Admiralty the day before moves me at this time to relate some few particular passages of the Governor's conduct and usuage to me with relation with that office since his arrival.

On or about the 24ᵗʰ day of February 1731 Mʳ Burrington (I was told) caused his Commission as Governor of this Province to be published at Edenton I was then gon a voyage after admiralty perquisites near two hundred miles by water, and when I returned home on the 7ᵗʰ of March my wife shewed me a letter she had received from the Governor dated the 26ᵗʰ of February for the lent of her chaise which She told me She readily granted, and a Servant with it, to fetch his big belled wife (as he termed her) out of Virginia

On the 8ᵗʰ of March I waited on the Governor at Edenton where after some previous discourse in the Council chamber that evening before Chief Justice Smith relating to the affairs of the Admiralty, the Governor told me the Court of Admiralty here was his Court I replyed that I thought it was the Kings Court as all Courts were that was under his Majesties Government no he said it was his Court or words of near that purport whereupon I dropt the discourse finding it did not please At this time and before there was a suit depending in the Court of Vice Admiralty on a Libel and Complaint of Sir Richard Everard when Governor against one Miles Gale and Chamberlaine for presuming to hoist an Union Flag on four several dayes in Defiance (as it was given out) to Sir Everard on the Court of Admiralty and when the Marshall of Admiralty was going on board the sloope two brothers to serve a citation on Gale and Chamberlaine thereupon presented a gun at his brest and used other violence (as set forth to me by the said Marshal on oath) which compelled him to retreat on shore and for this contempt he the said Chamberlaine was cited to appear at a Cort of Vice Admiralty

On the 9ᵗʰ of March after my being Qualifyed a Member of Council by his Majesties appointment) the Governor repeated his former discourse, that the Court of Admiralty here was his Court ading withall that I must not hold Courts without his leave I was surprized to hear him talk after that Manner because my commission did impower me to hold Courts &c in any part of this Province, wherefore I was resolved to do my Duty and according to the appointment I had made to hold a Court and take cognizance of the Offences committed by the said Gale and Chamberlaine (which Court to the best of my memory was on the 10ᵗʰ of March aforesaid) when the Court was opened the Governor came

in placing himselfe at a considerable distance from the Bench and during
the proceedings with a displeased bow he told me I ought to give the
Defendants longer time whereupon the Court was adjourned till next
day   After I got out of Court the Governor followed me with a countenance full of wrath and coming up with me in a violent manner he
expressed Himselfe, vizt G—ds bl—d Sir what do you mean? you were
not to go on so, you are not to hold Courts without my leave &c   The
Chief Justice by this time came up with us and endeavoured to moderate matters, and afterwards declared to me that he was very sorry the
Governor should use me so and that the parties had applyed to him for
a prohibition which he thought he could not grant in those cases, by
reason they seem to appear properly within the Jurisdiction of Admiralty
On the 11th of the said month the Court met according to adjournment
and for further Deliberation (but more to prevent those extreams which
I found was like to be the consequence if I proceeded to judgment on
the offenders) I ordered the Court to be adjourned to Friday following and
then I returned to my Plantation   On the 14th of said March Mr Chief
Justice Smith and Coll. Jones made me a visit   Coll Jones then delivered me a message, by order he said of the Governor, not to hold Courts
of Admiralty without his leave, and that the Governor said he doubted I
should be ruined for what I had don already he also told me he heard that
the Governor did intend at my next sitting if I offered to persist in that
affair to come into Court thrust me out of the seat and resume the seat
as Judge himselfe, and this account I had likewise from others which
gave me reason to beleive it was true, wherefore to prevent the mischiefs
that might attend such violence as well as a contempt of the Court of
Admiralty which I expected would afterwards be made by the Populace
I forebore sitting in Judgment again on those offenders Gale and Chamberlaine, who as well as several other masters of vessels (I have been
told) the Governor gave leave that they might hoist a flag at mast head
when they pleased and this indulgence I beleive is true and found my
beleife on the observations I made the first year of the Governors
arrival, when Flags at the mast heads of vessells seem to me to be more
commonly wore than any other colours, don often in the harbour of
Edenton in sight of the Governor for several days together, especially by
Miles Gale who not only appeared as Admiral of the Sea but also a sort
of Lord paramount at land he being permitted to display a flagg on the
top of his house at many times and for days together in sight of the
Governor This Illegal use of the flagg and other forbidden colours
hath given great offence and vexation to the Commander of his Majesties

ships of war in America wherefore and for other reasons I presume it is
forbidden by his Majesties 93 Instruction thō to vessels commissioned
by the Governor of the Plantations, consequently those who have no
such commission are offendors in a large degree, how far the Governor
hath complyed with his Majesties 70ᵗʰ or that 93ʳᵈ Instruction or how
well I have deserved for endeavouring to prevent a breach thereof and
supporting the Jurisdiction of Admiralty here (as in the case recited of
Gale and Chamberlaine) I shall humbly submit to your consideration of
my Lords Commissioners of Admiralty and to my Lords for Trade and
Plantations

By the Copy transmitted to me by from Mᵣ Secretary Popple of Mᵣ
Burrington's letter without date to the Board of Trade he hath thus
expressed a complaint "was made to me also by Edmond Porter Esqᵣ
"Judge of the Admiralty against several persons for an intended Riot
"and Combination of a great number of persons intending to assassinate
"him or obstruct him in the execution of his office upon which I prom-
"ised him if he would draw up the Complaint in form that the persons
"might be served with Copies, I would appoint a day for hearing but
"the Judge having offered nothing further upon his Complaints, I con-
"clude he has dropt it, by what I can learn there was no Riot intended
"nor any design to hurt him"

What the Governor means by intended Riot I know not but I should
think when a great number of people (some of them privately armed)
mete on an unlawfull design and assemble themselves into the Court
House the very hour a Court of Admiralty was to sit and then and there,
revel, drink, sing and dance stamp shout and alternately set up in the
seat of Justice two mock Judges in dirission of the Admiralty and declare they would continue them Judges, by which means and other
bloudy designs as was apprehended they gave a Rout to the Court of
Admiralty on the 7ᵗʰ of January 17 30 (that was in pursuit of Admiralty
perquisites belonging to the Crown) as appears by several original depositions now by me: whether those were riotous proceedings I leave to
others to judge—I did often complain to the Governor on his first coming
as well as afterwards, concerning that abuse, desiring it might be examined in Council, and he did as often make light of it, and advised me to
make matters up with those who I had so accused, he did also at his
first coming and several times afterwards offer his service to interpose in
my behalfe to prevent those suits which he sayd would otherwise be
brought against me for some former proceedings of mine as Judge of
Admiralty, I told him that I knew nothing that I had committed in

that Station but what I could answer before impartial Judges, whereupon he replyed it is very well and seemed displeased which I then and do yet apprehend proceeded from my not entirely throwing myselfe on him for protection against the malice of those who did believe the Governor at the same time was stirring up to bring such against me in order to compel me to a resignation to his will and pleasure) the consequence whereof I dreded more than the misfortunes which might attend me if I did not submit to his proposal, and to. the two following reasons 1st because it would have fixed and imployed a guilt in me to desire his Excellency to screen or protect me from Justice   2^{ndly} I did expect during the Governors Administration that I must become after that a mear puple or a tool to him both in and out of Council Courts of Chancery and Admiralty and perhaps be constrained to vote Judge and Act very often against the light of my own conscience

After this Digression I must beg leave to go back to the subject matter of the aforesaid Riot and my application to the Governor   as before observed I found it was in vaine to say any more to him in private and therefore I drew up a Memorial concerning that affair dated May the 7th 1731, and delivered it the same day at the Council Board praying that proper Subpœnas might be issued out for my Witness and a day assigned me to maintain my charge,   the Governor I remember took up the said Memorial and perused it afterwards in a slight manner,   he told me I must apply to the Chief Justice, and this Memorial or petition was not so much as read out by the Clark of the Council, whereupon I was obliged to take it again without the least prospect of having a hearing in Council before the Governor though he hath asserted to the Board of Trade "that he offered me to appoint a time for hearing"'   The Governors extrarodinary behavor in that affair and his interfering with my proceedings in the Admiralty Courts against Miles Gale and Chamberlaine as before recited, is by Mr Smith (I hear) complained of to his Majestie, and is made two Articles of his charge against his Excellency, therefore I shall at this time forbear inlarging as I could do in many other perticulars of the Governors conduct since respecting that business— Mr Joseph Jenoure Mr John Lovick and Edmund Gale being three of the persons accused with the Riot aforesaid on the 7th of January 1730 (as appears by several depositions now by me) and giving a Rout to the Court of Admiralty here   and as I did apprehend Mr Lovick and Gale not being appointed members of Council agreable to the Kings 7th & 9th Royal Instructions was therefore the foundation of my 2^d and 3^d Exceptions dated the 19th of Feby 1731   Humbly offered to the consideration of my Lords for Trade and Plantations. How regular it was in the Governor after my suspension of Judge of the Vice Admiralty to commission Mʳ Gale in my stead who had been so judiciously accused by me and had lent a hand to vote me from that office without obliging him to give me Security as is directed by his Majesties 69. Instruction I leave to my superiours to Judge. It is very probable if Mʳ Gale had no prejudice to me at that time (as I am very well assured to the contrary) it was an inducement to him to vote me out of an office, that himself might have a promise of or did at least expect to enjoy against this Choice of Edmᵈ Gale to be Judge of Admiralty I did hear that Mʳ Ashe, Mʳ Rowan and Mʳ Harnet did dissent, thō I doubt not but it is represented in the transmitted Copies of the Council books to be the unanimous opinion and choice of the Council)

The next thing I beg leave to observe upon is that part of the Governor's Letter to the Board of Trade wherein he hath thus expressed "Complaint was also made to me against the Judge of the Admiralty "for many illegal and arbitrary proceedings in that Court against all "law and common right" I presume the complaint he means was that which was introduced by the Council Board on or about the 10ᵗʰ of May 1731. by Mʳ William Little in behalfe of himselfe and others amongst which Number of complainants (of whose names Mʳ advocate Little hath made bold to make use of) he mentions Robert Foster Esqʳˢ and William Makev Esqʳˢ those Epithetts of Esqʳˢ I suppose Little thought proper to bestow on the complainants that they might be thought by their Representations to the Board of Admiralty as men of Rank and Consequence though one of them Clerk of a precinct &c and the other a Tanner by Trade and Deputy Marshall under Halton In those complaints Little has likewise appeared as well for the dead as the living and accuses me in the 6 and 7 articles of his charge for proceedings in the Admiralty at Port Beaufort (which were three several proceedings against thee Sloops) and also one other proceeding at Bath Town against one West, all which four proceedings I do in the presence of God declare (how right or wrong so ever they were transacted) they were Courts of Admiralty held by my Deputy Mʳ Patrick Maule in the County of Bath, whilst I was in the County of Albemarle, above a hundred miles distant from the three first Trials as near sixty miles from that of Wests Tryal, whether such Jesuitical and false blending of things were not calculated for an other Meridian and using me very ill I refer to my Lords of Admiralty to whom those complaints I hear have been transmitted in order no doubt to prejudice my conduct, by inducing their

65

Lordships to beleive that all the Courts mentioned by Little were Courts held by me in person

Mr Maule my Deputy is a man of lerning and has a plentiful fortune, if he hath don amiss, am I to answer for it) and ought not he to have been called on to answer his own proceedings instead of me   No, that Method I suppose the Governor and Little thought would not be so well it was best to sadle me not only with my own failings (as was pretended by that of other men too—I must further observe that this long complaint of Mr Littles was brought into the Council Chamber, to the best of my Memory in two or three days after I had prefered my Memorial to the Governor on the 7th of May as aforesaid, together with a List of those accused with a Riot and design of murthering me the 7th of Jan^{ry} 1730 &c   by which black list it appeared that Mr Little himself was the second man accused, but that my Memorial was rejected by the Governor as before observed, and Mr Littles complaint (though for matters of less consequence) the Governor caused to be received or ordered it to be read out by the Clerk, and I do believe it was afterwards by his order only entered in the Council book as a matter of record against me, tho the Majority of Council then present did argue that complaints against a Judge of Admiralty lay more properly before his Excellency as Vice Admiral or words to that purpose, and I presume that Mr Little thought so to because his complaint is directed to no other person than the Governor   after all which to cause that complaint to be entered in the Council Book as I hear it was, is in direct breach (as I conceive) to his Majesties 50th Instruction, who is graciously pleased to direct, that all orders made in Council be first read and approved in Council, before they are entered upon the Council book   I must beg leave also to observe that this complaint of Mr Littles which I beleive in the beginning was no otherwise designed than as a scare-crow, the better to secure or at least to deter my vote in Council when matters relating to the Kings lands and the vast sums of money received by Little as purchase money for Lands &c during his being several years Receiver came to be inquired into) lay as it were like a rod over me from May til the 4th day of November following, until after I had so repeatedly given such seeming offence in Council to the Governor by giving an opinion squaring with my conscience thô opposite often to the Judgment of his Excellency as set forth in my Memorial to the Lords Commissioners for Trade and Plantations dated February 19th 1731   I desire it may also in a most perticular manner be Remembered that this Complaint which had laid dormant for near six months, untill I had been at a very great Expence in going from place

to place in my shallope not less than four hundred miles in pursuit of
the Kings naval stores, cast away in a ship called the Lovely Molly
Anne, and had bound over (the Governor's new favorite) Roger Kenyon
of Bath Town, to our General Court, for a Trial for the fellony in selling,
shiping off and otherwise embezelling the said Stores. I say let it be
Remembered that it was after all this, and Kenyons peace offerings of a
charriot &c. to Mr Burrington, that that lurking false and artfull complaint of Littles was a fresh roused up on the fourth day of November
1731 It was on that day also that the Governor layd the foundation
for my Suspention as Member of Council, alledging as appears by the
Council book that I had asserted a falsehood in my paper called my dissent against the choice of Mr Lovick and Gale to be Members of Council This single article of falsehood was all that his Excellency charged
me with on the 4th of November between which time until the 20th of
Jany the day of my Tryall and suspention as Judge of Admiralty,
I was gon to Core sound and Cape Fair and at no Council with
the Governor Consequently could give no offence in Council as set forth
in the Governor's 1st 2d and 3d charges yet I have afterwards experienced
that his Excellency was so fertile in his Invention or rather so full of
prejudice to me that he hath tacked to his first former charge, four other
charges

The usuage which I received on the Tryal and suspension of me as
Judge of the Admiralty and Member of Council vizt the Governor's
refusing to grant me time that day to put in an answer to the complaint
of Mr Littles as prayed for, his throwing a paper into the fire after I told
him it related to my defence, saying he would serve a bushel of them in
the same manner, and the great passion and prejudice which he discovered
to me during those Tryals are truly and justly set forth in the deposition
of Coll. Moseley Mr Ashe and Mr Montgomery the Attorney General to
which I refer Only I beg leave in support of my Exceptions against
the legality of those Mr Burrington's suspentions to make this further
observation, that by the attested copy of a paragraph from the Council
book, it appears on the 20th of Jany vizt "His Excellency the Governor
"further asked the advice and opinion of the Council, whether so bad a
"man as Mr Porter was proved to be should be continued a member of
"Council within this Province Thereupon the Council (it says) were
unanimously of opinion that the said Edmond Porter was not fit to sit at
this Board &c Is not this a plain prejudging both in the Governor and
such of the Council who did so vote? And when they had so prejudged
me they brought on my Tryal the next day for a further judgment.

Give me leave also to observe a little on the words before mentioned in the Council book viz' "that they (the Council) were unanimously of opin- "ion that the said E. Porter was not fit to sit at this Board" I believe there is no man so hardened a Sinner as to say, that either M' Ashe, M' Rowan or M' Harnet did vote for my suspention as Member of Council, how comes it to pass than, that the records of that Tryal sets forth on the 20th of Jan'y "that the Council were unanimously of opinion that the "said Edmond Porter was not fit to sit at this Board" And that after such their unanimous opinion, that three of them the next day voted against my suspention as member of Council? When these absurditys come to fall under the consideration of my Lords of Admiralty and the Board of Trade, I hope their Lordships will see plainly what dependance they can have on the Truth of those Copys transmitted them from the Council book I can say much on this head, and where the sence of things have been basely perverted and made nonsence in the Council book (as observed by M' Ashe's deposition a Member of his Majestys Council) As also entrys in the Council book that had never been Transacted in Council and other very substantial Matters intirely left out perticularly what relate to the proceedings against Colonel Moseley Coll Moore and other persons in Council about lands in Jan'y 1731, after Coll Moore had come near two hundred mile to answer the same which copious answers of Coll. Moseley's and Coll Moore I could not find in the Council Book but left out as I sopose by reason it contained matter about Land which related to the Governor himself Indeed It bears the name of the Council book and that is all but in my opin- ion It may more properly be called the Governors Political Diary— I do further assert that I was present in March General Court 1732, when the Governor came within the Bar of the Court about a quarter of an hour before the Court was adjourned, and in great pas- sion demanded the Deputy Marshal Makey to take hold of Coll Mose- ley and bring him out of the Court before him when M' Moseleys hand was on the book going to take the oaths to his Majesty, accordingly the said Marshall did take him out of Court and afterwards carried him prisoner to the Governor's house I was also present with Colonel Moseley at July General Court following before the Cort house dore when M' Mackey came up to us and took M' Moseley prisoner a second time (as he the Marshal sayd by the Governor's order for speaking in a cause which was brought by the Governor against me) whereupon Col Moseley went into Court again and applyed himselfe to the Judges and they declared they were not displeased with any thing he had said in that business or words to that Effect. Notwithstanding all which the Deputy Marshall by those Orders carried him away to the Common Goal and Mr Moseley was afterwards on a Habeas Corpus discharged from his confinement In October Court following Mr Little superceed Mr Paylin as Chief Justice and all the Assistant Judges were removed and a new set commissioned in their Room And I heard that all this choping and changing was don and consented too, by the Governor and Council of three only present vizt Lovick Gale and Mr Phenny How far such a conduct corresponds with his Majesties 5th and 44 Royal Instructions or the safety and security of his poore subjects in this Province is most humbly submitted. The Governor in his Letter to the Board of Trade dated Septer 4th 1731 represents me to their Lordships to be under many prosecutions and actions in those perticulars and at that time he hath vouchsafed to say right for all which prosecutions and Indictments I shall ever have cause to remember Governor George Burrington and the Grand Jury that found those Indictments, many of the said Jurors having been accused in the Plot of the 7th of Janry against my life and giving a Rout to the Court of Admiralty and therefore it could not be supposed that they would do otherwise, for those who would endeavour to take away my life no doubt but would destroy my reputation or fortune, neither were they a qualified Grand Jury according to the Laws of this Province but on the contrary I am very well assured they were packt for that Extra purpose. Also what the Governor hath related as to my objections in writing (or rather my opinion as set forth in the preamble of my assent) against the choice of Mr Lovick and Gale is True, the title of which said objections begin in these words "The opinion of Edmond Porter in Humble manner to his Excellency" the sense of which as but an opinion was a just and necessary application throughout the whole of those objections, wherefore then could I give such offence to his Excellency or wherein was the unfare reasoning or great falsity; the point seems to be given up by the Governor that there was six qualified Members of Council at that time in the Province vizt. Messrs Rice, Jenoure, Halton, Ashe, Harnett and myself, this if I understand numbers is six, wherefore then did his Excellency appoint Mr Lovick and Edmond Gale when he knew it exceeded the number seven (so strictly limmitted by his Majesty's 7th and 9th Instructions) If his Excellency thinks he had a Power to appoint as many members of Council as he pleased why did he put that previous question to me the 27th of July 1731 and afterwards make that opinion (which perhaps he would have termed a contempt if I did not give) a charge against me for suspention! As to the Truth of the several other parts alledged in his Excellency's Letters to the Board of Trade I am a Stranger too, and if I may speak with plainess neither do I believe any part or paragraph of them to be true, vizt where he insinuates or charges some of the Members of Council with Foolery and villainy! or that I ever asked his Excellency to be a party in any unlawfull Quarrels of mine or to screen me from any prosecutions! or that frequent Tumults or Riots, or that any Tumult or Riot hath hapned since the arrival of his Excellency headed by me or any other person or persons whatsoever to my knowledge! or that I had prevented the former Council, General Courts or Precinct Courts Sitting! or that I ever prevented any one Member of Council, by thought, word, or deed, from attending the Governor, for the Nomination of a New Chief Justice as set forth by his Excellency! Or that I did ever know, or hear of any qualified Member of Council that was dead at the time the Governor dated his letter to the Board of Trade Neither did I ever hear of any number or part of a 1000 Indians of the five Northern Nations, or any other Nation of Indians that was arrived in this Province mentioned in the said Letter! Or do I think I merit to be so continually called an Infamous or contemptable Fellow by the Governor Or do I remember that I ever insisted or gave an opinion (when the enquiry of Pattents for Lands granted by Sir Richard Everard) that nothing more ought to be enquired into than the words spoken by Sir Richard Everard against the King. For when things that related to Lands was discoursed of in Council the Governor seemed to think I was to forward in those matters, for which I have been discountananced by his Excellency both in and out of Council   I conclude this long Narrative (which I could not well contract in less compass and answer the perticulars of Mr Burrington's several charges and his two Letters to my Lords) If his Excellency would exercise more moderation and less sander and enquire narrowly into the Titles of the Stagpark, How old feilds the Burger and other Lands and the many thousand pounds purchas money for Lands received by Mr Little it might prove of greater advantage to his Majesty's Revenue in this Province than to pursue my ruin, or to reduce me to that great poverty mentioned in his Letter to my Lords Commissioners for Trade and Plantations, and however contemptable his Excellency would represent my circumstance to be I should be loth to exchange interest with him in this Province, (set aside about fifty or sixty thousand acres of land which he holds at Cape Fair whereof not one acre in my opinion is legally acquired) and notwithstanding Mr Burrington hath treated me in his representation as a mean and contemptable fellow, it may be remembered that on the first day of this Instant May I was elected at Edenton a Member of Assembly for the ancient precinct of Chowan in the County of Albemarle (in which precinct the Governor and myself resides) against all the force and power, he or his friends could make to the contrary, Wherefore how far the Governor's Enviduous Epithetts and character of me and others in this Province, savours of malice and untruth, is most humbly submitted to the Right Honble the Lords Commissioners for Trade and Plantations.

E PORTER

The foregoing Narrative of Edmond Porter Esqr he saith is founded partly on his own knowledge and other parts on his beleife and observation as set forth in the preamble and contents of the said Narrative to the Truth whereof the said Edmond Porter made Oath on the Holy Evangelists the fifteenth day of May 1733 before me

JOHN MONTGOMERY
Attorney General

Extract of the Council Journal of North Carolina relating to Mr Porter's not being fit to sit at that Board with Mr Porter's observations thereof

NORTH CAROLINA—ss.

Extract from the Council Journal 20 Jany 173¼

His Excellency the Governor further asked the Advice and Opinion of the Council whether so bad a man as Mr Porter was proved to be should be continued a Member of Council within this Province

Thereupon the Council were unanimously of Opinion that the said Edmond Porter was not fit to sit at this Board

(Vera Copia)   NATH. RICE. Secretary

The above Copy will discover the previous question put by the Governor on the 20 of Jany 173¼ which led some of the Council vizt Mr Jenoure, Mr Halton Lovick and Edmond Gale to prejudge me, and altho it Says it was the unanimous Opinion that I was not fit to sit at the Council Board, Mr Ashe Mr Harnett and Mr Rowan (of his Majesties appointment) did vote against my suspention, as appears by the several Inclosed Depositions

Observations ℔ E PORTER

NORTH CAROLINA—ss.

Extract from Governor Burrington's charge against Edmond Porter
    Esq⁰ in the Council Journal 21 Jan⁷ 173½

He hath behaved at the Council Board with so much Insolence to me
that the Council hath taken Notice of his rude Behaviour in these Minutes and have entered it as their Opinion that he is too bad a Man to sit
at the Council Board &c

    Copia Vera   NATH RICE. Secretary

    This paper will confirm that prejudging which was made on me the
20 day of Jan⁷ 173½ after which the next day the Governor and the
same four prejudging Councellors proceeded to a second Judgment and
then to suspention of me as Member of Council

                            Observations ♒ E. PORTER.

———

Extracts Relating to Cap Burrington's Suspending M⁷ Porter

    After the Governor on the 20ᵗʰ of January had pronounced sentence
of of suspention on E. Porter as Judge of Admiralty the following Entry was made in Council which by permission of the Clark I took from
the rough after his Excellency had left departed the room

    Vizt His Excellency the Governor further asked the advice and opin-
ion whether so bad a man as M⁷ Porter should continue to sit as a member of Council within this Province, thereupon the Council are of opinion that the said Edward Porter was not fit to sit at this Board, the
Governor thereon gave M⁷ Porter time to the last Tuesday in March
next, but at the Instance of M⁷ Porter the same is to be heard to-morrow
four of the Clock in the afternoon

    A True Copy Test   E. PORTER

    To the above entry and opinion, assented vizt Joseph Jenoure, Robert
Halton, John Lovick and Edmund Gale the other members dessenting
vizt M⁷ Ashe, M⁷ Rowan & Cornelius Harnet

    After the aforesaid Prejudging me, the Governor the next day brought
on my Trial for a further Judgment as will appear by the following Proceedings

                                         E. PORTER.

Thursday Eleven a clock att night

I complain against Mr Porter as a Member. of Council.

1th Because he has made it his whole Endeavour ever since my arrival to perplex and obstruct all proceedings in Council by raysing unnecessary disputes and cavils.

2dly That when his opinion has been asked upon affairs of the greatest consequence wherein the Peace and quiet of the Province has depended he hath asserted direct falshoods with an Intention to embarras and perplex the administration

3^ly He hath behaved at the Council Board with so much insolence to me that the Council have taken notice of his rude behaviour in their Minutes and have entered it as their opinion that he is too bad a man to sit at the Council Board.

4^ly That the Council having upon a very full examination of the vile behaviour as Judge of the Court of Admiralty given their opinion that he deserves a suspention from that office and he being suspended accordingly I think it cannot be proper to continue him a member of Council when as such he must sit as a Judge in the Court of Chancery for this Province.

5^ly That he being a person of very ill fame and character and now under many prosecutions and indictments not only for his barbarous proceedings as a Judge but for Tumults, Riots and other disorders I think it would be a reflection on his Majestie's Council here to have such a proffligate person sit with them, and therefore ask the opinion and advice of this Board whether the said Edmund Porter ought not to be suspended from being a member of his Majestie's Council for North Carolina.

According to my promise I now send you a charge & design to give in & lay before the Council to morrow every man present att the Council day knows how long I satt here (viz) from morning to nine att night. I am Sir

Your humble servant

GEO BURRINGTON.

Edmund Porter Esqr

N^o CAROLINA.

Friday following Thursday 11 'oth clock at night

The Answer of Edmund Porter to the Complaint of His Excellency Geo Burrington Esqr Governor &c.

His Excellency exhibiting a charge against me setting me forth as a very heinous person, and yet alledging no particular facts, urged me (that I might acquit myself and convince the world that I merited not such Titles as in the charge are given me) to an immediate answer, which I shall make in as few words as I can, hoping no advantage may be taken of any slip which may happen in a thing so hastily conceived and delivered

1 As to the first charge, I observe it is so general (no particular fact being alledged against me) that I know not how to answer to it otherwise, than that it will serve to be applyed to any of the Council who differing from the Governor in opinion shall raise disputes thereon

2 As to the 2nd I also observe that the generality of the charge admits no charge

3 As to the 3 charge I observe that it is also very general saving as to the notice the Council have taken of my Behaviour and the opinion they have already before any charge exhibited against me, delivered thereon and entered in Council which plainly shews that they vizt Such of the Council as have so done have prejudged me, How far this conduces to their Qualifications of being my Judges in the present case I shall leave to others to Judge

4 I must patiently bear the harsh terms the Governor is pleased to bestow on me in this Article and as to the proceeding of the Governor in my case as Judge of the Admiralty and the opinion of the Council as to my meriting a suspention from that office I shall only say that I thought it hard considering how unavoidably I was detained from appearing sooner (being frozen up with my vessel far from Edenton and not possible to come to it any otherwise than by water which detained me till Wednesday last in the afternoon from my Plantation) that I should so immediately on my very first appearance be pressed to a hearing and that after examination of the Evidence of the Complaints against me I was not allowed time to produce those in Defence, this I expected because (as I moved last night) I remember well it was the method observed in the complaint between Sir R Everard and Mr Lovick against each other But of this I shall take more particular notice at another place As to the reason given by his Excellency that because I am suspended as a Judge of the Admiralty it is not therefore proper I should be continued a member of Council, I beg leave to observe that supposing I were fully convicted of the Charges against me as Judge of the Admiralty, yet those facts were all done before my being in the Council I would therefore beg leave to make this Query Whether after I am nominated by his Majesty of his Council in this Province and qualified according to law, Facts done before, nowaies respecting that office may

be exhibited against me and allowed as sufficient reasons for turning or throwing me out of Council And if the Governor and Council shall be of that opinion I hope it may be a standing rule and that others may be also examined as to past actions of their life before their being in Council as well as me

5 As to the fifth Article I must observe as before the generality of the charge and the language bestowed on me (as yet I hope one of his Majesty's Council) by his Excellency, in the present case my Judge, at least one of my Judges, As to the Prosecutions, Indictments &c against me, I beg leave to say that others have been indicted before me, and that every one accused is not to be concluded guilty and therefore this is no reason for suspention or for throwing on me such hard names, if it were it would be an easy matter to make the most innocent person deserve it and to have bestowed on him the titles of one of ill fame and character and a proffligate person

To conclude as your Excellency hath been pleased to suspend me as Judge of Vice Admiralty I think it a most insupportable grievance that after I put in my first paper yesterday praying reasonable time to make answer to the complaint of Mr Little your Excellency not only overruled the same But my second paper produced on the Board your Excellency in great heat threw into the fire thô I told you it related to my defence

Delivered at the Council Board this 21st day of January 1731 Humbly praying that this my answer be entered in the Council Book

Signed   E PORTER.

Answer to Governor Burrington's charge.

Mr Edmund Porter praying us to commit to writing what he remembered to have heard the Governor say after having suspended him from being one of his Majesties Council in North Carolina. We do declare and give under our hands that on January the 21th 173½ at Edenton in the Council Chamber, after His Excellency George Burrington Esqr Governor had put the Vote to the Council then sitting whether they consented to the suspension of Edmund Porter Esqr and the Majority of the Council vizt Joseph Jenoure Robert Halton, John Lovick and E. Gale Esqr consenting to his suspension (those who dessented being John Baptista Ashe, Mathew Rowan & Cornelius Harnet Esqr) immediately thereon we heard the Governor say he doubted not but he should have him sending some very humble messages quickly, the other vizt Mr Porter answered, he would be cut to pieces for it, the Governor replyed, he might not perhaps come at first himself, but he would be sending his wife

BAP⁹ ASHE
CORN⁹ HARNET

The above is the hand writing of M⁹ Gale a Member of the Council appointed by His Majesty

We the Subscribers do hereby testify and declare that we were present in Council on or about the 30 of March 1733 when M⁹ Edmund Porter delivered to his Excellency a Paper of which the within is a true Copy, he having given us the same to be read before he put it in, desiring our Notice that if there should be occasion, he might have our Testimony thereon

NATH RICE.
BAP⁹ ASHE.

18ᵗʰ July 1733

M⁹ Porter's Letter to Governor Burrington acquainting him he has received a packet from the Secretary of the Board of Trade containing accusations against him

To His Excellency George Burrington Esq⁹ Governor Captain General &c

SIR,

I think myself obliged to inform your Excellency that I have received a packet from the Secretary of the Board of Trade, containing charges or accusations against me extracted from letters of your Excellency's together with a letter from M⁹ Secretary Popple, by order of the Lords Commissioners of Trade and Plantation wherein he acquaints me he is directed to transmit to your Excellency likewise Copies of a Representation and other papers containing complaints which I have made against your Excellency and that their Lordships may be enabled to make a judgment of the true state of the affair, he has by their commands acquainted your Excellency that their Lordships expect you should return to them such depositions and proofs in your own behalfe, as you should think convenient, giving me at the same time full liberty or any other person concerned to make affidavits before any Judge or other Magistrate of what they know concerning the subject matter of the said complaints, and that such Judge or Magistrate be likewise injoined to summon such persons as the complainants respectively shall name, in order to give their Testimony in this affair, and your Excellency he informs me, is further directed to interchainge with me true copies of the proofs and affidavits, so soon as they shall be made, directing me to observe the like on my part, Twenty days being allowed us to make our replys respectively, by affidavits or otherwise to be in like manner interchangeably communicated to each other and afterwards transmitted to their Lordships without loss of time, pursuant to the aforesaid directions of their Lordships, I presume to acquaint your Excellency thereof, and that I am ready and intend immediately to proceed in the affair

I am your Excellency most obedient servant

E. PORTER

Edenton March 30ᵗʰ 1732 }
delivered at the Council Board }

Mr Edmund Porter maketh Oath on the Holy Evangelists that the foregoing paper is a true Copy of what he delivered when the Governor was present at the Council Board on the day of the date thereof since which time the Deponent Sayeth he has had no answer thereto from the Governor as he did expect and doth beleive that his Excellency hath no design or desire to proceed in the form and manner prescribed by the Lords Commissioners for Trade and Plantations, Wherefore he is constrained to transmit to the Board of Trade the Several Deponents Depositions and Papers relating to his complaints against Governor Burrington.

E PORTER.

Jurat coram me
19° Die Julii 1733 NATH. RICE

I hereby certify that in Obedience to an Order from the Lords Commissioners for Trade and Plantations touching Governor Burrington and Edmund Porter Esqrs their complaints against each other, at the Instance of the said Edmund Porter I summoned Mr John Conner Attorney at Law to give his Testimony in relation to the said complaints, who accordingly appeared before me, but refused to answer to any Interrogatories, saying he would neither swear for nor against the Governor

NATH RICE Sec

7ᵗʰ April 1733

Four Letters from Gov. Burrington to Mr Porter with Mr Porter's
Remarks—Recd with Mr Porter's Letter of 15 Aug 1733

Letters from Governor Burrington to Mr Porter.

May 3rd 1725.

DEAR SIR

I have talked with the old Mr Crisp who will not part with his hors
under a price of eight each   nothing besides will fetch them   the price of
whip law is £7 10s in bills and Grindstone 2 5 In the same   I design
to begin my journey through Bertie next Wednesday   I recommend diligence to you dureing my absence   att my return will not fail to see
whither you have industrious (or no)   In mean time

    I am

        Your most humble servant

            GEO BURRINGTON

                  Sunday Noon

DEAR SIR

I have thought much concerning the discourse we have had together
about the Levy am entirely of opinion it cannot lawfully be raised
without the Assembly, for then there would be no occasion for Assemblys
(as Gale says there is none) therefore I have told all people I have
talked with, that no money can be lawfully demanded nor paid before
so ordained by the Assembly   every body is of the same opinion here   I
design for Bertie tomorrow where I shall preach the same Doctrine as I
hope you will in your Neighbourhood   att my return to this place shall
acquaint you with the success of my journey,   my humble respects to
Madam Porter

        I am Sir, your humble servant

    The young Knight is clapt   G B.

                  August the 17th 1725.

DEAR SIR,

I take the oportunity of Mrs Loyds visit to let you know that I set
out this morning for my journey into the Lower precincts,   I doubt not
but the Gentry will be in motion   if they have any meetings with the
voters of Chowan your Prensence will quash and defeat their ill designes,
the Knight and his honest company seem much disquieted and low in
spirit   they talk (especially Gale) that there is no occasion for an Assembly they will have none &c   but this I take for a fetch to make us

slaken our diligence in promoting the choice of good men to serve their Country in the Ensueing Assembly which must be chosen and meet according to the Fundamental Constitutions of Carolina as you well know, I am sure nothing shall be wanting on my part to rescue the administration out of the hands of these rogues therefore beleive my journey will take me up a fortnight att my return you shall be sure to hear if there is anything worth notice the way I go. If you have any leisure in the mean while I hope will employ some of it in drawing up an address for the Proprietors for the Assembly men to sign It is absolutely necessary to have it ready by the time if you think it necessary to send one

          I am Sir
              Your most obedient friend
              and humble servant
                      GEO BURRINGTON

NOTE.—Mr Burrington under his own handwriting on the other side says vizt "I am sure nothing shall be wanting on my part to resque "the administration out of the hands of these rogues" It is to be observed this letter was wrote the first year of Sir Richard Everards Government when Mr John Lovick was his principle and only adviser and at that time the Secretary and one of the Council under the late Lord Proprietors therefore must be comprehended by Mr Burrington's letter to be one of the Rogues therein mentioned thō he has now thought fit to appoint him a Member of the King's Council for this Province

                                E. P

Remarks vizt

The 4 inclosed Letters are of Governor Burrington's hand writing wrote about 7 years past thō he pretended to the Board of Trade that he knew little of me before his last coming over' this is so far from Truth, that it will appear by one of these Letters dated May 3d 1725 he was so very obliging (at my first comeing with my family to settle here) that he was cheapning and buying hors, whip saws and grindstones for my negroes to work with, at a time when he was actually Governor under the Lords Proprietors and therefore would have been rude in me to have put his Excellency on so mean an Office It is a Maxim in Law that where the credibility of an Evidence or Accuser is disproved in one point, the Testimony is usually invalid in the whole If their Lordships are pleased to judge of things by the same rule I am sure of being safe against all the Machinations, Calumny and Detraction of his Excellency

Coll Moseley's after dinner

DEAR SIR

I am sorry you could not favour us with your good Company today, Shall not be able to wait on you till after the Court is broke up, we are now drinking your health all happiness attend you

I am sincerely

yours

GEO BURRINGTON

[B P R O NORTH CAROLINA B T VOL. 9 A 43.]

LETTER FROM CAPTAIN BURRINGTON TO LORDS OF TRADE OCTOBER 5th 1733.

MY LORDS,

I have the honour to send your Lps the Journal of the late Assembly, the reason they were not dispatched sooner was that I could not obtain the short Journal of the Upper House from the Secretary's Deputy before the fifth day of this month

There was a fair prospect that business would be done by the late Assembly, before Mr Smith returned in last June, but this man by the Advices he brought from England, or invented himself, so much confused the Lower House that Moseley and his faction confounded the other Members, and nothing could be done, they carried their impudence so far, I thought myself obliged to dissolve them The Report of their Committee I did not see till some weeks after the Dissolution, it was wrote by Moseley the speaker, the original is in my Custody, I purpose to have it examined into when the Council meets, and shall be able (I think) to expose the Paper & its Author.

Smith's Letter to the Assembly, is a sequel of his Articles of Complaints against me, and shews the inconsiderate villany of a man that will put his name to anything a sett of subtle Rogues write for him

Mr Rice his paper in the Journal will be answered the next Council, and his folly and falsehood made apparent

It has been thought by many people in this Province a way to Preferment by opposing me and obstructing the Administration, the behaviour of some of His Majesty's Officers has been of singular use to Moseley and his Gang, thereby he has not only hitherto prevented an examination and enquiry into his roguery and frauds when Surveyor General, but has those officers entirely under his own direction

The Province is in perfect Peace and Quietness, and this a year of the greatest plenty ever known in North Carolina, The Summer proved sickly, but very few have dyed There will be abundance of New Settlers in the approaching winter come from the Northern Provinces, this intelligence I have received from many already come in

I am (with due Respect)

Your Lordships

most humble

and most obedient servant

GEO BURRINGTON

N Carolina
the 5th October 1733

[FROM NORTH CAROLINA LETTER BOOK OF S P G]

MR. LAPIERRE TO THE BISHOP OF LONDON

New Brunswick in Cape Fear alias
Cape Fear Octr the 9th 1733

My Lord

As I had the honor to have been ordained by your Lordships predecessor in the year 1707 who recommended me to the Governor of South Carolina Sir Nath' Johnston, to entitle me to a parish called St Dennis in a French Colony which I was to serve till the death of the old settlers who did not understand the English tongue, so in the time of the new generation who understood the sd tongue in which they were born I became an Assistant to the Revd Mr Hazel in the Parish of St. Thomas next to my parish hoping of the two nations to make but one and the same people tho' they were a distinct parish they indifferently followed the English Church and the French as well acquainted with both languages And then seeing that my ministerial functions were not essentially required from a French Minister and hearing besides that in a province of North Carolina called Cape fear, alias New Hanover they wanted a minister the Inhabitants of that place sent for me and the Revd Mr

Garden your Lordship's Commissary in concurrence with the rest of the Clergy did actually consent that I should go and settle the divine service where it had never been   I readily complied to go thither with the proviso that they would inform your Lordship concerning my removal, but things succeeded otherwise than I expected the first year,   I was regarded and respected of the Inhabitants as St Paul was at the first by the Galatians   every one readily subscribed towards my salary, & tho' it fell short of near £100 Yet was I satisfied out of consideration to a new country which owed its good beginning less to the provision made by human Laws than to the good discretion of some conscientious inhabitants   the 2ⁿᵈ year the Gentⁿ of the Vestry thought fit to lay an assessment upon the parish that private subscribers should not be overburthened but this proved of none effect upon a mistake because what was called a parish was in reality no parish by law or act of public assembly therefore I was entirely left to the good discretion of the several Inhabitants against whom the vestry had no power of compulsion therefore I fell short of my salary the second time   the third year the Vestry I confess did me that justice to engage that satisfaction to me that might be denied by the public accordingly they promised me a certain sum to lessen my loss but this fell a great deal short of my necessary living   after the 3ᵈ year I served the people of Cape fear six months longer but received nothing for it only this answer Who put you to work?   then I thought it was time to ask for my discharge which after 3 times asking they granted me at last and took in my stead one Mʳ Richᵈ Marsden now actually performing the divine service among them, a man whose whole study always was to undermine me,   now my Lord I am left to my own shifting and I am forced to work in the field for my living and for fear this people of my former charge should in any wise endeavor to impose upon your Lordship's probity as I hear they petition for a new minister so I think myself in conscience bound to declare my mind that any Clergyman that has a mind to come thither at their request will find a lawless place, a scattered people, no glebe, no parsonage to receive him without which Govʳ Burrington told them that no minister should ever be sent to them from the Society nor from your Lordship   however my Lord there is a certain Colony in this province that requires my help upon promise of subscribing towards my maintenance with whom I will with your Lordship's good leave apply upon any reasonable terms sooner than to see the country destitute of the light of the Gospel   the bearer my Lord can testify the truth of what I do here set forth before your Lordship whose most obd't servant and dutiful son I ever profess to be in the Gospel of Christ

JOHN LAPIERRE

[B. P. R. O. NORTH CAROLINA. B. T VOL. 9 A 44.]

CAPTAIN BURRINGTON TO LORDS OF TRADE

NORTH CAROLINA the 12th of Novr 1733

MY LORDS OF TRADE,

With this your Lordships will receive the Journal of the Lower House of Assembly There was but one Councillour attended, so that Assembly fell for want of an Upper House Mr John Lovick a member of Council deceased before the meeting of the Burgesses, several more of of the Council I hear are very ill, In my next I am apprehensive I shall inform you of more vacancys in His Majesty's Council here

> I am
> > My Lords
> > > with due respect
> > > > Your Lordships
> > > > > most humble
> > > > > > & most obedient servant
> > > > > > > GEO BURRINGTON

[B P R O NORTH CAROLINA B. T VOL. 9 A 34.]

To the Right Honourable the Lords Commissioners of Trade and Plantations

The Representation of Gabriel Johnston Esqr Governor of North Carolina

Sheweth,

That William Smith Esqr Chief Justice of North Carolina presented a memorial to your Lordships July 13 1732 concerning the validity of the Laws of North Carolina, & praying that your Lordships might referr the said petition, to the Attorney and Solicitor General for their opinion.

That the said petition has never yet been referred, nor nothing done in consequence of it That it is of great moment to the said Mr Johnston to be rightly advised about the contents of the said Chief Justice's memorial

He therefore hopes your Lordships will be pleased to referr it to the Sollicitor General now, he being just ready to depart for his Government.

[B P R O North Carolina B T Vol. 21 p 214]

Mr SECRETARY POPPLE TO ATT' & SOL' GEN'
6 DEC. 1733

To John Willes Esqr and Dudley Ryder Esqr His Maj. Attorney &
Solicitor General

GENTLEMEN,

Mr Smith Chief Justice and Chief Baron of North Carolina having
presented a Representation to My Lords Commiss'r for Trade and Plantations stating some difficulties he labours under with respect to the Laws
of that Province I am commanded to send you the inclosed copy of the
said Representation and to acquaint you with their Lordships desire of
your opinion thereupon as soon as may be

I am

Gentlemen

Your most humble Serv't

Whitehall   ALURED POPPLE
    December 6th 1733

[B P R O North Carolina B. T Vol. 21 p 215]

Mr SECRETARY POPPLE TO Mr ATTORN' GEN' WILLES
11 DEC 1733

Mr Willes Attorney General

SIR,

Having laid your letter of yesterday's date before my Lords Commiss'r for Trade and Plantations I am commanded to send you the charter granted by King Charles the 2nd to the Proprietors of Carolina their
Lordships not knowing of any other authority vested in the said Proprietors to establish laws or constitutions than that contained in the said
charter

I am likewise to acquaint you that there were originally eight Proprietors of Carolina seven of whom have surrendered their rights to the
Crown

And in answer to your third Query "Where the power of making
laws for that Province is now vested" I am commanded to send you an
Extract of the Commission given to the Governor of North Carolina

under the Great Seal of this Kingdom which is to the same effect as those given to the Governors of all other Plantations under the immediate protection of the Crown

I am

Sir

Your most hum^ble Servt

Whitehall   ALURED POPPLE
Dec 11th 1733

P S. I am to desire you will please to return the inclosed printed charter when you transmit your Report

———

[B P R. O North Carolina B T Vol. 9 A 35.]

———

Lincolns Inn Decr 30th 1733

Sir,

Before Mr Sollicitor and I can give our opinions on the representation of Mr Smith which you was pleased to send us, we want to be more particularly informed of the authority by which the late Lords Proprietors of North Carolina made the fundamental constitutions therein mentioned. We should be glad likewise to be informed whether all or only some of the said Lords Proprietors have surrendered up their rights to the Crown, and in whom the power of making laws for that Province is now vested When we have received your answer, the Lds Commissioners for Trade and Plantations shall have our opinion as soon as may be   I am

Sir

Your very humble servant

J. WILLES.

———

[B. P R. O B T Journals. Vol. 43. p 6]

———

BOARD OF TRADE JOURNALS.

Whitehall Tuesday Jany 16 173¾

Present

Mr Bladen.   Sir O Bridgeman
Mr Ashe   Mr Brudenell

A Memorial and Remonstrance of two gentlemen of the Council and the Attorney General of North Carolina against Capt. Burrington Govr of that Province was read And the Board agreed to consider further thereof

[Page 48.]

WHITEHALL Tuesday April 3. 1733.

Then were read four papers from Mr Rice and Mr Ashe containing complaints against Capt Burrington Govr of North Carolina

[Page 50]

Thursday April 5th 1733

A letter from the Duke of Newcastle dated the 27th of last month signifying his Maj^{ty} appointment of Gabriel Johnstone Esqre to be Govr of North Carolina was read And the Secretary laying before the Board the Draught of a Commission accordingly a Representation thereupon and a letter for inclosing the same to the Duke of Newcastle were sign'd

[Page 71]

Thursday May 24th 1733

Mr Johnstone appointed Govr of North Carolina attending the Board desired he would let them have a state of the blank Warrants for Grants of Land which had been granted by Sir Richard Everard the late Govr of that Province and he promised to perfect the said state as soon as possible

[Page 85]

Tuesday June 19th 1733.

The following copies of Orders in Council were laid before the Board & read

*   *   *   *   *   *   *

Order in Council of the 10th May 1733 approving the Draught of a Commissⁿ for Gabriel Johnstone Esqre to be Govr of North Carolina

[Page 86.]

Wednesday June 20th 1733.

The Naval Officers List of ships entered and clear'd at Port Beaufort in North Carolina from Christmas 1730 to Michaelmas 1732 was read

[Page 103.]

Tuesday July 17th 1733.

Mr Johnstone appointed Govr of North Carolina attending his Observations upon the Draught of his Instructions were read and the Draught of his general Instructions and of those which relate to the Acts of Trade being agreed The Draught of a Representation thereupon was order'd to be prepared [page 105] which was agreed and sign'd as also a letter for inclosing the same to the Duke of Newcastle on 18th July

[Page 109]

Wednesday July 25ᵗʰ 1733.

A Representation from Capt. Burrington Gov. of North Carolina containing the present state and condition of that Province was read and the Papers referred to in the said Representation dated the 1ˢᵗ of Jan⁷ 173⅞ was laid before the Board

Minutes of Council from 28 March 1732 to the 8ᵗʰ Novʳ following

[Page 146.]

Wednesday Novʳ 28ᵗʰ 1733

The Memorial of Gabriel Johnstone Esqᵐ praying that the Representation of Mʳ Smith Chief Justice of North Carolina relating to the validity of the laws in that Province may be referred to the Solicitor General for his opinion thereon was read and directions were given for sending a copy of the said Representation to Mʳ Attʸ & Mʳ Solʳ Genˡ for their opinion thereupon in point of law.

[Page 156.]

Tuesday December 11ᵗʰ 1733

The Secretary laying before the Board a letter he had received from the Attorn⁷ Genˡ stating some difficulties with regard to the Memorial of Mʳ Smith relating to the laws of North Carolina (read 12 July 1732) and sent to Mʳ Attorn⁷ Genˡ the 28th of the last month the same was read and Directions were given for making an Answer thereto.

[Page 165.]

Thursday Decʳ 20ᵗʰ 1733.

Copy of an Order in Council of the 2ᵈ Aug 1733 approving the draught of Instructions for Gabriel Johnstone Esqʳ Govʳ of North Carolina was read

[FROM THE MSS RECORDS OF NORTH CAROLINA COUNCIL JOURNALS.]

COUNCIL JOURNALS

N° CAROLINA—ss.

At a Council held in the Council Chamber in Edenton the 29th day of March Anno Domini 1733

Present

His Excelly George Burrington Esqr Govr &c

The Honoble { Nath Rice   Jno Baptta Ashe } Esqrs Members
            { Robt Halton Jno Lovick   }   of His
            {   Edmd Gale   } Majestys Council

His Excelly the Governr laid before this Board some Praragraphs of a Letter from Mr Popple Secry to the Rt Honoble the Lords of Trade & Plantations (wrote by their Lordships command) in answer to several matter laid before their Lordships by His Excelly, This Board thereon prayed time till to morrow morning to Consider the sd Letter

Fryday March 30th

Present

His Excelly George Burrington Esqr Govr &c

The Honoble { Nath Rice   Jno Baptta Ashe } Esqrs Members
            { Robt Halton John Lovick   }   of His
            { Edmd Gale   Will Owen   } Majestys Council

This Board having Considered the Letter laid before them yesterday by his Excelly the Govr are Unanimously of Opinion that it is for His Majesty's services and the Good of this Province that an Assembly be called   Thereupon His Excelly the Governour by and with the advice and Consent of His Majesty's Council doth order that writts Issue returnable on the third of July next requiring the Freeholders of the several precincts & Towns within this Province to meet at the usual Places on the First Tuesday in May next to choose their Representatives to sit in the next General Assembly to be held at Edenton

A Paper was read at this Board signed by Mr Rice & Mr Ashe which is as follows Vizt N° 1

His Excelly the Governr thereon gave in a paper in Answer thereto which was also read & is as follows Vizt N° 2

Mr Rice & Mr Ashe filed a Paper in the Council Office the 11th of Novr last which was now read Vizt N° 3

His Excelly thereon caused His Answer thereto to be read which was in these words Vizt N° 4

Read the Petition of the Inhabitants of Edgecombe prec⁴ which is in these Words Vizt No 5

Read the Petition of the Inhabitants of Bertie prec⁴ in these words Vizt N⁰ 6

N⁰ CAROLINA—ss

At a Council held at the Council Chamber in Edenton the 3ᵈ day of April Anno Domini 1733

Present

His Excelly George Burrington Esqʳ Govʳ &c

The Honoble { Nathˡ Rice   John Lovick } Esqᵐ Members
{ Robt Halton   Edmᵈ Gale } of His
{ Jno Bapᵗ⁸ Ashe   Wᵐ Owen } Majestys Council

Read the Petition of the Inhabitants of Craven precinct in these words N⁰ 7

Ordered that a New Comⁱ pass the Seal for a Court of Oyer and Terminer to be held on the second Tuesday in June next directed to the Chief Justice &c

Ordered that a New Comⁱ of the Peace pass the seal constituting and appointing Mʳ Owen Esqʳ Robt Turner, Robt Peyton Benjⁱ Peyton Churcil Reading Samˡ Sinclare Richᵈ Wᵐ Silvester Henry Crafton Roger Kenyon Wᵐ Carruthers Wᵐ Willis Edwᵈ Adley Wᵐ Dunbar Franⁱ La Mare Gentˡ Justices of the Peace for the Precᵗˢ of Beaufort and Hyde

Ordered That a Commission pass the Seal Constituting and appointing Thomas Lovick Esqʳ John Nelson Richᵈ Rustell Enock Ward Richᵈ Whitehurst Joseph Bell Nath Taylor Arthur Mabson Ebenezer Harker Shaddock Charles Cogdale & George Cogdale Gent Justices of the Peace for the precinct of Curratuck

Ordered that a Commission of the Peace pass the Seal of the Colony Constituting and appointing Daniel Shine Thoˢ Martin John Powell Thomas Master Jacob Sheets Martin Franks Jno Fornville John Slocomb John Bryan Cornⁱ Loftin Simon Bright and James Green Gent Justices of the Peace for the precinct of Craven

A Representation of Thomas Blount King or Chief man of the Tuskarora Indians by Mʳ Francis Pugh one of the Commissioners for Indian affairs was read in these words Vizt No 8

This Board taking the same into Consideration are Willing that the Supponees do live with the Tuskarooroes in case both parties agree to the same, and that the Chowan Indian Indians have Leave to live with the Tuskarooroes Indians provided King Blount Will Recieve them

His Excelly the Governour acquainted John Montgomery Esq' Attorney General that he was going to take some Depositions relating to him and that he might be present at the Examination   M' Attorney thereon prayed to be allowed Councel to assist him which was accordingly Granted   Whereupon M' Attorney prayed M' Moseley might be allowed to be Councel for him which was also Granted

---

NORTH CAROLINA—ss.

At a Council held at the Council Chamber in Edenton the 3d day of July 1733

Present

His Excelly George Burrington Esq' Gov' &c.

The Honoble { Nath Rice   John Lovick } Esq'' Members of
            { Jno Bap'' Ashe   Edm'' Gale } His Majestys Council

This Being the Day the General Assembly was to have met at Edenton and there being but four members of the Upper House present who were unwilling to do business without a greater number the Council thereon advise the Governour to prorogue the Assembly to the next day Whereupon His Excelly the Governour by and with the advice and Consent of His Majestys Council doth Prorogue the General Assembly of this Province till to morrow being the fourth instant and they are hereby Prorogued accordingly

---

NORTH CAROLINA—ss

At a Council held at the Council Chamber in Edenton the 6th day of August Anno Dom 1733

Present

His Excelly George Burrington Esq' Gov' &c

The Honoble { Nath Rice   John Lovick } Esq'' Members
            { John Bap'' Ashe   Edm'' Gale } of His
            {   W'' Owen   } Majestys Council

His Excelly the Governour acquainting this Board that the General Assembly had addressed him that Major Stephen Goold Rec' of the Impost Duty on the Tonage of Vessells for Port Bath might be Compelled to give Suff' Security for the monies he had rec'ed for the Publick in s⁴ Office and His Excelly the Gov' also acquainted this Board that the said Goolde was in Custody of the Marshall until he gave good security for the same and desired the Opinion of the Council thereon who were unanimously of Opinion that ye said Goolde remain in Custody untill he gave security in the Sum of £800 currt money of this Province that he pay or cause to be paid the Powder money he hath rec̄ed since his appointm⁴ to the said Office when thereunto Lawfully required

Then the Council Adj⁴ till to-morrow

Tuesday August 7ᵗʰ

Present

His Excelly George Burrington Esq' Gov' &c

The Honoble { Nath¹ Rice   John Lovick ⎫ Esqⁿ Members
John Bapᵗᵃ Ashe   Edm⁴ Gale ⎬ of His
Wᵐ Owen ⎭ Majestys Council

Read the Petition of the Inhabitants of Beaufort precinct in these words Vizt

Read a Petition of the Inhabitants of Carteret precinct in these words Vizt N° 2

Read a Petition from the Inhabitants of Onslow Precinct presented by Mr Ford who made Oath that the same was a True Copy from the Original Petition now in his Custody signed to by all the People whose names were subscribed to the said paper or by their order to him which is in these words Vizt N° 3

Ordered that the several Recⁿ of the Powder money within this Province do attend before this Board with their accounts on the first day of next Biennial Assembly and that notice thereof be given to each of them by sending a Copy of this Order

Read the Petition Edward Mitchel Ordered that Mʳ Kenyon have Notice to attend at the Council in October next, N° 4

The Petition of the Chowan Indians setting forth &c N° 5

Ordered that Aaron Blanchard attend this Board at their Sitting in October next and that in the mean time the said Blanchard is hereby Ordered to committ no waste in yᵉ said Indians Land

By order

R FORSTER C C

[B. P R O Am & W Ind Vol. 22. p 199]

LEGISLATIVE JOURNALS.

NORTH CAROLINA—ss

At a Council held at the Council Chamber in Edenton the 3ᵈ day of July 1733.

Present

His Exce⁽ˡˡʸ⁾ George Burrington Esqⁿ Governor &c.

The hon⁽ᵇˡᵉ⁾ { Nath Rice   John Lovick } Esqⁿ Members of His
         { Jno Bapᵐ Ashe   Edmᵈ Gale } Majesty's Council.

This being the day the General Assembly was to have met at Edenton and there being but four Members of the Upper House present who were unwilling to do business without a greater Number, the Council thereon advised the Governour to prorogue the Assembly to the next day Whereupon his Exce⁽ˡˡʸ⁾ the Governor by and with the advice and consent of His Majesty's Council doth prorogue the General Assembly of this Province till to morrow being the fourth instant And they are hereby prorogued accordingly

At a General Assembly begun to be Held for His Majesty's Province of North Carolina at Edenton the 4ᵗʰ day of July 1733

Present

His Ex⁽ˡˡ⁾ George Burrington Esqⁿ Governor &c

The hon⁽ᵇˡᵉ⁾ {   } Esqⁿ Members
         {   } Majesty's Council.

His Excellency the Governor commanded the attendance of the Lower House, who came and told the House he presented Col. Edward Moseley then speaker, who his Excellency approved of and then delivered his Speech which is in these following words viz

GENTLEMEN OF BOTH HOUSES,

Upon my first arrival after I had taken the charge of this Government for the King I called an Assembly, and as directed by His Majesty's Instructions I proposed to them several things to be enacted for the regulation of the Province, but was not so happy as to obtain their Complyance with them, which if then agreed to and settled, I am satisfied would have been much better for the Country and might have been a means of gaining His Majesty's further favour about the Rents, which People are so desirous should be made easy to them

That Assembly proposed to pay the King's rates in Rice & Tobacco at a rated price, in lieu of Proclamation money which His Maj^v offered to receive them at instead of sterling   As I did not think myself impowered to make any further concessions, without knowing His Majesty's Pleasure, for that reason and some others thought it not necessary to call another Assembly before I had made a report of the state of this Country to the Lords Comm^{rs} for Trade and Plantations, and was honoured with an Answer from them. Which I very early did, with great care and faithfullness, but their Answer came not to my hands till the 26th day of March last, when I issued writts for this Assembly

I must now acquaint you, that by a fresh direction I am restrained from passing an Act for the payment of Quit Rents in any other specie, but in Proclamation money, and I am ordered to take care that the Officers Fees be paid in Proclamation Money also, how far the obedience of this Assembly to the King's Instructions may induce His Majesty to grant further Ease or Indulgence to the People in their rents, I leave you to consider

It is expected as may be seen in the 19th Instruction (which I shall cause to be layd before you) that there should an Act be passed to oblige all possessors of Lands in this Government to register the same in the Auditor's Office, which is the more reasonable since His Majesty is not only graciously pleased to permit me to pass an Act for remitting all arrears of rents due when the King compleated the purchase of Carolina, but also to quiet People in the possession of their Lands, a favour that I hope this Assembly will endeavour to merit.

I am commanded by the 75th and following Instruction to take especial care that the Publick Service of the Church of England be duely maintained and that a competent Provision be made for the Ministry, Lands assigned them for Glebes, and convenient houses built thereon, The little Provision hitherto made for supporting the publick worship seems to be a reproach to the County, and prevents many good People from coming here to settle   It certainly becomes you to provide some more decent means to maintain the Clergy, and to appropriate money for the Building a church, or Chappel in every parish, which in most places are now wanting

I think it would prove for the ease and benefit of the People if the Power of the Precinct Courts was enlarged, and better provision made for Jurys which one of my Instructions directs me to recommend

I will not burthen you at this season with to many things for your consideration but I cannot help recommending to you to do something for the encreasing the Products of this Country which will gradually beget more industry among the People and will best promote a British Trade that is so much wanted here, and which we ought always to encourage, and for this end I think it would be well to exempt all Vessells that come from Great Britain from the payment of Powder money, and that your own Commodities for that Trade were under better Inspection and Regulation

GENTLEMEN

I conclude with heartily wishing there may be that harmony and good agreement between you, that the Country at this time has occasion for, I hope you meet together with such good dispositions, that no particular interests and Views, no Heats, no Divisions may hinder your joyning with me in promoting the Wellfare of this Country which I assure you I have equally at heart with the best men herein, and sincerely promise you my concurrence in everything that shall be for His Majesty's Service & the good of this Province

GEO BURRINGTON

The House adjourned till to morrow morning

Thursday July 5th
The House met again
Present as before
Received the following Message from the Lower House vizt

To THE HONOBLE THE COUNCIL

Ordered That Capt William Downing, Mr Cullen Pollock, Colo Henry Bonner, Mr Arthur Williams, Major Robt Turner, and Mr Thomas Smith be a Committee to joyn such Members as shall be appointed by the Upper House as a Committee of Claims.

AYLIFFE WILLIAMS Clk Gen Ass

By Mr Swann
   & Mr Burnham

Resolved That John Bapta Ashe, Edmond Gale, and William Owen Esqrs be and they are hereby appointed a Committee to joyn with such Members of the Lower House as are appointed to make a Committee of Claims.

By Order
ROBERT FORSTER, Clk Upper House

Adjourned till to morrow morning Ten of the Clock

Friday July 6
The House met again
Present as before
Adjourned till Monday morning Ten of the Clock

Monday July 9
The House met again
Present

The hon^{ble} { Nath Rice   John Lovick } Esq^{rs} Members
         { Jn° Bapt° Ashe Edm⁴ Gale } of His
         { Wm Owen } Maj^{ties} Council

Received the following Message from the General Assembly vizt

Read the Petition of Thomas Murphy setting forth that a Ferry by order of Craven Court was established at or near the said Murphy's which he has constantly kept and very lately the Precinct Court hath appointed another Ferry above said Murphey much out of the way and much to the said Murphey's prejudice And the subject matter of the said Petition appearing to be true by the Testimony of some of the Members of this House.

Ordered That the Ferry be & remain at said Murpheys.

Sent to the Governor and Council for concurrance
By order.
A WILLIAMS Clk Gen Ass.

By Mr Chas Sawyer
  & Mr John Sawyer

This House thereon sent the following Answer thereto

Mr SPEAKER & GENT OF THE GENERAL ASSEMBLY

It is the opinion of this House that the subject matter of the said Petition (if not to be provided for by a special Law for that purpose) may more properly be recommended to the Precinct Court to be regulated as the opinion of the Gen: Assembly, with which this House is ready to concurr.
By order
ROB^t FORSTER ₱ Clk of the Upper House

Received the following Message from the General Assembly vizt

TO HIS EXCELL^y THE GOVERNOR & COUNCIL

It being represented to this House by the Members from divers parts of the Province that the Publick Roads and Bridges in general are much

out of repair whereby the traveling to the General Court and Assembly
is rendered difficult

This House humbly desire the Speaker that he will be pleased to
direct the Magistrate ... that they do take effect ... and that
the Roads and Bridges be forthwith repaired and Ferrys duly kept and
that the same be constantly kept up, that upon any failure by the Overseers or People who are to labour on the said Roads the Justices to see
that the Laws relating to Roads, Bridges and Ferrys be put in force and
all delinquents duly fined.

By order

A. WILLIAMS Clk Gen Ass.

By Mr Jno Sawyer
    & Mr Chas Sawyer

Which being read the same was concurr'd with and sent down to the
General Assembly

Received the following Vote from the General Assembly viz:

To His Excell' the Governor & Council

The Council House and the House the Assembly sits in wanting
repair

Voted That Col. Edward Moseley, Col Henry Bonner and Mr Charles
Westbeere be Commr to agree with workmen for the repairing those
Buildings, and that when the same repairs are perfected the said Com-
missioners or any two of them have Power to draw on the Publick
Treasurer for payment of the Workmen.

Voted That Mr Christopher Becket have £12. Paper money as now
current ℗ annum for his care in keeping the Doors & Windows of the
Council House and Assembly House when those Houses are not used.

Sent to His Excell' the Governor and Council for concurrence

By order.

A. WILLIAMS Clk. Gen: Ass.

By Mr Chas Sawyer
    & Mr Jno Sawyer.

To which Vote this House made the following Endorsement thereon

Mr Speaker & Gent: of the Gen. Assembly

This House are ready to concurr with the within Vote Provided a
certain sum be set or mentioned to limit the Commissioners in their
Draught and that they render Account to the Gen: Assembly of the
expences. This House likewise recommends to the consideration of the

General Assembly that they would include the Repair and care of the Goal in the same Vote.

By order.

ROBᵗ FORSTER ⅌ Clk Upper House.

Received the following Vote from the General Assembly vizᵗ

To His Excellʸ the Governor & Council

Thursday July 5ᵗʰ

Voted That the several Powder Recᵉʳˢ do lay their Accounts before this Assembly by Wednesday next.

A. WILLIAMS. Clk. Gen: Assembly.

Sent by Mʳ Jnᵒ Sawyer &
Mʳ Chaˢ Sawyer.

Which being read the same was concurr'd with.
Received the following Message from the General Assembly vizᵗ

To His Excellʸ the Governor & Council.

This House taking into consideration the Affair of the New Precincts lately erected. This House desires to have a Conference with His Excellency and the Council concerning the same.

By order

A. WILLIAMS Clk. Gen: Assembly.

Sent by Mʳ Winn &
Mʳ Kenchen

Which was read and concurr'd with, and agreed that a Conference be held thereon to morrow morning.

Resolved That His Excellency have notice of this Conference.

Received the following Vote from the General Assembly vizᵗ

To His Excellʸ the Governor & Council

The old Paper Money which was brought in and accounted for at the Assembly held in April 1731. being carefully sealed up and lodged in the hands of the Publick Treasurer.

Voted That the same be brought and layd before the Assembly to morrow in order that the same may be destroyed.

Sent to the Governor & Council for Concurrence

By order

A. WILLIAMS. Clk. Gen· As.

By Mʳ Jnᵒ Sawyer &
Mʳ Chaˢ Sawyer.

Which was read and Concurr'd with.

69

Read the following Message from the General Assembly viz[t]

To His Excell[y] the Governor and Council

Col Thomas Swann Treasurer of Pasquotank and Col Thomas Pollock Treasurer of Bertie being dead this House recommends unto his Excellency the Governour and Council M[r] James Lockhart to be Treasurer of Bertie and M[r] John Solly to be Treasurer of Pasquotank

Sent to His Exce[lly] the Gov[r] & Council for concurrence

By order

AY WILLIAMS Clk of y[e] General Assembly

By M[r] John Sawyer &
    M[r] Cha[s] Sawyer

Which being read this House sent the following Answer thereto viz[t]

M[r] Speaker & Gent of the Gen[l] Assembly

This House proposes M[r] John Palin in the room of M[r] John Solley named by your House, for Treasurer of Pasquotank which if agreed to this House will concurr with the Vote

By order

ROB[t] FORSTER [$\mathscr{p}$] Clk of y[e] Upper House

Adjourned till to morrow morning

Tuesday July 10th

The House met again

Read a Bill for an Act entituled an Act to repeal the Act of Assembly entituled an Act for raising a Publick Magazine of Ammunition upon the Tonnage of all Vessells trading to this Government past at the Biennial Assembly in the year 1715 the first time and past

His Excellency the Governour returned an Endorsement on the Vote of both Houses for destroying the old Paper money accounted for in the Assembly held in April 1731 viz[t]

I concurr provided two (or more) Members of the Council be present to take an account of Bills and see them destroyed

GEO. BURRINGTON

Resolved That the same be sent down to the General Assembly And that John Bapt[a] Ashe and John Lovick Esq[rs] Members of this House be present to see the said Bills destroyed

His Excellency the Governour returned an Endorsement on the Message of the General Assembly relating to Murphey's Ferry viz[t]

I am of opinion Mʳ Murphey's Ferry and Martin Frank his Ferry are both very usefull and therefore neither ought to be suppress'd.

GEO BURRINGTON

Ordered that the same be sent down to the Gen Assembly

His Excellency the Governour was pleased to send the following Endorsement on the Vote of the General Assembly for repairing the Council House, Assembly House and Goal and was concurr'd with by this House vizᵗ

I consent to sign a Warrant for the sum mentioned to be layd out in repairing the Council House, Court House and Goal, and if you think proper to allow a salary for taking care of those Edifices, I concurr therewith and will appoint a proper person for that Service

Ordered that the same be sent down to the Gen Assembly

His Excellency the Governour was pleased to send the following Endorsement on the Message from the General Assembly for appointing Treasurers in the room of Col. Swann and Colᵒ Pollock deceased, vizᵗ

I am of opinion New Precinct Treasurers ought not to be appointed in the place of those lately deceased before the King's pleasure is known in respect to the Bills issued in the year 1729

GEO BURRINGTON

Ordered that the same be sent down to the Gen Assembly
Adjourned till to morrow morning

Wednesday July 11ᵗʰ

The House met again

His Excellency the Governour was pleased to send the following Endorsement on the Vote of the General Assembly for the Powder Receivers to lay their Accounts before the Assembly vizᵗ

The Council or General Assembly ought to address me to give Orders to the several Receivers of the Powder Money (if they desire to inspect their Accounts) to attend at the time appointed for that purpose & not to vote it should be done

GEO BURRINGTON.

Ordered That the same be sent down to the General Assembly.

His Excellency the Governour was pleased to return the following Endorsement on the Message of the General Assembly for a Conference on the affair of the New Precincts vizᵗ

The Members of His Majesty's Council I deem to be sufficient to hold the intended Conference concerning the New Precincts therefore have no intention to be present

GEO BURRINGTON

Ordered that the same be sent down to the General Assembly

Read a Bill for an Act Entituled an Act to repeal the Act of Assembly Entituled an Act for raising a Publick Magazine of Amunition upon the Tonnage of all Vessells trading to this Government past at the Biennial Assembly in the year 1715. a second time & past without amendments

Mr Speaker & the Gent of the General Assembly waited on his Excellency the Governour in Council and returned an Answer to his Excellency's Speech in the following words viz't

To His Excell'y George Burrington Esq'r His Maj'y Cap'n General & Governor in Chief of North Carolina

MAY IT PLEASE YOUR EXCELL'Y,

This House having taken your Excellency's Speech into our most serious consideration and having duly examined the conduct of the Assembly in April 1731, We cannot but be of opinion that the Assembly went as far as it was possible towards a complyance with the Royal Instruction concerning the Quitt Rents and Fees in as much as the want of Gold and Silver Currency is so well Known in this Province, and now at this last Election, Our Principals throughout the Province having recomended nothing more earnestly to us, than that we should not consent to burthen them with such payments as it is impossible for them to make

We take notice that your Excellency is pleased to say that that Assembly proposed to pay His Majesty's Rent in Rice and Tobacco at a rated price in lieu of Proclamation money w'ch His Majesty offered to receive instead of sterling, We find by a due inquiry into the matter that the Assembly did endeavour to comply with the Royal Instruction as near as possible and therefore as there seemed to be no probability of such payments to be made in Gold and Silver they offered a just equivalent But that the rents are due in Sterling as your Excellency seems to intimate or even in Proclamation money, We humbly beg leave to differ in Opinion and we hope to be able to support this our Opinion.

The Rents reserved in the Grants of Land are not said in the Grants to be payable in sterling money or any other, and in all equitable construction we think the money reserved must be understood the money of the Country and so the Law hath always been taken nor has Sterling money or Proclamation money been ever recovered on any specialty but where those have been specifically named & expressed

But to shew that the Rents and Fees are payable only in the current money of the Province we desire it may be remembered, That before any Paper money was currant in this Province there was always acts of Assembly declaring the Prices of the products of the Country to pass as money in all respects as well for Quitt rents as any other Payments and when the paper money was established, it was provided that the same should be currant in all payments, excepting for purchase of Lands. So that we think it is very plain that the rents are not payable either in sterling or Proclamation Nor doth it seem to us by anything yet laid before the House that His Majesty offered to receive Proclamation money for rents in lieu of Sterling It doth indeed appear that His Majesty proposes that your Excellency should pass a Law to remit the Arrears of Rents due from this Province to the time of perfecting His Purchase (which he was given to understand was very large) in case the Assembly would by the same Law provide that all Possessors of Land should register their Grants in the Auditor's Office, that the Quitt rents payable for the future should be in Proclamation money, and the Fees of the Officers should be settled in Proclamation money, We give His Majesty our hearty thanks for such a mark of his paternal Care shewn to us in the Offer of remitting so large an Arrear as was thought to be due from the Province but at the same time we humbly beg leave to represent that by a diligent inquiry of the Members of this House who came from the several parts of the Province we cant learn that the Arrears (if any due) are worth collecting because we all very well remember that the Collections have been very constantly made and some have even now produced to the House receipts for the year 1730 Since His Majesty purchased the Province, Indeed we think His Majesty's offer to the Province of S⁰ Carolina in the like case was very wisely accepted as we are told it has been in regard they owed 15 or 16 years Arrears for altho' Gold and Silver might be something scarce there yet by their large and extensive Trade they might be able to procure it tho' at some difficulty when they had so great an indulgence as the remittance of 15 or 16 years But in this Province we have no prospect of gaining Silver or Gold sufficient for such purposes Our Trade very much cramped by the bad Navigation and the excessive Fees taken by Naval Officers and Collectors the like not heard of in any of the British Dominions as far as we can learn. And at the same time such Fees taken without any colour of Law

Concerning the Tenure of the Lands in the County of Albemarle in particular, We humbly conceive the Right hon^ble the Lords Commissioners for Trade and Plantations, have not a true account of the state and condition of the Lands in that County by what they are pleased to say of the Deed of Grant being in the nature of a temporary Power of Attorney revokeable at pleasure which they say the Lords Proprietors seem to have done by their Instructions to Govr Eden We therefore beg leave to represent the Case of the Tenants of Albemarle County as it appears to us When His Majesty King Charles the Second granted the Province of Carolina to the Lords Proprietors there were divers persons in possession of Lands within the bounds of the Charter who held their Lands by Grants from the Government of Virginia and therefore in the Royal Charter there was a saving of those persons Rights; The Lords Proprietors in laying out the Province into eight Countys called that eigth part of the Province lying next to Virginia by the name of Albemarle County within which County it was that those persons dwelt who held Lands by Virginia Grants and as the Lords Proprietors proposed to grant the Lands of their Province on harder terms than the King's Subjects held theirs in Virginia the Inhabitants of Albemarle County by their humble Applications to the Lords Proprietors obtained the Deed of Grant dated May 1st 1668 whereby the Lands of that County were to be granted to all new-comers for the future (who had right to take up fifty acres for each person in their family) on the same Terms and Tenures as the People of Virginia held their Lands, As by the same Deed will more at large appear But all the other Lands in the Province were to be granted at their Lordships and their Successors Discretion and therefore they sometimes gave directions to grant their other Lands at a high Quitt rent, and at other times on payment of purchase money, with reservation of small Quitt Rents payable yearly But their Lordships never attempted to infringe the Deed of Grant, what was intended to be done by the directions to Governour Eden respected only the other Lands and not those of Albemarle County, As appears both by their Lordships directions which mention only the Sale of Lands, and not the granting of Quitt Rents which Distinction was always made between Albemarle County Lands and the other Lands of the Province, This also appears from the constant practice of their Lordships Officers, who notwithstanding the aforesaid Order or any other, granted the Lands in Albemarle County agreable to the Deed of Grant aforementioned without the least Checque from the Proprietors.

As the principal and most valuable Lands in the County of Albemarle are already granted, we humbly hope that if such a construction were to be put upon the Deed of Grant as that it were revokeable, as we trust such construction will not be made, yet that His Royal Majesty will be graciously pleased to confirm the same Grant unto His good Subjects of the said County of Albemarle and direct that all the vacant Land in the same may be granted as hath been heretofore accustomed agreable to the Deed of Grant, Altho' this is the case of His Majesty's Subjects and Tenants of this Province and that no such like encouragement as a remission of 15 or 16. years rent was offered us the Assembly readily came into His Majesty's Proposals and by a Bill for an Act consented that the Officers Fees should be settled in Proclamation money or just equivalent thereto And even to comply with the Payment of Proclamation money for the rents, and for want thereof a just equivalent as also to register the Grants in the Auditor's Office. Wherefore we humbly hope your Excellency and the Council will joyn with us in making a true state of the Poverty of this Province and their inability to comply with a Proposal for payment to be made in Proclamation money and that His Majesty will be graciously pleased to direct an equivalent may be ascertained in the same Law for those we represent have given us in charge not to burthen them with such payments as they can forsee no possability of complying with

We are sorry to find that your Excellency should have any reason for so long a disuse of Assemblys, it being now above two years since any sat to do business, and altho' with respect to the Affair of the Quitt rents your Excellency might not think fit to treat with an Assembly on that head until you had the royal Instructions, yet give us leave to observe that the Affairs of the Province in our humble opinion required the meeting of an Assembly before this time, not only for our Application to His Majesty towards the good & happy settlement of this Province but also for the suppressing the many Oppressions which have so loudly been complained of through the whole Province which could no other way so properly be represented as in an Assembly

We are of opinion with your Excellency that a British Trade ought by all means to be encouraged, we will therefore do everything in our Power to promote that in particular as also all other Trade in Generall, and as the Powder money laid on Vessells was found to be the only expedient for raising a Magazine in the time of Indian War, as that occasion ceased some time past we propose to ease the Trade of that Burthen, which has so loudly been complained of by the Traders to this Province

And as a further encouragement we propose that a sum be paid out of the Publick Treasury to the Commissioners for the severall Inletts towards Bouying and Beaconing the Channels

We propose to take into our consideračon the hardships of the People living in the remote parts of the Country and to give them such Ease with respect to the Courts as may be of use to them

By the Laws passed in 1729 which we understand are under His Majesty's consideration we think a very good provision was made for establishing the several Vestrys to build churches, Purchase Gleebs and to make ample Provision for the Clergy, at the same time proper provision was made for the payment of Jurys. We shall therefore forbear to do anything relating to those matters untill we shall be informed of the Royal pleasure concerning those Laws

Your Excellency's kind wishes that a good harmony may be between us, and your promise of a concurrence in everything that shall be for His Majesty's Service and the good of the Province gives us the utmost satisfaction when we reflect on the heavy grievances this poor Country hath long laboured under, not only by exorbitant Fees we have had so just reason to mention to your Excellency at this time, as well as it hath been heretofore, but likewise from the Pervertion of Justice by evil and wicked Officers (we are sorry we are forced to say of your Excellency's appointment and approbation) especially by William Little Chief Justice and his Assistants, which particular grievance we promise ourselves will now be remedied by the arrivall of Mr Chief Justice Smith who we have good reason to believe to be a Gentleman of great honour and integrity not only from his having His Majesty's approbation but from his behaviour ever since his first arrival in this Province.

We assure your Excellency we are met with the best Disposition to promote His Majesty's Service and the Wellfare of the Province which we think ought to be inseparable, and as there doth not seem to be the least appearance of any particular interest or view among us, so we shall studiously avoid anything that may look like Heat or Division

By order of the House

EDWd MOSELEY, Speaker

The House adjourned till to morrow morning

Thursday July 12th The House met again
Present His Excelly in Council
Read the Petition of William Little Esqr Chief Justice in these words viz.t

North Carolina—ss.

To His Excell[y] George Burrington Esqre Captain General & Governour
in Chief. and the hon[ble] the Council now sitting in Assembly

The Petition of William Little Chief Justice

MAY IT PLEASE YOUR EXCELL[y] & THIS HONÕBLE BOARD

In the Address of the Lower House of Assembly to the Governour's
Speech, I find myself named in a manner I think very unjust and injurious to my Character among their pretended grievances they have
charged me in the Office of Chief Justice and the Assistant Justices with
pervertion of Justice, such a charge I conceive ought not to have been
made without giving some instance of it, but that they have not pretended to do, for reasons I submit. As the charge is great so in Justice
ought the proof to be, instead of that there is none, only some persons
undertook (as I am told) of their own knowledge to make it good, as tho'
it was not necessary that something should be made appear to that House
before they could justly pass such a grievous censure, This must be
allowed a very falacious way to build so weighty a charge upon, had I
ever took such a latitude in judging I might have justly been accused of
Oppression and pervertion of Justice   There was an attempt something
like this against me at a former Assembly when I was Attorney General
(by the same men too that stirred up this) when an Artifice was used to
prevent my then clearing it, in hopes something might stick by the bare
charge, for some time at least, for the next Assembly I was acquitted
by the Journal of the House, and made the falsehood of it apparent
and yet without taking notice of that, I am told that this accusation was
the principal thing repeated and urged now against me, in the Debate of
the House upon this present charge, and tho' this is a charge against me
as Chief Justice.

I therefore beg that this accusation of the House may not be permitted
now to pass over without being inquired into, that it may be seen how
utterly groundless the complaint is. I am sensible this Board as an
Upper House will not erect & assume to themselves a judicial Power of
trying Causes or convicting Offenders nor do I know any instance of
such Tryals Once indeed the House here took upon them to impeach
two great Peers of the Land, but that I believe will not be thought a
precedent   But if the Board cannot proceed in it as a Court, yet as Governour and Council they have Power to examine into the conduct and
behaviour of Officers and to remove, suspend, condemn or censure a
Chief Justice or any other Officer that truly merits it, as I hope they will
take occasion to shew

70

For my part if this charge against me be thought true, I freely own I ought to be removed, I therefore beg a day may be appointed for hearing it, and that I may have timely notice of the particular Facts if they have any to charge against me, and that the House may be directed to make good their Complaint which now being only a charge in general can only in as general terms be denyed, which I do in the most solemn manner, and with a confidence usual to Innocence

To be arraigned on the seat of Justice is what I thought even envy would not attempt against me, having acted with all good Conscience as my own heart assures me, and I am at a loss how such a charge could possibly be framed against me, I have been recollecting but cannot make myself sensible of having committed one material Fault in the station, much less am I conscious of anything in the least that can merit the name of pervertion of Justice which my soul abhors with the utmost disdain, and could anything like it be made appear I shall be content to stand condemned for ever But if they fail in making good their charge, as I know assuredly they must, what recompence, what reparation can I have

Bodys of men have a Priviledge that when refuted none takes it nor can they be called to account, but in all Justice the more tenderly then should they use their Power without partiality and without prejudging

I am not insensible the secret springs their Reports rise from, and could easily retort so as might take off all edge from their charge but shall waive it, I will shun everything that may look like bringing a railing accusation or recriminating, since I know my own Innocence I shall the more easily keep temper and decency especially to the worshipfull the House that have now espoused the cause. But the Gentlemen that have been thus unhappily led to censure and condemn me unheard or without one proof or instance of any corrupt judgment or injustice I have done in the Office, must give me leave to think I have had exceeding hard measure, God send it may never be measured back to the contrivers of it, I thank God I have not done so by any man but in everything before me have at all times judged impartially so may God judge me and them at last But perhaps the Gentlemen may intend by my perverting justice only the Crime of taking Fees in Bills at four for one, if that be all that is meant, I shall have very little to say to it, I therefore intreat the House may be more particular in stating Facts, and those that effect me particularly, and as they have been pleased thus to single out my name that they will please to let me stand single in my defence

As to the taking exorbitant Fees so much complained of in the Address, for my part I must solemnly aver, that I never taxed nor took myself any other than by the Table of Fees the Law has appointed, nor have I ever insisted that they should be paid in money but was always ready to receive them in any of the rated Commodities of the Country as they are rated by Law, of which there are one and twenty several species of the produce of the Country so the Oppression could not be so violent as is pretended, nay I should have been content to have received them even in Pitch and Tar, nor should have ventured to refuse what the Law has provided. When the Fees have been paid in Bills as the People chose to do at four for one as an equivalent rather than money, I have taken care they should be received at no higher advance than four for one, tho' I am told, others design to take six for one, and if four for one be thought too high, and I have committed an error in it, I am not alone (tho' only I am personally named) if it be a crime no doubt the Assembly will vote it illegal to receive them so, and that will affect all without condemning it in one and not in another It is well known the Fees are taken so in the Precinct Courts as well as in the General Court, which the Country in all parts is sensible of and which their Principals I believe are most agrieved at tho' the House hath not mentioned them

For my part it was not I that begun it, the Practice was established before my time, Mr Chief Justice Smith and the other Officers took them so, but if the House intend me the honour of setting me at the head of the charge I shall beg leave to decline it. I intended soon to have quitted the place, nor was I ever fond of the Office of Chief Justice it was not my seeking but it was the pleasure of the Governour & Council nay I may say by His Excellency's commands that I took it. And tho' they would now endeavour to wound the Governour (for it) thro' me I have the pleasure to think I have done no dishonour to the appointment, further, modesty forbids me to say.

I have been for some time determined to retire from all publick Business, that I may (if it shall please God) recover from my long illness I have undergone I shall not therefore undertake the defence of the cause, but I choose to leave the charge to my successors be it Mr Smith or any other, who no doubt will soon make the People easy in the matter.

I shall therefore conclude with importunately repeating my Prayer that if the House have anything to alledge, on any other head than that of four for one, they may assign the Particulars, and that a day may be appointed for hearing it before this Board

This honourable Board where tho' I have often appeared for favour to others (as my accusers may know) yet for myself I ask none only for justice to my injured Character and I do not in the least doubt it from this honourable Board who are not to be led away with Heat & Clamour, Prejudice, Passion or Private Pique

To your Excell'y therefore & your Honours I most humbly but most cheartfully submit myself & my Cause and shall ever remain in all duty &c.

July 12th 1733   W LITTLE

Ordered That a Copy of the said Petition be sent down to the General Assembly.   Absent the Governour

Read a Bill for an Act entituled an Act to repeal the Act of Assembly entituled an Act for raising a Publick Magazine of Ammunition upon the Tonnage of all Vessels trading to this Government past at the Biennial Assembly in the year 1715 the third time and past

Ordered That the Bill be engrossed

Adjourned till to morrow morning

Friday July 13th
The House met again
Received the following Vote from the General Assembly viz't

To the Upper House

Voted that the sum of Ten pounds be paid out of the Publick Treasury to the Rev'd Mr Boyd for his sermon preached before the Assembly this day and that His Excell'y the Governour be desired to issue his Warrant for payment of the same

Sent to the Upper House for Concurrence
                              By order
                                        MOSELEY VAIL ⅌ Clk

Which was read and concurr'd with

Received the following Message from the General Assembly viz't

To the Upper House

Reported from the Committee of Propositions & Grievances that the Committee have had several complaints laid before them and sundry Petitions from divers Inhabitants setting forth that divers free People, Negroes & Molattoes residing in this Province were taken up by the Directions of Thomas Bryant, James Thompson, Benjamin Hill, John Edwards, Thomas Kerney and William Lattimoor of Bertie Precinct

Benjamin Peyton and Robert Peyton of Bath County Justices of the Peace and others and by these Justices bound out until they come to 31 years of age contrary to the consent of the Parties bound out

The said Committee further report that these practices are well known to divers of the said Committee and that they fear that divers Persons will desert the settlement of those parts fearing to be used in like manner so unlawfully

It is therefore humbly recommended by the said Committee that a vote pass this House declaring the illegality of such a practice and that all such Persons so taken from their Parents or Guardians be returned to their respective parents or to those under whose care they were, and that those Magistrates who have bound out such Persons and those to whom they have been bound do attend at the next Biennial Assembly to answer for such their doings. With which Report the House concurr'd and Ordered the same to be sent to the Upper House for concurrance.

By order

MOSELEY VAIL ℈ Clk

Which was read and the following Message returned in Answer viz't

MR SPEAKER & GENT OF THE GEN ASSEMBLY

As to the Message touching the Report of the Committee relating to the practice of binding out Free Negroes and Molattoes till they come to 31 years of age contrary to the Assent of the Parties and to Law This House are of Opinion that the Justices of Peace who have so acted may be ordered to attend the Assembly this Session if time will admit if not that then it be recommended to the next Biennial in order that such an illegal practice may be exploded In the mean time this House are ready to concurr with the General Assembly in earnestly recommending the matter to the Courts of Law, so that speedy Justice may be done and that the Parties injured may have relief

By order.

ROBt FORSTER ℈ Clk Upper House.

Received the following Message from the General Assembly viz't

TO THE UPPER HOUSE

Reported from the Committee of Propositions & Grievances that the register of writings for Beaufort and Hide Precincts being dead, one Benjamin Peyton hath possessed himself of the writings and book belonging to that Office pretending a Commission from the Governour for the same and hath carryed them from Bath Town contrary to order

of that Court which forbid the moving them from Town and that it is
much to be feared by the Magistrates and Inhabitants of those Precincts that the same may be imbezled by the said Peyton he being a Person of very ill fame & character   It is the opinion of this Committee
that the Assembly do address his Excellency the Governour that if he
has granted such a Comission he would be pleased to recall it, and that
he would direct the Books and Papers belonging to that Office may be
kept at Bath Town as by Law it was provided they should be   This
House concurrs with the Report of the Committee divers of the Members of this Assembly very well remembring that the said Peyton when
he was formerly Marshal of Bath County attended this House at the
Assembly begun in April 1731 when it appeared to the Members divers
whereof are now present that he had erased or caused to be erased the
name of a person duly chosen and returned for Newbern Town and
inserted or caused to be inserted another person not duly chosen

The House concurred therewith & ordered to be sent to the Upper
House for Concurrance

By Order

MOSELEY VAIL ℘ Clk

Which was read and the following Message in Answer thereto returned,
Viz:

Mr SPEAKER & GENT OF THE GEN ASSEMBLY

This House having your Message relating to Mr Peyton and the Registry of Beaufort and Hide under their consideration are desirous you
would let them have the evidence which has been produced to you of
the fact

By order

Rt FORSTER ℘ Clk Upper House

Adjourned till to morrow morning

Saturday July 14th   The House met again

Read a Bill for an Act entituled an Act for Enlarging and confirming
the Jurisdiction of the Precinct Courts the first time and passed with
Amendments.

Read a Bill for an Act entituled an Act to prevent the annoying or
stopping up of Harbours or Navigable Creeks or Rivers in this Province the first time and past with Amendments

Adjourned till Monday morning

Monday July 16ᵗʰ   The House met again.

Read a Bill for an Act entituled an Act for Enlarging and Confirming the Jurisdiction of the Precinct Courts the second time and pass'd with Amendments.

Adjourned till to morrow morning

Tuesday July 17ᵗʰ   The House met again
Adjourned till to morrow morning

Wednesday July 18ᵗʰ   The House met again
Present
His Excellʸ George Burrington Esqʳ Governour &

The Honᵇˡᵉ { John Baptᵃ Ashe   Edwᵈ Gale.   } Esqʳ Members of
{ John Lovick   William Owen   } His Majˢᵗʸˢ Council

His Excellency the Governour commanded the attendance of the General Assembly who came in a full Body and His Excellency the Governour delivered the following Paper which he read and is as follows vizᵗ

GENTLEMEN OF BOTH HOUSES.

I opened this Assembly with a very kind Speech and sincerely recommended to you Unanimity and to proceed without heat or Passion, I proposed several things to you for the good of the Country which I always endeavoured to promote, but there having been so much time frivolously spent or worse, I find it to little purpose to keep you longer together.

Mʳ SPEAKER & GENT OF THE LOWER HOUSE

You from the beginning have discovered such a spirit that I early doubt whether any good might be expected from you, but have waited patiently to see what might be effected, but finding my good intentions to no purpose, I only tell you I am heartily sorry to see heat and Party prevail so much among you, I assure you that is not the way to serve your Country, tho' you have an opportunity thereby to serve yourselves and display piques & prejudices.

You have artfully and falsely endeavoured to represent the Government under me as grievous and oppressive, tho' every man in the Province knows the contrary, unless you will call His Majesty's Instructions grievous, which my steady adhering to, has been the occasion of raising all this Faction

As to my disuse of Assemblys as you maliciously terme it, there past not two years between the last Assembly & the chooseing this tho' I think the frequency of their meeting unless they would proceed with more temper and justice, is of no other use than to promote party and faction, and to give some People an opportunity to pursue their own malice and envy under the Umbrage of an Assembly   Bodys of men cannot blush, and that's your advantage, One of the most furious among you (I am told) declared he should not have attended this Assembly but purely to oppose the Governour, and that he came on purpose to plague him   I wish there had been no more Incendiarys amongst you, and that all the others had the Country's good more in their thoughts   I condemn not all, for I believe there are some well meaning honest men amongst you, but even those bore down or carryed away by the false zeal & clamour of the rest, an instance of which sufficiently appeared in the management of your Answer to my Speech,   it was drawn by the most inveterate Member, and no sooner brought into the House, but pushed on with a noise and violence that stifled all opposition and that was called, Nemine Contradicente

If Assemblys in this Province proceed in the manner you have done with heat and partiallity, they themselves will grow the greatest grievance and oppression to the Country,   Burgessing has been for some years a source of Ives and occasion of disturbances, which has deterred good men from being Candidates or entering the lists of noise and Faction wch every common observer knows.   Neither doth the King's Instructions that only Freeholders should vote find any weight in your Elections tho' always inserted in the Writts

As to the affair of the Chief Justice, I have already acquainted you I would appoint a day for hearing and making good the charge, but as you seem to waive it I appoint the 30th day of this month for the said hearing at the Council Chamber, where you or any other People may attend to make good the Charge   His Petition layd many days before you without any notice taken thereof, but yesterday on a sudden heat without regarding me or his station, you insolently presumed by your Surgeant to take him into custody for a pretended contempt found in the Petition by him delivered to the Upper House, tho' all unbiased Men do allow it was wrote with as much Decency and Temper as the Charge would admit of

You have also presumed to take into Custody the Receiver of the Powder money for Port Roanoake, tho' under very sufficient security who had my orders agreable to His Majesty's Instructions not to make up any Publick Accounts but before me in Council

You have denyed to conform to His Majesty's Instructions concerning the payment of the Quitt rents, thō by calling you again together I give you another opportunity of accepting His Majesty's most gracious favour in allowing them to be passed in Proclamation money instead of Sterling, Nay, you have denyed they are due or ought to be paid in any money at all, but of your own making

You have offered but three Bills all this time, one of which is so inconsiderable as not to be worth mentioning One other for Enlargeing the Power of the Precinct Courts, which I recommended to you, you took care to clogg with such Clauses as you must know I could not possibly assent to.

I also proposed to you for the encouragement of the British Trade to relieve their ships from paying the duty of Powder money, and you have brought in a Bill which has past both Houses for taking the said Duty wholly of all Vessels

I am informed you have refused to admit several Members of your House legally chosen and returned by the proper Officers, pursuant to the ancient and constant Practice of the Province and as you are but part of a House, my allowing your proceedings, or orders would be giving up an undoubted right of His Majesty's which has never been contested before this time.

For the aforesaid reasons I dissolve this Assembly and it is hereby accordingly dissolved

GEO BURRINGTON

A true Copy Exam⁴ by

R⁰ FORSTER ⅌ Clk Upper House

NORTH CAROLINA—ss.

At a General Assembly began and held at Edenton for the said Province July yᵉ 3rd 1733

MEMBERS RETURNED

Chowan	Perquimons	Pasquotank
Colᵒ Edwᵈ Moseley	Mʳ Richᵈ Skinner	Mʳ Chⁿ Sawyer
Colᵒ Henry Bonner	Mʳ Samˡ Swann	Mʳ Gabˡ Burnham
Edmd Porter Esqʳ	Mʳ Zebulⁿ Clayton	Mʳ Jnᵒ Sawyer
Collen Pollock Esqʳ	Mʳ Chⁿ Denman	Mʳ Jerᵐᵏ Symons
Capᵗ Wᵐ Downing	Capt. Richᵈ Sanderson	Coloᵉ Thoˢ Swann

Curratuck	Bertie	Beaufort
Mr Fran^s Morse	Mr Jam^s Castlelaw	Maj^r Robt Turner
Mr John Mann	Capt George Winn	Doct^r Patr^k Maul
Mr John Etheridge	Mr Arth^r Williams	
Mr Stephⁿ Williams	Mr Isaac Hill	Hide
Mr Thos White	Mr Wm Kinchen	Mr Thos Smith
		Mr Wm Barrow

Craven	Carteret	New Hanover
Mr Wm Handcock	Mr Ch^s Cogdal	Mr Jno. Swann
Mr Evan Jones	Mr Jos^h Wickers	Mr Jno. Porter

Edenton	Bath Town	Newburn Town
Mr Ch^s Westbeer	Mr Jno Lahey	Mr Walter Lane

Mr Ayliffe Williams produced a Dedimus from his Excellency the Governour to qualify the Members of this House and the following Members qualified accordingly vizt

For Chowan—Col^o Edwd Moseley Col^o Henry Bonner Mr Collen Pollock Edm^d Porter Esqr Capt Wm Downing For Edenton—Mr Ch^s Westbeer For Pequimons—Mr Richd Skinner Mr Saml Swann Mr Zebulun Clayton Mr Charles Denman For Pasquotank—Mr Ch^s Sawyer Mr Gabriel Burnham Mr Jno Sawyer For Beaufort—Doct^r Patrick Maul Maj^r Robt Turner For Craven—Mr Wm Handcock Mr Evan Jones For Curratuck—Mr Francis Morse For Bertie—Mr Arthur Williams Mr Isaac Hill Mr William Kinchen Capt George Winn For New Hanover—Mr John Swann

The aforementioned Members being qualified several Gent. that were elected for the New precincts of Onslow Edgecombe and Bladen appeared and the House of Opinion that they ought not to qualify as Members the House intending to take the same into Consideration to Morrow

Sent the following Message to the Upper House

The House being qualified are ready to wait on your Excellency

A WILLIAMS Cth Genl Assemb^{ly}

Sent by Edm^d Porter Esqr
  & Mr Col^o Pollock

The Messenger of the Upper House came to acquaint this House, His Excellency the Govr was ready to receive them

Whereupon the House attended

The Members waited upon the Governour who directed them to choose their Speaker and he would be ready to receive him this Evening

The House thereupon returned and Unanimously chose Col⁰ Edward Moseley Speaker

Sent the following Message

To his Excell⁷ the Gov⁷ in Council

This House have chose their Speaker and are ready to present him to your Excellency

By Order

A WILLIAMS Cᵗʰ Genˡ Assembly

Sent by Mʳ Westbeer
    & Mʳ Denman

The Messenger of the Upper House came to this House and informed the House that his Excell⁷ the Gov⁷ was ready to receive their Speaker

The House thereupon attended with their Speaker and there not being Members of the Council sufficient to make an House His Excell⁷ was pleased thereupon to prorogue the Assembly untill to Morrow, which is accordingly prorogued

A WILLIAMS Cᵗʰ Genˡ Assemᵇʸ

Wednesday July yᵉ 4ᵗʰ

The House met pursuant to Yesterday's Prorogation and there appeared Mʳ Thoˢ Smith Member for Hide precinct who took the Oath by law appointed and subscribed the Declaration

Received a Message from the Gov⁷ That he was ready to receive the Speaker Whereupon the House waited upon his Excell⁷ who approved of the Speaker and made a Speech, which the House obtained a copy off and returned Where the same was read again Vizᵗ

Gentl. of Both Houses,

Upon my first Arrival after I had taken Charge of this Government for the King I called an Assembly and as directed by his Majesty's Instructions, I propos'd to them several things to be enacted for the Regulation of the Province, but was not so happy as to obtain their Complyance with them, which if then agreed too, and settled, I am satisfied would have been much better for the Country and might have been a means of Gaining his Majesty's further favor about the Rents, which People are so desirous should be made easy to them

That Assembly proposed to pay the King's Rents in Rice and Tobacco at a rated Price in Lieu of proclamation Money which his Majesty offered to receive them at instead of Sterling As I did not think myself impowered to make any further Concessions, without Knowing his

Majesty's Pleasure, for that Reason and some others I thought it not necessary to call another Assembly, before I had made a Report of the State of this Country to the Lords Commissioners for Trade and Plantations, and was honoured with an Answer from them Which I very early did with great care and Faithfulness, but their Answer came not to my hands till the 26th day of March last, when I issued Writs for this Assembly

I must now acquaint you, that by a fresh Direction, I am restrained from passing an Act for the payment of Quitt Rents in any other Specie but in Proclamation money, and I am ordered to take care that the Officers Fees be paid in Proclamation Money also   How far the Obedience of this Assembly to the Kings Instructions may induce his Majesty to grant further Ease or Indulgence to the People in their Rents I leave you to consider

It is expected, as may be seen in the 19th Instruction (which I shall cause to be laid before you) that there should an Act be passed, to oblige all Possessors of Land, in this Government to register the same in the Auditors Office, which is the more reasonable since his Majesty is not only graciously pleased to permitt me to pass an Act for remitting all Arrears of Rents due when the King compleated the Purchase of Carolina, but also to quiett People in the Possession of their Lands, a Favour that I hope this Assembly will endeavour to Merrit.

I am commanded by the 75th and following Instruction to take especial care that the Publick Service of the Church of England be duly maintained and that a competent Provision be made for the Ministry, Lands assigned them for Gleebs, and convenient Houses built thereon,   the little Provision hitherto made for supporting the Publick Worship, seems to be a Reproach to the Country and prevents many good People from coming here to settle   It certainly becomes you to provide some more decent Means to maintain the Clergy and to appropriate Money for the building a Church or Chappel in every Parish, which in most Places are now wanting

I think it would prove for the Ease and Benefit of the people if the power of the precinct Courts was inlarged and better Provision made for Juries, which One of my Instructions directs Me to recommend

I will not burthen you at this Season with too many things for your Consideration but I cannot help recommending to you to do something for the Encreasing the Products of this Country, which will gradually beget more Industry among the people and will best promote a British Trade that is so much wanted here and which we ought always to encourage, and for this End I think it would be well to exempt all Vessels that come from Great Britain from the payment of powder Money, and that your own Commodities for that Trade were under better Inspection and Regulation

GENTL

I conclude with Hearty wishing there may be that Harmony and good Agreement between you, that the Country at this time has Occasion for, I hope you meet together with such good Dispositions, that no particular Interest and Views, no Heat, no Divisions may hinder your joining with Me in promoting the Wellfare of this Country, which I assure you I have equally at Heart with the Best Men herein, I sincerely promise you my Concurrence in Everything that shall be for his Majesty's Service and the Good of this Province

GEO. BURRINGTON.

Ordered That Mr Edmond Porter Mr Collen Pollock Mr John Swann Mr Charles Denman Mr Gabriel Burnham Capt William Downing Mr Charles Westbeer Doctr Patrick Maul and Mr Arthur Williams be a Committee to consider his Excellency's Speech and draw up an Answer thereto.

And whereas we perceive by his Excellency's Speech that he has received fresh Directions and Orders concerning the Quitt Rents and ffees. The House thereupon sent the following Message to his Excellency

TO HIS EXCELLENCY THE GOVERNOUR

Your Excellency in your Speech having been pleased to mention your Receit of fresh Instructions concerning the Quitt Rents and ffees this House desires your Excellency would be pleased to communicate to this House Copies of those Instructions relating to the Quitt Rents and ffees, that the Committee appointed to consider the Speech and make answer thereto may be the better enabled to make their Report to the House.

A WILLIAMS Ch Genl Assembly.

And thereupon his Excellency caused to be delivered to this House the two following Paragraphs. Vizt

My Lords having referred several Questions upon the Acts of this Province to his Majesty's Council for their Opinion in Point of Law, An answer to that part of your Letter, must yet be deferred for some time. But I am now to acquaint you with Respect to that part of your Letter, where you ask the opinion of the Board whether the Receivers of his Majesty's Quitt Rents may not accept of an Equivalent for Proclamation Money, That you are steadily to adhere to your Instructions upon all Occasions, and therefore when any Act shall be passed, it must be enacted that his Majesty's Quitt Rents be punctually paid in Proclamation Money And if it shall appear that there is not money sufficient to answer the said payments, His Majesty may then, upon a proper Application agree to take an Equivalent in the products of the Province

I am likewise to inform you that the grand Deed of 1668 from the Lords Proprietors, which you mention as pleaded by the people against paying any higher Quitt Rents than are paid in Virginia, can only be understood as a Temporary Letter of Attorney from the Lords Proprietors revocable at Pleasure, as in effect it was many years ago, when they directed their Govr Mr Eden to grant no Land without reserving One peny $\mathcal{P}$ Acre, however as the paying 4 Shills Proclamation Money p^r Hundred Acres, is well as paying all officers Fees in the said Currency and registring all Grants of Land, are by your Instructions made the Terms upon which his Majesty has been graciously pleased to declare he will remitt the paym^t of the Arrears of Quitt Rents. His Majesty's Officers may soon have Directions to collect the said Arrears unless the people do speedily think fitt to comply with his Majesty's Terms, which are calculated for their Advantage and for quieting them in their Possessions

Two Paragraphs of a Letter from the Board of Trade dated Augt 16th 1732

Ordered The several Returns for the Members of this Assembly be laid before this House

Which was done accordingly, excepting for the Precinct of Curratuck and the New precinct of Onslow

Mr Charles Cogdal Mr Joseph Wickers being returned Members for Cartaret precinct took the Oaths and subscribed the Declaration according to Law for their Qualification

The House taking into Consideration the Affair of the New precincts.

Ordered The same be referred to the Committe appointed to consider the Governour's Speech, that they examine presidents and report to the House their Opinion concerning the same

Mr Ayliffe Williams produced his Excellency's Commission for being Clark of the Lower House of Assembly Also Mr John Richards produced his Excell^{cy} Commission for being Sargeant of the Lower House of Assembly

This House conceiving that the appointing the aforementioned Officers has always appertained to this House

Ordered That the Consideration thereof be referred to the Comitte aforesaid to examine Preceedents and report to the House their Opinion concerning the same

A WILLIAMS C^{lk} Genl Assembly

Adjourned to 9 a Clock }
  to Morrow Morning }

Thursday July 5th

The House mett pursuant to Adjournment

Ordered That the Committe appointed to make Answer to the Governour's Speech be a Committe of Propositions and Grievance and that any of the Members of this House may join the said Committe

Ordered That Capt Wm Downing Mr Collen Pollock Co^ll Henry Bonner Mr Arthur Williams Maj^r Robert Turner and Mr Thomas Smith be a Committe to join such Members as shall be appointed by the Upper House as a Comitte of Claims

A. WILLIAMS C^{lk} Genl Assem^{ly}

Sent by Mr Swann &
    Mr Burnham

Voted That the several Powder Receivers do lay their Accounts before this Assembly by Wednesday next.

Adjourned to 9 a clock to Morrow Morning

Friday July 6th

The House met pursuant to Adjournment. And there appeared Mr James Castelaw Member for Bertie precinct who took the Oaths and Subscribed the Declaration by Law appointed for his Qualification

Mr Edmond Porter from the Committe appointed to answer his Excell^y the Governour's Speech made Report that the Committe had sundry Times considered the same & agreed to a Draught of a Report, which was read and laid on the Table

The said Report was read again and being fully debated and considered.

Voted. Nemine contradicente that the said Answer be accepted which is as follows. Vizt

To His Excell^y George Burrington Esqre His Majesty's Capt Genl and Govr in Chief of North Carolina

MAY IT PLEASE YOUR EXCELL^y

This House having taken your Excellency's Speech into our most serious consideration and having duly examined the Conduct of the Assembly in April 1731 We cannot but be of opinion, that the Assembly

went as far as it was possible toward a Complyance with the Royal
Instruction concerning the Quitt Rents and ffees, inasmuch as the want of
Gold and Silver Currancy is so well known in this Province, and now at
this last Election our Principals throughout the province having recommended nothing more earnestly to Us than that We should not consent
to burthen them with such payments as are impossible for them to make

We take Notice that Your Excellency is pleased to say that that Assembly propos'd to pay his Majesty's Rent in Rice and Tobacco at a rated
price in Lieu of Proclamation Money, which his Majesty offered to
receive instead of Sterling   We find by a due Enquiry into the Matter,
that the Assembly did endeavour to comply with the Royal Instruction
as near as possible and therefore as there seemed to be no Probability of
such payments to be made in Gold and Silver, they offered a just Equivalent—But that the Rents are due in Sterling as your Exce^lly seems to
intimate, or even in Proclamation Money,   We humbly beg Leave to differ in Opinion and We hope to be able to support this our Opinion

The Rents reserved in the Grants of Lands are not said in the Grants
to be payable in Sterling Money or any other, and in all equitable construction We think the Money reserved must be understood the Money
of the Country and so the Law hath always been taken, nor has Sterling Money or Proclamation Money been ever recovered on any Specialty,
but where those have been Specially named and expressed

But to shew that the Rents and ffees are payable only in the Currant
Money of the Province We desire it may be remembred, that before any
Paper Money was currant in this Province there was always Acts of
Assembly declaring the prices of the Products of the Country to pass as
Money in all respects as well for Quitt Rents as any other Payments,
and when the paper Money was established, It was provided that the
same should be currant in all payments, excepting for Purchase of Lands
So that we think it very plain, that the Rents are not payable either in
Sterling or Proclamation   Nor doth it seem to us by anything yet laid
before the House that his Majesty offered to receive Proclamation Money
for Rents in Lieu of Sterling   It doth indeed appear that his Majesty
proposes that your Exce^lly should pass a Law to remitt the Arrears of
Rents due from this province to the time of perfecting his Purchase
(which he was given to understand was very large) in case the Assembly
would by the same Law provide that all possessors of Land should register their Grants in the Auditors Office, that the Quitt Rents payable
for the future should be in Proclamation Money & the ffees of the Officers should be settled in Proclamation Money   We give his Majesty our

Hearty thanks for such a mark of his Paternal care shewn to us in the offer of remitting so large an arrear as was thought to be due from the province, but at the same time We humbly beg leave to represent that by a diligent Enquiry of the Members of this House who came from the several parts of the province, We can't learn that the Arrears (if any due) are worth collecting, because We all very well remember that the Collections have been very constantly made and some have even now produced to the House Receits for the Year 1730 Since his Majesty purchased the Province. Indeed, We think his Majesty's offer to the province of South Carolina, in the like case was very wisely accepted, as We are told it has been, in regard they owed 15 or 16 years arrear, for altho' Gold and Silver might be something scarce there, yet by their large and extensive Trade, they might be able to procure it, tho at some difficulty, when they had so great an indulgence as the Remittance of 15 or 16 Years. But in this Province We have no prospect of gaining Silver or Gold sufficient for such purposes, Our Trade being very much cramp'd by the bad Navigation and the excessive ffees taken by Naval Officers and Collectors the like not heard off in any of the British Dominions as far as We can learn, and at the same time such ffees taken without any Colour of Law

Concerning the Tenure of the Lands in the County of Albemarle in particular we humbly conceive the Right Honble the Lords Commissioners for Trade and Plantations have not a true Account of the State and Condition of the Lands in that County, by what they are pleased to say of the Deed of Grant being in the Nature of a Temporary Power of Attorney revocable at pleasure which they say the Lords Proprietors seem to have done by their Instructions to Governour Eden We therefore beg leave to represent the case of the Tenants of Albemarle County as it appears to us. When his Majesty King Charles the second granted the province of Carolina to the Lords Proprietors there were divers persons in possession of Lands within the Bounds of the Charter, who held their Lands by Grants from the Government of Virginia and therefore in the Royal Charter, there was a Saving of those persons Rights, the Lords Proprietors in laying out the Province into Eight Counties, called that Eighth part of the province lying next to Virginia by the name of Albemarle County within which County it was that those persons dwelt who held Lands by Virginia Grants and as the Lords Proprietors proposed to grant the Lands of their Province upon no harder Terms than the King's Subjects held theirs in Virginia, the Inhabitants of Albemarle County by their humble Applications to the Lords Proprietors obtain'd the Deed

72

of Grant dated May the first 1668 Whereby the Lands of that County were to be granted to all New Comers for the future (who had Right to take up fifty acres for each person in their Family) on the same Terms and Tenures as the people of Virginia held their Lands as by the same Deed will more at large appear   But all the other Lands in the Province were to be granted at their Lordships and their Successors Discretion, and therefore they sometimes gave Directions to grant their other Lands at a high Quitt Rent, and at other times on payment of Purchase Money with Reservation of small Quitt Rents payable Yearly   But their Lordships never attempted to intring the Deed of Grant, what was intended to be done by the directions to Governour Eden, respected only the other Lands and not those of Albemarle County as appears both by their Lordships Directions, which mention only the Sale of Lands and not the Granting of Quitt Rents which Distinction was always made between Albemarle County Lands and the other Lands of the Province, this also appears from the Constant practice of their Lordships Officers, who Notwithstanding the aforesaid Order, or any other, granted the Lands in Albemarle County agreeable to the Deed of Grant aforementioned without the least cheque from the Proprietors

As the principal and most valuable Lands in the County of Albemarle are already granted, we humbly hope that if such a Construction were to be put upon the Deed of Grant as that it were revocable, as we trust such Construction will not be made, Yet that his Royall Majesty will be graciously pleased to confirm the same Grant unto his good Subjects of the said County of Albemarle and direct that all the Vacant Land in the same may be granted, as hath been heretofore accustomed agreeable to the Deed of Grant   Altho this is the case of his Majesty's Subjects, and Tenants of this Province, and that so such like encouragement as a Remission of 15 or 16 Years Rent were offered us, the Assembly readily came into his Majesty's proposals, and by a Bill for an Act consented that the Officers ffees should be settled in Proclamation Money or a just Equivalent thereto, and even to comply with the payment of Proclamation Money for Rents, or for want thereof, a just Equivalent, as also to register the Grants in the Auditors Office Wherefore we humbly hope your Excellency and the Council will join with us in making a true State of the poverty of this Province and their Inability to comply with a proposal for payment to be made in Proclamation Money   And that his Majesty will be graciously pleased to direct an Equivalent may be ascertained in the same Law For those we represent have given us in Charge not to burthen them with such payments as they can foresee no possibility of complying with

We are sorry to find that Your Excellency should have any Reasons for so long a disuse of Assemblies, it being now above two Years since any sate to do Business, and altho with Respect to the affair of the Quitt Rents Your Excellency might not think fit to treat with an Assembly on that Head, untill you had the Royall Instructions, Yet give us leave to observe that the Affairs of the Province in our humble Opinion required the Meeting of an Assembly before this time, not only for an Application to his Majesty toward the Good and happy Settlement of this province, but also for the suppressing the many Oppressions, which so loudly have been complained of thro the whole province, which could no other way so properly be represented as in an Assembly

We are of opinion with your Excellency that a British Trade ought by all Means to be encouraged, We will therefore do everything in our Power to promote that in particular, as also all other trade in general, and as the Powder Money laid on Vessels was found to be the only expedient for raising a Magazine in the time of the Indian War, as that Occasion ceased some time past, We propose to ease the Trade of that Burthen, which has been so loudly complained of by the Traders of this Province, and as a further Encouragement We propose that a Sum be paid out of the publick Treasury to the Commissioners for the several Inletts towards Bouying and Beaconing the Channels

We propose to take into our Consideration the Hardships of the people living in the Remote parts of the country and to give them such ease with Respect to the Courts as may be of use to them

By the Laws pass'd in 1729 which we understand are under his Majesty's Consideration, We think a very good Provision was made for establishing the several Vesteries, to build Churches, purchase Glebs, and to make ample provision for the Clergy At the same time proper Provision was made for the payment of Juries, we shall therefore forbear to do any thing relating to those Matters untill We shall be informed of the Royal Pleasure concerning those Laws

Your Excellency's kind Wishes that a good Harmony may be between Us, and Your Promise of a Concurrance in everything that shall be for his Majesty's Service and the Good of the province gives Us the Uttmost Satisfaction, when We reflect on the heavy Grievances this poor Country hath long Laboured under, not only by the exorbitant ffees, We have had so just reason to mention to your Excellency at this time, as Well as it hath been heretofore, but likewise from the pervertion of Justice by Evill and wicked Officers (We are sorry We are forced to say, of Your Excellency's appointment and Approbation) especially by Wilham Little Chief Justice and his Assistants, which Particular Grievance, We promise ourselves, will now be remedied by the Arrival of M[r] Chief Justice Smith who we have good reason to believe to be a Gentleman of great honour and Integrity not only from his having his Majesty's Approbation but from his Behaviour ever since his first Arrival in this Province

We assure your Excellency We are met with the best disposition to promote his Majesty's Service and the Wellfare of the Province, which we think ought to be inseparable and as there doth not seem to be the least Appearance of any particular Interrest or Views among us, So We shall studiously avoid anything that may look like Heat or Division

Ordered The same to be fairly transcribed for this House to wait on his Excellency therewith

The Committe of Propositions and Grievances laid before the House the following three papers which are as followeth Viz[t]

This House being made sensible that divers of the Members of the Assembly held in April 1731 had requested M[r] Chief Justice Smith, when he proposed to go for England to do the Country what Service he could touching certain Grievances and this House being Satisfied that the said M[r] Chief Justice Smith has been very Serviceable to this province in setting forth their Grievances

Voted Unanimously that M[r] Porter and M[r] Castelaw do wait on the said M[r] Chief Justice Smith and give him the thanks of this House for such his Service done to the Country and that they assure him that this House will take those his Services into their further Consideration

By Order

A WILLIAMS Clk Gen[l] Assembly

NORTH CAROLINA—ss.

George the Second by the Grace of God of Great Britain &c. King &c
    To the provost Marshal or Deputy Greeting

Whereas by the Consideration of our Chief Justice and his Assistants of our General Court began and held at Edenton on the last Tuesday of October last it was ordered in the Suit brought by John Bryant against William Whitehead, that the Plaintiff having discontinued his Suit should pay Cost, which Cost has been taxed, in the whole including this Writt besides Marshall's ffees the sum of two Pounds Eight shillings and ten pence proclamation Money or Equivalent as rated, whereof Execution remains to be done   We command you therefore to take the

Body of the said John Bryant and him in prison safely to keep without Bail or Mainprize untill he hath paid or Satisfied the same together with your own ffees hereof fail not and make return of this Writt with your Doing thereon

Witness William Little Esq' Chief Justice at Edenton this 20th day of Nov'' 1732.

Test Alexander Weight D M

W" LITTLE C"

Received of John Bryant ten pounds Bills of this Province of North Carolina for an Execution against him dated the 20th of November 1732 as Witness my Hand this 25th of December 1732

Remains 4'bll 7'   ALEXANDER WEIGHT D. M

Received the following Message from the Upper House

M' SPEAKER AND GENT. OF THE HOUSE OF BURGESSES.

Resolved That John Baptista Ash Edmond Gale and William Owen Esq' be and are hereby appointed a Committe to join with the Members of the Lower House as are appointed to make a Committe of Claims.

By Order
ROB' FORSTER C'' of y'' Upper House

Adjourned to 9 a Clock to morrow morning

Saturday July 7th

The House met pursuant to adjournment

The Council House and the House the Assembly Sitts in wanting Repairs

Voted That Col' Edward Moseley Col' Henry Bonner and M' Charles Westbeer be Commissioners to agree with Workmen for the Repairing those buildings, and that when the same Repairs are perfected the said Commissioners or any two of them have power to draw on the publick Treasurer for payment of the Workmen

Voted That M' Christopher Beckett have twelve pounds paper Money as Now currant ℔ Annum for his Care in keeping the Doors and Windows of the Council House and Assembly House when those Houses are not used.

Sent to his Excell' the Gov' and Council for Concurrance.

A WILLIAMS C'' Gen' Assembly

By M' Ch' Sawer &
M' Jn' Sawyer

Read the petition of Thomas Murphy setting forth that a Ferry by Order of Craven Court was established at or near the said Murphy's which he hath constantly kept And very lately by the said precinct Court hath appointed another Ferry above the said Murphy's much out of the Way, and much to the said Murphy's prejudice, and the Subject Matter of the said Petition appearing to be true by the Testimony of Some of the Members of this House,

Ordered That the Ferry be and remain at the said Murphy's.

Read the petition of the Inhabitants in the District between Terrapine Hill and Arkill's Bridge in Chowan precinct concerning an Order obtained in the precinct Court of Chowan Relating to a Road from Terrapine Hill to Mr Edmond Gale's

Ordered That this House will take the same into Consideration on Monday next and that in the Mean Time Mr Edmond Gale and the parties interrested have Notice thereof

Read the Petition of the Commissioners for Buoying and Beaconing of Ocacock Inlett and Channel

Ordered That the Consideration of the said Petition be referred untill the Powder Receivers Accounts of Port Bath are laid before the House

Capt William Downing from the Committe appointed to consider the case of the New Precincts made Report that the Committe hath sundry Times considered the same and agreed to a Report which was read and laid on the Table

The said Report was read again

Voted That the same be accepted which is as followeth Vizt

That when the province of Carolina was at first divided into Eight Counties, each County was to have been a Government, and for some Years that Eighth Part of the province, lying next to Virginia was known and distinguished by the Stile and Title of the Government of the County of Albemarle, and by those Constitutions bearing date 1698 agreed to by the Lords Proprietors and the Representatives of the People it was provided, that as the Country shall increase the Representatives shall also be proportionally increased if the Commons do so desire

The Scheme of each County, being a Government not taking effect by Reason of the Small progress made in setling the Country the province became divided into two Governments Vizt North and South Carolina

For the Government of North Carolina there was no Representatives of the People, but such as represented the County of Albemarle untill the Year 1697 when the County of Bath being the County adjourning to Albemarle had two Representatives allowed to sitt in the Biennial Assembly

As the Settlements encreased to the Southward the Governour and Council took on them at sundry times to divide the same into four precincts Viz^t Beaufort Hide Craven and Carteret and each of those precincts had two Representatives to sitt in the Assembly

In the Year 1722 the precinct of Chowan one of the precincts in Albemarle County having extended itself very far, it was thought advisable to erect a New Precinct to the Westward of Chowan River by the Name of Bertie, which was done by Act of Assembly in the Year 1722 and five Representatives allowed to that Precinct by that Assembly

In July 1729 the Governour and Council assumed a Power by Order of Council to erect a New Precinct to the Southward by the name of New Hanover adjoining to Carteret Precinct, and that Precinct sending Representatives to the Biennial Assembly in Nov^br 1729 those Representatives were not admitted by the Assembly to sitt and Vote untill an Act passed that Session for erecting that precinct.

At the same Assembly in the Year 1729 the Governour Councill and Assembly erected another Precinct in Albemarle by the Name of Tyrril

Thus the Way and Manner of Enlarging the Number of the Representatives is brought down to the Case of the New Precincts now under Consideration

Whereon We observe

1^t That Onslow Precinct is entirely taken out of Carteret and New Hanover Edgecombe Chiefly out of Bertie and Bladen out of New Hanover

2^ly We are of Opinion that a Method of enlarging the Number of Assembly Men by Order of Governour and Council is not agreeable to the Constitution, that the Representatives of the People are the proper Judges what Encrease is necessary, nor ought any Encrease to be made without their Assent

3^ly Should any Encrease be made without their Assent, it would alter the Form of Representation and make the Lower House to depend on the Governour and Council and be subject to what alterations they pleased to make, by dividing old precincts or erecting New lines from which many Absurdities would follow, as We conceive.

4^ly We find this power assumed by the Governour and Council is no ways agreeable to the practice of our Neighbouring Government of Virginia, for there, as it appears by their printed Acts, the same is done by Governour, Council and Assembly

5^ly Nor do we find that any power is given to the Governour and Council of this Province by the Royal Commission to Act in such Affairs without the Assembly

Upon the whole We humbly propose it to the House as our Opinion that the Members returned for the New precincts be not admitted, the Assembly not having been consulted in or agreed to such an Increase

The Committe are also of Opinion that it may be proper for the House to have a Conferrence with the Governour and Council concerning the subject Matter of the New Precincts

Mr Porter from the Committe appointed to consider the case of the Officers appointed for this House by the Governour made Report that the Committe hath several times considered the same and agreed to a Report which was read and laid on the Table

The said Report was read again

Voted The same be accepted which is as followeth   Vizt

This Committe has with great Dilligence Examined the Books of the Assembly and do find that it has been the constant practice of the House to name and appoint all their Officers Such as Clerk, Sargeant, Messenger and Door Keeper, Nor can we find that the Lords proprietors or their Governours ever attempted to Name or appoint those Officers or any of them   We are indeed informed, but not so fully as to give satisfaction in that case, that the Clerk of the House of Commons in England (by Custom) is appointed by the Crown   Therefore as we find the practice here, has ever been for the Assembly to choose those Officers, 'tis our Opinion that it will be most prudent for this House humbly to address to his Majesty that he will be graciously pleased to continue to the Assembly such priviledges, as they have hitherto enjoy'd and which has never been disputed   But if his Excellency will not permitt the Ancient Liberty and Priviledges of this Assembly that in Such case this Committe is of Opinion rather than to prejudice or retard the Business of this Session (untill his Majesty's pleasure be known) to admitt of the said Officers appointed by the Governour, saving to this House their Ancient Rights and Priviledges

The Answer to the Governour's Speech being fairly transcribed was read and examined

Resolved This House wait on his Excellency the Governour therewith on Monday next

Adjourned to 9 a Clock on Monday morning

Monday July 9th
The House met pursuant to Adjournment
And there appeared Mr John Mann Member for Curratuck, who took the Oath and Subscribed the Declaration by Law appointed for his Qualification

To His Excell^y the Govr and Council

It being represented to this House by the Members from divers parts of the province, that the publick Roads and Bridges in General are much out of Repair, whereby the travelling to the General Court and Assembly is rendered very difficult

This House humbly requests his Excellency that he will be pleased to direct the Magistrates in the Several precincts to take effectual care that the Roads & Bridges be forthwith repaired, and Ferrys duly kept, and that the same be constantly Kept So, and that upon any failure of the Overseer or people, who are to labour on the said Roads, the Justices do see that the Laws relating to Roads, Bridges and Ferrys be put in force and all Delinquents duly fined

By Order

A WILLIAMS C^lk Genl Assembly

Sent by Mr Jno Sawyer and
        Mr Ch^s Denman

Which was returned with the following Endorsem^tt Viz^t Read and Concurr'd with in the Upper House

By Order

R^t FORSTER C^lk Upper House.

In the Months of November January and February last I travelled thrô most of the precincts in this Government and to my great satisfaction found much labour had been bestowed the last Year in making New Roads and repairing the old and that the roads were in very good Condition, abundance of Bridges having been newly made therefore I desire to be informed in what part of the province the bad Roads mentioned in Your Message are, that I may know what Magistrates, I shall have Occasion to write to for performing what you desire On this subject

GEO· BURRINGTON

To his Excell^y the Govr and Council

The old paper Currancy which was brought in and accounted for at the Assembly held in April 1731 being Carefully Sealed up and lodged in the Hands of the Publick Treasurer Voted. That the same be brought and layed before the Assembly tomorrow in order that the same may be destroyed.

Sent to the Govr and Council for Concurrance

By Order

A WILLIAMS C^lk Genl Assembly.

By Mr Jno Sawyer &
    Mr Ch^s Sawyer

To his Excell'' the Gov' and Council

Col° Thomas Swann Treasurer of Pasquotank and Col° Thomas Pollock Treasurer of Bertie being dedd this House recommends unto his Excellency the Governour and Council Mr James Lockheart to be Treasurer of Bertie and Mr John Solley to be Treasurer of Pasquotank

Sent to the Gov' and Council for Concurrence

By Order
A WILLIAMS C'k Gen' Assembly

By Mr Jn° Sawyer &
    Mr Ch° Sawyer

Sent to the Gov' and Council the Vote of this House of July the 5th concerning the Powder Receivers

By Mr Jn° Sawyer &
    Mr Ch° Sawyer

The House taking into Consideration the great Increase of Vermin

Ordered that Doc' Patrick Maul Mr Zebulun Clayton and Mr Gabriel Burnham be a Committe to prepare a Bill for the Destruction of Vermin and that the same be laid before the House on Wednesday next

To his Excell'' the Gov' and Council

This House taking into Consideration the Affair of the New precincts lately Erected This House desires to have a Conference with his Excellency and the Council concerning the same

By Order
A WILLIAMS C'k Gen' Assembly

Sent by Mr Geo. Winn
    Mr Wm Kinchen

Read the petition of the Inhabitants of Bear River and the lower parts of Neuse River praying to be Erected into a New precinct

Ordered The same to lye on the Table for the Consideration of the House

Received the following Message from the Upper House concerning the petition of Thomas Murphy

Mr Speaker and Gent' of the Gen' Assembly

It is the opinion of this House that the Subject Matter of the said petition (if not to be provided for by a special Law for that purpose) may more properly be recommended to the precinct Court to be regulated, as the opinion of the General Assembly with which this House is ready to concurr

By Order
R. FORSTER C'k of y° up' House

To the Hono^ble the Council.

This House concurs with Your Message concerning the Ferry at Murphy's.

Voted That the same be referred to the precinct Court of Craven and that the said Court do regulate the same agreeable to the Vote of this Assembly

Sent to the Upper House for Concurrance

By Order

A WILLIAMS C^lk Genl Assembly

By Mr Art^r Williams &
Mr Isac Hill

Mr John Etheridge & Mr Stephen Williams Members for Curratuck appeared who took the Oaths and Subscribed the Declaration by Law appointed for their Qualification.

Received from the Upper House the Vote of this House concerning the Repairs of the publick Buildings &c together with the following Message (Vizt)

Mr Speaker and Gentl. of the Genl Assembly

This House is ready to concur with the within Vote provided a certain Sum be Sett or mentioned to limitt the Commissioners in their Draft, and that they render Accounts to the General Assembly of the Expences. This House likewise recommends to the Consideration of the General Assembly that they would include the Repairs and Care of the Goal in the same Vote.

By Order

R FORSTER C^lk of ye Upper House

This House agrees with the Upper House that the Commissioners be limitted to the Sum of Two hundred pounds for repairing and fitting the Council House the Assembly House and for repairing fitting and enlarging the Goal, and that the Commissioners do render an account of the expences to the General Assembly

By Order

A WILLIAMS C^lk Genl Assembly

Sent by Mr Handcock &
Mr Jones

Received from the Upper House the Message of this House concerning the Recommendation of the two persons to be Treasurers in the Room of the deceased which was endorsed as followeth Viz^t

Mr Speaker and Gentl of the Genl Assembly

This House proposes Mr John Palm in the Room of Mr John Solley named by your House for Treasurer of Pasquotank which if agreed to, this House will concurr with the Vote

By Order

R FORSTER C^{lk} up^r House

Which was sent back to the Upper House thus Endorsed (Viz^t) This House concurrs therewith

By Order

A WILLIAMS C^{lk} Genl Assembly.

Sent by Mr Mann, &
    Mr Etheridge

The House this day according to Order took into Consideration the petition of the Inhabitants of the district between Terrapine Hill and Arkills Bridge And the House having heard Mr Edmond Gale thereon, who had Notice to attend It is the opinion of the House that the p^tcinct Court of Chowan had no power to excuse the said Mr Gale and others from Working on the Road from Terrapine Hill to Arkills Bridge

Voted The same be referred to the precinct Court of Chowan who are hereby directed to see that the said Mr Edmond Gale and others do work on the Road aforesaid

Sent to the Upper House for Concurrance

By Order

A WILLIAMS C^{lk} Genl Assembly

By Mr Williams &
    Mr Morse

This House understanding that the Council is adjourned

Resolved That this House will wait on his Excellency the Govr with the Answer to his Speech to Morrow Morning

Adjourned to 9 a Clock to Morrow Morning

Tuesday July ye 10th

Met according to Adjournment

A Bill for an Act intituled an Act to repeal the Act of Assembly entituled an Act for raising a publick Magazine of Ammunition upon the Tonnage of all Vessells trading to this Government, passed at the Biennial Assembly in the Year 1715 Read in the House the first time and pass'd

A WILLIAMS C^{lk} Genl Assembly

Sent to the Upper House by Mr Porter &
    Mr Westbeer

Col⁰ Henry Bonner and Cap⁺ William Downing were sent by this House to his Excellency the Governour to lett him know the House was ready to wait on him with an Address in answer to his Speech   They reported to the House that his Excellency said he would receive the House in the Council Chamber to Morrow at 12 a Clock

The Vote of this House concerning the Destroying of the old paper Currency was returned from the Upper House with the following Entrys and Resolves thereon

Read and Concurred with in the Upper House

By Order

R FORSTER C^{lk} of the Upper House

I concurr provided two (or more) Members of the Council be present to take an account of the Bills and see them destroyed

GEO BURRINGTON

Resolved. That the same be sent down to the General Assembly and that John Baptista Ash and John Lovick Esq^{rs} Members of this House be present to see the said Bills destrov'd.

By Order

R. FORSTER C^{lk} of ye up^r House

Received the Vote of this House in Concurrance with the upper House respecting the Ferry at Murphy's with the Following Entry from the Governour

I am of Opinion Mr Muphy's Ferry and Martin Franks Ferry are both very usefull and therefore neither ought to be supprest

GEO. BURRINGTON

Adjourned to 9 a Clock to morrow Morning

Wednesday July ye 11th

Met pursuant to Adjournment

A Bill for an Act entituled An Act to repeal the Act of Assembly entituled an Act for raising a publick Magazine of Ammunition upon the Tonnage of all Vessels trading to this Government past at the Biennial Assembly in the Year 1715 Read the second time and past

Sent to the Upper House by Col⁰ Bonner &

Cap⁺ Downing

The House appointed Mr Speaker Mr Porter Mr Downing Mr Castelaw Doct^r Maul to speak on the Conference with the Upper House of the Subject Matter of the New precincts and that any other Member may

Speak as he shall See Occasion That the said Managers of the Conferrence shall be guided by the Report of the Committe agreed to by this House

Received the following Message from the Governour.

I am of opinion that New precinct Treasurers ought not to be appointed in the places of those lately deceased before the King's pleasure is known in Respect to the Bills issued in the Year 1729

GEO. BURRINGTON

Received from the Upper House the Votes &c of this House concerning the publick Buildings with the following Entries thereon Vizt

Read in the Upper House and Concurred with.

By Order
R. FORSTER Cth of ye upr House

I consent to sign a Warrant for the Sum mentioned to be laid out in Repairing the Council House Court House and Goal and if you think proper to allow a Sallary for taking care of those Edifices I concurr therewith and will appoint a proper Person for that Service

GEO BURRINGTON

Received from the Upper House the Bill for an Act entituled an Act to repeal the Act of Assembly entituled an Act for raising a publick Magazine of Amunition upon the Tonnage of all Vessels trading to this Government past at the Biennial Assembly in the Year 1715

July ye 11th

Read in the Upper House a Second time and pass'd

By Order
R FORSTER Cth upr House

Received from the upper House the Message of this House concerning a Conference about the New precincts with the following Entries thereon (Vizt)

Read in the Upper House and concurr'd with and agreed that a Conference be held thereon to Morrow Morning   Resolved that his Excellency have Notice of this Conferrance

By Order
R FORSTER Cth uppr House

The Members of his Majesty's Council I deem to be sufficient to hold the intended Conferrance concerning the New p'cincts therefore have no Intention to be present

GEO: BURRINGTON

This House according to his Excellency's directions waited on him in the Council Chamber this day at noon, where the Address in Answer to his Excellency's Speech was read and delivered to him after which his Excellency retired

And then this House proceeded to a Conferrence with the upper House concerning the New Precincts.

The House returned from the Conferrence with the Council and Mr Speaker reported to the House.

That on the said Conferrence it appeared to be the Sense and Opinion of the Council and this House that the Several precincts should be ascertained, in Order that at the next biennial Election they should return Members to serve in that Assembly

This House concurrs with the Report

Voted That the precinct of Edgecombe to be bounded by the Country Line and Roanoak or Morattock River to the Rainbow Bank from thence to   Shall Send   Members to Serve in the next biennial Assembly

Received from the Upper House the Vote of this House concerning Powder Receivers with the following Entries thereon Vizt

Read and Concurred with in the Upper House.

By Order

R. FORSTER Clk upr House

The Council and General Assembly ought to address me to give Orders to the several Receivers of the Powder Money (if they desire to inspect their Accounts) to attend at a time appointed for that purpose, and not to Vote it should be done

GEO BURRINGTON

The Publick Treasurer according to Order lay'd on the Table the Box Containing £9555 2.6 old paper Currancy that was lodged with him at the Assembly in April 1731 Jno Baptist Ash and John Lovick Esqrs Members of the Council who were present at the Sealing of the said Box at the Assembly in April 1731 came from the Upper House and they together with the Members of this House carefully examined the said which was found Corded and Sealed in the same Manner it was when lodged in the Treasurers Hands.

Thereupon according to the Directions of his Excellency the Governour, Council and Assembly the same Paper Currancy was publickly burnt and destroyed in the Street between the Court House and Council House Several Members of the Council Most of the Members of this House and divers other persons being present

Mr John Lakey Member for Bath Town appeared who took the Oaths, Subscribed the Declaration by Law appointed for his Qualification

A Bill for an Act entituled an Act to prevent the Annoying or stopping up of Harbours, Rivers or Navigable Creeks in this Province

Read in the Lower House the first time and past with Amendments

       A WILLIAMS Clk Genl Assemly

Sent to the upper House by Mr Etheridge &

       Mr Skinner

Adjourned to 9 a Clock to Morrow Morning

Thursday July ye 12th

The House mett according to adjournment.

Ordered That the thanks of this House be given to the Reverend Mr Boyd for his Sermon preached before the House this Day

Voted That the Sum of ten pounds be paid out of the publick Treasury to the Reverend Mr Boyd for his Sermon preached before the Assembly this Day And that his Excellency the Governour be desired to issue his Warrant for Payment of the Same

Ordered the Same be Sent to the Upper House for Concurrance.

Reported from the Committe of Propositions and Grievances

That the Register of Writings for Beaufort and Hyde precincts one Benjamin Peyton hath possessed himself of the Writings and books belonging to that Office pretending a Commission from the Governour for the same and hath carried them from Bath Town contrary to an Order of that Court, which forbid the moving them from Town and that it is much to be feared by the Magistrates and Inhabitants of those precincts that the same may be imbezelled by the said Peyton he being a Person of Ill Fame and Character

It is the Opinion of this Committe that the Assembly do address his Excellency the Governour that if he has granted such a Commission he would be pleased to recall it and that he would direct the Books and Papers belonging to that Office may be Kept at Bath Town as by Law it is provided they should be

This House concurrs with the Report of the Committe Divers of the Members of this Assembly very well remembring that the said Peyton when he was formerly Marshal of Bath County attended this House at the Assembly begun in April 1731 when it appeared to the Members divers whereof are now present, that he had erased or caused to be erased the name of a person duly chosen and returned for Newburn Town and inserted or caused to be inserted another Person not duly chosen.

The House concurred therewith and Ordered to be sent to the upper House for Concurrence.

Reported from the Committe of Propositions and Grievances that the Committe have had several Complaints lav'd before them, and sundry Petitions from divers Inhabitants setting forth that divers free People Negros and Mullatos residing in this Province were taken up by the Directions of Thomas Bryant James Thomson Benjamin Hill John Edwards Thomas Kerney and William Lattimore of Bertie Precinct Benjamin Peyton and Robert Peyton of Bath County Justices of the Peace and others, and by those Justices of the Peace bound out untill they came to 31 years of Age contrary to the consent of the parties bound out

The said Committe further Report that these practices are well known to divers of the said Committe and that they fear that divers persons will desert the settlement of those parts fearing to be used in like Manner so unlawfully.

It is therefore humbly recommended by the said Committe that a Vote pass this House declaring the Illegality of such a Practice, and that all such Persons so taken from their Parents or Guardians be returned to their Respective Parents or to those under whose Care they were and that those Magistrates who have bound out such persons, and those to whom they have been bound do attend at the next biennial Assembly to answer for such their Doings   With which Report the House concurred and ordered the same to be sent to the Upper House for Concurrence

The Bill for repealing the powder Act was read the 3rd time and pass'd.

Sent to the Upper House by Mr Smith &

Mr Skinner

Received from the upper House the Bill for Repeal of the powder Act Endorsed, Read the third time in the upper House and pass'd

Ordered The same be Engrossed

A Petition of William Little Esqr Chief Justice directed to the Governour and Council was sent from the Council to this House

Ordered that the same lye on the Table for the Consideration of the House

The following Address was sent to his Excellency the Governour

TO HIS EXCELLENCY THE GOVERNOUR.

When this House pass'd a Vote July ye 5th 1733 that the Several powder Receivers should lay their Accounts before this Assembly by the 11th of the Month and sent the same to your Excellency and the Council for Concurrance We received the same Vote concurred with in the Upper House, but to our Great Surprize instead of receiving your Excellency's Consent You are pleased to Send the following Message Viz'.

The Council or General Assembly ought to address Me to give Orders to the Several Receivers of the powder Money (if they desire to inspect their Accounts) to attend at a time appointed for that purpose and not to Vote it should be done

We humbly beg leave to remind your Excellency at the same Session of Assembly in 1715 when the Act was pass'd for raising a Magazine of Ammunition on the Tonnage of Vessels, an Act also pass'd entituled Public Treasurers to give Account, wherein it is expressly provided that all persons whatsoever within this province (be they of what Quality or Condition Soever) that formerly have been now are or hereafter shall be Treasurers, Collectors or Receivers of Publick Moneys, now raised or hereafter to be raised by the Authority of the General Assembly, or who by any Ways or means have are or shall for the future be possessed of the same or any part thereof shall from time to time and at all times be hereafter accountable to the General Assembly or to such Commissioners as shall or may be appointed by the Authority of the Same and to no other person or persons whatsoever

Wherefore we think this Assembly has not proceed'd otherwise than agreeable to that law, but whether the Vote of the House concurred with by the Council is with a Design to inspect only, or for other purposes, We think the Assembly ought to have those Accounts laid before them, and that without Delay Because We have great Reason to believe that Money is in very unsafe Hands and may be lost

And that We may discharge the Trust reposed in Us as Representatives of the People We desire Your Excellency to let Us Know who are the Receivers of the powder Money, by whom and when appointed, and what Security they have given for the faithfull Discharge of their Offices For those formerly appointed by the Assembly (Some of whom We understand Your Excellency has been pleased to displace) gave very good and satisfactory Security, and duly accounted with the Assembly and paid to the Assembly the Moneys due or those Accounts agreeable to the Law before recited

                         By Order

                              JN° LEAHY D C¹ᵏ

Sent by Maj' Turner &
      Mr Smith

Adjourned till to morrow Morning 9 of the Clock.

Friday July 13th
Met according to Adjournment
Received a Message from the Clark in these Words.

Mr SPEAKER AND GENTLEMEN,

My Health will not permitt Me to wait on the House, I should be very much obliged to any Member that would be so good to take the Minutes and am Gent^l

Your most humble Servant

A WILLIAMS.

July ye 13th 1733

Read the petition of William Little Chief Justice which was sent from the Upper House July ye 12th In these Words.

N° CAROLINA—ss

To his Excell^y George Burrington Esqr Capt Gener^l and Govr in Chief
And the Hono^{ble} the Council now Sitting in Assembly
The Petition of William Little Chief Justice

MAY IT PLEASE Y^r EXCELL^y & THIS HONO^{ble} BOARD

In the Address of the Lower House of Assembly to the Governour's Speech I find myself named in a Manner I think very unjust and injurious to my Character

Among their pretended Grievances they have Charged me in the Office of Chief Justice and the Assistant Justices with Pervertion of Justice, such a Charge I conceive ought not to have been made without giving some Instance of it, but that they have not pretended to do, for Reasons I submit

As the Charge is great, so in Justice ought the proof to be, Instead of that there is none, only some persons Undertook (as I am told) of their Own Knowledge to make it good as thô it was not necessary that something should be made appear to that House before that could justly pass such a grievous Censure, this must be allowed a very fallacious way to build so weighty a Charge upon, had I ever took such a Latitude in judging I might justly have been accused of Oppression and pervertion of Justice

There was an attempt something like this against me at a former Assembly when I was Attorney General (by the same Men too that stirred up this) when an Artifice was used to prevent my then clearing it, In hopes something might stick by the bare Charge, for sometime at least for the next Assembly I was acquitted by the Journals of the House, and made the Falshood of it apparent and yet without taking Notice of that, I am told that this Accusation was the principal thing repeated and urged now against me in the Debate of the House upon the present Charge, and thō this is a Charge against me as Chief Justice

Therefore I beg that this Accusation of the House may not be permitted now to pass over without being enquired into, that it may seen how utterly groundless the Complaint is.

I am sensible this Board as an Upper House will not erect and assume to themselves a Judicial power of trying Causes or Convicting Offenders, nor do I know any Instance of such Tryalls, Once Indeed the House here took upon them to impeach two Great peers of the Land, but that I believe will not be thought a preceedent But if the Board cannot proceed in it as a Court, Yet as Governour and Council they have power to examine into the Conduct and Behaviour of Officers, and to remove, Suspend, condemn or Censure a Chief Justice or any other Officer that truly meritts it, as I hope they will take Occasion to shew

For my part if this Charge against me be thought true I ffreely own I ought to be removed, I therefore beg a Day may be appointed for hearing it, and that I may have timely Notice of the particular Facts, If they have any to charge against Me and that the House may be directed to make good their Complaint which now being only a Charge in General can be only in as General Terms be deny'd, which I do in the most Solemn Manner and with a Confidence usuall to Innocence

To be arraign'd on the Seat of Justice, is what I thought even Envy would not attempt against me, having acted with all good Conscience as my own Heart assures Me, and I am at a loss how such a Charge could possibly be framed against Me I have been recollecting but cannot make my Self Sensible of having committed One material Fault in the Station much less am I conscious of anything in the least that can meritt the Name of perverting Justice, which my Soul abhorrs with the utmost Disdain, and could anything like it be made appear I shall be content to stand condemned for Ever But if they fail in making Good this Charge, as I know assuredly they must, what Recompence, what Reparation can I have.

Bodies of Men have a priviledge, that when refuted, none takes it, nor can they be called to an Account but in all Justice, the more tenderly then should they use their Power without partiality and without prejudging

I am not insensible the Secret Spring these Reports rise from and could easily retort So as might take off all Edge from this Charge but shall waive it, I will shunn everything that may look like bringing a railing Accusation or Recriminating. Since I know my own Innocence I shall the more easily keep Temper and Decency especially to the Worshipfull the House that have now espoused the Cause. But the Gentlemen that have been thus unhappily led to Censure, and condemn me unheard, or without one Proof or Instance of any Corrupt Judgment or Injustice I have done in the Office, must give Me Leave to think I have had exceeding hard Measure, God Send it may never be measured back to the Contrivers of it, I thank God I have not done so by any Man but in everything before Me have at all times Judged impartially, so may God judge me and them at last.

But perhaps the Gent¹ may intend by my perverting Justice only the Crime of taking ffees in Bills at four for One, if that be all that is meant, I shall have very little to say to it, I therefore entreat the House may be more particular in Stating Facts, and those that concern Me in particular, and as they have been pleased thus to single out my Name, that they will please to let me stand Single in my Defence

As to the taking exorbitant Fees so much Complained off in the Address, for my part I most Solemnly aver that I never taxed nor took myself any other than by the Table of Fees the Law hath appointed, nor have I ever insisted that they should be paid in Money, but was always ready to receive them in any of the rated Commodities of the Country as they are rated by Law, of which there are one and twenty Several Species of the produce of the Country, so the Oppression could not be so violent as is pretended, Nay I should say have been content to receive them even in Pitch & Tarr nor should have Ventured to refuse what the Law has provided

When the ffees have been paid in Bills, as people choose to do at four for One as an Equivalent rather than Money I have taken care they should be received at no higher Advance than four for One, thô I am told others design to take six for One, and if four for one be thought too high and I have Committed an Error in it I am not alone (thô I only am personally named) if it be a Crime no doubt the Assembly will Vote it illegal to receive them So, and that will affect all without condemning it in one and not in Another It is well known the ffees are taken so in the precinct Courts as well as in the General Court which the Country in all parts is Sensible off, and which their principals are most agrieved at, thô the House hath not mentioned them, for my part it was not I that began it, the practice was established before my time,

Mr Chief Justice Smith and the other Officers took them so, but if the House intends Me the Honour of setting me at the Head of the Charge, I shall beg leave to decline it.

I intended soon to have quitted the place, nor was I ever fond of the Office of Chief Justice, it was not my Seeking, but it was the pleasure of the Govr and Council, Nay I may say by his Excellency's Command that I took it, and thô they would now endeavour to wound the Governour for it through Me I have the pleasure to think I have done no Dishonour to the Appointment, further Modesty forbids me to say

I have been for some time determined to retire from all Publick Business, that I may (if it shall please God) recover from my long Illness I have undergon I shall not therefore Undertake the Defence of the Cause, but shall choose to leave the Charge to my Successor be it Mr Smith or any other, who no doubt will soon make the people easy in the Matter

I shall therefore conclude with importunately repeating my prayer, that if the House has anything to alledge on any other head than that of four for One, they may assign the particulars and that a day may be appointed for hearing it before this Board This Honoble Board where thô I have often appeared for Favour to others (as my Accusers may know) yet for myself I ask none, only for Justice to my injured Character, and I do not in the least doubt it from this Honorable House, who are not to be led away with Heats and Clamour, Prejudice, Passion or private Pique

To Your Excellr therefore and your Honrs I most humbly but most chearfully Submit myself and my Cause

And shall ever remain in all Duty &c

                              W LITTLE

July 12th 1733.

Ordered That Mr James Castelaw Mr William Downing Mr Isaac Hill Mr Arthur Williams Mr Charles Westbeer Doctr Patrick Maul and Mr John Swann be a Committee to consider the petition of Mr William Little and that they Report to the House their opinion concerning the same

The vote of the House concerning the practices of the Justices and others in Bertie precinct and other places concerning the taking up and binding out Divers Free people contrary to their Will sent to the Upper House for Concurrance

Also the Bill for Enlarging the Jurisdiction of the precinct Courts

Also the Bill to prevent Damages done to the Harbours.

Sent to the Upper House by Mr Leahy &

Mr Handcock

The Vote of the House concerning the Writings belonging to the Registers Office of Beaufort and Hyde precincts sent to the Upper House for Concurrance. Also the Vote for £10 to be paid to the Reverend Mr Boyd

By Mr Wicker &

Mr Cogdal.

The House being Sensible that Mr Mackey the Marshal has received four times more ffees than by Law appointed, It was moved and voted that Mr Mackey do attend and give Account by whose directions he received such ffees, He attended and answered that the ffees he takes on Executions Granted from the General Court, those Executions direct him to take Proclamation Money or an Equivalent in Bills at four for One That the others Fees he takes without Execution, he has taken the same by Mr Halton his Principal's Directions and that he constantly accounted with Mr Halton for one half thereof

The House being made sensible that Edmond Gale Esqr who acted as Deputy Collector and for Naval Officer on his Excellency's Arrival in this Government did put in practice the taking four times the ffees by Law appointed for those Offices Voted the said Mr Edmond Gale be desired to attend this House to declare by whose Advice and Directions he took and received those large ffees.

He attended and was asked the Question, who answered that it was by the Governour's Directions, He applyed to Mr Speaker who he said was by when he was directed, which Mr Speaker confirm'd

Mr Forster Deputy Secretary and Clark to the Council was directed to attend and the like Question being put to him he declared he was so directed by the Governour

Mr Little the Chief Justice was likewise directed to attend, and the like Question being put to him, he acknowledged he had directed the Officers by Executions to receive Proclamation Money or an Equivalent at four for One, the Question was repeated, in in particular whether he had not been advised and directed by the Governour to take such ffees, he gave in the following Answer in writing and declined to answer further.

This House having made a Charge against me, and I have petitioned a Day to be assigned to make Good the Charge, and I conceive this Question affects that Charge and may be leading before the Tryal, and besides I think it must be a great Reflection to think I have done things on the

Seat of Justice by the direction or bidding of any Man I therefore pray the House would not use the Question to me, had they done it before they pass'd their Censure I should have been glad to have been heard

Adjourned to 3 of the Clock afternoon

Met according to adjournment.

M' Church the Powder Receiver of Currratuck being removed out of the Province, his Accounts sworn to before M' Etheridge was produced at the Table

Ordered That they remain among the papers of this House to be further Considered when the other Powder Receivers Accounts are laid before the House

Read the Petition of the Upper Inhabitants of the N° side of Pamptico River praying to be exempt from the pamptico Road and that they be ordered to make a New Road from Tranters Creek toward Morattock

Ordered That the Consideration of the said Petition be referred to the next Assembly and that in the Mean time Notice be given of this petition to the Lower Inhabitants of Pamptico River working on pamptico Road

Sent the following Message to his Exce^{lly} the Govr

MAY IT PLEASE YOUR EXCELLENCY.

This House yesterday desired Your Excellency to let this Assembly know who are the Receivers of the Powder Money, by whom and when appointed, and what Security they have given, We Repeat our request to Your Exce^{lly}, and that the Bonds (if any) be forthwith lodged in the Secretary's Office, We are the more Importunate because if it shall appear that some of the Securities are Insufficient, as We have some Reason to suspect they are, this House in Conjunction with your Excellency and the Council may pass an Order for taking these Powder Receivers into Custody untill Satisfactory Security be given and accounts duly made up.

By Order

MOSELEY VAIL pro C^{lk}

Sent by M' Porter &
Col° Bonner

Received the following Message from the Upper House

M' SPEAKER AND GENT' OF THE GEN' ASSEMBLY

As to the Message touching the Report of the Committe relating to the practice of binding out free Negroes and Molattos 'till they come to 31 Years of Age contrary to the Assent of the parties and to Law

This House are of Opinion that the Justices of the Peace that have so acted may be ordered to attend the Assembly this Session if time will admitt, if not, that then it be recommended to the next Biennial in Order that such an Illegal practice may be exploded   In the Mean time this House are ready to concurr with the General Assembly in earnestly recommending the Matter to the Courts of Law, So that Speedy Justice may be done and that the parties Injured may have Relief.

By Order.
R FORSTER Cth upp^r House.

This House concurrs therewith

Ordered That the Justices of those precincts do take Care that Relief be given the Parties injured, and that the Parties concerned do attend at the next Assembly, and that the Representatives of Bertie and Beaufort Precincts do cause Copies of those Votes to be delivered to the Justices at the next precinct Court that Justice may be done

Received the following Message from his Excell^y the Govr

The time has not been sufficient for Me to do all that you desired in Your Message of Yesterday; the Respective Naval Officers are the Receivers of the Powder Money in all the Ports of this Government, their Securities are in the Secretary's Office, if they are not thought sufficient, or if any likelyhood appears of Loss to the publick, I am willing to use any means for Prevention

The Dates of their Commissions I Know not.

GEO BURRINGTON

The House sent to Mr Forster the Deputy Secretary to desire that those Bonds may be laid before the House for their Inspection

Accordingly he produced Mr Halton's Bond for port Brunswick Mr Wm Little and Mr Robt Forster as Securities Mr Ayliffe Williams Bond for Port Roanoak Mr Geo Martin Security these two Bonds is £500 each Currant Money, Mr James Winright's Bond for port Beaufort, Mr Richd Rustul and Mr William Badham as Securities in £500 Sterling, but for port Bath the Deputy Secretary said he had no Bond

Ordered That Copies of the above mentioned Bonds be taken and lodged among the papers of this House, and the Bonds be returned into the Secretary's Office

Sent the following Message to his Excell^y the Govr

MAY IT PLEASE YOUR EXCELL^y

By the Directions of this House Mr Forster the Deputy Secretary attended with the powder Receivers Bonds and on Examining him We find the Bonds for Port Beaufort hath two Securities in £500 Sterling, the Bonds for Port Brunswick and Port Roanoak are for £500 Currant Money and the last but One Security, but for Port Bath he had no Bond

We think it was a great Omission that the Bonds for Port Roanoak and Port Brunswick were not for Sterling Money as well as Port Beaufort and We think there ought to be two Securities for Port Roanoak, both which Omissions We hope Your Excellency will cause to be rectifyed.

And as there appears no Bond for Port Bath We desire Your Excellency to Send Your Warrant to bring the Powder Receiver for Port Bath before You and that he be committed to Safe Custody untill he give Bond in £500 Sterling with two sufficient Securities for the faithfull Discharge of that Office and to render just and true Accounts thereof according to the Law of this Province

By Order

MOSELEY VAIL D C^{lk}

Received the following Message from the upper House.

Mr SPEAKER AND GENT^l OF THE GEN^l ASSEMBLY.

This House having yours relating to Mr Peyton and the Registry of Beaufort and Hyde under their Consideration are desirous you would lett them have Evidence which has been produced to you of the Fact

By Order.

R. FORSTER C^{lk} up^r House

Received the following Message from his Excell^y the Govr

The Vote of your House passed the 5th of this Month that the Receivers of the Powder Money should lay their Accounts before the Assembly on the Eleventh was irregular and impracticable Irregular because you ought first to have applyed to Me to give those Officers Orders to produce their Accounts to be laid before You for Inspection Impracticable because some of the Receivers live at so great Distances from this Place, that it was not possible for me to give them so much as Notice of your Vote, which came not to my Hand before the 10th Day of this Month

The Answer I returned to your Vote on this Occasion was such as I ought by my Instructions to give, Your House has no Power to call for any Accounts but by Application first made to Your Governour

If the Kings Instructions are contrary to some Laws of this Province, the Governour must act in Obedience to the Kings Commands, therefore you must not be Surprized that whatever Your Law directs contrary to my Instructions is not taken Notice of Me

I am very willing to have the Accounts lay'd before your House and will give Instant Orders that the Powder Receivers be forth coming on any Day you Desire, but when they were appointed I know not, their Commissions will shew the time, the Remainder I answered Yesterday in Return to Your last Message.

GEO BURRINGTON

Ordered. That the Consideration thereof be referred until Tuesday Morning next and that in the meantime His Excellency be desired to let Us have an Inspection or a Copy of his Commission and those Instructions which are supposed to be contrary to the Law of this Province.

Sent the following Message to his Excellency the Govr

MAY IT PLEASE YOUR EXCELLENCY

By your Excellency's last Message to this House in Relation to the Powder Receivers You are pleased to say "If the Kings Instructions "are contrary to some Laws of this Province, the Governour must Act "in Obedience to the Kings Commands, therefore you must not be sur- "prized, that whatever your Law directs contrary to my Instructions "is not taken Notice of by Me

We desire your Excellency will be pleased to lett this House have a sight of your Commission or a Copy thereof, as also of such Instructions as Your Excellency thinks are contrary to our Laws, because this House has Voted to take your last Message before mentioned into their Consideration on Tuesday next

By Order

MOSELEY VAIL D Clk

July ye 14th 1733.

Sent the following Message to the Upper House

When this House sent the Bill relating to precinct Courts with the Clause relating to the Appointment of Justices for the precincts which We find you have left out. That Clause was proposed as the best Expediment to prevent so many Evil Magistrates from being appointed, as We find there hath been these few years past, Many are the Grievances complained of by Oppressive Magistrates in Bertie and Beaufort, divers whereof are persons of very ill Fame and Character an Instance whereof was by this House laid before You with Respect to Mr Benjamin Peyton of Beaufort Precinct when We sent up the Vote concerning the Registry of Writings for that precinct, since that a Discovery has been made to this House that the said Peyton took Recognizance from One William Larner in a £1000 Sterling with Robert Peyton Senr and Edward Travis as Securities each in £500 Sterling for the said Larner's Appearance at the General Court to answer a Charge made against him for Counterfeiting the paper Currancy of this Province and since that in the Absence of the said Larner the said Peyton made no Return of that Recognizance to the General Court, but of One acknowledged by the said Larner without out Sureties, When at the time of his causing that Recognizance to be wrote the said Larner was out of the province

Sent by Mr Burnham &
    Mr Sawyer

Received the following Message from his Excelly the Govr

I will send a Copy of Some Instructions that Laws of this Province are not agreeable to

GEO BURRINGTON

Adjourned 'till Monday Morning

Monday July ye 16th
Met according to Adjournment
A Province Bill of Forty Shillings belonging to Humphry Smith of Craven precinct was produced to this House defaced by falling into a pot of Soup So as not to be legible, of which proof has been made on Oath before a Magistrate.

Voted That the Treasurer of Craven precinct do Exchange the same
Sent to the Upper House for Concurrance
By Mr Burnham &
    Mr Sawyer

Voted That Mr Speaker Collen Pollock Edmond Porter Esqm Colo Henry Bonner and Mr Charles Westbeer be appointed Commissioners to be joined by Members of the Upper House for taking and stating the Accounts of the Powder Receivers and that they or any four of them make Report of and lay the same before the next Assembly

The Bill concerning precinct Courts &c. Read a Second Time and past with Amendments.
Sent to the Upper House by Mr Burnham &
    Mr Sawyer

Received the following Message from the Govr

If the Secretary or his Deputy did not take proper Security from the Receivers of the powder Money according to the Law of this Province made and provided on that Occasion, the Secretary is answerable for the Omission

I am of the same Opinion with your House that the Securities ought to have been alike for every part, why it is otherwise the Secretary must account for, nothing shall be wanting on my part to rectify his Omissions.

How it came to pass that the Receiver of the Powder Money for Port Bath had the Commission delivered to him before he gave the proper Security I know not, but as Several Papers of very great Consequence have been mislaid, lost, or Stolen out of the Secretary's Office, I am at a Loss, what to say further, before the Receiver of port Bath is examined, for my own part I will take the utmost Care the Publick shall not suffer My Warrant as you desire shall be issued to bring the said Receiver forthwith to this Town to be dealt with according to Law

GEO BURRINGTON

This House having received the above Message from his Excellency, It is Ordered that the Secretary have a Copy thereof and that he be desired to give an Answer to so much thereof as concerns him or his Deputy

Adjourned to to Morrow Morning 9 of the Clock.

Tuesday July 17th
Met according to Adjournment.
Sent the following Message to the Govern^r

MAY IT PLEASE YOUR EXCELLENCY,

Mr Ayliffe Williams being Commissioned by Your Excellency to administer the Oaths to the Members of this House, He was sent to Yesterday to Administer the Oaths to One of the Members that is not qualifyed to which he returned Answer that he was Sick and could not attend. The like Message was sent this Day to which he returned the like Answer.

Your Excellency is desired to appoint Some other Person to administer the Oaths, that can attend

By Order
MOSELEY VAIL D C^a

The Bill concerning Harbours &c Sent to the Upper House
By Mr Etheridge &
Mr Mann

Received the following Message from his Excellency the Governour

Mr SPEAKER AND GENT¹ OF THE GEN¹ ASSEMBLY

I wish it was possible for Me to return you thanks for your Answer to the Speech I made at the Opening this Assembly, but as you know it is not due, nor to be expected, I go on to answer Several Matters and positions lay'd down in Your Answer for Facts, or Colourable pretexts why will not pass Acts of Assembly in Obedience to his Majesty's Instructions

You say in your Answer that the Assembly in 1731 went as far as it was possible towards a Compliance with the Royal Instructions concerning Quitt Rents and ffees, thõ it is well known that if the Quitt Rents and ffees were to be paid in the Manner prescribed in the Bill framed for that purpose by that Assembly they would not amount to One third of Proclamation Money

Notwithstanding in the next paragraph you write that upon a due Enquiry You find that the Assembly did endeavour as near as possible to comply with the Royal Instructions, and suppose an Impossibility of paying Rents and ffees in Gold or Silver But this ought to be supposed or mentioned to Me because I well know that Six times Cash is every Year carried out of this Government into Virginia to purchase Negros and British Commodities.

The Rents reserved are in Sixpences and Shillings, what Money they are, and their Value is known even by Boys bred at the Blew-Coat Hospital and in all Equitable Construction ought and must be understood Sterling Money of Great Britain a rated Commodity or a Bill cannot be understood by the Laws of England a Lawfull Tender in Satisfaction for a Debt or Quitt Rent, albeit many knavish and Vile Frauds have been carryed on in Some Colonies in America under Colour of Law to enable the Inhabitants to pay their Just Debts at Home with small Expence .

In opposition to the Hope You have of being able to support your Opinion that his Majesty's Rents are not due in Sterling Money nor Even Proclamation, I offer my Self to maintain and prove that the King's Rents in this Province are due and ought to be paid in Sterling Money of Great Britain But his Majesty having been pleased to offer an Acceptance in proclamation Money upon certain Conditions set down in the 19th Article of my Instructions and the Assembly having disregarded and slighted his Majesty's Favour in that Respect, I am in much doubt whether any Abatement may be obtained for the future and believe the Quitt Rents of this Province will be collected in Sterling Money only

I admire how it came into Your Thoughts to imagine the ffees paid to the Collectors and Naval Officers in this Government are larger than in the Neighbouring Governments when the Contrary is So well known for the largest Vessels that come into this province, the whole amount of the Collectors ffees do not exceed the Value of Sixteen Shillings Sterling the like Vessels pay a Moidore in Virginia. The Assembly in the Year 1722 a time when there was no Governour in the province altered by an Act of Assembly the ffees paid to the Gov' and Naval Officers for Ships Entering and Clearing before that alteration Each Vessel not belonging to the Country paid to the Governour and Naval Officer £1 17 6 Sterling and You all know as well as my Self that less than the Value of twenty Shillings Worth of Goods (I mean Sterling) will now pay those ffees, and for that Reason the Assembly in 1731 would not put the ffees of the Naval Office on the old Establishment, thõ it was proposed to them The Collectors and Naval Officers have a Right to demand and take their ffees in Bills at the Rate Set upon them

What you have wrote in Your Asnwer to my Speech concerning the Grand Deed is confused and will be unintelligable to all people not well versed in the Affairs of this Country, althõ you conceive the Lords of Trade have not a Right Information in that matter, I think you are mistaken, and to convince the Representatives, I shall cause to be read to them, what I wrote to the Board of Trade about the Grand Deed.

As the Assembly in 1731 would not pass One Bill in Obedience to his Majesty's Instructions, I saw no Necessity, or even Occasion to call another before I received Directions from the Lords of Trade to Several Matters of Great Consequence I laid before them in a letter dated the 1st of July 1731 their Lordships Answer came not to my Hands before the 26th of last March, I was in Expectation of receiving the said Answer a Year Sooner and therefore deferred calling an Assembly I know not any Affairs of the Province so urgent to require the meeting of an Assembly Since the Sitting of the last, I have been in every Precinct of this Province and have not heard the Complaint of any Oppression Since I came into North Carolina I must own Abundance of Men made loud Complaints to Me of Grievous Frauds and Cheats put upon them by a former Surveyor General and his Deputies, therefore I Sincerely desired if I knew how, to Cause Restitution to be made to these deluded Sufferers

If I understand the intended Law in 1729 for enabling Vestries to build Churches purchase Gleebs and make provision for the Clergy, the true Meaning of it is, that None of those Good things should be effected

I cannot think Your House in Earnest in pretending this Country Suffers by the ffees now taken, because they are not half the Value of those paid in the Neighbouring Governments

Your Charge against Mr Chief Justice Little and his Assistants for pervertion of Justice, I take to be a Calumny invented by some ill disposed persons, who have conceived a Dislike to him and them for their Great Abilities and faithfull Discharge of their Duties. But if your House has any Accusation to make against those Gentlemen or any other Officer in this Government I will assign You a day for hearing, and promise to do all that can be required of Me, that Justice may be done To this Article I require your immediate Answer.

I cannot pass by what You say in Relation to Mr Smith without observing the Contradiction and partiality of your House Mr Little, is accused, as Chief Justice for pervertion of Justice, for no other Reason, that I can learn, but taking Proclamation Money or an Equivalent for his ffees; and Mr Smith hath the thanks of your House and is recommended for his former Integrity in that Office thō he Sat but one Court, and the principal Business he did was the Establishing those very ffees in that Court, which now causes so heavy a Charge against Mr Little You gentlemen are strangers to Mr Smith and his Character, which I too well know, but as I shall be necessitated to be more particular about him in another place, I shall neither trouble you nor my Self further about him at present.

                              GEO BURRINGTON

Ordered That Mr Smith have a Copy of so much thereof as Relates to him and he is desired to give an Answer thereto.

The following is the paper referred to in the Governour's Reply

The Grand Deed from the Lords proprietors to the County of Albemarle in 1668 Your Lordships Secretary says, can only be Understood as a Temporary Letter of Attorney revocable at pleasure and that in Effect it was revoked in an Order to Mr Eden to grant no Lands under One penny ℔ Acre Quitt Rents I cannot tell whether Your Lordships considered the Copy of the Grand Deed incerted in the Journals of the House of Burgesses, nor what Information has been given you of the supposed Order to Governour Eden, and as it is an Incumbent Duty on Me truely to represent things, I am under a Necessity of stating that Affair in another Light than Your Lordships seem to apprehend it

The Great Deed of Grant from the Lords proprietors to the County of Albemarle, still carefully preserved, was dated May y° 1ˢᵗ 1668 and Entered in the publick Records of the Government, being a Grant of So much Land to any person settling therein, according to the Condition and tenure of the Grant this hath from time to time been always held as firm a Grant as the proprietors own Charter from the Crown, and the people have always claimed it as an undoubted Right, by Virtue of that Grant upon their complying with the Conditions of it. They plead that a Charter or Grant from the proprietors to the people of any part of the Country is as valid as their Grant or Deed to any particular persons would be and no more revokable, and thõ the genèral Deed is general without naming any particular persons, yet every particular person full-filling the Condition Entitles himself then to a part of the Grant, and it becomes a particular Right, and Title to him, and thõ the proprietors Establishment in point of Government might be revocable, Yet Grants of Land cannot be revoked. And that the grand Deed has been always looked upon as a firm and absolute Grant of the Lands in Albemarle County (on Condition) they further Evidence by every patent made out since to each particular person in the County For this Grant by the Grand Deed and peoples complying with it is made the Consideration expressed in each private Grant, the form of the Patents in Albemarle County running thus, His Excell⁷ &c Know Ye that We &c according to our Great Deed bearing date the 1ˢᵗ day of May 1668 do give and Grant —— Acres &c and after the Land is described and bounded it's added, which is due for the Importation of One person for every fifty Acres &c which Importation was made a Right and being proved entitled People to so much Land under the General Grant of the Grand Deed and upon it a Warrant from the Governour issued to the Surveyor General to measure and so much Land where the Claimant laid his Rights (that is where Ever he chose to have it laid out to him) and on the Return of the Survey a Patent was made out for it Still referring to the Grand Deed (as I just now mentioned) So that the patent is but a Confirmation of their previous Conditional Right by the Grand Deed, and a Concession of it, and the people further plead that the Grand Deed is confirmed by a Law of the Country, still unrepealed among the Body of their laws that establishes the forms of particular Grants or Patents under the Grand Deed and what Rent is to be reserved in it. So that by the charter from the Crown to the Pro-prietors and their Heirs and Assigns and by the Grant from the Proprie-tors to the County of Albemarle by their Grand Deed on Such Conditions and Rents Viz⁴ the same as in Virginia (which is two Shillings for every hundred Acres) and this Confirm'd and established by a Law Still in Force, which provides that Patents should issue under the Grand Deed to Albemarle County, upon those Conditions and on that Rent reserved, the People still claim it as their undoubted Right in Albemarle County to take up Land on those Conditions and on that Rent. Upon the whole they conclude that altho the Grand Deed from the Proprietors to Albemarle County was a Grant or Condition to be fulfilled, yet is an absolute Grant and what was never in the Lords Proprietors Power to revoke, if they had been desirous so to do, but they never did attempt to revoke the said Grand Deed And as to the supposed Order to Governour Eden mentioned by your Lordships Secretary, I am persuaded that Your Lordships have been misinformed in that particular for I can find no such Order, nor can I learn that Ever such Order came here, but am in the most positive Manner assured there was not, nor was there Ever any Grants made at the Rent of One penny p' Acre nor any patents ever issued at an higher Rent than two Shillings ℔ Hundred Acres, which is the same as the Quitt Rents of Virginia which being made in Tobacco or Money at the Choice of the Tenants, the People here claim a Right of paying in the Same Manner, but this Affair is not Yet come in Debate because the King's Receiver has not been in this Government, nor any Quitt Rents collected Since my Arrival.

The Bill relating to precinct Courts came from the Upper House. Past with Amendments.

Received the following Message from the Governour

If M' William's Illness continues, another fit Person shall be appointed to Qualify Your Member

GEO BURRINGTON

M' Secretary by his Deputy M' Forster delivered in the following Answer to the Request of the House

M' SPEAKER AND GENT' OF THE GEN' ASSEMBLY

In answer to Your Message of yesterday touching the Powder Money with his Excellency's Answer to your Message to him upon that subject I take leave to inform you that (the Gov' now Keeping the Seal) Commissions do not pass thro' my Office as formerly, when the Seal was in the Secretary's Custody, and particularly the Commissions to the powder Receivers were not expedited by Me or my Deputy, who denies to have either Countersign'd or deliver'd them out to the parties appointed by his Excellency to that Office, or to have had any other concern therein, then writing out by his Excellency's Command the Form of such Commissions

I do not find that the Law relating thereto directs Me to take Security on that occasion, thô, if it did, it must necessarily be Understood, that it were to be done upon Signification from the Governour of such Commission issuing, but having received no Notice or Direction from his Excellency in Relation thereto I apprehend I am in no wise Answerable for the Omission

His Excellency by Implication Taxes Me with want of Care in the Execution of my Office, for that Several Papers of Consequence have been lost, mislaid or stolen out of the Office, which I humbly conceive to be beside the Question, and not at all to the purpose, since his Excellency does not pretend to have lodg'd a Bond for Port Bath with Me, which therefore could not be lost or mislaid by Me, but as it is easy for Me to prove the Charge groundless and without foundation, No Material Papers having been lost out of the Office since I have been Secretary of the province, Notwithstanding the ill provision there is for the safe and well keeping thereof, So it is easy to discern with what View it was made and incerted (not very pertinently as I have shewn) in his Excellency's Answer

NATH. RICE.

Mr William Downing reported from the Committe that they had considered Mr Little's Petition and come to a Resolution thereon which Resolution was read in these Words.

Resolved. That it appears to the Committe that the said William Little hath treated the Lower House of Assembly not only with Ill Manners, but with Insolence and contempt in that Scandalous and invidious Libel which he calls a Petition in which he accuses the House of acting in a very unjust and injurious Manner, and affirms that, had he done as the House has done, he might have justly been accused of Oppression and pervertion of Justice, He insinuates as if there were a Secret Conspiracy in the House against Him

Such Scandalous Expressions reflecting on the Dignity of this House highly deserves it's censure

This House might now (as Mr Little Seems to request) proceed to a Charge in Relation to his many and great Crimes, but that we conceive that he has greater Trust on the Support of those who had commissioned him, than on his Own Innocence, for We cannot but observe that he seems to triumph on the Expectation of being acquitted by the Council, One of which he is nearly related to and another one of his Assistants mentioned to be guilty with him of pervertion of Justice

Therefore We conceive this House will take a proper time (of which themselves are best Judges) to form their Charge and make it good against the said William Little for Pervertion of Justice, Oppression and Extortion notwithstanding all that the said William Little hath said in his Libel

Which Resolution was read and unanimously approved

Ordered That the Sargeant attending this House do immediately take Mʳ William Little into his Custody and him safely keep untill to morrow Morning and that he then bring him before the House to Answer for his Affronting the House by sundery Reflections exprest in his petition now before the House

By Order of the Genˡ Assembly

July yᵉ 17ᵗʰ 1733.

This House having pass'd a Vote the 5ᵗʰ of this Month that the several Powder Receivers should lay their Accounts before this Assembly by the 11ᵗʰ of this Month of which Mʳ Ayliffe Williams Clerk of this House, who Acts as powder Receiver for Port Roanoak had sufficient Notice, the same Vote being entered by him in the Journal of this House and the said Mʳ Ayliffe Williams having hitherto failed to lay his Accounts before this House, and the House being informed that he is departing this province

Ordered That the Sargeant attending this House do immediately take the said Mʳ Ayliffe Williams into his Custody and him safely keep untill he shall be discharged by this House.

Mʳ William Barrow Member for Hyde precinct took the Oaths and subscribed the Declaration by Law appointed for his Qualification

Adjourned till to Morrow Morning 9 of the Clock

Wednesday July yᵉ 18ᵗʰ

Met according to Adjournment

Ordered That Collen Pollock Edmond Porter Esqᵐ Capᵗ William Downing Mʳ Arthur Williams Mʳ Isaac Hill and Mʳ John Leahy be a Committe to consider the Reply made by the Governour to the Answer this House made to his Speech and make an Answer thereto and Report the Same to the House

Adjourned 'till the Afternoon

Met according to Adjournment

M' Smith delivered in his Answer in the following words which was read

MR. SPEAKER AND GENT' OF THE ASSEMBLY.

I have the Favour of a Message from You containing a paragraph of a Paper sent to you by his Excellency the Governour in which he bears so hard on my Conduct that You very justly concluded, I ought to vindicate my Self of those Imputations; I thought I had so fully answered all his Excellency's Charges against Me that I expected no further Trouble from him on that Head, but finding that he still goes on to vilifie Me purely to create Jealousies between your House and the Officers in General and my Self in particular, I should be very much wanting to my Character did I not clear my Self from those Malitious Groundless Insinuations. The Governour Seems to insinuate that you gave me the Thanks of your House for the same thing that you censured M' Little when it plainly appears by your Journal that you passed that Vote in my Favour purely for the Services I did you in Representing to His Majesty the many Grievances and Oppressions you laboured under from his Excellency's Administration, Whereas Your Charge against M' Little is for Notorious pervertion of Justice, things entirely different in my Opinion, but I have had so many Instances of his Excellency's Regard to Truth that I am not at all surprized at it, he is further pleased to observe that I established those ffees you now complain off, which is so far from Truth, that M' Speaker and Several Others can attest that most of the Officers had Orders from the Governour to take Proclamation Money or four for One Some Weeks before the General Court he mentions in his paper, and for Once I appeal to his Excellency himself if he did not insist upon the Officers paying one hundred and fifty Guineas to two Gentlemen at Home for Procuring that Instruction, which Orders ffees to be paid in Proclamation Money, declaring that he had given his Bond for it, which as I was Satisfyed to the Contrary from the known Honour and worth of those Gentlemen, So when I mentioned it to them in London, they declared it was utterly false· I think his Excellency has forgot himself, when he says I established those ffees at that Court in which I presided as Chief Justice, for I am sure no Order of that Sort was made as will appear by the Records, unless foisted in; His Excellency goes on to inform you, that he knows Me and my Character too well, as to my Character it is well known amongst Gentlemen of worth and Honour, and indeed I was in Hopes, that his Excellency would Scarcely have contradicted himself so flatly, since it is notorious to the principal Members of your House and also of the province, that not only at my first Arrival but even to the time I refused to comply with his Arbitrary and Illegal Measures, he gave Me a Character both for Integrity and Ability far beyond what I either desired or expected His Excellency seems to hint, that he must take notice of Me in another place what place he means I know not, but I have so fully exposed his practices in every Place that his Menaces now are both Vain & empty, but when I consider what a Low State he hath brought himself to in the Opinion of all Men by his Strange and unaccountable Actions, my good Nature so far gets the Better of Me as to move my pity more than my Resentment

As You have a great Deal of Business upon Your Hands I must ask Pardon for taking up so much of Your time, but the Falsity and the Ungenerous View with which that Paper was contrived made it somewhat Necessary for Me to answer it fully, to conclude tho his Excellency upon all Occasions expresses his Contempt of the Assembly I shall always esteem it a particular Favour to have the approbation of the Representatives of the people of this province

Wm SMITH

The Committe made Report in these Words following which was read and unanimously approved Viz.

The Committe are of opinion that nothing his Excellency has yet said is sufficient to alter the Opinion of the House concerning the Money the Quitt Rents are to be paid in, as the People of England well know what is meant there by shillings and pence, so it is as well known in this and other provinces that by shillings and pence is meant the Currancy of those provinces and not Sterling or proclamation Money unless such are expressly mentioned

The Committe are of Opinion that the Bulk of Trade of this Province is carried on by Vessels under 50 Ton, and the Instance his Excellency gave of the ffees in that province was not well chosen because by their printed Laws now before the Committe, it appears that the Naval Officers ffees for such Vessels is but 10 Shi^{ll} and the Collectors 7^s 6^d and in the province of New England, where most of our Commodities are carried they are much less than in Virginia, nor can the Committe learn that the ffees are near so large in any province as are taken in this What his Excellency says of 20 shi^{ll} in Goods at first in London being sufficient to pay the Officers ffees, is what we can't admitt to be true, but were it So, we think it is not to the purpose in the present dispute, For the Complaint of the House is, that four times more is taken than is by Law appointed, and we find this practice early introduced by the Governour (Viz') within a Day or two after his arrival as appears by the Declaration made by the Officer to the House

The Committe are so far from agreeing with his Excellency when he asserts that the ffees offered to be paid by the Assembly in April 1731 would not amount to One third Proclamation Money, that it will be evident by the propositions of that Assembly to make the ffees on the like Establishment as they were before paper Money was Currant, that the same was in effect equal to Proclamation Money, for so the Council declared the ffees were before paper Money was made, The Committe think it very strange that after his Excellency has declared that what the House said in their Answer to his Speech of M' Little Chief Justice and his Assistants pervertion of Justice, he takes to be a Calumny invented by some Ill disposed persons, he goes on to tell the House he will appoint a Day for hearing, and required an immediate Answer to that part.

The Committe can't be of opinion that it is proper for them, after so much said by the Governour in excuse for M' Little to proceed to a hearing before him and the Council now present being but five Members, One of those he is nearly related to, another one of his Assistants equally charged with M' Little, and a third a Party Complaining

His Excellency Seems to be much concerned at what the House said concerning M' Chief Justice Smith, the Committe do not conceive that M' Smith had the thanks of the House for what M' Little is accused, We think his Excellency has misrepresented that Matter, what the House had principally in View on that Occasion was the difference between Integrity in the One and pervertion of Justice &c. in the other Officers of the General Court. As to the Oppressive Article the Fees, We think it very apparent, that it was not M' Smith that Establish'd them because his Excellency directed the taking such large Fees from the Vessels at least a Month before the General Court Sate. We are informed that when M' Smith discerned how the Laws of the province ran concerning Fees, he directed the Clerk to take no other Difference, than such as had been proposed by the Assembly

Whether M' Smith is so well known to the House as to his Excellency We conceive is not material, for when the Country was found to labour under Such Oppression and pervertion of Justice, When the Governour of a province would be the Arbiter of his own Differences, and take the Goods he pretended a Right to out of the possession of another, and burn the House another built towards gaining possession of Land he wanted, when attempts were made to recover by due course of Law Satisfaction for such Goods took away by the Governour, for the Chief Justice and his Assistants in such a Case to pervert Justice by giving Judgment that the party injured by a Governour had no Relief here, And when Measures were taken by the same Justices at the Governour's Instigation to prevent the Injured Party from seeking Relief Elsewhere by Imprisonment Excessive Bail and refusing to read his Petition wherein the Hardships of his Case was shewn When Persons upon the least Displeasure were called 200 Miles to answer to Trifles, when ffees were unaccountably multiplied in all Cases. When people were turned out of their possessions by those who had no Right to take up Lands by the Royal Instructions, when none were admitted to take Lands on the Royal Instructions thô they were ready to comply therewith unless they would pay the Governour 2s 6d Silver Money for every 50 Acres, thô such demand was no ways warranted by the Laws of this province or the Royal Instructions, when free people were taken up by the Magistrates and placed in a state of Servitude little inferior to Bondage against their Wills

In short when all the Laws of the province were in a Manner Disregarded, all the Courts of Justice in a Manner Stopt, when Injustice, Oppression and Arbitrary power had almost over run the whole province, It was surely high time (in the opinion of the Committe) to rejoice at any alteration that was likely to be made in the Courts of Justice or elsewhere

The Committe have reason still to be of opinion that the Right Honble the Lords Commissioners of Trade had not a Right Information of the affair of the Lands In Albemarle County and the Deed of Grant, when they understood it in the nature of a temporary letter of Attorney revokable &c and the Method his Excellency has taken to shew us, that the House was mistaken in that Opinion, rather confirms Us, because by that paper laid before the House with his Reply, it is apparent his Excellency thought as the House did, for that Paper wrote to the Board of Trade, since the Receit of that Instruction does not only say That he is persuaded their Lordships have been misinformed But much pains is bestowed therein to shew, that his Excellency is much of the same Opinion with the House concerning the Deed of Grant.

The Committe is much surprized at what his Excellency says that he well knows that Six times more Cash is every year carried out of this Government to Virginia to purchase Negros and British Goods than is necessary to pay the Rents and ffees.

If this be true there must yearly go out of Virginia at least £9 000 if the ffees should be left out of the Computation. For the Rents alone We think will not be short of £1 500 ℔ Annum if duly collected, for the Grants issued before the Kings purchase and for Lands his Excellency has granted Warrants for by taking the ffees into Computation, as they are now so extravagantly taken, the sum would be prodigiously Swolᵃ The Committe have made diligent Enquiry, and We can scarce find any other way that Cash is brought into the province but from Virginia, and that by the Borderers, who sometimes receive it for provision carried thither, the sum brought into the province or carried out We conceive to be very small, and not sufficient to pay half the Rents, of the province, and is not to be come at, by those who live at any Considerable Distance from the Line, for those who take such pains to carry Provisions to Virginia at the Charge of a great Land Carriage, do it Chiefly to lodge Money there to purchase Slaves, which are difficult to be bought any other way The Trade being so much injured as We conceive by the Heavy Burthens on the Traders who come by Water and by the Bad Navigation. This Report of your Committe is humbly submitted to the House by

    COLLEN POLLOCK   E. PORTER   W DOWNING
    ARTHʳ WILLIAMS   ISAAC HILL   JNO LEAHY
July yᵉ 18th 1733.

In regard the Clerk has not attended the House by Illness and otherwise, It is the Direction of this House that the Speaker keep the papers to form the Journal by and that they be then delivered to the Clerk if he is able to receive them and is in the province

Mʳ SPEAKER AND GNᵗ OF THE HOUSE OF BURGESSES

I require Your immediate Attendance in the Council Chamber.
                  GEO BURRINGTON

The House accordingly attended his Excellency in the Council Chamber where the Governour made the following Speech

GENᵗ OF BOTH HOUSES

I opened this Assembly with a very Kind Speech and sincerely recommended to You Unanimity and to proceed without Heat or Passion, I proposed several things to You for the Good of the Country, which I always endeavoured to promote, but there having been so much time frivolously spent, or wore, I find it to little purpose to keep you longer together

Mr SPEAKER & GENT' OF THE LOWER HOUSE.

You from the Beginning have discovered such a Spirit that I early doubted whether any good might be expected from You, but have waited patiently to see what might be effected but finding any good Intentions to no purpose, I only tell you I am heartily sorry to see heat and Party prevail so much among You. I assure you that is not the way to serve Your Country thô you have an opportunity thereby to serve Your Selves and display Picques and prejudices

You have artfully and falsely endeavoured to represent the Government under Me as grievous and Oppressive thô every Man in the province Knows the Contrary, unless you will call his Majesty's Instructions Grievous, which my Steady adhering to has been the Occasion of Raising all this Faction.

As to my Disuse of Assemblies as you malitiously term it there past not two Years between the last Assembly and the chusing this, thô I think the frequency of their Meeting, unless they would proceed with more temper and Justice, is of no other Use than to promote party and Faction and to give some People an opportunity to pursue their own Malice and Envy under the Umbrage of an Assembly Bodies of Men cannot blush and that's your advantage One of the most furious among you (I am told) declared he should not have attended this Assembly but purely to oppose the Governour, and that he came on purpose to plague him I wish there had been no more Incendiaries amongst You and that all the others had their Country's Good more in their Thoughts. I condemn not all, for I believe there are some well meaning Honest Men amongst You, but even those bore down or carried away by the false Zeal and Clamour of the Rest; and Instance of which sufficiently appeared in the Management of your Answer to my Speech, it was drawn by the most inveterate Members, and no Sooner brought into the House, but push'd on with a Noise and Violence that Stifled all Opposition and that was called Nemine Contradicente

If Assemblies in this province proceed in the Manner You have done with Heat and partiality, they themselves will grow the greatest Grievance and Oppression to the Country, Burgessing has been for some Years a source of Lies and Occasion of Disturbances, which has deterred good Men from being Candidates, or entring the Lists of Noise and Faction, which every common Observer Knows Neither doth the Kings Instruction that only ffree-holders should Vote find any Weight in Your Elections, thô always incerted in the Writs.

As to the Affair of the Chief Justice, I have already acquainted You, I would appoint a Day for hearing, and making good the Charge, But as you seem to waive it, I appoint the 30ᵗʰ Day of this Month for the said hearing at the Council Chamber, where You or any other people may attend to make good the Charge. His petition laid many Days before you, without any notice taken thereof, but yesterday on a Sudden Heat without regarding Me or his Station You insolently presumed by your Sargeant to take him into Custody for a pretended Contempt found in the Petition by him delivered to the Upper House, Thō all unbiassed Men do allow it was wrote with as much Decency and Temper as the Charge would admitt off

You have also presumed to take into Custody the Receiver of the Powder Money for port Roanoak, thō under very sufficient Security, who had my Orders agreeable to his Majesty's Instructions not to make up any publick Accounts but before Me in Council

You have denyed to confirm to his Majesty's Instructions concerning the payment of the Quitt Rents, thō by Calling you again together, I gave You another Opportunity of accepting his Majesty's most Gracious Favour in allowing them to be paid in proclamation Money instead of Sterling, Nay you have denied they are due or ought to be paid in any Money at all, but of your own making.

You have offered but three Bills all this time, One of which is so inconsiderable as not to be worth mentioning, One other for enlarging the power of precinct Courts, which I commended to You, you took care to clog with such clauses, as you must know I could not possibly assent to

I also proposed to You for Encouragement of the British Trade to relieve their Ships from paying the Duty of Powder Money and you have brought in a Bill which has passed both Houses for taking the said Duty wholly of all Vessels

I am informed you have refused to admitt Several Members of your House legally chosen and returned by the proper Officers, pursuant to the Ancient and constant practice of the province, and as you are but part of an House, my allowing your Proceedings or Orders would be giving up an undoubted Right of his Majesty, which has never been contested before this Time.

For the aforesaid Reasons I dissolve this Assembly and it is hereby accordingly dissolved.

July yᵉ 18ᵗʰ 1733   GEO BURRINGTON
Nᵒ Carolina.

    True Copy Examined
By me   WILLIAMS Clk Genˡ Assembly

NORTH CAROLINA—ss.

Att a General Biennial Assembly begun att Edenton for the said Province the 5th day of November 1733.

MEMBERS RETURNED

Chowan	Perquimons	Pasquotank.
Col Edwd Moseley	Mr Chas Denman	Mr Gabril Burnham
Colo Henry Bonner	Mr Richd Skinner	Mr Jere Symons
Collen Pollock Esqr	Mr Saml Swann	Mr Chas Sawyer
Capt. Wm Downing	Capt Rd Sanderson	Mr Jno Sawyer
Edmd Porter Esqr	Mr Zebula Clayton	Mr Caleb Sawyer

Bertie	Edgecombe	Beaufort
Mr Jams Castellaw	Capt Wm Whitehead	Mr Patrick Maull
Mr Ar Williams	Dr Davy Hopper	Mr Robt Turner
Mr George Winn		
Mr Isaac Hill		
Mr John Harrold		

Hide	Bath Town	Edenton
Mr Thos Smith	Mr John Leahy	Mr Cha Westbeere
Mr Wm Barrow		

Accordingly there mett Col Edwd Moseley, Col Henry Bonner Mr Chas Westbeere, Mr Arthur Williams, Mr George Winn, Mr Gabrill Burnham, Mr Jeremiah Simons, Mr Chas Sawyer Mr Caleb Sawyer, Mr Samuell Swann, Mr Charles Denman, Mr Richard Skinner, Members of Assembly who took the Oaths and subscribed the Declaration by Law appointed for their qualification Which oaths &c were administered by Mr Ayliffe Williams appointed so to do by a Dedimus from his Excellency the Governor

Ajourned to 9 of the clock to morrow morning

Tuesday Novr 6th
Met according to Adjournment
Present as before
There appeared Doctor Patrick Maull Member for Beaufort and Captain William Downing Member for Chowan, who took the oaths and

subscribed the Declaration by Law appointed for their qualification, and took their seats in the House accordingly.

Present Dr Patrick Maull & Capt Wm Downing

Adjourned to 9 of the Clock to morrow morning

Wednesday Novr 7th

Met according to Adjournment.

Present as before

There appeared Mr John Harrold Member for Bertie, Mr Zebulan Clayton and Capt Richd Sanderson Members for Perquimons, who took the oaths and subscribed the Declaration by Law appointed for their qualification

Present Mr John Harrold, Capt. Richard Sanderson and Mr Zebulan Clayton

Adjourned to 9 of the Clock to morrow morning.

Thursday Novr 8th

Mett according to Adjournment

Present as before

Mr Thomas Lowther Member for Curratuck appeared who took the Oaths and subscribed the Declaration by Law appointed for his qualification   Present Mr Thomas Lowther

The Clerk received the following letter from his Excellency the Governour which he read in these words vizt

November 8th 1733.

Sir,

I have given myself the trouble to write a Paper for the use of the present Burgesses, which I will send to be read in their House, or cause to be read to them in the Council Chamber forthwith, as they like best.

Notifie the above & send me an imediate Answer.

I am your humble servant

GEO BURRINGTON

To Mr Williams

    Clk of the Assembly

To which the Burgesses made Answer they were ready to wait on his Excellency And immediately went to the Council Chamber Where the Governour made the following Speech (vizt)

Gentlemen

I am sorry you are deprived of the oportunity of serveing your King and Country at this time for want of a sufficient Number of the Council to make an Upper House

Some weeks after the dissolution of the late Assembly, I was shewn by the Clerk of the said Assembly, a Report from a Committee signed by six Members, and approved by that House, tho' I am informed but few Members were then present, and so great noise in the House while the Paper was reading, that it was impossible for the Members, not in the Secret to understand or comprehend the same, this Report containing several matters layd down or suggested which I look upon as very injurious to me and my character, as well as extreamly false, and scandalous in themselves, I think myself obliged in vindication of my reputation to make some answer to them

The first Article concerning what money the King's Quit Rents ought to be paid in, will certainly be fixed by the Lords of Trade and Plantations and His Majesty's most hono^ble Privy Council in England Because there is not any appearance that an Assembly here will act conformable to His Majesty's Instructions on that Head

The Committee were much mistaken in giving it as their opinion that the Bulk of the Trade of this Province is carried on by Vessels under Fivety Tons Burthen, the contrary plainly appears by the respective accounts of the several Collectors, and naval Officers; Whatever the Committee might read in old printed Laws of Virginia, the smallest Vessell that enters and clears in that Government pays 20^s sterling Governour's dues, a Pistole to the Collector besides Permits, which generally come to 7^s 6^d and the Naval officers Fees are the same, or very near, Ships above a hundred Tons, Pay a Movdore to the Collector, about the same to the Naval Officer, and 30^s sterling to the Governour. And all disinterested Persons do allow that the Port charges are much higher in Virginia, then in this Province, difference of money considered, Further Mr Gale Collector at Roanoake assured me, he has offered forty masters of Vessells belonging to the New England Governments to pay all their Port charges in his District, for a Bill payable there, of so much mony as Vessels belonging to this Government pay in that Country, and that no one of those Masters would ever imbrace his proposal That the Committee will not admit a well known truth that 20^s worth of Goods bought in England, being sufficient, to pay all the Fees due to the Collectors, and Naval Officers in this Province, for entring and clearing a ship, I cannot help but I am able to produce several accounts and receipts of things I have purchased, for which I have pay'd in the Province Bills more than 20^s for what cost but one in England The Committee say the Complaint of the House is, that four times more is taken then by Law appointed this I deny, for the Officers take the Bills as all other Men do, and as they were rated when issued; Moseley Vail nephew to the late Speaker, being now Clerk of Chowan Precinct Court, takes the Fees belonging to his Office at four for one, which surely Mr Mosely would not suffer, if it were unlawfull, or oppressive to the Country, What is wrote in the last part of this Paragraph of a Declaration made by an Officer of my introduceing the practice &c of taking four for one, the Officer (viz't Mr Edmund Gale) denys, and the said Declaration fathered upon him, was the Ofspring of a Member of that House noted for leaseing The time mentioned a day or two after my Arrival, being then and long after extreamly busied, was too short a time for me to be apprized of the nature and Value of the Bills then newly emitted For my own part I received no Fees in many weeks after my comeing into the Country

I acknowlege that the rated Commodities before the year 1715, were then equal to Proclamation money, tho' somewhat sunk in Value since, but the adding rice to the former rated Commoditys at 11ˢ ⅌ hundred, as intended by the Assembly in 1731, before any Act passed to make the same merchantable, and the Officers to pay 10 ⅌ Cent for collecting, what they could not in all likelyhood sell, would be their ruin, for in the draft of the Act, nothing is said in what condition the rice is to be delivered for Fees, and People for anything I can see therein might have paid it in the Hulls (if the Bill had passed) in which condition it had not been of more Value then Oats, Therefore I still say that Assemblys intended settlement of Fees would not have amounted to above one third of Proclamation Money

I have many strong reasons still to believe that taxing Mr Little the Chief Justice and his Assistants with Perversion of Justice was a Calumny invented by wicked men, on the contrary have heard Mr Little much applauded by great numbers, for his impartial behaviour in the Office he executes, and much praised, and admired for his excellent knowledge in the Law; And as to his Assistants it is agreed by all unprejudiced men, they are the best that ever sate in this Province with any Chief Justice, and I affirm I have not heard of any Complaint made against Mr Little or the Assistants, but by the late Assembly, and Mr Ashe, I can say more, not the least reflection on any of their Proceedings. Weak and fallacious are the reasons the Committee give why they did not think proper to proceed to charge Mr Little before me in Council, because the Allegations they had to produce against him must have been entered on the Council Journals, and if myself and the Council had not acted becoming our duty it would have been matter of just complaint, nav the very Journals would have exposed us, it does not appear by the Journals of the late Assembly that any Person in the Council did complain to the Lower House against M' Little or any one of his Assistants, it must be judged a very extraordinary matter for a Member of the Upper House to slight those with whome he sate, and lay his Complaints before the Lower House

I do not think it necessary to make the Burgesses of this Country the Judges of my differences with M' Smith, they will be heard in another place, certainly it must be thought impertinent in the Assembly to mention the said Smith in the Answer to my speech in the manner they did, The Articles against me he signed and delivered to the King doubtless will be inquired into, and Smith's villanys in due time set forth and detected, in the mean while I declare to all men on my own knowledge, that Smith is a stupid inconsiderate blockhead, a perfidious creature, a Promise breaker, a horrible lyar, a most ungrateful wretch that has not one good quality in him, and what the Committee say in respect to his taking Fees the contrary has been proved in the Depositions taken in support of my Answer to the Articles of Complaint he delivered against me, and are entered in the Council Journals May 17ᵗʰ 1732 The value Smith's pretended friends in this Country have for him is sufficiently manifested in the respect they shew him at this time, when for want of better accommodation he is forced to live in an Ale House, and eat and drink upon Tick like a poor sailor out of imployment When the men who have so grosly imposed upon this fellow have no further occasion for him, they will laugh at and slight him, and then he may find time to ruminate on, and repent his past wicked conduct and vile Deportment

The next Article is very unaccountable and such stuff as I never read before, but when examined and answered will be found to reflect on the Composers themselves, and not on me, Who is it that finds the Country labours under oppression and Perversion of Justice, No Man in the Country has made known any such thing to me, till the sitting of the last Assembly, It is not said in this part of the Report, such and such things were done by a Governour of a Province, nor the Province nor Governour named, but craftily ushered in with When the Governour of a Province would be Arbiter of his own differences &c The Goods next mentioned by what follows are a Mare of mine and a Colt foaled on my Grounds, that a man who worked upon my Plantation att Cape Fear, sold to Capt Hugh Blaning for fivety Pounds in Bills (£5. sterling) but the said Captain being assured by several People that the

Mare and Colt belong'd to me, he did not drive them to his Plantation but left them at Mr Harnetts, In August 1732. I vas att Cape Fear and being informed by Captain Blaning and others of the sale aforesaid after some discourse, he (Blaning) was fully satisfied, and convinced the said Mare and Colt were my Property, and delivered them to my People, altho' Mr Ashe did much persuade him to the contrary, As appears by an attested writing of the said Blaning's. At the time when this happened, I was within a few miles of the Place, where Mr Ashe lived, but Mr Ashe did not lett me know then, that he had any claim to this same Mare and Colt neither did he make the least mention of his pretentions before the October Court following, then he was pleas'd to tell me in the Council Chamber (most of the Members then present) that my Servants had mark'd two Mares belonging to him, which surprized me because our Lands were far distant, after some questions he told me he claimed the Mares my workman had sold Blaning, he had bought them he said of the said Workman, to which I answered if he pretended a right to those Mares, I would try the cause with him next Court, and give security so to do, and employ'd a Lawyer (vizt Mr Osheale). The next day Mr Ashe had the impudence to produce to the Court an information against me as a Criminal, for taking up and misbranding the Mare & Colt, which I was informed the Court said they had no Power to take Cognizance off, as brought in that manner, but my Lawyer at the same time acquainted the Court, and Mr Ashe then present, that he was impowered by me, and would try the cause in any manner Mr Ashe pleased, as to the right of the Mares, but Mr Ashe declared he did not intend to proceed in that manner, but to sue for a Tort, as he expressed himself, and gave it under his hand But Mr Ashe's information that he delivered to the Court, being very vile and scandalous, my Lawyer brought it to me, and I complained to one of the Assistants of the abuse, who thereon issued a warrant to take up Mr Ashe, who refuseing to give Bail, was committed, but about an hour after his committm^t he was brought before the Chief Justice by an Habeas Corpus, and admitted to Bail, and the sum mentioned in the Recognizance very small, considering the greatness of his Offence, these goods as they are called, were never in Mr Ashe his possession, therefore the writers of the Report are guilty of a falsehood, in setting down that they were.

And now for the House that was burnt

When I was formerly in this Country, I purchased ten thousand acres of Land on the N. E. branch of Cape Fear River, in two parcels of five thousand acres each, and paid near 20 years quit rents for the same, and

78

did leave my Receipts and Warrants in the hand of Mʳ Edward Moseley, Sir Richard Everard then Governour of this Province did sign one
Patent for five thousand acres dated the 30ᵗʰ July 1725, but could not
be prevailed upon to sign the other, before he certainly knew I was appointed Governour of this Country by the King, so that the second Patent bears date the 6ᵗʰ of April 1730, Mʳ John Porter Junʳ was the
Deputy Surveyor who survey'd the said Lands for me, there was with
him when he made the survey Mʳ William Flavel another Deputy Survevor, and one Mʳ John Worth, who survey'd the said Lands as directed,
but some years after this, Contrivances were set on foot, to take away
from me the best part of the first five thousand acres, & accordingly
Mʳ John Porter Junʳ did obtain a Patent in the name of Roger More
Esqʳ for himself from Sir Richard Everard for one thousand acres of
the said land, being all within my Bounds, and the marks fixed by him
and Mʳ Flavell the other Surveyor, Mʳ Samuell Swann, one other Patent
within my Bounds also of six hundred, of which Mʳ Moseley has a part ;
These two men Mʳ Moseley's nephews, & Mʳ Roger Moore himself a
Patent for 640 Acres within my Bounds, but this last Gentleman was
so fully convinced of my right to that land that he delivered up his
Patent to me, But to return to the House that was burnt on my Land,
Being at Cape Fear in 1731 it was the common discourse among the
People that lived in those parts how basely these men endeavoured to
defraud me of my Land, and that Mʳ John Porter and Mʳ Samuell
Swann, were endeavouring to sell those lands belonging to me, they had
repatented, but no man would buy them (because it was very well known
no one had any real title to them but myself) tho' those Lands are very
good, and commodiously situated, during the time I remained at Cape
Fear word was sent me that Mʳ John Porter would raise a logg house as
an affront to me upon my Land, upon which I gave him notice that if he
did, I should cause it to be fired, sometime after, I was at that place, and
finding a logg House of five unbarked green pine loggs in height, without either Chimney, plaistring or other labour used in building Houses,
I ordered my Negros to fire the covering of this House or Hog sty, the
loggs being quite green, would not burn, it is a very common Practice
for the People in this Province to burn their Houses, as being a cheaper
way then pulling them down, But what struck most upon me in
the Affair of this Logg House, was the fate of a former Governour
who was also one of the Lords Proprietors at the same time,
I mean Seth Southwell Esqʳ who being surprized on his own
Plantation and clap't into a Logg House, by the late Mʳ Pollock

& others and there kept Prisoner until he renounced the Government and took and subscribed a strange oath too long to be here incerted It is not unlikely but some People in this Country might have the same intentions to me, if I would have suffered the Logg House to have remained covered, I have been told by many that M' Moseley contrived the method to defraud me of the Lands above mentioned, and that his Nephew John Porter has often times declared he gave his Uncle Moseley a very good Negro for his management in that affair, what M' Moseley had of his other Nephew M' Samuell Swann I have not yet heard, but so far have I been from any unwillingness to try this affair in a legal way, that I began the suit myself, to this I add that I have often declared, in the most publick manner that I scorned to take any advantage by being a Governour in matter of right or property, that if any man had a personal difference with me, when ever I was desired would cross the line of this Government with him, and give any satisfaction could be demanded of a Gentleman. I observe upon what has been abovesaid that M' Ashe and M' Moseley his uncle are men of surpriseing conduct and ingenuity, that out of their own detestable frauds and crimes, can find matter to accuse & caluminate me

I now proceed to the remainder of the Paragraph Article by Article.

No Persons have been called from Cape Fear to this place upon trifles as suggested, some have been summoned upon weighty matters by order of Council, and but very few, (an Assembly has nothing to do in such matters) there hath been but one trifling Fee to the Marshall added to the former since I came into the Country, and I believe that not paid As many People in this Province had been imposed upon by Surveyors some years since, who had on their own Authority without warrants survey'd much Land, about a year after I came M' Rice the Secretary laid Warrants on some of those Lands, upon which the matter was argued in the Council, and it was the opinion of the Council, the former Possessors were intruders, so M' Rice had the Land, As I know not of any People turned out of their legal Possessions, nor no man has complained but in respect to M' Rice, nor the Committee given one instance of such proceedings as they suggest, I look upon that Article as put in to swell the Paragraph, When was that time, when none were admitted to take up Lands unless they would pay 2ˢ 6ᵈ silver for every fifty Acres, I affirm and can prove by hundreds of men, and my own Secretary, that I have received for that Fee all sorts of Provisions dead or alive, and many sorts of goods, or anything that was offered (Bills excepted,) some Cash I have received but in the space of near three years the whole amount is short of two hundred Pounds, includeing the Fees for takeing up Land and all others, the Governour of this Province hath no Fee for signing Warrants for Land, nor for the Patents but 2ˢ 6ᵈ has been certainly paid them for every fivety Acres of Land taken up (not purchased.) When I was Governour for the Proprietors, the then Secretary received it of me, no man complaining, Sir Richard Everard had the same, and all Governours before us, as far as I can be informed, The Assembly that sate in 1731 thought 2ˢ 6ᵈ too small for that Fee, therefore in the draft of a Bill for payment of Quitt Rents and Officer's Fees they augmented it to three shillings, yet the other Fees were all left as they stood before Lands are taken up in this Government at one third of what the Charges arise to in the neighbouring Countrys, and the Fees accrueing to the Governors here, are the most inconsiderable of any Government belonging to the King, and altho' the Committee are pleased to say the Fee taken for Lands is not warranted by any Law, yet I am sure it is as lawfull for a Governour to receive it as any other Fee whatsoever I know not what the Committee mean about free People being taken up by the Magistrates &c if it doth not refer to the Negro children bound apprentices by the Justices in Bertie Precinct, the first knowledge I had of that matter I received from the late Assembly, and having inquired thereinto am informed that several free Negroe and Molatto Children were bound Apprentices, pursuant to an Act of the 5ᵗʰ of Queen Elizabeth, which said Act is continued in full force here, by an Act entituled an Act to preserve the Queen's Peace within this Government, I have no Power to set aside the Proceedings of the Precinct Courts, if any one is injured there, they may apply themselves to the General Court for redress.

When I came into this Province I found the Laws disregarded the Courts of Justice stop'd, and indeed Injustice Oppression arbitrary and admiralty Power, had realy overran the whole Province, but since my Arrival the General Court has been duly held, now and then there has been a failure in some of the Precinct Courts, by Mr Rice the Secretary's not appointing Clerks of those Courts in time, or nominating such scandalous fellows, as the Justices would not admit to act, but this no ways effects me. Mr Rice is my declared enemy, and open Maligner, therefore I take not upon myself to answer for his misdoings and neglect, I seriously declare that to the best of my knowledge and memory, neither myself or any man in the present administration of this Government has acted in an arbitrary or illegal manner, for which reason the Committee or any others are desired (if they can) to produce any particulars of such proceedings in me, or the rest of the Gentlemen, now in any post or imployment in this Government, that the just may be distinguished from the unjust.

In regard to the Grand Deed, be it known, that I acquainted the Lords of Trade and Plantations, when they had under consideration what Quitt rents should be paid for Lands thenceforth taken up in this Country, that the Lords Propriet" soon after their own Charter granted by King Charles the 2ᵈ had under their hands and common seal, given and confirmed to the Inhabitants of Albemarle (The whole Province of North Carolina being so called at that time) a Deed by which they obligated themselves, their heirs &c to grant Lands in this Country upon the same conditions and terms as then used in Virginia, whereupon their Lordships were pleased to order the Books relateing to Carolina which had been given up by the late Proprietors for His Majesty's service to be delivered to me to examine, that the said Deed or copy (if discovered) might be examined, I desired Colonel Halton to assist me in peruseing the said books, but after three days labour, our search proved in vain for we could not find any Copy of that Deed, or anything relateing to it in a letter to their Lordships of the 1ᵗ of July 1731, I wrote among other matters, concerning the Grand Deed (which I forbear to recite because any one that desires a transcript may have it applying to my Secretary) To that part of my letter the late Assembly saw the Answer I received from their Lordship's Secretary. I frankly declare it has always been my own opinion the Grand Deed was good, and ought to remain in force, but I may be mistaken, and the King's Attorney & Solicitor General, or Mʳ Fane Council to the Board of Trade, a most learned lawyer, may be able to prove it a temporary letter of Attorney or void in itself, since the King's purchase, which will put a final end to the said Grand Deed.

As the Committee are pleased to express themselves surprized at what I wrote in a message to the late Assembly that six times more Cash is carried out of this Country into Virginia to purchase Negros and British Commoditys then is sufficient to pay the King's Quitt rents, after duly considering this Article I don't perceive the least occasion to receed from what I then wrote; but will give some reasons to support my assertion, which I hope will convince the Committee and all others concerned in writing the Report of the truth of what I then lay'd down Many men of good understanding & knowledge have assured me, that in a year when Mast abounds fivety thousand fatt hoggs are supposed to be driven into Virginia from this Province, and allmost the whole number of fatted Oxen in Albemarle County with many Horses, Cows & Calves, much barreled Pork is also carried into Virginia, a considerable quantity of Pitch, Tar, Tobacco, Dear skins and Beaver skins and sold there for money, add to these the Trade carryed on by Perianquas from this Government to Norfolk Town, In hides, tallow, Bees wax, Mirtle wax, Feathers, Beef, Pork, Butter, Chees &c. the whole amount of the export (in my opinion) cannot come to less than fivety thousand pounds Virginia money one year with another, therefore it cannot be so difficult to pay the King's rents in cash as the Report suggests. I agree with the Committee, that if the King's rents were well collected and paid, they would not fall short of £1500 a year, But I am not of their opinion that those that live at any considerable distance from Virginia, cannot procure mony, for that end because Mr Rowan one of the Council told me that he had sold Irish goods for mony at Bath Town, and received, and caryed to Ireland above one hundred Pounds silver mony in a voyage, Cash is brought into Cape Fear River from the West Indies, and other Places, more then is sufficient to pay the Quitt rents due from that side of the Province What is meant by heavy burthens on the Traders wants explanation, for I know not what these burthens are If a Port was opened and a Fort built on Ocacock Island, and a small Garrison kept there, large Vessells might there load and unload in security and small Vessells carry the merchandize about the Country, and then this Province would have equal advantages by their Ports (being never frozen) with any Province in His Majesty's Dominions in North Carolina.

As all the Committee of the late house of Burgesses that sign'd the Report I have now answered, are again chosen, I advise them to consider if they were not grosly imposed upon in being made Tools to sign a Paper the writeing of other Men, so vile in itself and void of truth

GENTLEMEN,

I repeat my concern that you are prevented from rectifying the misdoings of the two former Assemblys, and wish you all a safe return to your several Plantations

GEO BURRINGTON

Edenton
   The 8th of Novr 1733

The Burgesses return'd to their House and ordered the same to be entered, and then departed

WILLIAMS. Clk of the Gen Assembly.

1734.

[B. P. R. O. NORTH CAROLINA B. T VOL. 9 A 37]

LINCOLNS INN. January 7ᵗʰ 1733

SIR,

The Charter which you sent us referrs to another which is prior, and which it will be necessary for us to see.

We likewise desire to have a Copy of the Fundamental Constitutions of the Late Lords Propᵐ for at present it does not appear to us by any thing that we can find in the Charter which you sent us, By what authority those Constitutions were made, nor how far they are at present in force   When the first Charter, and a Copy of these Constitutions are sent to us, there shall be no delay on our part   I am

Sir
Your very humble servant

J WILLES.

(Endorsed)

Recᵈ }
Read } 7ᵗʰ Janʳʸ 173¾

[FROM NORTH CAROLINA LETTER BOOK OF S. P G]

MR. LAPIERRE TO THE BISHOP OF LONDON

NEW HANOVER ALIAS CAPE FEAR IN Nᵒ CAROLINA
April 23ᵈ 1734

MY LORD:

I had the honor in my last to inform your Lordship about the present state of Cape fear both Civil and Ecclesiastical   I was the first minister of the Church of England that came to these places to preach which I did during three years and a half and at last frustrated of the best part of my salary was obliged to ask for my discharge then forced to work in the field to help to maintain my family afterwards compelled by necessity to sell my house & land & lastly my movables so that at this time I am no better than a mendicant   I have been 3 years out of place depending and living upon my own substance but every now and then exercising

my functions gratis among some of the dispersed families 'tis true my
Lord I had several invitations from abroad for vacancies to be supplied
but the Letters directed to me fell into the hands of our Gentlemen who
made no scruple to suppress them as I have found it out since, lest my
complaints of their proceedings should reach too far last of all I went
further northward to a new colony called New River consisting of above
100 families all poor people but very desirous to have the holy worship
set up amongst them Gov' Burrington and one Mr John Williams being
the chief encouragers it is a thriving place and likely in few years to
become a flourishing parish, there is a vast number of children among
them to be instructed and if this place falls to my lot I shall make bold
my Lord to send you a larger and more satisfactory account both of Cape
fear and of that new place. Your Lordship's pastoral Letters my Lord
which the Rev'd Mr Garden sent me I dispersed among the people of
Cape fear but to little purpose for some of the chief Inhabitants had
already been secretly seduced by the favorers of one Chub and by means
of such seducers and underhand dealers many have learned to quibble
and cavil about the holy scripture and as their belief so is their manner
of life in public incest or polygamy the first of which in a great man was
the first occasion of my gradual depression and degradation in their mind
when I spoke against it till at last they substituted in my room after I
took my discharge one Mr Rich'd Marsden formerly a preacher in Charles
town in South Carolina who declined appearing before Comissary Johnson and the rest of the Clergy to shew his credentials, afterwards my
Lord Portland's Chaplain in Jamaica then an incumbent in Virginia in
a parish called Princess Ann and of late a traficant to Lisbon, and sometime after his return promoted by a few Gentlemen to be Minister to
Cape fear without any popular election a man of an indifferent character
and causing by the violence of assesments great murmurings among the
people before they can get a qualified vestry and the said Rich'd Marsden
belonging to Liverpool pleads that he was ordained by one of your Lordship's predecessors much about the time that I was sent to So. Carolina
under Queen Ann 1707 one Mr Hall being the Bishop's Secretary and
a Cape fear Gentleman had since agreed to send to Your Lordship for a
Minister and to have him qualified a Missionary by the Hon'ble Society
this my Lord is left to the prudent discretion of that Hon'ble Body and
to Your Lordship's mature consideration that their bounty should not
be misapplied nor a clergyman ensnared by their fair words there being
no rules nor laws in the place for Church or State and the people being
most of them stated men and very substantial planters but unwilling to

Contribute towards the building of Churches and glebehouses or to the handsome maintenance of a minister all captains of ships who have been here will depose the same. My Lord I am Your Lordship's most humble servant and most dutiful Son in the Gospel,

JOHN LAPIERRE

[B. P. R. O. Am & W Ind Vol. 23. p 285.]

N. Carolina June the 1st 1734.

MAY IT PLEASE YOUR GRACE

Haveing lived in this Province some years without receiving any mony from the King, or the Country, was constrained to sell not only my household goods, but even linnen, plate and Books, and mortgage my Lands, and stocks the many sicknesses that seized me, and their long continuance, have greatly impaired my constitution and substance, my affairs and health being in a bad condition, I humbly desire my Lord Duke will be pleased to obtain his Majesty's leave for my return to England

I am
with profound Duty
my Lord Duke
your Grace's
most humble
and most devoted servant

GEO BURRINGTON.

[B P R. O. North Carolina B T Vol. 9 A 56]

N. Carolina 1st June 1734

My Lords,

Since my last letter to your Lordships Mr Owen one of the Council in this Province departed, some others were very like to dye but my escapeing death was unexpected by all who saw me, by the decease of Messrs Lovick and Owen and the refractoriness of others who will not come to

Council when summoned, there has not been one held in ten months. it is near three years since I sent your Lordships a list of persons that I thought proper to fill up the Council but as yet am unacquainted what your Lordships design in that affair

My Secretary will have the Honour to present this letter I assure your Lordships he is very capable of giveing a perfect account of the state and condition of this country

I have the Honour to remain with great Respect
   My Lords
    your Lordships
     most humble
      and most obedient servant
        GEO BURRINGTON

[B. P R. O Am & W Ind Vol. 23 p 286]

No CAROLINA the 17ᵗʰ of September 1734

MY LORD DUKE

Last year Mr Fury gave me intelligence, that his Majesty had appointed a new Governour for this Province, impatiently I expected his comeing (being very desirous to be rid of my charge) and notwithstanding the horrible villainys, Rice Smith and Montgomery had carried on against me, in this Country, and in England, I refrained from giveing them disturbance, or molesting them in any respect, onely hopeing by your Grace's Justice and goodness that when I returned to England an examination of my conduct and behavior, and theirs might be obtained, but these wicked men in defiance of Law, reason and my authority as Governour, have lately been guilty off, and committed the most impudent actions and crimes, an account of some of them (after due examination) shall be incerted in the next Council Journals. I have been necessitated, for the preservation of my own life, and peace of this Countrey to suspend Mr Rice the Secretary, from his place in the Council

May it please your Grace I hope speedily to receive the King's leave for comeing home the affairs of this Province will prove difficult to the Lords of Trade without my assistance I am humbly of opinion it would be for his Majestys service if the Board of Trade stayed till my return before they make the alterations in the Instructions that are requisite for the proper regulation of Government in North Carolina.

There lives not a man who honours the Duke of Newcastle or has a more entire submission to his will and pleasure then

His Grace's
  most humble
    and most devoted servant
      GEO BURRINGTON

[B. P. R. O. NORTH CAROLINA B. T. VOL. 9 A. 56.]

GOV. BURRINGTON TO LORDS OF TRADE
17 SEPT. 1734.

N. CAROLINA 17th of Sepr 1734.

MY LORDS,

Being directed by the ninth Instruction to give your Lordships notice If I suspend any Member of the Council in this Province without acquainting the other Councillors therewith and allso to render your Lordships my reasons for so doing I trouble your Board with this Letter to inform your Lordships that yesterday I suspended Nathaniel Rice Esqr Secretary of this Province from his Seat in Council, the reasons for so doing were, the preservation of my life, and the peace of this Country lately there was a villainous contrivance to murder me, I have reason to think and beleive Mr Rice was deeply concerned in that wickedness I design to send your Lordships a clear account of this matter in the next Sett of Councill Journals.

My Lords many times the Councillors have been summoned several Courts have passed when the Council ought to sit and meet in Court yet I have not been able to make up a sufficient number of Members to hold a Council nor Court of Chancery since July Court last was twelve months. therefore Mr Halton and Mr Ashe are summoned to appear att the Council Chamber the 25th of this month to shew cause why they have absented themselves. it is allmost two years that Mr Halton has neglected comeing to Courts or Council Mr Ashe and Mr Rice more than a year. I purpose soon to fill up the Council to the number limited by the Instructions that the business of the Countrey may be carried on in the usual Course, which I hope will prove to the good likeing of the Lords of Trade and Plantations

I am
  Your Lordships most humble
    and most obedient servant
      GEO BURRINGTON.

[B P R O Am & W Ind Vol. 23 p 287]

N Carolina the 7th of October 1734.

May it please your Grace

I had the honour by a letter dated the 17th of September to give my Lord Duke of Newcastle an account that I was obliged to suspend Nathaniel Rice Esqr secretary of this Province, from being one of the Council, for the preservation of my life, and the peace of this Province

Mr Robert Halton another Councillor, haveing been often summon'd, and admonished of his neglects hath failed comeing to any Court or Council, this month compleats two years therefore by a letter wrote to him the 26th of last month I suspended Mr Halton for willfully absent-ing himself from the Councils, without shewing cause, being thereunto required   Rice and Halton being suspended, there remained Mr John Ashe and Mr Edmund Gale and no more, who had sate as Councillors in this Province   To fill up the Council to the number prescribed in his Majesty's seventh Instruction I swore on the 27th past Coll Benjamin Hill, Coll Francis Pugh, Coll· Henry Gaston Coll McRora Scarbo-rough and on the 29th Coll Daniel Hanmer, Members of the Council, all these Gentlemen have good estates (for this Countrey) I believe they will act with honour and integrity, and becomeing the station of Coun-cillors,   the last named of these Gentlemen is also appointed Chief Jus-tice of this Province in the room of Mr William Little deceased, Coll. Hanmer was bred to the profession of the Law is nephew to Sir Thomas Hanmer in great esteem with the people of this Countrey and thought the only man capable of executeing the Office of Chief Justice in this Province Mr John Montgomery the Attorney General was suspended on the 29th of last month for the many villanys by him pertetrated Mr John Hodgson a very good Attorney is appointed to succeed him   My Lord it would take up too much of your time to read the long history I can write of the wickedness, villanys, follys and madness, Smith, Rice and Montgomery have been guilty of in this Province the detestable method of lyeing, and inventing slanders and calumnys (these men have so long used) against me deserves more then ordinary punishment. The Council Journals contain but a small part of what I am able to prove against them, I am of opinion even therein may be found enough to convince any reader that they are unfit persons to be imployed in offices of Trust   If it is your Graces pleasure, to order these scoundrels att this time fled from Justice to be restored to their former places, this Countrey will be in the greatest Confusion   send what Governour you please

Mr Lovick and Mr Little being dead, it clearly appears that they were falsely accused by Porter and others of profiting themselves, in the sale of Lands to pay for running the Line between this Province and Virginia, both dyeing much in debt

The Kings Instructions compell me to trouble your Grace with this letter.

> My Lord Duke
>> (with the greatest submission)
>> I am, your Grace's
>>> most humble and most devoted servant
>>>> GEO BURRINGTON

[B P R O. North Carolina. B. T Vol. 9 A 56.]

GOVᵣ BURRINGTON TO LORDS OF TRADE
7 OCT 1734

N. Carolina the 7ᵗʰ October 1734.

My Lords,

I did myself the Honour to inform your Lordships in a letter dated the 17ᵗʰ of last month that I had suspended Nathaniel Rice Esqᵣ Secretary of this Province from his place in the Council and my reasons for so doing were, the preservation of my life and peace of this Countrey. Mr Robert Halton another Councellor haveing been frequently sent for to Council and to attend the Courts, for two years together, and often admonished of his neglects, but still willfully absenting all the time and refuseing to shew cause for his said neglects I thought fit for his Majesties service to suspend him by letter the 26ᵗʰ past.   Then there remained Mr Ashe and Mr Gale in this province, and no others who had sate in the King's Council.

On the 27ᵗʰ of September last I swore Coll Benjamin Hill, Coll Francis Pugh, Coll Henry Gaston, Coll Mac Rora Scarborough into the Council and on the 29ᵗʰ Coll . Daniel Hanmer (nephew to Sir Thomas Hanmer) to whom I have given the Commission of Chief Justice of North Carolina vacant by the death of William Little Esqᵣ   Mr John Hodgson is made Attorney General in the room of John Montgomery, suspended on the 29th past for the innumerable villainys he has committed   I forbear writeing more of the said John att this present referring your Lordships to the Council Journals but promise to send the Board of Trade a much fuller account of this man and his companions in villainy Smith and Rice when thereunto required

Mr Lovick and Mr Little being dead it is now manifest beyond contradiction that they did not profit themselves by selling the lands, as was falsely suggested to his Grace of Newcastle, and Lords of Trade. Both these Gentlemen dyed much in debt and left no money to pay their Creditors.

My Lords I daily expect the Kings leave for my return to England when it arrives shall make haste to London,   hope to inform my Lords of Trade of all that is necessary for his Majesties Service in N Carolina and endeavour to prove myself

> Your Lordships
> most humble
> and most obedient servant
>
> GEO BURRINGTON

[B. P R O B T Journals, Vol. 44 p 129]

BOARD OF TRADE JOURNALS.

WHITEHALL. Thursday Augt 1st 1734
At a Meetg of H M. Comrs for Trade & Plantns
Present

| Mr Docminique | Mr Pelham |
| Mr Bladen. | Sir Ar Croft |

The following letters from Captain Burrington Govr of North Carolina were read and the papers therein referr'd to were laid before the Board, vizt

Letter from Capt. Burrington dated 20th Feby 173½ with

Minutes of Council of 26 July 1731 to 22 Janry 173½

Letter from Capt Burrington to the Secry dated 27th May 1732.

Letter from Capt. Burrington to the Secry dated 2 Novr 1732

Letter from Capt. Burrington dated 14 Novr 1732

Letter from him dated May 19th 1733 containing a state of that Government

Letter from Capt. Burrington dated 5 Oct. 1733

Letter from Capt. Burrington dated 12 Nov. 1733 giving account of the death of one of the Council

And then was read also a letter from M[r] Rice and M[r] Ashe two of the Council of North Carolina dated April 20th 1733 relating to Gov[r] Burrington's proceeding to appoint several new Precincts and thereby making an alteration in the Constitution of the Legislature with their objections to it the Governor's Answer and their reply

Letter from M[r] Rice and M[r] Ashe dated 20th April 1733 with a copy of their Remonstrance to Gov[r] Burrington his Answer and their reply all relating to the issuing of Warrants for Lands in that Province

The case of M[r] Moseley concerning Warrants for lands in North Carolina

The objections of M[r] Rice and M[r] Ashe against M[r] Owen's being admitted of the Council of North Carolina together with their affidavit of Gov[r] Burringtons refusing to suffer their objections to be entered

Deposition of M[r] Montgomerie Att[y] General of North Carolina relating to several abuses he has suffered from Capt Burrington

Letter from M[r] Porter one of the Council in North Carolina to the Sec[ry] dated 15th August 1733 relating to his suspension from the Council and Office of Judge of the Admiralty Court there by Capt. Burrington

List of Papers received with M[r] Porter's letter

Three depositions of M[r] Moseley Montgomerie and M[r] Ashe relating to the misbehaviour of Capt Burrington and to the dispute between him & M[r] Porter

Narrative upon oath of Edmund Porter Esq[re] relating to his complaint against Capt. Burrington

A Certificate from M[r] Rice Sec[ry] relating to the denial of M[r] Conner Attorn[y] to give his testimony against M[r] Burrington and 3 other papers relating to the dispute between M[r] Burrington & M[r] Porter

Order'd that M[r] Johnstone the present Gov[r] of North Carolina be desir'd to attend the Board on Tuesday morning next.

[Page 123.]

Wednesday July 24th 1734

M[r] Shelton attending acquainted the Board that he had a Warrant from the late Lords Proprietors of Carolina granting him 12,000 acres of land but that the Gov[r] having lately refused to give directions to the Surveyor to set out the said land he desired the Board would please to

order the Gov' to set out the said land   The Board upon this acquainted
M' Shelton that the Draft of a Law to settle the Quit rents of the Province upon which in great measure the validity of the Grants from the
late Lords Proprietors would depend was now under consideration before
the Attorney and Solicitor General and that the Board would take M'
Shelton's Warrant under consideration so soon as the said Draft of an
Act should be agreed And in the mean time order'd that a letter should
be wrote to the Attorney and Solicitor General to remind them thereof

[Page 182.]
WHITEHALL Tuesday Aug' 6ᵗʰ 1734

M' Johnston attending as he had been desir'd the Board took again
into consideration the several letters & papers from Capt. Burrington
read at the last meeting and gave M' Johnston directions upon such parts
of them as were not answered.

[Page 134]
Thursday August 8ᵗʰ 1734

M' Shelton Sec'ʸ to the late Lords Proprietors of Carolina attending
the Board desired he would inform them what he knew concerning the
deed of Grant from the said Proprietors to the County of Albemarle
in North Carolina 1668 And he said that the Lords Prop' would never
consent to that deed nor had ever sign'd & that they had constantly
given Instructions to their Governors directly against it   That they
had often wrote to their Governors not to grant any land under that
pretended deed which supposing it had been sign'd could never be look'd
upon any otherwise than as a temporary letter of Attorney from the
said Lords Proprietors to their then Governor

[Page 181]
Wednesday November 6ᵗʰ 1734

An Order of the Com'' of Council of Nov. 1ˢᵗ 1734 referr'd to the
Board M' Shelton's petition & a warrant from the late Lords Prop'
granting him a Barony in South Carolina & praying a confirmation of
the same was read & directions were given for prepar' Dft of a Report
in favor thereof—which was sign'd on 19ᵗʰ Nov 1734

[FROM THE MSS RECORDS OF NORTH CAROLINA COUNCIL JOURNALS.]

COUNCIL JOURNALS.

NORTH CAROLINA—ss

At the Council Chamber in Edenten the 15th day of April Anno Dom 1734

Whereas by the Departure of His Excelly George Burrington Esqr His Majesties Governour in Chief of this Province, the Government thereof devolved upon the Honoble Nathaniel Rice Esqr pursuant to His Majesties Royal Instruction declaring that upon the Death or Departure of the Governour out of the Province, the first Councellor shall take upon him the Administration of the Government with the Title of President and Commander in Chief thereof   And whereas all the Members of His Majesties Council Reside above Two Hundred miles from the seat of Government so that they could not have notice to be present the said Nathaniel Rice being first Councellor took & Subscribed the several Oaths by Law Enjoyned for Qualification of Publick Officers in presence of us the subscribers and caused publication thereof to be made by Proclamation and therein continued all officers Civil and Military in their respectives post and Employments & then took upon him the administration of the Government.   The Honoble the President thereupon Directed Summons to Issue to the Members of His Majesties Council to meet at the Council Chamber in Edenton on Monday the 20th day of May next

W SMITH
J MONGOMERY Atty Genl

NORTH CAROLINA—ss

George the Second by the Grace of God of Great Brittain France and Ireland King Defender of the Faith &c

To our Trusty and well beloved Nathaniel Rice Esqr Greeting

Out of the assurance we have of the Loyalty Prudence and Ability of you the said Nathaniel Rice Do hereby Constitute and Appoint you (During our Pleasure) Secretary of our province of North Carolina, hereby Authorizing you and Giving you full power and authority to be present at all meetings of our Governour and Council and of our Assemblys and to keep an Exact Register of all their acts Proceeding and

Orders, and also to Recieve from the Surveyor General all Certificates of Lands by him sett out and Surveyed, According to the warrants to him Directed, And to Draw up all Conveyances and Assurances of Lands to be granted pursuant to our Instructions Given to our Governor of our said province, thereon, and to cause the same when duly Executed to be Enrolled, And Generally to Do and Perform all Other acts usually done by other secretarys or that to the Duty of said Office shall belong, And we do hereby further Impower you to recieve all Fees Perquisites and advantages whatsoever to the said Office of Secretary belonging or any-wise appertaining In Testimony whereof we have caused these our Letters to be made Patents Witness our Trusty and well beloved George Burrington Esqr Governor of our Said province at Edenton under his hand and Great Seal of our said Province the Eleventh day of May In the fourth year of our reign Anno Domini 1731

GEO BURRINGTON [SEAL.]

Entred from the Original by me
Wm IRVIN
Examined & Compared with the
Original ⅌ me
Jno RICE

[B P. R. O B T North Carolina Vol 9 A 61]

LEGISLATIVE JOURNALS.

At a General Assembly begun & held at Edenton for the said Prov-ince Novr the Sixth 1734

MEMBERS RETURNED

Chowan	Pequimons	Pasquotank
Col Edwd Moseley	Mr Zeb Clayton	Mr Gab Burnham
Col Cullen Pollock	Mr Saml Swann	Mr Cho Sawyer
Col Henry Bonner	Mr Cho Denman	Mr Cala Sawyer
Capt Wm Downing	Mr Richd Skinner	Mr Jer Simons
Mr Thos Luten	Mr Jos Long	Col John Palin

Currituck	Bertie	Edgecombe
M' H White	M' T Castellaw	M' W Whitehead
M' G Bowers	M' Ar Williams	M' J Spiers
M' J Mann	M' G Winn	M' Bar Macquinny
M' T Etheridge	M' J Dawson	M' D Hopper
M' Lew' Jenkins	M' J Hodgson	M' J Millikin

Beaufort	Hyde	Craven
M' Ed Saller	M' Sam Sinclaire	M' Wal' Lane
M' R' Turner	M' W'' Cording	M' D' Shine

Carteret	New Hanover	Onslow
Col Thos Lovick		M' J Starkey
M' J' Winright		M' J Williams

Bladen

Edenton	Bath Town	Newburn Town
M' W'' Badham	M' Rog' Kenyon	M' S Powell.

Received the following Order from y' Gov' & Council

His Excell' the Gov' was pleased to Nominate and Appoint Col Macrora Scarborough & Col Dan Hanmer to Administer the Oaths by Law Appointed for Qualification of Publick Officers to the Members of the present General Assembly of this Province as also to the Clerk of the said House.

Whereupon the following Members appeared and were Qualifyed (before the said Col Scarbrough & Col Hanmer, M' Anderson the Deputy Clerk of the Crown reading the Oaths) viz'

Col Ed Moseley Col Henry Bonner M' Thos Luten M' W'' Badham M' Cha' Denman M' Rich' Skinner M' Joshua Long M' Arthur Williams M' Geo Winn M' John Hodgson M' Gab Burnham M' Cha' Sawyer M' Jer Simons M' Caleb Sawyer M' Tho' Lovick M' John Powell M' Rob' Turner M' Ed Saller M' Roger Kenyon M' Sam' Sinclare M' James Millikin M' Daniel Shine M' Walter Lane M' James Winright M' J'' Starkey & M' Abraham Blackall Clerk of Assembly

The House Adjourned till tomorrow Morning nine o'clock.

ABR BLACKALL C'' of Assembly

Thursday Nov' y' 7'''

The House met according to Adjournm'

The House being directed by His Excell' to choose their Speaker. Unanimously made choice of Col Ed Moseley to be Speaker, And by

His Excell'ʸ direction the House waited on Him in yᵉ Councill Chamber & presented their Speaker, When the Governour made the following Speech to the Council and Assembly viz'

GENTLEMEN OF THE UPPER AND LOWER HOUSES

You are now called together to consider and Act for the good and Welfare of this Province   many of the Burgesses now Chosen by long Experience and Acquaintance with them, I know to be Gentlemen possessed with requisite Understanding for the due discharge of the Trust their Country has reposed in them Insomuch that I Entertain hopes great Matters may be effected at this Time for the benefit of North Carolina.

GENTLEMEN OF THE UPPER HOUSE.

The Signal proofs you have given of your knowledge in Business, and readiness to Serve your King and Country merit great Commendation   I cannot doubt, (Gentlemen) of your Diligence during the Sitting of this Assembly to promote the passing such Acts, as are recommended or required in the King's Instructions

GENTLEMEN OF THE LOWER HOUSE

In the former Assembly I recommended many things which I thought would conduce to the Honour & Prosperity of this Country,   the said Assemblys took so little notice of what I laid before them that I do not now name any matter in particular, to your consideration but may in a few days, if I find you are disposed to do business,   In General I wish and Earnestly desire, your ready complyance with such things as His Majesty requires in His Instructions or has ordered me to recommend to you   Transcripts of them, the Clerk of your House now has in his profession I suppose, if not, you may be furnished with them on the first Message to me

GENTLEMEN OF BOTH HOUSES.

I expect you will behave in such manner as the King may be satisfyed with your proceedings and the Country receive great benefits by the good Laws which (I hope) you will now frame & enact

My ready concurrence I am sure you cannot doubt nor shall not stand in need of

GEO BURRINGTON

The Assembly returned to their own House & having obtained a Copy of the Govᵣ Speech Ordered that it be read in the House in the afternoon

Divers Members appearing that have not yet been Qualifyed.

Ordered that the Messenger of this House do wait on the Members of Council appointed to Administer the Oaths, & desire they would be present at their Qualification, accordingly Col. Scarbrough and Col Hanmer appeared and Mr Zebulon Clayton Mr Samuel Swann and Mr William Cording were Qualifyed

The House Adjourned till three O'Clock in the afternoon

ABRA BLACKALL C^th of Assembly

The House met according to Adjournment

Mr James Castellaw Mr John Dawson & Mr Lewis Jenkins were Qualifyed before Col Scarbrough and Col Hanmer His Excell^cy Speech being read according to Order

Mr Thos Luten Mr Charles Denman Mr Gab^l Burnham Mr James Castellaw Mr Lewis Jenkins Mr Robt Turner Mr Walter Lane & Mr William Badham were appointed a Comittee to make an Answer thereto And then the House Adjourn^d till to Morrow morning ten of the Clock

A BLACKALL C^th of Assembly

Friday Morning Novr ye 8th

The House met according to Adjournment

Read the Petition of John Harrell Setting forth that he was duly elected a representative for Bertie precinct but the Marshall had returned Mr John Hodgson in his room he humbly prays ye Poll may be inspected.

Mr John Hodgson being present in the House having heard the same petition, the list of the Poll was produced and being examined and cast up it was found to be in Mr Hodgson favour It being moved in the House by divers Members that a bill be brought in to declare that none but freeholders should Elect and Chuse Members of Assembly Ordered that Mr Zeb Clayton and Mr Saml Sinclare be a Committee to prepare and bring in a bill for that purpose agreable to His Majesty's Royall Instruction

Col Scarbrough & Col Hanmer brought from the upper House a bill for an Act entituled an Act for the better and more effectual encouraging and promoting the Trade of this Province

Ordered that the bill be read to Morrow Morning

The House adjourned till tomorrow morning at nine of ye clock

Saturday Morning Nov' y° 9th

The House met according to adjournment

The Bill entituled an Act for the better and more effectual encouraging and promoting the Trade of this Province was read a first time and passed.

The House on reading the above Bill entered into a Debate concerning the Pilotage and being informed that Cap' Miles Gale was willing to undertake the Pilotage at and near Ocacock The House sent for him and on his appearance before The House and declaring his Willingness to undertake the Pilotage he was directed to lay his propositions before the House on Monday next

Ordered that the powder receivers Accts be laid before the House and also the Treasurers Accts on y° eighteenth Instant Mr Wm Badham reported from y° committee for drawing up an Address to His Excell' which was read and after some amendments made. Ordered that the same be fairly engrossed and that this House will wait on His Excell' with the same this afternoon

The House adjourned till three of y° Clock

Met according to adjournment

Col Cullen Pollock and Mr Wm Downing being returned Members and failing to appear Ordered that the Sergeant do wait on them to require their Appearance on Monday next

This afternoon Mr Speaker and Such of the Members as were present waited on His Excell' with the Address of this House which was in these words viz'

To His Excellency George Burrington Esq're His Majestys Cap' Gen' & Governour in Chief of North Carolina.

MAY IT PLEASE YOUR EXCELLENCY

We return you our hearty thanks for your kind Speech to us and are very glad you have conceived so good an Opinion of our Understanding & Capacity to serve this Province

We shall at this Juncture wave entering into any debate relateing to the Conduct of former Assemblys who (in our humble Opinion) have always had regard to the Interest of their Country But now most willingly Embrace this Opportunity, to demonstrate to your Excell' with what hearty Chearfulness we are met as well to Execute and discharge the Trust and Confidence reposed in us, And consult the welfare and benefit & prosperity of this province As also with due respect & regard to observe Obey and (as much as in us lies) comply with His Majestys Royall Instructions.

The Assurance Your Excell' hath been pleased to give us of your ready concurrence with both Houses in frameing and enacting Some good and wholesome Laws for the benefit and Advantage of this Province and agreable to the Circumstances thereof, which at this time are greatly wanted, makes us Strongly of Opinion and we persuade our Selves, that there will be a good Harmony and Understanding between both Houses. We on our parts will so Strenuously endeavour to promote, encourage and Advance the Trade of this province and the General good thereof, and also behave in such manner that His Majesty may be well Satisfyed with our proceedings and the Country fully convinced of our good intentions

By Order of the House

EDWARD MOSELEY Speak'

To which His Excell' made the following Answer

M' SPEAKER AND GENTLEMEN OF THE GENERAL ASSEMBLY

I accept of your Answer to my Speech very kindly and take this Opportunity of once more assuring the House of Burgesses, that I earnestly desire to see this Country well setled, by good and wholesome Laws. The Opinion I entertain of the Wisdom and good Intentions of the Members that Compose the General Assembly is grounded upon the real Meritt I know they are possessed off And Since the Council have made so handsome a declaration (in their Answer to my Speech) of readiness & zeal to serve the King, and you the representatives the like I hope there is not a possibility that our duty to the Kings most Excellent Majesty, in Obeying His Instructions, and Effectually doing good for this province Should be delayed or Obstructed, but that we shall with Agreement truly & sincerely so demean our Selves that the present Livers in this Country may have reason to thank us, at the end of this session and their posterity not only to Remember us with gratitude, but bless our Memorys for the benefits they shall hereafter enjoy by the Laws we pass in this Assembly

GEORGE BURRINGTON

The House adjourned till Monday morning nine of the Clock

A BLACKALL C'k of Assembly.

Monday Nov[r] y[e] 11th

Met according to adjournment

The House takeing into consideration y[e] Subject matter of the New precincts which had been considered of in the last assembly It is Ordered that Bills be brought in to establish three new precincts by the names of Edgecombe, Onslow, & Bladen with proper Boundaries so as not to Injure the Neighbouring Precincts and to Assertain y[e] Number of representatives for each prect And that M[r] Hodgson & M[r] Lane be a Committee for preparing the Bill

The House adjourned 'till three of the Clock

Met according to Adjournment

Read y[e] petition of the Inhabitants of Bear River &c praying y[e] same might be erected into a Precinct

Ordered that M[r] Sinclare & M[r] Lane be a committee to prepare a Bill for the same

Read the petition of y[e] Inhabitants of Hide precinct praying that they might have a Court and Magistracy erected in their precinct as other precincts have   This House is of Opinion that the said precinct ought to have a Court and the same priviledges as other precints in the Country of Bath have and enjoy

Sent to the Upper House for concurrence

By M[r] Sinclare &

    M[r] Cording

Read a Bill entituled a Bill for an Act Appointing that part of Bertie precinct which lies on the South Side of Roanoak river to be Establisht a precinct by y[e] name of Edgecombe

Sent to the upper House for Concurrence

By M[r] Sinclare &

    M[r] Cording

The House Adjourned to Tomorrow Morning nine of the Clock

                ABRA BLACKALL C[th] of Assembly

Tuesday Nov[r] y[e] 12th

Met According to Adjour[t]

Read the petition of y[e] Inhabitants of Pasquotank precinct, praying that the North East parish of the precinct aforesaid might be erected into a precinct

Orderd that M[r] Ch[o] Sawver and M[r] Gabriel Burnham be a Committee to prepare and bring in a Bill for the same

The erecting Tyrrll prec[t] by Act of the Biennial Assembly in the year 1729 not having been duly observed, it is Orderd to prevent any dispute concerning the same that M[r] Bonner & M[r] Luten do prepare & bring in a Bill to Establish y[e] same precinct

M[r] John Etheridge & M[r] John Mann appear'd and were Qualifyed before Col Hanmer & Col Gaston

The House adj[d] till y[e] afternoon

Met according to adjournment

Read a bill entituled a bill for an Act for erecting the west part of Carteret precinct from Bartrums Creek on Bogue Sound, and the East part of Hanover precinct from new Topsail Inlet & Creek in Bath County into a seperate precinct & parish by the name of the precinct and parish of Onslow

Passed the first time & Sent to y[e] Upper House

By M[r] Bonner &

M[r] Luten

Rec[d] from the upper House the petition the Inhabitants of Hyde precinct with the following endorsements

Monday Nov[r] y[e] 11th 1734

Read in the upper House & concurr'd with and Order'd that the same be sent to His Excell[y] for His Concurrence

By Order

R FORSTER C[lk] of the Upper House

November the 12th 1734

I concur with this petition   GEO BURRINGTON

Rec[d] from the upper House the Bill entituled a Bill for an Act appointing y[e] part of Bertie precinct which lies on the South side of Roanoake River to be Establisht a precinct by the name of Edgecombe passed in the upper House

Recd from the Upper House the Bill for an Act for the better and more effectual encourageing & promoting y[e] Trade of this province

Passed in the upper House

Read in the House certain propositions from the Inhabitants of y[t] part of the province commonly called Edgecombe precinct. Order'd that the same be taken into consideration on this day Sen'nights and that in the mean time any Member is allowed to frame such Bill as he thinks proper on the subject matter of the same

81

Read the first time a bill entituled an Act for the enlarging and Establishing the power and Jurisdiction of the precincts Court and the Magistrates thereof, and also to regulate divers proceedings therein and passed

Sent to the upper House

By Mr Bonner &

    Mr Luten

Read a Second time the Bill entituled a Bill for an Act appointing that part of Bertie precinct which lies on the South side of Roanoake river to be establisht a precinct by the name of Edgecombe and passed with amendments

Sent to the upper House

By Mr Bonner &

    Mr Luten

Read Capt Gales proposals for Buoying and Beaconing Ocacock Inlet

Ordered that the Same lye on the table till tomorrow Morning for further Consideration   Read a Second time the bill for an Act for the better and more effectual encouraging and promoteing the Trade of this province and passed with amendments

Sent to the upper House

By Mr Badham &

    Mr Clayton

Mr Speaker acquainting this House that by a letter from Col Maurice Moore of Cape Fair dated October ye 29th he was informed that His Excelly Gabriel Johnston Esqr His Majesty's Governr of this province arrived at Cape Fair ye 27th of October, to confirm which News Mr Speaker produced a letter of Govr Johnston's writing at Cape Fair Barr dated October ye 27th that was enclosed to him by Col Moore to be sent express to William Smith Esqr Chief Justice of North Carolina—whereupon it was proposed that this House should send two of the Members to wait on His Excellency to congratulate His Arrival

The House adjourned 'till tomorrow morning nine of the clock

                ABRA BLACKALL Clk of Assembly

Wednesday Novr ye 13th

The House met according to adjournment

Read a Bill entituled a Bill for an Act for erecting the North East parish of Pasquotank precinct into a Seperate precinct by the name of

              passed the first time

It being certifyed by Proclamation from His Exce[lly] Gov[r] Johnston that He hath publisht his Commission at Cape Fair in Open Council it is therefore unanimous Opinion of this House that they proceed no further in Business.

By Order
ABRA BLACKALL C[th] of Assembly

CPSIA information can be obtained
at www.ICGtesting.com
Printed in the USA
FFHW01n1418170918
48467447-52306FF

9 781277 089189